Muhammad Mors

The United Arab Emirates

A MODERN HISTORY

Makarem

First published 1978 in the UK by Croom Helm Ltd., 2 St. John's Road, London SW11 and in the USA 1978 by Harper & Row Publishers Inc., Barnes and Noble Import Division.

Second edition 1994 Muhammad Morsy Abdullah published by Hurtwood Press Limited, Silversted Westerham Hill, Kent TN16 2HY, UK.

This new edition 2007 published by Makarem G Trading and Real Estate LLC. Abu Dhabi, United Arab Emirates.

ISBN 0 903696 37 1

Printed and bound in Dubai

H.H. Shaikh Zāyed b. Sulṭān Āl Nihayyān
Father of Nation

H.H. Shaikh Khalīfa b. Sulṭān Āl Nihayyān

President of the United Arab Emirates

Contents

Foreword

Acknowledgements

Abbreviations

Introduction 13

1. The Trucial States and British Imperial Interests 21
   - I British Diplomacy in the Period of International Challenge, 1892–1918 23
   - II The Growth of British Interests between the Two World Wars 40
   - III The End of the British Imperialistic Era 71

2. Internal Changes 87
   - I Introduction 89
   - II The Trucial States between 1891 and 1918 90
   - III Changes in the Economy and in Political Attitudes: Cultural Development, 1892–1939 103
   - IV Important Political Changes during the Inter-War Period 113
   - V Decisive and Far-reaching Developments after the Second World War 133

3. Western Neighbours of the Trucial States 157
   - I Geographical Introduction 159
   - II The Qaṭar and Ottoman Dispute over al-'Udaid, 1871–1913 160
   - III The British and Ibn Sa'ūd's Policy towards the Trucial Coast up to 1939 168
   - IV Negotiations Concerning Abū Dhabī's Frontiers with Sa'ūdi Arabia, 1934–8 180
   - V The Post-War Period and the Agreement of 1975 199
   - VI Settlement of the Maritime Boundaries of Abū Dhabī and Qaṭar 212

4. Britain, Persia and the Trucial States 219

I The Qājār Period 221

II Ṣirrī, Ṭanb and Abū Mūsā Islands until 1921 233

III Britain's Attitude towards Persian Policy during the Rezā Shāh's Reign 246

IV The Search for a Settlement to the Islands' Dispute after 1945 273

5. Britain, Muscat and the Inter-State Boundaries 289

I A Historical Review of the Political Map 291

II The Frontiers between Muscat and the Trucial States 296

III The Inter-State Boundaries 307

6. Conclusion 317

Bibliography 325

Maps and Appendices 331

Index 357

Foreword

Dr Muḥammad Morsy Abdullah is unusual in coming to the history of the Gulf with a far greater equipment than the ordinary research student of Middle Eastern History, for he has spent nearly a quarter of a century in the Gulf States and has lived through many of the events which he has since discussed with participants or witnesses, often in colloquial Gulf Arabic. He draws, moreover on local family documents thus adding another dimension to official reports and diaries—to which of course he accords their proper appreciation. He has ranged also beyond British, French and German archives to consult Ottoman documents at Istanbul and American sources in Washington.

The highly sensitive issues still active in the contemporary history of the Gulf have been handled unemotionally with non-partisan objectivity, each statement carefully weighed but with a combination of discretion and tact in no way detracting from sincerity. His broadly-based study of the United Arab Emirates will at once be recognised for the authoritative reference that it is. Nowhere else can one find that intimate acquaintance with the mentality of the local people, their educational background, their religio-political thinking and writing, and the attitudes that have developed therefrom, especially, Dr Morsy maintains, in Abū Dhabī. It may come as something of a surprise to perceive that the 'Truce' the British imposed on the Gulf States, if essential to the movement of international shipping, and the Indian Government's non-involvement policy in their internal affairs, was not beneficial to the area. By contrast the post World War I growth of the strategic importance of the Gulf to Britain—notably in imperial policy in air communications, the history of which is perhaps little known outside official circles—did aid economic progress. Britain protected the then important pearling industry and supported the Gulf States *vis-à-vis* Iranian expansionist objectives up to the affair of the Islands on the very eve of Britain's withdrawal.

Dr Morsy points out that the ill consequences anticipated from the withdrawal did not take place. Yet there was real justification for such fears and so wise a monarch as the late King Faisal is reported to have demanded of a British official whether Britain intended to hand over the Gulf, like Aden, to the communists. The Labour Government responsible for the Aden débacle was replaced by the Conservatives and the late Sir William Luce, one of the most distinguished British officials with whom Dr Morsy was able to discuss the events leading to independence, was despatched to study the situation. The withdrawal was made with no background of broken faith. Dr Morsy, with Arab eyes, inclines to see a consistent British attitude over these years to Gulf affairs, and to give relatively small weight to the real division on foreign policy between the Conservatives and the Labour left.

Boundaries have played an important part in the recent history of the Gulf States, particularly, of course, in the Buraimī episode. Dr Morsy himself was involved in the mapping of Abū Dhabī and it was a happy coincidence that Julian Walker, who was responsible for the complex demarcation of boundaries in the area, spent his sabbatical year at the Middle East Centre while Dr Morsy was formulating his work.

The creation of the United Arab Emirates despite traditional divisions and the threat of externally sponsored subversion, and the Federation's present stability are highly creditable to the rulers—Dr Morsy is specially appreciative of the role played by its President, Shaikh Zāyed. Already this is a far cry from the first historic but uncertain discussion of the rulers at Dubai in January 1964.

February 1978

R. A. Serjeant
Faculty of Oriental Studies,
Middle East Centre,
Cambridge.

Acknowledgements

As this work is mainly based on my thesis for the Ph.D. degree at Cambridge University in 1975 entitled 'Britain and the Trucial States between 1892–1939', I wish to thank Professor R. B. Serjeant who guided me in the early stages of this study and afterwards continued to show interest and encouragement. My greatest debt of gratitude is to my supervisor, Dr R. Bidwell; he was most generous in the time he gave me, and his wide knowledge of the whole variety of sources and his familiarity with tribal matters and modern Arab history proved invaluable in all my discussions with him.

My thanks are also due to their Highnesses the Rulers of the Trucial States (now members of the Supreme Council UAE), the heads of tribes and the chiefs of certain families who gave me interviews and who shared with me their time and experiences, to the late Shaikh Khālid b. Muḥammad, ex-ruler of Shārjah, Shaikh Surūr b. Muḥammad Al-Nihayyān, Chairman of the Presidential Court and to the Ministers (UAE), the late Aḥmad b. Sulayyim, Aḥmad b. Ḥāmid, Māni' Sa'īd al-'Utaibah, Muḥammad Ḥabrūsh al-Suwaidī, Thānī b. 'Īsā, 'Abdullah 'Umrān and 'Abdullah al-Mazrūi. Also Shaikh Hādif b. Ḥumaid (Ḥamriyyah), Shaikh Suhail b. Māni' (at al-'Ain), 'Alī al-Shurafā (director of the Presidential Court), 'Abdullah al-Nuwais, Deputy Minister of Information, the late Judge Muḥammad Sa'īd b. Ghubāsh (Rās al-Khaimah), 'Abdullah al-Hūl (Chief of Police, Dubai), 'Abdullah, Muḥammad and Aḥmad, sons of 'Alī al-Maḥmūd, Ibrāhīm al-Midfa' and Mubārak al-Nākhī (all from Shārjah), the late Khalīfah al-Yūsuf, Nāṣir b. Midhkir al-Hājirī, the two experienced pearl-divers Ya'kūb 'Alī al-Qubaisī and Ḥusain Khalīfah b. Jiraiwish al-Qubaisī, the late 'Abdullah b. Ghamnūm (all from Abū Dhabī); 'Alī al-Tājir (Dubai), Aḥmad 'Alī al-Shīrāwī (Baḥrain), the late Muḥammad 'Alī al-Ṭāhir (Beirut), Qusai Muḥib al-Dīn al-Khatib (Cairo) and finally to the pioneer teachers, particularly Zuhdī al-Khaṭīb, Shaikh Muḥammad b. Yūsuf, 'Abd al-Qādir Hulayyil, Walīd Barzanjī, Nāṣir al-Ja'barī, Muḥammad Aḥmad Kayyālī, 'Alī al-Najār and Māhir 'Āshūr.

I would like also to thank the foreign scholars and personalities who gave me interviews and provided me with useful information, especially Sir Gilbert Laithwaite (India Office), Sir W. Luce and Sir Geoffrey Arthur (the last Political Resident in the Gulf), Mr E. F. Henderson (former Ambassador to Qatar), Mr J. P. Bannerman, Mr A. Reeve and Mr A. D. Harris (the Foreign and Commonwealth Office, London), Professor W. Dostal, Vienna University, Professor G. Rentz, Hoover Institute, Stanford University,

California, Dr Phebe A. Marr, Berkeley University, California, the American geological engineer the late Fred A. Davies (former General Manager of Aramco), Lafayette, California, Dr J. Wilkinson, Oxford University, Ambassador Daniel Van der Meulen, Grossel, Holland, Captain A. Bodger, Group General Manager of Gulf Air, Col. J. Briggs, Adviser to the Police Force, Dubai, Major M. Budd of the Trucial Oman Scouts, Dr Lt. Col. D. G. McCaully and Mr Julian Walker, former Political Agent in Dubai.

I must also express my sincere gratitude to Dr Susan Skilliter, Faculty of Oriental Studies, Cambridge, Dr Nejat Goyunc, Ankara University, and to two Turkish colleagues, Mr Muṣṭafā Bilge and Yūsuf Halacoglu in Istanbul, who have been most helpful in the reading and translating of the Turkish Archives, also to all those who assisted me in understanding the German documents, to all those who read the draft of this study, helping me to polish the English style, particularly Mr Barry Unsworth and Mr Nicholas Turner, and finally to Miss Stella Uttley who typed the manuscript. My thanks are also due to the two photographers Muḥammad and Yaḥya Badr.

I would like to pay tribute to the helpfulness of all the staffs of the libraries and official archives in the India Office and Public Records Office in London, the National Archives and Records in Washington, the Theological Seminary Library (Reformed Church of America), New Brunswick, New Jersey, the Hoover Library in Stanford, California, Politisches Archiv des Auswärtigen Amts, Bonn, Archives du Ministère des Affaires Étrangères au Quai d'Orsay, Paris, and especially the staffs of these three libraries in Cambridge, The Faculty of Oriental Studies, The Middle East Centre and Cambridge University. As most of my work during the last four years was in the India Office, I am most grateful to Mrs P. Tuson who was of particular help.

In addition, my deep gratitude goes to all my many colleagues and friends in responsible positions in the Government of the United Arab Emirates, who helped me in this work and are too numerous to mention individually. This appreciation would not be complete without an acknowledgement of my special debt to Dr 'Izz al-Dīn 'Ibrāhīm Muṣṭafā, Cultural Adviser to the President of the UAE, who generously took on the added burden of my responsibilities in the Centre for Documentation and Research, Abū Dhabī, in order to free me to pursue this study, and also to my wife, Nagwah, who has shared the trials of these last seven years of research. Finally, my thanks to Mr David Croom and his staff, particularly Miss Judy Bennett, for the enthusiasm they showed and the help they gave in publishing this work.

Abbreviations

AM	The Arabian Mission, Reformed Church in America.
APOC	Anglo–Persian Oil Company.
CAB	Public Record Office, Cabinet Files.
CENTO	Central Treaty Organization.
CID	Committee of Imperial Defence.
CO	Colonial Office.
DSA	Department of State Archives, National Archives and Records, Washington.
FA	French Archives (Archives du Ministère des Affaires Etrangères, Paris).
FO	Public Record Office, Foreign Office Files.
GA	German Archives (Politischen Archives des Auswärtigen Amts, Bonn).
GS	Government of Shārjah.
IOR	India Office Records.
IPC	Iraq Petroleum Company.
JRCAS	Journal of the Royal Central Asian Society.
MME Sub-Committee	Committee of Imperial Defence, Standing Ministerial Sub-Committee for Questions concerning the Middle East.
OA	Ottoman Archives, Istanbul.
OME Sub-Committee	Committee of Imperial Defence, Standing Official Sub-Committee for Questions concerning the Middle East.
PG Sub-Committee	Committee of Imperial Defence, Persian Gulf Sub-Committee.
Pol. Res.	Political Resident.
SGI	Secretary of the Foreign Department of the Government of India.
SNO	Senior Naval Officer, Persian Gulf (Royal Navy).
SSC	Secretary of State for the Colonies.
SSI	Secretary of State for India, London.

To

HH Shaikh Zāyed b. Sulṭan Āl Nihayyān,
- Founder of the United Arab Emirates.
With affection and gratitude for his encouragement and support

Introduction

Because my M.A. thesis had been written on 'The Relations between the First Sa'ūdī State and 'Omān during 1795–1818', and because I had spent the previous twenty-five years working in Qaṭar and on the coast of 'Omān, early in 1971 it was my original intention for my Ph.D. dissertation at Cambridge to extend my studies of the same area. After a few months spent exploring the main issues and problems in the modern history of Eastern Arabia and the Gulf, and consulting recent theses and other writings on the subject, it seemed to me that the United Arab Emirates on the Coast of 'Omān, known politically before 1971 as the Trucial States, while usually included in general surveys of 'Omāni and Gulf history, had never been accorded the separate and specific treatment that they deserve. Furthermore, from the late eighteenth century the Coast of 'Omān developed independently and strongly influenced British policy changes in the Gulf during the nineteenth century, assuming strategic importance between the two World Wars and after.

During the early months of study my work in the rich material in the India Office Library and the Public Record Office in London proved decisive in determining the period to be covered by my research into the history of the 'Omāni coast. Two factors persuaded me to take 1892 as its beginning; first, the two penetrating and well documented works on the area by Kelly and Lorimer, who ended their researches respectively at 1880 and 1905; secondly, because it was in 1892 that the British concluded the 'Exclusive Treaties' with the Trucial Shaikhs, treaties which continued to be the cornerstone of their supremacy in the region. Although it is impossible to make use of archives for research beyond 1945, because they are not available to the public, I decided to continue the period of study for the Ph.D. thesis which had ended at 1939, to the year 1971. My decision was influenced by three factors. First, as the British left the area in 1971, that year marked the end of a significant era. Secondly, the many published official documents, serious researches, the availability of sufficient newspapers and journals, and the possibility of interviewing important foreign and Arab personalities who had played a role in events, together with my own long experience in the Gulf, all combined to compensate for the lack of archives in giving a fairly accurate picture of the time. Thirdly, the many significant local events and the rapid changes and developments which took place in the short post-war years in the

Trucial States, which ended with the emergence of the United Arab Emirates, make it a crucial period in the history of the area.

The historical issues concerning the Trucial States in the years between 1892 and 1971 are treated in five chapters. In Chapter 1, 'The Trucial States and British Imperial Interests', I have dealt with the local and international challenge to Britain's supremacy before the First World War, which resulted in the conclusion of the 'Exclusive Treaty' of 1892. In this study I have tried to explain the role of this treaty during a time of international challenge to British supremacy and to the rights Britain assumed in the Trucial States. At the turn of the century other powers had very little real interest in the area and were mostly concerned with embarrassing Great Britain and pressuring her for concessions elsewhere. By 1914 this period of challenge had ended. Between the two World Wars Britain faced serious economic competition in the Gulf from the American oil companies and Japanese trading activity. In this period Britain's policy on the Trucial Coast changed from the negative one of denying the area to others to the positive one of securing air bases essential to imperial communications and the exploitation of oil concessions. Between 1892 and 1939 the British, with a few exceptions, maintained their traditional policy of non-interference in internal affairs.

Although the British left India in 1947, the Gulf area, an important centre for air communication, remained vital to British imperial interests, and when oil was discovered on the Coast the importance of the Trucial States was dramatically increased. This led to a fundamental change in Britain's traditional policy of non-interference, which dates from the early nineteenth century, and the British now became involved in local affairs. They established the Trucial 'Omān Scouts in 1950, the Trucial States Council in 1952, which encouraged a tendency towards union, and the Development Council in 1965, when the British were faced by Arab League activities on the Coast. In examining the few early cases of intervention before 1939, and the internal achievements and intervention in the post-war period, I have sought to understand and explain fully the growing British interests in the region.

During the fifties the British strengthened their base in Shārjah, and even more so in 1967, after their withdrawal from Aden. However, they left the Trucial States four years later and an end came to the British era of supremacy in the area.

Chapter 2, 'The Internal Changes', records the dismemberment of the Qawāsim Emirate during the nineteenth century as a result of British policy. In the early eighteenth century the Trucial Coast, influenced by a civil war in 'Omān, was divided into two parties, Himāwī and Ghāfirī. The Qawāsim family were the leaders of the Ghāfirī faction whilst the Āl Bū-Falāḥ, rulers of Abū Dhabī, were at the head of the Hināwī party. The growth of Abū Dhabī at the turn of the century prompted Britain to adopt a new policy of establishing a balance of power between the Ghāfirī group (including members of the former Qawāsim Federation) and the Banī Yās (Abū Dhabī).

This period, especially the years following the First World War, saw several economic, political and cultural changes on the Trucial Coast. The changing spirit of the time and the consequent modification of the reactions of the people and their rulers towards British policy is examined in a study of 'Abd al-Raḥmān b. Muḥammad, Head of Ḥīrah (1915–42), of Shaikh Sulṭān b. Sālim, Ruler of Rās al-Khaimah (1919–48), and of the unrest in Dubai and the opposition Movement of 1938.

In the post-war period this change accelerated and the Coast witnessed fundamental developments: the creation of Dubai Municipality, the first representative body in the area, which fulfilled the aims of the Movement of 1938 and modernised this town under Shaikh Rāshid b. Sa'īd Āl-Maktūm; secondly, the spread of modern education on the Coast, and particularly in Shārjah, as a result of Egyptian, Kuwaiti, Qaṭarī and Sa'ūdī activities in this field; thirdly, this genuine awakening, in addition to the spread of Arab nationalism, soon influenced political thinking and ended the previous isolation of the Trucial Coast which, since the fifties and especially after the rise of Nasser, became involved in Middle East politics; fourthly, the production of oil in Abū Dhabī in 1962 and later in Dubai and Shārjah, which placed the area in a prominent position in world economic and political affairs. The Emirate of Abū Dhabī, which for various reasons had previously existed in isolation, in 1966 began its soaring development under the rule of Shaikh Zāyed b. Sulṭān. In the later 1960s this urbanisation of Abū Dhabī attracted immigrants from neighbouring countries and the population increased dramatically, as had occurred in Dubai a few years earlier. Finally the most significant internal development on the coast of 'Omān in the period was the strong desire for unification amongst the emirates, particularly after the British had in 1968 announced their decision to withdraw from the Gulf. Although Sa'ūdī Arabia and Kuwait favoured a union of nine emirates, Baḥrain and Qaṭar declared their independence early in 1971 and the United Arab Emirates was born on 2 December that year under the leadership of Shaikh Zāyed b. Sulṭān Al-Nihayyān.

In this second chapter I have paid special attention to the political thinking of the inhabitants and particularly to their attitude towards the British and their policy. This local point of view has been almost completely neglected by non-Arab historians, partly, no doubt, because they had no real access to local sources that would have enabled them to document local attitudes. It may be noted that British policy throughout the nineteenth century had consistently ignored the feelings of the people and their rulers because its main interest was focused on security at sea. However, from the turn of the century this attitude gradually changed and the feelings of the inhabitants began to be a factor in British decisions, partly, at least, as a result of the interest in Arabia taken by Indian Muslims. The increase in British interest after the establishment of the airport at Shārjah in 1932, in addition to the discovery of oil and the growth of Arab nationalism in the area in the post-war period, all contributed to the greater attention Britain then gave to local feelings.

In Chapter 3, 'The Western Neighbours of the Trucial States', I have explained the various factors that influenced British decisions. Among these were Britain's own relations with these neighbouring countries and her interests there. The Qaṭar and Ottoman dispute over al-'Udaid between 1871 and 1913 is also discussed. When in 1933 Ibn granted the oil concession of al-Ḥasā to the Americans, a settlement of Abū Dhabī frontiers with Sa'ūdī Arabia became urgent. The negotiations from 1934 to 1938 between Britain and Sa'ūdī Arabia are studied in depth because of their intrinsic importance and because of the light they have thrown on the mechanics of British policy-making in the Gulf. It is fascinating to find high-ranking diplomats and senior members of the India Office arguing about a well used by a few Bedouins.

In the early years of the post-war period Aramco resumed its exploration in the Eastern provinces of Sa'ūdī Arabia and the western part of Abū Dhabī territory, an activity which renewed the frontier problem. This led to the Buraimī dispute which took place between 1952 and 1955. However, the problem remained dormant from 1955 until 1967, when talks began, for the first time in the history of this dispute, directly between the Ruler of Abū Dhabī and King Faiṣal of Sa'ūdī Arabia, whose kingdom during this period emerged under his wise leadership into a strong regional power. After lengthy negotiations an agreement was concluded in 1975, and this protracted dispute therefore came to an end.

Chapter 4, 'Britain, Persia and the Trucial States', examines the expansion of the central government's authority over southern Persia during the Qajar Dynasty, the fall of the Qawāsim Emirate at Lingah between 1887 and 1899, Rezā Shāh's establishment of a strong central government over the Persian coast and islands, and his nationalist régime which adopted an antagonistic attitude towards the British and their previous privileges in his country. Finally, Britain's advocacy of the Qawāsim's rights over the islands of Ṣirrī, Ṭanb and Abū Mūsā, to which the failure of the negotiations of an Anglo-Persian treaty between 1929 and 1935 was largely due. The emergence of contemporary Iran under Muḥammad Rezā Shāhanshāh as a dominant regional power could be considered one of the major events in Gulf politics in the post-war period. The British, after a long period of confrontation with Iran, succeeded during the 1960s in establishing cordial relations with Shāhanshāh. In 1968, the British, keen for stability in the Gulf after their projected withdrawal and anxious to secure their economic interests in Iran and the Arabian coast, now adopted the role of mediator, trying to find an acceptable solution between Iran, Shārjah and Rās al-Khaimah over Abū Mūsā and Ṭanb Islands. Iran and Shārjah finally came to an ambiguous agreement over Abū Mūsā in which neither party acknowledged the other's sovereignty. Failing to conclude the same agreement with Rās al-Khaimah, Iran occupied the two Ṭanb Islands on 30 November 1971, the last day of British protection.

In Chapter 5, 'Britain, Muscat and the Trucial States' Boundaries', the frontiers between the Qawāsim and the Sultanate of Muscat and 'Omān at Rūs al-Jibāl and the Shimailiyyah district on the Gulf of 'Omān are discussed. British recognition of the independence of Rās al-Khaimah in 1921 and Kalbā in 1936, and Britain's refusal to recognise the independence of Fujairah are elucidated. Between the two World Wars the granting of oil concessions created an awareness of inter-state boundaries and these became crucial after the Second World War. Since the 1950s, and because of the security needs of the exploration teams of the oil companies in the interior of the Trucial States, the British became completely involved in demarcating the boundaries. In 1952 they acknowledged the independence of Fujairah, which had a long history of revolt against the Qawāsim in their bid for independence, actually attained some decades earlier. In 1954 the Foreign Office detailed Julian Walker (Assistant Political Agent, Dubai) to map the frontiers between the Sultanate of Muscat and 'Omān and the Trucial States, as well as the inter-state boundaries within the latter. Initially, the shaikhs pledged themselves to accept the arbitration of the British Government and at intervals Julian Walker worked on the frontiers until 1960. In 1958, due to his efforts, an agreement was concluded between Abū Dhabī and the Sultanate of Muscat and 'Omān. In February 1963, the Research Department at the Foreign Office drew up the first Trucial States frontier map.

The main sources for this work came from the official archives and records of governments that had an interest in the area; these were supplemented by interviews with important persons on the 'Omāni coast, as well as talks with British and American scholars and officials who had worked in the area. This necessarily involved a great deal of travelling on my part to different parts of the Trucial Coast to collect information. My work in compiling the two maps of the United Arab Emirates in 1972 and 1976 proved of great value in understanding the land and the people. Furthermore, my trip in 1969 along the Persian coast of the Gulf between Bushire and Bandar 'Abbās, and particularly to the then sparsely inhabited town on Lingah which lies on this route, was very profitable. While in Dubai I made a point of visiting the eminent Persian merchants whose fathers had emigrated to this town from the Persian coast after the first wave of migration in 1887, and I found these talks most enlightening. Amongst a total of more than fifty local interviews, two men in particular, both widely read and knowledgeable, gave me valuable information: Ibrāhīm al-Midfa' in Shārjah and Aḥmad b. Sulayyim in Dubai. Ibrāhīm al-Midfa' was the secretary to the last three rulers of Shārjah and kept a number of important family documents, amongst them the letter sent by Ṭālib Pāshā al-Naqīb. Aḥmad b. Sulayyim took part in the 'Reform Movement' of Dubai in 1938, and after spending some years in India, came back as Director of Customs and was a Minister in the United Arab Emirates.

As most of the educated young men had left the coast for Doḥah after the Second World War to find a living in the newly established Department of Education, I met them there. In Doḥah I had interviews with the poet Mubārak al-Nākhī and with Muḥammad and Aḥmad, sons of the late philanthropist 'Ali al-Maḥmūd. While working in Doḥah some years previously, I had long discussions with the late Judge Muḥammad Sa'īd b. Ghubāsh which I recorded and was able to use for this work. As the two nationalist magazines, *al-Fath*, edited by the late Muḥib al-Dīn al-Khaṭīb,[1] and *al-Shūrā*, edited by the late Muḥammad 'Alī al-Ṭāhir, both had a great influence on the young generation on the Trucial Coast during the 1930s, I visited Cairo where they were published. There I found in the files of Muḥib al-Dīn the names of the subscribers in the Trucial States, which gave an indication of the identities of those who were influenced by nationalist ideas. I was most fortunate in meeting the late Muhammad 'Alī al-Ṭāhir in Beirut, where he spent his last years, and he provided me with a list of subscribers among whom I found the names of the same people of the Trucial Coast recorded in *al-Fatḥ* files. In Abū Dhabī I also met 'Alī al-Tājir, who knows the Coast well and has visited it frequently since 1938. It was on this local information that my study of the changes in the economy, the political attitudes and the development of culture was mainly based.

To complete this picture I went to the American Mission in Baḥrain, where I was advised to visit the Theological Seminary Library of the Reformed Church of America at New Brunswick, New Jersey. There I read their annual reports and quarterly magazines, which provided me with a wide range of information on the internal changes and social life of the Trucial Coast. In California I had long talks with Professor G. Rentz, an authority on the Arabian peninsula, particularly in the post-war period, and previously head of Aramco's Relations Department. He kindly arranged for me to meet two people Dr Phebe A. Marr, who has a wide knowledge and experience of the Gulf, and Mr Fred A. Davies, who worked in Baḥrain and al-Ḥasā in the early 1930s. He also advised me to see Mr Daniel Van der Meulen, former Dutch Minister to Sa'ūdī Arabia, whom I met in Grossel, Holland, and who provided me with useful background information regarding the life and activities of King Ibn Sa'ūd.

Finally, I had the privilege of meeting some important British people. In London I had a long talk with Sir William Luce (Political Resident in the Gulf between 1960 and 1966 in addition to his official mission in the Gulf before British withdrawal). At Oxford I met Sir Geoffrey Arthur (the last British Political Resident in the Gulf) and in Cambridge I met Julian Walker, who was on research leave In frequent discussions with the latter concerning the Foreign Office's map I was able to enrich my knowledge of the area. In the United Arab Emirates I met Mr Edward Henderson, an expert on frontier questions, particularly the Buraimī dispute; Major M. Budd, who served in the Trucial 'Omān Levies, the Trucial 'Omān Scouts and the Union Defence Force for twenty years; Dr D. G. McCaully, who was Director of the al-Maktūm Hospital in Dubai from 1949–64; and Mr J. Briggs, who commanded the Police Force in Dubai from 1959–75 and is now adviser to this force. In Baḥrain I talked to Captain Alan Bodger, who has managed Gulf Air for the last eighteen years.

As I have mentioned before, the main data was to be found in the official archives. Accordingly I visited Paris, Istanbul, Bonn and Washington. In addition, I had the opportunity of consulting the three volumes *Shārjah Title to the Island of Abū Mūsā*, written by M. E. Bathurst and Howard Chance (solicitors of the Supreme Court) in September 1971, and submitted to the late Shaikh Khālid b. Muḥammad, Ruler of Shārjah.

The interests of the Ottomans, the French and the Germans, which I found recorded in their archives, were all concentrated on the period which preceded the First World War. In addition to providing useful information on the tribes and on Turkish relations with the Trucial States, the Ottoman archives focus chiefly on the regard of the inhabitants for them as a great Muslim power. French activities in the Gulf were centred in Muscat, from where they obtained their information on the 'Omāni coast, whilst the German Consul in Bushire was the main source of information on this area for the Foreign Ministry in Berlin. Both French and German archives pay particular attention to local reactions to British policies on the Trucial Coast, something which is very important to our study, especially as it is not clear enough in the British records. In the archives in Bonn there was an extensive collection of cuttings from the press in India, Britain, France, Russia and Germany, which was very helpful in reflecting the different attitudes of the major powers towards events in the Gulf. On the other hand, the Americans had no interest in the region before the First World War. Their interest developed gradually between the two World Wars, and they were primarily concerned with oil questions, British policy in the Middle East and the Arab nationalist movement. Moreover, their reports in this period came from their consuls in Baghdād, Tehran, Aden and Cairo, all very remote from the Trucial Coast and therefore lacking complete accuracy. However, as their involvement in Gulf politics and economy expanded dramatically in the post-war period their reports became increasingly abundant and well-informed.

In fact, the diaries and reports written by the Residency Agent at Shārjah and the Political Resident at Bushire, which covered the main part of the period up to 1947 and which were kept in the India Office Library in London, constitute the main sources for this study. This wealth of historical material is unique both in being written on the spot and in having an official stamp.

However, it still represents the British point of view and needs to be balanced by local data. I found further valuable information on the inter-war period in the archives of the Public Record Office in London. At this time the developing British interests in the Gulf and the different crucial issues that emerged had increased the attention paid to the area by the Foreign Office, the Colonial Office and the Committee of Imperial Defence. Much of the rich information on the Trucial Coast was recorded in the Foreign Office files on Arabia and Persia. Also, in the files of the CID I found useful information recorded in the meetings of the Persian Gulf and the Official Middle East Sub-Committees (see Chapter 1, pp. 42, 44).

I hope that I have been able to explain the main features of the history of the United Arab Emirates between 1892 and 1971, particularly the increasing significance of the 'Omāni Coast in British Imperial interests, as well as explaining the interactions of internal affairs with the Sa'ūdi, Iranian and British policies. It would be of great satisfaction to the author if this work might in the future attract the attention of other scholars to the issues which it treats, and on which they may be able to throw further light.

M. Morsy Abdullah,
Abū Dhabī, February 1978.

Note

1. Muḥib al-Dīn al-Khatīb died in 1970 in Cairo and Muḥammad Alī al-Ṭāhir died in 1974 in Beirut.

1 The Trucial States and British Imperial Interests

I British Diplomacy in the Period of International Challenge, 1892–1918

II The Growth of British Interests between the Two World Wars

III The End of the British Imperalistic Era

1 The Trucial States and British Imperial Interests

I British Diplomacy in the Period of International Challenge, 1892–1918

The Exclusive Treaty of 1892

The British first came to the Gulf at the beginning of the seventeenth century. They came as traders, representing the East India Company, and for two centuries were entirely involved in peaceful commercial activity, centred mainly on Bandar 'Abbās and Bushire on the Persian coast, and Basṣrah in the Wilāyet of Baghdād. The military and political presence of the British in the area began only as an indirect result of the attack on their ships by Qawāsim zealots at the beginning of the nineteenth century. This brought about the British expedition of 1819 against Qawāsim ports on the coast of 'Omān, followed by the conclusion of the General Treaty of 1820 with the shaikhs of this coast, who undertook to refrain from piracy.[1]

In 1823 the first local Residency Agent was appointed in Shārjah to report to the British Political Resident in Bushire on affairs on this coast.[2] The conclusion of several treaties (1839, 1847, 1856) to abolish the slave trade on the Coast of 'Omān increased British involvement in the affairs of this area. In 1853 the British concluded the Perpetual Maritime Peace with local rulers, and the area, which had hitherto been referred to as the 'Pirate Coast', now became known in British official documents as the Trucial Coast.[3]

From this foothold in 'Omān British political and military power during the second half of the century extended northwest to Baḥrain and Kuwait. The principal purpose of British vigilance and control in the Trucial States was to secure a peaceful passage for their trade, which was concentrated mainly on the Persian coast, and in the 1870s the trade flourished after telegraph lines, postal and steamer services had been established there. During this period the supply of Indian goods to the Trucial Coast depended mainly on the port of Lingah, where the British steamship lines called regularly. Here, and particularly at Shārjah, Dubai, Rās al-Khaimah and Abū Dhabī a few Indian traders who were British subjects began to settle.[4]

The gradual development of British supremacy in the Gulf in the second half of the century elicited an antagonistic reaction from the two local powers, Persia and Ottoman. This did not disturb the British unduly, but when in the 1890s the French, the Russians and the Germans entered the field the British were for the first time aware of a threat to their long-standing supremacy. Lorimer, in his official Indian Government *Gazeteer*, connected the treaty of 1892 with Ottoman designs against the British in the Gulf after 1871, with Persian activities in 1887 and in particular with French interference in the Trucial States in 1890.[5]

In May 1871 the Ottomans had occupied al-Ḥasā and extended their influence to Qaṭar. Although the Turks had defined the aim of this expedition as only to restore the Sultan's power over Nejd, the British authorities in India were made increasingly uneasy by the Ottoman claims and by rumours of their sovereignty over the Trucial Coast, which had preceded and now followed this invasion. These suspicions were confirmed in June 1871, when the latest issue of the official Baghdād *Gazette* listed Baḥrain and eight towns in Trucial 'Omān as being part of the province of Nejd.[6] It was not only Turkish expansionism and the presence of Ottoman warships in the Gulf which disturbed the British; the Turkish attitude towards the Indian Government's engagements and treaties with the Trucial Coast also gave cause for disquiet. In the same month the British Ambassador in Constantinople, in response to a request from the India Office, furnished the Turkish Government with a copy of British treaties with the Arab chiefs of the Gulf, and the Turks refused to recognise or be bound by them[7] (an attitude which continued until 1913, when the Anglo-Ottoman Convention was signed). The troubles which ensued over al-'Udaid between the Shaikh of Abū Dhabī and the Shaikh of Qaṭar, who was encouraged by the Ottomans, in addition to an increasing tendency on the part of the latter to correspond directly with Shaikh Zāyed b. Khalīfah, ruler of Abū Dhabī, convinced the British of the need to review their previous relations and treaties with the Trucial shaikhs and to establish closer ties with them.[8]

A second factor which underlined the need for a new treaty with the Trucial States emerged in 1887, when the British authorities in the Gulf were annoyed by vigorous Persian political activities at Baḥrain, Qaṭar and the Trucial Coast. It was one of the major plans of the newly appointed Derya Begi (the Governor-General of the Gulf ports), Amīn al-Sulṭān, and carried out jointly by his representative at Bushire, Ḥājjī Aḥmad Khān, and his tax collector, Malik al-Tujjār. At the beginning of August 1887, Ross, the Political Resident, was engaged, on instructions from the British Minister to Tehran, in observing the visit of Baḥrain of Malik al-Tujjār, who informed him that Malik's superior, Amīn al-Sulṭān, was an ambitious man and that Malik's visit to Baḥrain could create trouble for the British. Whilst in Baḥrain, Ross received information that Ḥājjī Aḥmad Khān was visiting the Trucial Coast in the steamer *Khalder* of the Bombay & Persian Navigation Company. The Political Resident's steamer *Lawrence* was immediately despatched with the first Assistant Resident to Abū Dhabī, to observe the movements of Ḥājjī Khān in an attempt to ascertain his purpose. Ḥājjī Aḥmad remained with Shaikh Zāyed b. Khalīfah for a few days, after which he went to Dubai to express his condolences at the death of Shaikh Ḥashr and then returned to Abū Dhabī. He sailed directly to Lingah and arrived there on 13 September.[9]

The Residency Agent, Ḥājjī Abū al-Qāsim, was unable to give the captain of the *Lawrence* any details of Ḥājjī Aḥmad Khān's meetings with the shaikhs of Abū Dhabī and Dubai, which had been held in complete secrecy; it was revealed afterwards that they had sworn on the Qur'an to keep them highly confidential. It was not until the end of September that the first intimation of what had taken place came to the attention of the British authorities through the Sultan of Muscat, who passed it on to the British Political Agent. According to a letter about the visit from Shaikh Rāshid b. Maktūm to the Sultan of Muscat dated 14 September 1887, Ḥājjī Aḥmad Khān persuaded the Shaikh to accept a Persian agent on the same footing as the British Residency Agent. Hājjī Aḥmad's intention was that the chiefs of Abū Dhabī and Dubai would denounce the influence of the Christians, meaning the British, and bring their people under Persian authority. Shaikh Rāshid refused absolutely to discuss this with him and declined to give him an interview even in the private house of b. Dalmūk, an eminent and rich merchant in Dubai.[10] These facts provoked Ross's suspicion, but the probability of a Russian design behind the visit caused great concern. Precautions had been taken by Colonel Ross in December 1887 against Ottoman and Persian activities, obtaining from the shaikhs of the Trucial coast a written assurance that they would on no account correspond with or enter into an agreement with any government whatsoever, except the British, and that they would not, without the consent of the British Government, allow an agent of any other government to reside in their land.[11]

However, immediate provocation made it a matter of urgency to attach the shaikhs of Trucial 'Omān to the British Government by new and more stringent obligations. Two Frenchmen appeared on the Coast in 1891, whose motives were suspected of being political: one of them, a M. Chapuy, was described by Lorimer as 'half adventurer, half merchant and wholly intriguer'. The two Frenchmen visited the Shaikh of Umm al-Qaiwain three times, bringing gifts; the Shaikh was convinced of the advantages of flying the French flag, as did the Banī Bū-'Alī's tribe in Ṣūr, and he agreed to write a letter to the French Government, promising a good reception in his land for French citizens. Responding to this critical situation, Major Talbot, the new British Political Resident in the Gulf, suggested to the Government of India in November 1891 the conclusion of a formal agreement on the lines of the written assurance of December 1887, and this having been approved by the Government, an Exclusive Treaty was signed on various dates in March 1892 with the Trucial Shaikhs. The shaikhs bound themselves, their heirs and their successors to abide by the assurances of 1887, and undertook on no account to cede, sell, mortgage or otherwise give for occupation any part of their territory save to the British Government.[12] This treaty became the main pillar of British authority on the Trucial Coast and was to serve as a model for agreements signed in due course by the Shaikhs of Baḥrain, Kuwait and Qaṭar. (Turkish, Sa'ūdī and Persian activities on the Trucial Coast during this period will be discussed in detail in Chapters 3 and 4.)

The Effect of Foreign Rivalry on British Policy on the Coast

In the years from 1892 to 1914 the Gulf area became the scene of intense rivalry between the major European powers. The French, the Germans and the Russians not only sought free access for their commercial enterprises (as the Japanese and Americans were to do in the war-weary atmosphere of 1918–39 without exciting British hostility); they went further and challenged the British right to treat the Gulf politically as a 'British lake'. What especially aroused British anxiety at home and in India was the fact that all three powers were suspected by the British of attempting to establish naval bases in the Gulf; the French at Bandar Jiṣṣah in 1898, the Russians at Shahbār on the Persian coast in the late 1890s, and the Germans at their Baghdād Railway terminus at Kuwait, or at Baṣrah, in 1900. By firmness and diplomacy, as well as some coercive measures in the Gulf, the British contrived to emerge completely victorious. France in 1904, Russia in 1907 and Germany in 1912, all signed agreements formally recognising British supremacy in the area, and in 1913 the Ottomans followed suit.[13]

This struggle had an immediate effect on British policy on the Trucial Coast. This area had always, since the early nineteenth century, been intimately bound up with the safety of the British Empire in India. Now, when major European powers were seeking naval bases in the Gulf, this 500-kilometre stretch of coast, commanding the entrance to the Gulf and with numerous islands, acquired a greater strategic importance. The task of preventing the other powers from gaining any political, or even commercial, foothold on this coast entailed an increase in vigilance and supervision. The British were represented at Shārjah by their Residency Agent, Khān Bahādur 'Abd al-Laṭīf (1890–1919), who reported directly to the Political Resident in Bushire.[14] At the turn of the century British control in the Gulf produced some confusion in British machinery since the Political Resident was corresponding with two departments, the Foreign Office and the India Office;[15] as regards purely local affairs the Trucial Coast came under the jurisdiction of the Government of India, which had to consult the Foreign Office about relations of the Coast with Persia and the Ottomans. The differences of opinion and attitude between the Foreign Office and the India Office in the pre-1914 period will emerge repeatedly in this study. After 1902, when the Committee of Imperial Defence was established to form the missing link between the military and civil authorities, it also had its say; in 1904–5 it dealt with the strategic importance of the Musandam peninsula to Britain, and the Cabinet implemented its recommendations.[16]

During this contentious period affairs in the Gulf were influenced by three important British personalities: Lansdowne in London, Curzon in India and Cox in the Bushire Residency. Lansdowne was Viceroy in India from 1888–94 and Secretary for Foreign Affairs between 1900 and 1905.[17] The 'Lansdowne Declaration' of 5 May 1903 was a landmark in the British policy of firmness, as a positive threat to other powers and one to which they promptly yielded, and in the House of Lords, during a debate on the Baghdād Railway, Lansdowne laid down the broad lines of British policy: 'I say without hesitation, we should regard the establishment of a naval base or of a fortified port in the Persian Gulf by any other power as a very grave menace to British interests, and we should certainly resist it with all means at our disposal.'[18]

Curzon, Viceroy of India from 1899–1905, was an expert on Gulf affairs, of whom Lorimer said that he 'courted rather than feared responsibility', and that his methods were 'rapid and energetic'.[19] During his five years in India he frustrated French designs in Muscat in 1899, and arranged the signing of an Exclusive Treaty with Kuwait. In 1901 he was strongly in favour of declaring the Trucial Coast a British Protectorate, but as no serious foreign interference transpired in this area the idea was not suggested to the Foreign Office and the plan did not materialise.[20] In the same year he requested permission to visit the Gulf as a show of power, in answer to the visits of the Russian and French warships, and was finally given approval later in 1903; he then proceeded in the cruiser *Argonaut*, the largest ship to visit the Gulf before the First World War, accompanied by a flotilla of seven warships. On 18 November he inspected the inlets of the Musandam peninsula, which he considered of vital strategic importance in guarding the entrance to the Gulf. On 23 November he visited the Trucial States, where near Shārjah he received the shaikhs on board and addressed them with a speech in which he outlined the British policy of maintaining the *status quo*;

> If any internal disputes occur, you will always find a friend in the British Resident, who will use his influence, as he has frequently done in the past, to prevent these dissensions from coming to a head, and to maintain the *status quo*, for we could not approve of one independent Chief attacking another Chief by land, simply because he has not been permitted to do it by sea, and thus evading the spirit of his treaty obligations.[21]

Cox, Political Agent in Muscat from 1899–1904 and afterwards Political Resident in Bushire until 1914, may be considered as the ablest British representative in the Gulf. He helped to engineer the positive British policy and set it in motion, as will be seen repeatedly in this study.

French Activities Although none of the apparent threats from France, Russia and Germany were directed immediately at the Trucial Coast, their effects, as regards British reactions and policy, were felt mainly in that area.

French activities in the Gulf were centred in the Sultanate of Muscat. French citizenship and the French flag were granted to the inhabitants of Ṣūr; the French attempted to establish a coal depot in Bandar Jiṣṣah, south of Muscat, for their maritime line; they conducted extensive anti-British propaganda; and they played a large part in the flourishing arms trade in Muscat. The principal aim of the French in all four activities was to undermine British influence and extend their own.[22]

In 1894 the French reopened their consulate in Muscat, and Ottavi, their consul, established intimate relations with the Sultan, Faiṣal b. Turkī. It seems that the rupture in Muscat's relations with Britain between 1895 and 1899, due to French activities, had a direct effect on Zāyed b. Khalīfah, the close friend of Sultan Faiṣal b. Turkī, whose disaffection from Britain he began to share (see p. 99).

At the turn of the century Goguyer, a French ex-diplomat in Tunisia who knew Arabic well, established himself in Muscat and traded in arms. He became a nuisance to the British, writing fierce articles against them in the Paris paper *Dépêche Coloniale*. A secret bulletin sponsored by the French Foreign Ministry and called *Fatḥ al-Baṣāyer* ('Opening the Eyes') which later, in 1902, took the name *Murshid al-'Albāb* ('the guide of thoughts'), was circulated by post in the Gulf, India and the Trucial Coast, stirring up religious feeling against Britain. Also, *al-'Ahrām* specifically described by Lorimer as a pro-French Egyptian daily newspaper, shared in this campaign against British activities in the Gulf.[23] Although the campaign died gradually after the Anglo-French Entente of 1904, in which France recognised British supremacy in the Gulf, the resentment it had bred on the Coast continued and was to play a role in the 'Dubai Incident' of 1910 (see p. 33).

The French arms trade had far-reaching consequences in the affairs of Muscat and the Trucial Coast. It had begun in the 1880s and was originally handled by British and French companies; in the 1890s Muscat became its chief centre in the Middle East. In 1898 the British realised that the arms trade there was directly connected with the troubles on the Afghān–Indian border, so they advised the Sultan to establish an official force to control the traffic. Though the British firms were obliged to cease such trading the French merchants, especially Goguyer, increased their business, and as Goguyer was backed by French newspapers and some influential politicians of the Colonial Party in Paris, the trade continued until 1914, regardless of Britain's blockade of the Gulf between 1907 and 1913 and her constant protests to the French. The French tolerated arms trading in the Gulf because of a similar British trade in Morocco, which allowed the infiltration of weapons through the Algerian frontiers.[24]

Russian Activities The scene of Russian activities in the area up to 1890 was Persia, particularly its northern region, and throughout the nineties Russia showed signs of increasing interest in the Gulf and of anti-British activity in co-operation with the French. A Russian warship visited the Gulf for the first time in 1893, but what annoyed the British was the visit of Russian engineers to Bandar 'Abbās in 1895 to survey a possible rail route and terminus. In 1897 the Russians attempted to establish a coal depot in Bandar 'Abbās, but the British contrived to prevent this. Russian warships continued to visit the Gulf in 1901 and 1902, and in 1903 they were accompanied by French warships. The most important Russian enterprise was the short-lived Odessa Maritime Line, founded in 1903 by the Russian Government to connect that city with the Gulf ports.

This show of naval power at the turn of the century was to have its effect on British policy in the Lansdowne declaration and in Curzon's visit to the Gulf, both in 1903. The first immediate repercussion as regards the Trucial Coast, however, was a growing British awareness of the need to prevent any foreign power from establishing a commanding position at the entrance to the Gulf, and consequently of the strategic importance of the Musandam peninsula. As early as 1900 the question of acquiring naval bases and telegraph stations on the Musandam peninsula, to meet possible Russian aggression in these waters, had been raised in British official circles, and on 23 October 1902 the Government of India proposed that the old telegraph buildings at Elphinstone Inlet should be reoccupied by a native agent in charge of a British flag, and that the strip of coast between Dabā and Khūr Kalbā should be recognised as part of the territory of the chief of Shārjah. The Government of India explained that 'it had long been the policy to regard the territory [Musandam] as being under the sovereignty of the sultan of Muscat', but the establishment of a rival influence by the French at Muscat made it 'questionable whether it would not be expedient to treat the territory as independent'. This issue became a subject of discussion at the meetings of the Committee of Imperial Defence and much correspondence between the Foreign Office, the India Office and the Admiralty. In February 1903, with the concurrence of the Foreign Office and the Admiralty, the India Office informed the Government of India that HM Government 'agree that steps may be taken, when an opportunity occurs, of acting without attracting special attention, to re-occupy the old telegraph building at the Elphinstone Inlet.'[25]

As a result of Curzon's tour in the Gulf at the end of 1903, the Government of India, in a secret despatch of 21 January 1904, recommended the selection of suitable naval bases or coaling stations at the entrance to the Gulf. Fearing that a large Russian fleet, which was known to be in the vicinity on its way to the Far East, might enter the Gulf, the Government of India decided to erect the flagstaffs. Nothing was said, therefore, to the Sultan of Muscat, and Lieutenant Shakespear, the newly appointed Acting British Consul at Bandar 'Abbās, was entrusted with the task instead of the British Consul at Muscat. Shakespear accompanied the Captain of HMS *Sphynx* on 21 November 1904 and flagstaffs were erected at Elphinstone Inlet, Telegraph Island and al-

Ghanam Island. However, during the Russo–Japanese conflict in the Far East, the question of these flagstaffs was reconsidered by the Committee of Imperial Defence in its meeting on 23 February 1905, and the recommendation was made that 'the flagstaff on Telegraph Island might be maintained as a sign of continued occupation. One of HM ships should occasionally visit the island for this purpose and no flags to be hoisted'.[26] The Government of India was authorised to remove the two flagstaffs at Elphinstone Inlet and al-Ghanam Island and this was done in October 1905. The Russian threat, like the French, had not lasted long. The Anglo–Japanese treaty of 1902 and the Anglo–French Entente of 1904, in addition to the Japanese defeat of Russia at Port Arthur, all facilitated a British–Russian understanding and the conclusion of the treaty in 1907, by which Russia recognised British supremacy in the Gulf.[27]

The second immediate effect on the Trucial Coast of Russian activities during the period of challenge before 1907 was the positive policy which the British adopted towards attempted Persian expansion into the Trucial States. Simultaneously with their abortive attempts to gain a footing in the Gulf, the Russians had succeeded in acquiring an ever-growing influence in Teheran. For this reason the British continued to see the hand of Russia behind Persian activities on the Trucial Coast (see Chapter 4, p. 245).

German Activities German interests in the Gulf came from two directions: from East Africa, where they had a colony for the first time in 1884, and from the Ottoman Empire, which offered one of the best spheres for their enterprises and expansion.[28] These interests lay in the Baghdād Railway project, in the German firm of Wonkhaus and the Hamburg–Amerika Steam Navigation Company. The Germans were granted the Baghdād Railway concession in 1898. This project became an issue between the British and the Germans when the latter chose Kuwait as its terminus, and the British promptly reacted by concluding the Exclusive Treaty of 1899 with Kuwait. After lengthy negotiations between 1902 and 1911, Germany and Britain came to an agreement over the railway, according to which the line had to end at Başrah and the British became joint owners of the company.[29]

Adding to the British fears of German intrigue were the activities of the firm of Robert Wonkhaus, which had been founded in East Africa and had established a branch at Lingah in 1897 to trade in mother of pearl. Through energetic management it expanded rapidly and Cox viewed it and its agents with grave suspicion. When a member of the firm was assaulted in Baḥrain in 1903 he acted at once to forestall any German pretext at intervention.[30] The British in the Gulf, from Cox down to the clerks of commercial houses, believed that the Wonkhaus firm was not merely an energetic business rival but a direct representative of German political imperialism. When in 1906 the Hamburg–Amerika Line, one of the biggest of the steamship companies, extended its services to the Gulf, thus offering a serious challenge to a long-standing British monopoly, Wonkhaus became its agent, and the British press in London and India launched a bitter attack upon the company. The *Times of India* claimed, 'no one will be so foolish as to imagine that the decision to run a line to the Persian Gulf is based on commercial principles'; to the editor 'the purpose was entirely political',[31] fully backed by the German State and connected with the Baghdād railway issue. It was in this climate that Wonkhaus acquired a red oxide concession on Abū Mūsā Island in 1906.

In 1898 Shaikh Ṣaqr b. Khālid, ruler of Shārjah, departed on a pilgrimage, entrusting the administration of his emirate to his uncle, Sālim b. Sulṭān; while he was away Sālim granted a concession to mine red oxide on Abū Mūsā island to Ḥasan Sumaiḥ and his son 'Abdullah, who both lived at Lingah and claimed to be British subjects, and to their partner 'Abd al-Laṭīf, the Residency Agent at Shārjah. In the original agreement, which was drafted by 'Abdullah Ḥasan, Sālim was mentioned as the owner of Abū Mūsā island. On his return from pilgrimage, Shaikh Ṣaqr was informed of the concession, which he confirmed, granting the annual concession rent to Sālim.[32] For the first few years the project remained a local matter, but the business assumed a wider significance in British circles when on 1 June 1906 the sales manager, Ḥasan Sumaiḥ, entered into a contract with Wonkhaus to deliver from 2,000 to 3,000 tons of red oxide per year for four years, during which time Wonkhaus was to have the entire monopoly of the product, with the option of renewing the contract when it lapsed. Ḥasan kept the transaction secret, and it was not until 16 December 1906 that, after repeated requests, he sent a copy to his partner 'Abd al-Laṭīf, who now found himself in a very embarrassing position. 'Abd al-Laṭīf immediately notified Cox and the Shaikh of Shārjah of the situation, asserting that he had had no complicity in the contract.

As soon as Cox had received 'Abd al-Latīf's news about the Wonkhaus contract he expected trouble. The red oxide of Abū Mūsā would be a suitable excuse for German interference and would have made an ideal freight for the steamers of Hamburg–Amerika Line, which arrived in the Gulf laden with construction material destined for the Baghdād railway but lacked return cargoes. Moreover, if Abū Mīsā proved to be commercially valuable, new claims to sovereignty might be made by Persia. Cox sent a message to Shaikh Ṣaqr reminding him of his treaty pledges and on 21 February 1907 the Shaikh accordingly cancelled Ḥasan Sumaiḥ's concession. On 27 August Cox was instructed by the Government of India, on his own recommendation, to warn the Trucial Shaikhs that the grant of a concession of any sort to mine or otherwise exploit any portion of their territory was considered as falling within the scope of Article III of the treaty of 1892.[33]

Ḥasan Sumaiḥ and Wonkhaus denied Shaikh Ṣaqr's right to terminate the concession, for Ḥasan Sumaiḥ claimed that the grant had been made by the Shaikh's uncle, the original owner of Abū Mūsā island, so he continued to work the mines, ignoring the cancellation. Shaikh Ṣaqr delivered a final order to Ḥasan Sumaiḥ that all work on the island was to cease within a period of ten days, i.e. by 3 October 1907, and Cox meanwhile obtained the approval of the Government of India to remove Ḥasan Sumaiḥ's workmen by force. On 22 October Lt Gabriel, Vice-Consul of Bandar 'Abbās, arrived at Abū Mūsā on board the *Lapwing*, with several dhows in tow, filled with Shaikh Ṣaqr's men. Sumaiḥ's men, numbering nearly 100, were removed to Lingah and their huts destroyed.

This incident produced great excitement in British and German newspapers. The first official German reaction was to send the Dragoman of their Bushire Consulate, Mirzā Ḥusain, to Shārjah, where he told the Shaikh on 28 November 1907 that Germany could not recognise the cancellation and threatened him with serious repercussions – a heavy claim for compensation. To avoid Persian interference, the negotiations over this dispute with the Germans were handled in London and not in Tehran. The case now entered a lengthy period of claim and counter-claim, with the exchange of supporting evidence and relevant documents, and the principle of compensation was eventually agreed upon in 1914, some months before the outbreak of the war. The determination of the actual amount was further postponed, as no compromise had been reached between the Board of Trade's £2,000 and Wonkhaus' £6,000. The war brought an end to further negotiations and Wonkhaus received no compensation at all.[34]

Arms Traffic, the Tightening of British Control, and the Dubai Incident of 1910

At the turn of the century the British met with resentment from the inhabitants of the coast of 'Omān. The British arms blockade in the Gulf was misinterpreted by the Arabs as being directed to the gradual disarmament of Arabia, with a view to its ultimate occupation and partition. They had no idea of the reasons which had compelled the British to enforce the blockade and would not in any case have been in sympathy with them. They could not understand why the arms traffic was untouched by the British in Muscat, where it was protected by treaties with foreign powers, while it was strictly prohibited in Dubai, where there was no such shield. The British for their part failed to understand that 'to the Arab his rifle is by far his dearest possession . . . because it is to him the only security for his life and property'. Arab irritation increased when in 1910 the British sent an armed vessel to patrol their coast. Anti-British feeling was aggravated by the French press campaign and Ottoman's Pan-Islamic propaganda. An American, the Reverend S. M. Zwemer, who visited the Gulf that year, attributed the anti-British feeling on the coast of 'Omān largely to the Egyptian newspapers *al-Mu'ayyad* and *al-Liwā* (brought by the BISN Company from Cairo to Dubai via Bombay) which had been inculcating in the population of Arabia a belief that the partition of Persia was soon to be followed by the partition of Arabia.[35]

The Dubai incident of December 1910 (since the turn of the century Dubai had grown into a major commercial and political centre) was ostensibly a matter of traffic in arms alone, but it involved wider economic and political issues, in particular the growth of British interests in this port and Britain's need at this period to tighten her control over the Trucial Coast in order to face international challenge. The incident also reflected a build-up of ill-feeling on both sides, the Arabs in Dubai and the British, represented by Cox and the captains of the blockade fleet. Cox's feeling towards the people and the Shaikh of Dubai were by 1910 distinctly sore: he had been repeatedly frustrated in his attempts to install there a British Political Officer, a telegraph station and a post office, the need for which was urgent because of increasing British interests in the town and the necessity of tightening political and administrative control over the coast of Omān in the face of the threat from other world powers, as had been done on the Persian coast at Bandar 'Abbās and Muḥammarah, and in Kuwait and Baḥrain on the Arabian side of the Gulf. Cox, in his report of 6 June 1908, after reviewing the existing British administrative arrangements in the Gulf, advocated the establishment of a Vice-Consulate at Lingah to meet the German activities of the Wonkhaus Company and to pay visits to the Coast of 'Omān when necessary. He wrote, 'The experience of the last two or three years makes me doubt whether it is safe to leave these backward Shaikhs longer in the charge of a native agent.'[36]

When in August 1910, at the time of Cox's tour of the coast, 'Abd al-Laṭīf the Residency Agent was about to retire owing to ill-health, some of the British Indians in Dubai expressed a wish for a British successor, but Shaikh Buṭī b. Suhail, ruler of Dubai (1906–12), consistently rejected Cox's approaches. Cox described him as 'less enlightened' and always difficult to deal with because he usually discussed Cox's proposals with his 'troublesome' relatives and advisers. When Cox received information in November 1910 that the coast of 'Omān had become the forwarding base for arms, he felt the time was ripe to renew his demand for the acceptance of a British Political Agent of Dubai. Anticipating the Shaikh of Dubai's objection to his proposed Agent, Mr New, Cox decided to take with him for moral support one of HM ships from the large fleet already in the Gulf to blockade the arms traffic. Mr New was on the point of leaving for Dubai with Cox and Rear-Admiral Slade, Senior Naval Officer, when the Dubai incident occurred and upset all of Cox's calculations.[37]

In 1910 Rear-Admiral Slade and his captains were much annoyed by the news that Dubai had become a centre of arms traffic; British warships had almost completely blocked the traffic by sea from Muscat to the ports of Balūchistān and Persia, and enterprising dealers had evolved another route. Camels with arms and ammunition were sent overland from Maṭrah to the Trucial Coast, to Abū Dhabī, Dubai and Shārjah, whence they were shipped by native craft to Persia and Qaṭar. Cox observed that it was to the recently arrived shopkeepers, immigrants from Lingah and now living in Dubai, that the British were indebted for this troublesome traffic. A continual stream of caravans carrying rice from the newly emerging port of Dubai to the hinterland of 'Omān, was laden with arms on the return trip, and the Trucial Coast took over from Muscat as the principal arms distributing centre.

To stop this new leakage caused the British great trouble. They had devoted four years of strenuous effort, in an exhausting climate, in the attempt to stamp out the traffic and were being driven to increasingly desperate measures, such as burning dhows proved to have been used for gun-running. Slade now gave instructions that contraband arms in Dubai must be seized, with or without the Shaikh's assistance. One small incident on 20 December 1910 not only increased the Arab's misunderstanding of the British arms blockade, but heightened the mistrust and tension between the two sides. Lt. Noakes RN, at the head of a boat party patrolling the coast at Dubai, called upon Shaikh Buṭī b. Suhail to ask his permission and co-operation in searching various houses for arms. Unaware of Muslim tradition in Dubai of the sanctity of an Arab house and of the awkward position in which he therefore placed the Shaikh as an Arab ruler, Noakes thought that the Shaikh's hesitation was a means of delaying a search while the arms were removed. Finally he was allowed to make a perfunctory search, which proved fruitless and served only to provoke further hatred and antagonism on both sides.

On 23 December 1910 Captain J. V. Dick of HMS *Hyacinth* heard the story of this incident from Lt. Noakes and was angered by it. He further received intelligence that a consignment of arms had arrived in Dubai and was stored in the houses of Aḥmad b. Dalmūk and Thānī b. Khalaf. Dick 'decided that it was my duty to endeavour to find them and that the only prospect of success lay in immediate action'. On 24 December, therefore, relying on the general instructions of Rear-Admiral Slade, without waiting for authorisation and disregarding the considerable risk involved, Dick landed with a strong armed party of 100 men in the early morning to search the two houses. He notified the Shaikh of his intention and forty men went to Aḥmad b. Dalmūk's house and sixty proceeded to Thānī b. Khalaf's. As Captain Dick insisted on searching the two houses a serious fight broke out. Ten Arabs were killed and five injured in front of Thānī b. Khalaf's house, while two were killed at b. Dalmūk's. The British lost five men and nine were injured. To cover the retreat of the British landing party several shells were fired from HMS *Hyacinth*, killing a further twenty-five Arabs and damaging numerous buildings.

At this stage the Shaikh interfered, but it was only with difficulty that he stopped the fighting, which could have turned into a massacre. The *Hyacinth* hastened to Bushire to give a report, arriving on 26 December. The Shaikh ordered the tide pole, erected by Captain Dick on his landing to be pulled down.[38]

When Cox and Rear-Admiral Slade arrived in Dubai on 28 December 1910 with the two warships *Odin* and *Lawrence* and the *Hyacinth*, the town was in a state of panic and the people anticipated immediate hostilities. At the beginning the Shaikh refused to come aboard on seeing Cox's flag until he had received a safe conduct in writing.

The Shaikh repudiated Dick's assertion of his complicity and accused the landing party of having begun hostilities. He refused to re-erect the pole and insistently refused to receive a British Officer as Resident's Agent at Dubai. The Rear-Admiral and Cox agreed that political, commercial and arms traffic requirements demanded the appointment of a British Officer and the establishment of a post office and wireless station, and so, on 30 December 1910, a six-point ultimatum, expiring in forty-eight hours, was presented to the Shaikh in writing demanding:

1. The immediate replacement of the tide pole.
2. The acceptance of telegraph installations.
3. The delivery of 400 serviceable rifles.
4. Payment of Rs. 50,000 as a fine.
5. Acceptance of a British Officer as Agent, together with a small personal guard.
6. Acquiescence in the establishment of a sub-post office of the Indian Postal Department.[39]

The Shaikhs of Shārjah and Umm al-Qaiwain tried to intervene and persuade Cox to mitigate the terms of the ultimatum, but in vain. Meanwhile, as Cox expected the Shaikh of Dubai's council to object to the British Agent, he cabled the Government of India, asking for permission to occupy the town for a short period (after first bombarding it), and to leave Mr New later as Agent with a strong guard. The ultimate resort to bombardment was supported by Rear-Admiral Slade. Cox left for Bushire and on 1 January 1911 the Rear-Admiral reported that the Shaikh of Dubai complied with four demands but, according to the will of his people, refused to accept the British Political Agent and the telegraph station. Slade left Dubai on the 10 January 1911. By the end of February 1911, as all was still reported quiet, the armed boat stationed at Dubai was withdrawn and a coastal patrol was introduced in its place.[40]

The Dubai incident figured prominently in the English and Indian newspapers and provoked an important exchange of official correspondence. To the *Times of India* the incident came as a complete surprise. They could not understand how the Trucial Coast, which had been at peace with Britain for more than half a century and which had undergone these sobering influences of trade, should suddenly become the scene of bitter fighting. Muslim opinion in India was so sensitive to any British involvement in Arabia that the Government was forced to pay attention.

On 2 and 3 January 1911 the Government of India sent cables to Cox which condemned Captain Dick's search without the presence of the Shaikh and without authorisation. The fine demanded by the ultimatum appeared onerous and the attempt to install a British Agent by bombardment was criticised. The need to reassure the Arabs that the British had no intention of weakening their independence was stressed and Cox was instructed that 'the establishment of telegraph, post office and British Agent, should be deferred till the situation quietened'. This incident shows clearly the kind of liberties a strong naval Captain or a Political Resident could take on the grounds of the difficulty of the situation and inadequate communication. Slade, in his report to the Admiralty of 2 January, blamed the Shaikh's behaviour and stressed the need for a British Political Officer in Dubai. He suggested that if Dubai were to be coerced again a simple bombardment would not suffice to reduce a resolute enemy to submission and advised that a military force of at least 1,000 men, including artillery and sappers, should be sent to occupy the town. The whole of the pearling fleet, consisting of some 350 dhows, could easily be destroyed. Slade continued: 'it is very doubtful, however, whether the Arab would be forced by these measures to give in, and if he did not submit, all that would have been accomplished would be the destruction of a town and industry which it is to our advantage to maintain'. He concluded that in his view the operations had been 'somewhat hastily undertaken' and he had now given orders to prevent a repetition of such action without reference being made to himself or to the Political Resident at Bushire.

On 8 January 1911 Cox sent a detailed letter to the Government of India, in which he admitted that he was not prepared to maintain that Captain Dick's action, without the presence of the Shaikh, had been prudent. However, in view of the Shaikh's negligence Cox justified Captain Dick's action and had no choice but to support him in order to encourage the initiative of all the commanders of HM ships in these waters. Cox explained his failure to consult the Government before presenting an ultimatum by saying that the people of Dubai did not understand deliberate methods of justice and it would have been difficult to prolong a decision while attempting to exchange telegraphic communications with the Government by wireless, which was liable to interruption from atmospherics at any moment in the most uncertain weather which prevailed at the time. He defended the extent of the fine imposed (on his recommendation) and the number of rifles to be surrendered as he knew the Shaikh could easily afford these impositions. Cox denied any basic desire to install an agent by bombardment, but tried to exploit the incident as a pretext for appointing one. He insisted on the location of one in Dubai, and suggested that when the Commander-in-Chief next visited the Gulf he could carry out the installation of the British Agent with the necessary ships and men: 'in order to bring him [the Shaikh] and the intractable section of his followers to their knees, it might be necessary to occupy the town for a short period after first dominating it by bombardment.' This suggestion was once again rejected by the Government of India.[41]

The most important long-term effect of the incident was to provoke hatred among the local people against the Indian traders and British firms. In October 1912 Shaikh Buṭī b. Suhail refused to let Muḥammad 'Ismā'īl, a Muslim Indian, agent of Gray, Paul and Company, land in Dubai. After being delayed for some hours, the ship took him to Bandar 'Abbās. Cox was informed of this incident by the agent of BIC. On 9 October Cox wrote to the Shaikh expressing his surprise at this refusal to allow him to land. Moreover, he sent his First Assistant, Captain Birdwood, to Bandar 'Abbās, to accompany Muḥammad 'Ismā'īl to Dubai with a reprimanding letter, demanding that the Shaikh should receive them at once.[42] The Shaikh defended his refusal by saying that Muḥammad 'Ismā'īl had a bad reputation and was known to interfere in local politics and to be involved in local intrigues. Moreover, he had received a petition from various merchants in the town requesting that the new Indian agent should be a man who was acquainted with local usages and customs, a proposal which Birdwood supported in his report to Cox. The Shaikh reported that there had been difficulties regarding the wages of the Arab boatmen in the late agent's time, and hinted at the possibility of taking over the landing arrangements himself.

The effect of the Dubai incident on the arms trade was minimal and short-lived. For a while the shaikhs on the Trucial Coast appeared to respect British prohibition. Throughout 1912 Cox never ceased to demand the installation of a British Political Officer as the most effective way of putting an end to the illegal trade and tightening British control. The Shaikh of Dubai, supported by the notables, stubbornly and consistently refused. In December 1912, Shaikh Buṭī b. Suhail died. The presence of rival claimants to the succession offered a suitable opportunity for effecting a bargain and, in spite of the traditional British non-interference policy, Cox was authorised to take advantage of the situation to press for the establishment of a telegraph station and post office at Dubai in return for Government support of the eventual successor to the chieftainship. From the British point of view, the attitude taken by the new chief, Shaikh Sa'īd b. Maktūm, towards their proposals was no more progressive than that of his predecessor.

At the end of 1913 the question of coercive measures against Dubai was again discussed in military circles in India. To Cox's surprise he received a telegram from General Brigade, Karachi, on 5 December: 'Kindly wire if rations be sent for detachment 95th Infantry proceeding Dubai and whether field of foreign service scale.' He replied at once that he was not aware that any expedition to Dubai had been sanctioned by Government and gave orders that the detachment should under no circumstances be disembarked at Dubai without further intimation to his office. As the arms trade died naturally in 1914 after the British closed the arms store in Muscat and confiscated all French arms, the expedition against Dubai did not appear again in Indian Government files.[43]

The Slave Trade

The continuation of the fanatical enforcement of her anti-slavery policy was one of Britain's main aims during this period on the Trucial Coast. Owing to the three treaties concluded by the British in 1839, 1847 and 1856 and the energetic efforts of the Political Residents and naval captains in suppressing the previously flourishing business, the slave market in this area was significantly diminished. This insistent policy was one of the major reasons for anti-British resentment on the 'Omāni Coast and it is important to note that this liberal and humanitarian activity was viewed differently locally, where the people felt no guilt about the trade and regarded the measures as oppressive and as unwarranted interference in internal affairs. Much of the ill-feeling arose from the fact that in their society slaves were well-treated and some of the more capable even attained such influential positions as governors and teachers, a situation very different from that in the Western Hemisphere.[44]

During the 1890s the dying trade began to revive when the French, with the intention of annoying the British, gave their flag and citizenship to the sailors of the port of Ṣūr in 'Omān. One of the early outcomes of the treaty of 1892 was that it prevented the shaikhs of the Trucial States and their subjects from receiving the French flag and so renewing their trade in slaves. On 31 August that year 'Abd al-Laṭīf, the Residency Agent in Shārjah, reported some remarks made in open council by the Shaikh of Dubai on the subject of Britain's refusal to allow slave trading by native Arabs, expressing his surprise that a British warship, coming upon an 'Omanī dhow under French colours unloading slaves at Rās al-Khaimah, had allowed it to carry on unmolested; he proposed 'taking the French flag and so escaping from the malice of the English'.[45]

The letter written by Ottavi, the French Consul in Muscat, on 26 February 1896, in which he mentioned Shaikh Zāyed's willingness to accept French protection, provides us with some further information. The Residency Agent had reported that Shaikh Zāyed b. Khalīfah had not prevented the introduction of slaves by certain members of the Banī Yās, and Colonel Wilson, the Political Resident, accompanied by HM ships *Lawrence* and *Lapwing* had imposed a fine of 2,100 piastres on the Shaikh under threat of bombardment. Zāyed complained about the incident to Sultan Faiṣal, who paid 1,100 piastres towards the fine. Ottavi gave an interpretation of the incident in his report, based upon the local rumours to the effect that 'Abd al-Laṭīf had been levying a 'tax' of ten piastres per slave from all the Trucial shaikhs, but Zāyed, impressed by the dignity of his position, had refused to pay, whereupon 'Abd al-Laṭīf reported the importation of slaves and provoked

Colonel Wilson's anger. Ottavi mentioned that although many local complaints had been sent to the Political Resident about the Residency Agent's corruption, Wilson's blind faith in 'Abd al-Laṭīf caused him to ignore them completely. It is ironic that the French Consul who was in charge of granting the French flag to the citizens of Ṣur should accuse 'Abd al-Laṭīf of being 'the biggest slave-dealer' in the Persian Gulf.[46]

As a result of Britain's continued efforts the slave trade virtually disappeared between the two World Wars. During this period Britain took further steps toward manumission, which once again created bitter resentment.[47]

The British and the Trucial States during World War I

As a result of the treaty of 1892 and the energetic and effective measures taken during the period of challenge, Britain was able during World War I to send expeditions and supplies from India to Baṣrah through the peaceful waters of the Gulf without fear of interruption. At the beginning of the war one of the precautions taken by the British to counter Turkish holy war propaganda was to gain the goodwill of the Arabs in Arabia, including the shaikhs of the Trucial States and their subjects. The Political Resident was empowered to transmit three notices to the shaikhs which were to be published as widely as possible in their territories for the information of their subjects and dependants, so that there might be no doubt as to the real causes leading to this dispute with Turkey. In order to assure the Arabs of Britain's respect for the Muslim holy places the notices said that as long as the Indian pilgrims proceeding to Mecca and Madīnah were not seriously interfered with, no hostile actions against the ports to Jeddah or the holy places would be taken by the British or Indian Governments or by their ships or soldiers. The notices asked the independent shaikhs of Arabia to consider their attitude towards the oppressors of Muslims, the Turks, who called themselves their protectors. All the British required was that order and quiet should be maintained in their territory and that they would not allow their subjects to be stirred up by agitators talking of *Jihād* (holy war). In this way, with a little patience, they would emerge unscathed from the trouble that now surrounded them. The shaikhs of the Trucial States were all with varying degrees of warmth, favourable towards the notices.[48]

Aware of Britain's interests in this area, McMahon, High Commissioner in Egypt, clearly pointed out in his correspondence with Sharīf Ḥusain of Mecca in 1915 the significant position of the Trucial States. He emphasised that the expected independent Arab state was to recognise Britain's special treaties and interests in the shaikhdoms of the Gulf. Moreover, in the same year Cox concluded a treaty with Ibn Sa'ūd to ensure his co-operation against the Turks. Pledges on the part of Ibn Sa'ūd not to interfere in the affairs of the Trucial States were included.

II The Growth of British Interests between the Two World Wars

British Political Control and Administrative Responsibilities

The study of British control and administration in the Gulf between the two World Wars reveals the growing importance of the area in British strategy. After 1921 the Colonial Office and the Air Ministry became increasingly involved in Gulf politics, in addition to the India Office, Foreign Office and Admiralty thus creating further confusion of British political control in the area. The establishment of the Ad Hoc Persian Gulf Sub-Committee in 1928–9 and the Standing Official Middle East Sub-Committee in 1930 succeeded in co-ordinating the policies of the different departments concerned.[49] The conflicting points of view expressed in the meetings of those departments over the designation of British control and policy in the Gulf, particularly in the Trucial Coast, is a matter of central importance to this study.

On 11 January 1921 the Prime Minister established an Inter-Departmental Committee chaired by Sir James Masterton Smith in order to outline a Middle Eastern Service in the Colonial Office for the administration of Iraq, Palestine, Aden and Arabia. The Committee recommended with reference to the Gulf area:

> That the Arabian littoral of the Persian Gulf should remain under the control of the Political Resident in the Persian Gulf, that this officer should be appointed at the present by the Government of India, but should be authorised to communicate direct with the Colonial Office on matters concerning the Arabian littoral; that the functions of the Government of India in respect of the Arabian littoral should be confined to administrative and purely local matters, and that the prior concurrence of the Colonial Office should be obtained by these to any measures of political significance; but the relations of HM Government with Ibn Sa'ūd should be conducted exclusively by the New Department through the Political Resident at Bushire in the first place.[50]

The Indian Government objected to these recommendations but without success. As a result of these arrangements the Political Resident corresponded with the following departments: the Colonial Office on questions of oil and matters affecting Ibn Sa'ūd except when he was in the Ḥijāz; with the Foreign office in his capacity as Consul General, Bushire; and with the Government of India for the internal affairs of the various states on the Arab littoral, for Kuwait, Bahrain, the Trucial States and Muscat.

The emergence in 1918 of the Royal Air Force[51] soon proved its strategic importance by its mobility and effectiveness. This can be clearly seen in the military operations in the post-war period in Yemen, Iraq, Trans-Jordan and

1. Shaikh Zāyed b. Khalīfah (1855 to 1909) Ruler of Abū Dhabī, surrounded by his sons and tribal chiefs.

2. The ruins of Shaikh Shakhbūṭ b. Diyāb's fort at Miraijib in al-'Ain in the eastern region of Abū Dhabī. Built in 1818 this is one of the earliest Al-Nahayyan buildings.

3; Shaikh Sulṭān b. Sālim al Qāsimī, Ruler of Rās al-Khaimah (1921 to 1948).

4. Muḥammad Sa'īd b. Ghubāsh, who graduated from al-'Azhar in the 1920s.

5. The British Expedition against the Qawāsim of Lingah in 1809.

6. A visit to Sir Rupert Hay, the Political Resident to Shaikh Shakhbūt, Ruler of Abū Dhabī, in the late 1940s. Second to the left is Shaikh Ḥāmid.

7. A gathering of the Trucial Shaikhs in the early 1950s. Shaikh Shakhbūṭ b. Sulṭān, Ruler of Abū Dhabī and Shaikh Sa'īd b. Maktūm, Ruler of Dubai, stand in the centre of the front row. In the back row from left to right are: Shaikh Zāyed b. Sulṭān (second from left); Shaikh Rāshid b. Sa'īd; Shaikh Aḥmad b. Rāshid; Shaikh Rāshid b. Ḥumaid and his son 'Ali and Shaikh Ṣaqr b. Muḥammad.

8. Shaikh Saʿīd b. Maktūm, Ruler of Dubai (1912 to 1958).

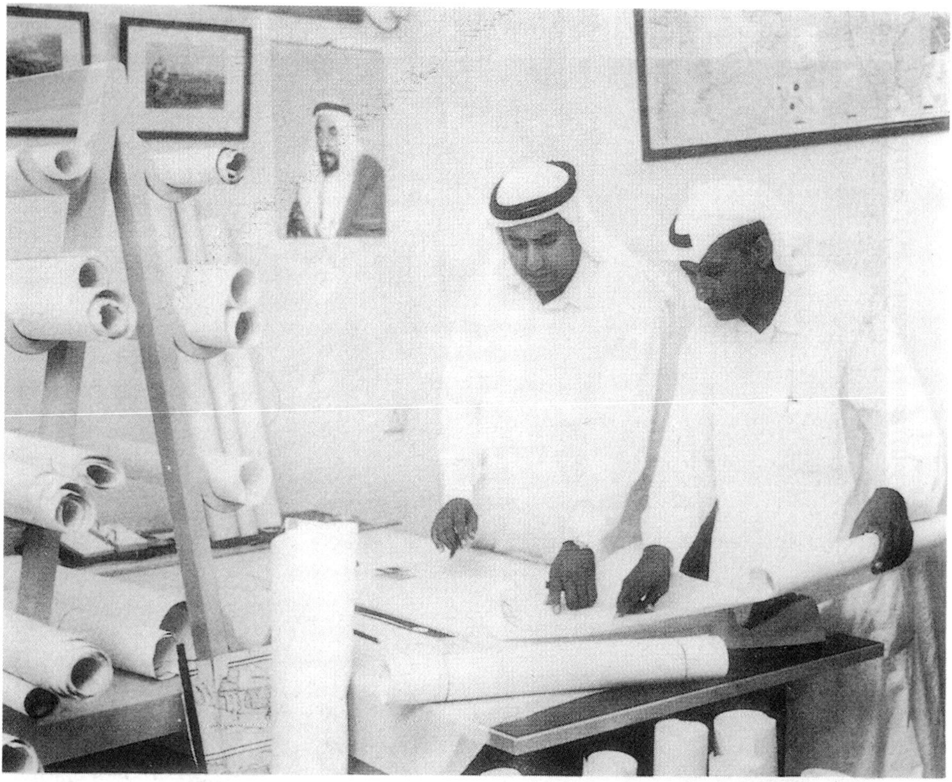

9. The Centre for Documentation and Research in the Ruler's Palace, Abū Dhabī. The Centre was established in 1968 and is the first of its kind in the Gulf.

10. The author recording local data in the Majlis of Shaikh Muhammad b. Buti in Tarif.

11. The declaration of a union between nine Emirates (the seven Emirates of the UAE, Baḥrain and Qaṭar) on 27 February 1968.

12. The signing of the 'Independence Agreement' on 2 December 1971. A historic occasion which created the new state of the United Arab Emirates.

along the Northern Indian borders. In addition the economics achieved by turning over the responsibility for defence from the Army to the Air Force were enormous.[52] In 1921 the RAF base recently established at Ḥabbāniyyah, near Baghdād, took over the defence of Iraq from the Army; five squadrons were stationed there in 1924 in fulfilment of treaty obligations to Iraq, for the protection of the oil fields and the national boundaries.[53]

On 30 June 1926 the confusion arising from so many departments dealing with Arabia and the Gulf was brought to the House of Lords' notice by Lord Lamington, who demanded that there should be a single department to co-ordinate and centralise British relations with Arabic-speaking countries in the Middle East.[54] Developments in the next two years in Persia and Sa'ūdi Arabia, together with the inauguration of the air route and the oil concessions, created radically new problems. The widely differing solutions offered by each department concerned made the Cabinet realise that the time had come for co-ordination.

So impressed was Colonel Haworth, the Political Resident (1927–8), by 'the rise of Ibn Saud and the insecurity to which a chain of air stations along the Arab coast might be exposed by internal dissensions and the danger of Saudi interference in the petty shaikhdoms of the Trucial Coast', that he suggested in his two letters of 30 April and 9 May 1927 that the long-established policy of abstention by HM Government from all but naval commitments should now be discarded. It should be replaced by a definite assumption of responsibility in the states concerned, for the orderly succession from shaikh to shaikh, for his maintenance in power, and for the protection of his territories by land as well as by sea. He proposed a greater degree of British interference in the Trucial States and support for them in order to ensure that they should not be absorbed by Ibn Sa'ūd. As a result, during the 1927 negotiations for a new treaty with Ibn Sa'ūd, the Government of India recommended the Foreign Office to embody in this agreement Article VI of the 1915 treaty, binding Ibn Sa'ūd to 'respect the position of the Arab Shaikhdoms in alliance with HM Government' (see Chapter 3, p. 178). The failure of the Foreign Office to enforce the literal interpretation of the article was a marked disappointment to the Government of India.[55] Furthermore, stressing the role of the Admiralty in the defence of the Gulf, Haworth proposed the occupation of some critical points on the Arab side at the mouth of the Gulf, like Khaṣab for instance, to convert it into another Gibralter.[56] At the same time, the Government of India stressed that the degree of control exercised for the last nine years by the Colonial Office was already too great and should be reduced, demanding that the Admiralty be entrusted once again with defending British interests, a service which they rendered effectively in the past.[57]

On March 17 1928 the Air Ministry presented to the Cabinet the Air Staff Memorandum, which highlighted the confusion of British control in the Gulf and aroused great concern. The existing system, whereby no important decision could be reached by the Colonial Office without first consulting and obtaining the concurrence of a number of other government departments, was criticised and the Memorandum recommended that the broad principles of air control, which was so novel, based on accurate intelligence and swiftness in decision and action, should be widely circulated among local British authorities. It was proposed that the Air Officer Commanding should be the sole authority for conducting air operations and deciding when they should be suspended and peace negotiations opened. But the question of simplifying and speeding up the machinery for political control in Arabia and the Gulf was the main theme. It was suggested that an inter-departmental sub-committee on the lines of Masterton's should be set up to carry out a detailed enquiry and outline solutions, and that Kuwait and the Trucial Coast should come under the complete control of a single department, the Colonial Office.

The security of the rich oil fields in Persia and Iraq and the protection of Imperial Airways routes through the Gulf were among the main points in another Air Staff memorandum to the Foreign Secretary on 29 May 1928. The Air Staff further stressed that the advent of air power created an explosive situation in the Gulf. Germany, it was true, had been eliminated from the problem, but the Russian danger remained in an aggravated form. Communist Russia had repudiated the Convention of 1907 and did not recognise the *status quo* in the Gulf, while Persia was so weak in a military sense that no reliance could be placed on her to fulfil the function of a buffer state. The development of air power and the cross-country vehicle increased the possibility of a sudden emergence of a Russian air menace in the Gulf at some future date.[58]

Therefore, on 25 June 1928 the Persian Gulf Sub-Committee of the Committee of Imperial Defence was set up by the Prime Minister to examine British policy in the Gulf. The Sub-Committee was composed of the Foreign Secretary, Lord Chancellor, Colonial Secretary, Secretary of State for India, Air Secretary, First Lord of the Admiralty, President of the Board of Trade and the First Commissioner of Works.[59] This committee held nine meetings between 2 July 1928 and 18 March 1929, with four main themes on their agenda. First, the Anglo–Persian negotiations for a treaty covering Persian claims to the islands of Baḥrain, Abū Mūsā and Ṭanb, the air agreement for the Persian coast route and British naval bases at Henjām and Basīdū. Secondly, the encroachment of Ibn Sa'ūd into the Trucial Coast and the raids of the Ikhwān in Iraq, Kuwait and the Trucial Coast. Thirdly, the question of declaring a Protectorate over the Trucial Coast. Fourthly, British political machinery in the Gulf and the Middle East.

During these nine months agreements on general lines of policy emerged and two important recommendations regarding political control were presented to the Cabinet. The Chiefs of Staff had arrived at the conclusion that 'the maintenance in the sense of supremacy in the Gulf was still essential to the security of India and Imperial interests; therefore no foreign power must be allowed to establish a naval base or fortified post in the Gulf or air undertakings within striking distance of it. Moreover the maintenance of the independence of Kuwait, Baḥrain, the Trucial States and Muscat was necessary for British purposes.[60] However, the Committee objected unanimously to Haworth's proposal of declaring a 'Protectorate' over the Trucial Coast. The Viceroy based his own objection of 15 October 1928 on two grounds, that it would provoke not only Ibn Sa'ūd and the Trucial shaikhs themselves, but also Arab opinion in general, and that it would overstretch British military commitments by requiring protection by land as well as by sea.[61] It was also accepted that the best breakwater for Ibn Sa'ūd and Persian encroachment would be the complete independence of the Trucial Coast, which the British must secure against both. The Committee also objected to the Air Ministry's insistent demand for control of air operations on the grounds that 'the Royal Air Force must remain the instrument of the political authorities, who, in the last resort, must decide when and in what manner that instrument should be used'. Owing to strong pressure from the Foreign Office the Committee recommended, subject to possible demands from Persia, that there should be two appointments, namely a Consul-General for Fars, stationed at Bushire, and a Political Resident for the Gulf stationed on the Arab littoral.[62]

At the final meeting on 18 March 1929, two main resolutions were passed. The aim of the first was to establish closer co-operation between the Political Resident in the Gulf and the Air Commander in Iraq. The Committee recommended that the Air Force in Iraq should be charged with the defence of British interests on the Arabian coast, in the same way as he had already applied to the Senior Naval Officer, Persian Gulf, for naval assistance. Furthermore the Air Officer in Iraq was advised that he should give every possible assistance to the Political Resident in the Gulf in the performance of his duties, and that he should acquaint the navy with all air operations undertaken or contemplated in the Gulf.[63]

Owing to a difference of opinion no conclusion was reached on the main item of their agenda concerning the co-ordination of British control, but a small committee was established under the chairmanship of a Treasury official, Sir Warren Fisher, to fill in this gap. Meanwhile in furtherance of the recommendation to transfer the Political Residency from Bushire to the Arab coast, Lieutenant-Colonel Barrett, the Political Agent in Baḥrain, on 22 July 1929 presented a comprehensive study in which he proposed Baḥrain as the most suitable place for the Residency in preference to Kuwait. A primary reason for choosing Baḥrain was its proximity to the Trucial Coast, which now required more attention than it had received from the Resident in the past. The Government of India was influenced to leave Bushire by two arguments, the fact that a Residency on the Arab side would consolidate its control there, now required by the Arabian air route, and the new situation created by the admission of American oil capital to Baḥrain (for which it blamed the Foreign Office). Although the Government of India realised that it must reconcile itself to this move at an appropriate time, the Residency was not transferred during the 1930s. On 9 September 1929 the Viceroy's letter shows us the sense of dignity that postponed this move, '. . . We must adjust ourselves to a new position, though it is still felt here that our quitting Bushire at such a juncture under Persia's pressure cannot be accompanied by some loss of dignity'.

In December 1929 Fisher's committee reported that two standing co-ordinating committees of the Committee of Imperial Defence, the one ministerial and the other official, should be set up to deal with such Middle East questions as might concern the two departments. On 14 July 1930 the establishment of these two sub-committees was approved in a meeting of the Committee of Imperial Defence. The Official Committee generally met under the chairmanship of the Permanent Under-Secretary of State for the Colonies. Each committee represented all departments concerned. The spadework was done in the Official Sub-Committee and the Ministerial committee was only to meet when the official one failed to reach agreement.[64] The Standing Official Sub-Committee had its first meeting on 25 February 1931 and came to an end on the eve of the Second World War on 14 August 1939, holding in all sixty-nine meetings, of which twenty-nine were concerned with the Gulf. The main issues were the abortive negotiations with Persia and those with Ibn Sa'ūd over Abū Dhabī and Qaṭar frontiers, the Imperial Airway's route and oil concessions in the Gulf.[65]

Three eminent protagonists rose to dominate the discussions in general and on the Trucial Coast in particular: G. Rendel, the Head of the Eastern Department in the Foreign Office between 1930–38, and G. Laithwaite and his successor J. C. Walton representing the India Office. In his memoirs Rendel gives us a clear picture of the different outlooks of the various departments:

> The Admiralty and the War Office were at that date still very sceptical about the value of air power and generally tended to line up against the Air Ministry . . . The Government of India found it difficult to believe that any of the recent internal changes in the Middle East could be permanent. Nor had they much faith in the stability of the new Persia, and they long hoped to be able to go on running the Persian Gulf under a virtual governor precariously established on almost hostile Persian soil. When we at the Foreign Office insisted on the impracticability of this they were inclined, with the support of the Admiralty, to think us defeatist. I generally found myself in closest sympathy with the Air Ministry.[66]

The year 1932 witnessed several important events in British administration and political control. First, the air agreement with Shārjah had far-reaching repercussions. The long-standing desire for a wireless station on the coast, repeatedly sought before the First World War by Cox, was now unintentionally realised. This further tightened British control, as it now became customary for T. Fowle, the Political Resident (1932–9) and Lieutenant-Colonel Loch, the Political Agent in Baḥrain (1933–9), to communicate over the air with 'Īsā b. 'Abd al-Laṭīf, the Residency Agent in Shārjah (1919–35).[67] Under the terms of the Airport Agreement with the Shaikh of Shārjah the British undertook to protect him from any form of aggression resulting from the airport being situated in his territory.[68] Thus the policy that had been unanimously rejected four years previously by the Persian Gulf Sub-Committee now became a necessity through force of circumstances. Secondly, the idea of moving the Residency from Bushire to Baḥrain, as well as the establishment of a naval base on the island three years later instead of Henjām marked a historical shift of British interests in the Gulf from the Persian coast, where it had lasted for more than a century, to the Arabian side. Reflecting the increased importance of the Trucial Coast in British Strategy in 1932, 'Īsā b. 'Abd al-Laṭīf was asked to communicate directly with the Political Agent in Baḥrain, who was now entrusted with day-to-day British affairs on the coast, instead of the Political Resident in Bushire.

Thirdly, the appointment of Fowle, who had long experience of Persia and the Gulf, to the Political Residency at Bushire proved an influential factor. At a time of crisis when Persia was challenging British supremacy, when American oil involvement was on the increase and when open unrest appeared in Qaṭar and the Trucial Coast, Fowle showed himself to be a firm official and an able British officer, similar in character to Cox but modified by the changed political climate of the inter-war period. During the previous decade he had been consul at Meshhad, Sistān and Kirmān,[69] at a time of strong nationalist feeling hostile to Britain; from this he developed an obstinate refusal to bend to such pressure. Fowle's independence of action was far less than Cox's for he was governed by the Official Middle East Sub-Committee, and wireless communication gave him far less freedom to act on his own; nevertheless his opinions held great weight and he was several times invited by the Official Sub-Committee to express them personally. Finally, in this year the old question of political control, a constant source of rivalry between the Colonial Office, Foreign Office and India Office, was raised again. Since 1925, when Ibn Sa'ūd invaded al Ḥijāz, the Foreign Office replaced the Colonial Office in all political dealings with him. Furthermore, in 1932 the Foreign Office had taken over the control of foreign relations with Iraq when that country became completely independent.

On 9 June 1933 the Colonial Office requested in a memorandum that they be relieved of all work in the Persian Gulf and proposed that these duties be taken over by the Foreign Office. On 10 June the Foreign Office prepared a memorandum to the Cabinet suggesting that they were the obvious department to take over dealings with the Arab States in the Gulf, basing their argument on two points: because the granting of oil concessions in the Gulf had now become an important Anglo–American issue, but also because the international importance of the principalities on the Trucial Coast had recently been greatly increased by the development of international air communications, with both the French and the Netherlands governments applying for permission for their aircraft to fly regularly over the area. In the India Office's memorandum they stressed the difficulty of drawing a fixed line between what was purely internal in the Gulf States and therefore administered by the Foreign Office. The main aim was to diminish the number of channels of correspondence of the Resident and to reduce the number of authorities whom he might be required to address. The arrangement eventually reached was that all correspondence from the Gulf at present handled by the Colonial Office should in future be dealt with by the India Office, and the Foreign Office should receive copies of all the relevant papers and should be kept in the closest possible touch with affairs. Decisions on matters of policy should continue to be taken in close consultation with the Foreign Office and the Middle East Sub-Committee.[70]

In 1934 Fowle's handling of an internal incident in Dubai raised a discussion initiated by the Air Ministry, over the traditional British policy of non-interference in inner Arabia. In September, after the failure of a murder plot against Shaikh Sa'īd b. Maktūm by his cousins, who had tried to depose him in 1929, a meeting was held in the town to overthrow the ruler. Meanwhile, Fowle was under pressure from the Air Officer Commanding in Iraq to obtain landing facilities for the Royal Air Force, which was charged with the defence of the Imperial Airways route. Fowle, impressed by the hostile attitude in the Trucial States regarding British military facilities, tackled the negotiations with great patience, a policy which was irksome to the military-minded air officers in Iraq. The Political Resident felt it important to support the friendly Shaikh of Dubai while underlining the fact that any lapse by the ruler in the protection of British lives and property would be regarded very unfavourably. On 21 October 1934 the Senior Naval Officer was asked to visit Dubai and he recommended that material help be given to the ruler. On 27 October Husain b. 'Amād, Assistant Residency Agent, came to Dubai in the British sloop *Lupin*, bringing a delivery of arms to the ruler and circulating in the town a message from Fowle which created the impression among the people that the British were once again openly supporting the ruler. On 30 October Lieutenant-Colonel Loch arrived in Dubai and had an immediate interview with Shaikh Sa'īd. A telegram soon arrived from Fowle ordering that the supply of arms and ammunition to Shaikh Sa'īd should at once be publicised along the coast in order that the whole population should learn of the British support for their friends, and on 31 October, at Fowle's request, British aircraft from Iraq several times flew low over the town. Following upon this the Shaikh ordered his cousins to show their obedience within twenty-four hours or be exiled, a threat which proved effective. Shaikh Sa'īd expressed his gratitude for the Political Agent's presence during this crisis and for the British show of force in his support. Loch commented that the British action had considerably strengthened their own position on the Trucial Coast.[71]

Once again the Air Officer Commanding in Iraq was exasperated by Fowle's cautious policy, which gave a show of support to the Shaikh without proper intervention in the internal affairs—he felt it would result in the further lowering of British prestige in the Gulf and so threaten the security of the air route. On 16 November Fowle wrote to the Government of India reporting the incident and explaining his opinion concerning British policy on the Trucial Coast. He stressed that Britain must keep to her traditional policy of non-interference in internal affairs and avoid taking action to prevent hostilities between shaikhs on land. The common objection of the shaikhs to granting air facilities was that they feared this would be the first step to the establishment of British administration over them.[72] Fowle's argument was supported by his superiors and the India Office, but immediately came under bitter attack from the Air Ministry, who were pressing for a policy of intervention. The controversy lasted a year and intensified after declaring of a 'Protectorate' over Qaṭar at the end of 1934. While the India Office advocated non-interference and the Air Ministry called for the exact opposite, each claimed to be the true interpreter of Curzon's speech on British policy in the Trucial States of 23 September 1903, which was regarded as the authority in this matter. Finally, on 24 September 1935, a special meeting of the Middle East Sub-Committee was convened, at which Fowle was present, to settle the question of British policy on the Trucial coast.

In developing the Air Ministry's ideas before the meeting, Air Vice-Marshal C. L. Courtney claimed that their views were consistent with Lord Curzon's speech in whose time the only action open to HM Government was by sea, but new air power permitted intervention on land as well as by sea. Courtney entirely agreed with the action taken by Fowle in the 'Dubai Incident' but he made it clear that 'they could not regard it as anything but intervention, though of a kind perfectly justifiable and consistent with Lord Curzon's speech'. They would therefore like to see the policy of HM Government restated in somewhat clearer terms. Colonel Fowle explained that if the safety of the air route could be assured with the present commitments of HM Government, he saw no need to extend them. Rendel began his speech pointing out that

> It seemed essential to recognise that the general situation in the Gulf, particularly from the international point of view, had been completely and fundamentally revolutionised by post-war developments. Lord

> Curzon's speech had been made at a time when the Persian Gulf had been virtually a British lake . . . There was no aviation, there was no oil, and there was little foreign trade. As a result, the limits of HM Government's action had been set solely by themselves. Today the Persian Gulf was one of the world's highways, bordered by strongly nationalist States, whose interest in the Gulf was real and active and the discovery of oil had led other foreign powers to take an increasing interest in Gulf affairs . . . he feared that, if HM Government tried to maintain a negative policy of non-intervention and minimum control, they might find themselves subjected to very strong pressure from foreign powers whose nationals wished to be allowed to enter the Persian Gulf for commercial exploitation, aviation, etc.

Rendel ended by supporting the Air Ministry's views. However, Captain Philips of the Admiralty expressed the idea that they were in general agreement with the views of Colonel Fowle and he suggested that the time had come to replace the native Agent at Shārjah, who had died recently, by an Englishman and this was subsequently agreed.

To the disappointment of the Air Ministry, the meeting concluded that there was no need for a new pronouncement or to adopt a new policy in the Trucial States, though the British Government must admit ultimate international responsibility for the affairs of the area. The Committee charged the Air Officer in Iraq that intervention on land in the Trucial States had become an additional commitment which he might in certain circumstances be called upon to meet.[73]

On 5 May 1936 another meeting of the Official Middle East Sub-Committee was held to discuss the transfer of the Political Residency from Bushire to Baḥrain, but although the Government of India agreed to the Foreign Office demand for the move, Fowle proved stubborn and declared that it was not a matter of urgency. As a result the transfer was postponed till after the Second World War.[74] In 1937, the Government of India agreed to the appointment of Captain J. B. Howes as the British Political Officer in Shārjah. This delay occurred because it was thought that the life of an Englishman might be in danger from the Arabs of the Trucial Coast; nevertheless his post was transferred to Baḥrain during that summer and the new Residency Agent, 'Abd al-Razzāq, resumed charge in his absence.[75] In this year the conclusion of the oil concession with Dubai, which was followed in 1938 by oil agreements with the other shaikhs, implied the extension of British protection on land as well as on sea. Thus the possibility which had been dismissed a decade earlier had now become a reality owing to the increasing British interests in the Trucial Coast.

The Military and Civil Air Routes

On 1 April 1918 the Royal Air Force came into being by the amalgamation of the Royal Flying Corps with the Royal Navy Air Services. The new force was soon to prove its strategic importance by its mobility and effectiveness, clearly seen in military operations in the post-war period in Southwest Arabia, Iraq, Trans-Jordan and along the North India Border. In addition an enormous saving was achieved by turning over the responsibility for defence from the Army to the Air Force. Accordingly the Air Ministry sought to establish many bases, in the interests of Imperial defence, along a line from the Cape to Cairo and from Cairo to Singapore.

In 1932 the RAF, recently established in Ḥabbāniyyah near Baghdād, took over the defence of Iraq from the Army. Five squadrons were stationed at Ḥabbāniyyah in 1924, in fulfilment of treaty obligations to Iraq, for the protection of the oil fields and the general protection of the country's frontiers from outside interference.[76] In May 1924 the first service aircraft landed at Baḥrain and Ibn Sa'ūd objected 'on the grounds that it caused consternation among his subjects'. Sir Hugh Trenchard, Chief of the Air Staff, considered that 'a rupture of the Persian Gulf link would be just as grave a disaster to the Air Force as the closing of the Suez Canal would be to the Navy'.[77] Therefore in the late 1920s the need for military air bases and facilities for the RAF in the Gulf was a matter of paramount importance.

Meanwhile, Imperial Airways were arranging for the start of an air service between Cairo and Karachi as a further step towards a full air link between London and Australia. In January 1927 the airline began operations between Cairo and Baṣrah with stops at Gazah, Ruṭbah and Baghdād. The command of the Air Force in Iraq was asked to help the airline in conducting an air survey of the Gulf area with a view to locating suitable landing grounds.[78]

Consequently the British Consul in Jeddah, the Ambassador in Tehran and the Political Resident in the Gulf were soon involved in negotiations with the local authorities in order to obtain air facilities. In fact the establishment of the air route in the Gulf was fraught with many difficulties, and none were greater than the sensitive nationalist feelings in Persia, the hostile attitude of the Ikhwān (the Muwaḥḥidīn zealots, called *Wahhābīs* by their enemies), and the suspicions of the Trucial shaikhs of British interference in their local affairs. In the minds of the shaikhs the situation was aggravated, for although the recent operations of the Air Force on the frontiers of Iraq and Trans-Jordan were viewed as effective by the British, they were regarded by the shaikhs as disastrous in respect of tribal warfare. The repeated negotiations with Ibn Sa'ūd proved completely abortive and those with the Shah of Persia took some years before reaching a restricted agreement on the Imperial Airways route.[79]

The Trans-'Omān Expedition, conducted in 1927 by the Royal Air Force in Iraq and accompanied by Bertram Thomas, was the most important one attempted on the Trucial Coast in planning the new route. The expedition started from Ṣuḥār on 12 May and in addition to Thomas consisted of three RAF officers: Squadron-Leader C. H. Keith, Flight-Lieutenant T. V. O'Brien and Pilot-Officer C. W. Switzer. They were escorted by twenty-seven members of the Banī Ka'b tribe, twenty of the Banī 'Umar tribe and twenty of the Maqābīl tribe, who supplied transport animals. The trip ended at Shārjah on 3 June after investigating suitable landing grounds for the proposed airline route on the Arabian coast. Thomas's report to the Political Resident on 13 June is of great significance for our study, since it reveals the attitudes of the rulers as well as the tribes in the hinterland of the Trucial Coast towards the British and the air route. Unfortunately for Thomas and the expedition, the visit coincided with an extreme peak of 'Ikhwān anti-western fanaticism which was temporarily out of control, even of Ibn Sa'ūd himself (see Chapter 3, pp. 172–3). The attitude of the 'Omānīs and the shaikhs of the Trucial Coast was outlined in three letters which gave a clear indication of the difficulties Thomas and the expedition were to face on their mission.

The first of these letters was sent by 'Īsā b. Ṣāliḥ of inner 'Omān to Sayyed Nādir b. Faiṣal Āl Bū-Sa'īd before the expedition left Muscat, asking for information concerning British aims in connection with the air route. The second letter was addressed by the Shaikh of Shārjah to Sālim b. Dayyīn, Shaikh of the Banī Ka'b, in Ṣuḥār at the start of the expedition. Thomas himself, in his book *Alarms and Excursions in Arabia*, quotes this letter without naming its author: it shows clearly the religious feeling of the inhabitants that made them hostile towards the designs of the British, whom they regarded with suspicion and considered as infidels. The Shaikh of Shārjah writes: 'I hope you may not do any harm to the Muslims but do what pleases them and God. Probably the Nasara [Christians] will come to you and ask you to do for them something which will bring bad consequences for you and us. I advise you before anything happens and advise you to keep the honour and dignity of Arabs'. The third letter was from Aḥmad b. Hilāl, representative of Shaikh Ṣaqr b. Zāyed of Abū Dhabī, from whom Thomas had expected help. He was unco-operative and replied to the Wālī of Ṣuḥār: 'Please note that Shaikh Ṣaqr has not sent us any information . . . The western people are destructive and we fear their greed and they have no friends'.

Thomas was obliged to avoid Buraimī, which was an important halt in the original itinerary of the expedition, due to the strong objections of the shaikh of the oasis, who said that their 'intrusion was unwanted . . . that the country belonged to God, themselves and Ibn Sa'ūd'. Accordingly Thomas changed the route to Maḥdah, the main town of the Banī Ka'b tribe. He reported that at Buraimī 'Our messengers had met with a hostile reception, had in fact been pursued out of the town, and returned frightened and full of dire forebodings'. The expedition therefore was forced to make a survey of Maḥdah as being the only suitable area available for their plans in the interior, and in their report recommended it as a landing ground. Thomas attributed the hostility of the inhabitants towards the air route to a belief that the project would lead to a tightening up of British control which was regarded by the shaikhs as inimical to their interests. In addition, the arrival at Buraimī of one of Ibn Sa'ūd's agents at the time of this expedition and his growing influence among the Bedouins contributed towards the hostile attitude.

Therefore the RAF Officers recommended the route Ṣuḥār–Maḥdah–Abū Dhabī instead of Ṣuḥār–Buraimī–Abū Dhabī. Thomas, well informed of local affairs, suggested that it was advisable to abandon the interior route totally owing to the attitude of the tribes, who were completely under Ibn Sa'ūd's influence; their opposition was in his opinion beyond British control. On the other hand he was in favour of a coastal route since British sea power could break down tribal opposition there at any moment. However, Thomas tentatively sounded out Sālim, the Shaikh of the Banī Ka'b, about the possibility of the Royal Air Force using Maḥdah as a landing ground. Sālim, who was well disposed towards the British, expressed his fears of reprisal by Ibn Sa'ūd, but made his final agreement subject to two conditions: first, no foreign troops to be quartered there, for this would discredit him in the eyes of the Arabs, and secondly, he could never agree to Maḥdah being used for operations against Arab tribes.[80]

This expedition encountered so much hostility and suspicion that the British decided to abandon for the time being the prospect of establishing landing grounds on the Trucial Coast. Extensive efforts were now directed towards Tehran in connection with a proposed Persian coast air route.

In 1929 three important developments took place in connection with the air route: the conclusion of the air agreement with Persia; the extension of the defence responsibilities of the RAF in Iraq to include the Gulf; and the establishment of air facilities for the RAF at Rās al-Khaimah. In March of that year the long negotiations with the Persian Government brought a temporary solution to the quest for an air route, when authorisation for weekly flights in each direction along the Persian coast for a period of three years was granted to Imperial Airways. The Persian Government made it clear that after the expiry, if the air line wished to continue to fly through Persia it must follow an air corridor soon to be established through Tehran in the north of the country.[81]

Since the RAF stationed in Iraq was commissioned to assist in the establishment of the air route in the Gulf, the Air Ministry became more and more involved in Gulf politics and administration.

In March 1929 No. 203 Flying Boat Squadron arrived from London at their permanent base in Baṣrah and within a month began to cruise in the Gulf. Their main tasks were two-fold: first, to select landing grounds and refuelling bases for the Arabian route, for which the British still had high hopes as an important alternative to the recently acquired Persian coast route: secondly, they sought to establish refuelling stores, flying boat anchorage and wireless telegraphy stations for themselves, since they were entrusted with the responsibility for the defence of the airways route. The officers found that the creek at Râs al-Khaimah was the most suitable place for flying boat anchorage, with a fine stretch of perfectly flat gravel nearby which seemed to be a ready made landing ground for Imperial Airways. They decided to visit Rās al-Khaimah, to examine thoroughly 'its facilities for aircraft and to negotiate terms under which the Shaikh would permit fuel supplies to be kept for its safe custody'. However, Shaikh Sulṭān b. Sālim, Ruler of Rās al-Khaimah, totally refused to discuss the matter owing to strong opposition by his people. In June, although the Political Agent accompanied the flying boats on their second visit to Rās al-Khaimah, the negotiations again proved abortive.

Consequently in May 1930 it was decided to adopt a firm policy and locate a fuel barge at Rās al-Khaimah. It was towed to the creek by a motor boat of HM sloop *Cyclamen*. The Shaikh's men arrived and threatened to fire on the motor boat and the barge was left on the shore. Immediately the Political Resident, accompanied by two sloops, arrived at Rās al-Khaimah and after exercising moral and physical pressure, including the seizure of pearling dhows and a blockade by sea, ultimately induced the Shaikh to accept the petrol barge and to guarantee its safety as a facility for the flying boat squadron.

Early in 1931 the Persian Government specified the corridor for international air services which followed the route Iṣphahan–Yezd–Tehran, but Imperial Airways, for technical and economic reasons, found the route impossible to operate and the need for the alternative Arabian route became a matter of urgency. The Shaikh of Râs al-Khaimah was approached on the matter of further landing facilities, but it was not pressed owing to the last minute possibility of striking a bargain with Persia in order to extend the three-year agreement for the coastal route.[82] However, the subject of an Arabian air route occupied the early meetings of the Standing Official Sub-Committee for questions concerning the Middle East which had been established the previous year by the Committee of Imperial Defence. The Air Ministry recommended that Imperial Airways should use flying boats similar to those in use in the Royal Air Force. Two reasons for this recommendation emerged during the discussions: first, the political and military difficulties which would result from the emergency landing of an aeroplane among hostile tribes on the Trucial Coast and al-Ḥasā; secondly, sea anchorage would preclude the possibility of an awkward political situation should requests for landing rights be made by the French and the Dutch companies who used only land craft.

However, the situation changed fundamentally at the end of the year when Persia showed a definite reluctance to extend the three-year agreement.[83] As a result of surveys by Air Ministry representatives they found Rās al-Khaimah to be the most suitable place for an intermediate resting stage on the Trucial Coast, Baḥrain and Gwāder being convenient halts for fuelling purposes, while Kuwait and Yās Island formed emergency refuelling stations *en route*. It was proposed to anchor a vessel at Rās al-Khaimah to serve as a rest house for passengers, as a stores depot, a wireless station, and as permanent quarters for a few operators and mechanics. The India Office considered that a sum of £3,000 would be sufficient, because of the depression in the pearling industry, to secure the goodwill of the Shaikh of Rās al-Khaimah and the local notables.

As the Admiralty raised objections to the choice of Rās al-Khaimah, and the Treasury refused to pay any expenses without a ministerial sanction, an urgent meeting of the Official Middle East Sub-Committee was held on 2 November 1931. Rendel, for the Foreign Office, opened the session by informing the members that the current situation required that they should proceed immediately with the establishment of the Arabian route, 'unless HM Government was prepared to see the air service to India definitely interrupted'. He suggested that Biscoe, the Political Resident, who was expected to visit the Trucial Coast in mid-November, should be instructed to re-open negotiations with the Trucial shaikhs immediately. Then the Admiralty representative, Captain Cunningham, who was closely concerned with the question of the protection of army landing places or rest houses on the Arabian coast, objected to the Trucial Coast route and the construction of air facilities at Rās al-Khaimah, on the grounds that the Coast was in a constant state of unrest owing to the rivalries of the various local chieftains, adding that 'at Rās al-Khaimah the proposed floating rest house would be moved in an enclosed lagoon within easy rifle range of the palm groves on the shore, and very liable to attack, particularly by any discontented local elements who wish to involve the local Shaikh in trouble'.[84] Cunningham suggested that the island of Abū Mūsā, some sixty miles west of Rās al-Khaimah, where the problem of defence was simple, would be an alternative rest stage. Since there was a difference of opinion between the Admiralty and the Air Ministry, besides the demand of the Treasury for Cabinet authorisation, it was decided to re-examine the various points of view within three days and to prepare a memorandum for the Ministerial Middle East Sub-Committee.

At the meeting of 5 November 1931 Rendel stated that the conflicting points of view would create considerable apprehension among the Ministers concerned, and that the Admiralty point of view strongly opposed the establishment of an Arabian air route with stopping places on the Trucial Coast. He suggested that the Admiralty should either subscribe to a general statement of approval for the Arabian route, in case no viable alternative emerged, or actively dissent from the majority recommendation and produce a minority report suggesting some alternative course of action. Finally a compromise was reached that the future agreement with the Shaikh should either be of a temporary nature or that it should be subject to the approval of HM Government.[85]

In November and December 1931 the Ministerial Sub-Committee made important decisions. On 17 November the Arabian route was agreed to, the Political Resident was authorised to begin negotiations with the Trucial shaikhs, and the Departments concerned were asked to provide an estimate of the cost of the new line. In early December, the Treasury gave its estimate of £20,000 capital outlay plus recurrent expenditure of £30,000 a year. They conceived that it would prove cheaper to pay a substantial rent to the Persian Government rather than to become involved in an expensive and risky substitute on the Arabian coast. The Secretary of State for Air described the estimate as exaggerated; in the opinion of his advisers and the Managing Director of Imperial Airways this figure was not likely to be reached.

On 17 December the Ministerial Sub-Committee agreed to an initial capital cost of £17,000–£20,000 and a recurring cash expenditure of £15,000–£17,000 per annum on operating charges. Secondly, 'the Air Ministry should be authorised to sanction the despatch of an Imperial Airways Officer to make a complete and detailed survey of a civil air route along the Arabian shore'. Lieutenant-Commander B. W. Galpin, RN (Retired) was sent. Concurrently, Lieutenant-Colonel Biscoe visited the Shaikh of Rās al-Khaimah seeking facilities for a night stop, and reported on 20 December the complete failure of negotiations. Biscoe found it useless to make further efforts there, as the Shaikh, although himself showing some disposition to come to terms, was powerless in the face of local opposition.

Negotiations therefore began with the Shaikh of Dubai, with a view of using the creek there instead of Rās al-Khaimah. However, Shaikh Sa'īd b. Maktūm was 'also unwilling to accept responsibility for affording the desired facilities'. On 15 February 1932 a meeting was held at the Air Ministry to discuss the crucial situation, which was alleviated slightly by Persia granting an extension of three months, until the end of May, for the Imperial Airways agreement. Meanwhile, the Company gave its own estimate for operating the Arabian line as £26,000 for annual cost and £28,500 for initial capital expenditure.

March 1932 proved to be a key month in the development of the Arabian air route. First, according to reports received from Tehran, any further hopes for the Persian coast route had gone. Rendel, realising the vital need to open the Arabian air route, commented, 'should our air service to India be interrupted, even temporarily, the Persians would consider that they had dealt a definite blow to British influence in the Gulf and scored an important diplomatic success. This would make it all the more difficult for HM Government to deal with the Persians in future'. Secondly, on 10 March Commander Galpin, according to new instructions from Imperial Airways to investigate landing grounds instead of sea anchorages, sent a cable to the effect that after examining possible facilities at Dabā and Shārjah, he considered Shārjah the most suitable place. At a meeting held at the Air Ministry on 21 March, Imperial Airways presented their proposal to use land planes, for economic and technical reasons, instead of flying boats agreed on a year ago, and suggested Shārjah as a suitable field. This came as a surprise, particularly to the Air Ministry.

At the meeting of the Official Middle East Sub-Committee held on 5 April to discuss this change, Rendel revived the problem which had been raised a year ago, regarding possible French and Dutch requests to use the proposed landing facilities. He said, 'This would involve other countries getting a footing in the Persian Gulf . . . and the possibility of the despatch of a foreign vessel to the Gulf and the establishment of a permanent footing there must be faced'. For the India Office Walton pointed out that 'When the time comes for a decision, it might, from the local political point of view, be preferable if possible for HM Government to endeavour to exclude foreign aircraft, relying on the exclusive nature of our treaty relations with the Trucial Shaikhs.'[86] However, the meeting accepted the proposal to operate the Arabian line immediately with land aircraft. Biscoe, recently returned from annual leave, was asked to open new negotiations with the Shaikh of Shārjah, but as he was suffering from angina pectoris and unfit to engage in any difficult operations he had been advised by his doctor not to return to the Gulf. But he insisted on doing so, because he felt that the successful opposition which the shaikhs had shown during the past five months would seriously affect British prestige on the Trucial Coast.[87] Moreover, it had become a matter of pride to achieve what had become 'one of the romances of the British Empire'. It was necessary also to overcome the obstruction of 'Īsā b. 'Abd al-Laṭīf, who was unlikely according to local informants to welcome British personnel with wireless facilities in his 'parish'. Biscoe visited Shārjah in April 1932, but the Shaikh, who was under pressure from his family and the Shaikhs of Dubai and Rās al-Khaimah, refused to grant facilities. However, b. Kāmil, the Wazīr and a wealthy pearl merchant who had travelled abroad and visited Paris, saw this as an opportunity to ameliorate the Emirate's financial position and to request that the ships of the British India Steam Navigation Company should call at Shārjah as well as Dubai. Influenced by this argument, Shaikh Sultan b. Ṣaqr sent an encouraging letter to Biscoe, expressing his willingness to renegotiate that matter.[88]

On 3 May the Political Resident visited Shārjah with two flying boats and, seeing that the Shaikh had fallen once again under the influence of the opposition, threatened to proceed with the air route without his consent and without paying him any subsidy. Shaikh Sulṭān yielded and Biscoe cabled the Indian Government on 7 May, giving them the good news and suggesting that forty guards should be immediately enlisted by the Residency Agent, 'Īsā b. 'Abd al-Laṭīf, and that the 'Rest House' should be surrounded by a wall. Both house and aerodrome would be clear of the town and under the cover of naval guns.[89] Furthermore, in this month the Persians agreed to extend their air agreement from the end of May to the end of September.

In June 1932 Biscoe worked on a draft air agreement that would satisfy

Shaikh Sulṭān b. Ṣaqr and visited Shārjah. He found to his disappointment that the Shaikh's brothers were still trying to obstruct the agreement and that the Shaikh was under additional pressure from Dubai, whose people feared that the mail boats would transfer their port of call from there to Shārjah. The signing of the agreement was again held up, but the Shaikh promised to allow an engineer to be sent down and to collect building material for the 'Rest House'.[90] On 14 July the Political Resident instructed H. R. P. Dickson, the Political Agent in Kuwait, to join him in another attempt to have the Shaikh sign the agreement. Unfortunately Biscoe died on board HMS *Bideford* when they were on their way to the Trucial Coast, but Dickson decided, after the funeral, to continue the journey to Shārjah and tackle the air agreement himself. After three strenuous days of negotiations Dickson succeeded in getting the Shaikh's signature on 22 July after sunset. At the end of the negotiations the Shaikh asked for a one gun salute as he left the *Bideford*. The Captain refused, quoting Admiralty regulations which forbid all salutes after the sun has set. Dickson's reply showed the patience and diplomacy he had needed to succeed: 'For God's sake, don't start making difficulties now. Fire all the guns you have—if necessary, with live shells—but let us get the Shaikh Sulṭān's signature'.[91]

In this agreement—to last for eleven years—the Shaikh had to enlist thirty-five guards, their salaries to be paid by the British Government. Eight hundred rupees would be paid to the ruler each month from the first day of landing, and three hundred rupees paid for the 'Rest House'. The British Government would give him a loan to build the 'Rest House' and the monthly payment would be deducted from the loan. In addition the Shaikh would be given a subsidy of five hundred rupees per month from 1 July 1932 onwards. Five rupees would be paid for every plane landing, but Royal Air Force planes were exempted. In accordance with the treaty of 1892, it was decided that the representative of Imperial Airways should not in future have direct contact with the Shaikh, but through the Political Resident.[92]

The agreement had immediate repercussions. Steamers of the British India SN Company began to call at Shārjah, much to the chagrin of the inhabitants of Dubai, who now realised too late the chance that had been missed. Ironically, Shaikh Sulṭān b. Ṣaqr, Ruler of Shārjah, who five years previously had written to the Shaikhs of Banī Ka'b and Buraimī to warn them against co-operating with Thomas' mission, was now the only ruler who consented, under some pressure, to the air agreement with the British. In fact his letter of 1927 had been written when the Ihkwān movement in Sa'ūdī Arabia was at its height and his people were greatly influenced by them. If King Ibn Sa'ūd had not suppressed this wave of religious fanaticism in 1930, Shaikh Sulṭān could not have considered signing any agreement. Even so, in Shārjah itself, while some welcomed the air agreement, others for religious reasons opposed it bitterly and migrated to Rās al-Khaimah.

At the beginning of October 1932 the first Imperial Airways plane inaugurated the Arabian route and landed at Shārjah on its way to India.[93] Now the need arose for occasional landing grounds and air facilities for the Royal Air Force and Imperial Airways. Early in 1934 the Shaikh of Dubai gave refuelling facilities and sea anchorage in a four-year agreement. Ṣīr Banī Yās and Abū Dhabī islands were also chosen. In December 1934 Colonel Loch, the Political Agent in Baḥrain, visited Shaikh Shakhbūt, the Ruler of Abū Dhabī, who had repeatedly refused to grant any air facilities, and threatened to prevent Abū Dhabī boats from proceeding to the pearl fisheries, an act which would severely affect the Shaikh and his people. Finally, on 13 February 1935 the Shaikh signed an agreement accepting a petrol tank on Sīr Banī Yās and the establishment of a landing ground on the island and one near Abū Dhabī. However, Shaikh Shakhbūt insisted in this agreement that the British must not interfere in his internal affairs, and that foreigners had no right to enter the town without his permission. In July the Abū Dhabī landing ground was ready to receive planes.[94]

The renewal of air agreements on the Trucial Coast reflected the current climate of internal politics and the changing attitude towards the British. Early in 1938, when the British insisted on their policy of manumission of slaves on the Trucial Coast and demanded the deportation of two Arab traders from Dubai (see Chapter 2, p. 129) who were accused of involvement in arms traffic, the newly elected Majlis decided on 27 March that in retaliation the air agreement was not to be renewed. However, within a year Shaikh Sa'īd had regained control and overthrown the Majlis; the agreement was then prolonged.[95] In fact the Arabian air route and its recent establishment on the Trucial Coast, together with the oil concessions, had fundamentally changed the position of the Trucial Coast in British strategy. Reviewing the meetings of the Committee of Imperial Defence and their discussions of defence schemes on the Arab side in the Gulf before the Second World War, one realises that the safety of the landing grounds and refuelling had become a matter of great concern, a situation that had only emerged in the inter-war years.

The Appearance of American and Japanese Economic Enterprises

American Activities As from 1890 the evangelistic and medical activities of the American missions of the Dutch Reformed Church in Baḥrain, Kuwait and Muscat represented the only sphere of United States interest in the Gulf. American popularity amongst the Arabs was engendered by their successful educational institutions in the Middle East and President Wilson's doctrine regarding the right of all nations to complete independence and self-determination. Although the disagreement between the United States and France and Britain on post-war policy resulted in America returning to her previous isolation, the inter-war period witnessed a great extension of

American economic activities throughout the world. American enterprises in the Middle East, centred on oil, soon involved the Gulf area.

One of the main areas of disputes over oil between Britain and the United States during the 1920s was Iraq. The Turkish Petroleum Company there, shared by British, German and Ottoman capital, had been established before the war and had been granted a concession in 1914. After the defeat of Germany and Turkey, the company became a complete British monopoly. At this time the powerful American oil companies, with seven decades of experience, huge capital resources and sophisticated technology were under the temporary misapprehension that the United States oil reserves would soon be exhausted, thus leaving them unable to meet the growing demands of an expanding domestic industry. The State Department in Washington soon came under strong pressure from these companies to protest against French and British discrimination in the occupied Ottoman areas. When the American senate was informed that France and Britain had signed the San Remo petroleum agreement in April 1920, which gave the French a share in the Turkish Petroleum Company, it reacted indignantly. The State Department in its various memoranda to the British Government between 1920 and 1922 put forward the 'Open Door' policy as a condition of United States recognition of the French and British mandates in the Middle East, threatening otherwise to retaliate with the closure of all areas under American influence to British oil operations.

When it became clear that the Foreign Office would have to yield, a representative of British oil interests took the initiative and met a delegate of an American Consortium of five oil companies. A settlement was reached which was soon presented to their respective governments. The American group was given a share of 23.5 per cent in the Turkish Petroleum Company in Iraq, equal to that of the French, the Anglo-Persian Oil Company and the Royal Dutch Shell Company. In 1924 the Government of Iraq confirmed the previous concession to this company under its new shareholders. By 1928 the British were feeling the need to limit the scope of the US companies in the Gulf and succeeded in gaining acceptance of the 'Red Line Agreement' by which the members of the American Consortium were prohibited from prospecting individually in the former Ottoman territories in Arabia. Exploitation was now to be undertaken jointly in the name of the whole company, which in 1929 adopted the new name of the Iraq Petroleum Company.[96]

However, Britain was not completely successful in confining American activities in the Gulf. The Americans succeeded in acquiring conclusive concessions covering Baḥrain in 1928 and al-Ḥasā in 1933. It was not without strenuous effort that the British in 1934 settled their disputes with the Americans over the oil of Kuwait on a fifty-fifty basis.[97] In fact, the swift American gains in a comparatively short period were facilitated by various factors within the British camp, important among which was the unpopularity in the area of the Anglo–Persian Oil Company, in which the British Government had a predominating interest. In the early 1920s, in spite of heavy British pressure (Cox, Arnold Wilson, now Director-General of APOC and Knox, the Political Resident), Ibn Sa'ūd, the Shaikhs of Kuwait, Qaṭar and Baḥrain consistently refused to give oil concessions to this company.[98]

Amīn al-Rīḥānī, the naturalised American Arab traveller who was respected by the State Department in Washington as an authority in Arab affairs, was touring Arabia in 1922. Sincerely devoted to his native land as well as to the country of his adoption, Rīḥānī believed that the introduction of American capital and modernisation would be to the advantage of the Arab countries. When in 1922 Major Holmes, a New Zealand mining engineer representing the Eastern Syndicate, a British firm without much capital, came to 'Uqair and asked Ibn Sa'ūd for an oil concession Rīḥānī supported his request. In his report to the State Department of 27 October 1923, Rīḥānī wrote, 'Now, the writer is, on general principle, against the Abadan monopoly and has succeeded in convincing the Sultan that it is better to his interest to grant the concession to an independent company that had no connection with the British Government.'[99] In a report of 28 March 1924 Lt. Colonel A. P. Trevor, the new Political Resident, explained the general attitude in the Gulf towards APOC:

> At present any ill-wishers of the British or of the Anglo–Persian Oil Company never lose an opportunity of impressing upon their hearers that the Anglo–Persian Oil Company is a Government concern and that to grant a concession to this company is tantamount to giving it to Government: that they have hitherto always looked to the Government to deal impartially with Arab matters, that they cannot hope for Government to do so when the interests of the Anglo–Persian Oil Company come up against those of the Arabs.[100]

As a result of this attitude, Holmes, as representing a small private firm, succeeded in obtaining concessions in al-Ḥasā in 1922, in Baḥrain in 1923 and in Kuwait in 1925.

A second factor in the British failure to compete effectively with the Americans at this time, in spite of their apparent political advantage, was an absence of serious desire to extend their own oil production on the Arabian Coast. There were three reasons for this: first, recent sporadic surveys in 'Omān, Qaṭar and Kuwait had convinced them that there were no further oil prospects to exploit; secondly, the capital and the energies of IPC and APOC were absorbed by the construction of the pipeline to the Mediterranean and the extensive activities of APOC in Persia; and thirdly, Britain's immediate domestic needs were already adequately met by the rich wells in Iraq and Persia. British interest in gaining oil concessions on the Arabian coast lay in a purely dog-in-the-manger anxiety to exclude the

Americans for they had no real intention of using any oil concessions they might acquire in this area. For this reason, when Holmes, who as we have seen was short of capital, attempted to persuade IPC, APOC and other British financiers to take an interest in the Baḥrain and al-Ḥasā concessions, he failed.

The consequent lack of unity between the various British interests involved was the third factor favouring American success. After the First World War APOC was putting pressure on the British Government to assist them in obtaining an oil monopoly on the Arabian coast by the strict enforcement of the shaikh's pledges. Accordingly, Cox and the Political Resident, acting on instructions from the Colonial Office, attempted to discredit Holmes and tried unsuccessfully to persuade Ibn Sa'ūd and the shaikhs to cancel his concessions.[101] Holmes was virtually driven to approaching the American companies. In 1928 the Standard Oil Company of California bought the Baḥrain concession. This constituted a material contravention of the treaty of 1892 and so put the British in an awkward position. This question became a matter of discussion between the Colonial Office and the US State Department. The British insisted on the 'nationality clause' and it was agreed finally that Standard Oil of California should take up the concession through an operating British subsidiary registered in Canada. The top managers in Baḥrain and Canada must be British and all dealings with the Shaikh of Baḥrain were to be conducted through the British Political Agent.[102] This solution to the nationality clause problem became the pattern for American and international oil companies who would shortly begin to operate in Kuwait, Qaṭar and the Trucial Coast.

The heat of Anglo–American competition at this time emerged in the letters of Alexander Sloan, the US Consul in Baghdād, who clearly saw all British activities as connected with oil. Sloan observed the travels in 'Omān of Bertram Thomas, the British Financial Adviser to the Sultan of Muscat, with great concern, and in 1931 he reported that, although he understood that Thomas's expeditions were undertaken privately they were also said to have been watched benevolently by the British Government. In another report to his Government he wrote, quoting the British representative in Baḥrain of the Mesopotamia and Persia Corporation (whom he met on his visit to Baḥrain in January 1931 when Thomas arrived after his historic crossing of the Empty Quarter), 'British officials stationed in the Persian Gulf were well aware of the fact that Mr Thomas had not been sent to act as financial adviser to the Sultan of 'Omān solely, but that his main duties there were to explore the interior and to try and locate for the Anglo–Persian Oil Company oil seepages reported to have been discovered by Arab caravans in that section of Arabia'. He added that British officials were also aware of the fact that an APOC tanker had picked Mr Thomas up at Muscat and had landed him at Dhofār, and that his journey, while ostensibly undertaken as an exploratory trip over an unknown portion of Arabia, was also taken to obtain all possible information for the APOC.

This interpretation of Thomas's trips was not confined to American diplomatic and commercial circles. Dr Dame, an American medical missionary, informed Sloan during his visit to Baḥrain that Thomas, during his five years' stay in the Sultanate of 'Omān, had paid little attention to his duties as financial adviser, but had seemingly seized every opportunity to make trips into the interior of the country.[103] The British, for their part, became suspicious of the activities of the American medical missionaries, the only Americans in the area with ready access to the shaikhs and other notables, and kept a careful eye on their movements. The Political Resident who had forbidden access to the area to all foreigners without a visa, now imposed particularly severe restrictions on the visits of American medical missionaries to Qaṭar and the Trucial Coast.[104]

In 1932 the Americans struck oil in Baḥrain. This came as a complete surprise to the British and marked a turning point in the oil industry in the Gulf. There were two immediate effects. The Shaikhs were deeply impressed by the Americans' superior efficiency in the field of oil production, which for years to come influenced their willingness to co-operate with US companies, and the British promptly developed a lively interest in oil on the Arabian side of the Gulf, though as yet they still failed to take the competition seriously enough to prevent the granting of the al-Ḥasā concession by Ibn Sa'ūd to the Standard Oil Company of California in 1933.

In the next two years Anglo-American tension over Kuwait grew. The American Gulf Oil Company sent Major Holmes as a representative to the Shaikh of Kuwait and APOC sent Chisholm, its manager, with an interpreter, Ḥājjī 'Abdullah Williamson, who was to play a part in the oil exploration and negotiations on the Trucial Coast in the later 1930s.[105] During these negotiations enmity arose between Holmes and Williamson, who had close friendship with the Kuwaitis and discoursed with them in their own tongue.[106] British authorities in the Gulf tried to influence the Shaikh to prefer APOC and the Americans promptly retaliated by again threatening to penalise British oil interests in areas under American influence. Finally the Foreign Office, keen to maintain American friendship, agreed in 1934 (with much resentment from the India Office) to allow free competition in Kuwait, and the dispute ended in joint participation in a Kuwait concession to be owned and financed equally by the two companies.

In 1934 the demand for oil and Anglo-American competition shifted southwards to Qaṭar and the Trucial Coast. The British now felt, in the Gulf as well as at home, that they must move with more energy and determination if the oil concessions in these remaining areas were not to slip inevitably into American hands with serious economic and political consequences.

Japanese Activities The competition offered to the British by the Japanese was less formidable than that from the US, and was focused, particularly during the 1930s, on trade, shipping and oil transportation. One reason for Japanese popularity in the Gulf was that the Arabs saw them as representing the liberation of the East from the Western yoke. After the First World War Japan had emerged as a major power with a strong navy and industry. Japanese manufactured goods and cotton textiles now found a healthy market in the Gulf. In the early 1930s the Japanese Company of Mitsubishi, the Yamashita Steamship Co. and the maritime line Mitsue Bussan Kaisha Ltd, established agencies in Baḥrain and many visits by their representatives were recorded.[107] In 1933 the Department of Overseas Trade, in discussing the Japanese activities with Fowle, the Political Resident (1932–9), stressed that 'We are losing very valuable time—and probably trade—in a most vulnerable spot. As you know, we are keenly exercised about the intensity of Japanese competition, particularly with our cotton trade, and the Persian Gulf has hitherto formed a not inconsiderable market for that industry'.[108]

The American construction of a new oil camp at Dhahrān in al-Ḥasā encouraged Japanese trade. It was Japan who supplied cement and construction material for the camp through their new agents in Baḥrain, Yūsuf Kanū and Muḥammad Yatīm, both eminent local merchants who had long and intimate ties with British interests. These two merchants now saw their way to establish strong commercial relations with the Americans and with Japanese companies, and were very soon to play a role as American intermediaries for oil concessions with the chiefs of the Trucial Coast. In the later 1930s Japanese tankers appeared in the Gulf alongside the British and American vessels transporting Baḥrain oil, the majority of which was now directed to Japan.

Japan's concern with oil came very late. On 13 April 1938, Sir Reader Bullard, the British Minister in Jeddah, reported that the Japanese Ambassador in Cairo had visited Ibn Sa'ūd in Riyādh, presenting very generous offers for oil, which, however, King Ibn Sa'ūd had refused.[109]

Oil Concessions

The story of the search for oil on the Trucial Coast really begins in late 1935. It was the last area in the Gulf where Anglo–American oil rivalry between the wars was played out. The recent American success in obtaining 100 per cent concessions in Baḥrain and al-Ḥasā and 50 per cent in Kuwait, owing to the compromising policy of the Foreign Office, had caused strong reactions in British official circles and within the British oil companies. The new and positive British official policy regarding oil concessions which had begun in Qaṭar two years earlier was also practised in the Trucial Coast.

As already mentioned, in the post-war years APOC put pressure on the Colonial Office to reserve areas in the Gulf, including the Trucial Coast, as a monopoly for their future exploitation. Accordingly, between February and May 1922 each Trucial shaikh gave a written undertaking to Colonel A. P. Trevor, the Political Resident (1920–24), that if oil were found in their territory they would not grant a concession for it to any foreigner except to the person appointed by the British Government.[110] Although APOC was the only oil company given access by the Colonial Office to the Trucial Coast in 1925, they handled their opportunity carelessly, coming to the false conclusion that there was no oil in the area and this influenced their policy till the early 1930s. Realising Arab hostility to their own company, APOC conducted all investigations in the name of one of their subsidiaries, D'Arcy Exploitation. On 19 October 1925 two APOC geologists, G. M. Lees and Washington Gray, and one botanist, Mr Fernandez, accompanied by 'Abdullah Williamson, had visited Shārjah on their way down to Muscat in the Company's steamer *Khūzistān*. They proceeded to Rās al-Khaimah where, owing to the hostility of the tribes, they spent only one day and moved on to Khaṣab, where they passed three days surveying the mountains.

It was not only the carelessness of the company and the incompetence of the geologists, who were given no real chance of exploration that was involved; also involved was the India Office policy of excluding all oil concession hunters, whether British or foreign, because of the backward character of the area and the risks involved, an attitude which continued until the early 1930s. On 4 February 1926 Lieutenant-Colonel F. B. Prideaux, Political Resident (1924–7), expressing the general attitude of the India Office, criticised the visit of the three men, which had taken place without his permission.

> It is impossible for any European to land and start on a journey of exploration in any of the Chiefships without the previous consent and support of this Residency . . . the Residency can obtain the Shaikh's consent to geologists making excursions—say of 30 or 40 miles into the interior in order to correlate the geology on the southern side of the Gulf with the known facts as to the geological conditions on the Persian side, but there is no likelihood at present of any of the six chiefs issuing to any one an Exploration Licence [*sic*] in connection with a concession to bore for oil.[111]

This was also made clear by a circular from the Political Resident in Bushire the same day, stressing that all Europeans were forbidden to visit the Trucial Coast, owing to lack of accommodation and prevailing insecurity; accordingly no requests to explore for oil, specifically those of APOC and the Eastern Syndicate, could be met for the time being.[112]

The discovery of oil in Baḥrain and the inauguration of the Arabian air route in the same year gave a new significance to the Trucial Coast and Qaṭar in British policy. At a meeting of the OME Sub-Committee between 1932 and 1934, criticism of the Foreign Office's compromising policy through the India Office and the Admiralty led to the acceptance of a fundamentally different approach to the oil concessions in Qaṭar and later in the Trucial Coast. A brief study of the methods exercised in Kuwait and Qaṭar will give us a clear idea of this new policy. In April 1932, after diplomatic approaches by the United States Government, the British Cabinet, on advice from the Foreign Office, decided that it was for the Shaikh of Kuwait alone to decide whether or not he would refuse to allow the oil concession to go to non-British interests. In a meeting on the OME Sub-Committee on 2 December Rendel refused even to sanction a personal communication from Fowle or Dickson to advise the Shaikh on where his interests lay between APOC and the American Gulf Oil Company. He stated that it might be necessary to publish correspondence at a later date and that such an intimation to the Resident might well be regarded as weighing the scales in favour of APOC. He added,

> In view of the present state of Anglo–American relations, and of the numerous problems of world importance for the solution of which Anglo–American co-operation was essential, the Foreign Office could not agree to any action likely to provoke an accusation of bad faith or sharp practice which could not afterwards be proved by the correspondents.[113]

Fowle and Dickson therefore did not interfere in any of the long negotiations, which ended in the formation of a mixed company, half American and half British, to which the oil concession was granted in May 1934.

On 25 August 1932 Shaikh 'Abdullah b. Jāsim, Ruler of Qaṭar, granted APOC a two-year option on oil exploration and, repeating his request of a decade earlier, asked the British for protection. Because of the prevailing British policy of not extending commitments in the Gulf, his request was once again neglected.[114] During 1933 several interdepartmental meetings were held at the Colonial Office, at one of which Fowle was present, to discuss British policy in the Gulf. Mr Hearn the representative of APOC expressed the wish of his company for a visit to Qaṭar to extend their oil option into a long-term concession, something which had been neglected for more than a decade. 'He thought that if the APOC did not move quickly there was a danger that Major Holmes and his associates would forestall them and obtain a concession for American interests'. He was anxious to avoid the same situation arising in Qaṭar as had arisen in Kuwait. When Hearn stressed that APOC was only acting on behalf of IPC, Rendel found his proposition acceptable in view of the fact that while the former company was an all-British concern the latter was an international one. The Admiralty supported Hearn, for they far preferred IPC to the American interests working with Major Holmes.

As a result of these meetings APOC was given permission to deal directly with Shaikh 'Abdullah. After this experience of the dealings in Kuwait, which he bitterly criticised, Fowle requested that he might be able to give political support to APOC, without which he felt sure they would fail in their negotiations. In August 1933 the Shaikh, encouraged by his private secretary Muḥammad al-Mānī', who had strong sympathies for Ibn Sa'ūd, interrupted the negotiations and visited Riyādh. Fowle saw that the Shaikh's favourable attitude had changed on his return, and he was informed that during his visit the Shaikh was under strong pressure to give the oil concession to the Americans. In October 1933 Fowle reminded the Shaikh of his treaty obligations, which angered him greatly. Fowle advocated a firm policy, pointing out that it would not be a rejection of the 'Open Door' policy, since IPC—to which any concession obtained would be immediately transferred—contained an American element.[115]

In the winter of that year a great deal of correspondence passed between the India Office and Foreign Office. In a memorandum of 16 December 1933 Laithwaite stressed Qaṭar's importance for the Trucial Coast and for general British strategy in general saying:

> The Shaikhdom of Qatar is of particular importance because of its geographical position on the southern littoral of the Persian Gulf. The establishment of a non-British oil company in Qatar, particularly if identical or closely associated with the American company to which Ibn Saud has granted the Hasa concession, must inevitably sooner or later react unfavourably on the position of HM Government in the vitally important Shaikhdom of Bahrain. It will inevitably prejudice in an increasing degree as time goes on the position of HM Government in the semi-barbarous areas of the Trucial Coast.[116]

In January 1934 on realising the possibility that Ibn Sa'ūd might give active support to the Standard Oil Company to secure the Qaṭar concession, Fowle asked for authorisation to threaten the Shaikh of Qaṭar that he would not be permitted to grant a concession to any company that was not at least partly British. Arguing that the main reason for the Shaikh's refusal to grant a concession was his fear of retaliation from Ibn Sa'ūd, the only inducement likely to turn the scale in favour of APOC would be an undertaking to give the Shaikh protection against landward aggression.

On 23 February the Committee of Imperial Defence held a special meeting to discuss this question and recommended that 'HM Government are prepared to give the Shaikh a guarantee in respect of unprovoked aggression by land in return for the grant by him of an oil concession to the Anglo-Persian Oil Company (acting for the Iraq Petroleum Company)'.[117] Between 2 and 4 April Fowle and Loch visited the Shaikh but met with difficulties in negotiating a concession because of recent offers from Standard Oil of California. They discovered that a certain Dr Thomas from the American Mission in Baḥrain, who had left on their arrival, had attempted to influence the Shaikh in favour of the Americans. He tried to instil the idea that the

Americans were the richest people in the world while the British were merely poor but politicians. When Fowle threatened the Shaikh, the latter asked for a written document of protection.[118] A meeting of the OME Sub-Committee on 12 April approved Fowle's energetic policy and sanctioned its continuation. However, it took a further year of negotiations before the final written guarantee of protection was completed. This elicited an immediate protest from King Ibn Sa'ūd.[119]

During this year the scene moved from Qaṭar to the Trucial Coast. In May Philby and Holmes on behalf of the Americans sent letters to the Shaikh of Dubai and other shaikhs on the Trucial Coast in order to obtain oil concessions. An Indian clerk working for Holmes asked for a visa from Baḥrain to visit Dubai and Abū Dhabī and on being questioned stated that Major Holmes intended to send him to negotiate oil concessions on the Trucial Coast; his visa was cancelled immediately. Aware now of the American's moves, Fowle realised that the moment was critical and good relations must be actively cultivated with the shaikhs and their families, so instructions to this effect were sent to Loch and to the Residency Agent in Shārjah. Since it had been proved that American medical officers had involved themselves in oil matters in Qaṭar, they were forbidden access to the Coast and the British now undertook to send their own doctors, another sign of their intention to secure the people's goodwill. In December 1934 the Assistant Surgeon, R. Holmes, accompanied the Political Resident on his tour to carry out medical work and during his visit a year later Dr Holmes was accompanied by the Medical Officer of the Royal Air Force. These visits continued until a permanent clinic was established in Dubai in 1939.[120]

The Americans' obvious intention of extending their oil activities to the Trucial Coast and the shaikhs' own interest in the potential oil resources in their territory, combined with the new official British policy as seen in Qaṭar, caused new energetic policies of expansion in the British oil companies. A new subsidiary called Petroleum Concessions Ltd was established in October 1935 with headquarters in Baḥrain, with Major Stephen Longrigg as Managing Director. This company created an affiliate called Petroleum Development (Trucial Coast). Longrigg described the aim of these two as being one of prudent self-defence against uncontrolled operation by outsiders rather than self-aggrandisement of the IPC.[121] In November 1935 the new company succeeded in obtaining options in Rās al-Khaimah, Shārjah, Abū Dhabī and Dubai for two years; in January 1936 the Shaikh of 'Ajman finally agreed, but the Shaikh of Umm al-Qaiwain refused because his payment was not equal to that of Abū Dhabī. In this month Ḥājjī 'Abdullah Williamson accompanied the geologists as an interpreter on their visit to the Trucial Coast.[122]

A successful diplomatic approach was made to Holmes, who then became the representative of Petroleum Development in the coming negotiations with the Trucial Shaikhs.[123] Although it was advantageous to take Holmes from the Americans, it created great enmity with Williamson who, nearing the age of retirement, had hoped for the appointment himself and not the part of a mere interpreter. On 31 May 1936 Holmes visited the Coast for the first time and found the shaikhs unfavourable—he met with no success. For more than a year the negotiations proved difficult because of the Qawāsim shaikhs' general preference for an American company, in which they were guided by sympathy for Ibn Sa'ūd. The personal enmity between Holmes and Williamson and the attempts of both to discredit the other was another factor that endangered an agreement. At the same time the Americans were still in correspondence with the shaikhs, and their agents were merchants in Baḥrain who in the past had intimate ties with the British and who had established good personal relations with the Trucial shaikhs.[124] As in Qaṭar, it would not have been possible to gain any concessions without the same policy of interference and the firm approach of the Political Resident. In June 1936 Holmes paid a second visit but found the Trucial shaikhs displaying care and caution in their business dealings and he did not succeed as he had anticipated. In September Holmes, accompanied by Loch, visited the Coast with a draft agreement, which the Shaikh of Dubai asked to study, but they succeeded in obtaining from the shaikh a house for the Company's representative.

In December 1936 an Indian Muslim, 'Ajīb Khān, visited the Coast with the secret intention of attempting to gain an oil concession for Standard Oil of California. When Lloyd Hamilton, the representative of the Baḥrain Oil Company, approached the Foreign Office and India Office for permission to visit the Coast, he was informed that in this area priority had been given to 'Petroleum Concessions' in which the Americans were a partner and he must wait his turn. Viewing these proceedings from a distance Fowle became increasingly annoyed with the delays and on 14 January 1937 he sent a letter to Loch asking him to press Holmes to speed up his negotiations, paying particular attention to Umm al-Qaiwain and Kalbā, where there was the greatest risk of American intrusion.[125] Accordingly Holmes visited the Coast on 27 January to resume negotiations, and Loch followed him. Unknown to them their position was being undermined by Williamson, who would view any failure by Holmes with pleasure. Unaware that the official British oil policy in the Trucial States was fundamentally different to the one he had known in Kuwait, he wrote in a letter of 4 February 1937 to the Shaikh of Rās al-Khaimah that the British Government 'would neither press nor force anyone and that the Shaikhs ought to know that they are quite at liberty to choose whatever suits them'. When he added 'We understand that Major Holmes wants to obtain concession of Kalba, Wadi al-Ghoar and also Umm al-Howsh. My brother, you know the necessary arrangement in this connection. We have sent a man of Sharjah on our behalf to Kalba in order to persuade your cousin not to agree to those terms which may bring disadvantage'.

In his letters of February and March 1937 Holmes mentioned that the shaikhs had now come to an arrangement whereby negotiations should only be carried out with the Shaikh of Dubai and that the rest would follow suit. It also became evident that they were well informed about the agreements in Qaṭar, Ḥasā and Kuwait, for when Holmes next visited the Shaikh of Dubai the latter talked about safeguards, drilling obligations and a paid representative appointed by himself in London. However, by the middle of March 1937 general agreement had been reached on all but three points. The Shaikh objected that the draft he had been given in September 1936 differed greatly from the one with which he was now presented. He also insisted that the annual payment of Rs. 25,000 should be dated from September 1936 and on a representative in London. Although Holmes explained that the British Government and Fowle would not agree to a representative, the Shaikh was adamant. On 19 March 1937 the company agreed to the payment condition.

As the expiry date of the two-year options drew nearer, Holmes concentrated on trying to have them extended; the shaikhs refused, with the exception of the Shaikh of Dubai, who extended his to 31 December 1937 only. On 11 March 1937, during Loch's visit to the Coast, his clerk 'Alī secretly obtained hand-written copies of Williamson's letter to the Shaikh of Rās al-Khaimah mentioned above, and others to him from K. S. Yūsuf Kānū and Ḥusain Yatīm in Baḥrain and K. S. 'Amād, a relative of 'Īsā b. 'Abd al-Laṭīf, who in 1935 had hoped to be appointed as Residency Agent in Shārjah after 'Īsā died, though the British chose 'Abd al-Razzāq, a native of Kuwait. On 26 March 1937 the Shaikh of Dubai wrote to 'Abd al-Razzāq informing him that 'Abdullah Williamson had been refused entry into Dubai because he had been creating misunderstanding between the Shaikh and his friends and intriguing in internal affairs; he disclaimed all responsibility for Williamson's safety in his country. Williamson therefore left in a few days for Baḥrain, where he accused Holmes and 'Abd al-Razzāq of plotting against him. 'Abd al-Razzāq, on the other hand, ascribed the difficulties that Holmes was facing to the activities of these four persons. He enclosed copies of their letters to the shaikhs and wrote to Loch saying,

> The danger of their activities can be easily foreseen and unless they are soon stopped, they will not only do harm which will be detrimental to the interests of the British companies, but will greatly damage the British policy on the Trucial Coast and will make things very difficult for the government to deal with.[126]

On 30 March, in a mood of disappointment, Holmes telegraphed the company in London that the Shaikh's final word was that he would defer his decision for a further week to give the company an opportunity to reconsider its decision. He stressed that the shaikhs generally believed that the

Americans were prepared to offer better terms than the British company and that they would welcome an excuse to enter into negotiations with Standard Oil. He added, 'Standard Oil California are communicating privately with Rulers and Rās al-Khaimah Ruler wrote to Dubai Ruler yesterday, stating that he intended writing to Standard Oil Baḥrain asking them to be ready to send their representative to discuss concessions when the present option expired'.[127]

Not satisfied with the slow negotiations and aware of recent information and rumours from the Coast, Fowle sent a circular letter to the Trucial Shaikhs informing them that the California Oil Company had approached certain shaikhs in the Coast, and that this Company had been officially notified that Petroleum Concession Ltd had prior rights in the area and HM Government could not therefore approve of any negotiations between the shaikhs and the California Oil Company.[128] On 8 April the Secretary of State for India, also impatient for a settlement, telegraphed Fowle that if the Shaikh of Dubai attached importance to the appointment of a London representative and Petroleum Concession agreed, the Government of India need not interfere. He added, 'there does not appear to be any objection in principle particularly in view of Kuwait precedent. It is increasingly desirable to get Dubai concession disposed of'. Immediately, Fowle asked the Shaikh of Dubai and Holmes to meet him at Baḥrain. With the company's concurrence in the question of London representation the Shaikh stated that he was now willing to sign, but he insisted that he must sign in the presence of his notables, so Fowle secured from him the promise that he would sign the concession within a fortnight of his return to Dubai.

The agreed period ended in May, but no news was received, which worried both Loch and Fowle. On 15 May the latter received information from Loch that the Shaikhs of Rās al-Khaimah and Shārjah were endeavouring to prevent the Shaikh of Dubai from signing. At a meeting at Shārjah with Shaikh Māni' b. Rāshid, head of the opposition party in Dubai, present, they decided to ask Shaikh Sa'īd b. Maktūm to reject the draft concession completely in favour of the Americans. On 18 May Fowle telegraphed Hickinbotham, the new Political Agent in Baḥrain, that unless the British took drastic action, Standard Oil might have a good chance of capturing Trucial oil. He asked Hickinbotham to proceed directly to Dubai and if the Shaikh refused to sign he should inform him that his promise to the Political Resident was binding, and HM Government would not give him permission to grant a concession to any other company. Regarding the Shaikhs of Shārjah and Rās al-Khaimah Fowle proposed teaching them a lesson to mind their own business by unofficially telling 'Abd al-Razzāq

> to stop all travel papers to them and their subjects. The result of this would be that their merchants will not be able to visit Bombay for sale of pearls. No reason will be given for this action but Rulers will doubt-

> less connect cause and effect. If an excuse is necessary at any time in the future arms' traffic or smuggling into India can be cited.[129]

Fowle added 'get hold of Mana and on my behalf try to frighten him on the same lines as I did with Salih al Mana at Doha'. A day later Hickinbotham cabled that he would fly to Dubai on 20 May and suggested that an unusual number of sloops, say two, should be sent to Shārjah and that an RAF flight arriving on the same day should be detained two days before proceeding to Aden. Should the Shaikhs of Rās al-Khaimah and Shārjah prove difficult, Hickinbotham asked permission that the sloops might cause as much trouble as possible to the pearling fleet by bringing dhows belonging to these shaikhdoms to Shārjah and searching and detaining them on the pretext of suspected traffic in slaves. 'This will affect people who will bring pressure to bear on the rulers.' Before Hickinbotham left, Fowle informed him that he was reluctant to ask the Navy and thought that the non-issue of travel papers would alone be sufficient.

On 22 May Shaikh Sa'īd b. Maktūm signed the agreement with Holmes in the presence of Hickinbotham. The duration of this agreement was seventy-five years; the Shaikh was given Rs. 60,000 on signature and the company had to pay Rs. 200,000 within sixty days of the discovery of oil in commercial quantities. In addition, the company would pay annually Rs. 30,000 rupees and guarantee the annual payment of not less than Rs. 90,000 on the discovery of oil. Three rupees was decided as the price of every ton and two annas per 1,000 cubic feet of natural gas produced and sold. Holmes informed the Shaikh that the company would open an account for him at the Eastern Bank in Baḥrain. Further, Hickinbotham officially notified the Shaikh that should he wish to grant permission to a bank to open a branch or agency in Dubai he would have to obtain HM Government's agreement before entering into any negotiations with the bank.

Although he received congratulations from the British oil companies, Fowle felt the struggle was not over, for the other shaikhs had to be roped in, which would be no easy task. Fowle expressed his dissatisfaction with Petroleum Concessions' procedures and the general situation in his telegram to the Secretary of State for India on 25 May, mentioning also that on 23 May, after the signing, Holmes had received a telegram from the company saying that they could not authorise him to sign unless Article 13a stood as previous drafted. Fowle telegraphed to Hickinbotham that the change could be made only if the Shaikh agreed, which he did not. He added,

> whole conduct of Dubai negotiations on part of the Company and Holmes has been unsatisfactory and that Shaikh has signed concession is due as much to his personal promise to me as to any effort on the part of the company. Holmes has been most dilatory and I have good evidence that Hajji Williamson also employed by the company on the

> Trucial Coast has been intriguing on behalf of California Arabian Standard Oil Company and against Shaikh of Dubai who has asked that he should not be allowed back in Dubai territory.[130]

He further criticised Holmes' and the company's inefficiency in having no draft agreements drawn up for the other shaikhs whose options were to expire shortly. He suggested that the company headquarters in London be approached on the following points: that their conduct to date had been unsatisfactory and must be remedied and that they telegraph details for the other concessions to Holmes immediately; 'unless the company bestir themselves, there is a distinct danger of the remaining Trucial Coast shaikhdoms and of Muscat being captured by the California Arabian Standard Oil Company'.

At the end of the month Fowle and Hickinbotham studied the means by which they could use the travel documents more effectively to coerce the Shaikhs of Shārjah, Abū Dhabī and Rās al-Khaimah. Holmes now asked the company to relieve him because of ill-health and Ernest O. Parkes, who succeeded him on 17 September signed an agreement for seventy-five years with the Shaikh of Shārjah, the first to yield quickly.[131] However, the negotiations with Abū Dhabī proved difficult, as the Shaikh informed them in February 1938 that he declined to consider any concession unless identical with that granted by Ibn Sa'ūd. Not surprisingly, he was accused of conniving in the slave trade by the British authorities, who were at the time under pressure regarding slavery in Arabia; he was told 'that slave trading goes on through his territories, therefore he was deprived of the good offices of HM Government' and in March all travel papers for himself and his subjects were stopped. In April, when the Shaikh of Rās al-Khaimah asked for travel documents for himself and some of his dependants he was told they had been postponed until he apologised to the naval officer to whom he had failed to offer his respects on his last visit. On 8 December 1938 Longrigg visited the Coast and succeeded in signing an option with the Shaikh of Rās al-Khaimah to explore for oil, for two and a half years but without drilling. The Shaikh of Kalbā granted a concession for seventy-five years on 30 December.[132] Fowle's efforts were finally successful before he left his office in the Gulf in 1939 when in January the Shaikh of Abū Dhabī awarded a concession for seventy-five years, and a five-year exploration licence for 'Ajmān, but Umm al-Qaiwain refused to grant a seventy-five-year concession until 20 March 1945. In 1938 and 1939 exploration teams on the Coast, accompanied by Ḥājjī Williamson, were active in the hinterland.[133]

III The End of the British Imperialistic Era

Britain's interest in the Gulf from the early seventeenth century was primarily commercial. The British had entered the area only as traders, representing the East India Company, but after 1798 international rivalry and local challenge involved Britain in the internal politics of the Gulf, and this brought about the eventual establishment of her political and military supremacy. It is worth noting that the Trucial States were the first Arab territory into which Britain extended her authority in 1820 and the last area in which she relinquished it in 1971. During that period of 150 years the importance of the Gulf and Trucial States in British strategy was intimately connected with the Indian Empire, and the Gulf was administered by representatives of the political and military service of the Government of India, which exercised a powerful and decisive influence on British policy.

Although the British withdrew from India in 1947, the Gulf and Trucial States had by this time become vital to British strategy on their own account, for Gulf oil had become Britain's greatest single source of energy from abroad, and had developed as a major element in the sterling area's monetary system. The Gulf had also assumed great importance as a link in international air communications. Nevertheless, in 1968 the British Government declared its historic decision to withdraw from the Gulf and did so in 1971, and a new phase began in the long history of the area. Although Britain lost her political and military presence, she maintained her position as a leading economic power. Britain returned to her position with regard to commercial transactions particularly in the newly established oil industry, and the change took place in a climate of genuine international free competition, and mutual respect and equality between Britain and the Gulf States.

British withdrawal was precipitated by international, local and domestic factors. After World War II the international climate of decolonisation within and outside the United Nations was one of the causes which led Britain to relinquish her Imperial responsibilities. Simultaneously the United States and the Soviet Union arose as the two major political and economic powers, a situation which soon influenced Britain's position in the Middle East and the Gulf. Although Britain and the United States allied to curb threatening Soviet ambitions in Iran and the Gulf, Britain faced bitter economic rivalry there from the American oil companies. Furthermore, in the post-war period Britain's interests came into conflict with those of the two ambitious local Gulf states, Sa'ūdī Arabia and Iran, and her position there was further weakened by the spread of modern Arab nationalism which was increasingly felt throughout the area.[134] However, it was an anti-colonial change in British public opinion, combined with economic crises at home, which gave rise to her new 'East of Suez' policy, which were the main factors in forcing her decision in 1968 to withdraw from the Gulf and the Trucial States.

In studying Britain's position and interests in the Trucial States during the post-war period we shall deal with two main issues. First, we shall examine the development of events in the Gulf and Trucial States during the period, and as the treaty of 1892 remained the main tie between the two parties, it is important to discuss to what extent they held to the articles of the treaty in the midst of the stormy events of those years. Secondly, we must discuss the changes which occurred in Britain's administrative and political control within the area, and her reasons for adopting a new policy of direct interference in certain fields in the internal affairs of the Trucial States.

An early conflict of interests developed between the British and American oil companies, Iran, Sa'ūdī Arabia and the oil-producing states in general. During the Second World War the US State Department showed much interest in Sa'ūdī Arabia's oil and began actively to support the American oil companies in the Gulf, who in 1948 denounced the 'Red Line' agreement, declaring their willingness to negotiate independently of the British with the rulers of the states.[135] Between May and June 1949 the Trucial shaikhs proclaimed their rights over the continental shelf, thus increasing the importance of the Trucial States in British oil policy, their long coastline extending from al-'Udaid to Rās Musandam.[136] However, this added another factor to an early conflict with Sa'ūdī Arabia, when Aramco exploration teams entered Abū Dhabī territory in 1949, and thereby reopened the frontier dispute between Sa'ūdī Arabia and Abū Dhabī. The Sa'ūdīs, confident in their new alliance with the United States, presented their own ideas about their frontiers, claiming two thirds of Abū Dhabī territory, while Britain in fulfilment of her commitment to the 1892 treaty, as well as defending her own interests in the Trucial States and Abū Dhabī's historic rights, stubbornly refused to accept those claims.[137]

At this time Britain was also faced with mounting nationalistic feeling in Iran and the Arab oil states of the Gulf, focused on the injustice of the previous oil agreements which had been granted under unfavourable political and social conditions. In 1948 Venezuela imposed on the operating companies within her territories the principle of an equal sharing of oil profits, and within two or three years the system of profit-sharing had spread to Sa'ūdī Arabia, Iraq and Kuwait, replacing the fixed 'per-ton' royalty system. In Iran the refusal of the Anglo–Iranian Oil Company to accept the equal division of profits brought about the Iranian antagonism which ended in the nationalisation of the company in 1951.[138] This conflict over oil matters was soon to be felt in the Trucial States. Shaikh Shakhbūt, after declaring his rights over the continental shelf in 1948, granted the Superior Oil Company of California a concession at sea, and this at once created a dispute between the Shaikh and Petroleum Development (Trucial Coast), which claimed that its concession covered the same area, while the Shaikh insisted that its offshore limit was only three miles of regional waters. Britain referred the dispute to arbitration which resulted in favour of the Shaikh. However, the Superior Oil Company in March 1953 relinquished the concession to a new company, Abū Dhabī Marine Areas Ltd (ADMA), owned two thirds by British Petroleum and one third by Compagnie Française des Pétroles, for a period of seventy-five years.[139]

The Gulf Aviation Company, which considerably increased British interests in the Gulf and the Trucial States, was founded by a British pilot, Frederick Bosworth, in March 1950 with BOAC participation. Regular services between Baḥrain, Dhahrān, Doḥa and Shārjah were initiated during the first year; Abū Dhabī, Dubai and Muscat were included later.[140] Gulf Aviation played an important part in supplying the needs of the various oil companies operating in the Gulf and Trucial States, and played a major role in connecting the Gulf ports; in 1970 it was developed into the national airline of the independent states of the United Arab Emirates, Baḥrain, Qaṭar and the Sultanate of 'Omān.

In the midst of the turmoil which accompanied the nationalisation of the AIOC in 1951, Britain had to face another dispute in the Gulf. In 1952, the Sa'ūdīs, challenging Britain, sent a detachment of police to Ḥamāsā village in al-Buraimī area, where they hoisted the Sa'ūdī flag (see Chapter 3, p. 209). This audacious act was met by a strong British determination to maintain her traditional supremacy in the area, and groups of the Trucial Omān Levies were stationed at al-'Ain in the al-Buraimī region. As a result, following the failure of the Geneva Arbitration of 1955, the Sa'ūdīs were obliged to withdraw from the oasis; Sa'ūdī Arabia ended diplomatic relations with Britain, and Sir Anthony Eden, who was visiting Washington at this time, explained Britain's action to his American allies. Arab nationalism and anti-colonialism were now coming increasingly into prominence, and, combined with widespread resentment at earlier British policy in Palestine, the Arab World became united in support of the Sa'ūdīs in their confrontation over Buraimī.[141]

In these years Nasser became the spokesman of the militant Arab nationalism, identified with 'neutralism', which was of course anti-British and anti-treaty. The Suez crisis in 1956 produced strong reactions in the Gulf, particularly in Baḥrain, which Palgrave, the British adviser since 1927, was obliged to leave in 1957. Furthermore, even young students in the schools of the Trucial States demonstrated, expressing their sympathy with Egypt in her fight against the Israeli invasion and British and French collaboration. It was only after strenuous military efforts that the British, once again showing their stubborn determination not to abandon their former allies and, with them, their traditional influence in the Gulf, aided the Sultan of Muscat and suppressed the revolt in 'Omān and the Green Mountains between 1957 and 1959.

This stormy tide of anti-British feeling in the Gulf area during the fifties was crowned by news of oil production in Abū Dhabī's territory, when in the summer of 1958 the wells of Umm al-Shaif, twenty miles east of Dās Island showed the presence of oil in commercial quantities. A year later oil was also found at Murbān field in the mainland south of Ṭarīf by Petroleum Development (Trucial Coast). It took little time to construct the pipeline to Dās Island and to Jabal Dhannah on the mainland, where storage tanks were built, and on 3 July 1962 the first oil tanker left the territorial water of Abū Dhabī, near Dās Island. On 15 December 1963 another oil tanker, carrying Abū Dhabī mainland oil left the new harbour of Jabal al-Dhannah. In 1965 Petroleum Development (Trucial Coast) changed its name to Abū Dhabī Petroleum Company (APC) and an amending agreement for a fifty-fifty share of profits was signed with Shaikh Shakhbūt.[142]

The challenging tide of Arab nationalism fomented by Cairo, Damascus and Baghdād began to ebb in the Gulf in the early sixties. The Kuwaiti incident of 1961 and differences and realignment in the Arab world were the main factors in bringing this about. Britain, who realised that Kuwait was now in a position to look after her own affairs, answered the Kuwaiti demand for independence. Qāsim's immediate attempt to claim for Iraq the newly independent state and Britain's rapid reaction in defending her rights had a favourable effect on British interests in the Gulf and resulted in other Arab protectorates becoming more cautious about early independence, for their own special reasons. Furthermore, the conflict between the Iraqi revolution and Nasser, together with the withdrawal of Syria from her union with Egypt, created serious differences in the Arab revolutionary camp. Moreover, the rift between Sa'ūdī Arabia and Egypt over Yemen after 1962 had a direct effect in reconciling Britain with Sa'ūdī Arabia; diplomatic relations between the two countries were resumed, which helped to solve many of their previous problems, thus paving the way for a British decision to withdraw from the Gulf. The Shah of Iran, too, who thought that Nasser's next step after Yemen might well be against him in the Gulf, soon allied his country with the British, so that they might face the coming threat together. This strengthened Britain's friendship with Iran, re-established after 1955, and facilitated her eventual withdrawal.

The tide of active Arab nationalism reached the Trucial States in 1965 after a decade of radio and newspaper propaganda from the Arab lands, particularly Cairo, Damascus and Baghdād. Unrestricted Iranian immigration into the Trucial States, which was repeatedly denounced by these countries, and Britain's failure to involve herself in internal reform and development in the area became matters of discussion in the Arab League in 1964. A special committee for Gulf Affairs was established and Dr Sayyid Nowfal, the Assistant Secretary-General, visited the Trucial States in November and was welcomed by the shaikhs and the people with great enthusiasm. It was decided to establish an 'Arab Fund' to which Kuwait, Iraq and Sa'ūdī Arabia were asked to become the principal contributors. In his report, Dr Nowfal recommended that a centre representing the Arab League should be established in Shārjah to look after the new projects. Shārjah was chosen because the ruler, Shaikh Ṣaqr b. Sulṭān, had shown much interest in Arab League activities on the Coast.

The British, who thought that these recommendations would undermine their position in the area and were contrary to the articles of their 'treaty' with the shaikhs, vigorously resisted them. In March 1965 the Trucial States Council convened and W. Luce, the Political Resident in the Gulf, was present. The shaikhs decided to establish their own new fund and welcomed the aid offered by the Arab League, as it would then come under their supervision. In May, when Dr Nowfal revisited the Coast, he became aware of a certain change in attitudes among the rulers and he detected a tension which had not been apparent before. In June the British contributed two million pounds sterling to the newly established Trucial States Development Council. Shaikh Ṣaqr b. Sulṭān, who had become greatly involved in the Arab League project, was sent into exile. On the other hand the Arab countries differed in their policy with regard to aid. Iraq did not pay; Kuwait insisted in giving aid only to the Arab League fund and not to the Trucial States Development Council—and Qaṭar and Sa'ūdī Arabia decided to finance special projects on the Coast directly. The Sa'ūdīs took over a project to build the coastal road connecting Dubai with Rās al-Khaimah, which was completed in the next few years.[143]

The Arab defeat in 1967, together with the question of the liberation of Arab-occupied land, afterwards patched up Arab differences. The Arab Gulf oil states played a major role at this time of need and largely contributed to the rebuilding of the economy and armed forces of the Arab states in confrontation with Israel. The most important effect of the defeat was that Egypt became completely absorbed in the Arab–Israeli conflict and left the Arab Gulf problems to Sa'ūdī Arabia, Kuwait and Iraq, thus facilitating Britain's policy of reconciliation between the Arab Gulf States and Iran, which was fundamental to their forthcoming decision to withdraw.

From 1960, after OPEC was formed, the oil-producing countries began to adopt a common stand and exerted a rapidly growing influence on the oil scene. ADMA's 1953 agreement was revised in November 1966 to incorporate the fifty-fifty profit-sharing principle. The new supplemented agreement provided for expanding royalties in line with standard OPEC financial agreement and for periodic relinquishments of unexploited land. In the same month another agreement was signed with Abū Dhabī Petroleum which also provided for expanding of royalties. The 13,000 square kilometres relinquished by Abū Dhabī Petroleum Company under the 1965 amendment to its oil concession agreement, was awarded in January 1967 to a consortium comprising the Italian ENI group, Philips and Aminoil. Furthermore, after ADMA relinquished the area specified by the 1966 amendment to its old concession, a consortium of three Japanese firms won the concession for forty years in the same area. On 14 May 1968 a third agreement for thirty-five years was reached between Abū Dhabī and a consortium of Mitsubishi firms for oil exploration in an area of 6,500 square kilometres. The terms of these new oil agreements were considered at that time to be the most advantageous secured by any Middle Eastern state and were the subject of lively comment in the oil industry press. Meanwhile the Dubai Oil

Company, a consortium of American Continental Company, Compagnie Française des Pétroles, Spanish and German oil companies discovered oil at sea in Fateh field in June 1966, and the first tanker left Fateh in September 1969.[144]

From these recent developments in the Gulf oil industry emerged an important fact which influenced British strategy in the Trucial States. The industry had become an international enterprise in which the oil-producing countries received a fair share. Negotiation and mutual respect of rights between both parties became the only guarantee for the British and foreign enterprises and not the presence of military forces, which offended national dignity and provided bitter attacks by Arab nationalists. Japan secured her trade and interests in the Gulf through friendly relations. In addition Britain's decision not to use force in the Iranian crisis in 1951, and her experience of the failure of military action during the Suez crisis of 1956, strengthened the growing opinion that the use of force in local oil disputes would be ineffective. Furthermore the traditional military equipment used to fortify the British bases at Shārjah and Baḥrain after the British withdrawal from Aden in 1967 would have been inadequate in the event of international conflict with the threat of nuclear power.

However, Britain's main cause for withdrawal from the Gulf could be explained by studying her economic and domestic situation between 1966 and 1968. There was a growing conviction that Britain's interests were primarily European and that she was no longer a world power. In July 1966, as a result of continued economic deterioration, the Prime Minister announced steps designed to curb expenditure, particularly overseas, and a major reconsideration of Britain's role east of Suez began. In April 1967 the Labour Party Defence and Overseas Policy Committee took a decision in principle to reduce the forces in the Gulf, the area where the Committee recommended that Britain should now fortify her military position.[145]

On 18 November 1971 sterling was devalued. In the same month the British left Aden, and Roberts, Minister of State at the Foreign Office, visited the Gulf States, giving assurances that Britain would remain in the Gulf as long as necessary to maintain peace and stability. Barely two months later the worsening economic situation and the increasing political strength of those who argued for early withdrawal obliged the Prime Minister to make a different announcement, so that on Tuesday, 16 January 1968, which some British called 'Black Tuesday', Harold Wilson announced that British forces would withdraw not only from the Far East but also from the Gulf by the end of 1971.[146]

Many of the British representatives in the Gulf deplored this sudden volte-face. They believed that the decision was premature and would create instability because of the lack of cohesion among the shaikhdoms and the unresolved disputes both between themselves and with their larger neighbours, Sa'ūdī Arabia and Iran. In June 1970, Edward Heath, who had succeeded Wilson as Prime Minister, recalled Mr Luce from retirement to re-examine, in full consultation with the shaikhs, Sa'ūdī Arabia and Iran, the problems of British withdrawal from the Gulf, and find satisfactory solutions.[147]

The British Government's announcement of withdrawal set new forces in motion within the Gulf. Direct negotiations between Abū Dhabī and Sa'ūdī Arabia slowly progressed and released the tension between both countries. In February 1968 Abū Dhabī and Dubai formed a federation and invited the rulers of Qaṭar, Baḥrain and the Trucial States to join it and participate in the discussions relating to the future of the area. In January 1969 the Shah of Iran made his historic speech to the effect that Iran would not use force to reclaim Baḥrain and that she would listen sympathetically to the wishes of the inhabitants of the island in determining their future. The desire of the Baḥrainis was examined by the United Nations, which endorsed their desire for independence on 11 May 1970. The discussion between the nine Emirates to form a union failed and consequently Baḥrain and Qaṭar declared their independence in August and September 1971 respectively.[148]

It was only in the dispute over Abū Mūsâ and Ṭanb islands that British diplomacy was unable to find a solution satisfactory to both parties. On 30 November, the last day of British protection, Iranian troops landed on Abū Mūsâ and occupied half of it, while the two Ṭanb Islands were taken by force. On 2 December the United Arab Emirates, comprising the seven Trucial Shaikhdoms, was proclaimed an independent state. Contrary to many commentators at the time and also to Lord Curzon's warning in the past, British withdrawal was not followed by a political vacuum and disorder. In retrospect, many British officials who were initially against their government's decision to withdraw their forces from the Gulf, reassured by the current peaceful development and progress of the area, have accepted that the timing was right after all.

The second object of our study is the fundamental changes in British administration and political control which had taken place on the Trucial Coast between 1945 and 1971. In 1947, when the British withdrew from India, the historic role played in Gulf affairs by the India Office and by the Secretary of State for India came to an end. The Foreign Office, with its wide understanding of international and local changes in the Gulf, now undertook the responsibility for British interests in the area, and in contrast to the traditional India Office policy of non-interference, which had lasted for more than a century, now took an active part in reforming the internal affairs of the area, particularly in the Trucial States.[149], [150]

In 1946, before the Foreign Office took over, the Government of India implemented the decision of the Middle East Sub-Committee taken a decade before, and transferred the political residency from Bushire to Baḥrain. The residency being in Baḥrain, the British authorities were now in a position to supervise and control the affairs of the Trucial States, which was more in keeping with their growing interests in this area. Other important modifications were soon to follow in the structure of British political representation, as analysis of the list below will show (see Appendix, pp. 348-9).

Political Officers (Shārjah)

1945–6	Captain R. C. Murphy	Residency Agent
1946–7	Captain J. E. Hudson	Jāsim al-Kazmāwī
1948–9	Mr J. N. Jackson	

Permanently Resident

1949–51 Mr P. D. Stobart
1951–2 Mr A. J. Wilton
1952–3 Mr M. S. Weir

(20 May 1953 post raised to status of Political Agents)

Political Agents (Dubai)

1953–5 Mr C. M. Pirie-Gordon
1955–8 Mr J. P. Tripp

Political Officers (Abū Dhabī)

1955–8 The Hon. M. S. Buckmaster.[151]

First of all, in 1949, the political officer who was then stationed at Shārjah, owing to the growing importance of the Coast, now began to reside there throughout the year rather than in cold weather only, as he had done previously. This ended the office of the Residency Agent which had been held by local people representing Britain since 1823, the last of whom was Jāsim al-Kazmāwī (1945–9).[152]

The list also shows another significant fact, that Murphy and Hudson—who were the last appointments made by the Government of India—were captains seconded from the army, whilst Jackson and Stobart, the new appointments of the Foreign Office, were civilians, career diplomats from the regular foreign service. This brought an end to a long line of political representatives such as Miles, Ross, Cox and Fowle, chosen from the army and trained by the External Political Department of the Government of India. Furthermore, the growth of British interests in the area was reflected in the decision implemented on 20 May 1953 to raise the status of the political representation from that of Political Officer to that of Political Agent. The seat of the British political representative was simultaneously transferred from Shārjah, where it had been located for the last 130 years, to Dubai owing to the latter's gradual emergence over the past five decades as the commercial centre of the Coast. In the meantime, the Emirate of Abū Dhabī expanded and in 1955 the British Government appointed another

Political Officer there, the Hon. M. S. Buckmaster, to represent her growing interests. In 1961 this post was raised to that of Political Agent. These two Political Agencies remained unchanged until the British withdrew in 1971, the last two representatives being Mr J. F. Walker (1970–71) in Dubai and Mr C. J. Tredwell (1968–71) in Abū Dhabī.

In 1953 a British Court was established for the first time within the Political Agency in Dubai as a result of the increased number of British Indian subjects residing in the area. Assistant Judge Maudsley was the first in Dubai and came under the Senior Judge of the Gulf based at Baḥrain. For some years to come it was the Political Agent himself who assumed the position of judge in addition to his other responsibilities.[153]

The new policy of Britain's involvement in the internal affairs of the Trucial States which the Foreign Office had adopted was confined to certain fields. In May 1949 McCaully, former member of the Indian Medical Service, was appointed in charge of the al-Maktūm hospital in Dubai.[154] In March 1951 the Trucial 'Omān Levies, later to be called the Trucial 'Omān Scouts, was established for internal security. This new force was commanded by British officers and completely under the control of the Foreign Office. Initially it took Shārjah airport as its headquarters and moved afterwards to Ḥīrah, where local recruitment raised its number to 100 by the end of the year. This single rifle squadron was to develop into five squadrons by the late fifties, operating with an annual budget of half a million pounds sterling. By the time the British left the Gulf, the budget had grown to £3.5 million to support a force of 1,500 men. Britain also provided the Abū Dhabī and Dubai governments with officers to build up their new police forces in the late fifties, and Abū Dhabī Defence Force in 1964.[155]

As inter-state boundary disputes now threatened to impede oil operations in the Trucial States the British Government attempted to find a solution to these problems. Between 1955 and 1959 (see Chapter 5, p. 295), the Political Agency having secured the acceptance of the shaikhs to stand by its arbitration, a wide study and investigation were conducted. The shaikhs were informed of the British judgements and accordingly in 1963 the Research Department of the Foreign Office drew up the political map of the Trucial States.

Contrary to her traditional policy of maintaining the *status quo*, in the post-war period Britain realised that her interests would be secured by strengthening ties between Trucial shaikhdoms. In 1952 the Trucial States Council was set up in order to bring the rulers closer together in the hope that they might form some political and economic association in the future. In this year two meetings were held and these were presided over by the Political Agent. The council had no written constitution and no executive and policy-making powers, but was merely consultative and advisory. A Jordanian, Ahmad Bīṭār, was in 1964 appointed legal adviser to the Council.[156] In 1965, due to Arab League activities on the Coast and its proposal to accelerate reform in the area, the Council extended its activities to internal welfare and the Trucial States Development Council was established. In 1966 the Political Agent withdrew from the chairmanship of the Council and Shaikh Ṣaqr b. Muḥammad, ruler of Rās al-Khaimah, was elected president.[157] Initially the development budget depended mainly on British aid, but Abū Dhabī's contribution to the development of the Coast increased considerably after 1966, when Shaikh Zāyed b. Sulṭān assumed power. He contributed 50 per cent of the Trucial development budget for the year 1967–8 and 90 per cent of the budget for the year 1968–9.[158] The numerous meetings of the Trucial States Development Council soon created a common cause among the shaikhs and became one of the main factors facilitating the emergence of the United Arab Emirates in 1971.

Notes

1. Despite the unusual series of violent incidents which accompanied the Portuguese presence in the Indian Ocean and the Gulf Area, the Portuguese were the first to regard as piracy the liberating activities of the Imāms of the Ya 'āribah dynasty in 'Omān and East Africa. At the turn of the eighteenth century, British travellers and officials of the Bombay government followed their example, describing the attacks of the Qawāsim against their ships in the same terms. In his thesis, *The First Sa'ūdī Dynasty and 'Omān*, the author reached the conclusion that these attacks were motivated more by economic, political and religious factors than by piratical ones. The Qawāsim, mainly maritime traders, were quite aware of the struggle the British had once waged against the Portuguese, the Dutch and the French for the monopoly of the Gulf trade, the consequences of which they now felt, expressing their resentment in this way. Moreover, in 1798 the Government of Bombay made an alliance with the Sultanate of Muscat and 'Omān as a precautionary measure against the expected invasion of India by Napoleon. The Sultan of Muscat, who was meanwhile engaged in fierce local war with the emerging independent Qawāsim Emirate, benefited from this agreement. Due to the former pact and British aid to the Sultan of Muscat in his expeditions against the Qawāsim on Qishm Island in 1805 and 1809, the Qawāsim found themselves forced into direct conflict with the Government of Bombay. Finally the Qawāsim adopted the Unitarian principles of the reformer Shaikh Muhammad Ibn 'Abd al-Wahāb and became the naval power of this religious movement. Henceforth, encouraged by the increasing power of the first Sa'ūdī dynasty, the Qawāsim had the audacity to attack the British at sea. (M.Morsy Abdullah, 'Omān and the First Sa'ūdī Dynasty', Cairo, 1978.
2. V. G. Lorimer, *Gazetteer of the Persian Gulf, Oman and Central Arabia*, Calcutta 1908–1915, republished by Gregg International, Westmead, England, 1970. I Historical Part I A, 17, 29, 94, 110, 167, 662–71, 678.
3. J. B. Kelly, *Britain and the Persian Gulf*, London, 1968, p.363, Lorimer, op.cit., p.719.
4. Lorimer, ibid., pp.238–40; Lorimer, II Geographical A, p.1098.
5. Lorimer, I Part I A, ibid., pp.730, 737–9. R. Kumar, *India and the Persian Gulf Region, 1858–1907*, London, 1965, p.104.
6. O.A., Hususi, No. 117, 29 Safar 1317H. (11 July 1899) and No. 96, Gumazi el-Evvel 1317H (18 September 1899). Kelly, *Britain and the Persian Gulf*, p.729.
7. Kelly, ibid., pp.807–13. Kumar, op.cit., pp.117, 121.
8. Lorimer, I Part I A, op.cit., p.730.
9. IOR, P/3276, Ḥājjī Aḥmad Khān to the Sultan of Muscat, 13 September 1887.

10. IOR, P/3276, Printed Correspondence (1887–88). Col. E. C. Ross, Pol.Res. Bushire, to A. Nicolson, H.B.M. Chargé d'Affaires at Tehran, 30 October 1887.
11. IOR, J. A. Saldanha, *Precis of the Affairs of the Persian Coast and Islands, 1884–1905*, Calcutta, 1906, pp.57–8.
12. Lorimer, I Part I A, op.cit., p.738.
13. B. C. Busch, *Britain and the Persian Gulf 1894–1914*, London and California, 1967, pp.68, 117–18, 189–90, 336–9, 365.
14. D. Hawley, *The Trucial States*, London, 1970, p.328.
15. P. Graves, *The Life of Sir Percy Cox*, London, 1941, p.93.
16. Busch, op.cit., pp.262–5.
17. Lord Newton, *Lord Lansdowne*, London, 1929, pp.56, 190, 344.
18. Hansard, IV series 121, HoL, 5 May 1903, Col. 1348.
19. Lorimer, I Part A, op.cit., p.320.
20. Earl Ronaldshay, *The Life of Lord Curzon*, London, 1928, II, p.45–50. IOR, R/15/1/14/14, Report of British Relations with an increasing influence over Trucial Chiefs, 26 February 1901–12 December 1902.
21. FA, Asie Oceanie, N.S., Mascate X. (Letters from French Consuls in Baghdād, Bombay, Mascate and Bouchir on Curzon's visit to the Gulf). Lorimer, I Part II, op.cit., p.2639.
22. Lorimer, I Part I A, op.cit., p.547; FA, Asie Oceanie, N.S., Mascate IV, Consul, Bouchir, au Ministre Develle, Paris, 23 Novembre 1893.
23. Lorimer, ibid., pp.339–40; FA, op.cit., Mascate V., Ottavi à Delcasse, 10 Mars 1900 (enclosed copies of Fatḥ al-Baṣāyer).
24. FA, Asie Oceanie, N.S., Mascate XXIII, Directeur de Louis Dieu et Cie., au Ministre des Affaires Etrangères, Paris. 3 Février 1913, and Mascate XX, Ambassade de France à Londre au M. Pichon, Paris, 28 Février 1910.
25. Lorimer, I Part I A, op.cit., pp.300, 302, 310, 325–38; FA, Asie Oceanie, N.S., Mascate XVII, Ministre des Affaires Etrangères à Ministre de la Marine, Paris, 28 Février 1902; FA, ibid., Mascate IV, Vice-Consul à Bouchir au Ministre à Paris, La Russie dans le Golfe Persique, 18 Juin 1899.
26. IOR, L/P & S/10/23, British Flagstaffs, 10 to Governor-General of India, 19 May 1905 and Cox to SGI, 24 September 1904 and FO to 10 15 March 1905, and SNO to Commander-in-Chief, East Indies, 25 November 1904.
27. G. P. Gooch, and Temperley, *British Documents on the Origins of the War, 1898–1914*, IV, London, 1929, pp.6–8–23.
28. Lorimer, I Part I A, op.cit., pp.310–11.
29. Busch, op.cit., pp.108–10, 254, 377; B. G. Martin, *German Persian Diplomatic Relations*, 'S–Gravenhage, 1959, pp.60–1, 147–8.
30. GA, Turkei 165, bd. 26, Listermann, Vice-Consul Bushire to Fürst von Bülow, 12 July 1906; GA Turkei 165 bd. 25, Report from Listermann, Vice-Consul Bushire, to Bülow, 7 June 1906; E. Staley, 'Business and Politics in the Persian Gulf, the Story of the Wonkhaus Firm', *Political Science Quarterly*, 48(1933), pp.372, 376, 380.
31. GA, Turkei 165 bd. 26, Report from Listermann, Vice-Consul, Bushire, to Fürst von Bülow, Berlin, 12 July 1906.
32. FO, 371/532, Dispute over Abū Mūsā Red-Oxide, 'Memorandum for Communication to the German Ambassador' by FO, with Appendices, 27 May 1908.
33. IOR, L/P & S/10/127, Abū Mūsā Red-Oxide, 'Abd al-Laṭīf, Shārjah, to Cox, 28 February 1908, Ruler of Shārjah to Ḥasan Sumaih, 17 February 1907; Cox to 'Abd al-Laṭīf, 21 March 1908; and Listermann, German Vice-Consul to Shaikh Saqr b. Khālid, 19 November 1907.
34. Busch, op.cit., p.372.
35. *Times of India*, 31 December 1910.
36. IOR, L/P & S/10/406, Persia, Lingah Vice-Consulate, Cox to SGI, 29 May 1909; Cox to GI, 6 June 1908.
37. IOR, L/P & S/10/115, Dubai Incident, Cox, Bushire to SGI, 8 January 1911; Cox, Bushire, to SGI, 8 January 1911.
38. IOR, ibid., Capt. Shakespear, Kuwait, to Pol. Res., Bushire, 20 December 1910; Cox, Bushire, to SGI, 8 January 1911; J. D. Dick, Captain *HMS Hyacinth* to the Commander-in-Chief, East Indies, 31 December 1910; Cox, Bushire, to SGI, 8 January 1911;

DSA, American Consulate Muscat, Salim al-Khajah, Lingah, to American Consul Muscat (enclosed letter from Shaikh Buti to Sultan of Muscat).

39. IOR, L/P & S/18B/196, Arms Trade in the Persian Gulf, 1913; pp.14-5; IOR, L/P & S/10/115, Admiral Slade, *Hyacinth* at Bushire, to the Secretary of the Admiralty, 2 January 1911; GA, Turkei No 165, bd 33, Listermann, Bushire to Dr von Bethmann Hollweg, Berlin, 13 January 1911.
40. DSA, Box 10075, Report to the American Ambassador in Constantinople on Political Conditions in the Persian Gulf, Muscat, 10 January 1911.
41. IOR, L/P & S/10/115, Slade to Admiralty, 2 January 1911; Cox to SGI, 8 January 1911; 10 to FO, 6 January 1911.
42. GA, Turkei 165, bg. 33, Listermann, Bushire, to Dr von Bethmann Hollweg, Berlin, 13 January 1911.
43. IOR, R/15/1/14/32, Cox to Shaikh Buṭī b. Suhail, 9 October 1912; Residency Agent to Cox, 19 October 1912; Vice-Consulate, Lingah to Cox, 9 October 1913; IOR R/15/1/270, telegram General Brigade, Karachi to Pol. Res., 5 December 1913; telegram Cox to General Brigade, 5 December 1915; Cox to Major C. C. R. Murphy, Intelligence Officer, 22 January 1914.
44. R. Hay, *The Persian Gulf States*, Washington, 1959, pp.38–9. Kelly, *Britain*, pp.411–12.
45. IOR, R/15/1/0/183, Residency Agent, Shārjah to Pol. Res., 13 August 1892.
46. FA, Asie Oceanie, N.S. Mascate 3, Ottavi à Ministère des Affaires Ētrangères 26 Février 1896.
47. R. J. Said, 'The 1938 Reform Movement in Dubai', *Al-Abhath*, XXIII, December 1970, pp.254.
48. IOR, L/P & S/10/463, German War, Pol. Res. to All Shaikhs in the Persian Gulf, 11 November 1914.
49. IOR, R/15/1, Introduction by P. Tuson, p.4.
50. IOR, L/P & S/11/193/768, Middle East, Report of the Inter-departmental Committee, 31 January 1931, p.4.
51. Institute of International Affairs, *Political and Strategical Interests of the United Kingdom*, London, New York, Toronto, 1939, pp.276–7.
52. P. Sassoon, 'Air Power in the Middle East', *JRLAS*, 20(1939), pp.398–9.
53. IOR, L/P & S/10/1268, Persian Gulf, Political Control, 1829–37, Memorandum of H. Trenchard, Chief of Air Staff, 8 May 1928.
54. Hansard, V. Series 64, HoL. 30 June 1926, Col. 679–82.
55. IOR, L/P & S/10/1271, establishment of Protectorates in the Gulf, Haworth to SGI, 30 April and 9 May 1927; I.O. Memorandum on the Trucial Chiefs, 1908–28, 4 October 1928, p.3.
56. IOR, L/P & S/10/1273, Persian Gulf Political Control, Telegram from Viceroy to SSI, 17 October 1928.
57. CAB, 16/94, Memorandum by Colonial Office, 31 October 1928.
58. IOR, L/P & S/10/1268, Memorandum of H. Trenchard, Chief of Air Staff, 8 May 1928; Air Ministry to Secretary of State for Foreign Affairs, 29 May 1928.
59. CAB, 16/94, composition of the PG Sub-Committee, 24 September 1928.
60. CAB, 16/93. PG Sub-Committee, Table of Meetings and Minutes of Meetings on 24 October 1928, p.6; Minutes of Meeting on 12 November 1928, p.5.
61. IOR, L/P & S/10/1271, Memorandum by the Secretary of State for the Colonies, 2 November.
62. CAB, op.cit. Minutes of Meeting on 22 November 1928, p.7.
63. CAB, 16/93, Meeting No. 8, 18 March 1929.
64. IOR, L/P & S/10/1274. Removal of Residency from Bushire, Pol. Res. to SGI, 17 August 1929 (enclosed Barrett Study); Telegram from Viceroy, 9 September 1929; Report by a Sub-Committee on Political Control, 12 December 1929.
65. CAB, 5/2 & 3 & 4, Minutes of Meetings between 1931–39.
66. G. Rendel, *The Sword and the Olive*, London, 1957, pp.61–2.
67. Hawley, op.cit., p.228.
68. CAB, 51/3, Meeting No. 37, OME, Sub-Committee, 8 November 1934.
69. *Who was Who*, 1929–1940, London, 1941, p.470.
70. IOR, L/P & S/10/1273, Memorandum of the FO to the Cabinet, 10 June 1933; Memorandum of 10 19 June 1933.

71. IOR, R/15/1/14/43, Unrest at Dubai and SNO Report, 22 January 1935 & Pol. Agent, Baḥrain to Pol. Res. 7 November 1934; Pol. Res. to SGI, 16 November 1934.
72. CAB, 51/8, Memorandum of OME Sub-Committee, Fowle to SSI, 16 November 1934, pp.2,3.
73. CAB, 51/3, Meeting No. 43, OME Sub-Committee, 24 September 1935, pp.1–13.
74. Rendel, op.cit., p.103.
75. Hawley, op.cit., p.328.
76. Sassoon, op.cit., pp.397–9.
77. CAB, 16/93, PG Sub-Committee, Minutes of Meeting, 24 October 1928.
78. Burchall, H., 'The Air Route to India', *JRCAS*, 14(1927), p.15.
79. H. R. P. Dickson, *Kuwait and Her Neighbours*, London, 1956, p.345.
80. IOR, L/P & S/11/294, B. Thomas to Pol. Res., 13 June 1927; Appendices A and B; Appendix D and p.6, 11, 13–14, 36–7.
81. H. Burchall, 'The Political Aspect of Commercial Air Routes', *JRCAS* XX, January 1933, pp.77–8.
82. G. W. Bentley, 'The Development of the Air Route in the Persian Gulf', *JRCAS*, XX, April, 1933, pp.177, 180, 182.
83. Burchall, January 1933, op.cit. pp.82–4, 182.
84. CAB, 51/2, Eastern Air Route, OME Sub-Committee, Meeting No. 12, 2 November 1931.
85. CAB, 51/2, OME Sub-Committee, Meeting No. 13, 5 November 1931.
86. CAB, 51/1, MME Sub-Committee, Memorandum by Financial Secretary to the Treasury, 10 December 1931; Memorandum by the Secretary of State for Air, 16 December 1931; Report by Rendel, 10 May 1932.
87. Dickson, op.cit., pp.346–8.
88. Bentley, op.cit. (comment), pp.184, 187. Dickson, op.cit., pp.345, 348.
89. CAB, 51/8, Telegram Pol. Res. 7 May 1932.
90. Bentley, op.cit., pp.184–5.
91. Dickson, op.cit., p.349.
92. IOR, L/P & S/18/B 471, Air Agreement of Sharjah.
93. C. Belgrave, *Personal Column*, London, 1960, p.76.
94. CAB, 51/8, Fowle to SGI, 10 July 1935, p.278.
95. Said, op.cit., p.260.
96. John A. De Novo, *American Interests and Policies in the Middle East 1900–1939*, Minneapolis, 1963, pp.29, 177–87. Hurewitz, op.cit., 11, 161.
97. S. L. Longrigg, *Oil in the Middle East*, London, 1954, pp.101–2, 108, 111.
98. B. Shwadran, *The Middle East, Oil and the Great Powers*, London, 1956, pp.371, 385–6.
99. DSA, Box 10076, Edward M. Groth, Beirut, to Secretary of State (enclosed a report from Amīn al-Riḥānī), October 1923.
100. IOR, L/P & S/10/989. Persian Gulf, Oil Concessions, Pol. Res. to SSC, 28 March 1924.
101. DSA, Decimal Files, Box 7056, A. Sloan, American Consul Baghdād to Secretary of State, Washington, 14 March 1931. 10 L/P & S/10/989. Pol. Res. to SSC 29 October 1924; Under Secretary, CO to 10, 13 March 1925; Telegram Pol. Res. to the Secretary of State for the Colonies, 7 March 1925.
102. IOR, L/P & S/10/18/B 456. Dubai Agreement.
103. DSA, Decimal File, Box 7056, A. Sloan, Baghdād to Secretary of State, Washington, 14 March 1931.
104. DSA, Decimal Files, Box 7067. Murray, Chief, Division of Near Eastern Affairs to American Embassy, London, 1 December 1932 and 8 June 1934.
105. Williamson was a British adventurer who as a boy had sailed from Bristol in 1884 to the Western Coast of the U.S. and ended up at Aden, where he joined the British police. In 1890 he became a Muslim and departed for the Gulf, where he lived among the Bedouins near Baṣrah. When the British occupied the town he joined Cox's Intelligence Service. After the war he was employed by APOC and because of his knowledge of Arabic and local customs he accompanied their survey parties on the Arabian side. His employment with APOC lasted for thirteen years, ending in 1937 when he reached the retiring age of sixty-five and the company awarded him a generous

pension. The biography *Arabian Adventure, the Story of Hājjī Williamson* has to be used with great caution.

106. Shwadran, op.cit., pp.285–90. W. E. Staton-Hope, *Arabian Adventurer, The Story of Hajji Abdullah Williamson*, London, 1951, pp.328–9.
107. IOR, L/P & S/12/3767, Baḥrain News and Intelligence Reports. Japanese activities beginning from April 1934.
108. FO, 371/16967, Letter on Fowle's Meeting at the Department of Overseas Trade, 5 October 1933.
109. IOR, L/P & S/12/2115, Oil Concessions in Sa'ūdī Arabia, Bullard to FO, 13 April 1939.
110. IOR, L/P & S/10/1271, 10 Memorandum on 'The Trucial Chiefs, 1908–28', 4 October 1928.
111. IOR, L/P S/10/994, Prideaux to SGI, 4 February 1926.
112. IOR, L/P & S/12/2115, Circular of Pol. Res., 4 February 1926.
113. CAB, 51/2, Meeting No. 21, OME Sub-Committee, 2 December 1932.
114. CAB, 51/3, Meeting No. 42 of OME Sub-Committee, 24 September 1935, 11.
115. IOR, L/P & S/10/994, Provisional record of a meeting, Colonial Office, 26 May 1933; Extract from Kuwait Intelligence Summary for October 1933.
116. CAB, 51/3 Memo of Meeting No. 29, OME Sub-Committee, 23 February 1934.
117. CAB, ibid., Minutes of Meeting.
118. IOR, L/P & S/13/3767, Persian Gulf Diaries, 1933–41, 1–15 April 1934.
119. CAB 51/3, Meeting No. 31, OME Sub-Committee, 12 April 1934; Meeting No. 42, 24 September 1935.
120. IOR, L/P & S/12/3767, 16–31 May 1935, 16–31 January 1937, 1–15 December 1934, and repeated afterwards to 1939.
121. Longrigg, op.cit. pp.113, 115.
122. IOR, R/15/675, Petroleum Concessions 1936–37, Residency Agent to Pol. Agent, 15 January 1936.
123. Before Petroleum Concessions could proceed to obtain its oil concessions from the shaikhs of the Trucial States, agreements had to be concluded with the British Government according to previous practice in Baḥrain. The company was asked to lay down in these agreements that in every aspect it should be solely British: registered in Great Britain and presided over by a British Chairman. Not only this, but even in the Trucial States, their dealings with the shaikh were to be made through the Political Resident, but a British representative and all their employees were also to be British, or else subjects of the shaikh—other nationalities should be employed only with the approval of the Political Resident. The approval of HM Government had to be acquired for the designated representative, who would have to agree to the Political Resident's wishes and to those of the shaikh. In the case of civil aircraft, the company had to abide by the general regulations made by the shaikh on the advice of the British Government. The company was not to occupy the sites chosen for British defence purposes and for wireless installations. Moreover, should there be war, the British Government would exercise pre-emption rights, and would assume control of the whole company, which would conform to all directions issued by the British Government. IOR, L/P & S/12/3767, 16–31 May 1936.
124. US Foreign Relations, op.cit., 1929 III, American Chargé d'Affaires, London, to Secretary of State, 30 May 1929. Staton-Hope, op.cit., pp.325–8.
125. IOR, op.cit. 1–15 June 1936, 16 December 1936 – 15 January 1936; Pol. Res. to Pol. Agent, Baḥrain, 14 January 1937.
126. IOR, R/15/1/675, Williamson to Shaikh Sultan b. Salim, 3 February 1937; Holmes to Pol. Agent, 27 March 1937; Residency Agent, Shārjah to Pol. Agent, 31 March 1937; Shaikh Sa'īd to 'Abd al-Razzāq, 26 March 1937; 'Abd al-Razzāq to Pol. Agent, 31 March 1937.
127. IOR, ibid., Telegram, Holmes to Skliros care Petconcess, London, 20 March 1937.
128. IOR, L/P & S/12/3767, 16–31 March 1937.
129. IOR, R/15/1/675, SSI to Fowle, 8 April 1937; Fowle to SGI, 12 April 1937; Loch to Fowle, 15 and 18 May 1937; Fowle to Loch, 18 May 1937.

130. IOR, ibid., Fowle to Hickinbotham, 20 May 1937; Fowle to Pol. Agent 27, May 1937 (in answer to Pol. Agent telegram of 18 May); Fowle to SGI 25 May 1937; Fowle to SGI 25 May 1937; personal letter from W. Fraser (APOC) to Fowle, 24 May 1937.
131. IOR, ibid., 25 May 1937; Fowle to Pol. Agent, 18 May 1937; Pol. Agent, 18 May 1937; Pol. Agent to Fowle, 27 May 1937; Fowle to SGI, 25 May 1937.
132. IOR, L/P & S/12/3767, 1–16 March 1938, 1–15 April 1938 and December 1938; reports on the years 1938–39.
133. Longrigg, op.cit., pp.115–16.
134. J. Marlowe, *The Persian Gulf in the Twentieth Century*, London, 1962, pp.185–207.
135. Shwadran, op.cit., p.353.
136. S. Chubin and S. Zabih, *The Foreign Relations of Iran*, Berkeley, California, 1974, p.282.
137. J. B. Kelly, *Eastern Arabian Frontiers*, London, 1964.
138. M. S. Al-Otaiba, *OPEC and the Petroleum Industry*, London, 1975, pp.29–31.
139. C. Mann, *Abu Dhabi, Birth of an Oil Sheikhdom*, Beirut, 1969, pp.89–90.
140. Belgrave, op.cit., pp.164–75.
141. Kelly, op.cit. (Eastern Arabian Frontiers), pp. 175–206, 261–3.
142. Mann, op.cit., pp. 92–3.
143. S. Nowfal, *Imarat Sahih Oman*, Cairo (2nd Edition), 1972.
144. M. Morsy, *Two Glorious Years in the History of Abū Dhabī*, Beirut, 1968, pp.33–7, 101–7.
145. P. Darby, *British Defence Policy East of Suez 1947–1968*, London, 1973, pp.304–21.
146. Darby, ibid., p.325.
147. E. Monroe, *The Changing Balance of Power in the Persian Gulf* (The report of an international seminar at the Centre for Mediterranean Studies, 1972), New York, 1972, pp.13–5.
148. J. D. Anthony, *Arab States of the Lower Gulf*, Washington, 1975, p.45, 74, 98.
149. Hawley, op.cit., pp.170–2.
150. In 1864 Pelly, the Political Resident, submitted a report to the Government of India in which he explained that Britain's policy of non-interference and keeping the peace in the Gulf only at sea had engendered the mistrust and hatred of the local inhabitants, who looked upon the British as no more than a punitive and unjustifiable police force. He suggested that the political residency should be transferred from Bushire to Khaṣab in the Musandam peninsula, where a British colony could be established to serve as an example of modern civilisation – educationally, economically and socially. In his opinion, peaceful relations and intercourse between this British community and the Arabs of the Trucial Coast would change the pattern of behaviour of the latter and lead to an appreciation and understanding of British efforts. However, the Government of India was reluctant to involve itself in such responsibilities and thus ignored the report. Lorimer, IA, op.cit., pp.252–60.
151. Hawley, ibid., pp.328–9.
152. Hawley, ibid., p.328.
153. Hawley, ibid., p.179.
154. Hawley, ibid., p.231.
155. Hawley, ibid., pp.174–5, 248.
156. Hawley, ibid., pp.176–8.
157. Hawley, ibid., p.228.
158. Morsy, op.cit., p.114.

2 Internal Changes

I Introduction

II The Trucial States between 1891 and 1918

III Changes in the Economy and in Political Attitudes: Cultural Development, 1892–1939

IV Important Political Changes during the Inter-War Period

V Decisive and Far-reaching Developments after the Second World War

2 Internal Changes

I Introduction

A study of the internal changes in the Trucial States is necessary to an understanding of the modern history of this area for four basic reasons. First, such a study should reveal the effect of British policy on internal political, economic and cultural affairs. Secondly, it should provide a very suitable examination of the British traditional policy of 'non-interference' and its application in this part of Arabia; in those instances when Britain did resort to interference, and these increased greatly in the period between the two World Wars and after, it is quite essential that the accompanying circumstances should be studied. Thirdly, a consideration of internal changes in the Trucial States is fundamental to explaining the partial reversal in British policy towards Abū Dhabī and the Qawāsim occurring between 1892 and 1914. After favouring Abū Dhabī and attempting to weaken the Qawāsim throughout the nineteenth century, the British changed their attitude towards both for a number of reasons which will be explained below. Fourthly, it is useful to understand the reactions of the various shaikhs and their people towards British policy and actions in the region.

The area that extends from Khūr al-'Udaid to Rās Musandam has been known locally as the Coast of 'Omān since the beginning of the eighteenth century. During that century inner Arabia and 'Omān were for diverse reasons in a state of unrest, which was expressed in waves of tribal migration towards the coastal regions of the Gulf. Notable among these migrants were the Qawāsim, who settled at Rās al-Khaimah and Lingah, and the Banī Yās, who took Abū Dhabī as their capital. At that time the Coast of 'Omān witnessed the development of small villages and settlements into large and important towns. From medieval and later Arabic sources (for example, the manuscript of Ibn Mājid), it seems that Abū Dhabī, Dubai, Shārjah, 'Ajmān, Umm al-Qaiwain and Rās al-Khaimah were small villages whose few inhabitants had gathered there for the pearl diving, already a long-established occupation, and to supply the needs of the caravans on their route along the coast between 'Omān and al-Ḥasā.[1] Other tribal branches from inner 'Omān began to populate the Coast, entering into alliance with either the Qawāsim or the Banī Yās federations. Moreover, 'Omān was in the eighteenth century divided into two political factions, the Ghāfirī and Hināwi, and the Qawāsim took the leadership of the former group on the Coast, while the Banī Yās assumed that of the Hināwī in the area.

In 1908 Lorimer gave us a detailed description of the towns and the social life in the emirates of this coast. According to his estimates, the total population of the Trucial States, including the Coast of 'Omān, the Shimailiyyah district on the Gulf of 'Omān, the Buraimī oasis in the interior and the Shiḥūḥ area at Rūs al-Jibāl was 105,000.[2] In the nineteenth century, although the emirates on the coast were only recently established and their population was small, they soon occupied an important position in British strategy in the area as well as in local politics. In the last census in the United Arab Emirates of 1976, total population amounted to more than half a million.

II The Trucial States between 1891 and 1918

The Dismemberment of the Qawāsim Emirate

The powerful Qawāsim shaikhs, who adopted Muwaḥḥidīn (Unitarian)[3] principles and gave the name of their family to a federation of tribes on the Coast of 'Omān at the end of the eighteenth century, lost much of their authority after the destruction of their capital, Rās al-Khaimah, and of their naval force by the British expedition of 1819. Encouraged by this decline in prestige and by the action of the British in concluding treaties with each shaikh on the Trucial Coast individually, 'Ajmān, and 'Umm al-Qaiwain were able to declare and maintain their independence. As a result Rās al-Khaimah and Shārjah were physically separated and the two independent states within their emirate later proved to be a thorn in the flesh of the Qawāsim.[4] The federation of tribes disappeared and the earlier unity of the Qawāsim with their branch at Lingah on the Persian coast was weakened. The new Qawāsim federation, greatly reduced in size, now consisted of the towns of Shārjah, Ḥīrah, Ḥamriyyah, Jazīrat al-Hamrā, Rās al-Khaimah, Rams and Sha'am on the Trucial Coast and Dabā, Khūr Fakkān, Fujairah and Kalbā in the Shimailiyyah district on the Gulf of 'Omān. It also included the fertile oasis of Dhaid, which had strategic importance in the interior of the emirate. Shārjah and Rās al-Khaimah, as the two main towns had a mixed population from many different tribes.[5]

Shaikh Sulṭān b. Ṣaqr (1803–66),[6] who dominated the politics of the Coast in the first half of the nineteenth century, took Shārjah as an alternative capital and it grew rapidly, particularly after the British chose it as the base of their local Residency Agent in 1823. It was the main political and economic centre of the Coast of 'Omān until the end of the century. During this period the power of the Qawāsim in local politics as well as within their own state continued to decline. By 1892 disputes among the sons of Sulṭān b. Ṣaqr had divided his state, giving rise to rebellions in the causes of independence in different parts of the previously united emirate, particularly in Rūs al-Jibāl, Ḥamriyyah and Fujairah.[7]

Throughout the century many factors contributed to the progressive decline of the strong Qawāsim federation, but most important among them was its conflict with Britain. The Qawāsim were reluctant to recognise the maritime peace imposed by the British in 1820 and defied their authority, possibly obliging the British to use forceful measures to establish their superiority over them.

A few simple facts of geography help to explain the dependence of the Qawāsim upon their naval power in controlling the various areas under their rule, and to show to what extent the Qawāsim were weakened by the destruction of their navy by the British. As the Qawāsim Emirate was divided by the Ḥijr mountains into two parts, one on the Coast of 'Omān and the other on the Gulf of 'Omān, the revolts of the Shiḥuḥ and Sharqiyyīn tribes, who controlled the main passes through these mountains, were crucial to the history of the emirate. Not only did their enmity entail a loss of a part of the Qawāsim's state, but it did prevent any land communication between Shārjah and the Shimailiyyah district.

In 1855, when the Shiḥūḥ tribe in Rūs al-Jibāl revolted against Qawāsim sovereignty, Shaikh Sulṭān b. Ṣaqr was unable to subdue them by land and therefore tried to blockade their ports. Captain Felix Jones, the Political Resident, ordered Shaikh Sulṭān to stop sending troops by sea; the Shaikh protested and the Government of India in 1859 supported the Political Resident's attitude. Since the British repeatedly forbade the Qawāsim to use naval power after 1858, the Shimailiyyah district also became semi-independent, a further step towards the dismemberment of the Emirate. Moreover, the strong ties between the Qawāsim and the Sa'ūdīs aggravated the British opinion against them, but as the second Sa'ūdī State (1824–92) declined, the position of their allies, the Qawāsim, also weakened.

The enmity which prevailed from early in the eighteenth century between the Qawāsim shaikhs, who led the Ghāfirī tribes on the Coast of 'Omān, and the Sultans of Muscat, who were part of the powerful leadership of the Hināwī party, had the effect of weakening Qawāsim authority after 1820. When rivalry began after 1823 between the Qawāsim and the Banī Yās, who belonged to the Hināwī party, the Qawāsim Emirate found itself encircled by two strong hostile neighbours, Muscat and Abū Dhabī. The Qawāsim's weakness in the face of the new Hināwī opposition encouraged first the Shiḥūḥ and then the Sharqiyyīn to revolt against their Qasimī rulers. Both these tribes were Hināwī in politics and Sunnī Shafi'ī in sect. When the Qawāsim rule had been strong the few Hināwī tribes within their federation, which was dominated by tribes of the Ghāfirī party adopting Wahhābī doctrines, were unable to form a threatening opposition. With the weakening of the Qawāsim's authority, the Shiḥūḥ and the Sharqiyyīn found an opportunity to rebel with the encouragement and help of the Sultan of

Muscat and the emerging Hināwī power of the Banī Yās under Shaikh Zāyed b. Khalīfah, Ruler of Abū Dhabī.[8]

Although there was a tendency towards separatism among the sons of Shaikh Sulṭān, those who governed Shārjah considered themselves heads of the Emirate and as such responsible for its overall safety. They were Khālid b. Sulṭān (1856–68), Sālim b. Sulṭān (1868–83), Ṣaqr b. Khālid b. Sulṭān (1883–1913) and Khālid b. Aḥmad b. Sulṭān (1913–24). Khālid b. Sulṭān, who established himself in Shārjah in 1861, succeeded his father as Shaikh in 1866, and was able to extend his authority over Rās al-Khaimah by expelling his brother Ibrāhīm. However, at the beginning of his rule Fujairah revolted, refusing to continue payment of a tribute to the Qawāsim ruler. The Sharqiyyīn tribe consisted at that time of many divided branches with no single leader, scattered among the villages on the Gulf of 'Omān and in the Ḥijr mountains and valleys. The strength of their desire for independence was shown by their unanimous support for Fujairah's defiance. Shaikh Khālid's hopes of unifying the Qawāsim and restoring their former authority were shattered for two other reasons: the British destruction of his fort at Zūrā (because of his alliance with the Sa'ūdīs), and the opposition he encountered from Shaikh Zāyed b. Khalīfah. In 1869, Shaikh Khālid received a mortal wound in single combat with the Shaikh of Abū Dhabī and died a few days later on 14 April.

Sālim b. Sulṭān followed his brother as Ruler of the Qawāsim in Shārjah without serious opposition, since Khālid's son Ṣaqr was not of age. Sālim, like his brother Khālid, was anxious to stop the weakening and dismemberment of his emirate, but his use of both diplomacy and force to this end during the seventeen years of his rule proved fruitless. The renewed revolt of the Sharqiyyīn in Fujairah at the beginning of the 1870s constituted the crisis of his rule. The scene of conflict between Shaikh Sālim and the Sharqiyyīn was Dabā. Dabā was made up of three parts: in the north the village of Dabā al-Bay'ah, inhabited by Banī Shuṭair, a Shafi'ī branch of the Shiḥūḥ tribe who considered themselves subjects of Muscat; in the south Dabā al-Ghurfah, inhabited by the Sharqiyyīn tribe; and in the middle, Dabā al-Ḥiṣn, inhabited by Wahhābī Shiḥūḥ, loyal to the Qawāsim, whose representative occupied the fort there.

The Shaikh of Fujairah formed an alliance with Ṣāliḥ b. Muḥammad of the Shiḥūḥ in Dabā al-Bay'ah. The Qasimī force was besieged in Dabā al-Ḥiṣn by the Sharqiyīin and the Shiḥūḥ, and Shaikh Sālim, unable to send reinforcements, attempted to reach a friendly settlement. The result was that Shaikh Ḥamad b. 'Abdullah accepted peace and promised to pay tribute to Shārjah.

This settlement did not please the Sultan of Muscat, who encouraged the Sharqiyyīn tribe to resume their rebellion. The Sharqiyyīn and the Shiḥūḥ again besieged Dabā al-Ḥiṣn. Infuriated, Shaikh Sālim sent a force of 800 Qawāsim by sea, who took the fort of al-Ghurfah, killing thirty-six and capturing thirty of the rebels. This show of force put a temporary end to the disturbance.

In the spring of 1879 the people of Fujairah rose again. At the head of a deputation, Shaikh Ḥamad went to Shārjah to explain the demands of the Sharqiyyīn. Sālim exiled the members of the delegation to imprisonment on Abū Mūsā and then occupied the fort of Fujairah. After Shaikh Ḥamad b. ʻAbdullah, the headman of Fujairah, had succeeded in escaping from the island and had arrived at Muscat in April, he asked the Sultan, Turkī b. Saʻīd, to take Fujairah under his protection. The Sultan and Miles, the Political Agent, discussed the question. Turkī claimed the ownership of the Shimailiyyah district and protested against the unjust policy of Shaikh Sālim in this area. As the dispute was now assuming serious proportions, with the possible involvement of Muscat, Abū Dhabī and Dubai, the British felt obliged to lay down a definite policy. Ross, the Political Resident, convinced that the Shimailiyyah district should remain within the Qawāsim Emirate, ordered Miles to advise the Sultan not to interfere in the area.

At the beginning of 1880 Ḥamad b. ʻAbdullah returned from Muscat and led a fresh rising at Fujairah, driving the Qawāsim garrison out of the fort. Ross now warned Sālim b. Sulṭān not to attempt the recovery of Fujairah by sea, advising him instead to proceed with negotiations. The Government of India agreed with Ross' point of view that the whole of the Qasimī coast on the Gulf of ʻOmān from Dabā to Khūr Kalbā, and also the coast of Rūs al-Jibāl from Dabā to Musandam, 'should be deemed subject to the operation of the Maritime truce'. Sālim protested against the British restrictions at sea, and asked to be allowed to operate by land with the support of a British man-of-war off Fujairah, requesting also that the Sultan of Muscat should be restrained from helping Shaikh Ḥamad b. ʻAbdullah. These demands show that Sālim hoped to receive the same British favour and help in subduing his rebellious subjects as Zāyed b. Khalīfah had enjoyed in his dispute with his subjects, the Qibaisāt, at al-ʻUdaid in 1878. Sālim visited Colonel Ross in Bushire and reluctantly accepted his decision that the Shaikh of Rās-al-Khaimah, who had good relations with the Sharqiyyīn tribe, should arbitrate.

The dispute was settled at the end of 1881. A written agreement was reached giving Sālim suzerainty over Fujairah, and Ḥamad b. ʻAbdullah once again agreed to the payment of customary tribute. Although Sālim had re-established nominal authority over Fujairah, his policies, his use of force, and his unfriendly relations with the Ruler of Rās al-Khaimah made him unpopular in the whole emirate. In 1883 he went to stay on the island of Abū Mūsā, leaving his nephew, the young Shaikh Ṣaqr b. Khālid, as regent.

Shaikh Ṣaqr, now aged twenty, deposed his uncle during the latter's absence, proclaimed himself Ruler, and due to his popularity was recognised by the inhabitants of Shārjah and the British Government. Ṣaqr b. Khālid, whose reign lasted thirty years, drew from his uncle's failure the lesson that the solution to the problems of his emirate could not be simply military, but must be diplomatic as well. In particular it was necessary to cultivate the friendship of the British, and to end their long-standing suspicion of the Qawāsim. Several factors contributed to the success of Shaikh Ṣaqr in his efforts, and a fundamental change in the British attitude towards the Qawāsim emerged during his reign. First, at the end of the century, the Qawāsim no longer posed the same threat to the British as they had decades before, and their allies the Sa'ūdī Rulers had gone into exile in 1891. Secondly, the Persian occupation of Lingah and Ṣirrī in 1887 and the Persian policy of encroachment against the Qawāsim brought about a *rapprochement* between Shaikh Ṣaqr and the British, who saw Russian instigation behind the Persian move. Thirdly, the growing French influence in Muscat by the turn of the century also contributed to the development of the British–Qawāsim *rapprochement* and caused the British to review the question of the Sultan's sovereignty over the Musandam Pensinsula and his claims to the Shimailiyyah district. Also, in 1884 Ṣaqr made an attempt to re-establish authority over Ḥamriyyah, whose independence had been proclaimed by Saif b. 'Abd al-Raḥmān in 1875. Ṣaqr invited Saif to Shārjah and in his absence appointed Saif's brother Ḥumaid to the chieftainship. Saif returned to Ḥamriyyah and because of his popularity was able to expel his brother. Ḥamriyyah therefore remained semi-independent.

Persian aggression towards Lingah and Ṣirrī produced several significant changes in the internal politics of Shaikh Ṣaqr. In particular it made him settle his differences with Shaikh Sālim and come in 1889 to a new agreement which gave his uncle the larger revenue of Abū Mūsā island and the office of adviser to Ṣaqr. Ṣaqr also found it prudent in 1895 to enter into an alliance with Zāyed b. Khālifah, which was to prove very useful to Shārjah over the next few years. In August 1900 Ḥumaid b. 'Abdullah, the Ruler of Rās al-Khaimah and father-in-law of Ṣaqr b. Khālid, died, and the latter took the opportunity to re-annex the town and district to his emirate. At first he appointed his cousin Ḥamad b. Mājid as Governor, but a few months later he replaced him with his own son Khālid. When Ṣaqr b. Khālid took control of Rās al-Khaimah, the relations between Fujairah and Shārjah again became tense, so that in 1901 Fujairah revolted and the rising spread to other villages in the Shimailiyyah district and the mountains. Ṣaqr b. Khālid then induced the Naqbiyyīn tribe in the Shimailiyyah district and the Mazāri' in Rās al-Khaimah (both Ghāfirī) to attack the villages of the Hināwī Sharqiyyīn. Therefore, in February 1902 Shaikh Ḥammad, to stop this aggression, put himself under the protection of the Shaikh of Dubai.

The matter was referred to the British authorities, and on the advice of the British a meeting between Shaikh Ṣaqr and the Shaikh of Fujairah took place on 12 September in which both pledged to accept the arbitration of the British. It took some time for the latter to reach a definite agreement, since the issues involved in the Shimailiyyah district were very delicate indeed from the point of view of British strategy. Meanwhile Ṣaqr led an attack against Fujairah by the Banī Qatab and Banī Ka‘b, and after a siege of twelve days a temporary truce was made by Sulṭān b. Muḥammad, the Shaikh of the Na‘īm at Buraimī.[9]

In November 1903, in a speech at Shārjah, Curzon gave the Government of India's decision which exhibits how a new British policy towards the Qawāsim was emerging as a consequence of the changed circumstances. He said: 'You are all of you aware that the strip of coast known as the Batinah Coast [read Shimailiyyah] on the opposite side of the Oman Pensinsula, is under the authority of the Chief of the Jowasimis. Nevertheless his authority is contested in some quarters. It is desirable that these disputes should remain undisturbed'.[10] Not satisfied with this decision, Shaikh Ḥamad b. 'Abdullah sought the direct help and protection of Zāyed b. Khalīfah, but Zāyed, who not only had an alliance with Shārjah but also at this time was in need of the friendship of the Qawāsim because of his ambitions in the interior, would not provide the active help expected by Fujairah.

Although in reality the Sharqiyyīn governed themselves in the Shimailiyyah district, Britain's recognition of the Qawāsim's rights of sovereignty over the area was extremely important to the nominal unity of the Emirate. On the occasion of Curzon's visit to the Coast the Government of India again showed its new attitude towards the Qawāsim when Shaikh Saif b. 'Abd al-Raḥmān, the headman of Ḥamriyyah, vainly sought recognition of his independence, explaining that the reason for his request was the failure of the Shaikh of Shārjah to protect the village against attacks by its neighbours. Britain's support of Shārjah's rights over Ḥamriyyah and Fujairah convinced Shaikh Ṣaqr of her good intentions towards him. In 1904 Shaikh Saif died and was succeeded by his son, 'Abd al-Raḥmān b. Saif, who ruled until 1921, and was able eventually to obtain partial recognition for the independence of Ḥamriyyah.[11]

On 23 June 1908 'Abd al-Laṭīf, the Residency Agent, described the dissatisfaction of the elders of the Qawāsim family with Ṣaqr b. Khālid, whom they considered weak; in particular they pointed to his inability to suppress the revolt in Fujairah. They were afraid that if he continued to govern all the Qawāsim's territories, the survival of the whole Emirate would be endangered. The issue focused on Rās al-Khaimah. When Ṣaqr b. Khālid's son, who had been his representative there since 1900, died in March 1908, the elders thought that the town and its hinterland should be governed individually. As governor they proposed Shaikh Ṣalim b. Sulṭān, the ex-ruler of Shārjah, who was currently in retirement in Ḥamriyyah. Ṣaqr complied and deputed his uncle to replace his deceased son, unwisely in the view of the British authorities, who remembered Sālim as 'one of the principal figures in the Abū Mūsā drama' (see Chapter 1, p. 31). Sālim, an able and aggressive ruler who succeeded in putting down disorder in the area, soon became the effective independent ruler of Rās al-Khaimah. Between 1910 and 1921 the question of whether to recognise an independent Rās al-Khaimah became an issue for the British.[12]

In 1913, when Shaikh Ṣaqr b. Khālid died and his son Sulṭān was still a minor, Khālid b. Aḥmad succeeded in Shārjah, where he ruled until 1924[13] Fujairah continued to strengthen its position in the mountains and the Shimailiyyah district. In 1944 the Shaikh of Fujairah visited Umm al-Qaiwain to strengthen his alliance with it, an action which the British resented. In accordance with its traditionally hostile policy towards Shārjah, Umm al-Qaiwan aided the Za'āb, the Shaikh of Ḥamriyyah and Fujairah.[14]

The Growth of Abū Dhabī under Zāyed b. Khalīfah

In the eighteenth century the Abū Dhabī Emirate was concentrated on four centres, Līwā,[15] Abū Dhabī village, Dubai village and some islands in the extreme west, notably Dalmā and Ṣīr Banī Yās. The Banī Yās encompassed a federation of tribes—Āl Bū-Falāḥ, al-Hawāmil, al-Maḥāribah, al-Mazārī, al-Sūdān, Āl Bū-Muhair, al-Rimīthāt, al-Qibaisāt and al-Marar. The Emirate of Abū Dhabī, which had grown in size and strength in the nineteenth century, now reached the zenith of its power, under Zāyed b. Khalīfah (1855–1908).[16] A gallant warrior by nature, Zāyed had also, during his refuge in Dubai,[17] learned the art of ruling, which enabled him to dominate internal policies in the Trucial States, to extend his authority over the hinterland to 'Ibrī in the Dhāhirah area, and to gain official British recognition for his sovereignty as far as al-'Udaid in the west. Following a revolt against the ruler, Sa'īd b. Ṭaḥnūm in 1855, the elders of Abū Dhabī summoned the young Zāyed b. Khalīfah to assume power in the Emirate.

The early attitudes of the Banī Yās towards Britain, the Sa'ūdīs and the Sultans of Muscat, differed markedly from those of the Qawāsim, and broadly determined the subsequent history of their emirate during the nineteenth century. Since Abū Dhabī's economic interests lay mainly in the date groves at Līwā and in the pearl fisheries around Dalmā island, far from the navigation channel of the Gulf, the Banī Yās, unlike the Qawāsim, had no conflict with the British at sea. Again unlike the Qawāsim, they remained Mālikī, and did not adopt the Muwaḥḥidīn doctrines. In fact, the extreme bravery of their resistance to the massive Sa'ūdī invasions of 1800–14, under the leadership of Shaikh Shakhbūt, earned them, despite their small numbers, a place among the leaders of the Hināwī party in 'Omān. It earned them, too, friendly relations with the Sultans of Muscat, especially Sa'īd b. Sulṭān (1806–56). This friendship became a traditional part of the external policy of Abū Dhabī and made an important contribution to the growth of the Emirate during the century. In the British punitive expedition to the Coast in 1819, the towns of Abū Dhabī and Dubai did not suffer the bombardment launched upon the Qawāsim ports, Rās al-Khaimah and Shārjah. In contrast with the Qawāsim, Abū Dhabī's dealings with the British and their representative in Shārjah were remarkably untroubled.

After the fall of the first Sa'ūdī State in 1818, the Sultan of Muscat regained his nominal authority over the autonomous Buraimī oasis, where there were six villages inhabited jointly by the Na'īm, a Ghāfirī tribe who had adopted the Tawhīd (Unitarianism) faith, and by the Dhawāhir, a Hināwī tribe who kept their Shāfi'ī beliefs. After Shaikh Shakhbūṭ b. Diyāb, now a major Hināwī leader, had resigned power in 1816, he went during the 1820s to the territory of the Dhawāhir tribe in the oasis, where he planted palm groves and built the fort of Muraijib as his residence. The alliance which he now formed with the Dhawāhir initiated an extension of the power towards Buraimī of the successive Rulers of Abū Dhabī in the next few decades, a challenge which brought strong opposition from the Na'im tribe, and from the Ghafalah and Banī Qatab Bedouin tribes, who formed the fighting elements of the Qawāsim.[18]

During the first fifteen years of Shaikh Zāyed b. Khalīfah's long reign a series of events contributed to his success in establishing himself as the dominant ruler in the area. The three local powers—the Sultanate of Muscat, the Qawāsim Emirate and the second Sa'ūdī State—declined in the hinterland. When Shaikh Zāyed b. Khalīfah, in single combat, killed Shaikh Khālid b. Sulṭān in 1868 he gained much prestige and respect among the Bedouin tribes. This marked a change in the balance of power between the Qawāsim and the Banī Yās, to the extent that the succeeding rulers of the Qawāsim, Sālim b. Sulṭān and Ṣaqr b. Khālid, gave up their traditional rivalry with Abū Dhabī and earnestly sought the friendship of Zāyed. The collapse of the second Sa'ūdī State after the death of Imām Faiṣal b. Turkī in 1865 had given Shaikh Zāyed an excellent opportunity to extend his authority unopposed over the whole Dhāhirah area. In June 1869 Zāyed and the Imām 'Azzān b. Qais, Ruler of Muscat (1868–70), co-operated to occupy the forts of the Na'im in Burainī and expel the Sa'ūdī force.[19] A strong alliance was established between them, and in February 1870 'Azzān b. Qais entrusted to Shaikh Zāyed b. Khalīfah the defence of the Na'īm villages in Buraimī which belonged to Muscat, in addition to the Dhawāhir part of the oases which he already controlled.[20] Moreover, the Ottoman occupation of al-Ḥasā in 1871, although it represented a powerful threat to the boundaries of Abū Dhabī, had the effect of strengthening its ties with the British, whose strategy now required an assertion of Abū Dhabī's rights over al-'Udaid (see Chapter 3, p. 161).[21]

During the 1870s and 1880s, Shaikh Zāyed b. Khalīfah's authority in the interior continued to increase gradually. In 1874 he attacked the Na'īm tribe who sought the protection of the Ruler of Dubai. Also in that year Zāyed tried to improve his relations with the Sultan Turkī with whom there was some friction owing to his refusal to aid him against Imām 'Azzān. Zāyed visited Muscat and advised Shaikh Sāliḥ b. 'Alī, head of the strong Hināwī tribe of al-Ḥirth and Turkī's leading opponent, to settle his dispute with the Sultan and remain in the interior. However, strong ties were re-established in 1888 on the accession of Turkī's son Faiṣal, who now entrusted Zāyed with maintaining order in al-Dhāhirah between Buraimī and 'Ibrī.[22]

In 1880 Shaikh Zāyed went on a pilgrimage to Mecca, where he consolidated the traditional relations between the Rulers of Abū Dhabī and the Sheriffs of Mecca.[23] On his return, he sent his son Khalīfah to Baḥrain to cement the Āl Bū-Falāḥ friendship with the Āl Khalīfah, the ruling family there. On his way, Shaikh Khalifah visited Doḥah, where he persuaded Khādim b. Buṭī, the head of the Qibaisāt, to bring his tribe back to Abū Dhabī, an enterprise which was of great importance to Zāyed, since the Qibaisāt had ties of marriage with the Āl Bū-Falāḥ and constituted at this time the main workforce in the pearl-diving trade at Abū Dhabī. The suddenness and secrecy of the Qibaisāt's departure from Doḥah angered Jāsim and fighting broke out between Abū Dhabī and Qaṭar, lasting from 1880 to 1890. Although these prolonged wars were fought mainly in Qaṭar territory and the western part of Līwā, they had an impact on Zāyed's plans to extend into the Ghāfirī areas on the Trucial Coast, where his endeavours to form alliances with the Ghāfirī emirates, and to obtain recognition of his authority in the hinterland by the Banī Qatab and by the Na'īm tribe of al-Buraimī, were disturbed in 1888. As a consequence a loose and informal alliance of the Ghāfirī tribes did come into being, based on the expectation that Ibn Rashīd, the Wahhābī leader, was about to arrive on the Coast of 'Omān.[24]

In 1890 the Banī 'Irār at al-'Ain, the largest village in the Dhawāhir area of Buraimī, revolted against Shaikh Zāyed, and the revolt was soon aided by a coalition of the Na'im with the Shaikhs of Shārjah and 'Ajmān—but with the help of Shaikh Rāshid b. Maktūm and Sultan Faiṣal b. Tūrki, Zāyed suppressed the revolt in April 1891. The Na'im tribe was forced to acknowledge the sovereignty of Zāyed, who reinforced their attachment to him by marrying the daughter of their shaikh. In a still more definite assertion of the Banī Yās presence at al-Buraimī, Zāyed's son Khalīfah began a date plantation in al-Mas'ūdī in the north of the oasis; Mas'ūdī was to become one of the settlements of the al-Buraimī area. Besides this, members of the Banī Yās bought land and houses at al-'Ain, which would grow as a result until it rivalled the village of Buraimī itself. Meanwhile, in 1897 Zāyed decided to strengthen his authority in the Buraimī area by building a new fort at al-Jāhilī in the Abū Dhabī sector of al-Buraimī oasis. He appointed Aḥmad b. Hīlāl to represent him permanently in the oasis, and in this capacity Aḥmad served Zāyed's sons and grandsons also, holding the office of Governor until his death in 1936.[25]

The turn of the century witnessed both the zenith of Zāyed b. Khalīfah's power in his successful unification of the Coast by alliance and the beginnings of British opposition to his scheme. At this time various factors led to an estrangement between Abū Dhabī and the British authorities, who after 1900 acted increasingly to restrain Zāyed's ambitions. An early factor in the cooling relations between the parties could have been his close alliance with the Sultan of Muscat. It seems that the rupture in Muscat's relations with Britain between 1895 and 1899 had a direct effect on Zāyed's attitudes. In his report to Paris on 26 February 1896 the French Consul in Muscat wrote that he had received two letters from Shaikh Zāyed, encouraging the French to establish commercial and political relations with him, and offering Abū Dhabī as a port of call for the Messagerie Maritime.[26] However, the British ultimatum to Faiṣal in February 1899, which forced him to abandon his friendship with the French, had the effect of closing that option for Zāyed as well. Zāyed's communication with the French remained unknown to the British authorities, but in 1900, when he again violated the treaty of 1892 by entering into correspondence with the Persians, it was no secret from the British, who reacted with strong disapproval and began to feel that Zāyed had overstepped the mark; this was reflected in their policy towards him in the last few years of his life.

Another important factor contributing to the change in the British attitude towards Zāyed was that his aggrandising plan conflicted with the current British policy of maintaining the *status quo*, underlined in Curzon's speech in 1903 (see Chapter 1, p. 27). Cox's two visits to the Trucial Coast in 1902 and 1904 revealed to him the unexpected growth of Zāyed's power, which humiliated his Ghāfirī neighbours, the previous masters of the area,[27] and he concluded from the attitude of the Ghāfirī group towards Ibn Sa'ūd and his proposed visit in 1905 that if the British did not retain the balance of power on the Coast and stop Zāyed's trespassing on his neighbouring Ghāfirī shaikhs, who were Wahhābī, they might seek help from Ibn Sa'ūd, a situation full of danger to British interests.

Two incidents in particular illustrate most clearly the way in which British policy, guided by Curzon and conducted by Cox, hindered Zāyed's ambitions: the first concerned his Zūrā project, and the second his dispute with the young Shaikh Rāshid b. Aḥmad, Ruler of Umm al-Qaiwain.

To maintain his ascendancy over the Bedouin tribes, Zāyed now needed some bases within their territory. He saw in the island of Zūrā a safe asylum for the flocks and herds of his dependent tribes and an excellent base for his own operations in the event of hostilities with tribes lying at a distance from Abū Dhabī. Zūrā was a sandy tract in the sea extending between 'Ajmān and Ḥamriyyah, and separated from the mainland by a comparatively deep channel. In February 1895 Zāyed obtained British permission for the Bedouin tribes he had collected to use the island as a depot for provisions.[28] On 28 May 1897 'Abd al-Laṭīf, the Residency Agent, passed on to the Political Resident a request from Sulṭān b. Nāṣir, the head of a section of the Sūdān tribe which had recently migrated from 'Ajmān, first to Shārjah and now to Dubai. Sulṭān b. Nāsir, who was also Zāyed b. Khalīfah's father-in-law, asked to be allowed to colonise Zūrā. Although the Residency Agent recommended Sulṭān b. Naṣīr as a rich pearl merchant and a man of peace, he also reported the suspicion with which the neighbouring rulers and tribes, especially the Banī Qatab, viewed Zāyed's designs, so the British delayed giving an answer.

Concerned at the delay, Sulṭān b. Nāṣir sought and obtained the written permission of the Shaikh of 'Ajmān to settle on the island with his tribe. Furthermore, he asked his son-in-law Zāyed to protect him from the neighbouring Bedouins. Zāyed encouraged the project, seeing in the Shaikh of 'Ajmān's consent a new opportunity to realise his earlier plans for Zūrā. On 27 December 1898 he informed the Residency Agent that Sulṭān b. Nāṣir had begun to build there, and that the settlement was under his protection.[29]

In July 1900 Ṣaqr b. Khālid, the Shaikh of Shārjah, and 'Abd al-'Azīz b. Ḥumaid, the new Shaikh of 'Ajmān, complained to the British about the building on Zūrā, on the grounds that Sulṭān b. Nāṣir was a Hināwī, closely attached to Shaikh Zāyed, whereas Zūrā was in the midst of Ghāfirī territory. The immediate British response was to instruct Zāyed, in a letter of 6 October, to stop the enterprise completely. This revocation intensely annoyed Zāyed, who saw himself thus deprived of one of the chief means on which he had counted for the extension of his influence over the Coast of 'Omān. Ṣaqr b. Khālid, concerned not to damage his alliance with Zāyed, sent a special messenger to Abū Dhabī to explain that his objections did not imply any hostility towards Zāyed himself. The Shaikh of 'Ajmān, on the other hand, was more forceful in his resistance. He insisted that anyone living on the island must do so as his subject, and he began to build a fort on the mainland facing Zūrā. He also wrote to his relative Shaikh Sulṭān b. Muḥammad, head of the Na'īm in Buraimī, to arrange that the Na'īm should attack Abū Dhabī territory in the oasis if Zāyed tried to enforce the settlement on Zūrā.

By the end of the year war was imminent. The Shaikh of Shārjah was induced to side with 'Ajmān, and the two Shaikhs sent arms and provisions to the Na'īm in Buraimī. On the other side, the Sultan of Muscat sent aid to Shaikh Zāyed, who had the support of Dubai and Umm al-Qaiwain. On 9 February 1901 Zāyed expressed his surprise at the Political Resident's change of attitude on the question of Zūrā and said he had not been accustomed to such treatment from the British. Umm al-Qaiwain and Dubai tried to reach a peaceful settlement to the dispute. Zāyed, who felt his prestige among the Bedouin had suffered, insisted that Shārjah and 'Ajmān must recompense Sulṭān b. Nāṣir and himself for their outlay on the settlement at Zūrā, a sum of $20,000, otherwise he would have no alternative but to establish the colony by force. The Residency Agent advised him not to use force but to seek a solution through British channels.[30]

Over the next few years, Zāyed wrote several times to the Political Resident, but none of his letters was answered. In March 1905, Cox made a personal inspection of Zūrā and, influenced by his conviction of the necessity of maintaining the *status quo*, came to the conclusion that the proposed settlement should not be authorised unless it was with the unanimous consent of all the Trucial shaikhs, which he was unlikely ever to obtain.

The second incident began after a dispute with the Banī Qatab tribe. In 1904 Zāyed demonstrated his influence in the interior by obliging the Banī Qatab to pay blood money for killing two citizens of the town of 'Ibrī on the southern edge of the Dhāhirah province. In the same year the long-established friendship between Abū Dhabī and Umm al-Qaiwain was put in doubt by the accession as shaikh in the latter emirate of Rāshid b. Aḥmad (1904–22), a young man of ability and forceful character, who made overtures to the lawless Banī Qatab.[31] Early in 1905, the Banī Qatab, motivated by enmity towards the Na'īm of Buraimī, occupied the hills at the head of Wādī Ḥattā, and, assisted by funds from the Shaikh, built a fort to command the road, which enabled them to control the village of Maṣfūṭ. As this action also affected the neighbouring village of Ḥijrain, which belonged to the Shaikh of Dubai, he called on Zāyed to help him against the Banī Qatab. In August of the same year a quarrel arose at Māzim between the Balūch colony there and their neighbours, the sedentary Banī Qatab group. Since Māzim was in the Dhāhirah province, which had been entrusted by the Sultan of Muscat to the Shaikh of Abū Dhabī, the Balūch appealed to Zāyed. At this point, in September 1905, a meeting of all the Trucial shaikhs was held at Dubai, presided over by Shaikh Zāyed, in an attempt to settle the problem of Wādī Ḥattā. It was decided that the fort should be destroyed and Maṣfūt returned to the Na'īms; and Zāyed advised Shaikh Rāshid b. Aḥmad not to encourage the adventures of the Banī Qatab, advice which Rāshid promised to follow. Zāyed also tried to induce the nomad Banī Qatab not to join their kinsmen in the assault on Māzim in the south.

However, Rāshid at once broke his promise by engineering a reconciliation between the Banī Qatab and Shārjah and 'Ajmān, thus clearly using the Ghāfirī Banī Qatab to split the alliance dominated by Abū Dhabī; the Bedouin of Banī Qatab attacked the fort of Māzim, killing some Balūchi. In December 1905, during his visit to the area, Cox, who considered that the affairs of the Dhāhirah province were not part of the responsibilities of the Ruler of Abū Dhabī, tried to persuade Zāyed to turn his attentions instead to the threat posed by the new Sa'ūdī revival in Nejd,[32] but Zāyed neglected to follow Cox's advice. Infuriated by the outrages of the Banī Qatab and the audacious challenge of Rāshid b. Aḥmad, early in 1906 Zāyed collected his forces and prepared to move against the Banī Qatab. Unable to enter into a war with Abū Dhabī, Rāshid persuaded the shaikhs of the various branches of the Banī Qatab to go in a delegation to Dubai and ask Shaikh Butī to mediate for them. Zāyed demanded a fine of 200 camels for the misdemeanours of the Banī Qatab, a penalty which was well beyond their means, and the Shaikh of Umm al-Qaiwain asked that the fine be reduced, but Zāyed did not answer. The Banī Qatab then appealed to all the other Trucial shaikhs to mediate for them, but they refused. Counsels of moderation eventually prevailed and a general meeting of the rulers of the Coast was held at Khawānīj, near Dubai. At the end of April 1906 a written agreement was drawn up defining the spheres of tribal influence of the shaikhs of Abū Dhabi and Umm al-Qaiwain: the Banī Qatab, the Ghafalah and Banī Ka'b were assigned to Rāshid, while Zāyed was recognised as governing the Na'īm Shaikh of Darīz in the Dhāhirah, Fujairah and the Shiḥūḥ tribe.[33]

In November 1906, not content with this settlement, Zāyed collected and armed his adherents in preparation for an attack on Falaj 'Ālī in Umm Al-Qaiwain territory, where Shaikh Rāshid was building a fort. Rāshid, who was determined to resist Zāyed, asked the British for two guns to mount on the fort. The situation took on wider dimensions from the British point of view when it was reported that Goguyer, the French arms dealer, had visited Umm al-Qaiwain. Cox then sent a strong remonstrance to both shaikhs. In January 1907, Rāshid led a delegation of the Banī Qatab to Zāyed's camp in the interior in an effort to appease his anger, but after being hospitably entertained for several days he was suddenly seized and put in chains, while the Banī Qatab were allowed to leave. Soon the Banī Qatab declared war on Abū Dhabī and Dubai and sent a message to the Shaikh of Shārjah, as one of the heads of the Ghāfirī, warning him not to ally himself with Zāyed. In February Zāyed marched to the Khawānīj, where he joined forces with the Shaikhs of Dubai, Shārjah and 'Ajmān.[34]

Cox reacted forcefully and on 18 February went to Shārjah in person with two warships. He insisted on the immediate and unconditional release of Rāshid, and undertook to make a satisfactory settlement when this was done. The Shaikh of Shārjah came on board with Zāyed's answer. At first Zāyed refused to release his prisoner without certain guarantees, but on 20 February Cox delivered a final warning that if Zāyed's prisoner was not released by noon on the following day, he, Cox, would communicate directly with the Government of India—the usual preliminary to a bombardment. Thereupon Zāyed released Rāshid, who went aboard Cox's ship. After long discussions, presided over by Cox, involving the Shaikhs of 'Umm al-Qaiwain, Shārjah and Dubai, the matter was successfully concluded and an agreement was signed on 25 February, the main articles of which were as follows: the Shaikh of Umm al-Qaiwain pledged himself to dismantle the fort at Falaj 'Āl 'Alī, return the camels belonging to the Shaikh of 'Ajmān and undertook not to interfere between the Shaikh of Shārjah and the heads of Ḥamriyyah and Fujairah. Shaikh Zāyed agreed not to attack the Banī Qatab at Falaj 'Āl 'Alī, who were under the protection of Shaikh Rāshid as long as they stayed where they were and did not join their kinsmen beyond the boundaries of Umm al-Qaiwain. However, as an earnest of his good intentions, Zāyed did not, in the event, insist on the destruction of the fort at Falaj 'Āl 'Alī. In a letter to the Government of India on 28 February 1907 Cox explained his position: although it was an internal matter, he said, he had interfered, not only because Zāyed had been in technical breach of the Maritime Truce when he had sent Rāshid's retinue to Abū Dhabī by sea. In view of the delicacy of the situation which had become clear to him during the talks, he asked the Government of India to endorse his position and refrain from more severe measures against Zāyed, which he considered would only weaken his prestige among the Shaikhs.[35]

Rāshid's determined stand, and the involvement of Cox in the developing situation had amounted to a setback to Zāyed's plan for the unification of the area under Abū Dhabī. During the reign of his sons, Shaikh Taḥnūn (1909–12) and Ḥamdām (1912–22), the Abū Dhabī Emirate contracted until eventually it was confined within its traditional boundaries.[36]

III Changes in the Economy and in Political Attitudes: Cultural Development, 1892–1939

Changes in the Economy

There were four main developments in the economy of the Trucial Coast between 1892 and 1939: the growth of the pearl trade from the end of the nineteenth century, the emergence of Dubai in 1903 as the main port of the coast, and the decline of the pearl industry, followed by the new revenues derived from the rent of the Shārjah airport and the conclusion of oil concessions during the 1930s. The main sources of income for the inhabitants of the Trucial States were agriculture, pearl fishing, maritime commerce and shipbuilding. The rich cultivated areas were limited to Līwā Oasis, reckoned to have 33,000 date trees, the al-Buraimī area with 60,000 date trees, the Sīr area with 25,000 trees, Dhaid village and Falaj al-Mu'allā.

When we review the available trade statistics of the Trucial Coast at the turn of the century it becomes apparent how dependent the inhabitants were on pearl fishing for the means of purchasing the ordinary necessities of life—rice, tea, coffee, sugar, textiles and wood—which they did not themselves produce. At the end of the nineteenth century Abū Dhabī owned the largest diving fleet on the coast with 410 boats, followed by Shārjah with 360, Dubai 335, Umm al-Qaiwain 70, Rās al-Kaimah 57 and 'Ajmān 40. As the richest of the pearl fisheries in the Gulf lie between the Qaṭar peninsula and Dubai, the island of Dalmā in Abū Dhabī's water became the centre for provisions and for the pearl market during the diving season, an economic factor which also added to the political weight of the state of Abū Dhabī during this period.[37] The British authorities, however, strongly supported the inhabitants of the Arabian shore in their claim to exclusive fishing rights, which they had exercised from time immemorial. Although the lucrative arms traffic supported some adventurers and immigrants before World War I, the Government of India was aware that pearling had become the major source of income for the inhabitants of the Trucial Coast. Cox objected to any foreign interference in the Arab monopoly and was convinced that the intrusion of foreigners supplied with dredgers and diving equipment would, if the undertaking succeeded, drive thousands of Arabs to gun-running, slaving and piracy for a living. He explained these dangers to the Arab rulers in a letter in 1906, warning them against granting the French and German companies concessions in pearl fishing. He repeated this warning in a letter dated 20 July 1911.[38] Consequently, with the help of the British, who wished to encourage the pearl industry along traditional lines, pearl fishing remained during this period an Arab monopoly, and the introduction of modern equipment was prohibited.

One of the immediately noticeable results of the importance of the pearl trade was the influential position which its merchants came to occupy in internal politics; among these men were b. Khalaf al-Utaibah and Ḥāmid b. Buṭī in Abū Dhabī, b. Dalmūk, Shaikh Māni' b. Rāshid, Sālim b. Miṣabbaḥ, b. Bayāt and b. Badūr in Dubai, b. Darwīsh, Ḥumaid b. Kāmil and 'Alī al-Maḥmūd in Shārjah, b. Lūtāh in 'Ajmān and Nāṣir b. Rāshid in Umm al-Qaiwain. Many of them exercised great political power behind the scenes, preferring for this purpose an accommodating ruler to one with strong views of his own.[39] Moreover, it was these pearl merchants who financed the internal wars between states. On the other hand, as the rulers' revenues were not as great as those of the pearl merchants, although almost entirely dependent on customs, fishing licences and levies on date groves, they also profited from the booming economy. Their main source of income at that time was the levies they collected from every pearling boat according to its size. As a result of the affluence, the rulers were able to strengthen their control over the Bedouins by giving their chiefs regular annual presents.[40]

The second important development was the rise of Dubai. Between 1873 and 1902 the bulk of the Indian trade came to the coast through the port of Lingah, but after 1903, when the steam navigation companies began to call at Dubai, the port underwent an unprecedented development. It soon became the chief pearl market of the Gulf after Baḥrain and occupied in this respect the place formerly held by Lingah. Other factors also contributed to the prosperity of the port of Dubai during this period. Burckhardt the German-Swiss traveller, who visited Dubai in February 1904 during a voyage in the Gulf, reported that the Shaikh of Dubai had abolished the 5 per cent customs duty and declared Dubai a free port. Burckhardt was not therefore surprised to find German and British merchandise abundant in the markets of the city. He explained that the influx of immigrants from Lingah, who were attracted by this far-reaching policy of the ruler, were causing the rents of houses and shops to increase, from which the Shaikh and the inhabitants profited greatly.[41] The unrest prevailing in the Sultanate of Muscat between 1895 and 1920, which blocked the roads between the port of Muscat and Maṭrah and the interior, enabled Dubai to supply inner 'Omān with provisions.

The composition of the inhabitants in the principal towns of the coast was an indication of the different economic activities there. The pure tribal

Arabs, who can be regarded as the aristocrats of this society, limited themselves to fighting, pearl fishing and the dhow trade, which were thought to be truly honourable occupations. As a result, the few Persians who had originally settled on the Coast, in addition to the many Arab Hūle[42] and Persians, who had migrated more recently, monopolised the activities of shopkeeping and retail trading and some of them became extremely rich. The Banians who made their appearance on the Coast after 1865 as representatives of the British and Indian firms in Bombay, dealt in textiles and took to banking, providing the pearl industry with the necessary loans, since Muslims, bound by a religious law, could not practise usury.[43]

The number of Banians and Persians in the towns reflected a flourishing economic situation. According to a study presented to the Political Resident by Ḥajjī 'Abd al-Laṭīf, the Residency Agent, in 1901 the number of Banians in Dubai was 52, in Abū Dhabī 39, in Shārjah 76, in Rās al-Khaimah 9, in 'Ajmān 4 and in Umm al-Qaiwain 3; whilst the Persians were 500 in Dubai, 96 in Abū Dhabī, 89 in Shārjah, 30 in Rās al-Khaimah, 20 in 'Ajmān and 20 in Umm al-Qaiwain.[44]

The flourishing economy of the Trucial Coast, based as it was on a system of advance payments at high interest rates, had fallen into the hands of the Banians and some Persian merchants, a state of affairs which, though concealed for a time by the general prosperity, was later, during the 1930s, to prove disastrous. The earliest signs of the decline of the pearl trade were reported in July 1929 when sixty pearling boats in Dubai were unable to proceed to the fishing banks for lack of advances. The report also mentioned that Muḥammad b. Bayāt was declared bankrupt, being in debt for Rs. 600,000, and Muḥammad b. Aḥmad b. Dalmūk was in debt to Ḥajjī Muḥammad 'Alī Zainal in Bombay because the sale of his pearls had been delayed in Paris. He was obliged to obtain a loan of Rs. 200,000 from a Banian in Bombay named Gaushamdeshk, at an interest rate of 36 per cent.[45] This difficult year was followed by another.

During the 1930s many Banians, particularly in Dubai and Shārjah, sent complaints to the Political Resident, asking him to use his influence to obtain the repayment of their debts by leading pearl merchants. Protection of the Banians' claims and property on the Trucial Coast was one of the main causes of British interference in the internal affairs of the emirates between the two World Wars. As there was no order in council to judge the claims of the Banians in these emirates, the Political Resident held the shaikhs personally responsible for ensuring the repayment of the debts. The process was prolonged throughout the 1930s, most settlements being a compromise amount paid in long-term instalments.[46] The depression had an immediate effect, not only on the merchant classes but, in consequence, on the rulers too, whose authority over the Bedouins now weakened since, owing to a shortage of money, their traditional presents were not forthcoming. Between 1928 and 1934 the Bedouins of the 'Awāmir, Manāṣir and Banī Qatab periodically raided the towns on the coast, and it was sometimes dangerous to travel outside these towns without an armed escort.[47] The majority of the Banians left the coast during the economic depressions.

The final major development in this period was the improvement in the economic situation brought about by general world improvement and the establishment of new external sources of income. The 1932 agreement concerning the airport at Shārjah affected not only Shārjah but much of the Trucial Coast. Shaikh Sulṭān b. Ṣaqr insisted that ships of the British India Steam Navigation Company should call at Shārjah as well as Dubai as a condition of granting the airport facilities. Soon Dubai became a refuelling station for flying boats and considerable fuel stores for the land planes station at Shārjah were put ashore there. Various emergency landing facilities were later provided by Abū Dhabī, Rās al-Khaimah and Kalbā.[48] During 1937–9 oil concessions were granted, and although oil revenues were not at first substantial, it marked the beginning of a new period of prosperity for the Trucial Coast. For the first time the rulers had an independent, comfortable income compared with the previously rich merchants who were still suffering financially, since the pearl trade never regained its former prosperity. This new fact had far-reaching political repercussions in the internal history of the coast.

Cultural Advances

From a study of the several interviews by the writer with the educated elders on the Coast of 'Omān, it is apparent that early in the twentieth century there began a cultural awakening which was without precedent in the modern history of the Trucial States. During this period an important manuscript on the history of the Coast was written by 'Abdullah b. Sāliḥ al-Muṭawwa', a citizen of Shārjah, a map of the pearl-fisheries was published in 1941 by Shaikh Māni' b. Rāshid, a member of the ruling family in Dubai, and many poets began to establish themselves, among them Sālim b. 'Alī 'Uwais, Mubārak b. Saif al Nākhī and Mubārak b. Ḥamad al-'Ukailī from Shārjah and Aḥmad b. Sulṭān b. Sulayyim from Dubai.

Three main factors contributed to this cultural revival. First, the flourishing economy of the 'Omānī Coast at the beginning of the twentieth century. Secondly the opening of the Suez Canal in 1869 and the development of steam navigation routes in the late nineteenth century which reconnected the Gulf with Egypt after a rupture of about three hundred years. As the Gulf before World War I had no Arabic printing press, one finds that the majority of extant books of the period had been printed in Cairo. New lines of communication also brought to the Gulf, with the mail, Cairo daily newspapers and literary magazines, thus creating a political awareness within the educated groups on the Trucial Coast. The establishment of a fortnightly maritime service between Dubai and Bombay in 1902 intensified the influence of both Cairo and Bombay. In 1924, the desert route between Damascus and Baghdād was opened, creating new links between the Trucial Coast and Syria, Lebanon, Palestine and Egypt. One of the monthly nationalist magazines, *al-Fatḥ*, was sent from Cairo to its subscribers on the Trucial Coast by this desert route to Baṣrah, then steamer to Dubai.[49]

The third factor was the role which Bombay played at the end of the nineteenth century; Bombay had by then progressed after two centuries of British rule from a small unimportant village into a large modern city, which to the Arabs of the Gulf reflected European civilisation. Bombay remained the main centre for medical treatment until the beginning of World War II. Furthermore it was the main market for pearls, where all the rich Arab merchants of the different Gulf states gathered after the pearl fishing season. Large Arab businesses had established agencies in Bombay and a small Arab community had grown up in the city, among which were the well-known families of al-Bassām, Āl Ibrāhīm and al-Quṣaibī. With the co-operation of his Arab colleagues, Muḥammad 'Alī Zainal, a wealthy pearl merchant, built an Arab school there. Arab visitors to Bombay, meeting together in the city, quickly became aware of the political situation in different parts of the Gulf. It was to Bombay, in 1915, that the British banished Ṭālib Pasha Naqīb from Baṣrah, as well as 'Abd al-Wahhāb Zayyānī from Baḥrain in 1923. Moreover, the important Arab reformers and writers—Rashīd Riḍā in 1912, Ḥāfiz Wahbah in 1913, Muḥib al-Dīn al-Khaṭīb in 1915, Amīn al-Rīhānī in 1923 and 'Abd al-'Azīz-Tha'ālibī in 1923 and 1936—all spent some time in Bombay as guests of the wealthy Arab residents.[50] During this period in Bombay there was a printing press publishing traditional Arabic books, particularly the Qur'ān and the Ḥadīth, financed by the Nizām of Hyder'abād. There were also three bookshops selling Arabic publications. Most private libraries on the Trucial Coast had books published in Bombay as well as books from Cairo. It was also in Bombay that Shaikh Māni' b. Rāshid found the printing facilities for his map of the pearl fisheries of the Gulf.[51]

About 1903 three important schools, the Taimiyyah school in Ḥīrah, the Aḥmadiyyah school in Dubai and the b. Khalaf school in Abū Dhabī were established. The Taimiyyah school was financed by 'Alī al-Muhmūd, a wealthy and philanthropic pearl merchant in Shārjah and was mainly concerned with religious teaching. The school enrolled 200 students from Shārjah itself and 120 boarding students from other towns, Rās al-Khaimah, 'Ajmān, Za'āb, Ḥamriyyah and Umm al-Qaiwain; both education and accommodation were entirely free. Students had their lessons in the traditional way, sitting on the ground. It is clear that for the old Qawāsim federation Shārjah had become the cultural centre, a fact which gave her a reputation for intellectual eminence on the Coast lasting throughout this period. The teachers came mainly from Nejd, the centre of the Unitarian teachings. The Aḥmadiyyah school was financed by another wealthy philanthropist, also a pearl merchant, Muḥammad b. Aḥmad b. Dalmūk, who named the school after his father. Students at this school contributed small fees for their education, but, as distinct from the Taimiyyah school, they sat at desks during lessons. The teachers came mainly from Lingah and al-Ḥasā and later from Zubair. In Abū Dhabī another enlightened and very rich pearl merchant, Khalaf b. 'Utaibah founded a school and entrusted the teaching to Shaikh 'abd al-Laṭīf b. Ibrāhīm, a member of the Āl Mubārak family, famous as scholars of the Mālikī teachings in al-Ḥasā.[52] The religious scholar 'Abd al-Laṭīf encouraged his cousin 'Abd al-'Azīz b. Ḥamad, in 1915, to teach in the Aḥmadiyyah school in Dubai, where he remained until 1941. Shaikh Aḥmad al-Raḥbānī, who came from Nejd, concentrated his activities in the sphere of education at Rās al-Khaimah, and taught Muḥammad b. Ghubāsh, who later became one of the eminent scholars of the Trucial Coast. Shaikh Aḥmad al-Raḥbānī died in 1918 at Rās al-Khaimah.

In 1911 'Alī al-Maḥmūd established a new school at Ḥamriyyah and made 'Abd al-Wahhāb al-Wuhaibī and his brother 'Abd al-Ṣamad responsible for the teaching, together with 'Abdullah b. 'Abd al-Azīz. The two brothers came from Nejd and had graduated from al-Azhar University and studied in the Seminary school of Muḥammad Rashīd Riḍā. 'Abdullah b. 'Abd al-'Azīz was also originally from Nejd and was an enthusiastic religious reformer, but left the school after a short time to preach to the Banī Bū 'Alī tribe in J'alān. Around 1913, Ṣāliḥ b. Muḥammad al-Khilaifī, a Nejdī educated in Egypt and Iraq, where he specialised in mathematics, was brought to Shārjah by 'Alī al-Maḥmūd to teach his subject, but he shortly moved to Dubai, where the wealthy merchant Sālim b. Miṣabbaḥ Āl Ḥimūdah gave him financial assistance to set up a small school, called al-Sālimiyyah, which remained open for about twelve years. When it closed, Ṣāliḥ al-Khilaifī returned to Shārjah to teach in the new school al-Qāsimiyyah.

In 1915 'Ali al-Maḥmūd asked the eminent scholar, Muḥammad 'Abd al-'Azīz b. Māni', who had received his education in Nejd and was a student of the reformer Muḥammad 'Abduh in Egypt and the Scholar al-Alūsī in Baghdād, to come to Shārjah to teach in his school. However, during his visit to Doḥah in Qaṭar on his way to Shārjah, Shaikh 'Abdullah b. Jāsim, Ruler of Qaṭar, asked him to stay and open a school there, which continued from 1915 to 1938 and inaugurated modern education in Qaṭar, producing all the educated elders of the state.

Subsequently, 'Alī al-Maḥmūd paid for twenty students from various towns to study at Doḥah, where they spent five years. The most important among these students were Muḥammad b. Sa'īd b. Ghubāsh from Rās al-Khaimah and Mubārak b. Saif al-Nākhi from Shārjah.

The period after World War I witnessed further advances in education. In 1921 another mission of students was sent by 'Alī al-Maḥmūd from his school to Doḥah to study with Ibn Māni'. Four new schools were opened, three in Dubai and one in Shārjah. Muḥammad 'Alī Zainal, a wealthy merchant trading at Bombay and Hijāz, established the Falaḥiyyah school in Dubai, to which teachers from Iraq were brought. This school played an important part in the development of modern teaching in Dubai. The al-Sa'ādah school, too, was set up in Dubai by two merchants, Muḥammad b. 'Ubaid al-Bidūr and Yūsuf Sirkāl. 'Ubaid b. Nabūdah founded a third school in Dubai called the 'Modern School', but it was closed after only six years. In Shārjah it should be particularly noticed that under the influence of post-war changes in the area, teachers at the Qāsimiyyah school which had begun in 1917 now came from Zubair in Iraq as well as from Nejd. 'Abdullah al-Muzayyin became the director of the Aḥmadiyyah school in Dubai. In 1926, a significant step towards the broadening of education was 'Alī al-Maḥmūd's decision to help an intelligent young student, Muḥammad b. Ghubāsh from Rās al-Khaimah to continue his advanced studies at al-'Azhar; after four years Ibn Ghubāsh returned to occupy the position of judge in his town. In the same year 'Alī al-Maḥmūd helped two other students 'Abdullah al-Qāsimī and 'Abd al-'Azīz b. Rāshid from Nejd, to go to this university in Cairo, thus furthering his reputation as a man deeply concerned with the advancement of education throughout the area.

As all these schools and educational activities were badly affected by the decline of the pearl industry after 1927 and many were forced to close, all the teachers who had come from beyond the Coast of 'Omān now went back to their own countries. When the financial situation improved in the late 1930s it should be noted that the few schools which were re-opened were directed and run by the younger generation from the Trucial States, who themselves had received their education during the first two decades of the century when schools had flourished in the area. The re-opening of the schools in Dubai and the financing of education generally, were among the main achievements of the reform movement of 1938. When the council of Dubai (*Majlis*) established an education department, it appointed a Director-General of schools. A list of the teachers in the schools of Dubai is found among the Council's documents and it is noticeable that the majority of them were also local citizens.[53]

Political Attitudes

By 1892 the city-state unit, whose formation was begun during the nineteenth century, was well established on the Coast. 'Omān knew political unity during the Ya'āribā dynasty, which ruled the country between 1624 and 1749, but a civil war took place during 1718–49 and split the country between the Hināwī party, headed by Mubārak b. Khalaf al-Hināwī, and the Ghāfirī party, led by Muḥammad b. Nāsir al-Ghāfirī. The division was merely political, not a traditional tribal one, as both the Hināwī and the Ghāfirī parties contained tribes of the 'Adnānī and Yemenī origin. The Āl Bu-Sa'īd dynasty, which followed the Ya'āribā in 'Omān, failed to restore

'Omānī unity and two independent federations emerged at the end of the eighteenth century on the Coast of 'Omān: the Qawāsim federation with its capital at Rās al-Khaimah, and the Banī Yās federation centred on Abū Dhabī.

The dismemberment of 'Omān went a stage further after the British expedition to Rās al-Khaimah in 1819. The British refused to regard Shaikh Sulṭān b. Ṣaqr (1803–66) as the representative of the whole Qawāsim federation, or Shaikh Shakhbūṭ b. Diyāb as the sole representative of the Banī Yās, and they therefore concluded the treaty in 1820 with each shaikh within the Qawāsim and the Banī Yās federations individually. In the ensuing years the Qasimī family at Shārjah and Rās al-Khaimah failed to re-establish the authority of the federation over 'Ajmān and Umm al-Qaiwain, which became totally independent. In 1833 the Āl Bū-Flāsah, a branch of the Banī Yās, also set up an independent state at Dubai. At the end of the nineteenth century divisions along the Coast of 'Omān again became apparent. Rās al-Khaimah itself became independent between 1869 and 1900[54] and the Sharqiyyīn tribe revolted successfully against the Qawāsim in the mountainous area surrounding Fujairah. In 1913 an Immamate appeared at Nizwā in inner 'Omān, and it gained its internal independence from the Sultan of Muscat by the terms of the Sīb treaty in 1920.[55]

These events illustrate a tendency towards political dismemberment in 'Omān, which resulted in a fragmentation of loyalties from large to smaller units, particularly in the towns on the Coast, where political allegiance now centred on the city-state. Owing to migration between the states, the composition of the cities by the end of the nineteenth century had become a mixture of both parties, and these new immigrants came to focus their loyalty on the local ruling family, with the result that their adherence to the old Hināwī and Ghāfirī parties gradually faded. On the other hand, in the interior the Hināwī and Ghāfirī factions retained the political loyalties of the Manāsīr, 'Awāmir, Khawāṭir, Banī Qatab and Shawāmis tribes, who lived apart in the desert and maintained direct relations with the tribal groups of inner 'Omān, where the Hināwī–Ghāfirī division still dominated politics.

Although the British policy of isolating the whole area from foreign contact was one of the factors that retarded development, the British did not censor the Arabic newspapers and literary journals and this had a great effect. Some awareness of world developments was gained too from the merchants who frequently visited Baḥrain and Bombay. But changes were slow and limited in effect to a small number of the inhabitants in the coastal cities. The decline in the pearl trade, which forced the closure of most of the schools after only a few decades, prevented the wider expansion of education. Furthermore teaching within the schools was mainly conducted on traditionally religious lines. The strong tribal influence prevailing on the Trucial Coast and even in the cities, which were divided into sub-tribal residential quarters, also contributed to hinder progress, but the changes that began to occur at this time created the nucleus of intellectual thought and the basis for great educational, social and political advances after World War II.

One of the most important issues confronting the Arabs of the Trucial Coast, as well as their neighbours in the Gulf, was their attitude towards the Ottomans. The political thinking of the people of the coast was dominated by a religious rather than a national identity, and in this they were influenced by the Cairo newspapers *al-Mu'ayyad* and *al-Liwā*, which described the Ottomans as leaders of Islam and defenders of the faith (see Chapter 1, p. 32). The Persian merchants of Lingah who had immigrated to Dubai, being Sunnī, also fervently supported the Ottomans, an attitude which strengthened the same feeling on the Coast. As early as 1876 the Ottoman Consul in Bombay reported to the Sublime Porte that thirteen Sunnī merchants, representing towns on the Persian Coast, had given him a large sum of money which they had collected for the Ottomans and had written to the Calif expressing their willingness to fight with the Turks against their enemies.[56] At the beginning of the twentieth century Khājah 'Abd al-Raḥīm, an important immigrant with literary interests, subscribed to *al-Ḥabl al Matīn*, an Islamic paper published in Calcutta which propagated Islamic unity.[57] The Turkish wars in the Balkans had a direct impact on the inhabitants of the Trucial Coast: we read in a monthly report of the Persian Gulf Residency of 30 October 1912 that the declaration of war between the Turks and the Balkan States had practically paralysed the despatch of pearls to London or elsewhere, as long as the war continued. In January 1913 the Residency Agent, 'Abd al-Laṭīf, furnished Cox with the news that Shaikh 'Abd al-Laṭīf b. Ibrahīm Āl Mubārak, a scholar from al-Ḥasā (which was under Ottoman rule by this time), and director of Khalaf al-'Utaibah's school in Abū Dhabī, had visited Dubai and that at his suggestion the inhabitants had collected subscriptions to aid the Turkish Government and were remitting them by instalments. The total amount was Rs. 43,000.[58] Although the British maintained a strict surveillance over the Trucial Coast, secret correspondence was exchanged between important persons in Shārjah and Baṣrah. A letter dated 1913 in the possession of the al-Midfa' family shows that Ṭālib al-Naqīb, president of a committee set up in Baṣrah to raise funds for the Ottoman navy, corresponded with the 'Mayor' of Shārjah, 'Abdullah Ḥasan al-Midfā', asking him to collect money and send it to Baṣrah.

Ibn Māni''s scholarly teachings and liberal religious ideas had perhaps their greatest impact on the Trucial Coast through his school in Doḥah, which attracted many young students from the Coast. Ibn Māni' enriched contemporary religious thinking through the broad scope of his studies, and helped his students towards an understanding and appreciation of the ideas of Muḥammad 'Abduh and Rashīd Riḍā. These Islamic reformers were concerned with the decline of the Muslim society and the growth of the West, and advocated the purification of the Islamic society. Ibn Mānī''s former students occupied leading positions during the 1930s as judges, teachers and businessmen, and some of them produced important poetry.

After World War I the political map of the Middle East changed, and new states, based on Arab national identity, emerged. The revolts against the French and British mandates in Syria and Iraq aroused strong interest and sympathy on the Trucial Coast. During this period two important men visited the Gulf: Amīn al-Rīḥānī, the Arab writer, and Tha'ālibī, the Tunisian nationalist leader. Tha'ālibī, who in 1923 met Shaikh Rāshid b. Mānī', head of the future Dubai reform movement, in Bombay, was invited by him to visit Dubai during his tour of the Gulf. This visit was an occasion for nationalist and literary celebrations, held by members of the ruling family and the wealthy merchants. Aḥmad b. Sulayyim, a young student at this time, composed a poem of welcome for Tha'ālibī, which was read at the house of Shaikh Mānī' and he still remembers Tha'ālibī's remark, 'My son, do not forget that you are a young Arab poet, and your poem should in future embrace the wider Arab struggle for liberation and progress.'[59]

The Palestinian cause, which was a main factor in uniting Arab feelings in the Middle East, occupied the political attention of the Coast too, particularly that of educated young people. In response to the Palestinian Islamic Congress in Jerusalem in 1930, a meeting was held in the chief mosque in Shārjah at which two young educated men, Mubārak al-Nākhī and Ibrahīm al-Midfa', gave enthusiastic nationalist speeches and money was collected for the Palestinian cause.[60] Two Cairo magazines, *al-Fatḥ*, edited by Muḥib al-Din, and *al-Shūrā*, edited by a young Palestinian refugee, Muḥammad 'Alī al-Ṭāhir, cherished nationalist revolutionary sentiments and eulogised the heroes and martyrs of the Palestinian, Syrian and Iraqi struggles. Some articles published in these journals were sent anonymously by young liberals in the Coast of 'Omān, notable among whom was Mubārak-al-Nākhī, and articles and news reports about the Coast were sometimes sent from Muscat or Bombay to avoid detection by the British. Teachers, particularly in the Falāḥ school in Dubai spread the extreme nationalist sentiments existing in Iraq. At this school, for the first time, a boy scout group was established which paraded frequently in the narrow streets of the town, carrying flags and chanting Arab nationalist songs, applauded by their parents and citizens. On 27 June 1930 it was reported in the Monthly Summary of the Political Residency that an Iraqi traveller and journalist, called Yūnis Baḥarī, came to Kuwait and from there went on to Baḥrain; he wished to visit the Coast of 'Omān in order to complete a book on the Gulf.[61] Bertram Thomas, in talking about the Shiḥūḥ revolt in 1930 in Rūs al-Jibāl, mentioned the unrest which the nationalist magazines and newspapers caused on the Trucial Coast:

Local unrest is largely nourished from abroad, as I was told by a

> neighbouring chief, perhaps the most enlightened of the Trucial hierarchy. In post-war years Egyptian, Indian and Iraqi newspapers devoted to politics have come to circulate in 'Omān and are the medium for the news of world unrest, a contagious germ.[62]

During the 1930s social changes occurred on the Coast. The traditional 'Omānī style of clothing was modified to include such adaptations as buttons, and many men exchanged the white headband for black. Some young men began to shave their beards, wear modern wrist watches rather than pocket watches and shoes brought from Bombay rather than sandals. Jackets also began to be seen in the towns. With the establishment of an aerodrome at Shārjah in 1933 with continuous flights from there, the people witnessed an important aspect of modern European technology which encouraged progressive elements in society. Shārjah airport was frequently visited by the rulers of the Coast, accompanied by the notables of their towns, to witness the landing and taking off of aeroplanes. Baḥrain, where the British established a modern administration, customs and security force, was held up as a fine example of modernisation. By 1938, owing to their income from oil concessions, all the shaikhs had bought cars, and some wealthy merchants owned them too.

Reviewing the available collected poetry, one sees a true reflection of the fundamental change in political, social and cultural attitudes during this period. Arab unity was the dream of these poets, who began to express an affinity with the larger political entity of 'Omān rather than the enclosed city-state. They combined nationalist sympathies with Islamic sentiments, and important events in the Arab world found a great response in their literature. Resentment of British control of the Coast was expressed in the work of Shaikh Sulṭān b. Sālim, Ruler of Rās al-Khaimah, who showed a certain defiance towards the British authorities. During the 1930s there was insecurity outside the towns, on account of Bedouin raids on the surrounding areas, and the rulers who tolerated such disturbances were bitterly criticised in many poems; this wish for a secure urban way of life was a strong factor in the development towards a modern society. Internal reform, justice and modern education were praised, whilst stagnation within society was denounced. The reform movement of 1938 in Dubai, headed by Shaikh Mani' b. Rāshid also provides a good example of the changing spirit of the time.

IV Important Political Changes during the Inter-War Period

A study of the careers of 'Abd al-Raḥmān b. Muḥammad and Sulṭān b. Sālim, in conjunction with an analysis of the Dubai reform movement of 1938 covers many of the internal political events in the emirates of the Trucial Coast. It also underlines the significant developments in economic, cultural and political attitudes taking place in this region in the inter-war period, and modifications in the traditional British policy of non-interference can be more easily understood. As Britain's strategic and commercial interests on the Coast grew she became more involved in the internal affairs of the States: her change in policy led the rulers to fear for the autonomy of their states, and they became suspicious of all British schemes and proposals. The Arabs of the Trucial Coast, dominated by religious concepts, tended to regard the Political Resident's position as they had done throughout the nineteenth century; they still addressed him as 'the Consul of the Magnificent Caesarean State'.[63]

It is necessary to say a few words about the role of the Residency Agent which was held throughout this period by 'Īsā b. 'Abd al-Laṭīf. He was the third generation of his family to hold the office, and the appointment of his grandfather, Ḥājjī 'Abd al-Raḥmān, had taken place in 1866. This family, therefore, was for nearly seventy years the immediate representative on the spot of the British Empire, and its members played a great part in shaping British policy. They could control what information reached their superiors and by exaggeration or suppression could present the picture that suited them and their own interests. By now they were immensely rich merchants with special links in Dubai. 'Īsā himself had a strongly autocratic personality and was not prepared to overlook anything which might reflect on his authority. The hostility which broke out against him on some occasions was motivated more by tribal and personal considerations than by nationalist feelings. The general resentment at Britain's position on the Coast, which was shown in some of the events of the period, was still based on religious rather than nationalist sentiments, and modern Arab nationalism, adopted in addition to their religious zeal by some elements of the young generation, had as yet a very limited effect.

'Abd al-Raḥmān b. Muḥammad, Head of Ḥīrah

Ḥīrah in the 1920s was a part of the Emirate of Shārjah, lying between its capital and 'Ajmān. It had a population of about 2,000, belonging mainly to the Āl Bū-Shāmis section of the Na'īm tribe.[64] On 16 June 1920 its Shaikh, 'Abd al-Raḥmān b. Muḥammad, in response to a plea for help from the family of a murdered Bedouin whose killer had taken refuge in 'Ajmān, became involved in a dispute with Shaikh Ḥumaid b. 'Abd al-'Azīz (1908–28), ruler of 'Ajmān. This dispute soon widened to include the Shaikh of Shārjah, Khālid b. Aḥmad (1913–24), who was opposed to 'Abd al-Raḥmān's behaviour. As a result, 'Abd al-Raḥmān was advised by the British to leave the Coast and reside in Baḥrain.

On 11 October 1920 'Īsā represented to the Political Resident that 'Abd al-Raḥmān was a pearl dealer who owed British subjects Rs. 20,000 but had found it impossible to earn enough in Baḥrain to pay these debts. 'Īsā's view therefore was that 'Abd al-Raḥmān should return to Khān village, but be confined there under the supervision of its Shaikh, Muḥammad b. 'Ubaid.

Meanwhile, after various wanderings, 'Abd al-Raḥmān was staying in Dubai, and on hearing this his relations and followers brought him back to his own village, Ḥīrah, in December, a move which was immediately opposed by Shārjah and 'Ajmān. With the Shaikh of Rās al-Khaimah's mediation, the Shaikh of Shārjah declared that although 'Abd al-Raḥmān should now leave Ḥīrah, he would be granted formal permission to return in one month's time. The negotiations failed and as some ten Indians were reported to be in Ḥīrah, to whom the Arabs, including 'Abd al-Raḥmān, owned money, it was possible that fighting might endanger the lives and property of those merchants.

The SNO was therefore instructed to go to the Trucial Coast (where he arrived at Shārjah on 5 January 1921) to effect a compromise between 'Abd al-Raḥmān and the Shaikhs of Shārjah and 'Ajmān. The SNO proposed that 'Abd al-Raḥmān should declare himself a subject of Shārjah and should reside for one month in the capital, after which time he could return to his village to carry on his business and pay off his debts without molestation. 'Abd al-Raḥmān had to promise not to incite further trouble and both parties were to sign written agreements to this effect in the presence of the SNO. A meeting was arranged between Khālid b. Aḥmad and 'Abd al-Raḥmān on board the SNO's vessel on 8 January 1921, when the agreement was signed.[65]

Although after the agreement the Shaikh of Shārjah's relations with 'Abd al-Raḥmān improved, a popular rising against him was in preparation, which would once more involve 'Abd al-Raḥmān. Khālid b. Aḥmad was a mercenary man, and this, together with the unjust way in which he had deprived Sulṭān b. Ṣaqr, the young son of the popular ex-ruler Ṣaqr b. Khālid, of his inheritance, alienated the people of Shārjah from him. In 1919 Sulṭān b. Ṣaqr had left Shārjah for Dubai, accompanied by his brothers and his maternal grandfather Khamīs b. Sālim. In March, 1923, the young claimant to the Shārjah chieftainship, Sulṭān b. Ṣaqr, who was still in Dubai, married a daughter of Shaikh 'Abd al-Raḥmān of Ḥīrah and though a peaceful man, found in his father-in-law a strong champion. Worried by this alliance, Khālid b. 'Aḥmad of Shārjah soon seized the watch towers of Ḥīrah, but he and his men were driven out by 'Abd al-Raḥmān on 19 July. At the beginning of August, the people of Shārjah opposed their Shaikh and refused to attack Ḥīrah on the grounds that the inhabitants were their fellow-tribesmen. Khālid then asked 'Īsā to intervene, and 'Īsā sent a representative to Ḥīrah where the inhabitants complained to him about the injustice of their Governor, 'Abdullah b. Aḥmad, brother of the ruler. In September 1921 both parties, Khālid and 'Abd al-Raḥmān, signed an undertaking not to molest or intrigue against each other. It seems that 'Īsā was displeased with the conduct of 'Abd al-Raḥmān, whom he had previously supported. After a complaint from Shaikh Khālid, Colonel Trevor sent a warning to 'Abd al-Raḥmān in December to obey his ruler.

This communication was a turning point in 'Abd al-Raḥmān's attitude towards 'Īsā. Soon afterwards, in January 1924, the people of Ḥīrah arrested Shaikh Khālid's new Governor and relations between the two sides once more became strained. Furious, Khālid besieged Ḥīrah with the aid of the Shaikh of 'Ajmān and prepared to bombard it. The notables of Shārjah instantly requested 'Īsā to intervene. Hearing a rumour that Sulṭān b. Ṣaqr was to come to the defence of Ḥīrah, 'Īsā asked the Shaikh of Dubai to keep Sulṭān in his town and managed also to keep the Shaikh of 'Ajmān from interfering. 'Īsā asked for a three-day truce, during which he persuaded 'Abd al-Raḥmān, whom he now described as a 'troublesome plotter', to leave Ḥīrah for Dubai, with which arrangement he was not happy. A new Governor, Sa'īd b. Mājid, was appointed to Ḥīrah. Colonel Trevor approved 'Īsā's action and instructed him that if 'Abd al-Raḥmān appeared again in Shārjah territory, Shaikh Khālid should either imprison him or banish him to some distant place.[66]

Although in exile, 'Abd al-Raḥmān still remained a threat to the Shaikh of Shārjah, since he had joined his son-in-law in Dubai. Khālid built a high tower in the fort of Shārjah, which looked over the interiors of the houses in the vicinity, something which was contrary to the tradition of the inhabitants. Totally disillusioned with Khālid's rule, the notables of Shārjah sent a signed letter to Sulṭān b. Ṣaqr in Dubai by a secret messenger, pledging their support for a revolt against the ruler, and their obedience to Sulṭān. After a secret arrangement with the inhabitants of Shārjah, Sulṭān b. Ṣaqr and his brothers, with the help of 'Abd al-Raḥmān, occupied the towers outside the town on the night of 1 November 1924. (The local rumours also mention some private arrangements with 'Īsā b. 'Abd al-Laṭīf.) Next day the inhabitants joined in the fighting. 'Īsā sent a messenger to Sulṭān b. Ṣaqr and the elders of Shārjah, telling them that the revolt would endanger British subjects and warning them of their responsibility if looting broke out in the market. On 3 November Sulṭān b. Ṣaqr made assurances of the safety of British subjects and undertook to be responsible for them; then the citizens of Shārjah attacked the fort in the centre of the town. It would seem that all the inhabitants of Shārjah supported Sulṭān since those fighting on his side were estimated at 3,000 whilst Khālid had only thirty men in the fort. On the fourth day Khālid sent out some men, who burned sixty houses and bombarded the town with guns. It was recorded that during the attack eight people had been killed, five of Khālid's men and three of Sulṭān's.

On 8 November Sulṭān b. Sālim, the Qāsimī Ruler of Rās al-Kaimah and 'Abdullah b. 'Ali b. Hiwaiden, the Shaikh of Banī Qatab, came to Shārjah to stop the fighting and arrange a settlement, and three days later the British sloop *Cyclamen* anchored near the port. On 21 November 'Abd al-Rāḥmān b. Sa'if, Shaikh of Ḥamriyyah, and 'Īsā b. 'Abd al-Laṭīf, joined Sulṭān b. Sālim and b. Hiwaiden, and a settlement was signed that day by both the parties in the dispute as well as the mediators. Sulṭān b. Ṣaqr was proclaimed Ruler of Shārjah (1924–51) on condition that he honoured Khālid's debts to the Banians and agreed to pay Rs. 60,000 to his brothers as their share of the inheritance which Khālid had withheld. Khālid b. Aḥmad was allowed to keep his belongings in Shārjah untouched. On this occasion it seems that, as a gesture of gratitude, Shaikh Ṣaqr gave his father-in-law a document of autonomy in Ḥīrah.[67]

On 11 October 1925 however, while 'Īsā and his cousin, Ibrāhīm Rajab, were visiting the port in Shārjah on official business, shots were fired at them, injuring Ibrāhīm, who later died at the Residency House. Shaikh Sulṭān b. Ṣaqr made a brief investigation and then ignored the whole matter. 'Īsā's opinion was that the bullets had in fact been aimed at him for the reason that in July and August he had insisted on the Political Resident's demand to fly the British flag from the Residency House in Shārjah. The audacity of the murder shocked 'Īsā and made him fear for Britain's prestige on the Coast. On 15 November 1925 HMS *Cyclamen* arrived at Shārjah; the SNO blamed Sulṭān b. Ṣaqr for his laxity and, after making enquiries among the Banians the next day, he found out that the plot was 'Abd al-Raḥmān's doing. Shaikh Sa'īd b. Maktūm tried to act as intermediary between the SNO and the Shaikh of Shārjah. On 19 November the SNO ordered 'Abd al Raḥmān to reside in Rās al-Khaimah for four weeks, and a letter was sent to its Ruler asking that he be kept under his surveillance. On 20 November the SNO, Captain M. Parry, requested that Sulṭān b. Ṣaqr should continue investigating the matter. 'Abd al-Raḥmān left Shārjah for Rās al-Khaimah the following day with a messenger from Sa'īd b. Maktūm.

The confinement of 'Abd al-Raḥmān in Rās al-Khaimah had serious repercussions. On 26 December the notables of Shārjah, who had expected that 'Abd al-Raḥmān would be totally exiled from the Coast by the British, sent a petition to the Political Resident, expressing their regret at the incident and promising to satisfy 'Īsā if 'Abd al-Raḥmān could remain in either Rās al-Khaimah or Dubai for a year. Correspondence followed between the Political Resident and the Government of India and on 13 February 1926 the former made the following proposals:

1. that the Shaikh of Shārjah should pay blood money to the relations of the murdered man in addition to Rs. 3,000 fine;
2. that the Shaikh should be called upon to exile 'Abd al-Raḥmān to India and should pay his maintenance during the period;
3. that if the Shaikh refused these terms the village of Ḥīrah should be returned to 'Ajmān.[68]

On 12 April the Government of India agreed in general to the Political Resident's proposals but did not approve of condition three, being of the opinion that the transfer of Ḥīrah to 'Ajmān was likely to lead to prolonged troubles on the Trucial Coast.[69] The Shaikh of Shārjah at first refused to comply with the surrender of 'Abd al-Raḥmān, but finally accepted the Government of India's decision. The British, at that point, decided to exile 'Abd al-Raḥmān to Aden for four years. At the beginning of June the SNO visited Rās al-Khaimah in HMS *Triad* but Shaikh Sulṭān b. Sālim refused to surrender 'Abd al-Raḥmān and insisted on the personal arrival of Shaikh Sa'īd b. Maktūm of Dubai as a guarantee. On 11 June Sa'īd and his brother Jum'ah came to Rās al-Khaimah and Sulṭān explained to them that he could not risk stirring up the Bedouins of Āl Bū-Shāmis against him as would be the case if he surrendered 'Abd al-Raḥmān to the British. He asked for 'Abd al-Raḥmān to be tried in a Shārjah court. After three fruitless days the SNO decided to leave, angered by the Shaikh of Rās al-Khaimah's attitude.

On 15 June Parry sent a telegram to the Political Resident asking for authorisation to bombard Rās al-Khaimah, but the Resident objected to bombardment, fearing that no amount of shelling would effect the surrender of 'Abd al-Raḥmān, pointing out also that the safety of Indians had to be considered.[70] On the next day Sa'īd b. Maktūm managed to see the notables of Rās al-Khaimah and 'Abd al-Raḥmān b. Muḥammad himself. The latter had no knowledge of the reason behind the SNO's arrival, but when informed by Sa'īd, he surrendered himself at once, leaving Rās al-Khaimah the next day. In Shārjah the SNO asked the Shaikh to pay Rs. 3,000 blood money for the death of 'Īsā's cousin, in addition to Rs. 150 monthly to the British for the care of 'Abd al-Raḥmān in Aden.[71]

In a series of letters, beginning in 1928 when economic depression was felt on the Coast, Sulṭān b. Ṣaqr appealed to the British to allow 'Abd al-Raḥmān to return to the Coast, explaining that his exile was a financial burden on himself and the pearl merchants at Shārjah, particularly after the Emirate's loss of Dhaid and the money he was obliged to pay to Khālid b. Aḥmād as a result of the two previous settlements.[72]

After Shaikh Sulṭān had given assurances of 'Abd al-Raḥmān's good conduct, the Political Resident reduced his exile by one year, allowing him to return to Shārjah in June 1929. However, the hatred for 'Īsā in Shārjah did not abate. 'Īzā reported that the Shaikhs of Rās al-Khaimah and Shārjah, who were cousins, had tried to intrigue with Ibn Sa'ūd and were united in anti-British activities. On 31 January 1931 Shaikh Sulṭān b. Ṣaqr and his father-in-law put guards around the Residency House, but on the advice of the notables of the town they were called off. Sulṭān's justification for his action was that he suspected 'Īsā, who was in contact with Khālid b. Aḥmad against him, of harbouring the ex-ruler in the Residency House in preparation for a *coup*. 'Īsā, in his report to the Political Resident, gave another explanation: the cause of Sulṭān's aggression was that three slaves had been inside the Residency seeking manumission.

'Īsā felt that his life was in danger and urged that some form of retaliatory action was necessary if British prestige were to be maintained and her policy of encouraging the manumission of slaves enforced on the Trucial Coast.

He explained that the Shaikh's conduct had deliberately challenged Britain's position. As a result of the incident 'Īsā left the next day for Dubai, where he met the SNO on the latter's arrival on 25 February. Influenced by discussion with 'Īsā, the latter suggested a heavy fine and the confiscation of weapons; 'Abd al-Raḥmān should be exiled a second time and his village, Ḥīrah, completely destroyed; Shaikh Sulṭān b. Ṣaqr should be deposed and Khālid b. Aḥmad reappointed as ruler. The Political Resident did not agree with this severe recommendation but ordered only that 'Abd al-Raḥmān be surrendered for exile.

At that time Britain was considering negotiations for air facilities and did not wish to endanger her relationship with the Trucial shaikhs. So when Sulṭān refused to hand over 'Abd al-Raḥmān, according to Arab tradition which he could not violate whatever the consequences, the Political Resident merely changed this condition to a fine of Rs. 2,000 and one hundred guns to be handed over within four days. The Political Resident felt this punishment was equal to the exile of 'Abd al-Raḥmān, as it would inflame popular feeling against the Shaikh, who would have to collect this amount from his wealthy merchants. It was extremely difficult for the Shaikh to find this amount because of the financial crisis, but when the notables of Shārjah asked for the fine to be reduced, the SNO threatened bombardment. Sulṭān managed to levy the full amount only in the last hour of his four-day limit.[73]

The long friendship between the ruler of Shārjah and his father-in-law, 'Abd al-Raḥmān, ended in the later 1930s when 'Abd al-Raḥmān claimed independence, like many dependent shaikhs at that time, hoping thereby to gain valuable oil concessions. 'Abd al-Raḥmān tried to use as justification the document of independence which he had been given more than a decade earlier by the Shaikh of Shārjah. The Political Agent in Baḥrain reported in September 1937 that 'Abd al-Raḥmān had approached him, but had been discouraged in accordance with instructions from Fowle.[74] On 27 March 1938 the Residency Agent reported that after the Shaikh of Shārjah's failure to defend the Emirate against the raids of the 'Awāmir tribe there had been increasingly frequent demands for Khālid b. Aḥmad, the ex-ruler, to be reinstated.[75] In January 1939 'Abd al-Raḥmān built a large tower to defend his village, an action which worsened the relationship.[76] Soon the events associated with the reform movement in Dubai were to widen the growing split between the two old friends. When Shaikh Māni' b. Rāshid was obliged to leave Dubai for Shārjah in April 1939 after the collapse of the reform movement, the British immediately advised Sulṭān b. Ṣaqr to refuse him asylum in Ḥirah, ignoring the advice of the Residency Agent 'Abd al-Razzāq, who sought by intimidation to prevent all the rulers from giving Māni' and his followers protection. Consequently the Shaikh of Shārjah, co-operating with the Shaikh of Dubai, prevented the citizens of Ḥīrah from visiting his town. Because of this, 'Abd al-Raḥmān threatened to take forceful measures against the notables of Shārjah.[77]

The enmity between Sulṭān b. Ṣaqr and ‘Abd al-Raḥmān which these petty incidents induced continued to dominate their relationship. Further rupture was ensured when ‘Abd al-Raḥmān accepted Shaikh Khālid b. Aḥmad, the ex-ruler of Shārjah, as resident in his town. On 10 August 1942 ‘Abd al-Raḥmān died and was succeeded by his son Saif as the head of Ḥīrah.[78]

Shaikh Sulṭān b. Sālim, the Ruler of Rās al-Khaimah (1919–48)

In June 1908 the fifteen-year-old Sulṭān b. Sālim had shown signs of an adventurous spirit when, after his father had been involved in disputes over the government of Rās al-Khaimah, he had occupied the fort of Shārjah. His father, who did not approve of that rash act, forced him to leave the fort,[79] and he spent the following years in Ḥamriyyah. In July 1919 Shaikh Muḥammad, the elder son of Shaikh Sālim, abdicated the government of Rās al-Khaimah in favour of his younger brother Sulṭān.[80] Sulṭān gained an outstanding reputation, not only because of his long reign but also because he became a symbol for the growing opposition to British policy amongst the younger generation in the Trucial States.

The career of Shaikh Sulṭān b. Sālim illustrates the changing political attitudes towards the British on the Trucial Coast between the two World Wars. He was a subscriber to one of the largest Islamic and nationalistic magazines *al-Fatḥ*, published in Cairo, which provided him with news of recent cultural and political developments in the Arab world. Like the other Wahhābī inhabitants of Rās al-Khaimah, Sulṭān had great sympathy and admiration for King ‘Abd al-‘Azīz of Sa‘ūdī Arabia. The growth of the Sa‘ūdī kingdom gave great moral strength to the Qawāsim and had some effect on their dealings with the British. Sulṭān's awareness of this and other changes in the Middle East made him the most sensitive of the Trucial shaikhs to British involvement in the internal affairs of the Coast. He became very suspicious of any proposals from the British, and his temperament made Britain's relations with him exceptionally difficult, so that between 1926 and 1935 they were greatly strained, beginning in 1926 when he refused to surrender ‘Abd al-Raḥmān b. Muḥammad of Ḥīrah to the SNO who had come to Rās al-Khaimah to escort him into exile. Shaikh Sulṭān had been disappointed by the agreement of Sulṭān b. Ṣaqr, ruler of Shārjah, to the exile of ‘Abd al-Raḥmān, a surrender to British pressure of which Sulṭān b. Sālim showed his disapproval by inciting the head of Āl Bū-Shāmis tribe against him.[81] Sulṭān's stand built up a good reputation for him beyond Rās al-Khaimah, particularly among the educated men on the coast of ‘Omān.

However, although appreciated for his external policies his autocracy at home stirred up much discontent within the Emirate, a feeling which grew with time, resulting in his enforced abdication in 1948. Sulṭān was thought to be the owner of some of the largest date groves on the coast, and he had a modern launch for his personal use; he also ran a prosperous business in Dubai. Nevertheless, he was not a generous man and stopped the traditional payments to the elders of the Qasimī family of the Emirate. He treated one of his relations, Khālid b. Khālid b. Ṣaqr, the young nephew of the ruler of Shārjah, so badly that he was obliged to take refuge in the Residency Agent's House in Rās al-Khaimah in 1927 and then to return to Shārjah. His main supporter, 'Alī b. Saif, was not popular among the other citizens of Rās al-Khaimah, aggravating the grievances felt at Sulṭān's rule.[82]

On 10 September 1928, during the Dubai dhow incident with the Persian Customs authorities near Ṭanb (see Chapter 4, p. 257), the SNO visited Rās al-Khaimah, where a meeting with Shaikh Sulṭān b. Sālim took place on board his ship. Their talks revealed the Arab evaluation of the political situation in the Gulf, and the changes they witnessed, but were unable to understand fully, British policy towards Persia at that time. Britain's lenient attitude towards Persia's nationalistic ambitions, for international considerations, were interpreted by the Arabs as a sign of decline in British hegemony. The SNO noticed that the Shaikh was flying a Turkish flag from his launch instead of the usual Trucial one. In the words of the SNO the Shaikh was 'definitely surly and he was inconveniently frank'. When asked if he could produce documents in proof of his ownership of Ṭanb island the Shaikh's reply was to the following effect:

> What is all this business about having to find documents to prove that Ṭanb belongs to me? When you wanted to put a lighthouse on Ṭanb you had no doubt in your mind about who owned it because you asked the Shaikh of the Qawāsim tribe for permission; you would not have asked him if anybody else owned it. What is happening to England these days? You seem to be frightened of Persia. If you are not frightened of Persia, why don't you tell them honestly to mind their own business or else you punish them the same as you would punish me. If you are frightened of Persia, it means that you are no longer any good as a nation and the Trucial treaties are no longer worth anything. Why do you argue with the Persians? From what I hear, Persia thinks she has become a big nation and is as good as England. If that is so, then England must be really a small nation. Why do you not go to war with these Persians and finish with them? Is England just a bully that can hit a small people like a Coast tribe, but is afraid of Persia?

When the SNO explained that Britain had fought and won the last war but policy was now only patience in order to prevent bloodshed, the Shaikh's reaction was that this policy, although aiming at peace, was really inspired by fear. This attitude was particularly clear when the Shaikh openly put the question: 'How much more of the Gulf will you give up to the Persians?'[83]

The year 1929 marked the next stage of the rapidly worsening relations of

Sulṭān b. Sālim with the British. At the beginning of this year occurred the events which developed when the RAF proposed to establish a petrol depot in a barge at Rās al-Khaimah, events which are described earlier in this book. A second event occurred at the end of September 1929 which also contributed to this worsening of relations: the Political Resident reported that to his astonishment the Shaikh of Rās al-Khaimah was complaining that he was not paid for the ships which passed the lighthouse on Ṭanb.[84] The Political Resident commented that the idea of gaining money from the lighthouse was a new one and surely not the Shaikh's own. In fact, his demand was a manifestation of the desire for recognition of the Qawāsim's rights, ignored by the British in the past. Also in November, the British authorities were annoyed by an attack on the Residency Agent's House in Rās al-Khaimah, where a woman had taken refuge, while the Shaikh made no objection to her family taking her home by force. 'Īsā complained to the Political Resident at such unprecedented audacity and the violation of his official status. On 26 November HMS *Crox* came to Rās al-Khaimah and Shaikh Sulṭān was obliged to fine the attackers twenty lashes to satisfy the SNO.[85]

Two further issues now added to the misunderstanding between Britain and Rās al-Khaimah: negotiations in December 1931 for a civil aerodrome for Imperial Airways, and Persia's claims to Ṭanb and Abū Mūsā islands. Shaikh Sulṭān b. Sālim initially refused to grant civil air facilities in his Emirate. His reluctance was chiefly based on the fear that the obtaining of air facilities would be the first step towards the establishment of British administration over the Shaikhdom. When the Shaikh of Shārjah agreed to Britain's proposals for an airport, Sulṭān b. Sālim accused him of selling his country to the British. The Shaikh of Shārjah, however, shared Sulṭān b. Sālim's fear, and was careful to insert a clause in the airport agreement which stated that the granting of the aerodrome in his territory in no way entitled the British to interfere in his internal affairs. Shārjah's air agreement was bitterly opposed by many of the elders,[86] who left for Rās al-Khaimah, where they found welcome and encouragement. Sulṭān b. Sālim was so worried that Britain would take action against him that he now refused to board any British ship. The SNO reported on 10 June 1932 that when he had visited Rās al-Khaimah, he had been told by a deputation of three notables headed by the ruler's cousin that the Shaikh was busy in the hinterland. He understood from them afterwards that the Shaikh had not come on board because he was angry with the British for their hostility towards him and his subjects. In answer, the SNO had reminded the ruler's cousin that the day might come when Rās al-Khaimah would badly need the good offices of the British Government in supporting her against her neighbours.[87]

Sulṭān b. Sālim continued in his refusal to board any British ship, and did not attend the general meeting of the Trucial rulers held on board a British ship in Dubai on 23 September 1933. There the Political Resident

16. A meeting of the Abu Dhābī Executive Council presided over by Shaikh Khalīfah b. Zāyed.

14. Shaikh Sulṭān, Ruler of Sharjah, replacing the traditional red and white flag of Sharjah with the Federal flag – a further step, towards actual

15. Shaikh Zāyed the Supreme Commander, taking the salute at the celebration to commemorate the unification of the Armed Forces. To his right Shaikh Khalīfah b. Zāyed, Deputy Supreme Commander, to his left Shaikh Muḥammad b. Rāshid, Minister of Defence, to the extreme left, Shaikh Sulṭān b. Zāyed the Commander General of the Armed Forces.

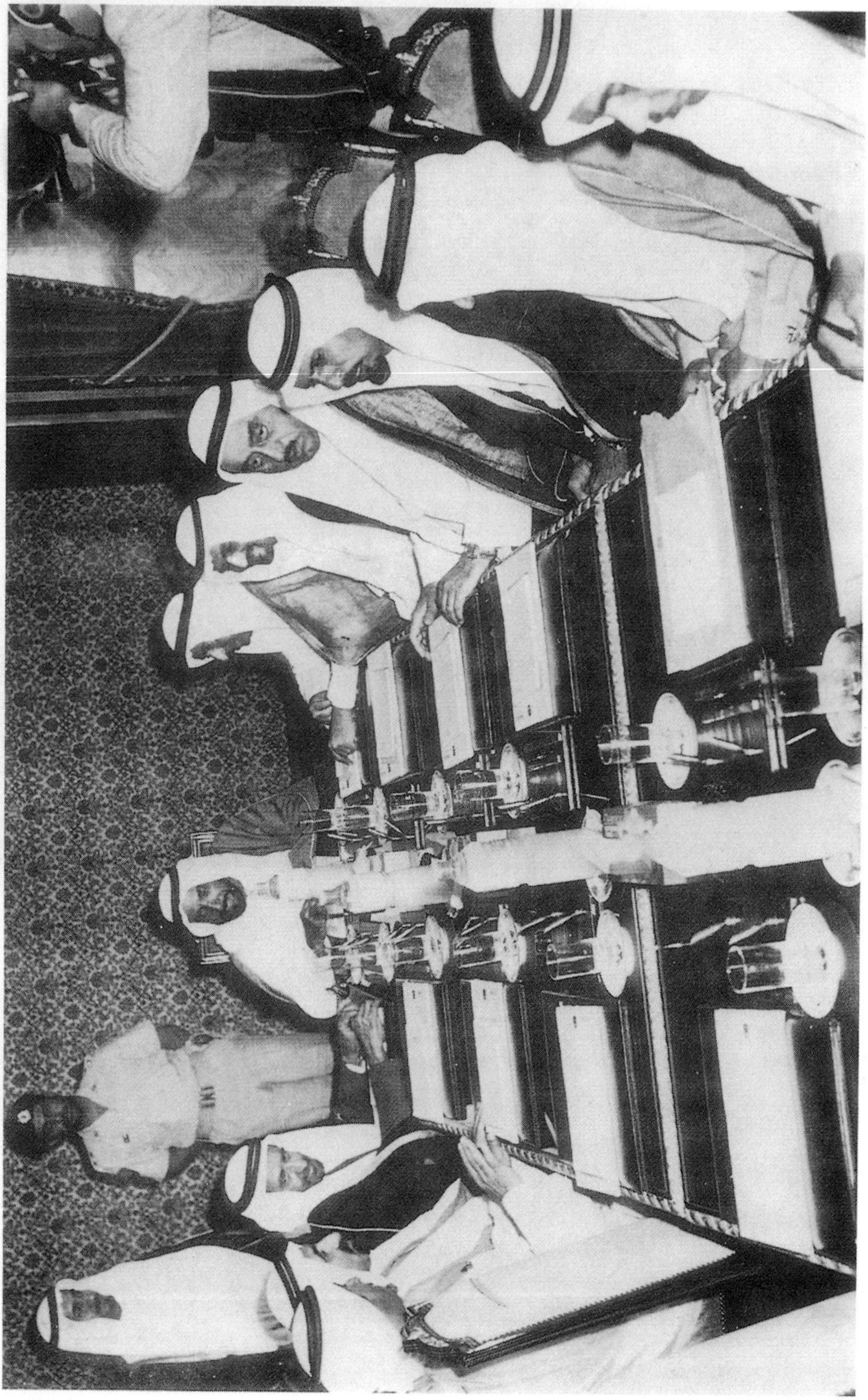

gave a speech reminding the shaikhs that Britain had protected them against the encroachments of their neighbours and asking them to keep their undertakings to the British not to communicate with any foreign power, particularly the Sa'ūdīs, except through the mediation of the British. This speech was followed by a display of the new air force in the Gulf, organised by Captain Welch, the Commander in Iraq.[88]

The Anglo–Persian negotiations over the Islands of Ṭanb and Abū Mūsā created unfounded Arab suspicions about Britain's attitude, which began to show more openly her uncompromising policy towards Persia. In October 1933, the British learned that Shaikh Sulṭān b. Sālim had received a letter from Tehran regarding Ṭanb island. On 21 October the SNO went to Rās al-Khaimah to investigate the matter but Shaikh Sulṭān b. Sālim refused to board the *Triad* and efforts to assure the Shaikh of his safety and persuade him to change his mind proved useless. The Shaikh showed willingness to board a British ship only if a court of high officials, not the Political Resident, agreed to listen to his case for the lease of the lighthouse on Ṭanb, his complaints about British confiscation of his ships (see p. 52) and their use without reasonable payment of his land and inlets for emergency landing by the pilots of the Imperial Airways. In his report of 23 October 1933, giving an account of the Shaikh's behaviour, the SNO wrote that his refusal to board a British warship was an attempt to get British representatives to visit him first and thus acquire even more local prestige. Through the Residency Agent the SNO had reminded the Shaikh that not long ago he had prevented the headman of Rams from severing his allegiance to Rās al-Khaimah and that, but for the British, his people would be slaves of the Persians as were the Arabs at Lingah, whom he could see almost daily arriving on the Arab Coast to escape from Persian interference. The SNO concluded his report by saying that the time had come when the Shaikh should be brought to heel as regards his duties in calling upon Political Officers and HM ships, and he warned that if action were not taken immediately the situation was likely to lead to trouble on the Trucial Coast, where the Shaikh's studied contempt for British authority had been noted. It was a matter of interest to his brother shaikhs, who were waiting to see what action would be taken by the British Government.[89]

The most serious crisis between Britain and Rās al-Khaimah occurred over the ownership of Ṭanb Island. On 17 September 1934 the British, disappointed with the failure of their long negotiations with Persia, instructed the Navy in the Gulf that any Persian naval vessel found at Abū Mūsā or Ṭanb without proper notification should be made to leave, by force if necessary. Britain's lowered prestige on the Arab Coast, due to British tolerance of the Persian Navy during the past few years, particularly in Rās al-Khaimah, was instantly improved. At the beginning of 1935, the British suspected that the Shaikh of Rās al-Khaimah was in direct correspondence with Persia, but this was soon found to be false. On 29 March Shaikh Sulṭān

b. Sālim explained to the British why Maḥmūd, his representative on Ṭanb, had left the island, and the reason for the lowering of his flag. In the past, when Rās al-Khaimah had enjoyed a considerable income from pearl-fishing he had not asked the British for rent for the lighthouse to pay his employees on Ṭanb, but now, after the decline of the pearl trade, his financial position had changed completely. Although he had informed 'Īsā about this the previous December, no help had been forthcoming. In April 1935 Sulṭān b. Salim nevertheless complied with the ultimatum he had received from the Political Resident and agreed to rehoist his flag on Ṭanb.[90]

Between 1935 and 1937 British records show that Sulṭān b. Salim began to co-operate with the British over the RAF barge and Imperial Airways and this effected an improvement in their relations; when Sulṭān and Sa'īd b. Maktūm discovered that the airport in Shārjah had improved the economy of the Emirate, they showed signs of regret at their previous refusal. The British, who were now hoping to conclude oil concessions with the Trucial Shaikhs, among them Rās al-Khaimah, also tried to show a spirit of tolerance and co-operation towards him.[91]

However, the incident at Kalbā stirred the Shaikh's anger against the British and vice versa. On 8 December 1936 Britain accepted for strategic reasons the *de facto* independence of Kalbā, since the Shaikh of Shārjah had proved himself powerless to govern it.[92]

On 4 May 1937, after the death of Sa'īd b. Ḥamad and the interference of the Qawāsim shaikhs in the affairs of Kalbā, concerned about the safety of the petrol store at Kalbā and British facilities acquired at independence, the Political Resident gave instructions to the Qasimī rulers not to involve themselves in the question of the Shaikh's successor, who should be chosen by the people of the town. Sulṭān b. Sālim received appeals from his nephew, Ḥamad b. Sa'īd, from Sālim b. 'Abdullah, head of the Naqbiyyīn tribe, and from Barūt, the guardian, to defend them against the interference of the Qawāsim of Dabā and Shārjah, but asking him not to come to Kalbā for the time being. They were particularly worried about Khālid b. Aḥmad, who, secretly supported by Umm al-Qaiwain, had sent his brother 'Abdullah to make arrangements for his taking over the control of Kalbā. Contrary to the instructions of the Political Resident and the wishes of Barūt and his party in Kalbā, Sulṭān b. Sālim considered Kalbā's affairs as a family matter in which he, as an eminent member of the Qawāsim, had greater rights than Barūt the slave. So he sent letters to Barūt asking him to prepare a list of all Shaikh Sa'īd b. Ḥamad's belongings. He wrote also to Sālim b. 'Abdullah, appointing him Governor of Kalbā and Khūr Fakkān. Moreover, at the beginning of June, ignoring the Political Resident's advice, he made his way to Kalbā through al-Qūr pass, a long route to take, but one that lay within his own territory.

As soon as his departure from Rās al-Khaimah was known, the conflicting jealousies and ambitions in the surrounding emirates rose to the surface. On

9 June 1937 the Bedouins of Banī Qatab, who dominated the entrance to the al-Qūr pass, invited by Umm al-Qaiwain, occupied strategic positions there and other groups of the tribe raided the town of Rās al-Khaimah. The Sharqiyyīn tribe blocked al-Hām pass, cutting the shortest route between Rās al-Khaimah and Kalbā. Meanwhile in Kalbā, Barūt and Muḥammad b. Maṭar, head of the Za'āb tribe, had left for Muscat to ask the Political Agent for help against Sulṭān b. Sālim, who, when he arrived, found himself surrounded by enemies who made it difficult for him to return to his town by land.

On 17 June the Political Resident, angry at the conduct of Sulṭān b. Sālim, instructed the SNO to go immediately to Kalbā and seize him. On 21 June the SNO arrived at Kalbā and, owing to Sulṭān's difficult position succeeded in taking him on board. The Political Resident, when informed that Sulṭān had agreed to go on board, instructed the SNO to make directly for Baḥrain, where Sulṭān would be detained in a comfortable house but not allowed to receive any visitors, not even the Shaikh of Baḥrain.

Although the Political Resident considered Sulṭān's action very serious, the ruler had been of great help to Britain in the previous two years, and so, in the hope of concluding an oil concession with him, the Political Resident thought Sulṭān should return to Rās al-Khaimah. Sulṭān had to give an explanation of his conduct to the Political Agent in Baḥrain and received from him a severe warning not to interfere in Kalbā again. On 25 June an interview took place between the Political Agent and Sulṭān and two days later he was taken back to Rās al-Khaimah, but his reaction to British conduct in the affair was one of extreme displeasure. On 10 July he sent a strong protest to the Political Resident, expressing his disappointment at his treatment after all his co-operation; he considered his compulsory visit to Baḥrain an imprisonment without cause; he insisted that the affairs of Kalbā were an internal matter in which the British, according to their treaties, had no right to interfere. As Kalbā was a Qasimī Emirate, ruled by his cousin, it was not fair that he should be instructed by the Political Resident not to interfere, and it was only right that he should be concerned with its government. The care of the young Shaikh could be entrusted to him rather than to the slave accepted by the British. Sulṭān therefore stated that he was going to complain to the British Government about the injustice of his detainment and the Political Resident's policy.[93]

This final breach of trust between Shaikh Sulṭān b. Sālim and the British continued owing to his obstinate refusal to conclude an oil concession with a British company and his preference for dealing with an American firm. Although Dubai had signed her agreement in May 1937 and Shārjah in September of the same year, Sulṭān agreed only to an option and delayed signing until December 1938 (see Chapter 1, p. 69).

Sulṭān b. Sālim gained something of a reputation amongst the young generation, but his internal policy in the Emirate created some resentment.

This was the main cause which led the Qawāsim family in Rās al-Khaimah to replace him in 1948 by his nephew Shaikh Ṣaqr b. Muḥammad.

The Opposition Group and the Majilis of 1938 in Dubai

Although the uprisings in Dubai of 1929 and 1934 against Shaikh Sa'īd b. Maktūm were personally motivated by his cousins in order to seize power, the short-lived movement of October 1938 to March 1939 adopted some reformist ideas unprecedented on the Trucial Coast, giving it a particular importance. The new Majlis, viewed in terms of its brief existence, would be a matter of little significance, but when placed within the context of the social and political conditions of the Trucial Coast in 1938 it assumes dimensions which go far beyond the effectiveness of the council itself.[94] Shaikh Sa'īd, who was well known as a strong personality and a wise diplomat, managed to retain power during these critical events, and his son Rāshid bravely championed his father's rights as the legitimate ruler and defeated the opposition groups. However, Rāshid, when he became ruler two decades later, realised the reformist ideas of the opposition group in his own way and proved himself the builder of modern Dubai.

The summer of 1928 witnessed two incidents, in Shaikh 'Ubaid b. Jum'ah's dispute with the Persian authorities at Hanjām and the Persian seizure of the Dubai dhow near Ṭanb, which greatly aroused the anger of his people and prevented imprudent reprisals. There were in Dubai at that time two attitudes towards this problem: one agreed with the Shaikh and the other, led by his cousins (Mani' b. Rāshid and his brothers, and Sa'īd b. Buṭī and his brother), demanded that Dubai be released from her treaties with Britain.[95] As a result, at the beginning of 1929 Sa'īd found it very difficult to get support amongst the notables of Dubai. Although the Ruler's traditional consultation with the heads of families in Dubai existed only in an advisory form, it had a good deal of influence on Sa'īd's decisions. In April, Sa'īd b. Maktūm offered to resign and this was not at first refused by the elders of Dubai, but Ḥissah bint al-Murr, Sa'īd's wife, a remarkable lady and an outstanding figure in both politics and business, was very much opposed to the Shaikh's resignation.

On 15 April 1929 a meeting of sixty persons was held under the leadership of Muḥammad b. Aḥmad b. Dalmūk, the prominent pearl merchant, who resented British policy and was also a strong ally of Māni' b. Rāshid, his son-in-law. At this meeting Māni' was proclaimed Ruler of Dubai,[96] and in accordance with custom at the accession of a new ruler on the Coast at this time, Māni' informed 'Īsā b. 'Abd al-Laṭīf, the Residency Agent in Shārjah, of his election.[97] 'Īsā, an intimate friend of Shaikh Sa'īd, anticipated trouble with Māni' and Muḥammad b. Dalmūk. Moreover, he was influenced by Sa'īd's wife's refusal to accept the resignation and decided to oppose Māni'. HMS *Lupin* was anchored at Shārjah at that time and 'Īsā forthwith informed her captain, J. M. Allyne, of the recent events in Dubai. 'Īsā and the captain proceeded immediately to Dubai that same day and there met Shaikhs Mānī‘ and Sa‘īd. In a telegram that evening, Captain Allyne informed Haworth, the Political Resident, that Sa‘īd had been forced to resign and was therefore still the legitimate ruler. Sa‘īd informed Allyne that in order to prevent bloodshed he had not resisted and he added that about half of the notables had come to him after choosing Mānī‘ to say that they had been forced to agree though, in fact, they supported Sa‘īd.

After many meetings during the night, the Captain signalled the details to Boyed, the SNO, and to Haworth next day, saying that from fairly reliable information it appeared that the reason for the attempt to eject Sa‘īd was his alleged enforcement of the payment of his subject's debts to the Indians, and general submission to all the wishes of HM Government. He added that Sa‘īd was friendly with the Bedouins, to whom he paid considerable subsidies, and it seemed probable therefore that fighting would break out in the town. For the safety of British subjects and interests in Dubai, he asked for permission to interfere and stop the fighting and the best way to do this, he thought, was to induce the weaker side, whom he considered to be Mānī‘ and his party, to withdraw their claims by affording the maximum British support to the stronger, in his opinion Sa‘īd. At the same time, the Captain informed both Mānī‘ and Sa‘īd that the matter had been referred to the Political Resident and the British authorities.

Boyed, the SNO, agreed with the point of view of Captain Allyne entirely. He strongly urged full British support for Shaikh Sa‘īd, explaining that from his personal experience during 1928 Sa‘īd's wisdom was a predominant factor in keeping the Trucial chiefs and the Coast quiet. On 17 April 1928, without consulting India, Haworth cabled his answer, informing the Captain that if the Shaikh really had the majority, as his cable reported, the Shaikh should be able to reassert his position. The Political Resident, unwilling to intimidate the notables, concluded that if this were not the case it was against British policy to attempt to bolster up Sa‘īd.

On the morning of the 18th, after a meeting of 400 persons, had been held in Dubai, ‘Īsā reported that they had decided Sa‘īd should remain the Ruler of Dubai. In the afternoon, Shaikh Sa‘īd, accompanied by his two brothers, Ḥashr and Jum‘ah, together with Ḥashr b. Rāshid, brother of Shaikh Mānī‘, visited the Captain on board *Lupin*. He was saluted by three guns on leaving the ship in recognition of his legitimate position. On the afternoon of the 19th the Captain returned Sa‘īd's call at his fort, and Mānī‘ was asked by ‘Īsā to be present, though Mānī‘ sent word that he was not well. In the evening, Captain Allyne sailed away in *Lupin*.[98]

In spite of several attempts at reconciliation, the cousins and some of the powerful elders of the town did not forget that Sa‘īd's-continued rule had been imposed on them in 1929. As mistrust between the two sides increased, Sa‘īd, encouraged by his son Rāshid, began to rally the support of the Bedouins of Āl Bilsh‘ar, a branch of the Manāṣīr tribe who had been living in the hinterland of Dubai and were loyal to Shaikh Sa'īd, an action which alarmed his opponents. In these charged circumstances, on 23 September 1934, the cousins tried unsuccessfully to assassinate the Shaikh. With the moral and physical support of Fowle, Sa'īd was able to regain his power and obliged his opponents to show their obedience in November of that year (see Chapter 1, p. 46).

Three main factors caused the Dubai movement of 1938: first, the growth of the ruler's power; secondly, the insistent demand of the notables in Dubai for control of the oil revenues; and thirdly, the impact of the political and nationalist press between the two World Wars. Between 1934 and 1938 British interests in Dubai increased greatly, in particular after the conclusion of the oil concession in 1937. Security and stability became essential for the safeguarding of the air route and the oil exploration teams. Thus the need for a strong ruler was paramount in British policy. The economic depression and increased political awareness among the inhabitants of the Coast both contributed to the opinion, voiced strongly in Dubai, that the oil revenue should not be regarded as the ruler's personal income but that its benefits should be shared by the whole community.

Realising the role Britain had played in past events, Māni' tried to better his relations with the British authorities. Sa'īd also saw the importance of friendship with the British and consolidated his good relationship with them. On a visit to Baḥrain on 6 November 1935, Māni' called on the Political Agent and praised the modern developments on the island which had been carried out with the help of the British, 'the friend of the Arabs'.[99] The improvement in relations between Māni''s faction and the British was aided by the death of 'Īsā b. 'Abd al-Laṭīf in 1935 and the subsequent appointment as Residency Agent at the beginning of 1936 of 'Abd al-Razzāq, who had no personal commitments on the Coast, though the family of Shaikh Sa'īd preferred that 'Īsā's nephew, Ḥusain 'Amād, be appointed, so that they might retain their hold on the post. 'Abd al-Razzāq arrived on 16 May and it was reported that a secret meeting had then been held at Dubai to discuss a refusal to recognise 'Abd al-Razzāq's appointment. Māni' b. Rāshid intervened and cautioned them to refrain from such activities.[100] 'Abd al-Razzāq did not wield the great influence on British opinion that 'Īsā had done, since a further British representative, Captain J. B. Howes, was appointed in 1937 to the post of Political Officer in Shārjah, at least during the cold weather. The British authorities therefore became more accurately informed of the internal situation on the Trucial Coast.

The appointment of 'Abd al-Razzāq instead of Ḥusain 'Āmād was quickly felt by Shaikh Sa'īd, and realising that it would take time to establish an intimacy similar to that which he had enjoyed with 'Īsā, he turned to internal diplomacy. On 19 January 1938, as Governor of Dīrah, he appointed Shaikh Sa'īd b. Buṭī, who began to carry out a programme of municipal reform in his area. Māni' and his brothers resented the appointment since it meant that a former ally was working with the ruler. Sa'īd's plan had the desired effect, causing mistrust between the two families of the opposition.[101]

However, the good relations established between Māni''s party and the British during the previous few years deteriorated because of Māni''s opposition to the terms of the oil concession, and two minor events which took place at the beginning of 1938 exemplified the rupture. The first of these again drew Māni''s party into conflict with Britain. At the beginning of 1938, the year in which Fowle took various measures to punish those who opposed the conclusion of the oil agreement, 'Abd al-Razzāq, under British instructions, encouraged manumission and the number of slaves gaining freedom from the Agency was so great that the slave owners in Dubai threatened to attack the British Agency in Shārjah. On 27 February Fowle approached Shaikh Sa'īd with the demand that he should deport two men—Khalaf 'Alī al-Zamānī, a Kuwaitī merchant, and Rayyis Muḥammad Rasūl, a Persian from Lingah—who were involved in the arms traffic. The Shaikh's promise to carry out this demand provoked demonstrations against him on 14 March 1938.[102] At a meeting in Dubai the notables passed two resolutions: manumitted slaves should be returned to their owners; Khalaf and Rayyis should not be deported. The notables also decided that Sa'īd should not renew the civil air facilities granted to the British without their agreement.[103] On 24 March Weightman, the Political Agent in Baḥrain, flew to Dubai and attended a meeting with the notables the next day, at which he explained British policy very firmly; however, in response to strong pressure, the Ruler asked Weightman to pardon Kahlaf and Rayyis, but this was refused and the Shaikh was again obliged to agree to deportation. B. Dalmūk, supported by Shaikh Jum'ah, brother of the ruler, raised the question of manumission, but this remained unsettled. Consequently, on 27 March, before Weightman's departure, the notables convened again and decided that the air agreement was not to be renewed.[104]

The second incident, which accelerated growing opposition to the ruler concerned Shaikh Rāshid, eldest son of Shaikh Sa'īd. Rāshid had attempted to extend the area of his business in transport services to include Dīrah, where he was challenged by his relative Maktūm b. Rāshid, brother of Māni', who ran a similar service to Shārjah. On 26 May, Rāshid attacked one of Maktūm's cars on its way to Shārjah, and Maktūm, infuriated, threatened to stop all cars belonging to Rāshid. The dispute soon began to assume serious proportions.[105]

Furthermore, opposition to the Shaikh was encouraged by the recent success of the movement in Kuwait, which had grown out of similar circumstances and with whose aspirations the people of Dubai sympathised, as well as by the current political demonstrations in Baḥrain.[106] Shaikh Sa'īd himself was inclined to reach an agreement with the opposition, but influenced by his wife and his son Rāshid, he ignored their complaints. At the end of June 1938 members of the Āl Bū-Flāsah presented a letter to Shaikh Sa'īd containing a number of demands: the abolition of the ruling family's monopolies over the landing of cargo and the taxi service and their replacement by fixed salaries; a budget for the welfare of the town; and the reorganisation of the Customs Department. Meanwhile the Āl Bū-Flāsah occupied certain towers in Dubai and Shaikh Sa'īd in consequence assembled his Bedouins in the town. The Political Agent asked 'Abd al-Razzāq to advise the ruler to concede some of the popular demands. On 15 August Shaikh Sa'īd was summoned to Baḥrain, where the Political Agent impressed upon him that it was in his own interests to keep his subjects satisfied by introducing necessary reforms in his shaikhdom.[107]

On 1 October, Fowle, the Political Resident, in order to strengthen Sa'īd's position, urged him to follow Weightman's advice to comply with the popular demand for reform and advised him to abolish the ruling family's monopolies. He advised Sa'īd that modern rulers must respond to the just demands of their people, otherwise they would lose their thrones. In conclusion he warned Shaikh Sa'īd that he would be held responsible for any injury suffered by British subjects.[108] Māni', too, received a letter from the Political Agent in Baḥrain on 7 October, which showed British anxiety over the unrest in Dubai and stated that Māni' would be held responsible for the safety of their subjects.

As the situation in Dubai was deteriorating, a sloop was sent to protect the property of British subjects. It arrived on 8 October, the same day that the majority of Āl Bū-Flāsah, led by Shaikh Māni', occupied the Customs House at Dīrah, taking complete control of that part of the town. The next day, Shaikh Shakhbūt of Abū Dhabī and 'Abdullah b. Muḥammad b. Hiwaidin, head of the Banī Qatab, arrived at Dubai to mediate between the two parties, but they failed to effect a settlement, as had Shaikh Sulṭān b. Sālim of Rās al-Khaimah, who had made a similar fruitless attempt at the beginning of the conflict.

When Weightman visited Dubai once more on 15 October he no longer totally supported Shaikh Sa'īd against the opposition, but negotiated a settlement between the factions, which was finally signed on 20 October. A Majlis, presided over by Sa'īd and composed of fifteen members, was to be selected by the notables and all decisions were to be ratified by a majority. This council would control the income and expenditure of Dubai, which had to contribute towards the general welfare of the state. However, Weightman made it clear to the Majlis that relations between Britain and Dubai would be conducted through the Shaikh alone and not through the Majlis.[109]

This move was hailed in the Iraqi newspapers, particularly in the *Sijil*, together with the news of the latest developments in Baḥrain and Kuwait. Between October 1938 and the middle of February 1939, the Majlis enthusiastically set about establishing an administration and eventually effected many social, political and economic reforms. In all publications the

Majlis was called 'the highest Council of Dubai'. By examining the correspondence between the Majlis and the ruler, the minutes of their meetings and the texts of the resolutions passed, the nature of the reforms and the attitude of the Majlis may be judged. The primary considerations revolved around the commercial life of Dubai, which was concentrated in the port. Staff to regulate the customs services in Dubai and Dīrah were elected, a tax of 2 per cent on imported goods was levied and an Arab director (a close relative of Māni') was appointed to replace the existing Persian director. A list of those allowed to be porters at the port was drawn up and their salaries fixed. Part of the revenue from the port was laid aside to finance municipal and educational projects. A council was set up to deal with each of these topics. Rāshid b. Māni' was placed in charge of education and 'Īsā b. Thānī became director of the municipality.

As the income from customs duties was not sufficient to cover the costs of the ambitious projects to enlarge the port of Dubai and to beautify the town, the Majlis decided that a financial subsidy should be provided out of the revenues from the oil concession and air agreement. The Majlis also paid attention to the security of the state and appointed men to patrol the desert and others to guard the town, particularly the market places. As part of its social reforms, the Majlis decided to give financial aid to the disabled and the elderly of Dubai. New terms like 'national duty', 'country' instead of 'city of Dubai', 'revolution for reform', which begin to appear in the documents of the Majlis, reflected a change in political attitudes under the impact of Dubai's new awareness of developing aspirations in the surrounding countries. An important insight into the nature of a ruler is given in the form of address which Māni' and his group adopted for the Shaikh in their letter asking for an elected Majlis in June 1938: 'To our cousin, who governs us by our will, our brother in blood and relation, the Shaikh whom we obey only when he is in the right, Sā'īd b. Maktūm.'[110]

Shaikh Sa'īd did not attend this Majlis after the first two meetings on 21 and 22 October, though Shaikh Māni' continued to request his presence and notify him of the agenda. A serious clash with the ruler occurred in March 1939, leading to an armed struggle at the end of that month and the final overthrow of the government. Sa'īd, aided by his son Rāshid, began to prepare a counter-attack, secretly assembling groups of Bedouins. Māni', aware of these endeavours, protested to Sa'īd, asking for his co-operation in ensuring the prosperity of the state. The main clash did not come until the end of February when Sa'īd refused to place the oil and air revenues in the hands of the Treasury. In answer, on 3 March 1939, the Majlis ordered fixed salaries for the ruling family, granting Sa'īd an annual income of Rs. 10,000, and bringing the revenue from oil and from the air agreement under its control. Sa'īd rejected these proposals, insisting on a percentage of the total income of the state. The Majlis then occupied Dīrah to enforce its demands.

The situation rapidly developed into fierce conflict. Both sides guarded their own areas and the Majlis prevented the Shaikh's armed men crossing the inlet to Dīrah.

On 29 March 1939, the occasion of the wedding of Shaikh Rāshid b. Sa'īd to Shaikhah Laṭīfah, an inhabitant of Dīrah, the Majlis relaxed its restrictions after a request from Sa'īd, and allowed men with weapons to enter the area to take part in the traditional gun salute and festivities. This opportunity was seized by Rāshid, since the Buṭī faction, the allies of Māni', were away from the town on a hunting trip. After crossing to Dīrah, Rāshid's armed men suddenly began their planned attack, seizing many of the members of the Majlis and their patrons. Shaikh Ḥashr b. Rāshid and his son were killed and Māni' was besieged in his house, from which he continued to fight for three days. Māni' sent his son Rāshid to the Residency Agent, 'Abd al-Razzāq, in Shārjah to inform him of the Shaikh's attack, but the Agent refused to interfere. Māni''s young daughter Ṣan'ah helped him during the struggle, covering him by gunfire while he fled unnoticed to Shārjah. Finally, half the members of the Majlis were able to reach Shārjah safely. The sons of Buṭī, receiving news of the fight, abandoned their hunting trip and went to Shārjah too.

On 1 April, when the fight was over, a British sloop arrived in the port. On the advice of Weightman, who flew to Dubai on 2 April, Shaikh Sa'īd announced a new advisory Majlis of fifteen members, five of whom had belonged to the previous one. Shaikh Muḥammad b. Ṣaqr, brother of the Ruler of Shārjah, together with the Ruler of Rās al-Khaimah, tried to act as conciliators, but Sa'īd refused. In June the Political Agent had Māni' and his followers moved to Rās al-Khaimah in order to avoid a violent outbreak between Dubai and Shārjah and in July Māni''s maternal relation, the Shaikh of Āl Bū-Shāmis, also offered him refuge in Ḥamāsā, where he sent his family; Māni' himself left for Bombay, arriving on 24 April 1940. Finally in May the same year Shaikh 'Abd al-Raḥmān b. Muḥammad invited Māni' to accept Ḥīrah as his home.[111]

A distorted account of this conflict soon reached neighbouring countries, particularly Iraq, where the press and the radio reported that the Shaikh of Dubai, encouraged by the British, had murdered the whole of the Majlis at a feast in order to suppress the liberal modernist movement. The Foreign Office, alarmed by these reports, asked the India Office for the facts, and after some correspondence it was decided that the Political Resident should provide an accurate account to be broadcast by the BBC. On 28 April 1940 the Political Resident provided the following text:

> Recently there has been democratic movement in the State of Dubai which is in special treaty relations with HMG. This was an internal matter and HMG however advised the Shaikh to associate his people with himself in his government according to immemorial Arab custom

by formation of a Council. The Shaikh did not take this advice and a Council was forced on him by the people which owing to maladministration later grew unpopular. At the end of March Shaikh Sa'īd with his supporters dissolved Council. In the course of disturbances two of the Shaikh's principal opponents, Shaikh Ḥashr and his son were killed. There were about ten other casualties, including wounded. Of the Council half of members remained at Dubai and the other half went to neighbouring state of Shārjah. HMG again advised Shaikh Sa'īd to rule with the aid of a Council and to establish also Majlis al-Tujjar which he has done. Five members of the old Council are in the new one.[112]

Māni' sent several letters to the Political Agent in Baḥrain, first complaining against the Residency Agent 'Abd al-Razzāq, who had spread the opinion among the Rulers of the Coast that it would be unwise to offer hospitality to Māni', as it was contrary to British will. During his exile, Māni' complained to the Political Agent that the map he was having printed in Bombay had been detained in the customs there, but on 24 May 1941, the Political Agent authorised the Gray Mackenzie Agency in Baḥrain to secure its release. While in exile, Māni' visited Baḥrain and Sa'ūdī Arabia, but finally died at Ḥīrah during the Second World War.[113]

Although the Majlis movement of 1938 was suppressed, Dubai witnessed reform and modernisation under the leadership of Shaikh Rāshid b. Sa'īd when he assumed power in 1958.

V Decisive and Far-reaching Developments after the Second World War

In the late forties and early fifties the whole of the Arab world was caught up in a movement of liberation from foreign rule. With it went a desire for social and cultural reform. During the same period in the Gulf, the nationalisation of the APOC in Iran, the beginning of the building of the modern states of Kuwait and Qaṭar, the development of the eastern part of Sa'ūdī Arabia and the rise of the nationalist and reform movement in Baḥrain were all signs of a significant break with the past. The tide of change in the Arab world and in the Gulf region soon had its impact on the Trucial Coast where the early indications of an awakening became visible. There was a desire, and also a determination, for improved conditions, both economic and cultural. This was the first main factor which engendered the changes that took place in the Trucial States between 1945 and 1971. These years can be divided into three periods according to the extent, rate and field of activity: the first period between 1945 and the end of the fifties, the second between 1960 and 1966 and the third between 1966 and 1971.

In the first period limited financial resources meant that change was slow and that projects were, for the most part, restricted. In the early fifties, individuals, and some whole families, dissatisfied with the situation at home, left the Coast and went to Qaṭar and al-Ḥasā in Sa'ūdī Arabia. This small-scale migration was due to several factors, namely, local political reasons, or the educational facilities and opportunities for lucrative employment in the oil-producing areas. At this time the lack of preparatory and secondary schools caused the more persistent students to go to Baḥrain, Qaṭar and Kuwait. On the Coast itself, some of the shaikhs and members of the ruling families demonstrated a desire for progress and development.

There were three fundamental developments during this early period: the beginning of modern education, the growth of modern Dubai and the results of the new British policy of involvement in the internal affairs of the area. In 1952 the Ruler of Shārjah sought help in the field of modern education from Kuwait, in 1953 from Egypt, and in 1958 from Qaṭar. Dubai followed Shārjah's example. Afterwards, all the other Emirates, except Abū Dhabī, received aid from Kuwait, Egypt and Qaṭar, and started their modern schools. By the end of the fifties, and after the gradual increase in these Arab countries' aid, progress in education became apparent throughout the Coast. The advance made in this field was particularly noticeable in Shārjah and Dubai.

Moreover, during this period Shaikh Rāshid b. Sa'īd was able to begin building modern Dubai, and in his own way more than realised the aspirations of the movement of 1938. The British Bank of the Middle East opened its first branch in the Trucial States in 1946 in Dubai. The establishment of al-Maktūm hospital in 1949, a joint project of the British and the Shaikh, made Dubai the only centre for modern medical treatment in the area during the fifties, while the transfer of the British Agency from Shārjah to Dubai in 1954 gave to Dubai an added political significance. As Dubai's progress in the first three decades of the twentieth century was due to her port, Shaikh Rāshid now focused his attention on regaining its former trade. Restoring and developing the port, he showed his skill in economic matters, and created an expanded source of income for his future projects. He borrowed 400,000 dinars from Kuwait to begin the renovation of the old port and the clearance of the creek. In 1956 the Dubai police force was started and a new court began. Moreover, in this year Mahdī al-Tājir was seconded by the Government of Baḥrain to be the director of the Customs Department. Aḥmad b. Sulayyim, who had left Dubai for India in 1938, came back after the war to be welcomed by Shaikh Rāshid, and was later appointed Mahdī's deputy. In the next few years Dubai became the entrepôt and market for the Trucial States and Inner 'Omān and the Far East, due to the dramatic improvements and modernisation of harbour and port facilities, on which work began in the late fifties and continued throughout the sixties.

In 1957 Shaikh Rāshid founded the modern Dubai municipality, an administration which realised great achievements in the modern city. The Shaikh encouraged the private sector to help him in modernising and developing the growing city. In 1957 a private company, with the Shaikh as president, established an electric power station. Two years later, and in the same way, telegrams and telephones were introduced. In the late fifties, Shaikh Aḥmad b. 'Alī, the ruler of Qaṭar, financed three new projects: the water pipeline project from al-'Awīr wells to the city, the construction of asphalted streets within the town, and the building of the new bridge connecting Dīrah with Dubai proper. In 1958 the first modern airport was built in Dubai and Middle East Airlines and British Airways, the first lines to begin operating in the area, started services connecting the Trucial States with Beirut, London and the outside world.[114]

To carry these new schemes out new manpower from abroad was needed, and immigration from the Persian Coast, Pakistan and India began. At this stage, because of the general lack of modern machinery in the port and in the field of construction, it was mainly unskilled labour that was required and for that reason, as well as for political reasons, few Arabs were among the new arrivals. In the following years, immigration continued and increased.

In the fifties the new British policy of involvement in the internal affairs of the Trucial States was one of the main factors operative in bringing about change and modernisation. The new policy began with the al-Maktūm hospital in Dubai in 1949. After the war the British focused their attention on internal security and on the establishment of stable relations between the separate states. In 1951 the Foreign Office organised the small but important military force of the Trucial States. In 1952 the Trucial States Council was established which, with hindsight, can be seen as a step towards the future federation. In Dubai the British shared with the Shaikh the expense of maintaining the new police force. When a similar force, supported by Shaikh Shakhbūt, was established in Abū Dhabī in 1957, British officers led it as they did that of Dubai.

Between 1955 and 1959, as regards relations between the separate emirates, the British Government effected one of her major achievements in settling the inter-states frontiers and informed the shaikhs of her final arbitration. At this time such a step was essential for internal security and for the determination of oil concessions. In addition, the demarcation of the frontiers for the first time introduced to the area the concept of the modern state. However, in the late sixties the British had to confront the strong feeling of individuality created by their earlier move.

In the field of education the steps taken were limited. The British confined themselves to the foundation of the agricultural school in Rās al-Khaimah in 1957 and the setting up of a training school in Shārjah in 1958.

In the second period, between 1960 and 1966, the rate and dimension of modern development in Dubai steadily increased, largely due to the secure and growing annual income from the port, reaching the figure of 1.6 million BD in 1966.[115] Moreover, the transit trade in gold during these years caused a boom in private enterprise. In the field of education, Kuwait established the scientific section of the third and fourth years of secondary schooling in the city of Dubai. In 1964 the British set up the Dubai training school. Students, who had previously left to study in Kuwait and Qaṭar, now continued their education in universities abroad. In the year 1963–4 Kuwait established an office in Dubai for the supervision of her increasing aid to the whole Coast, which now extended to the field of health. From this point the administration of such aid came under the Gulf Department of the Kuwaiti foreign ministry, and under its direction a big, 100-bed hospital was built in Dubai, and another eighteen-bed hospital in Shārjah.[116] In addition, clinics were opened in the other emirates.

During this period Dubai took the lead in the modernisation of local government. In 1960 Shaikh Maktūm b. Rāshid, the heir-apparent, became chairman of the Lands Department. Shaikh Ḥamdān, the second son of Rāshid, was appointed chairman of the Dubai municipality and head of the Department of Health and Medical Services. Kamāl Hamzah was seconded by the Sudanese Government to Dubai in 1960 to become the director of the municipality; his great industry won him a considerable reputation, and his success encouraged other emirates, particularly Abū Dhabī, to bring in Sudanese experts after 1966. In 1961 a postal department was started. Dubai now focused attention on the development of oil production, and a Petroleum Department was established in 1962, headed by Mahdī al-Tājir, who became, at the same time, Director of the Emiri Court. From this date Aḥmad b. Sulayyim, Mahdī's deputy in the Customs Department, became the Director. At the same time, Major Briggs, a devoted police officer, was appointed Chief of Police and under him the force expanded from 80 to about 200 men during this period. Shaikh Muḥammad b. Rāshid, after completing his military training in England, became head of the Department of Police and Public Security. 'Abdullah al-Hul and Muḥammad Sa'īd were the first young trained officers from Dubai to join the police force a few years later.

Although oil production in Abū Dhabī was making progress in this period, it is important to remember that modernisation and development proceeded slowly and only on a small scale because of the policy of Shaikh Shakhbūt. Some steps in education were made in 1960. The police force, established in the late fifties, was expanded slightly, and a defence force came into being in 1965. However, Shaikh Zāyed b. Sulṭān, the representative of his brother at al-'Ain, initiated his programme of reform in the eastern region of Abū Dhabī. In order to increase cultivated land, with the small funds at his disposal at this time he constructed new underground canals and restored the old ones, which had been ruined by negligence. He also encouraged the introduction of modern education, and was a frequent visitor to the new school at al-'Ain.

In the other emirates it was only in the field of education that any noticeable progress was made. Shārjah took the lead in this field on the whole Coast, and in this emirate Kuwait set up the literary section of the two final years of secondary education. In 1962, the British introduced a commercial course at the previously established training school. The extension of Kuwaitī, Egyptian and Qaṭarī aid to the other emirates meant that education began to develop in these states as well; by 1965 there were 344 qualified teachers working on the Trucial Coast, 205 provided by Kuwait, 94 by Egypt, 36 by Qaṭar and 9 by Baḥrain.

With reference to Rās al-Khaimah, it is important to mention that with the keen interest of the ruler, Shaikh Ṣaqr b. Muḥammad, modern education flourished in this emirate. An example of his interest in this field is seen in his concern with the education of his own family: Shaikh Khālid b. Ṣaqr, the heir apparent, after completing his secondary education in Kuwait, continued his studies in England and the United States, while his other sons and his daughter also continued their studies to university level. When it came into being, this emirate provided the Federation with many young graduates, certain of them, namely Saif b. Ghubāsh, Sa'īd b. Ghubāsh, Muḥammad 'Abdul Raḥmān al-Bakr and Sa'īd 'Abdullah Sulmān becoming Ministers.

However, steps taken in the field of construction were for the most part limited. Unlike Dubai and Abū Dhabī, Shārjah and the other emirates as yet lacked new sources of income and hence depended mainly on British help. For the period 1956–66, British aid to the Trucial States only amounted to £853,000 in all, and although most of it was for construction projects, the sum allotted was in itself small and little was achieved. These emirates did not consider the limited British aid sufficient, so that when the Arab League offered assistance on a bigger scale in 1965 Shārjah and her neighbours responded with enthusiasm. The British prevented the involvement of the Arab League in the affairs of the Coast and counteracted by establishing the Trucial States Development Council, increasing their subsidy to £2 million for the Council fund.

As indicated above, modernisation started slowly during the fifties. It gathered some impetus in the early sixties, particularly in Dubai. The third and last period, between 1966 and 1971, is marked by two major developments: first, the rapid growth of Abū Dhabī, which now took the lead from Dubai, and secondly, the change in political thinking which led to the emergence of the United Arab Emirates under the leadership of Shaikh Zāyed in December 1971.

After Zāyed came to power in 1966, Abū Dhabī went through a stage of unprecedentedly speedy development: in September 1966, new departments were established in the administrative field and headed by members of the ruling family and other prominent figures as follows:

Shaikh Khalīfah b. Zāyed, Ruler's Deputy and Chairman of the Courts in the Eastern Province.

Shaikh Ḥamdān b. Muḥammad as Chairman of Public Works, Electricity, Water Supply, Health and Education Departments.

Shaikh Muḥammad b. Khālid as Chairman of Customs in addition to his appointment as Deputy Chairman in the Finance Department.

Shaikh Mubārak b. Muḥammad as Chief of Police and Public Security.

Shaikh Taḥnūn b. Muḥammad as Chairman of the Deputy of Agriculture and Mayor of al-ʻAin City.

Shaikh Saif b. Muḥammad as Chairman of the Municipalities and Land Registration.

Shaikh Surūr b. Muḥammad as Chairman of the Department of Justice.

Shaikh Aḥmad b. Ḥāmid as Head of the Department of Labour.[117]

Early in 1967 a legal adviser was appointed. At the same time the Department of Planning and Co-ordination was set up, and an able and experienced Director-General was appointed. Subsequently, a planning council was formed with the ruler as president. Abū Dhabī's budget between 1967–72 gives some idea of the rate and dimensions of the fundamental changes which took place in this emirate during these years: her budget for 1967 was 25 m. BD and in 1968 it was increased to 80 m. BD. For the 'Five Year Plan' 1968–72, the budget was 316.97 m. BD. Moreover, the growth of the administration is demonstrated by the increase in the number of trained employees: in 1966, there were barely 200 employees on the public payroll, but two years later the number had increased to 2,000, and by the mid-seventies the figure had reached about 5,000.[118] A comparison of these figures with the budget of Dubai and that of the Trucial States Council fund during this period (see tables in Appendix, p. 350) demonstrates how Abū Dhabī outstripped her neighbouring states.

From 1966 Shaikh Zāyed's programme of reform and his liberal policy encouraged the individuals and families who had left in the fifties, particularly from Abū Dhabī, to return home. He adopted the wise policy of sharing the responsibilities of his new government between members of the ruling family, notable local figures and certain graduates from the more prominent families. This was an example which was quickly followed in the other emirates. The trust the Shaikh showed in the young educated generation won him their affection and in due course they proved their reliability. In 1967 Aḥmad Suwaidī, the first young graduate from Abū Dhabī, was appointed chairman of the Emiri Court, which, under the guidance of Shaikh Zāyed, played a fundamental part in the affairs of the Trucial States and succeeded in establishing modern Abū Dhabī's reputation in the Arab, Islamic and outside world. In 1968 Shaikh Zāyed established the Centre for Documentation and Research at the Emiri Court to enrich studies of the Gulf and Arabia. Three additional advisers were appointed after 1968 to the Emiri Court, one political, another economic and the third cultural. Mānīʻ al-ʻUtaibah, another graduate, was appointed Chairman of the new Department of Petroleum and his colleague Muḥammad Ḥabrūsh al-Suwaidī became

Deputy Chairman of Finance. In addition, other new graduates were given positions of considerable responsibility.

In July 1971 Zāyed took further steps to reform Abū Dhabī's administration; he issued two decrees, one for the establishment of the first Cabinet in the state, and the other for the formation of the Consultative Assembly. Shaikh Khalīfah b. Zāyed, the Heir Apparent and Deputy Ruler, was appointed Prime Minister, Minister of Finance and Minister of Defence. The newly established Department of Information became a Ministry with Aḥmad b. Ḥāmid at its head.[119]

One of the Zāyed's major achievements during this period was the substantial development of the Abū Dhabī Defence Force: by 1971, with 10,000 men, it greatly exceeded in manpower the 1,500 of the Trucial Scouts, and comprising land, air and naval units, was equipped with more sophisticated weapons.

Shaikh Zāyed's great success in Abū Dhabī, together with his contributions to the development of neighbouring emirates, increased his popularity in the area. Abū Dhabī provided 50 per cent of the Trucial States Fund for the year 1967, and 90 per cent in 1968. In addition, Zāyed financed the building of roads, such as that connecting Shārjah with Dhaid, and that connecting Dubai with al-Khawanīq. He built houses and co-operated in the establishment of electricity and water supplies. In June 1968 Abū Dhabī opened an office in Shārjah, headed by the late 'Utaibah 'Abdullah al-'Utaibah, for the purpose of providing employment for the inhabitants of the emirates, not only in their own states but also in Abū Dhabī. In the 'Five-Year Plan', 30 million BD had been allotted to the emirates for further projects.

Moreover, Shaikh Zāyed extended help in education to the other emirates, for which Abū Dhabī began to build schools and employ teachers, particularly at Rās al-Khaimah, 'Ajmān, Fujairah and Umm al-Qaiwain.[120] Due to economic difficulties in Egypt, following the Arab–Israeli war of 1967, Shaikh Zāyed in 1968 took upon himself the responsibility for providing the salaries of teachers sent by Egypt. In the same year a section for the supervision of university studies abroad was established in the Department of Education and thenceforth financed the university studies of the majority of students from the Trucial Coast. To a great extent, this relieved Kuwait from the heavy commitment which she had shouldered since 1961. In 1971 the number of students sent from the Trucial Coast to continue their studies abroad was 111 in all, thirty-one from Abū Dhabī and the rest from the neighbouring states.

During this third and last period Dubai became, in 1969, an oil-producing state for the first time and thus found a great new source of wealth. Construction and modernisation in this city–state gathered momentum. Port Rāshid remained the main project, and was both deepened and expanded. Between 1966 and 1971 Shārjah also passed through a stage of constructional development and modernisation. In 1965, when Shaikh Khālid b. Muḥammad became ruler, this emirate, although leading in education, was only at the threshold of the modern age. Khālid, energetic and enterprising, was able to secure moderate sums of money from the Trucial States Development Fund and from Zāyed. On his own initiative he laid the foundation of Port Khālid in Shārjah, inaugurated a modern administration and established a police force. He gave the young graduates, who had recently returned from abroad, a share in the new administration. The state presented a promising place for foreign investment and soon witnessed a rapid growth in construction and modernisation. In the late sixties, Sa'ūdī Arabia built the road between Shārjah and Rās al-Khaimah. She also established a religious school in Rās al-Khaimah and provided it with teachers.

Between 1966 and 1971, and later, these major developments on the Trucial Coast accelerated migration into the area from India, Pakistan and the Persian Coast, particularly into Abū Dhabī, Dubai and Shārjah. The foreign elements greatly increased in the early seventies. The establishment of a modern administration after 1966 necessitated the employment of a considerable number of Arabs from abroad, and these began to constitute an important element in society.

Modernisation and the many new developments, constituting a break with the past, brought about a radical change in political thinking. The establishment of modern airports and direct contact between the Coast and the outside world put an end to the isolation of the inhabitants of the Trucial States. Progress in education, the influx of Arab and European settlers, the setting up of broadcasting and television stations and the expansion of the local press were all factors which contributed to a far-reaching change, not only in the social and cultural life, but also in political attitudes. The split and rivalry between the Hināwī and Ghāfirī factions, which had dominated internal politics on the coast in the past, now disappeared. The influence of a widespread and growing belief in greater Arab unity encouraged a local feeling in favour of a federation of the states, particularly strong among the young educated generation, who were prominent in propagating an idea, which led eventually to the creation of the United Arab Emirates.

In reality, many factors played a part in the emergence of the Federation. Shaikh Zāyed's known achievements in Abū Dhabī, his generosity to the other emirates, together with his outstanding personal qualities, made him a popular figure and an obvious leader. Moreover, the British, after their decision in 1968 to withdraw, adopted a policy of encouraging the formation of a political union. The Arab countries also gave their support to such a union.

The events which in three years led to federation began with the announcement in January 1968 of complete British withdrawal from the Gulf by the end of 1971. This decision brought the small emirates face to face with the responsibilities which would result from independence; it also posed the threat of a military and political vacuum in the region. Abū Dhabī and Dubai were the first two states to react positively. On 18 February 1968 Shaikh Zāyed b. Sulṭān and Shaikh Rāshid b. Sa'īd met at Semaiḥ, between the two states, to discuss the situation. Zāyed's tolerance solved the frontier problems between the two emirates, and the two rulers announced a union. The two shaikhs' belief in federation and their commitment to the idea smoothed the path towards its realisation. In their pact they agreed to invite the other shaikhs of the Trucial States and the rulers of Qaṭar and Baḥrain to hold talks on the future of the area; their response was immediate, and after the meeting of the rulers of nine states in Dubai on 25 February 1968 it was announced on 27 February that a federation of Arab Emirates had been settled.[121] Although this initial agreement was followed by many meetings in the next two-and-a-half years the nine states failed to effect the proposed federation. On 14 August 1971 Baḥrain declared her independence and on 1 September of the same year Qaṭar followed suit. As a result the seven Trucial rulers concentrated their efforts on reaching an agreement among themselves. On 2 December 1971 the United Arab Emirates was proclaimed, with Shaikh Zāyed as President and Shaikh Rāshid b. Sa'īd as Vice-President.

In accordance with the constitution, the executive power was given to the Supreme Council and the Cabinet. The Supreme Council consists of seven rulers and is the highest authority in the Federation. Shaikh Maktūm b. Rāshid was appointed Prime Minister and Shaikh Khalīfah b. Zāyed, his deputy. Legislation was under the control of a 'Federal National Council', comprising forty members appointed by the rulers for two years. The distribution of seats was as follows: Abū Dhabī and Dubai, eight each; Shārjah and Rās al-Khaimah, six members each; and 'Ajmān, Umm al-Qaiwain and Fujairah, four each.

In December 1973, to strengthen the Federal Government, it was decided to dissolve the Ministries in both Abū Dhabī and Sharjāh, replacing them with local departments. At the same time, the former Federal Cabinet, consisting of fourteen members, was superseded by a new Cabinet of twenty-eight. In Abū Dhabī, Shaikh Surūr b. Muḥammad, in addition to his other responsibilities, became Chairman of the Presidential Court, which was the former Emiri Court. Local police forces were amalgamated under Shaikh Mubārak b. Muḥammad, Minister of the Interior. Ḥimūdah b. 'Alī, an able and experienced police officer, was appointed Minister of State for Public Security. In 1976, the Higher Defence Council succeeded in unifying the different military forces in the Federation, the Union Force, and the other forces of Abū Dhabī, Dubai, Shārjah and Rās al-Khaimah. Shaikh Zāyed was nominated Commander-in-Chief, Shaikh Khalīfah b. Zāyed became his Deputy, and Shaikh Muḥammad b. Rāshid was given the Ministry of Defence. Shaikh Sulṭān b. Zāyed, who had recently completed his military training in England, became Head of the Armed Forces in the Western Region, the new name given to the Abū Dhabī Defence Force. Moreover, a high-ranking experienced Arab officer was appointed Chief of Staff for the Federal Armed Forces.

In the field of education the Federal Ministry in 1972 took over full responsibility for all educational matters in the Union. In July 1972 a Federal law was passed making school attendance obligatory for all children over six years of age, as a result of which the number of students in primary schools grew substantially. One of the biggest achievements was in evolving a new and unified educational system and curriculum. At this point, the Ministry, having expressed due gratitude, asked Kuwait, Baḥrain, Egypt and Qaṭar to cease their historic aid. In 1977, on the 'Day of Learning', it was stated that the Ministry intended to give greater attention to the promotion of technical training and also to religious education, and on the same occasion it was announced that the plans for the Federal University at al-'Ain were complete and that it would open at the beginning of the academic year 1977–8. The foundation of the University crowned the efforts made in modern education in the area.

One of the most significant social changes was the emergence of women's organisations in Abū Dhabī and certain other emirates, with the object of improving the social and cultural position of women within the limits of the Islamic concept. A union was formed under the patronage of Shaikhah Fāṭimah, the wife of Shaikh Zāyed, and it quickly established itself among Arab and international women's groups.

After 1971 modernisation became more rapid and developments multiplied in all the emirates. In the early seventies The National Oil Company of Abū Dhabī was established with Shaikh Taḥnūm b. Muḥammad as President. This Company placed considerable emphasis on industralisation of the state. At Ruwais, big petrochemical and steel plants were started. Although Dubai continued to make steady progress in the late sixties, it was not until the mid-seventies that she matched her early rapidity in growth, a development for which three factors were responsible: the establishment of the Federation, the augmentation of her income from oil and Shaikh Rāshid's efforts. Dubai began her industrialisation with big projects like the dry dock, the aluminium smelter at Jabal 'Alī and the gas liquefaction plant. In Shārjah, too, after Shaikh Sulṭān b. Muḥammad came to power in 1972, and event which coincided with the beginning of oil production there, the country has reached a stage comparable with the achievements of Abū Dhabī and Dubai.

The gigantic growth in oil revenues after 1973 enabled Abū Dhabī, which already provided 90 per cent of the Federal budget, to increase her contribution. As a result of which, modernisation has rapidly become a reality in the other emirates where Federal expenditure on roads, schools, houses, clinics, electrification, agriculture and fisheries has transformed the lives of the people. 'Ajmān, Umm al-Qaiwain, Rās al-Khaimah and Fujairah have now grown in size, and the numbers of their inhabitants have increased.

In the international field, the UAE in December 1971 became a member of the Arab League and of the United Nations. The new state adopted a nationalist policy and in company with Sa'ūdī Arabia, Kuwait and Qaṭar, contributed aid to the Arab countries adjacent to Israel. In the 1973 war, the United Arab Emirates played a major role when Shaikh Zāyed, in accordance with the other Arab oil producing countries, stopped supplying oil to the West during the fighting. Moreover, the generous help given to Islamic and underdeveloped countries gained the UAE an eminent position. According to a statement from Nāṣir al-Nuwais, Deputy Director of the Abū Dhabī Fund, the foreign aid given by Abū Dhabī reached 30 per cent of her annual budget. Foreign aid in Kuwait, Sa'ūdī Arabia and Qaṭar is around 10 per cent and in Iran 6 per cent whereas in developed countries the figure never exceeds 1 per cent of the annual budget.

History of Modern Education

Within recent years there have been a number of studies of the growth in construction and of the economy of the Trucial States as well as of the political structure of the Federation, but so far no survey of the development in modern education in the area, a primary factor in the changes of the post-war period, has appeared. Hence, to fill the gap, the following pages are devoted to the history of education in the Trucial States between 1945 and 1971. For the most part the material has been drawn from the annual reports of the Ministries of Education in Abū Dhabī, Qaṭar and the Federation and from interviews with the new graduates, the teachers and some prominent figures.

Modern education, as distinct from the traditional form, started in the Trucial States in the post-war period. It was one of the fields in which progress was rapid and education soon became a force in accelerating cultural and political change. The story of modern education between 1945 and 1972 is one of great endeavour and determination. One finds in it the considerable effort made by the shaikhs, the enthusiasm and keenness manifested by students and parents, the devotion of the Arab teachers who came from abroad and the substantial help given by Kuwait since 1953, by Egypt since 1954, by Qaṭar since 1958, by Baḥrain during the 1960s and by Sa'ūdī Arabia since 1967. Finally, we see the contribution of Abū Dhabī after Shaikh Zāyed came to power in 1966.

For the shaikhs, students, parents and teachers, education had become a race with time, and it had a nationalistic motivation. In the early fifties the lack of modern schools obliged the more insistent students to go to Baḥrain, where such schools had been established before the war, and to Kuwait where education had been developed since 1947. Later, they also went to Qaṭar, where education had its proper beginning in 1954. With grants from Kuwait and Qaṭar these students continued their studies at universities, mainly in Cairo, Beirut, Damascus and Baghdād. Two of the earliest students to leave in search of educational facilities, one from Rās al-Khaimah and the other from Shārjah, finally obtained scholarships in Leningrad. It is important to note that in the two decades after the war the difficult circumstances which confronted the students helped to form responsible characters. Such young graduates came back to their homeland in the Trucial States in the late 1960s to participate with members of the ruling families in establishing a new and modern administration. In the first and second cabinets of the UAE some of these graduates held posts as Ministers.

The progress made in education led inevitably to an awareness of the contemporary Arab nationalist movement, and the help offered by the other Arab countries strengthened the ties between the Trucial Coast and their Arab brothers. The teachers sent in from abroad, being Palestinians, Egyptians, Jordanians, Iraqis, Lebanese, Syrians, Sa'ūdīs, Baḥrainīs or Sudanese, awakened the previously isolated inhabitants of the Trucial States to the wider problems of the Arab World, of which the Trucial States now became a part. The educational beginnings coincided with Nasser's revolution in Egypt and the establishment of the new broadcasting station of the 'Arab Voice' in Cairo, which exercised a great influence and had a particular effect on the younger generation. At the time of the Suez crisis in 1956 there were demonstrations in the main cities along the Coast, and in Shārjah a group of young students tried to set fire to the British air base. Later, in 1958, the union of Egypt and Syria was warmly welcomed, while in the growing city of Dubai, a new quarter was given the name of Port Said and a new square was named after Nasser. At the end of the school year, sports days, which began in Shārjah in 1958 and in Dubai in 1959, became nationalist occasions. Enthusiastic speeches were made and Arab slogans on the themes of liberation and union were chanted by the students and the crowds.

Educational advances forged new ties of friendship among the states on the Coast, and for the first time, in the field of sport, matches were held between the school teams from different states. For financial reasons, Kuwait in 1963 established the arts section of secondary education in the Trucial States in Shārjah, and in 1964, Kuwait also opened the scientific section in Dubai; these were the first two secondary schools ever to have been founded in the Trucial States, and students travelled by bus from Shārjah to Dubai to attend classes in Dubai and vice versa. In discussing the role of education as a factor in the unification of the Coast, it is important to emphasise how the difficulties which faced the students migrating in search of learning brought about mutual co-operation and created strong bonds among them abroad, in Dōḥah, in Kuwait, in Cairo and in Baghdād. It was in Dōḥah, for example, that 'Abdullah al-Mazru'ī, Thānī b. Īsā' and Rāshid 'Abdullah from 'Ajman met and made friends with students from the other emirates, especially Abū Dhabī, Dubai and Rās al-Khaimah.

When Shaikh Zāyed became ruler, apart from the stimulus he gave to education in Abū Dhabī, substantial help was given to the other emirates, and the part he played in education along the Coast increased his popularity and strengthened his position as a leader amongst the newly educated generation.

Whereas in the past the teacher had been the main element in maintaining the traditional pattern, in the years from 1945 to 1972 the teacher, coming from abroad, became the agent of change, replacing the Muṭawwa' (religious teacher) who was, for the most part, one of the few educated persons in society, enjoying great respect. During the fifties life was still simple and traditional in the Trucial States. These were the golden days of the *Majlis* of the shaikhs and influential figures, where people gathered to relax and discuss their affairs in general. In such a society, when there was no other form of entertainment, the teacher was invited to the ruler's Majlis, where he mixed with the local people. The teacher's role went far beyond the school premises; he was frequently asked for advice. Certain of the more intelligent and more sociable teachers gained the confidence of the shaikhs and ultimately became their secretaries. But the modern teacher responded to the respect and enthusiasm he encountered, devoting himself to his work and to his students; when necessary, he taught sixty-five pupils in a single class and gave thirty lessons a week. Because of the lack of teachers, the directors of many schools themselves gave many lessons in addition to their other duties. Some of these early modern teachers are still remembered with affection and gratitude. In 1977, on the 'Day of Learning', the Ministry of Education honoured their names as well as other local teachers who had served during that period.

Detailed studies of the development of modern education in the more populated states of Abū Dhabī, Dubai and Shārjah provide us with examples of the efforts made by the shaikhs, the students and the teachers, and make us more fully aware of the help given by the other Arab countries. Shārjah was the pioneer in educational development. After the war, Muḥammad 'Alī al-Maḥmūd reopened his father's school, al-Iṣlāh al-Muḥammadī, which closed when the pearl industry collapsed, having lasted only a few years. Later, financed by the ruler, Shaikh Sulṭān b. Ṣaqr, this school became known as al-Qāsimiyyah, with Muḥammad 'Alī al-Maḥmūd as headmaster. It was here that the first educated generation of Shārjah, including such figures as the late Shaikh Khālid b. Muḥammad and his brothers and 'Abdullah 'Umrān and his colleagues began their studies.

Subsequently, in 1948, Muḥammad 'Alī al-Maḥmūd, because of his father's name in the field of education and in the pearl trade, was invited to Dōḥah to supervise the new school that had recently been established there. It was the income from oil which brought about this new development in education in Qaṭar. Later many other teachers, such as Mubārak al-Nākhī from Shārjah, Ibn Ghubāsh and Ibn Ḥajar from Rās al-Khaimah, also went to Dōḥah. Aḥmad Abū-Raḥīmah now became the headmaster of the Qāsimiyyah school.

In Shārjah football became popular and the school team benefited from watching the tactics of the British players at the air base. In this period sport and social clubs flourished in Shārjah; future cultural and nationalist clubs were not yet known. On the other hand, the 'Cultural Club', which despite its name was mainly for sport, was established in 1951. English lessons were included in the curriculum of al-Qāsimiyyah and some students, like the young Shaikh Sulṭān b. Muḥammad, had additional private lessons from English and Italian residents.

In 1952, in search of a more sophisticated education, Shaikh Sulṭān b. Muḥammad, 'Abdullah 'Umrān and his brother Taryam went to Kuwait. Similarly, 'Abdullah al-Maḥmūd, elder son of the late 'Alī al-Maḥmūd, who had already left Shārjah for al-Dammān in al-Ḥasā, took his son Sālim to attend school in Baḥrain. In a move to promote education further, Shaikh Sulṭān b. Ṣaqr, who had inherited his father's literary interests, sent his secretary, Ibrāhīm al-Midfa', to Kuwait to ask for teaching staff. Kuwait responded favourably and 'Abd al-'Azīz Ḥusain, the Kuwait Director of Education, visited Shārjah to look into the matter himself. He was received with great ceremony and enthusiasm, and at the Qāsimiyyah school the young Shaikh Sulṭān b. Muḥammad, only ten years old, delivered a welcoming address in English. 'Abd al-'Azīz Ḥusain was greatly impressed by what he observed and in the school year 1953–4 he sent three qualified teachers to Shārjah.

The year 1953 marked a turning point in the history of education in Shārjah. In this year, further help was given by Kuwait when a hostel was established there for the incoming students from the Trucial Coast. On the request of the ruler, Egypt also responded and sent three teachers to Shārjah in the next school year. In 1953 female education, which was regarded favourably by the religious and intellectual circles, took a step forward, when the wives of the Egyptian and Palestinian teachers in Shārjah started educating the girls according to the modern system. As a result, al-Zahrā primary school for girls, the first of its kind in the Trucial States, was founded. One of the pupils to benefit from this development was 'Aishah al-Sayyār, and when she obtained her degree in Cairo in 1969 she became the first female graduate of the Trucial Coast.

By 1955 modern education was well established in Shārjah and the students who had left earlier for Kuwait were encouraged to return home. In 1957, for the first time, students sat for the fourth year and final preparatory examination. In the school year 1958–9 one class at Qāsimiyyah was prepared for secondary education. Moreover, in the same year Qaṭar began giving educational assistance on the Coast; Qāsimiyyah expanded and had 375 students with sixteen teachers, three from Qaṭar, four from Kuwait and six from Egypt. One of the Kuwaitī deputation was the first headmaster to be appointed and one of the Egyptians was made his deputy. At this time Jāsim al-Midfa' was one of the local teachers. In the same year the

Ashbīliyyah, the second school for girls, was opened. The activities of this academic year were crowned by the holding of the first sports day on the Coast.

Two years later, in 1960–61, Qaṭar built the first new secondary school in Shārjah, which was named al-'Urūbah. At the end of this school year sixteen students from Shārjah went to Kuwait to complete the third and fourth years of their secondary education and they later formed the first group to be sent by Kuwait to university, all of them going to Cairo. Amongst them there was one who, after insistent requests, was accepted into the Military Academy. In Shārjah and Dubai enthusiasm for education caused a group of leading citizens, among them 'Umrān Taryam, Sulṭān b. 'Uwais and 'Umrān b. Sulṭān al 'Uwais, to set up a fund to help young students abroad. On his own initiative, Sulṭān b. 'Uwais also built a new primary school named Hiṭṭīn. Although the third and fourth years of secondary education in the arts section were now taught in Shārjah, for the next few years students still had to go to Kuwait to sit the final examination.

After independence Kuwait augmented her aid to the Trucial Coast, increasing the number of teachers and building fourteen schools, amongst them a preparatory school in Shārjah, which was founded in 1963. By 1965 education had made rapid strides, as demonstrated by the increase in the number of teachers; 60 from Kuwait, 40 from Egypt, 9 from Baḥrain and 9 from Qaṭar. As Kuwait had provided teachers, most of the books and most of the stationery, the Kuwaitī educational system and curriculum tended to dominate, except in Abū Dhabī, along the Coast and particularly in Shārjah. Kuwait and Qaṭar provided accommodation for the teachers they sent, but the ruler of Shārjah was responsible for the housing of the Egyptian deputation. However, it was only the head of the Egyptian deputation who was based in Shārjah. Kuwait and Qaṭar took Dubai as their centre. The third and fourth years of secondary education were, for the most part, the responsibility of the Egyptian teachers.

In the summer of 1966 the first graduates from Shārjah returned home. By now secondary education was well established there and in 1967, for the first time, the final examination was held there. In the same year, Shaikh Khālid b. Muḥammad, the ruler of the state, entrusted the new Department of Education to 'Abdullah 'Umrān, and important positions were given to the rest of the new graduates. In 1968, Kuwait provided a new, modern secondary school for the pupils from al-'Ubrūbah; this foundation was her last great achievement in this field in Shārjah; the old building was renamed the 'Abdullah Sālim Secondary School'.

During these years proper cultural clubs began to appear, the most important among them being al-'Urūbah, with Shaikh Sulṭān b. Muḥammad al-Qāsimī as its president. Shārjah also witnessed in this period the emergence of a local and nationalist press, the first of its kind in the area. The Urūbah Club published a monthly magazine, *al-Yaqazah* ('the Awakening'), and in

1969 Taryam 'Umrān started the weekly magazine '*al-Shurūq*' to be followed by *al-Khalīj*, the first daily newspaper on the Coast.

Since Shārjah was the pioneer in the field it was not surprising that the first Minister of Education in the formation of the Federal Government in 1972 was chosen from that state—Shaikh Sulṭān b. Muḥammad al-Qāsimī, a graduate in agriculture. After he became the ruler of Shārjah, 'Abdullah 'Umrān took over his position. Khalfān al-Rūmī, a graduate from Shārjah, was Deputy Minister.

In Dubai the Aḥmadiyyah school, which managed to survive the difficult economic situation of the thirties and early forties, kept alive the educational spirit in the post-war period; its survival was made possible because the local teachers stayed on. Furthermore, after 1945 Shaikh Rāshid b. Sa'īd took over financial responsibility. Although it was not until 1957 that Dubai received teachers from abroad—from Kuwait in that year, from Qaṭar in 1958 and from Egypt in 1959—by the late sixties this state was able to compete with Shārjah's achievements. Kuwait and Qaṭar established their representatives in Dubai. During the post-war period Aḥmad al-Mūsā, an employee in the Court of Shaikh Rāshid, was in charge of educational matters in the Emirate.

In the early fifties it was exclusively from the Aḥmadiyyah school that the young generation received their education. The headmaster was Muḥammad b. Nūr and the teachers included Muḥammad b. Yūsef and Muḥammad Ḍabawī. The foundation of the new British Bank of the Middle East and the coming of other modern innovations distressed Muḥammad b. Nūr and caused him to leave. His place was taken by Muḥammad Ḥamad al-Shībānī, one of the teachers. Following visits to the Ruler, 'Abdul Azīz Ḥusain, the Kuwaiti Director of Education, paid a visit to the school and one of the older pupils, 'Abdullah al-Hūl, delivered a welcoming address in Arabic. In the school year 1955–6 Kuwait sent one teacher to the school and new subjects such as English, science and geography began to be taught, and a group of boy scouts was founded. Prior to the coming of the Kuwaiti teacher the pupils were taught according to the level of the majority. Now, to bring the older students forward, the new teacher divided the boys according to their age and aptitude and gave private lessons to the older ones, coaching them to a higher level. However, on the sports day at the end of the year a somewhat over-enthusiastic speech given by the Palestinian teacher from Kuwait upset the British Agency and the school was closed before the final examination.

The efforts of the Kuwaitī teacher had generated great enthusiasm for modern education and the closure of the school served only to make some of the older pupils more determined, so that 'Abdullah al-Hūl, Muḥammad Sa'īd, Rāshid al-Kaytūb and 'Alī al-Maydūr, for example, left for Qaṭar. Shaikh Maktūm b. Rāshid encouraged them and provided them with a letter to Shaikh Khalīfah b. Ḥamad in Dōḥah, who received them cordially. They were given places in the hostel and were able to take and pass the final primary examination. In Dōḥah the students from Dubai were for the first time brought into contact with students from Abū Dhabī, 'Ajmān and Rās al-Khaimah. A few years later, when they went on to Kuwait to complete their secondary education, a first condition for the chance of a university place, they met other students from Shārjah. In general the students from Dubai and 'Ajmān showed themselves to be particularly industrious: having taken and passed the first year preparatory examination in June, at their own request they sat and passed the repeat of the second year examination in September, consequently beginning the third-year course in October.

After a lapse of one year, the Aḥmadiyyah school was opened for the year 1957–8 and Zuhdī al-Khaṭīb was sent by Kuwait to become the new headmaster. During five years he was fortunate in gaining the trust of Shaikh Rāshid, and through his endeavours and achievements gained a reputation. Following the policy of his predecessor, he enabled the more able of the older students to reach the second preparatory level. This step narrowed the gap in modern education between Dubai and Shārjah from four to two years. The Aḥmadiyyah school now had 503 pupils and ten teachers, nine of whom were local. In this year part of the palace was donated by Shaikh Rāshid for a new primary school, called al-Sa'īdiyyah, with places for 150 boys. Another primary school, al-Maktūm, was opened by Shaikh Rāshid in Jumairah in the same year, with three local teachers and sixty-one students.

In the year 1958–9 Qaṭar sent her first deputation of seven teachers to Dubai. That year saw a considerable increase in the numbers of students, particularly in the Aḥmadiyyah school, and the need for a new school became urgent. At a meeting held in the Sa'īdiyyah school the sum of 200,000 rupees was raised and the new school was named al-Sh'ab ('the people'); the Shaikh gave 50,000 rupees and the rest of the money came from the rich merchants. At this meeting, it was announced that a school for girls would be established and that Shaikh Rāshid intended to send his own daughter there. In fact, two schools for girls were opened, the Khawlah school in Dubai proper, and al-Khansā in Deira on the other side of the inlet. At the end of this year the first sports day was held in Dubai: two of Shaikh Rāshid's sons participated, Shaikh Ḥamdan heading the boy scouts and Shaikh Muḥammad leading the gymnastic team.

In the summer Rāshid visited Egypt and as a result, six Egyptian teachers were sent to Dubai for the school year 1959–60. That year the final preparatory examination was held for the first time in Dubai; Qaṭar increased her supply of teachers from seven to ten, amongst whom was Muḥammad al-Kayyālī, who became Deputy Director of the Aḥmadiyyah, and then Director for the next eleven years. Now the need for new buildings to house the two girls' schools already established, and a new secondary school became evident. Kuwait financed the building of the secondary school, and Qaṭar, after a visit by the late Shaikh Jāsim b. Ḥamad, the Minister of Education, provided buildings for the girls' schools.

In 1962 Jum'a al-Hūl and other students, having finished their secondary schooling in Kuwait, were sent to university in Egypt, where Juma'a chose to study medicine while his colleagues opted for police training, commerce or the arts. Although in the general field of modern education Shārjah was two years ahead of Dubai, this group, by their dedication, were able to complete their secondary education in Kuwait at the same time as 'Abdullah 'Umrān and his fellows from Shārjah.

In 1963 Kuwait established an office in Dubai for the supervision of her growing aid to the whole Trucial Coast, which now extended into matters of health. This office came under the Gulf Department of the Foreign Ministry in Kuwait, thus ending the great role played by Murshid al-'Usaimī, the rich Kuwaiti merchant who had settled in Dubai for the last two decades and had acted as intermediary between the Kuwaiti Ministry of Education and the Kuwaiti teachers on the Coast. Two of the first projects undertaken in Dubai by the new office were the building of a preparatory school to house the old Aḥmadiyyah school and the construction of a hospital in the Deirah quarter.

By 1965 secondary education was well established in Dubai, and Kuwait chose the capital as centre for the scientific section of the secondary stage on the Coast. There were now ten schools in the state, seven for boys and three for girls; the teachers numbered 137: 68 from Kuwait, 31 from Egypt, 16 from Qaṭar and 22 locals; the students numbered 3,572. In the following years a religious institution was founded, housed at first in the old Aḥmadiyyah building but later moved to new premises provided by Kuwait. The old Aḥmadiyyah building, which had been constructed in 1912, was now completely deserted. In 1971 the number of schools increased and reached eighteen; so had the numbers of both students and teachers, to 6,183 and 253 respectively.

Whilst modern education began in Shārjah and Dubai in the early fifties, a comparable movement in Abū Dhabī did not start until the early sixties, and it was then slow and limited. However, after Shaikh Zāyed b. Sulṭān became Ruler in 1966, the next five years brought growth unprecedented in the area, and by the time the UAE emerged in December 1971 Abū Dhabī was able to match achievements elsewhere.

In the early fifties, for various reasons, Shaikh Shakhbūt, the ruler of Abū Dhabī, refused to join Shārjah and Dubai in asking Kuwait and Egypt to send teachers. This attitude, together with other factors, caused some important families to leave the state, most going to Dōḥah and a few to Sa'ūdī Arabia. It was in Dōḥah that Aḥmad Suwaidī, Muḥammad Habrūsh al-Suwaidī, Māni' al-'Utaibah, 'Abdullah al-Nuwais, 'Aḥmad Mansūr and

Aḥmad Mūsā, with many other young Abū Dhabians received their primary and secondary education, and from there the majority were sent by Qaṭar to universities abroad.

In 1958, influenced by educational developments in the neighbouring states and persuaded by Thānī b. 'Abdullah, a prominent figure from Dubai, Shaikh Shakhbūt opened the al-Falaḥiyyah school in the town of Abū Dhabī in a small building presented by the British Agency. However, at the end of the school year Shaikh Shakhbūt decided to close the school, and the three Jordanian teachers were sent home.

In 1959 Shaikh Muḥammad al-J'abarī, Minister of Education in Amman, visited Abū Dhabī with a deputation collecting funds for the reconstruction of the dome of the al-Aqsā Mosque in Jerusalem. In the following year, the Ruler of Abū Dhabī, trusting in the integrity of the Minister, sent certain notable figures, namely, Abdul Jalīl al-Fahīm, Khalīfah al-Yūsuf and Darwīsh b. Karam with a request for more teachers. In the school year 1960–1, six teachers arrived in Abū Dhabī, the al-Falaḥiyyah school was reopened, and the new school of al-Baṭīn was founded, while in the Eastern region the al-Nihayyāniyyah school at al-'Ain was opened under the keen supervision of Shaikh Zāyed. Two years later a further nine teachers were employed. In 1963 the first school for girls was opened in the city of Abū Dhabī and in the following year a second school was established at al-'Ain.

By 1965 six schools had been founded in the Emirate, with places for 390 boys, educated by 27 male teachers, and 138 girls instructed by 6 male teachers, all following the Jordanian system and syllabus. Between 1960 and 1965 various figures were put in charge of education, the last two being 'Abdullah al-Qīwainī and Shaikh Khalīfah b. Muḥammad. An important factor in this period was the encouragement given by Shaikh Zāyed to *al-Nihayyāniyyah* school at al-'Ain; he visited the school, received the teachers in his Majlis, and attended the annual sports day. The school football team was of a high standard, and a group of boy scouts was started. Moreover, Shaikh Zāyed showed his appreciation of the efforts of the most devoted teachers, increasing their small salaries from his own purse, and his two sons, Khalīfah and Sulṭān, along with other members from the ruling family, such as Shaikh Surūr b. Muḥammad, received their early education there.

With Shaikh Zāyed's accession in August 1966 a new phase began: a new Department of Education was established under the presidency of Shaikh Ḥamdān b. Muḥammad, who took on this task in addition to his other responsibilities. Preparatory and secondary education now developed with the construction of highly sophisticated schools. To encourage attendance transport was provided for the pupils and they were given monthly allowances. In 1968 a considerable number of teachers from Baḥrain were employed. With the changing situation, the Jordanian system of education had to be adapted to the local needs. Successive widely experienced men of education were appointed as directors in the Department. Teachers' salaries were raised and the number of qualified teachers was increased by several times. The willingness to learn was not confined to the younger generation, since a great number of older people, both men and women, attended evening classes. When Abū Dhabī established her Council of Ministers Muḥammad Khalīfah al-Kindī became Minister of Education and by 1971, after a mammoth expansion, the number of schools in the Emirate reached 25, with 439 teachers and 7,897 students, exceeding in numbers those of Shārjah and Dubai. The budget for education was increased from 129,442 BD in 1967 to 2,911,449 in 1971.

The migration of some families to Qaṭar in the early fifties proved most beneficial to Abū Dhabī when Aḥmad al-Suwaidī and his fellow graduates returned in the late sixties. Moreover, the training which some young Abū Dhabians, like Himūdah b. 'Alī, received in the police force in the late fifties, and their further education in this field abroad, soon proved of value to the state. In the late sixties these newly educated and able young men shared with Shaikh Zāyed and other members of the ruling family in the renaissance of Abū Dhabī.

Notes

1. Ibn Majid, *Le Pilote des Mers de L'Inde de la Chine et de l'Indonesie*, Gabriel Ferrand, Paris, 1921, pp.137–140.
2. Lorimer, I Part I A, op.cit., p.403; II A, pp.260–61; II B, pp.14, 37, 1698, 1808.
3. These were the followers of Muḥammad b. 'Abd al-Wahhāb, called by their enemies Wahhābīs, and by themselves al-Muwaḥḥidīn and al-Muslimīn. U.A. Ibn Bishr, *Unwan al-Majd Fi Tavikh Nejd*, Beirut, 1967, p.330.
4. Lorimer, I Part I A, op.cit., pp.689–90; Part II, pp.1757–61.
5. The composition of the inhabitants of other towns, roughly speaking, was the 'Āl Bū-Shāmis tribe in Ḥīrah and Ḥamriyyah, the Za'ab tribe in Jazīrat al-Ḥamrā and Kalbā, the Ṭinaij tribe in Rams, the Naqbiyyīn tribe in Dabā al-Ḥiṣn and Khūr Fakkān, the Sharq'yyīn tribe in Dadnah, Zubūrah, al-Qurayyah, Fujairah and al-Ghurfah, and the Shiḥūḥ tribe in Dabā al-Bay'ah, Khaṣab and Sha'am. The Shiḥūḥ tribe also lived in Rūs al-Jibāl and the Sharqiyyīn tribe in the mountains of Ḥijr around the pass of Ḥam. The oasis of Dhaid was inhabited by both Banī Qatab and the Khawāṭir, who made up the Bedouin element in the Qawāsim Emirate, together with the Ḥibūs, Ghafalah and Mazāri' tribes who also extended south of Dhaid to Milaiḥih and Gharīf, thus dominating the two desert tracks from Dhaid and Dubai to Wādī al-Qūr in the extreme south of the Qawāsim Emirate. Some branches of the Banī Ka'b tribe which live in this area surrounding the entrance of Wādī al-Qūr also gave their allegiance to the Qawāsim shaikhs.
6. There were many other revolts and internal disputes of many kinds during this period, but this work is concerned primarily with those connected with the dismemberment of the Emirate in which the British were involved.
7. See the Qawāsim Family Genealogical Tree No. 1.
8. Lorimer, I Part I A, pp.723–27, 756, 759–63, 779–84.
9. Lorimer, I Part I A, op.cit., pp.424, 751, 761–63, 779–83.
10. Lorimer, I Part II, op.cit., p.2639.
11. Lorimer, I Part I A, op.cit., pp. 751–52, 762, IOR, R/15/1/14/47, Hamriyyah, 'Īsā to Pol. Res., 22 July 1922.

12. IOR, R/15/1/14/6, Arab Coast, 'Abd al-Latif to Pol. Res., 23 June 1908; Cox to SGI, 4 August 1912.
13. Hawley, op.cit., p.356.
14. IOR, R/15/1/14/37, Khālid b. Aḥmad to 'Abd al-Latif, 7 April 1914.
15. Līwā, which was the seat of the Āl Bū-Falāḥ, the ruling family of the Emirate, was a fertile area of fifty-two oases, extending fifty kilometres from west to east and situated among the high sand dunes of the interior. These villages were inhabited by two main tribal groups, the Banī Yās and the Manāṣīr, who had lived amicably together for generations and had established strong ties.
16. See the Āl Nihayyān Family Genealogical Tree No. 2.
17. Zāyed had been a refugee in Dubai with his maternal uncles of the Sūdān tribe after the assassination of his father.
18. J. B. Kelly, *Eastern Arabian Frontiers*, London, 1964, pp.36, 45–8, 58–60, 91, 96–9.
19. Kelly, *Britain*, pp.688–9.
20. The Government of the United Kingdom of Great Britain and Northern Ireland, *Arbitration Concerning Buraimī and the Common Frontier Between Abū Dhabī and Sa'ūdī Arabia*, 1955, I, pp.35–6. See Map No. 2.
21. See the Āl Maktūm, *Rulers of Dubai*, Genealogical Tree No. 3.
22. FA, Asie Océanie, N.S., Muscate II, Ottavi à Hanotaux, Paris, 3 & 5 Octobre 1895. (Enclosed with despatch 5 October a letter from Salih b. Ali to Shaikh Zāyed b. Khalifah, dated 25 July 1895.)
23. Mann, op.cit., p.64.
24. IOR, P/3276, From Ross, Pol. Res., Bushire to SGI, 8 October 1887; news communicated by the Residency Agent, Arab Coast, dated 7 October 1887.
25. Lorimer, I Part I A, op.cit., pp.735–6, 771.
26. FA, Asie Océanie, N.S., Muscate III, Ottavi Muscate, à Berthelot, Paris, 26 Février 1896.
27. UK Memorial, II, 113.
28. Lorimer, I Part I A, op.cit., pp.650, 746.
29. IOR, R/15/1/14/4, Correspondence re. Zoora, 'Abd al-Latif to Pol. Res., 28 May 1897; Zāyed b. Khalīfah to Pol. Res., 27 December 1889; 'Abd al-Latif to Pol. Res., 24 July 1900.
30. IOR, ibid., Ṣaqr b. Khālid to Zāyed b. Khalīfah, 31 July 1900; 'Abd al-Latif to Pol. Res., 29 October 1900; Zāyed b. Khalīfah to Pol. Res., 9 February 1901.
31. See the Āl Mu'allā, *Rulers of Umm al-Qaiwain*, Genealogical Tree No. 4.
32. Lorimer, I Part I A, op.cit., pp.746, 751–3.
33. IOR, R/15/1/14/28, Arab Coast, Residency Agent to Shaikh Zāyed, 14 March 1906; Cox to SGI, 28 February 1907.
34. Lorimer, I Part I A, pp.753–4.
35. IOR, R/15/1/14/28, Arab Coast, Cox to SGI, 28 February 1907 (enclosed a Memorandum and Terms of Peace); Graves, op.cit., pp. 95–6.
36. Hawley, op.cit., p.352.
37. Lorimer, II A, op.cit., pp.263, 323, 416–26; II B, pp. 1825–6, 1938; FA, Correspondence Commercials, Bouchir, Vice Consular, Bouchir à Ministre, Paris, 5 Juin 1889.
38. IOR, L/P & S/10/457, Pearl Fisheries, Cox to 'Abd al-Latif, 20 July 1911.
39. An example of this may be seen in the role of the merchants in the substitution of Shaikh Ṣaqr b. Khālid for Shaikh Ṣalīm of Shārjah in 1884.
40. Lorimer, II A, p.409.
41. GA Turkei 165, bd. 29, a copy of Von Herrmann Burckardt's talk in Berlin, 3 February 1906 (his trip is included in this volume).
42. This was the name given by the Arab inhabitants on the Arabian side of the Gulf to the recent Arab immigrants from the Persian Coast.
43. IOR, L/P & S/10/115 from Capt. Shakespear, Kuwait, to Pol. Res., Bushire, 20 December 1910.
44. IOR, R/15/1/14/14, Trucial Chiefs, Report on the Trucial Shaikhs and their principalities from 'Abd al-Latif to Pol. Res., 29 July 1901. Hay, op.cit., p.380.
45. IOR, R/15/1/14/49, Arab States, Monthly Summary, July 1929, March and July 1930.
46. IOR, R/15/2/B/17, Claims of the Virumal Valabdas of Dubai, 'Īsā to Pol. Res., 28 January 1931.

47. IOR, R/15/1/14/37, Arab Coast, 'Īsā to Pol. Res., 11 and 25 April 1928.
48. IOR, L/P & S/12/3827, Persian Gulf, Trucial Coast, Dubai. Events in October 1938 regarding the Imperial Air route.
49. As mentioned on the subscription cards of *al-Fatḥ* Magazine in Cairo.
50. H. Wahbah, *Khamsun Ama Fi Jazirat al-Arab*, Cairo, 1960, pp.11–12; M. A. Al-Khatib, *Memoirs*, Cairo; A. Rihani, *Around the Coasts of Arabia*, London, 1930, pp.262–3.
51. IOR, R/15/2/B/11, Mani' to Pol. Agent, Baḥrain, May 1941.
52. The scholars of the Āl Mubārak family frequented Abū Dhabī in the late nineteenth century, welcomed by the eminent Shaikh Zāyed b. Khalīfah. Shaikh 'Abd al-Laṭif was an intimate friend of the Ruler of Abū Dhabī, Shaikh Ḥamdān b. Zāyed, and was buried in 1923 in the capital of this state.
53. IOR, ibid., Resolutions of the Majlis regarding Education Department, 25 Ramadan 1357 (20 November 1938).
54. Lorimer, I Part I A, op.cit., pp.633, 759, 763, 772.
55. R. Wingate, *Not in the Limelight*, London, 1959, pp.88–92.
56. OA, Irade 1294H. (1877), Hariciye, 16643, From Ḥusain Hasib, Turkish Consul Bombay, to Minister of Foreign Affairs (Constantinople).
57. Lorimer, I Part I A, op.cit., p.348.
58. IOR, L/P & S/10/827, Bushire Monthly Reports 1912–1925, 'Īsā to Cox October 1912 and January 1913.
59. Private Interview with Aḥmad b. Sulayyim.
60. IOR, L/P & S/12/3767, News and Intelligence Report of 1 to 15 November 1937.
61. IOR, R/15/1/14/49, Monthly Summary, July 1930.
62. B. Thomas, *Alarms and Excursions in Arabia*, London, 1931, p.261.
63. IOR, L/P & S/12/3767, op.cit.
64. Lorimer, II B, op.cit., p.1758.
65. IOR, R/15/1/14/29, 'Ajmān Affairs, 'Īsā b. 'Abd al-Latif to Pol. Res. 29 June 1920; Pol. Res., to Shaikh of 'Ajmān, 26 July 1920; 'Īsā to Pol. Res. 11 September 1920; SNO to Pol. Res. 13 January 1921.
66. IOR, R/15/1/14/30, Arab Coast, Report from 'Īsā to Pol. Res. 22 July 1923; 'Īsā to Pol. Res. 17 January 1924.
67. IOR, R/15/1/14/37 Arab Coast, 'Īsā to Pol. Res., 19 November 1924.
68. IOR, R/15/1/14/40, Arab Coast, 'Īsā b. 'Abd al-Latif, to Pol. Res., 22 October 1925; 'Īsā to Pol. Res. 3 December 1925; Notables of Shārjah to Pol. Res., 26 December 1925.
69. IOR, R/15/1/14/30, Arab Coast, Shārjah. 'Ajmān Dispute, report by Pol. Res., 23 January 1934.
70. IOR, R/15/1/14/40, Arab Coast, 'Īsā to Pol. Res., 25 March 1926; SNO to Pol. Res., 17 June 1926.
71. IOR, R/15/1/14/40, 'Īsā to Pol. Res., 26 June 1926.
72. IOR, R/15/1/14/30, Residency Agent to Pol. Res., 16 October 1927 and 28 November 1928.
73. IOR, L/P & S/12/30/3, Shārjah and Rās al-Khaimah; SNO to Pol. Res., 11 February 1931; SNO to Pol. Res., 25 February 1931; Pol. Res., to SGI, 2 March 1931.
74. IOR, R/15/1/14/48, Ḥamriyyah, Pol. Agent to Pol. Res., 18 September 1937.
75. IOR, L/P & S/12/30/3, Shārjah Affairs Pol. Res. to SGI, 27 March 1938.
76. IOR, L/P & S/12/3767, 1 to 15 January 1939.
77. IOR, L/P & S/12/3827, Dubai Affairs, Residency Agent to Pol. Agent, Baḥrain, 27 May 1940.
78. IOR, R/15/1/14/2, Arab Coast.
79. IOR, R/15/1/244, Successions of Shaikhs of Rās al-Khaimah, Residency Agent to Cox, 10 June 1908.
80. IOR, R/15/1/14/6, Trevor to SGI, 22 December 1920.
81. IOR, R/15/14/40, 'Īsā to Pol. Res., 26 June 1926.
82. IOR, R/15/1/14/6, Arab Coast, 'Īsā to Pol. Res., 16 January 1927.
83. IOR, R/15/1/14/9, SNO to Pol. Res., 10 September 1928.
84. IOR, R/15/1/14/49, Monthly Summary 1929–31, June 1930.

85. IOR, R/15/1/14/38, Shārjah Residency, 'Īsā to Pol. Res., 28 November 1929.
86. Among them 'Ali al-Maḥmūd, 'Abdullah b. Aḥmad al-Mannā'ī, Saif b. Aḥmad al-Abdūlī and Sālim b. Khamis, the maternal uncle of the Ruler, Sulṭān b. Ṣaqr.
87. CAB, 51/8, Fowle to SGI, 16 November 1934.
88. IOR, L/P & S/12/3767, News and Intelligence Report of September 1933.
89. IOR, R/15/14/9, Ṭanb (1912–34), SNO to Pol. Res., 26 October 1933.
90. IOR, R/15/Y14/10, Ṭanb (1934–5), Sultān b. Salīm to Fowle, 29 March 1935; Ī'sā to Fowle, 10 April 1935.
91. IOR, L/P & S/12/30/3, SNO to Pol. Res., 10 June 1932. R/15/1/14/43, Pol. Agent to SGI, 16 November 1934.
92. IOR, R/15/1/14/38, A Circular from Pol. Res. to Pol. Agent, Muscat, 8 December 1936.
93. IOR, R/15/1/14/45, Kalbā Affairs, Pol. Agent, Baḥrain, to Residency Agent Shārjah, 4 May 1937; Residency Agent, Shārjah to Pol. Agent, Baḥrain, 5 May 1937; Residency Agent, Shārjah to Pol. Agent, Baḥrain, 8 May 1937 and 12 May 1937; Telegram Pol. Res., Bushire to Pol. Agent, Baḥrain 17 June 1937; Telegram from SNO to Pol. Res., 21 June 1937; Telegram Pol. Res., to Pol. Agent, 22 June 1937; Telegram Pol. Agent to Pol. Res., 25 June 1925; Sultān b. Salīm to Pol. Res., 10 July 1937.
94. Sa'īd, op.cit., p.247.
95. IOR, R/15/1/14/41, Capture of Dubai Dhow, SNO to Pol. Res., 23 August 1928.
96. Māni' was the son of the late Ruler, Rāshid b. Maktūm, who had died in 1894, when Māni' was very young. He was educated in the traditional national school in Dubai and was known for his literary interests. At his home in Dīrah, Māni' established a large library; moreover, he subscribed to many Arab newspapers and magazines. It took him three years to draw up his map of the pearl fisheries of the Gulf, printed in 1941 in Bombay. In politics he and his brothers co-operated with the sons of Buṭī b. Suhail, but were strongly opposed to the other ruling branch of Sa'īd b. Maktūm. Both families lived in Dīrah whilst Shaikh Sa'īd's family lived across the inlet in Dubai proper. Māni' was in trade and became a leading pearl merchant. He travelled extensively, mostly to Bombay on business, and gained a wide circle of friends, among whom the closest were Shaikh Ḥamad b. 'Īsā, Ruler of Baḥrain, and the wealthy merchant Muḥammad 'Ali Zainal in Bombay. In 1923 he met the Tunisian nationalist leader Tha'ālibī in Bombay and twice invited him to Dubai.
97. Sa'īd, op.cit., p.250.
98. IOR, L/P & S/12/3827, File 30/107, Dubai Affairs, SNO to Pol. Res., 21 May 1929; Captain J. M. Allyne *Lupin* to Pol. Res., 15 April 1929; Haworth to Allyne, 17 April 1929; Report of Captain Allyne, 21 April 1929.
99. IOR, R/15/1/14/41, SNO Report, 10 September 1928.
100. IOR, L/P & S/12/3767, 16 May to 15 August 1936.
101. IOR, R/15/2/B/13 News Report, January 1936.
102. IOR, R/15/1/227, Pol. Agent to Pol. Res., 15 March 1938; Residency Agent, Shārjah to Pol. Res., 15 March 1938; Pol. Res., to SGI, 21 March 1938.
103. Sa'īd, op.cit., pp.254–5.
104. IOR, ibid., Report of Pol. Agent on his visit to the Coast, 25 March 1938; Weightman to SGI, 27 March 1938.
105. IOR, L/P & S/12/3767, 16 May to 15 June 1938.
106. DSA, Decimal Files 1930–39, Box 7055, from J. C. Satterthwaite, Chargé d'Affaires, Baghdād, to Secretary of State, Washington, 14 September 1938. G.A Politik, Arabien, Grobba, Baghdād, to Auswertige Amt, Berlin, 7 Mars 1939.
107. IOR, L/P & S/12/3767, 16–30 June and 1–15 August 1938.
108. IOR, L/P & S/12/3827, Fowle to Shaikh Sa'īd, 1 October 1938.
109. IOR, L/P & S/12/3767, 1–31 October 1938.
110. IOR, R/15/2/B/31, Disturbances on the Trucial Coast, Letters from the Majlis to Shaikh Sa'īd.
111. Sa'īd, op.cit., pp.256, 261–2.
112. IOR, L/P & S/12/3827, IO to SGI, 29 April 1939; Fowle's text for broadcasting 12 April 1939.
113. IOR, R/15/3/B/11, Political Agency, Baḥrain, Mani' to Pol. Agent, 24 May 1941.

114. Hawley, op.cit., p.227, 237, 243–8; Anthony, op.cit., pp.154–5, 162.
115. M. T. Sadik and W. P. Snavely, *Bahrain, Qatar, and the United Arab Emirates*, London, 1972, p.210.
116. Sadik, ibid., p.100.
117. Sadik, ibid., p.106.
118. Anthony, op.cit., p.124.
119. Anthony, ibid., pp.124–6.
120. M. M. Abdullah, *Two Glorious Years in the History of Abū Dhabī*, Beirut, 1968, pp. 114–5.
121. Abdullah, ibid., pp.120–3.

Western Neighbours of the Trucial States

I Geographical Introduction

II The Qaṭar and Ottoman Dispute over al-'Udaid, 1871–1913

III The British and Ibn Sa'ūd's Policy towards the Trucial Coast up to 1939

IV Negotiations Concerning Abū Dhabī's Frontiers with Sa'ūdi Arabia, 1934–8

V The Post-War Period and the Agreement of 1975

VI Settlement of the Maritime Boundaries of Abū Dhabī and Qaṭar

Western Neighbours of the [illegible]

[illegible]

3 Western Neighbours of the Trucial States

I Geographical Introduction

Since Abū Dhabī occupies the entire western region of the Trucial States, its problems with western neighbours are of crucial significance for the study of the whole Trucial Coast. Between 1871 and 1913 the source of friction lay in Abū Dhabī's relations with Qaṭar and the Ottomans, but since 1923 the frontier dispute has been mainly with Sa'ūdī Arabia. During the first period, and also between 1933 and 1939, the main area of dispute was al-'Udaid, but after the Second World War the frontier problem spread eastward to cover Līwā oases and the al-Buraimī area.

The al-'Udaid area stretches east of the al-Jāfūrah desert and comprises five main areas. The first lies south of the Qaṭar peninsula between Wakrah and Khūr al-'Udaid, which includes the two wells of Sakāk and Ambāk built by groups of the Āl Murrah tribe, while the second comprises the al-'Udaid inlet and its small peninsula, with the ruins and wells of the al-'Udaid old city in the northeastern corner. The Qibaisāt tribe established themselves in Dalmā island as pearl divers and traders, and during the pearl season took water from al-'Udaid and set up a temporary camp near the wells, while the Maḥāribah, together with groups of the Manāṣīr tribe, used the al-'Udaid peninsula for pasture in winter. The third important area is al-'Uqal, a name which indicates that the wells have abundant water near the surface; they stretch from north to south, parallel to the coast and close to the track which connects Abū Dhabī with Qaṭar and are divided between the Āl Murrah and the Manāṣīr tribes. The wells of Sawdā Nathīl, 'Uqlat al-Manāṣīr, 'Uqlat al-Rimth and 'Uqlat al-Nakhlah belong to the Manāṣīr tribe, whilst Raghwān and Hilaiwīn belong to Āl Murrah tribe. The fourth area is al-Mijann, surrounded by the al-Yasāt and Ghāghah group of islands which were important during the pearl season. Ba'yā and Sil', famous for their sweet and abundant water, were used frequently by the Maḥāribah and Qibaisāt tribes, who had stone houses on Ghāghah island. The Mazārī', a branch of the Banī Yās, and the Manāṣīr tribe in winter roamed the hinterland of al-Mijann, where to the south lies the well of Bunayyān, owned by the Āl Murrah tribe. The fifth area is Sabkhat Maṭṭī, consisting of salt marshes that are for the most part uncrossable in winter, extending along twenty miles of coast and inland for fifty. The well of Ṣafq, twenty-five miles inland between the

Sabkhat Maṭṭī and Mijann, was of significance in the frontier discussion. Sabkhat Maṭṭī, particularly the northern part, is considered the *dīrah* of the Manāṣīr.[1]

The Līwā oases, which comprise fifty-two settlements fifty miles south of Dhafrah, run parallel to the Ṭarīf coast. They have abundant water wells and groves of palm trees in the depression below the high dunes. The oases are inhabited by members of the Banī Yās federation and the Manaṣīr tribe, both of which belong to the political Hināwī Party and the Mālikī Sunnī sect. The al-Kadan area south of Līwā oases is roamed mainly by the 'Awāmir tribe, whose *dīrah* stretches eastwards to Umm al-Zamūl wells, fifty miles south of Buraimī. Ten ancient forts, mainly in ruins, are still scattered throughout the villages of Līwā Oases, which in the later 1940s, when they became a subject of frontier dispute, were not fully populated, many of the inhabitants having migrated during the nineteenth century to Abū Dhabī. However, the owners of the palm groves from the Manāṣīr and Banī Yās tribes usually congregated in Līwā in the summer to gather the date harvest.

The Buraimī oasis, a fertile and populated area named after the largest of its nine villages, is the centre of a tract of land called al-Jaw. Its position at the head of Wādī al-Jizī makes it the meeting point of the routes connecting the Bāṭinah coast and inner 'Omān with al-Ḥasā and the towns on the Trucial Coast, Abū Dhabī, Dubai, Shārjah, and Rās al-Khaimah. Thus strategic and economic factors combine to give Buraimī local importance in 'Omān.

The nine villages of the Buraimī oasis were divided in the late eighteenth century between the Na'īm, the Ghāfirī and the Dhawāhir who are Hināwī. Of the three villages in the oasis which are now in the Sultanate of 'Omān, two, S'arā and Buraimī, are inhabited by Āl Bū-Khrībān, and the third, Hamāsā, by Āl Bū-Shāmis. Both these groups are branches of the Ghāfirī Na'īm tribe and are Hanbalī. They adopted the Wahhābī principles in the early nineteenth century after the Sa'ūdī occupation of the oasis, an event which influenced the history of the Buraimī area and the recent dispute concerning it. The Dhawāhir tribe own most of the remaining six villages, of which the important one is al-'Ain. Since the early decades of the nineteenth century some Banī Yās have been living in al-'Ain too, and on the two estates of al-Jāhilī and Mas'ūdī established by Shaikh Zāyed b. Khalīfah and his eldest son. Dhawāhir and the Banī Yās, who are Hināwī, did not espouse The Wahhābī doctrines but maintained their adherence to their respective Shāfi'ī and Mālikī sects. Thus the recent history of Buraimī, together with its economic and strategic factors, gives the area international importance in modern times.

II The Qatar and Ottoman Dispute over al-'Udaid, 1871–1913

To understand the fundamentals of the relations between Qaṭar and Abū

Dhabī it is important to go back twenty years before the true beginning of this study. For it was during the 1870s that the inland frontier between the two states was settled by the British, who in the 1880s conclusively suppressed all attempts by Qaṭar to challenge their decision, so that it remained effective until 1971.

In 1783 the Āl Khalīfah family had moved their capital from Zubārah in Qaṭar to Manāmah in Baḥrain. This, together with the subsequent sanguinary dispute within the ruling family, had the effect of weakening its authority over the tribes in the Qaṭar mainland, among whom a feeling of independence gradually developed and became apparent in the 1860s under the leadership of Shaikh Muḥammad b. Thānī and his ambitious son Jāsim, the founder of independent Qaṭar. This movement showed itself in the growing towns of al-Bid' (later called Dōḥah) and Wakrah, which lie near the pearl fishing islands of Dalmā and Ghāghah, owned by the Banī Yās of Abū Dhabī, who viewed the increasing strength of their neighbours with some apprehension. Therefore, when in October 1867 Shaikh Muḥammad b. Khalīfah, Ruler of Baḥrain, asked his close friend Shaikh Zāyed b. Khalīfah of Abū Dhabī to come to his help against a rising of his dependants at al-Bid' and Wakrah, Zāyed immediately complied.[2] This attack embittered relations between Qaṭar and Abū Dhabī for many decades to come. Relations became still worse after 1869, when Khādim b. Buṭī, the head of the Qibaisāt tribe in Abū Dhabī, after a dispute with Shaikh Zāyed, migrated with his tribe to al-'Udaid.

In July 1871 Shaikh Jāsim b. Thānī, dissatisfied with British policy, invited the Turkish authorities to place a guard at al-Bid.[3] The British took the view that this was contrary to assurances given to them by the Porte, thus verifying the rumour reported from Baghdād that a Turkish expeditionary force would eventually take possession of Baḥrain, Muscat and the Arab coast (see Chapter 1, p. 24). Meanwhile, earlier that year, Shaikh Zāyed had asked the British authorities for permission to act against his absconding dependants, the Qibaisāt, at al-'Udaid. As Jāsim b. Thānī had offered the Turkish flag to Khādim b. Buṭī, this local quarrel now took on a deeper significance in British circles. Colonel Pelly made comprehensive enquiries about the sovereignty of al-'Udaid, consulting especially the friendly Shaikh Muḥammad b. Thānī, and reached the conclusion that it came under the jurisdiction of the Shaikh of Abū Dhabī. Nevertheless, to avoid violating the Maritime Treaty and provoking Turkish intervention, Pelly denied Zāyed permission to send his forces by sea. It was not long, however, before it came clear to the British that the Turkish presence in Qaṭar had encouraged Shaikh Jāsim and Shaikh Mubārak b. Naṣīr, the claimant to the Emirate of Baḥrain, to defy their authority.

On 16 September 1876 Prideaux, the officiating Political Resident, in a detailed letter to the Government of India, expressed the view that the disorder in Qaṭar, al-Haṣā and al-'Udaid pointed to the urgent need for some kind of understanding between the British and the Turks over their respective areas of jurisdiction in the Gulf. He suggested that a line beginning at a point somewhat to the south of ‘Uqair would be very advantageous to British interests and would enable Britain to put an immediate end to the piratical spirit which was spreading among the Arab tribes. ‘In fact Prideaux was more than thirty years ahead of his time. The line of demarcation which he proposed, and whose eventual location he predicted with considerable accuracy, did not come into being until the Anglo–Turkish Convention of 29 July 1913.’[4]

To deal with the immediate problem, the trouble at al-‘Udaid, Prideaux recommended in February 1877 that he should be authorised to bring about a reconciliation between the Qibaisāt and Shaikh Zāyed. If this failed, Zāyed should be helped to reassert his authority over al‘Udaid by force. This proposal, which the Government of India welcomed as an opportunity to curb the spread of Ottoman influence over the Trucial States, was accepted in May 1877. In March 1878 Colonel Ross accompanied Zāyed in an attack on al-‘Udaid, and the Qibaisāt fled to al-Bid‘. In May the Grand Vizier protested to the British Ambassador in Constantinople about the British attack on al-‘Udaid, which he considered Turkish territory. It is clear from Ross's report of 20 January 1879 and from Viceroy Lytton's despatch on 22 May, that the Government of India felt the need to reach some definite agreement with the Turks about frontiers in the area and was prepared to acknowledge the Turkish presence in Qaṭar on condition that the Turks recognised British treaties regarding Baḥrain and the Trucial Coast. When Britain made those overtures the Turks failed to seize the opportunity and it never recurred.[5]

In fact the British abandoned their conciliatory attitude towards the Ottomans and in 1880 the Government of India gave its long-withheld permission for British Naval officers to pursue what they considered to be Gulf pirates into Turkish waters. (All disturbances and sea attacks recorded at that time were instigated mainly by political motives, but were described by the British authorities as acts of piracy.) Furthermore, Colonel Ross was authorised to deal directly with Shaikh Jāsim, ignoring the Turks. British authorities in the Gulf also felt the need for new agreements with Baḥrain and the Trucial shaikhs to secure British interests and authority, so they concluded a treaty with the former in 1880 and with the Trucial Coast in 1892. At the beginning of 1880 Zāyed sent his son Khalīfah on a conciliatory mission to Khādim b. Buṭī at al-Bid‘ and the Qibaisāt tribe returned to Abū Dhabī. On 16 November 1880 Jāsim sent a letter to Zāyed requesting payment of some debts incurred by Khādim b. Buṭī, who he claimed had secretly left al-Bid‘ with his tribe.

During the fishing season of 1881 several clashes rook place between members of the Qibaisāt tribe and the inhabitants of Wakrah, which gave rise to an exchange of letters between Shaikh Jāsim and the Political Resident.

Jāsim's most important letter to Ross was that of 11 May 1881, in which he stated his intention of rebuilding al-'Udaid as a home for his dependants. Ross replied on 19 May to the effect that the British had already decided that al-'Udaid belonged to the chief of Abū Dhabī and that it was therefore impossible to allow any of Jāsim's people to settle there. Ross ended by recommending Jāsim to abandon his plan. When on 1 June 1881 Jāsim repeated his request for possession of al-'Udaid, adding a protest that Zāyed had given his subjects orders to arrest the Qaṭarīs coming to Banī Yās islands, Ross became exasperated; he was convinced that Jāsim's plan had been instigated by the Turks. So on 30 June 1881 he warned Jāsim 'to dismiss the illusion totally from his mind', and instructed the Residency Agent at Shārjah to tell Zāyed to keep a careful watch on the movements of Jāsim and his followers at al-'Udaid and its neighbourhood. In July 1881 Ḥājjī Abū al-Qāsim visited Dalmā himself and asked the Indian traders from al-Bid' to collect all information about Jāsim's plans.[6]

Jāsim, irritated by Ross's forceful reply and despairing of ever being able to reclaim his debts, at the end of the year began sending groups of the Banī Hājir tribe to raid Abū Dhabī territory. Further, he now directed his enmity towards the Banian traders in al-Bid'. In a letter of 12 November 1881 and in subsequent correspondence, Ross indicated that Jāsim's irritation seemed to be caused by 'my refusal to permit him to occupy 'Udaid, and some other matters'. Ross's animosity became clear when he continued;

> This Jāsim had always shown a jealous and even a hostile spirit as regards British authority in the Gulf, and had been greatly instrumental in bringing the Turks to Dōḥah. This person further trades in pearls and other merchandise and, wishing to get the whole traffic of al-Bid' into his own hands, would gladly drive the Indian merchants from the place by any means in his power.

He explained that by this policy Jāsim had been trying to test whether under Turkish patronage he was secure against the British.[7]

Jāsim now directed his hostility against the British. He wrote to Ross on 30 January 1882, and again on 9 March, demanding that all the Banian traders should leave for Baḥrain. After an abortive visit by Mirzā Abū al-Qāsim, the Residency Agent in Baḥrain, to al-Bid', he reported to the British that Jāsim had been 'to some extent influenced and encouraged by evil advisers who told him the Europeans had been ejected from Egypt, and that his connections with the Turkish Government would save him from unpleasant consequences'. On 22 July 1882 all the Banians left al-Bid' for Baḥrain on HMS *Woodlark*. On 24 August 1882, fearing that other chiefs might adopt similar tactics and that the position of British subjects in the Gulf might be endangered, Ross asked the Government of India for permission to use force and require Jāsim to pay the Banians Rs. 50,000 in compensation, a demand which the Viceroy endorsed and forwarded to the Foreign Office. On 4 November 1882 the Foreign Office agreed to Ross's request but limited the compensation to Rs. 8,000 and emphasised that if force had to be used every effort should be made to avoid actual collision with any Turkish troops at al-Bid'. On 3 December 1882 Ross landed at al-Bid' from two ships, and after long and patient negotiations Jāsim paid the required sum.[8]

On 10 February 1883 the British Ambassador to Constantinople received from the Porte a protest against Colonel Ross's proceedings as contrary to international law, and calling for a refund of the idemnity exacted. On 7 May 1883 the British replied that they did not admit the Turkish claim to sovereignty in al-Bid'. On 16 August the Turkish Ambassador in London reasserted the Sultan's sovereignty over Qaṭar, and on 31 August Lord Granville, in accordance with a suggestion from the India Office, stated explicitly that HM Government was unable to accept the views of the Porte on this subject: they were not prepared to waive the right to deal directly with the Arab chiefs of the Qaṭar coast.[9] In the four following years the question of al-'Udaid and its frontier lay dormant. On 22 June 1886 the captain of a Turkish warship wrote to Shaikh Zāyed to say that Qaṭar was a port of Nejd, which belonged to the Mutaṣarrif of Baṣrah. The Wālī of Baṣrah, 'Alī Riḍā Pāshā had ordered Jāsim to rebuild al-'Udaid and Zāyed was warned that if he opposed the project in any way he would have to answer for it. On 8 July 1886 Zāyed wrote to Ross informing him of this development and explaining that Jāsim was creating trouble in the pearl fisheries.[10]

The years 1888 and 1889 witnessed important developments in the relations between Qaṭar and Abū Dhabī. The main events took place in Qaṭar, the Līwā oases and Dhafrah. At the end of March 1888 Jāsim attacked Bainūnah, the western part of al-Dhafrah, just to the east of Sabkhat Maṭṭī in Abū Dhabī territory. The Turkish warship, already stationed at al-Bid', took part in the transport of Jāsim's ammunition and provisions to al-Sil'. Jāsim returned from the expedition with 400 camels and twenty-two Abū Dhabī hostages; he had told his friend Rāshid b. Maktūm, Shaikh of Dubai, about the proposed raid but had carefully sent the message after he had put to sea. All this put Dubai, who based her diplomacy on wide friendship with her neighbours, in an awkward position. Shaikh Zāyed was the head of the Hināwī party on the coast of 'Omān, to which Dubai belonged, and Shaikh Jāsim was moreover an established friend. Rāshid b. Maktūm promptly informed Zāyed of Jāsim's intended attack, but it was too late. On 30 April 1888 Zāyed, considering the attack a flagrant violation of the maritime treaty, not only by Jāsim but by the Turks too, protested to Ross. On 5 May the Political Resident ordered the Residency Agents at Shārjah and Baḥrain to investigate and they both reported that the Turks had taken part and that Jāsim's armaments and supplies had been transported by sea.[11]

During this month the emissaries of Ibn Rashīd, Ruler of Jabal Shammar, appeared in Constantinople for the first time and were hospitably received.

The special attention paid to them was noticed by the British Embassy, but the significance of this did not dawn on them until a few months later, when the Government of India asked them to protest to the Porte about a proposed attack on 'Omān by Ibn Rāshid.[12] At the end of May 1888 Shaikh Zāyed prepared a well-planned retaliation, asking the Shaikh of Dubai, as well as the other Trucial shaikhs, to join him. Furthermore, he gave orders forbidding access to the pearl fisheries to all the inhabitants of Qaṭar—this mainly with the intention of excluding spies who might observe his movements. All the Hināwī tribes on the Trucial Coast at once rallied to Zāyed. The Ghāfirī shaikhs took a neutral stand but the Banī Qatab tribe responded. The Ruler of Dubai, on whom Zāyed really counted, sent some of his bodyguards and a few other men.

The group which the Ruler of Abū Dhabī had sent to Qaṭar headed by his son Khalīfah arrived in complete secrecy at dawn on 14 June 1888. They launched a surprise attack on the town and the bazaar, then quickly withdrew to prepare an ambush. Many of the pursuers were killed, among them Jāsim's favourite son, 'Alī.[13] Jāsim, inflamed, now widened the scope of his diplomacy in every direction to secure allies in an attack on Zāyed. He wrote first to 'Abdullah b. Thaniyyān, one of the notables of the refugee Sa'ūdī family, who had been a member of the Council of State in Constantinople for some years. He clearly reminded b. Thaniyyān that the extremely rich territory of 'Omān was a part of Nejd, which by rights belonged to Āl Sa'ūd. In the absence of Āl Sa'ūd, Zāyed had seized power there and was tyrannising the people, who, said Jāsim, had come to him for help. He asked b. Thaniyyān to approach the Porte and obtain their sanction for an invasion of 'Omān. Jāsim also made several subtle attempts through other channels to arouse Turkish interests in 'Omān.[14] At the same time he wrote to Ibn Rashīd, proposing an invasion of 'Omān and promising to help with money, ammunition and men. Being a Wahhābī and well acquainted with the local politics of the Trucial Coast, Jāsim tried to play on the religious elements among the Ghāfirī group in 'Omān and their traditional enmity towards Zāyed. He wrote to the shaikhs of the Na'īm in Buraimī as well as the Shaikhs of Shārjah, 'Ajmān, Umm al-Qaiwain and Rās al-Khaimah calling on them to join forces with Ibn Rashīd and himself when they invaded 'Omān. Lastly, he sent presents to his friend the Shaikh of Dubai, informing him of Turkish intentions, and assuring him of the safety of his town. He also wrote to Ross twice in June and again in July 1888, complaining bitterly of the Political Resident's partiality for Zāyed, which had the effect of encouraging him in his aggressiveness towards Jāsim.

Ross, who was already disturbed by the rumours of an impending invasion of 'Omān by Ibn Rāshid and by the increased Turkish guard at al-Bid', saw that this local quarrel was threatening to develop into a clash between Britain and the Ottomans. He sent three letters: the first to Jāsim b. Thānī on 8 July 1888, offering his condolences on the death of his son, denying his accusation of partiality and exhorting him to fulfil his maritime obligations towards the British and confine his quarrels with Zāyed to the land. His second letter was to the Residency Agent in Shārjah, on 1 August 1888, telling him to advise the Shaikh of Dubai to be wise enough to avoid involving himself in Jāsim's projects. The third letter was to Shaikh Zāyed on 10 August 1888 firmly pointing out his responsibility for the attack on Qaṭar by the Manāṣīr tribe; as for any situation which might develop from this, Zāyed was reminded that according to the treaty the British were bound to defend him only at sea and not on land.[15]

Between August 1888 and the end of the year a series of developments occurred which ended by forcing Jāsim to make his attack alone. First, the British made representations in Constantinople. In July the India Office asked the Foreign Office to make enquiries at the Porte about the rumoured invasion. On 19 September the British Embassy in Constantinople addressed a note to the Porte on this subject. The Porte denied all knowledge of a proposed invasion, but the Embassy pointed out on 1 October that the constant exchange of envoys and presents between Ibn Rashīd and Constantinople in recent months appeared to give substance to the rumour.[16] Ross went to Qaṭar and had an important meeting with Jāsim on 5 October. For the first time Jāsim asserted that al-Sil' in al-Mijann belonged to Qaṭar and not to Abū Dhabī. When Ross enquired about the rumoured invasion of 'Omān by Ibn Rāshid, Jāsim answered that it was true, adding that the project was sanctioned by the Porte. Ross gave Jāsim a harsh answer, telling him that his frontiers must not be extended beyond the limits of Wakrah. After this, on 28 October, Ross asked the Government of India to provide him with three warships to protect British interests in 'Omān if necessary.[17]

More fatal to Jāsim's plans for a large-scale invasion was the fact that Ibn Rāshid and the Sultan were unable to agree on the details of the project. Ibn Rashīd asked the Sulṭān to place the province of al-Ḥasā under his jurisdiction as a prize, but the Sulṭān wanted to turn Nejd into an Ottoman vassal province. In consequence, Ibn Rāshid repeatedly postponed his expedition and ended by abandoning it altogether. Thirdly, the two persons to whom Jāsim entrusted his diplomatic correspondence turned out to be opposed to his project. 'Abdullah b. Thaniyyān, as a member of the Sa'ūdī family and at enmity with Ibn Rashīd, did not welcome a project which might extend the latter's power. Instead of pressing Jāsim's case at the Porte, he advised Jāsim to make peace with Zāyed. Further, Jāsim had entrusted his main negotiations with Ibn Rāshid to Nāṣir b. Mubārak of the Āl Khalīfah family of Baḥrain, an intimate friend of Zāyed. Instead of recommending Jāsim's proposal to Ibn Rashīd, he advised him against it. In the end Ibn Rashīd gave no help beyond a request to the heads of the Banī Hājir tribe to support Jāsim.

By the end of December Jāsim had despaired of receiving effective help and decided to attack on his own. He now spread a rumour that Ibn Sabhān, the Governor of Ibn Rashīd in Riyādh, and 'Adb al-Raḥmān b. Faiṣal, the head of the Sa'ūdī family, were accompanying him in his attack. In fact he was alone and concentrated his attack on the Līwā oases on the southern frontiers of Abū Dhabī emirate. Meanwhile Dubai now united with Shaikh Zāyed and the Ruler of Muscat in a strong Hināwī group against the expected invasion by Ibn Rashīd. The Sulṭān of Muscat closed the passes in the mountains near Buraimī which gave access to the Bāṭinah coast. Zāyed mustered his forces in Abū Dhabī, obliging his enemy to make a long desert march and placing himself well against any surprise attack by the Banī Ghāfir.[18]

When Jāsim arrived in Līwā he found only old men, women and children, with a few Banī Yās and Manāṣīr warriors, whom he captured in Khannūr fort. On 8 March 1889, on the basis of accumulated reports, Ross wrote to the Government of India accusing Jāsim of atrocities at Khannūr. The Political Resident now adopted a new policy of mutual co-operation between the British and the Turks to put an end to the dispute; in addition, he asked for negotiations with the Turks to settle the question of Ottoman sovereignty in these areas.[19]

The Banī Yās, infuriated by Jāsim's behaviour at Līwā, blamed Zāyed for leaving the area undefended and asked for a retaliation. Zāyed, with the Ruler of Dubai and substantially aided by Muscat, prepared forces for an attack. In March, he asked the Ghāfirī tribes and shaikhs to join him, but all of them refused and it was discovered that Jāsim had been writing to them, appealing to their religious feelings as Wahhābī and exhorting them not to co-operate with Zāyed.

In April Jāsim sent two letters to Ross, in reply to his accusation of having sent military supplies to al-Sil' by sea. In both letters Jāsim repeated his assertion of October 1888 that al-Sil' belonged to Qaṭar, claiming that it was an established fact that the limit of 'Omān on his side was Dhafrah, which lies immediately to the east of Sabkhat Maṭṭī.[20] In the same month the Porte entrusted the defence of Qaṭar against Zāyed's expected invasion to General 'Ākif Pashā; on 6 May the general sent a letter to Zāyed, warning him not to violate Qaṭar territory, and it seems that this was effective. Although Zāyed, accompanied by the Shaikh of Dubai, reached the south of Qaṭar in June they limited their activities to punitive measures against some tribes there.[21]

Influenced by the effect of these disturbances on the pearl fisheries and on trade, Ross wrote to the Government of India on 18 February 1890 suggesting the need for a settlement with the Turks and when asked what Turkish rights he would recognise and under what conditions, and within what limits, Ross replied on 15 March that if Turkey were willing to respect British interests in 'Omān and Baḥrain, 'after frank explanations, to engage in co-operation in maintaining order by sea and land, I think that we might recognise Bid'a as a Turkish port and military outpost, *status quo* being maintained south and east of that point'. Nothing came of this, but Ross was careful to handle the situation with tact and moderation. At the beginning of 1890 the British asked the Ruler of Baḥrain to arrange a reconciliation between Jāsim and Zāyed and although neither of them responded at once, the dispute died naturally that year.[22]

During the 1890s the pattern of relationships between the Turks, Qaṭar and the British underwent a profound change. The Turks, in maintaining their uncompromising attitude to recent British overtures, lost another valuable opportunity and antagonised the British. Jāsim, on the other hand, responded to the tact and restraint which Ross had shown in his later dealings and appreciated the British attempt to effect a reconciliation between Qaṭar and Abū Dhabī. This, in turn, accelerated Jāsim's understanding with the British, who throughout the last twenty years had insisted on treating him as an independent ruler and not as a Turkish vassal.[23]

In 1902, simultaneously with an attempt to re-establish contact over Kuwait, the Turks tried to establish small administration units at Zubārah and al-'Udaid, but the project was abandoned when the British showed determination to prevent it, if necessary by force. Indeed the question of establishing formal protection over Qaṭar was proposed by Lord Curzon but vetoed by the Foreign Office.[24] At the same time Zāyed proposed to rebuild al-'Udaid. After protracted discussion, the British, wishing to avoid a serious breach of the *status quo* with the Turks, declined to involve themselves in either of these projects.[25] After the *coup* in 1908 and in consequence of the deterioration in the Turkish position in Kuwait, Qaṭar and the Balkans generally, the military junta in Constantinople agreed eventually to discuss spheres of influence in the Gulf with the British. On 29 July 1913, after two years of negotiations, the Anglo–Ottoman Convention on the Persian Gulf area was signed, bringing a rivalry of forty years' standing to an end. In this convention the Turks totally abandoned their claims to Baḥrain and Qaṭar and gained Kuwait as an autonomous territory within the Ottoman Empire. As the limit of the province of Nejd they agreed upon the 'Blue Line', which begins at a point on the al-Ḥasā coast south of 'Uqair, opposite Zakhnūniyyah island, and runs due south. Although this convention was not ratified, the 'Blue Line' was mentioned in the Anglo–Turkish Treaty determining the frontiers between Aden and Yemen which followed on 5 May 1914 and was duly ratified.[26] It is important to note that the 'Blue Line' was an arbitrary line dictated by the interests of two major powers and was completely unconnected with any natural tribal or geographical boundary.

III The British and Ibn Sa'ud's Policy towards the Trucial Coast up to 1939

Anglo–Sa'ūdī Relations

It is not proposed to give here a detailed history of Anglo–Sa'ūdī relations, but it is important nevertheless to summarise them in order to show how their fluctuations affected the British attitude towards Sa'ūdī policy in 'Omān.

To understand the development of relations between Ibn Sa'ūd and the British in the light of his growing strength and their changing interests it is possible to divide the period into four parts, 1902–14, 1914–18, 1918–29 and the 1930s.

Growing up at the turn of the century, 'Abd al-'Azīz b. Sa'ūd had been introduced to world politics and Western civilisation when a refugee in Kuwait and thus acquired a knowledge his ancestors in the interior had lacked.[27] His experience in Kuwait at a time of conflict between Mubārak and the Ottomans gave him faith in the paramount power of the British, a faith which was strengthened by the growth of Britain's influence in the Middle East after the First World War. Immediately following the daring attack in January 1902 on al-Riyādh, Ibn Sa'ūd wrote to Kemball, the Political Resident, telling him that although he had received overtures from the Russians he would prefer the friendship of Britain. Kemball's scepticism regarding Ibn Sa'ūd's chances of success, together with the Indian Government's policy of non-interference in the politics of the Arabian interior, combined to produce a negative response. Although Ibn Sa'ūd repeatedly solicited British help between 1902–14, the crucial period in his rise to power, he always met with refusal. It should be noted that Ibn Sa'ūd's dealings with the British at this time were always with the Government of India, through the Political Resident in the Gulf. As an example one may quote the telegram from the Secretary of State for India to the Viceroy on 30 September 1904: 'HM Government desire that it should be clearly understood that its interests and influence are to be confined strictly to the coast line of Eastern Arabia and that nothing should be said or done to connect them even indirectly with the warfare now in progress in the interior.'[28]

In 1906 Ibn Sa'ūd made indirect approaches through Shaikh Jāsim b. Thānī, Ruler of Qaṭar, and Shaikh Mubārak of Kuwait to the new Political Resident, Major Cox, to discover what might be the British attitude to his annexing al-Ḥasā and concluding an agreement similar to that made with the Trucial chiefs and the Shaikh of Kuwait. Cox felt that British aloofness from the politics of inner Arabia should not be too exaggerated, and in a letter of 16 September 1906 expressed the view that it would now be advantageous to reach an understanding with Ibn Sa'ūd. Writing on 9 November 1906 Lord Morley, Secretary of State for India, reiterated that British interests should be confined to the coast. Repeated approaches by Ibn Sa'ūd and Cox at the turn of 1906–7 met with the same objection, emphasised by the recommendation from the British Ambassador at Constantinople, Sir Nicholas O'Connor.

After the Young Turks' *coup d'état* of April 1909 Ibn Sa'ūd again experienced Turkish aggression the following year when he realised that his dispute with Ḥusain, the new Sharīf of Mecca, had been instigated by the new régime. In the spring of 1911 Ibn Sa'ūd met a British Official, Captain Shakespear, the Political Agent in Kuwait informally, and close personal relations were established. Although the report Shakespear made in May tallied with Cox's earlier reports, the India Office and the Foreign Office agreed to continue the existing policy unless the Government of India should propose a departure from it, when the question could be considered again.[29]

The British and Turkish negotiations of 1911–13 over the disputes in the Gulf culminated with the Anglo–Turkish Convention in which the Ottomans accepted the 'Blue Line' as the frontier of al-Ḥasâ and Nejd. Ibn Sa'ūd, left to his own resources by the British, waited until 1913 for the opportune moment to attack al-Ḥasâ when the Turks had evacuated most of their troops for their engagements in the Balkans. On 8 May 1913 he invaded al-Ḥasâ and a week later met Captain Shakespear again in the hinterland of Kuwait. Ibn Sa'ūd's sudden occupation of al-Ḥasâ created a delicate situation for the British, who now treated him with great caution. On 13 May Cox pointed out to the Government of India the discrepancy between the draft of the Anglo–Turkish Convention now under consideration, which assumed Turkish presence in al-Ḥasâ, and the fact that it was now occupied by Ibn Sa'ūd. Accordingly the Viceroy reported the situation to London on 31 May 1913, suggesting that

> the Turks acknowledge the realities and with our help to arrange to include in the convention a satisfactory solution of the problem, the basis being that B. Saud should be recognised as autonomous Ruler of Nejd under the suzerainty of the Porte, and that he should be accorded the right to accredit an agent to him as one of the maritime Rulers and make agreements with him, with the knowledge of the Porte, in connection with the suppression of arms traffic, slave trade and piracy, and our mission in the Gulf generally.

In June the Government of India and the Foreign Office thought it impossible at this late hour to raise the question of the status of Nejd without running the risk of wrecking the negotiations with Turkey.

In July Ibn Sa'ūd once again resorted to diplomacy with the Turks, who also sought to recover their position by diplomatic procedures, having no longer the military resources necessary for war. These negotiations opened officially in August and reached a delicate point in November 1913, when the Turks asked for access for their troops to Qaṭīf and 'Uqair on the coast of Ḥasâ and that Ibn Sa'ūd should bind himself absolutely to refer all matters of foreign politics to the Porte and to allow no foreign merchants or agents in his territory as now recognised. However, as these negotiations continued, Ibn Sa'ūd did not despair of the preferred British alliance. In order to open the way for an *entente* he asked Cox for an explanation of the British attitude towards him. Cox recommended that the two parties should meet, which they did at 'Uqair on 15 December, the participants being Ibn Sa'ūd, Shakespear and Trevor, the Political Agent in Baḥrain. 'Abd al-'Azīz then revealed the draft treaty with the Turks which was prejudicial to British interests. It was therefore agreed that Ibn Sa'ūd should postpone concluding the treaty with the Turks for three months, during which time he would await an answer from the British. But having concluded an Anglo–Turkish Convention in July 1913 Britain preferred an understanding between Ibn Sa'ūd and the Turks, with Ibn Sa'ūd under Turkish sovereignty, and therefore gave no answer. So in May 1914 Ibn Sa'ūd was obliged to conclude the Turkish treaty found during the war by the British among Turkish records at Baṣrah, by which he became, at least in name, a Turkish vassal and accepted the office of Turkish Wālī of Nejd.

When the war broke out in 1914 Ibn Sa'ūd was asked by the Sultan to harry the British attack on Baṣrah while the British tried to secure his support. Disappointment in his relations with the British during the previous decade, souring subsequent relations, delayed his response. Eventually, in January 1915 Ibn Sa'ūd disclosed in a discussion with Captain Shakespear that he was anxious for a signed treaty with a solid guarantee of his position under the aegis of Great Britain and of this he gave Shakespear a draft. Discussions occupied the rest of the year and the treaty was signed on 26 December 1915. Ibn Sa'ūd was recognised as independent Ruler of Nejd, Ḥasā and Qaṭīf and was guaranteed hereditary succession to his state; he in turn undertook not to interfere in Kuwait, Baḥrain, Qaṭar and with the Trucial shaikhs.[30]

In 1916, following British support against the Turks, Sharīf Ḥusain declared himself King of the Arabs. Ibn Sa'ūd viewed the move with apprehension and began to suspect British intentions in Arabia. In order to divert rivalry between the two, Cox invited Ibn Sa'ūd to Kuwait in November, when an agreement was reached by which Ibn Sa'ūd undertook to maintain a force of 4,000 in the field against Ibn Rashīd and was promised a monthly subsidy of £5,000 as well as adequate ammunition and arms. This, however, did not avail to reassure Ibn Sa'ūd, who was all too conscious of the central role and preferential treatment accorded to his traditional rival, Ḥusain. Although the British continually pressed Ibn Sa'ūd to launch an attack against Hā'il, Ibn Rāshid's capital, it remained intact till the end of the war.[31]

During the war the Foreign Office took Sharīf Ḥusain's side whilst the Government of India sponsored Ibn Sa'ūd, and at the Cairo Conference in April 1921 Britain decided that Ḥusain be recognised King of Ḥijāz while his son Faiṣal was helped to become King of Iraq. In the same year another son, 'Abdullah, was proclaimed Amīr of Trans-Jordan and Ibn Sa'ūd found himself encircled by enemies set up by the British,[32] so in immediate retaliation he proclaimed himself Sultan of Nejd and in July intensified his siege of Hā'il, which surrendered in November 1921. Then in 1922 the Ikhwān began their raids in Iraq and Trans-Jordan and thus threatened the newly-established British mandates, which made it necessary for Cox to proceed at once to 'Uqair for a meeting with Ibn Sa'ūd, who was now insisting on dealing direct with London, as King Ḥusain did, rather than via the Political Resident in the Gulf. Between them they reached a settlement over the frontiers of Kuwait and the adjacent boundaries of Iraq.[33] By the end of March 1924 the British Government, under public pressure, ended their subsidies to the Arab chiefs; this was a severe blow to Ibn Sa'ūd economically, but he was thereby released from any obligations to follow the British policy regarding Ḥusain.[34]

In September 1924, under Ibn Sa'ūd's orders, the Ikhwān made a successful assault on Tā'if and the road to Mecca lay open. On 5 October 1924 King Ḥusain, unable to resist, abdicated. In July 1925, when it became clear that Ḥijāz would fall into the hands of Ibn Sa'ūd, the British in Trans-Jordan occupied 'Aqabah and Ma'ān, previously part of Ḥijāz, passing them over to Amīr 'Abdullah, which provoked Ibn Sa'ūd.

In the autumn Ibn Sa'ūd personally supervised a tightening of the siege of Madīnah and Jeddah, and the leaders of the Ikhwān, still irked by his control, advanced north, cutting communications between Trans-Jordan and Iraq. Sir Gilbert Clayton was immediately sent by the British Government to convey to Ibn Sa'ūd that the damage to Britain's proposed trans-desert pipeline and to the newly opened motor and air route to Baghdād could not be tolerated. On 1 and 2 November 1925 the two men signed the treaties of Baḥrā and Ḥaddā which in general terms and for seven years settled the frontiers between Sa'ūdi territory and Iraq and Trans-Jordan respectively.[35]

In December 1925 Madīnah and Jeddah surrendered, and in January 1926 Ibn Sa'ūd was proclaimed King of Ḥijāz in the Great Mosque at Mecca. In the following January, feeling more confident, he assumed the title of King of the Ḥijāz and of Nejd and its dependencies. Although by 1927 the main issue between Ibn Sa'ūd and his neighbours, Iraq and Trans-Jordan had been settled, a major area of friction between him and the British remained. The terms of the treaty, which treated Ibn Sa'ūd as a Gulf shaikh under British protection, now seemed to him humiliating and not consonant with his new autonomous status as king, by conquest, of most of Arabia. To discuss this and other problems Clayton came again in the spring of 1927 and on 20 May the Treaty of Jeddah was signed, embodying substantial modifications of the British position, including recognition of Ibn Sa'ūd's complete independence and sovereignty over Ḥijāz, Nejd and its dependencies.[36] For the future, Ibn Sa'ūd's dealings with the British would be direct with the Foreign Office and its legation in Jeddah, not through the Government of India.

The treaty of Jeddah alienated the Ikhwān movement from Ibn Sa'ūd. Its leaders now viewed these agreements as well as the reorganisation of the state on modern lines as a breach of their principles. One main issue which occupied the British at this time was the proposed Imperial Airways route between Baṣrah and Karachi, to which the general feeling of the Ikhwān was violently opposed. When at the end of the year, the British built police posts at widely spaced intervals along the Iraqi frontiers, the Ikhwān associated them with the air route and also suspected that an attack had been planned against them by King Faiṣal of Iraq. The hasty Ikhwān annihilated one of these forward police posts and in January 1928 the Royal Air Force promptly retaliated, pursuing the fleeing Ikhwān into Sa'ūdi territory. This act elicited a bitter protest from Ibn Sa'ūd, for it had poured fuel on the flames of Ikhwān discontent, which developed at once into open rebellion against him. It was only after two years of tact, firmness, much money and effort, that Ibn Sa'ūd succeeded in completely suppressing the revolt in December 1929.[37]

The last period of our study of the relations between Ibn Sa'ūd and the British—the 1930s—is of prime importance, since it was during these years (1934–8) that negotiations took place for settling the frontiers between Abū Dhabī and Sa'ūdī Arabia. During this decade Ibn Sa'ūd achieved several political successes in the Arab world as well as more recognition internationally, and now, free from Ikhwān opposition, he started a wide programme of modernisation and unification of his vast realm, to which he gave the name Kingdom of Sa'ūdi Arabia in 1932. He also established better relations with his Arab neighbours, with Iraq in 1931, Trans-Jordan in 1933 and Egypt in 1936.[38]

During the early 1930s, the majority of the foreign consulates in Jeddah were replaced by legations, after the example of Russia and Britain. Emir Faiṣal, Ibn Sa'ūd's son and Foreign Minister, made a number of trips to the capitals of the world, including Moscow, to introduce his country to international society. The most significant international success was the US recognition of Sa'ūdi Arabia in 1931, achieved after several efforts by Ibn Sa'ūd's friend Amīn al-Rīḥānī in Washington and insistent requests on the part of his Foreign Ministry.[39] After the 1933 American oil concession in al-Ḥasā and the beginning of oil production in 1939 the State Department in Washington was under heavy pressure from the oil company to send a diplomatic representative to Sa'ūdī Arabia. It was not until February 1942 that a small permanent legation was established in Jeddah under the American Minister in Cairo.[40]

The enhanced strength of Ibn Sa'ūd's position among his Arab neighbours and in the international field gave added power to his dealings with Britain. The 1930s produced some misunderstanding between the two nations, but Ibn Sa'ūd, aware that the British were still the paramount power in the Gulf and in the Red Sea, no less than in the past, was statesman enough to continue avoiding any real breach of good relations. In this he was helped by the benevolent attitude of the Foreign Office towards his country, shown in many ways throughout this decade. Rendel, the head of the Eastern Department, speaking at a meeting on 29 June 1937, explained how it had been 'clearly to our British interest that Sa'ūdī Arabia should become as stable and prosperous as possible'.[41]

The issues that clouded Anglo–Sa'ūdī relations were the Imperial Airways route, oil concessions, the abortive negotiations over Abū Dhabī–Qaṭar frontiers and the Palestine question. Although Ibn Sa'ūd had suppressed the Ikhwān revolt he very cautiously maintained a steadfast refusal to yield to the persistent British demand for air facilities. In February 1933 Lloyd Hamilton, representing the California Oil Company and S. Longrigg, representing the Iraq Petroleum Company, arrived in Jeddah, both seeking oil concessions in Sa'ūdī Arabia. This was a momentous point in Anglo–Sa'ūdī relations. Ibn Sa'ūd was in urgent need of new sources of revenue to meet the growing demands of his kingdom, especially as in 1932 the British Government refused his request for a loan and rejected his offer of an oil concession. He was therefore more than willing to grant oil concessions in return for adequate payment. Although Ryan put pressure on Ibn Sa'ūd to secure the concession for IPC it was granted instead to the Americans, who agreed to pay an advance of £50,000 in gold.[42] This not only deprived a British oil company of a source of income but also introduced US State Department interest into Sa'ūdī Arabia; at the same time Britain lost an opportunity to bind the Sa'ūdi Government to them by an important new mutual economic tie.

Ibn Sa'ūd and the Coast of 'Omān

The first Sa'ūdī state (1744–1818) governed al-Buraimī and from there exerted some influence over the rest of 'Omān from 1800 to 1818. The second Sa'ūdī state (1824–92 ruled intermittently in Buraimī for thirty-six years between 1828 and 1839 and 1844 and 1869.[43] This was the heritage that inspired Ibn Sa'ūd at the beginning of his career to regain power over the Trucial States.

Towards the end of 1905 Cox received information that Ibn Sa'ūd had visited Qaṭar and had been welcomed there by Shaikh Jāsim b. Thānī, who had been supplying him with arms and provisions. It was reported that Ibn Sa'ūd was planning a visit to the Trucial Coast and to Muscat to explore the country of his forebears. This news met with varied reactions from the British and the coast of 'Omān. Ibn Sa'ūd in the interior was no threat to the British but for him to arrive at the Gulf coast was a different matter, for the people there were thereby reminded of the harm they had suffered from the Wahhābī a century before. Although Cox was the first British official to sympathise with Ibn Sa'ūd and foresee that he was destined to dominate the politics of the Arabian peninsula, even he was disquieted by the intended visit, whilst the reactions of the rulers and inhabitants of the Trucial Coast were coloured by memories of the past. Ibn Sa'ūd's recent rise to power was mainly welcomed by his sympathisers in Ghāfirī, Shārjah, 'Ajmān, Umm al-Qaiwain, Rās al-Khaimah and the villages of Āl Bū-Shāmis and Na'īm in Buraimī; but his successes at that time were not wholly appreciated among the Hināwī group in Abū Dhabī, Dubai and the Dhawāhir villages in the al-Buraimī area.

Alarmed by the proposed visit, the Shaikh of Abū Dhabī and the Sultan of Muscat, who together now governed the villages of the Buraimī oasis, met at once to discuss the situation. The Government of India decided that Ibn Sa'ūd should be warned against the visit to the coast and told that steps would be taken to frustrate it. Cox had conveyed this message to Ibn Sa'ūd through his friend Shaikh Mubārak of Kuwait.[44]

At the 1911 meeting with Shakespear, Ibn Sa'ūd for the first time revealed to the British his feelings regarding the history of this family in 'Oman, which he considered a Sa'ūdī sphere of influence. In the same year Shaikh Buṭī b. Suhail of Dubai, irritated by the British attack on his city, asked Ibn Sa'ūd for protection. It was not until the Sa'ūdī occupation of al-Ḥasā in May 1913 that Ibn Sa'ūd's designs on the Trucial Coast became apparent and, worried by Ibn Sa'ūd's expansionist moves, the Shaikhs of Abū Dhabī and Dubai met to study the situation. In August the Residency Agent reported that they had decided to mobilise their Bedouins and to take the initiative. Cox immediately advised the two shaikhs of the improbability of an attack by Ibn Sa'ūd and deterred them from provoking hostilities.[45] The submission to Ibn Sa'ūd of the Āl Murrah tribe, who had never accepted Turkish authority, was soon to contribute greatly to his influence on the coast of 'Omān.[46]

Cox and the Viceroy emphasised the urgent need for an amicable understanding with Ibn Sa'ūd. On 9 August 1913 Cox telegraphed to the Government of India that Ibn Sa'ūd

> is in a position to give a varying deal of inconvenience alike in regard to Oman, the Trucial Coast and Qaṭar, which inconvenience an innocuous modus vivendi, arranged if necessary with the knowledge of the Porte, would obviate. It is not a question of any desire to interfere in the politics of Central Arabia. Ibn Sa'ūd is now at the coast, and for us it is a question of a new menace to our interests in the Gulf sphere which we need either to sterilise or protect ourselves against.

The British Government agreed generally with the Government of India and approached the Porte to enter into a friendly exchange of views with Ibn Sa'ūd in order to regularise his relations with the British and the Trucial Coast. In December, in order to reassure the British, the Turks intimated to the Ambassador in Constantinople that Ibn Sa'ūd would shortly be named Mutaṣarrif of Nejd and thus come under Turkish control.[47] When Ibn Sa'ūd, Shakespear and Trevor met the same month at 'Uqair, Ibn Sa'ūd, in spite of his desire for British friendship, worried the other two by his open claims in 'Omān. In a memorandum of the interview this statement occurs:

> In the course of his remarks Ibn Sa'ūd pointed out that though he claimed Trucial 'Omān and Qaṭar as part of his ancestral dominions and could make his power felt there, he was quite willing to meet the wishes of the British Government in regard to them. He hinted that the only reason which restrained him from over-running Qaṭar and possibly

Trucial 'Omān after he had occupied Ḥasā and Qatif was his desire not to alienate the sympathy of the British Government.

Furthermore, Ibn Sa'ūd advised the British that as they were now in Qaṭar, his enemies might take refuge in some of the Trucial States and foment trouble, a situation which would necessitate reprisals and involve him in a confrontation with the British Government which he was anxious to avoid.[48]

Ibn Saūd's conquest of al-Ḥasā had an immediate effect on the Ghāfirī party on the Trucial Coast. We can see an early example of this in January 1914, when the Sultan of Muscat informed the Political Agent of his worries regarding correspondence between Ibn Sa'ūd and the Shaikhs of Umm al-Qaiwain and Buraimī. They had asked Ibn Sa'ūd to come to Buraimī and showed their willingness to help him against the Hināwī party. In Abū Dhabī in the same month Shaikh Ḥamdām b. Zāyed (1912–22) twice expressed his fear of Ibn Sa'ūd to Captain Knox, the Political Agent in Baḥrain, and on 4 October 1914 once again, this time revealing the correspondence and the secret emissaries between Ibn Sa'ūd and the people of 'Omān, giving warning also that if Ibn Sa'ūd intended to come to Buraimī he, the Shaikh, would attack him before he entered Abū Dhabī territory. He explained that the Bedouins who had fled from Ibn Sa'ūd to the Trucial Coast and Qaṭar had done so to escape the burdens he had placed upon them. He concluded his letter with a request for arms and ammunition.

This information stimulated the British to accelerate the negotiations with Ibn Sa'ūd. Eventually British diplomacy succeeded and discussions started in January 1915. The India Office suggested 'that the new treaty should contain a clause binding Ibn Sa'ūd, subject to eventual definition of boundaries, not to interfere with Kuwait, Baḥrain, Qaṭar and the Trucial chiefs'. The treaty which Ibn Sa'ūd signed in December 1915 emphasised two points: the first, non-interference on the Trucial Coast, and the second, the settlement of the boundaries between his territories and Abū Dhabī which was to be discussed later.[49]

Between 1918 and 1930 Ibn Sa'ūd's policy regarding the coast was influenced by two factors: his relations with Britain, and the internal affairs of his country, particularly the fanaticism of the Ikhwān. It was only after 1925 that Ibn Sa'ūd turned his attention actively to the Trucial Coast. Until then he had been totally involved in the west in clashes with King Ḥusain and in the conquest of Ḥijāz; also with the newly established Hashimite states of Iraq and Trans-Jordan in the north.

To gain the support of the Ghāfirī group, who were traditional Wahhābī, he sent teachers and judges from Nejd to Shārjah, 'Ajmān, Umm al-Qaiwain, Rās al-Khaimah and Buraimī, who dominated education, effecting a religious revival and producing strong sympathy for his cause. The two Islamic magazines *al-Manār*, edited by Rashīd Riḍā, and *al-Fatḥ*, edited by Muḥib al-Dīn al Khaṭib, printed in Cairo and read widely in these Wahhābī towns, favoured Ibn Sa'ūd and increased his popularity in these areas. However, early in 1920, at a meeting in Hufūf, the Political Agent in Baḥrain, aware of his tactics, reminded Ibn Sa'ūd of his obligations and advised him not to answer the letters from the Arabs of the Trucial Coast who were also bound by treaties with Britain. The response to Ibn Sa'ūd on the Coast, particularly in Shārjah, was warm and enthusiastic, but he was obliged by the firm British attitude to let this opportunity pass. The Political Agent in Baḥrain gathered from his intelligence, especially after the visit to Baḥrain of B. Khādim from Shārjah, that Ibn Sa'ūd was honouring his assurances at Hufūf and not responding to the demands of his sympathisers.[50]

In dealing with the Hināwī group, Ibn Sa'ūd's representative in al-Ḥasā, 'Abdullah b. Jilwī, employed subtle methods upon the tribes of Abū Dhabī, particularly the Mazārī' and the Manāsīr, living near the Sa'ūdi frontiers. To gain their allegiance, b. Jilwī depended mainly on the warlike Āl Murrah tribe, who in the last few years had joined the Ikhwān and for whom Ibn Sa'ūd had established the two villages of Sakāk and Anbāk, south of Qaṭar and near al-'Udaid in Abū Dhabī. In 1925 the Āl Murrah made a raid on al-Dhafrah, capturing 150 camels belonging to the Banī Yās. This coincided with the restlessness of the Ikhwān and their further exploits both before and after the fall of Medīnah and Jeddah in Hijāz. In the same year the *zakat* collector, Muḥammad b. Manṣūr, a member of Āl Murrah, appeared in al-Dhafrah, Bainūnah and Buraimī. The acceptance of Ibn Sa'ūd's right to exact this religious tax could be taken to imply submission of a kind to his sovereignty, and the Sa'ūdis in fact made this point thirty years later. Yet by restricting the *zakat* collection to the interior and avoiding the coastal area, he was able to extend his power by a means which was ostensibly entirely domestic and religious and beyond the control or criticism of Britain. Bertram Thomas explained Ibn Sa'ūd's tactics thus:

> It is not invasion that the tribes fear which prompts them to pay *zakat*. This spectacular method, which the first invader Abdul Aziz al-Wahhābī, used at the beginning of the nineteenth century is no longer necessary. Today it is the power of letting loose a strong tribe to raid a weaker Dhahirah one and carry off its camels without hope of redress or retaliation that is Ibn Saud's strength. Thus immediately before the arrival of Ibn Sa'ūd's *zakat* Collector, one of the Banī Yās tribes was raided by the Āl Murrah and lost 150 camels. Payment of *zakat* to Ibn Sa'ūd is therefore a kind of insurance against the raider. In al-Buraimi the Sa'ūdi Official *zakat* Collector, arrested and hanged a Hasawi refugee and notified the Shaikhs of Abū Dhabī and Dubai that Ibn Jilwī had taken the 'Awâmir and Durū tribes under the protection of the Sultan of Nejd.[51]

In February 1926 Ibn Jilwī sent a policeman to Shārjah in pursuit of a

Nejdi criminal, and the Political Resident, reviewing these activities, became convinced that Ibn Jilwī intended to absorb the Trucial Coast and Buraimī, an opinion which he expressed in a report of 9 June 1926, adding that it was not known for sure to what degree Ibn Sa'ūd was sponsoring his representative in al-Ḥasā. The Foreign Secretary wrote to the Viceroy on 21 August 1926 to say that 'it was decided, after considerable discussion, that no action should be taken in the matter, pending the conclusion of the new treaty, then in negotiation with him [Ibn Sa'ūd]'.[52]

Bertram Thomas's report to the Political Resident of 13 June 1927 is of importance regarding Ibn Sa'ūd's influence on the hostility to the British that then prevailed in the hinterland (see Chapter 1, p. 50). As a result, during the 1927 negotiations for a new treaty with Ibn Sa'ūd, Clayton, acting on instructions from the Foreign Office, prompted by the Government of India, aimed to embody Article VI of the 1915 treaty, which bound Ibn Sa'ūd 'to respect the position of the Arab Shaikhdoms in alliance with HM Government'.[53] Ibn Sa'ūd, knowing that he must abandon hope of British endorsement of his immediate ambitions, raised no objection to the draft Article on condition that the words 'maintain friendly relations with' should be substituted for the words 'refrain from all aggression or interference with' also that the words 'or under the protection of His Britannic Majesty' should be omitted. He maintained that the original wording was incompatible with his dignity as an independent ruler and the term 'interference' seemed to him to allow too wide an interpretation.[54] In the end, on 27 May 1927 the Article was agreed upon in the following form, somewhat to the disappointment of the Government of India, who tried in vain to retain the original terms: 'HM the King of the Hijaz and of Nejd and its Dependencies undertakes to maintain friendly and peaceful relations with the territories of the Kuwait and Bahrain, and with the Shaikhs of Qatar and the Oman Coast who are in special treaty relations with His Britannic Majesty's Government.'[55]

During the discussion which followed Colonel Haworth's suggestion in 1927–8 of a protectorate over the Trucial coast it was decided that fostering friendly relations with Ibn Sa'ūd on the basis of the 1927 treaty would be the most secure and only practicable solution for the protection of the Arab shaikhdoms. A protectorate over the Coast, on the other hand, would involve the British in trouble with Ibn Sa'ūd and encourage the Shaikh to adopt a provocative attitude towards the Wahhābīs, and the British might therefore find themselves in a position of great embarrassment. At the end of 1928 the idea of a protectorate was abandoned completely.[56]

There is much evidence of the Muwahhidīns' enthusiasm for Ibn Sa'ūd's cause, in the popular literature of the Trucial Coast and in official records. Early in 1919 Ṣāliḥ al-Mutaww'a, a judge in Shārjah, expressed in poetry the joy felt by his colleagues and himself at Ibn Sa'ūd's victory over King Ḥusain at Khurmah. This same scholar later wrote a work entitled *Uqūd al-Jumān Fī Sirat Al Sa'ūd Fī 'Omān* (Necklace of Pearls in the History of Al

Sa'ūd in 'Omān') a work which was anonymously and frequently quoted in the Sa'ūdī 'Memorial' of 1955.

On 4 April 1920, Philips, the Political Agent in Baḥrain, reported that Muḥammad b. Khādim, a notable from Shārjah, had arrived at Manāmah on his way to Ibn Sa'ūd, bringing a present of 'Omānī dromedaries. Philips had been told that b. Khādim had said that 'everyone along the Trucial Coast and in the hinterland of Oman especially was longing for the day when Ibn Saud would take them under his protection. They had all sent embassies and letters to the Iman [Ibn Sa'ūd] but the latter had put them off with promises, doing nothing.' B. Khādim was typical of many zealous personalities, particularly in Shārjah and Rās al-Khaimah, who championed the cause of Ibn Sa'ūd, most important among whom was 'Alī al-Maḥmūd, the rich and benevolent pearl merchant who financed the schools in Shārjah and Ḥīrah and brought the teachers for them from Nejd. He not only made his home a centre of pro-Wahhābī preaching, receiving the emissaries from Nejd, but he also helped to finance Ibn Sa'ūd in his campaign in Ḥijāz. The Residency Agent's reports of the time refer to him as the 'Head of the Najdi propaganda on the coast'.[57]

The audacious attempt of 'Abd al-Raḥmān b. Muḥammad on 11 October 1925 to kill 'Isā b. 'Abd al-Laṭīf, the Residency Agent, because he had insisted on flying the British flag from the Residency House in Shārjah, was symptomatic of Wahhābī hostility towards the British which had spread to the coast. The relation between this incident and Wahhābī enthusiasm was proved by a letter sent from the shaikh of the Āl Bū-Shāmis to 'Isā saying that he would complain to 'Abdullah b.ḥJilwī in al-Ḥasā regarding the prolonged retention of 'Abd al-Raḥmān without proof of his guilt. When Captain Barry, the SNO, came to take 'Abd al-Raḥmān into exile in the middle of June 1927, he took this opportunity of intimidating Wahhābī elements on the coast. On this journey he visited Umm al-Qaiwain and 'Ajmān to instruct their Rulers to break off relations with the Sa'ūdīs, and in Shārjah he requested 'Ali al-Mahmūd to come to the Residency House on 19 June. Out of respect for 'Ali al-Mahmūd's standing the ruler accompanied him to the meeting. There he was advised to cease these activities. In fact the firm British attitude and Ibn Sa'ūd's enforced failure to respond to the popular interest in his cause had the effect of gradually damping the enthusiasm of the early 1920s, which continued in the 1930s only in a restrained way.

On his accession to power, Shaikh Sulṭān b. Zāyed soon incurred the discontent of Ibn Sa'ūd by the firm attitude he took towards the infiltration of Sa'ūdī influence. He tried to prevent the *zabat* collection by Sa'ūdī officials in al-Dhafrah and Buraimī, and in December 1925 the Shaikh of Dubai received from b. Jilwī a letter expressing his displeasure with Shaikh Sulṭān. Although his son, Shaikh Shakhbūt, maintained friendly relations with b. Jilwī, he continued his father's policy and in 1931 violence broke out between the Hawāmil section of the Banī Yās the Sa'ūdi *zakat* collectors. This, together with Ibn Sa'ūd's abandonment of his immediate ambitions on the Trucial Coast and his concentration during the 1930s on the reorganisation of his country's domestic affairs, put an end to the levying of the *zakat* in the area.[58]

IV Negotiations Concerning Abū Dhabi's Frontiers with Sa'ūdi Arabia, 1934–8

One of the main areas of controversy between Ibn Sa'ūd and Britain which clouded their relations during the 1930s lay in the abortive negotiations over the southeastern frontiers of Sa'ūdī Arabia. Discussion of the frontiers between Sa'ūdī Arabia and the Trucial coast developed in 1934 as an inevitable outcome of boundary questions in Qaṭar and al-Ḥasā, caused by the urgent need of two oil companies, APOC and Standard Oil of California, to determine the boundaries of their respective concessions. For the purposes of this study we need to follow the development of affairs in detail from the beginning, since the main decisions which effectively shaped the outcome of the Trucial Coast frontier negotiations with Sa'ūdī Arabia were taken at this stage. The oil concession in Qaṭar precipitated urgent discussion in London of the need to determine the boundaries of this shaikhdom and British responsibility for protecting it against any aggression from Ibn Sa'ūd. This discussion coincided with an official American enquiry about the same frontier, for the American Embassy in Ankara had approached the Turkish Government, asking for any document regarding the boundaries of Nejd and al-Ḥasā. When the Turks failed to supply these, the Americans in February 1934 asked the British Embassy if they could furnish a copy of the Anglo–Turkish Treaty of 29 July 1913. The British Embassy referred to the Foreign Office.[59] Obvious American interest in the outcome of the discussions of the next four years had its inevitable effect on Ibn Sa'ūd and for the first time in his dealings with Britain he felt that he was not alone, in the sense that the issue affected a powerful third party with whom the British would not wish to come into conflict.

Early Solutions

At the beginning of 1934 the OME Sub-Committee was much exercised over determining the southern boundary of Qaṭar and preparing an answer to the American enquiry, and on 26 January 1935, Laithwaite prepared a memorandum which represented the settled opinion of the India Office after consultation with the Government of India and the Political Resident in the Gulf. It dealt mainly with the question of immediate concern. 'The Southern Boundary of Qatar and the Connected Problems'. In an historical analysis Laithwaite mentioned the 'Blue Line' of 1913 for Nejd province and the latest map of Qaṭar peninsula in 1933 by the IPC geologists (see Map No. 3).

He also referred to a line indicated to Ibn Sa'ūd by Cox in 1922, as reported by Colonel Dickson, who had accompanied Cox to the 'Uqair Conference. From all this Laithwaite concluded that two lines should be adopted: the first, the IPC line, as the southern boundary of Qaṭar, and the second, the 'blue line', for the eastern boundary of the Sa'ūdī Kingdom. Laithwaite clearly recognised that 'acceptance of Qaṭar boundary will admittedly leave an area of undetermined ownership between Qaṭar and the "blue line" of Nejd'.[60]

In his memorandum Laithwaite discussed three possible ways of eliminating this vacuum, either to grant the area to Ibn Sa'ūd, a solution to which he strongly objected for reasons already given, or to allow the Shaikh of Qaṭar or of Abū Dhabī to claim it, a solution which seemed of doubtful practicability; but he finally recommended that the tract should be regarded 'as indeterminate in ownership' and that 'if possible, raising the thorny questions of its boundaries to the west and of political contiol within it with Ibn Sa'ūd'. The fate of this area called Barr al-Qara, between the 'blue line' and Qaṭar, was a vital question and became the subject of protracted discussions between the Foreign Office and the India Office. Laithwaite's well prepared and authoritative memorandum not only had a great effect on the British reply to the American enquiry but also carried great weight in the early meetings of the OME Sub-Committee the same year.

In February three significant incidents took place: a telegram from Ryan, a visit by Cox to the India Office for consultation, and a meeting of the OME Sub-Committee. Ryan's telegram of 14 February commented on Laithwaite's memorandum: It should be difficult to gain Ibn Sa'ūd's acceptance of the 'blue line', and it would be unwise to fix the boundary of Qaṭar while the Sa'ūdī frontier remained undetermined. As regards the first point, Ryan felt that Ibn Sa'ūd would never accept the view that he was a successor to the Turks, whom he regarded as usurpers. Moreover, the settlements of the Āl Murrah lay to the east of the 'blue line' and those tribes were his subjects. Concerning the second point, the definition of the Qaṭar frontier might lead Ibn Sa'ūd to assume that the British recognised his sovereignty up to the other side of it. Further, a no-man's-land between Qaṭar and Sa'ūdī Arabia would encourage Āl Murrah raids on Qaṭar, for which Ibn Sa'ūd could not be held accountable.[61]

On 20 February 1934 Cox, who had been in retirement for eleven years, was invited to the India Office to discuss the conversation which had taken place between Ibn Sa'ūd, Major Holmes and himself in 1922. Although Cox was an Indian Government veteran, he boldly made a proposal at which even the Foreign Office would only hint at this time: 'If occasion arose in the future for a compromise it would be a reasonable course to assign to Ibn Sa'ūd, in view of his strong position at 'Uqair close by, that length of coastline with its hinterland [Barr al-Qāura] up to the "blue line".'[62]

On 23 February 1934 an emergency meeting of the OME Sub-Committee was convened to implement the decision of the Committee of Imperial Defence taken the previous day that 'a guarantee of protection should be offered to the Shaikh of Qaṭar'.[63] Regardless of Ryan's advice the Committee decided to fix the boundaries of Qaṭar within which Fowle, the Political Resident, should offer the Shaikh a guarantee of British protection. The boundary line was similar to that indicated in the IPC map, which ran just south of the fort of Salwā and the Sakāk settlement. When all this was conveyed to Fowle, he replied with an urgent telegram on 28 February 1934:

> Study of recent papers strengthened my conviction that it would be dangerous to define the southern boundary of Qatar as suggested if it is intended to hold Ibn Saud to the 'Blue Line' when the question of eastern frontiers arises. Nejd and Qatar were coterminous territories in 1913 Treaty and Ibn Saud may argue that adoption of HM Government of boundary now suggested for Qatar constituted renunciation of 'Blue Line'.[64]

On 4 March, after a meeting with Sir Samuel Hoare, Secretary of State for India, and Sir John Simon, Foreign Secretary, an answer to the American enquiries was sent to the British Ambassador in Ankara. This stated that the British Government regarded the 'blue line' of the Anglo–Turkish Convention of 1913 as being the southeastern frontier of Sa'ūdī Arabia, but having sent this answer, Rendel and the Foreign Office legal advisers, after studying the whole question of both Qaṭar and Sa'ūdī Arabia, found that 'the question was exceedingly complex and important points of policy were involved'.[65] Rendel, in a significant letter to Laithwaite of 16 March, mentioned that:

(a) the 'blue line', from the point of view of international law, was perfectly valid though not necessarily static, and could be used as a basis for bargaining. If it turned out that the tribes to the east of the 'blue line' owed definite allegiance to Ibn Sa'ūd, as had been mentioned in Ryan's telegram, it might eventually be desirable to offer Ibn Sa'ūd some concession as far south as Salwā, as Cox suggested.

(b) the convention of 1914 spoke of the 'blue line' as separating the Turkish territory from that of Qaṭar, which means that the territories to the east of the 'blue line' appertained politically to the shaikhdom of Qaṭar. The Foreign Office were therefore 'in favour of putting a positive claim and taking the British stand at once on the "blue line", not only as the eastern boundary of Saudi Arabia, but also as the dividing line between that Kingdom and the territories of southeast Arabia coming within our [British] sphere'.

(c) the highest authorities in the Foreign Office pointed out the danger that Ibn Sa'ūd might learn the contents of the British reply to the American enquiry and be justifiably provoked. They therefore recommend that an early communication should be sent to Ibn Sa'ūd in the same sense as that already sent to the Americans, in order to avoid 'a great deal of trouble later on.'

Five days later, on 21 March 1934, Ryan warned the Foreign Office by telegram of the dangers attendant upon the adoption of the 'blue line' as the Sa'ūdī frontier, so the Foreign Office called a meeting of the OME Sub-Committee, which reached five important conclusions. These were soon to have a radical influence on all discussions of the frontier between Abū Dhabī and Sa'ūdī Arabia:

(a) that the British Government must take their stand on the 'blue line';
(b) that the question of cession of the Barr al-Qara to Ibn Sa'ūd in return for a final settlement should be deferred for the present;
(c) that the intermediate area lying between the 'blue line' and the base of Qaṭar peninsula should be definitely claimed as territory within the British sphere of influence and appertaining to Qaṭar;
(d) that no claim should be put forward on behalf of the Shaikh of Abū Dhabī to the intermediate area;
(e) that the Foreign Office should prepare a draft telegram to Sir Andrew Ryan informing the Sa'ūdī Government officially of the request of the US Embassy at Ankara and the British reply.[66]

As a consequence of all these discussions and suggestions, on 28 April 1934 Ryan handed a British note to Fu'ād Ḥamzah informing him as a matter of courtesy that the Government of the USA had recently asked the British Government for information about the boundaries on Eastern Arabia and that the British had supplied them with copies of the Anglo-Turkish Conventions of 29 July 1913, and 9 March 1914. On 2 May 1934 Fu'ād Ḥamzah told Ryan verbally that the Sa'ūdī Government did not consider themselves in any way bound by the Turks' acceptance of the 'blue line' and on 13 May 1934 sent Ryan an official note to the same effect. News of this Sa'ūdī reaction reached the California Oil Company, and through them the State Department in Washington, which immediately asked its legal advisers to look into the matter. On 8 June the British Government again maintained in a note to the Sa'ūdī Government that the terms of the 1913 and 1914 conventions were legally valid and still binding. In a memorandum enclosed with a note of 20 June the Sa'ūdīs insisted that the Turks had had no right to settle the frontier question, as Ibn Sa'ūd had at that time already been in occupation of al-Ḥasā for three months. They explained that both Qaṭar and the Trucial Coast had no frontiers properly speaking, that they were only boundaries of individual towns and villages, these being situated mainly near the coast. The tribes of the hinterland all belonged to Sa'ūdī Arabia.[67]

This definite rejection of the 'blue line' had its effect on the British, who now began to re-examine the problem, with the result that the September meeting of the OME Sub-Committee found several useful studies and memoranda. At this meeting a division of opinion between the Foreign Office and the India Office began to emerge clearly.[68] The Foreign Office point of view was presented in three papers by Ryan and one by Becket, the second legal adviser. The India Office attitudes were expressed in two papers, one from the India Office itself and one by Fowle. The first of Ryan's papers was his July report on the personal reaction of Ibn Sa'ūd. The King, who had no previous knowledge of the 1913 convention, was considerably shocked by this sudden emergence of the 'blue line' and asked Ryan to visit him at Ṭā'if, where several meetings took place between 12 and 14 July 1934. The King completely rejected the idea that the coastal principalities represented true sovereignties: he did not claim them now (although the people there would have welcomed his sovereignty) because of his agreements with Britain, which he would not go back on. Ryan succeeded in persuading the King to send Fu'ād Ḥamzah to London in September to discuss the matter there.

On 30 July 1934 Ryan followed this report with an important memorandum on Anglo–Sa'ūdī relations. He now admitted that he could not

> personally believe in the undoubted legal validity of the 'Blue Line' . . . It appears to me further that the Anglo–Saudi Treaty of December 1915 destroyed the validity of the 'Blue Line' by substituting a new criterion for the determination of Ibn Saud's boundaries. He was to be recognised as independent within his ancestral limits.

He suggested that if a generous territorial concession were made to Ibn Sa'ūd in southeastern Arabia as a part of a general settlement from which the British obtained important advantages elsewhere, this concession would no longer be regarded as a surrender, but merely as a part of a bargain satisfactory to both sides. The advantages in question were the Kuwait blockade, the Trans-Jordan frontiers and the al-Ḥasa air route.

Ryan's third paper was a note of 12 September 1934, summarising his point of view on the whole subject. He concluded this note by saying

> there is no doubt that the attempt to impose on Ibn Sa'ūd the 'blue and violet lines' after twenty years of silence regarding them can only strike Ibn Sa'ūd as an attempt to trick him by legal subtleties today out of what we led him to expect when we wished to enlist his support in downing the Turks . . . we must sometimes be firm with him, but we should never do anything avoidable to inflame his suspicions or to drive him to seek the support of other powers.[69]

The fourth paper from the Foreign Office was a note prepared by Mr W. B.

Becket, dealing with the legal aspect of the question of the 'blue line'. Becket explained that

> the legal position had been re-examined and it now seemed clear that it would be most difficult for HM Government to establish an unassailable legal case. The reason for this was that the 'Blue Line' did not, as had first been supposed, mark a division between two areas under clearly defined sovereignties but the area immediately to the east of it was not demonstrably under any effective sovereignty, and might fall to be regarded as a political vacuum.[70]

The India Office contribution was a 'Historical Memorandum on the Relations of the Wahhabi Amirs and Ibn Saud with Eastern Arabia and the British Government 1800–1934'. This study reached some important conclusions. The main points of relevance here are:

(a) The Sa'ūdī ancestral claims had no proper and certainly no legal foundation. The Sa'ūdī were mere invaders who had occupied al-Buraimī intermittently between 1800 and 1871, after which their influence died completely for sixty-three years.

(b) They stressed the legality of the 'blue line' according to two facts:

(1) in May 1914 Ibn Sa'ūd had accepted the position of a Turkish Wālī;
(2) as successor to the Ottomans in the area he was now bound, in international law, to honour their commitments.

(c) Ibn Sa'ūd's recent activities east of the blue line and particularly in the Trucial Coast and Qaṭar amounted to a sort of blackmail.[71]

The recent activities of Ibn Sa'ūd in the Trucial Coast also formed the subject of the paper submitted by Fowle. Since Ibn Sa'ūd's claim to any part of the Trucial shaikhdoms depended on the tribute which he exacted, Fowle presented a study of *zakat*, in which he emphasised that this tribute was exacted under the threat of raids or other unpleasantness, and this, in his opinion, 'is the modern blackmail, or the ancient Danegeld, and is in no way a sign of submission to Wahhabi rule. Such tribute as is exacted by Ibn Saud in the territories East of the "Blue Line" is Danegeld pure and simple'.

On 13 September 1934, and at the beginning of the meeting of the OME Sub-Committee which was convened at the request of the Foreign Office, Rendel said that Fu'ād Ḥamzah was shortly arriving in London and it was therefore desirable to decide the main lines of policy to be followed. Ryan and Fowle, who were in England on leave, were invited to the meeting. Rendel summarised Becket's legal point of view, and then outlined the political factor: 'if the British took their stand rigidly on the "Blue Line" a first class dispute with Ibn Saud might well develop' about an area over which neither HM Government nor their Arab protégés claimed sovereignty. However, he pointed out that any large concession to Ibn Sa'ūd now would be regarded as a complete surrender to his pressure and would do considerable injury to British prestige. He therefore advocated Ryan's suggestion that concessions should be offered as a part of a bargain in exchange for some advantages for Britain. Fowle now expressed his dissatisfaction with this approach, suggesting that a second opinion should be sought from the Law Officers of the Crown. Rendel replied that Law Officer's opinion, whatever it might be, would be unlikely to affect the issue, which was mainly a political one. Rendel, who was convinced that no settlement would be reached until the British offered some concessions, now posed the question about the maximum territorial limits which the British could claim for the Trucial shaikhs in the hinterland. On this point Fowle and Walton, Assistant Secretary of the India Office, immediately agreed to collect up-to-date information, since the need to offer concessions now seemed to be established. Meanwhile it was agreed that the opportunity should be taken of Fu'ād Ḥamzah's visit to try to ascertain Ibn Sa'ūd's minimum desiderata. The conclusions of the meeting show a considerable change in the attitude of the Committee, particularly a new readiness to come to terms with Ibn Sa'ūd. The Sub-Committee eventually agreed:

> that the Foreign Office should explain to Fuad Hamzah that although the British Government regarded the 'Blue Line' as the only frontier with a definite legal basis, they would be prepared to discuss the whole question without preconditions and in a generous spirit, as part of a settlement giving HM Government their desiderata in other direction.[72]

Between 19 and 25 September 1934 Fu'ād Ḥamzah and Ḥāfiz Wahbah had seven meetings with Rendel and Ryan concerning the frontier question and other important matters, including the Ma'ān and 'Aqabah problem, the Ḥijāz railway and the payment of customs on Sa'ūdī goods in transit through Baḥrain. Rendel was expecting and eager to learn what frontier line Ibn Sa'ūd actually had in mind. When Fu'ād Ḥamzah claimed Sa'ūdī sovereignty over the Āl Murrah and Manāṣīr tribes, Rendel replied firmly that the British agreed over the Āl Murrah but that the Manāṣīr were completely under the sovereignty of the Ruler of Abū Dhabī. Fu'ād Ḥamzah was expecting a telegram from the King defining the Sa'ūdī point of view, but he left London before it arrived, and on 15 October Ḥāfiz Wahbah made its contents known to the Foreign Office. The King's claims in southeastern Arabia were to the whole of the inland desert as distinct from the more or less settled coastal belt. When Ḥāfiz Wahbah was asked whether the King claimed the whole of the Empty Quarter, he repeated that his telegram says 'to the desert generally as distinct from the coastal belt'.[73]

During October, November and December further investigations were undertaken and some suggestions emerged concerning the extent and nature of possible concessions to Ibn Sa'ūd. As a result of these three months of study some definite and considered proposals were to take shape by January 1935. Meanwhile, in October Bertram Thomas had been confidentially informed of the difficulties which had arisen in connection with the 'blue line', and on the 19 and 21 of October he discussed the general position with Rendel and Laithwaite. Thomas confirmed Fowle's idea that *zakat* represented no more than a mild form of insurance, carrying with it no suggestion of suzerainty or sovereignty; to him the tribal boundary was likely to be very much more satisfactory than a territorial one. However, he mentioned the fluidity of the tribal line due to the change which would occur in the loyalty of the tribes and the general political situation, for example, in the event of the death of Ibn Sa'ūd or Ibn Jilwī.

Thomas's last point had an immediate effect on Rendel's thinking. This appears clearly in his two letters to Laithwaite. In the first, dated 23 October 1934, he reconsidered his earlier idea of approaching the question on a simple tribal basis; he next proposed that the definition of a southeastern frontier for Sa'ūdī Arabia might be based on a number of factors, in particular the geography of the area.[74] In his letter of 7 November 1934 Rendel proposed a wide geographical belt of special desert area on the seaward side east and south of Ibn Sa'ūd's kingdom. Rendel next explained his idea of the 'Desert Zone': 'It would not be a "neutral zone" with so-called equal rights, nor a mere "no-man's-land" where there would be no rights at all, but an area—rather like a maritime zone—where rights would be personal and not territorial'.[75] This 'Desert Zone' would enable Ibn Sa'ūd to maintain his personal rights over the nomadic tribes in the loose and rather undefined way which Thomas had described, and at the same time would preclude him (or the British) from giving, e.g. any oil concession. He produced a detailed study explaining the extent of the area. On the west a line starting from the head of Doḥat al-Salwā and running due south to parallel 19, and thence in a west–southwesterly direction to the eastern boundary of Nejran. On the east a line running from the same point on the Doḥat al-Salwā in a southeasterly direction to the western corner of the Sabkhat al-'Amrah, thence due south to the intersection of meridian 51 and parallel 23 (where they supposed the well of Bunayyān to be). Thence in an east–southeasterly direction to the line intersection of meridian 55 and parallel 22. Thence due south to the line intersection of meridian 55 and parallel 20. Thence in a west–southwesterly direction following the edge of the limit of the sand dunes of the Empty Quarter to a point some miles due north of Tarīm in Ḥaḍramaut.[76]

Meanwhile Fowle and Dickson had met in Kuwait and decided that to settle frontiers on a tribal basis would be the most suitable solution, a proposal which Fowle communicated to Laithwaite on 1 November 1934. He and Dickson suggested a line beginning at Doḥat al-Salwā and extending due south to parallel 20, which would concede to Ibn Sa'ūd some forty-five miles of coast with its hinterland.[77] This line was later accepted in principle, with alterations made after Loch had pointed out in December 1934 that the line originally suggested would have excluded Sakāk and Ambāk, the two settlements of the Āl Murrah, over whom Ibn Sa'ūd exercised *de facto* sovereignty.

These considerations were endorsed by the Government of India and the Foreign Office. Accordingly there emerged what came to be known as the 'green line'. Rendel described this line in his instructions to Ryan on 16 January 1935 as follows:

> A line running from the head of Dohat al-Salwa to a point slightly southeast of Sakak (but leaving that place to Saudi Arabia) and thence to north western extremity of Al Uqal (leaving to Qatar and Abu Dhabi a strip of territory extending inland for no less than 25 miles to west head of Khor al Udaid). Thence due southwards via (but west of) Bunayyan to parallel 20 North whence it would gradually rejoin 'Violet Line'.[78]

All these studies of October and November 1934 were discussed at the meeting of the OME Sub-Committee of 8 November 1934 at which Rendel propounded his suggestion of the desert zone. The question was raised whether it would be necessary, in case Ibn Sa'ūd objected to this proposal, to recognise him as sovereign in the 'Desert Zone', subject to the condition that he would grant mineral concessions there only in consultation with and to companies approved by the British. Laithwaite definitely opposed the suggestion, which he described as 'most unwise'. However, the discussion continued in this direction and it was agreed that Ibn Sa'ūd might if necessary be offered full sovereignty over the western part of the 'Desert Zone' as far as meridian 52. It was recommended that this last proposal should be thoroughly examined. The area in question was eventually marked by what was known as the 'brown line'.[79]

At the beginning of January 1935, Laithwaite, the Government of India and Fowle showed great concern over the tactics to be employed in presenting the British offers to Ibn Sa'ūd, fearing that the Foreign Office attitude to Ibn Sa'ūd might be over-conciliatory. They urged that Ryan should initially 'aim at making the Saudies show their hand before we show ours . . . that subject to this he should first offer solution (a) [green line], then solution (b) [Desert Zone], which is that which would suit us best and only in the last resort solution (c) [brown line]'.[80] After consideration of the latest views of the India Office on tactics Rendel instructed Ryan on 16 January 1935 first to ask for clearer indication of Ibn Sa'ūd's desiderata; secondly to offer Ibn Sa'ūd in full sovereignty an area as far as the 'green line', thirdly if this should prove insufficient, to mention, as a possibility, the 'Desert Zone' proposal; fourthly, and only as a last resort, the 'brown line'.

As the area under dispute had not yet been reliably charted Ryan asked what maps the Foreign Office were using and which ones he should use in discussion with the Sa'ūdīs. The Foreign Office indicated that the maps found most useful for reference here were: (a) Hunter's two maps of Arabia[81]; (b) Philby's map of Rub'-al-Khālī; (c) Thomas's map of the same; (d) IPC map of Qaṭar.[82]

At first Ryan found the atmosphere unfavourable for negotiations and was unable to give effect to his instructions. The King had been upset when nothing seemed to emerge from Fu'ād Ḥamzah's visit to London, and his telegram was received unsympathetically at the Foreign Office. During February 1935 the situation was further clouded by Ryan firmly rejecting a request from Fu'ād Ḥamzah that the Trucial shaikhs should attend the frontier negotiations. However, on 1 March 1935 Ryan again asked Fu'ād Ḥamzah for a precise statement of Ibn Sa'ūd's desiderata concerning his frontiers, and eventually on 3 April 1935, Fa'ād Ḥamzah handed Ryan a Sa'ūdī memorandum. In this memorandum, in Qaṭar the line started on the west coast fifteen miles up the bay of Doḥat al-Salwā and after running eastwards reached the east coast some seven miles north of Khūr al-'Udaid. The Khūr al-'Udaid and al-'Uqal area was assigned to Ibn Sa'ūd. The line began again in al-Mijjan and Khūr Duwaihin and extended in a more or less southeasterly direction to pass south of meridian 23 just south of Līwā oases, and ended at the intersection of meridian 56 and parallel 22, then turned due south to parallel 19. It then ran west–southwest to the intersection of meridian 52 and parallel 27, and thence due west.[83] Three days later Ryan commented to his government that the Sa'īdū memorandum was based on their claim to areas frequented by Āl Murrah, Banī Hājir and certain sections of the Manāṣīr. Ryan, in accordance with his instructions, now presented the 'green line' proposal. The Sa'ūdīs rejected it outright.[84]

As an immediate consequence of this rejection, and having regard to the wide area they claimed in their memorandum, Rendel realised that the 'Desert Zone' with its conditions would obviously be turned down too. He therefore considered it more prudent to abandon the 'Desert Zone' proposal completely and to proceed straight to the next offer, the 'brown line', which might have a greater appeal to the King. The reason for calling an urgent meeting of the OME Sub-Committee on 15 April was specifically to seek its sanction to this change in the programme. At this meeting the main difficulty Rendel found in the Sa'ūdī memorandum was the claim to the Khūr al-'Udaid and al-'Uqal areas; for there were the strongest of objections to allowing Ibn Sa'ūd to gain access to the sea on the eastern side of Qaṭar or establish a position for himself as one of the Trucial Coast rulers. The meeting was in unanimous agreement that the whole of Khūr al-'Udaid and the land immediately behind it as far as Bunnayyān well belonged to Abū Dhabī and could not under any circumstances be given to Ibn Sa'ūd.

At this April meeting Rendel for the first time criticised the tactics of the India Office towards the negotiations and commented that

> it seemed open to question whether offering concessions step by step was really the wisest policy. If concessions were extracted from us one by one after much bargaining they might as well acquire a greater value, and our eventual agreement to them might well be presented as more of a defeat than if we made our offers more easily and more completely in the first instance and stuck to them more firmly . . .

Moreover, he was convinced that the need to reach a settlement with Ibn Sa'ūd was very urgent because the British knew by this time that their legal position was weak and unless some settlement were reached there might be great difficulty with the American oil company in Ibn Sa'ūd's territory. Rendel therefore explained that Ibn Sa'ūd might well have a strong case against the British if his boundaries were not defined. His advisers were quite shrewd enough to realise that if the British could not present an unanswerable case it would be worth Ibn Sa'ūd's while to demand international arbitration. To support his argument for an urgent settlement, which meant being more generous with Ibn Sa'ūd, Rendel pointed out that 'in any case Ministers had already decided in favour of trying an agreement with Ibn Saud about these southeastern frontiers'.

Major Osborne of the War Office drew attention to the fact that since the British were unwilling to make any concessions either around Khūr al-'Udaid in the north or in the Aden Protectorate in the south, they must be as generous as possible in the desert area in the east, so he suggested that the 'brown line' should be extended to meridian 56. Laithwaite stressed that the India Office were only prepared to agree to instructions which did not involve any negotiations about the boundary east of meridian 53. He pointed out that the situation might change very considerably in a few years in the event of Ibn Sa'ūd's death.[85]

From an analysis of this meeting's conclusions it is quite clear that the India Office was still having a major influence on the decisions reached, a situation which was soon to change. It was decided that Ryan should drop the 'Desert Zone' proposal and proceed instead with the offer of the 'brown line'. If this also proved insufficient, Ryan might, as a last resort, extend the concession eastwards as far as meridian 53.

On 18 April a telegram was sent to Ryan containing revised instructions based on the conclusions of the last meeting, but with a slight modification. Baggally, the Foreign Office legal adviser, expressed the uncertainty regarding the exact position of Bunayyān which necessitated this modification:

> on further consideration of the matter in the Foreign Office it was felt that the exact position of Bunayyan, which it was essential to maintain

the dominions of the Shaikh of Abu Dhabi, was too uncertain to permit to parallel 23 north being safely used to define the limit of the proposed concession. It appeared preferable to describe the line as 'running from a point on the "green line" to the south of and distant at least five miles from Bunayyan to the intersection of meridian 52 and parallel to 22.30.'[86]

Rendel's Efforts Towards a Compromise

In May 1935, the situation was worsened by the granting of an oil concession to APOC by the Ruler of Qaṭar contrary to the expressed request of Ibn Sa'ūd. The King protested to the British that the Shaikh had no right to grant concessions in territory claimed by the Sa'ūdīs. Ryan prudently suggested that the boundary question and other unsettled matters might be discussed in London with Fu'ād Ḥamzah, to which the King ágreed and invited Ryan to visit him in Riyādh on his return from his summer leave.[87]

Between 24 June and 8 July 1935 several meetings were held in London between Ḥāfiz Wahbah, Fu'ād Ḥamzah, Ryan and Rendel. At the one held on 24 June the British, according to plan, offered the 'brown line' proposal in its first and then in its second stage. These were rejected by Fu'ād Ḥamzah who explained during the subsequent meetings that the Sa'ūdī memorandum 'had worked out, after the most searching investigation, a carefully plotted and rational enquiry which took account of the political and tribal situation, and they were prepared to provide detailed evidence in support of their proposal'. Fu'ād Ḥamzah asserted that their demands were drawn up on the basis of the grazing grounds of four groups, in particular of the Manāṣīr and the widespread Āl Murrah tribe in the desert of al Rub'-al-Khālī, which acknowledged Sa'ūdī sovereignty. Rendel, in reply, stressing British objections to basing the frontier solely on tribal considerations, maintained that the Manāṣīr owed allegiance to the Shaikh of Abū Dhabī. Further, he could not agree to the exaggerated Sa'ūdī claim to the *dirah* of Āl Murrah. When Fu'ād Ḥamzah protested that the 'brown line' proposal wrongly deprived the Āl Murrah of their well at Bunayyān, Rendel replied that according to his official information this well belonged to Abū Dhabī. Fu'ād Ḥamzah insisted that Bunayyān belonged to Āl Murrah and in support of his contention he presented a letter on 2 July and on 8 July a memorandum, which included a list of 161 wells owned by the Āl Murrah, among them the well of Bunayyān. At this deadlock over the ownership of Bunayyān the discussion broke down.[88]

Although these meetings were abortive, the data presented by Fu'ād Ḥamzah had a profound influence on Rendel, who immediately asked the British authorities in the Gulf to provide him with detailed information on all the contested points. The early information now received from the Gulf, particularly Colonel Dickson's profound study of the Āl Murrah tribe and its *dirah* made it clear that the Shaikh of Abū Dhabī had no real claim to Bunayyān, that it was a predominantly Murrah well and that on this issue it would be necessary to give way. These facts greatly modified Rendel's view of the justice of the British case. Furthermore, there were new and serious political considerations of expediency, arising out of the changes in the international situation. The British Government were at this time confronted with a situation of great delicacy in the Red Sea area where the Italians were making strenuous efforts to extend their influence and undermine the British position, constantly making approaches to Ibn Sa'ūd.

The King's invitation to Ryan to visit Riyādh in the autumn offered a good opportunity for the British to take a conciliatory initiative. Rendel and Ryan immediately applied themselves to working out a detailed plan of a new frontier proposal, which they could put to the next Sub-Committee meeting for sanction, authorising Ryan to offer it to Ibn Sa'ūd during his visit. At the meeting of 24 September 1935 Rendel explained all the above considerations in detail, observing that 'it was therefore of major political importance that we should treat Ibn Sa'ūd as generously as possible over the grievance which he felt against us in this matter of the frontier'. Clauson commented that the India Office would not regard failure to reach an agreement with Ibn Sa'ūd over this question as necessarily disastrous. Rendel immediately proceeded to present his carefully prepared proposal and succeeded in gaining the sympathy of all present. He based his proposal on the reasonable maximum claims of Abū Dhabī, Qaṭar, Muscat and Aden, and the reasonable claims of Ibn Sa'ūd to sovereignty over certain tribes such as the Āl Murrah, bearing in mind questions of oil and protection. One of his main points was that the British should recognise the Āl Murrah *dirah* as Sa'ūdī territory, and therefore abandon their claims to Bunayyān. However, his proposed line left within Qaṭar the Jabal Nakhsh, which is the southern spur of the Jabal Dukhān and an integral part geographically of Qaṭar peninsula, as well as allocating the areas of Khūr al-'Udaid, al-'Uqal, al-Mijann and Sabkhat Maṭṭī to Abū Dhabī.

Clauson drew attention to the fact that the India Office maintained its original position: that it could not agree to the boundaries of the Trucial shaikhdoms being fixed, nor could it permit Ibn Sa'ūd to come right up to them. To this Rendel answered that it now seemed inevitable that the boundaries should be coterminous. As a tentative basis for discussion Rendel described his line as follows:

(a) Starting from a point on the coast, four miles to the northeast of Qaṣr al-Salwā, the line would run southeastwards to a point (which could be called Key point 'A') at the western end of Sabkhat al-'Amrah, discovered by Thomas.

(b) From this point the line would run due south to the point 'B', where it would meet the northern edge of the Murrah *dirah* west of Duwaihin wells, as defined in the latest information from Dickson.

(c) Thence the line might run diagonally direct to the intersection of parallel 22 and meridian 54, thus roughly following the northern limit of the Murrah *dirah* as shown by Dickson. It would be important, however, to be able to establish a good claim by Abū Dhabī to some definite feature in the neighbourhood of key point 'B' where the north–south line turned and began to run eastward. Possibly such a point might be found at the Duwaihin wells, as shown on Major Cheesman's map, or at the well of Ṣafq, which the Shaikh of Abū Dhabī claimed, although Fu'ād Ḥamzah had also put forward a strong Sa'ūdī claim to it.

(d) From the intersection of meridian 54 and parallel 22 the line would run due south to the point shown on Dickson's blue print as Sabkhat Mijðrā.

Finally the Committee agreed to reopen negotiations with Ibn Sa'ūd, offering a line based on Rendel's suggestion, leaving the precise position of points 'A' and 'B' and any other details to be determined in the light of further information from the British authorities in the Gulf.[89]

The seven weeks between this meeting and the next, on 11 November 1935, saw a great deal of investigation in the Gulf and discussion, correspondence and an exchange of telegrams between the Political Resident, the Government of India, India Office and the Foreign Office. The main areas on which the discussion was centred were al-'Uqal, Ṣafq, Sabkhat Maṭṭī, Līwā oasis and the extreme eastern limit of the line. In addition there were two important developments: a letter of instruction to Ryan and the claims presented by the Ruler of Abū Dhabī.

On 23 October 1935, before Ryan left London for Jeddah at the end of that month, the Foreign Secretary, Sir Samuel Hoare, gave him a letter of preliminary instruction, according to the conclusions reached at that time. Hoare instructed Ryan to reopen negotiations by informing the King that, as a result of the consultations with Fu'ād Ḥamzah in the summer, the whole question of the frontiers in southeastern Arabia had been fully reconsidered by HM Government. The new British offer had been worked out after consultation with their local authorities in Arabia and in the light of the detailed evidence supplied by Fu'ād Ḥamzah. The Foreign Secretary stressed that it was very important before offering the new line to express to the King in general terms the earnest desire of HM Government to go as far as possible to meet his wishes, explaining Britain's historical obligations in the areas south of Qaṭar and at Khūr al-'Udaid and al-'Uqual, where the British could not agree to his claims. He then described the proposed line as defined at the last meeting, adding that details regarding the precise position of points 'A' and 'B' would follow shortly.[90]

The second development was the discussion which took place at the end of October 1935 at a meeting between Loch and the Shaikh of Abū Dhabī in the presence of the latter's family, in particular his aged uncle, Shaikh Khalīfah b. Zāyed, who was experienced in tribal affairs. The Āl Bū-Falāh expressed their agreement on the following line as their frontier:

(a) a line running north from Qaṣr al-Salwā to the sea three-quarters of a mile away;
(b) a line running south-east from Qaṣr al-Salwā to Khūr al-'Udaid as far as meridian 51, leaving the rocky ground and the hill of Barr al-Qaṭar to Qaṭar and the sandy ground south to Ibn Sa'ūd;
(c) a line running approximately south from intersection (b) to Ḥilaiwīn, leaving Sabkhat al-'Amrah, Khufūs, Rimth, Farhūd, 'Uqlat al-Manāṣīr, Duwaihin and Naklah to Abū Dhabī, and Sakāk, Ambāk, Righwān and Ḥilaiwīn to Ibn Sa'ūd;
(d) a line running approximately southeast from Ḥilaiwīn to the intersection of meridian 53 and latitude 22, leaving al-Mijann, Ṣafq, Sabkhat Maṭṭī and Quraini well to Abū Dhabī;
(e) a line running east from latter end (d) to intersection of meridian 55 and latitude 22.

Shaikh Shakhbūṭ regarded Sakāk and Ambāk areas as having belonged to Abū Dhabī in the past but he recognised that they now pertained to Ibn Sa'ūd.

In a telegram dated 4 November 1935 Loch explained that the Abū Dhabī claim in the al-'Uqal area was based on the use by the Manāṣīr of its wells mentioned above, east of line 'c'. The coastal route to Dōḥaḥ, which was of vital importance to Abū Dhabī, ran through this area at some distance (and west of Sabkhat al-'Amrah) because of the marshy coast (which indubitably belonged to Abū Dhabī). Loch expressed the opinion that the British should support Abū Dhabī here, particularly to the west and north of Sabkhat al-'Amrah.

During these seven weeks several important changes were made in the proposed line. The subject of discussion was the line 'c' from the wells of Duwaihin to the intersection of parallel 22 and meridian 54, and also the well of Ṣafq, Sabkhat Maṭṭī and Līwā oases. Fowle and Loch, in their telegram and letters during this period, stressed the importance to Abū Dhabī of these three places.

After a discussion between the India Office and the Foreign Office it was agreed that a new key-point must be established in the neighbourhood of the well of Ṣafq to ensure that it and the whole of Sabkhat Maṭṭī be included in the territory of Abū Dhabī. When the British authorities in the Gulf were consulted about the precise position of Ṣafq, Loch, after studying the available information, replied that it lay at the western edge of Sabkhat Maṭṭī and about 100 miles inland. Calculating from this, Rendel suggested that the new key-point should be placed at the intersection of meridian 52 and parallel 23. However, Loch's information, based on local estimates, was soon found to be most inaccurate. To ensure the Līwā oases to Abū Dhabī it was suggested that the line should extend from the last key-point near Ṣafq to the intersection of meridian 55 and parallel 22.40.[91]

After receiving Loch's telegram of 4 November a meeting of the OME Sub-Committee was convened on 11 November. Although Loch's recommendations concerning al-'Uqal area were accepted his proposal to extend the Abū Dhabī frontier southwards to include Quraini well was rejected by Rendel, who suggested that the area offered to Ibn Sa'ūd should be extended eastwards as far as meridian 56, to which the India Office would not agree. After much discussion it was agreed to follow the line suggested by Rendel at the last meeting as far as point 'A'. Point 'B' was defined as between the wells of Hilaiwīn and 'Uqlat al-Nakhlah. From here the line was to run to the intersection of meridian 52 and parallel 23 near the well of Ṣafq. Thence it should run either directly to the intersection of meridian 55 and latitude 22, or first to the intersection of meridian 52.40 and latitude 22.40 and thence to the intersection of meridian 55.40 and latitude 22. However, after consultation with the Political Resident in the Gulf they decided upon a compromise line which ran from Ṣafq to the intersection of meridian 55 and latitude 22.30. Final instructions to this effect were sent to Ryan in Jeddah in a telegram of 18 November.[92]

On 25 November, Ryan met the King and gave Fu'ād Ḥamzah a note containing the new proposal. Next day Fu'ād Ḥamzah informed Ryan that the King found it impossible to accept a proposal which ignored Sa'ūdī claims in Jabal Nakhsh and Khūr al-'Udaid. A deadlock ensued.[93]

Despite the Sa'ūdī's discouraging response, Rendel remained eager to pursue the matter and was convinced that British imperial interests in the Middle East urgently required a settlement with Ibn Sa'ūd. At the meeting of 24 February 1936 Rendel reiterated his view.

During 1936 the threat posed by Italian activities in the Red Sea area following their Ethiopian expedition, the growing danger of European war and especially the increasing difficulties in Palestine, all served to strengthen Rendel's determination to work for a settlement with Ibn Sa'ūd. Between April and December 1936 a serious revolt broke out in Palestine and obliged Britain to ask King Ibn Sa'ūd and the Arab Rulers to mediate between themselves and the Palestinian leaders. Thus the Palestinian question for the first time became officially an Arab question involving Arab governments. Rendel, who appreciated the role played by Ibn Sa'ūd during the last crisis in Palestine in persuading the Palestinian leaders to abandon their campaign of violence, considered that the King's friendship was of vital importance.[94]

Accordingly, in November 1936, after the lapse of a year in which no serious move had been made by either side to reopen negotiations, Sir Reader Bullard, who had recently replaced Ryan, took advantage of improved Anglo–Sa'ūdī relations, brought about by Ibn Sa'ūd's help in Palestine, to raise the frontier question again. Fu'ād Ḥamzah, after obtaining the King's views, replied that there could be no question of the Sa'ūdī Government agreeing to any compromise over Jabal Nakhsh or Khūr al-'Udaid. In December 1936 Bullard suggested that Britain should consider whether further slight concessions at Ṣafq and on the borders of 'Omān and the Aden Protectorate might be offered.[95]

In 1937 the OME Sub-Committee held three meetings to discuss the south-eastern frontiers, during which Rendel gradually gained more support for his view. On 1 February 1937 Rendel addressed the Sub-Committee, posing the difficult question of Ibn Sa'ūd's demands for Khūr al-'Udaid and Jabal Nakhsh, but as the latter had been definitely included in the map attached to Qaṭar oil concession and had always been regarded as geographically part of Qaṭar, it was difficult to recognise Ibn Sa'ūd's claim. But, as regards Khūr al-'Udaid, it might be possible to offer the Sa'ūdī's free transit there. In support of this suggestion he said that 'From the strategical point of view he did not consider that objection need to be taken to Ibn Saud obtaining access to the Persian Gulf at Khūr al-'Udaid, since he already has an outlet on that Gulf to the west of Qaṭar peninsula and his acquisition of a further outlet of doubtful value to the east of that peninsula would not materially alter the strategical position'.[96] As Rendel was leaving on 19 February for a brief visit to the Gulf and Sa'ūdī Arabia in response to a royal invitation, it was decided after discussion that a meeting between him and the Political Resident should be arranged to discuss the frontier question with a view to making the greatest possible concession to Ibn Sa'ūd without violating British promises to the Shaikhs of Abū Dhabī and Qaṭar.

On 24 February Rendel arrived in Bushire, where he discussed the whole issue with Fowle. Afterwards he visited Baḥrain. While there he took the opportunity to fly for some six hours, in company with Fowle and Loch, over the disputed areas in the northern sector of the proposed frontier line, to identify the various geographical features.

On 21 March he met Ibn Sa'ūd at his palace in Jeddah, as well as Yūsuf Yāsīn, the King's secretary. Ibn Sa'ūd repeated his familiar argument that the whole of the coast had belonged to his ancestors and that the present Rulers would not deny it. He insisted that Jabal Nakhsh belonged to him and explained that in claiming Khūr al-'Udaid for Sa'ūdī Arabia he was thinking as much of British interests as of his own. No one else could govern that region and when crimes were committed there it was to him that the people applied for redress. Rendel then gave Ibn Sa'ūd his latest observations to the effect that Jabal Nakhsh was only a part of Jabal Dukhān in Qaṭar and he informed the King that the precise position of Ṣafq was under consideration at the Agency in Baḥrain, since it had been discovered to be much nearer the coast than had been supposed. Regarding al-'Udaid, the land immediately to the west of it afforded the only land passage between Abū Dhabī and Qaṭar, and it was far more important to Abū Dhabī than to

Ibn Sa'ūd to retain the caravan route and to keep a coterminous frontier with Qaṭar. Rendel's study of the documents convinced him that the Shaikh of Abū Dhabī had strong claims to Khūr al-'Udaid, which the British had formally recognised for the past sixty years, as shown particularly by Cox's letter of 1 December 1906 to Shaikh Zāyed b. Khalīfah.

Although the discussion was cordial the King showed great reluctance to agree to any further attempt to define the frontiers on the basis of Ryan's line. On 27 March Bullard wrote, commenting on Rendel's visit, that it would be useless at present to continue to urge Ibn Sa'ūd to accept the British point of view and suggested that a joint commission should visit the Jabal Nakhsh area and examine the physical features on the spot. He urged that Britain should examine carefully the possibility of giving Ibn Sa'ūd a royalty on any oil that might be struck in or near Jabal Nakhsh.[97]

After the failure of Rendel's visit, the Foreign Office suggested that an early meeting of the OME Sub-Committee should be called to discuss what attitude Britain should now adopt. On 29 June they met and Rendel explained that Ibn Sa'ūd now appeared more reluctant to reach a settlement than in April 1935. This was a result of recent developments in the Palestine question: if Ibn Sa'ūd should now appear to assign any territory in Arabia to the British he would be accused by his own people of giving Arab territory away to the foreigner. Rendel supported Bullard's suggestion that Ibn Sa'ūd should be given a share in the oil of Jabal Nakhsh as part of a frontier settlement. To this the India Office objected. The meeting agreed to Bullard's view that for the present it was not desirable to press King Ibn Sa'ūd to reach a settlement; but, should the oil companies concerned decide to work in any of the areas under dispute, it would be necessary to consider the question of a unilateral declaration by HM Government defining clearly the frontier which they proposed to observe. The meeting recommended that a joint Anglo–Sa'ūdī topographical mission should be sent to the area.[98]

In October 1937 Loch received reliable information that a party from the Standard Oil Company of California had established themselves at Qaṣr al-Salwā and were working to the east. On 8 November the OME Sub-Committee met, mainly to discuss this situation, Bullard and Fowle being present. The need for a unilateral declaration, as decided upon at the last meeting, had now arisen. After some discussion it was agreed that the communication to Ibn Sa'ūd should be made as conciliatory as possible and take the form of a statement to the following effect:

> HM Government had heard that the Standard Oil Company of California were prospecting in the neighbourhood of Qasr al-Salwa, that the view of HM Government with regard to the frontier question had already been communicated to King Ibn Saud and that they were still prepared to reopen negotiations for a settlement on the lines already indicated; that in the meantime they assumed that no attempt to pass

> the line would be made by the company so long as no agreement had been reached; but that since there had been some uncertainty as regards the geographical features HM Government proposed that a joint mission should be appointed to establish the exact nature and location of the physical features.[99]

On 4 December Bullard sent a note to the Sa'ūdī Foreign Minister embodying the whole statement. To avoid any misunderstanding, he restated the definition of 'Ryan's line', adding a modification in favour of the Sa'ūdīs at the key point of Ṣafq well, which the latest air surveys had proved to be only twenty-five miles inland. On 19 December 1937 the Sa'ūdī Government gave its answer: it had instructed the American company not to explore beyond the Sa'ūdī 1935 'red line' and it did not believe that the Trucial Shaikhs would allow their oil companies to cross this line, pending a final agreement on the frontier. Further correspondence on this point during the next two months failed to reach any agreement upon a *modus vivendi.*[100]

On 22 December the Cabinet took a decision which had a great influence on the subsequent conclusions of the OME Sub-Committee regarding the negotiations for a frontier settlement, deciding that various proposals should be considered 'for securing the goodwill of Ibn Saud'. The object of this would be 'to counteract as far as possible the inevitable ill effects on the Arab World of the present policy of HM Government in regard to Palestine.[101]

In the first week of February 1938 two letters were exchanged in Jeddah which without any conclusion brought four years of official correspondence to an end. On 3 February Bullard wrote to the Sa'ūdī Foreign Minister informing him that the British Government had gone as far as it could in offering concessions, and that 'Ryan's line' represented the limit of possible compromise. On 6 February Prince Faiṣal, the Foreign Minister, replied in the same sense from their side, citing Fu'ād Ḥamzah's line as the Sa'ūdī limit. The complete deadlock which ensued was not to be resolved until the question was reopened a decade later.[102]

However, the Foreign Office, still hopeful and eager to find a solution, continued their efforts throughout 1938 and succeeded in gaining wide acceptance for their proposals at three meetings. But it was now too late; there was no time to put their resolutions into action before the energies of the Foreign Office and all those concerned were completely absorbed by the outbreak of war and its preliminaries. On 3 February 1938 the Foreign Office circulated a note to the other departments for discussion at the next meeting. Its purpose was 'to examine the possibility of a concession in regard to one of the two places in dispute—the Khūr al 'Udaid'. After outlining the geographical and historical facts concerning Khūr al-'Udaid and the various British and Sa'ūdī interests involved, the note reached the conclusion that 'if on general political grounds it were considered desirable to meet Ibn Saud's claim to the Khor al-Udaid in return for a final settlement of the frontier question, it would still be necessary to find some means of inducing the Shaikh of Abu Dhabi to waive his right there'. The Foreign Office suggested the offer of some monetary compensation to the Shaikh either by the Sa'ūdīs, who were in financial straits, or by the British Government. Another suggestion was to convince the Shaikh that reaching a settlement with regard to his frontiers with Sa'ūdī Arabia would be of greater benefit to him than keeping a place 'from which he derives no revenue and over which he exercises no effective authority'. Finally the note stressed that the Shaikh of Abū Dhabī relied entirely on British support for the maintenance of his independence from Ibn Sa'ūd, and they were therefore doubtless in a position to bring considerable pressure to bear on him if this suggestion should be considered desirable.

On 7 February 1938, on the eve of the meeting of the OME Sub-Committee, the India Office prepared a comment on the Foreign Office note. On 8 February the Sub-Committee met and agreed to seek the opinion of the Government of India and Fowle on the possible cession of Khūr al-'Udaid to Ibn Sa'ūd. On 14 July 1938 the Committee of Imperial Defence, for the purpose of gaining Ibn Sa'ūd's friendship or at least his neutrality in the expected war, decided

> that with a view to the settlement of southeastern frontiers of Saudi Arabia on lines acceptable to Ibn Saud, the Foreign Office and the India Office should be authorised to take up the question of the cession by the Shaikh of Abu Dhabi of a strip of territory in the Persian Gulf known as Khur al-Udaid; that, should compensation in the form of a cash payment prove necessary, the expenditure of a sum tentatively estimated at £25,000 for this purpose should be provisionally authorised, subject to the usual arrangements for obtaining Treasury sanction.[103]

V The Post-War Period and the Agreement of 1975

World War II put an end to the frontier dispute between Abū Dhabī and Sa'ūdi Arabia. The war years passed calmly, but the calm merely preceded a storm. After the war their differences grew, mainly because of the discovery of oil at al-Ḥasā and the growing expectation of more oil in adjacent areas. Limited disagreement, which had been almost resolved before the war, now extended to a wide area. In 1949 the Sa'ūdīs laid claim to new and larger areas, so the British retreated to their earlier position, the 'blue line' of 1913, and the mood of the negotiations changed rapidly; friendly discussions ceased and were replaced by confrontation between 1952 and 1954. In 1955 the dispute was taken to international arbitration, but this failed. King Faiṣal's accession to power in Sa'ūdī Arabia in 1964 and Shaikh Zāyed b. Sulṭān's accession in Abū Dhabī in 1966 marked a new period in relations between the two countries. In 1967 direct negotiations began for the first time. Finally, after long and slow but progressive negotiations, a satisfactory agreement was signed in 1975.

Sa'ūdī–British relations were still, in the post-war period, an important and effective element in the frontier question, so the dispute during this period can be studied in three stages: the first, between 1945 and 1955, which ended with arbitration; the second, between 1956 and 1963, in which diplomatic relations were severed; the third, between 1963 and 1975 when direct negotiations between Abū Dhabī and Sa'ūdī Arabia took place and the matter was settled finally and peaceably.

In fact, the first stage (between 1945 and 1955), which ended with the unsuccessful arbitration of 1955, is especially significant. Great attention was given by both the Sa'ūdī and the British Governments to studying the area with a view to justifying their different claims to the hinterland, and the information thus collected finally supplied the data for those massive volumes, the Sa'ūdī, Abū Dhabī and Muscat 'Memorials' of 1955. The numerous volumes of the two 'Memorials' prepared by the Sa'ūdī and British Governments for the International Tribunal in Geneva in 1955 enrich our geographical, historical and legal knowledge of the hinterland of the Trucial Coast and are considered to be both comprehensive and scholarly. However, in the post-war period fundamental changes took place in the area, and there are still unrecorded facts regarding the wider dimensions of the dispute and the many other parties involved which might throw more light on the question.

The development of events in the dispute after 1945 will not be discussed here in detail, as were those of the 1930s; we will only explore the various avenues which it is hoped will lead to a better understanding of the history. In addition, a study of the development of the early reports as they grew during a decade and helped in compiling the 'Memorials' of 1955 is a matter of great concern to us, for it will not only explain how the data was gathered, thereby increasing our knowledge of the area, but will also reveal the general economic and political changes and the effective powers and factors behind the scenes. These were the American and British Governments and the oil companies, the internal affairs of the actual protagonists, Sa'ūdī Arabia and Abū Dhabī, and the change in British–Sa'ūdī relations after the Second World War.

After the Second World War American political and economic interests in Sa'ūdī Arabia increased and the Americans, seeing that they now had interests of their own at stake, became involved to some extent in the frontier question through Aramco. The cementing of an American political link with Sa'ūdī Arabia was the outstanding development of the war years. In February 1942 the protracted efforts of the California Oil Company to establish diplomatic relations between the United States and Sa'ūdī Arabia, which had begun in the late 1930s, were finally rewarded and an American Chargé d'Affaires was appointed in Jeddah. Then the American Government's

17. A friendly exchange of views between the Shah of Iran and Shaikh Zāyed.

18. Prince Fahd of Sa'ūdī Arabia and Shaikh Zāyed signing the Abū Dhabī/ Sa'ūdī Agreement of 1975.

19. Cordial talks between Shaikh Zāyed and Shaikh Khalīfah b. Hamad, of Qatar.

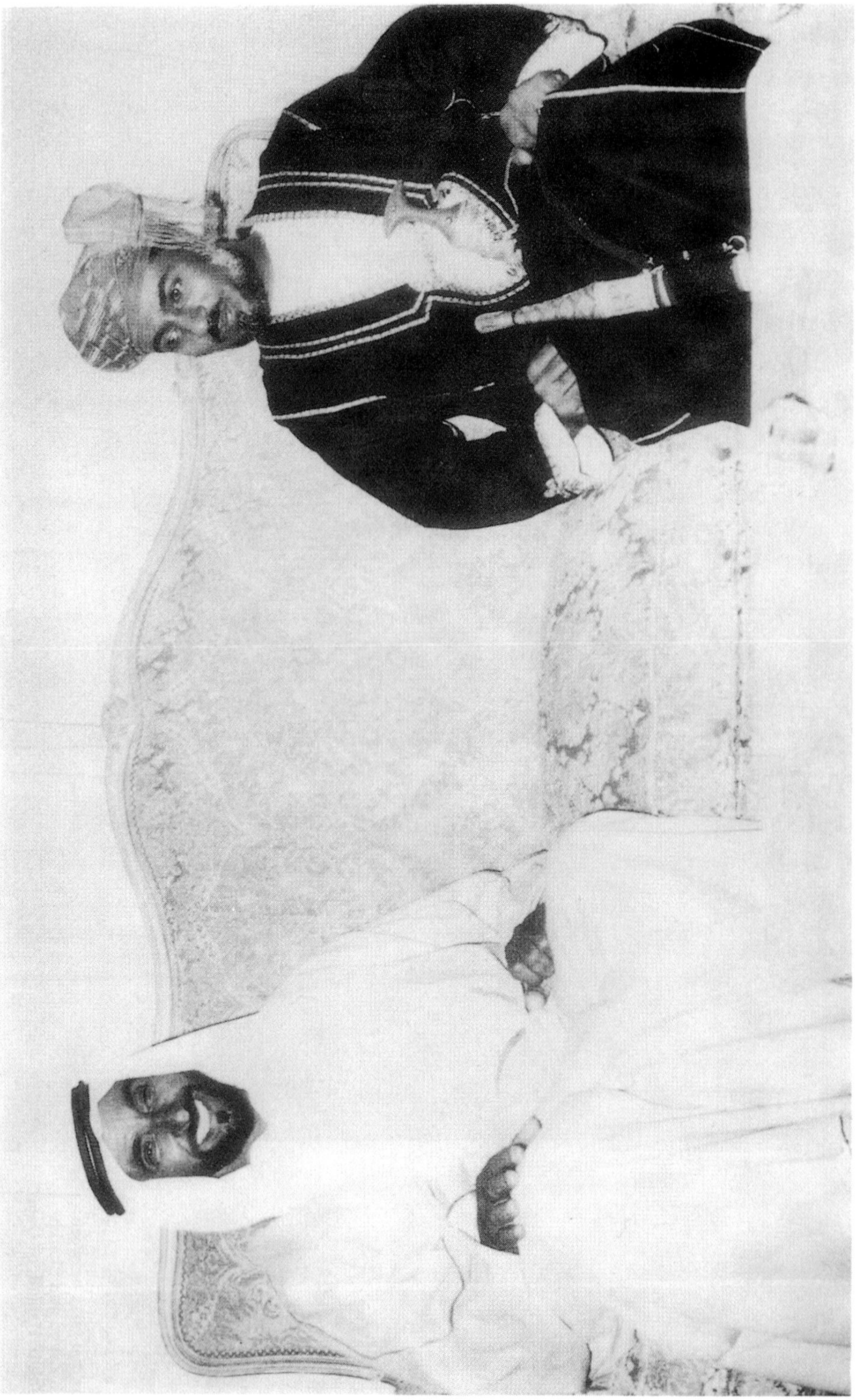

21. HH Shaikh Zāyed b. Sulṭān on his way to the first session of the Federal National Assembly in November 1977 accompanied by the new Chairman, Taryam Umran.

22. Shaikh Zāyed addressing the Federal National Assembly.

23. Shaikh Zāyed b. Sulṭān receiving a falcon's hood from a Dutch falconer at the opening session of the International Conference for Falconry and Conservation.

24. Shaikh Brigadier Sulṭān b. Zāyed presiding at the Falconry and Conservation Conference held in Abū Dhābī in December 1976.

25. Shaikh Zāyed and King Hussain visiting the Jordanian Front.

26. Discussions with Yasser Arafat of the PLO.

27. A march past of the Abū Dhabī Defence Force in 1969.

28. Sheikh Brigadier Sulṭān b. Zāyed, General Commander of the recently unified Armed Forces of the UAE presenting a medal.

attitude of indifference towards Sa'ūdī Arabia quickly changed to one of serious interest as it came to recognise the strategic role that Arab oil could play in their war effort. At that time there was a growing fear in the United States that American oil reserves were being rapidly exhausted and a newly-formed Inter-Departmental Committee in Washington recommended that the Government should take over the Sa'ūdī concession. If this step had materialised, it would have meant the Government's direct involvement in the economic affairs of Sa'ūdī Arabia.

Meanwhile, Ibn Sa'ūd's Government was in a state of economic crisis because of the interruption of pilgrimages and the cessation of British war subsidies. In an attempt to induce Ibn Sa'ūd to grant his oil concession to the United States Government, Roosevelt, in February 1943, exceptionally agreed to extend the Lend-Lease agreement to the Sa'ūdīs, who were not actually war allies. However, Aramco objected to this project and finally Congress, consistent with the American principle of free enterprise abroad, opposed it. Nevertheless, the American Government's interest in Sa'ūdī Arabia increased and in April 1943 America strengthened her diplomatic relations by promoting her representative in Jeddah to the status of Minister. In July an official invitation was extended to Ibn Sa'ūd to visit the United States. Furthermore, on 16 June 1944 the American Minister at Jeddah requested permission from the Sa'ūdi Government to open a consulate in Dhahrān. In 1945 the historic meeting between President Roosevelt and Ibn Sa'ūd took place on board an American cruiser in the Bitter Lakes, and from then on American influence in Sa'ūdī Arabia superseded British. In 1946 Sa'ūdī Arabia granted America landing facilities and an air base at Dhahrān and an American Military Mission took over from the British the training of the Sa'ūdī army. In addition, during the early post-war years the Marshall Plan for the reconstruction of Europe, the Korean War of 1950 and the nationalisation of the AIOC in 1951 all served to increase the need for Sa'ūdī oil as a means of implementing the foreign policy of the United States and this resulted in the strengthening of American–Sa'ūdī relations.

American oil investment in Sa'ūdī Arabia further cemented the links between both countries. During the war Aramco grew enormously, becoming a potent force. In 1936 successful exploration work induced the Texas Oil Company to take over half the shares of the California Arabian Oil Company and a decade later the immense size of their concession, the rich reserves and large expenditure on the construction of the pipeline to the Mediterranean, necessitated an amalgamation with two other major oil companies—Standard Oil of New Jersey and Socony Vacuum. This vast conglomerate not only competed with great power against neighbouring British companies, but also developed strategies which carried much weight in the State Department in Washington. An ambitious exploration scheme began in 1945, particularly after Truman's declaration on the 'Continental Shelf', and a research branch of the Relations Department was established. George

Rentz, a young American scholar and Arabist joined this branch and later took charge of it.

As mentioned earlier, the British Government and the British oil company, Petroleum Concession (Trucial States), were also main factors in the Abū Dhabī–Sa'ūdī frontier dispute and played a role as did, to some extent, the American Government, and to a larger extent the Aramco Oil Company. Although Britain was faced with American schemes and Sa'ūdī ambitions, she was determined to defend her traditional privileges on the Trucial Coast. Having shown willingness to give the Sa'ūdīs the al-'Udaid area in 1938, she now took a different stand and reverted to her traditional support for Abū Dhabī's claim in order to protect her own interests in the face of Sa'ūdī and American ambitions.

Petroleum Concession (Trucial States), which tried in vain to explore the hinterland of this area from 1937 onwards, was after the war determined to find oil. Although Petroleum Concession had no well-established or organised research branch as had Aramco, its archives on the interior were in the near future to prove richer, more accurate and more comprehensive than those of Aramco and the knowledge accumulated by the Foreign Office. As the Government of India, whose archives now became the property of the Foreign and Commonwealth Office, had in the past concentrated its attention on the Coast and had had its treaties with its shaikhs, British knowledge of the interior was to a large extent vague until the immediate pre-war years. In the late 1930s the oil company teams began to explore the hinterland, an activity which they continued in the post-war period and their repeated visits enriched the archives. Furthermore, the representatives of the oil company who were resident in Dubai throughout the year got to know the local people, cultivated a sympathy with them and were in fact better informed than the British political officers who, because of the heat and lack of accommodation on the coast, spent most of their time until 1951 in Baḥrain. Two personalities in the oil company became particularly well informed about the area and were soon to play a major role in collecting the data later used in the Abū Dhabī and Muscat Memorial of 1955. The first was E. F. Henderson,[104] the oil company's representative in Muscat together with Dubai after 1948, in Abū Dhabī in 1950 and finally in Baḥrain, responsible for political concessionary dealings. The second was 'Alī al-Tājir, who was on the staff of the company headquarters in Baḥrain and had frequently visited the Coast from 1938 on and had remained in Dubai after 1952. Hence 'Alī's conviction of the rightness of Abū Dhabī's and Muscat's cause grew, as did his enthusiasm in co-operating with Henderson to collect material for this cause.

Moreover, internal affairs and changes of fortune in Sa'ūdī Arabia, Abū Dhabī, the Trucial Coast and the Sultanate of Muscat in the post-war period had much influence on the development of the frontier question. Because of the power of Ibn Sa'ūd, Aramco was able to start oil operations unhampered by Bedouin raids. So the Sa'ūdīs received an increasing and steady income from oil. In 1940 the Sa'ūdī Kingdom's income from oil was $1.5m and in 1950 it reached $112m. In addition, the new fifty-fifty profit sharing agreement between Aramco and the Sa'ūdī Government improved the Kingdom's balance of payments. Furthermore, Al-Ḥasā production was augmented after 1951 as a result of a world-wide lapse in oil production following the nationalisation of the AIOC. However, Sa'ūdī Arabia was at this time on the threshold of modernising her administration and building the infrastructure of her growth and development. The need for a larger income became obvious, particularly since the Sa'ūdī economy depended almost entirely on oil. Much attention was now given to the Sa'ūdī continental shelf and the rich oil territories in al-Ḥasā, the Empty Quarter and adjacent areas.

But the economic and political situation on the Trucial Coast was very different from that in Sa'ūdī Arabia. The decline of the pearl industry during the 1930s deprived the Trucial Shaikhs of the substantial income with which they had secured the loyalty and obedience of the tribes in the hinterland. This economic decline reduced the political power of the rulers over their tribes, and movements favouring autonomy for individual tribes began to be felt in some parts of the interior, particularly in the Banī Qatab area at Jabal Fāyah. The establishment of the Imamate in Inner 'Omān after 1921 and the intermittent struggle for power between the Imamate and the Sultan of Muscat over al-Dhahirāh province encouraged autonomous feelings, particularly in al-Buraimī area, inhabited by the Āl Bū-Shāmis, the Na'īm, the Banī Qatab and the Banī Ka'b tribes. These areas were unfortunately the chief places of interest to the exploration teams of Petroleum Concession, which they had constantly endeavoured to reach without success since 1937. However, the British geologists were freely active in 1948–9 in Abū Dhabī territory, where peace prevailed and the authority of the ruler was strong. This was due mainly to the popularity of his younger brother Shaikh Zāyed b. Sulṭān who was in charge of the eastern hinterland area. In fact peace at al-'Ain in Abū Dhabī territory allowed the oil company to use it as the base for their explorations north and south.

The insistence of the British oil company on visiting the Jabal Fāyah, Jabal Hafīt and Jabal Fahūd areas in inner 'Omān, in addition to the creation of the Trucial Scouts and their station in al-Jāhilī, produced a tense atmosphere in the hinterland. The tribal chiefs considered these steps as a campaign against their autonomy, which they had enjoyed for two decades, so they viewed the rulers and the active British policy in the interior with great suspicion and much discontent. Finally, the Sultan of Muscat was able to extend his authority over al-Buraimī, when Aḥmad b. Ibrāhīm, the Minister of the Interior, was welcomed there for the first time in 1949. Nevertheless, the nomination of Shaikh Ṣaqr b. Sulṭān, the head of the Na'īm tribe in al-Buraimī, as the Sultan's representative accelerated the deteriorating situation, for he was not popular in the area, particularly among the Āl Bū-Shāmis in Ḥamāsā and their chief, Rāshid b. Ḥamad.

Changes in British–Sa'ūdī relations after the war affected the events relating to the frontier. Previously amicable relationships deteriorated rapidly. In fact the friendly relations which existed between the British and 'Abd al-'Azīz were founded not so much on goodwill, as was the case with the Hashemite kings in Jordan and Iraq, as on the wise and careful statesmanship of 'Abd al-'Azīz, who controlled his ambition and his people to co-exist with the overwhelming British power in the area at that time. In the post-war period this sort of relationship was badly shaken by the emergence of American power, for the Americans became 'Abd al-Azīz's new friends and British power was generally in decline. Discontent with British policy in Palestine on the part of 'Abd al-Azīz and the Arabs generally, and the eventual creation of the State of Israel in 1948, contributed to the deterioration of Sa'ūdī–British relations.

Thus, the American and British Governments and oil companies, the internal affairs of the actual protagonists, Sa'ūdī Arabia and Abū Dhabī, and finally the change in Sa'ūdī–British relations, were the factors which now influenced the development of its frontier problem in the post-war period. Dormant after 1939, it was reopened between 1947 and 1949 when Aramco survey parties penetrated the coastal region east of Qaṭar. This annoyed Shaik Shakhbūṭ, who complained to the recently established British Political Officer in Shārjah. In April 1949 a group of American geologists, accompanied by some armed Sa'ūdī guards, camped near al-Sil' in the al-Mijann area and on the 22 Sobart, the British Political Officer in Shārjah, accompanied by Shaikh Hazzā', Shaikh Shakhbūṭ's brother, handed the party a note insisting on their withdrawal. They left and on 25 April Aramco headquarters replied stating that this protest should have been directed to the Sa'ūdī Government since the oil company was not concerned in the political aspect of the frontier question.

This incident sparked off a frontier controversy and correspondence began between the Sa'ūdī and British Governments. The Sa'ūdīs protested to the British Embassy in Jeddah about Stobart's action, but Britain rejected the Sa'ūdī protest and asserted the validity of Abū Dhabi's sovereignty in the area. In September negotiations were reopened. On 14 October the Sa'ūdīs began their discussions to extend their boundaries beyond the Fu'ād Ḥamzah line of 1935, and feeling more confident because of their new wealth and alliance in addition to the instability of the tribes in the hinterland of the Trucial Coast, reverted to their initial stand of 1934, insisting that the whole of the inland desert of southeast Arabia was part of Sa'ūdī Arabia and that the Trucial Shaikhs' authority did not extend beyond their coastal belt. The Sa'ūdī Government's memorandum of 14 October claimed a huge area; all the mainland and half the coastline: from a point on the coast two kilometres east of Bandar al-Mirfa' the boundary ran in a straight line to the southwest until it reached latitude 23.36° north, from there due east until it intersected longitude 54.00° east, and from that intersection in a straight line to latitude 24.25° north and longitude 55.36° east.

An exchange of letters began between the British and Sa'ūdī Governments, in which one can see the weight of the post-war historical and legal studies of the area. On 30 November 1949 the British rejected the new Sa'ūdī claims as totally unrealistic, taking a firm stand on the terms of the Anglo–Turkish convention of 1913–14. As it was clear that the Sa'ūdīs were relying on historical arguments in presenting their claims, the British appended the text of a 'declaration' by 'Abdullah b. Faiṣal in 1866 in which, apart from collecting *zakat* (religious alms) according to ancient custom, he pledged that he would not interfere with Arab principalities in alliance with the British. On 10 December the Sa'ūdīs replied, refusing to accept the 'Blue Line' as a basis for discussion and declining to acknowledge Abdullah b. Faiṣal's 'declaration', which did not exist in their archives. Furthermore, they once again extended their claims into the Buraimī area, this time leaving no doubt about the fact that they considered this an integral part of their kingdom, and also the lands of the Imamate of 'Omān, which they declared were populated by the Sa'ūdī tribes. The Sa'ūdīs ended by suggesting that a thorough investigation should be made to determine accurately the loyalties of the tribes in the disputed area.

At this point, in January 1950, Rentz and his colleagues in the research branch of the Aramco Relations Department produced their first work, a lengthy study of 'The Eastern Province of al-Ḥasā'. This report consisted of two main parts. The first was a study of the areas of al-Ḥasā province situated to the east of the Salwā and stretching to the Trucial Coast, in which Rentz came to a geographical conclusion that al-Dhafrāh, Līwā and al-Khatam were all parts of al-Ḥasā. The second was a detailed statement on the tribes inhabiting these areas in which he reasserted that the Manāṣīr and the 'Awāmir were Sa'ūdī subjects. These two conclusions were soon to influence the frontier question. Rentz ended his report with a study of *zakat*, the collection and distribution of which was still one of the duties of the state in Sa'ūdī Arabia. With the assistance of the Exploration Department, which took an active interest in the preparation of this report, two maps of the Trucial States were prepared for the first time, one of al-Dhafrāh and the surrounding region, the other showing the areas included in the Sa'ūdī Kingdom. A third map was also produced, showing the position of these two areas within the Arabian peninsula. In these early attempts the position of many places was only approximate.[105] Rentz recorded that the system followed in the investigation and the kind of sources relied upon were open to error. He considered that his work was at a primitive stage and that further study would no doubt reveal more information. For example, he mentioned 149 settlements and villages in Līwā which even now comprises only 52. He based his first work mainly on interviews with Bedouins who happened to live, for political and financial reasons, in al-Ḥasā. He also depended on the Admiralty book on the Gulf printed in 1916 and the works of two British explorers, the books of Philby after 1933 and an article by Thesiger written in 1949.

Thesiger, the last British explorer in Arabia, reached the southern part of Līwā in December 1946, and in October 1948 he explored Līwā oasis. But Rentz was the pioneer scholar, inaugurating detailed research and study of this previously unknown and therefore unmapped area. Although he personally admitted to never having visited the area, the information collected from the tribesmen provided us for the first time with a very comprehensive picture which enriched our knowledge of all the hinterland.[106]

Regardless of the negotiations which began in September 1949, a *zakat* collector, Muḥammad b. Manṣūr, was extremely active in the hinterland of Abū Dhabī. When his men visited Līwā oasis on 10 April 1950 the British protested. On 11 May the Sa'ūdīs rejected the complaint and demanded to know on what historical basis the Shaikh of Abū Dhabī made claim to regions which had belonged to Bedouins who had long been subject to Sa'ūdī rule and had been paying *zakat* to their representatives throughout the whole period. To this the British replied in a detailed memorandum dated 24 July that it was the Sa'ūdī Government who had to prove their title to these lands and not the Shaikh of Abū Dhabī. On this occasion they reasserted that Ibn Sa'ūd had been a Turkish subject and he was therefore bound by the 'Blue Line'. Furthermore they denied that the collection of *zakat* from tribes in these areas claimed by the Sa'ūdīs constituted adequate proof in international law. In conclusion, the British agreed to a Joint Technical Commission, and if that proved ineffective the frontier dispute would then be submitted to international arbitration. On 22 September the Sa'ūdīs again denied the existence of the 1913 convention between Ibn Sa'ūd and the Ottomans, in which the former was considered a Turkish subject. They agreed however with the proposed Joint Frontier Commission and that meanwhile the *status quo* prevailing until October 1949 should be respected.

Although by April 1951 the British and the Sa'ūdī Governments, after exchanging many letters, had agreed that the Commission should begin activities the following autumn, neither side was optimistic about the achievement of a permanent settlement. Meanwhile, Emir Faiṣal, the Minister for Foreign Affairs, was invited to London for discussions on the maritime boundaries of Sa'ūdī Arabia with Kuwait and Baḥrain, and the territorial frontiers in the Lower Gulf were also discussed. Faiṣal put forward the idea earlier proposed by the Sa'ūdīs that a Round Table Conference of the shaikhs should be held.

On 28 January 1952 the Round Table Conference opened at Dammām. Emir Faiṣal led the Sa'ūdī delegation and the British delegation was headed by the Political Resident in the Gulf, Sir Rupert Hay, accompanied by the rulers of Qaṭar and Abu Dhabī. Shaikh Shakhbūṭ claimed as his boundary a line beginning at Sawdā Nathīl and running on a straight course to the southernmost tip of the Sabkhat Maṭṭī. From there the line ran approximately southeastwards to al-Quraini well, then northeastwards to Umm al-Zamūl wells. After several plenary and informal sessions the conference came to a stalemate in mid-February.

It became clear four years later that the Sa'ūdīs and Aramco had been active meanwhile in collecting documents and letters from the shaikhs in al-Buraimī area, some of whom visited Sa'ūdī Arabia. At the same time British Petroleum Concessions found, by mere chance in early 1952, an Arabic copy of Aramco's report on al-Ḥasā and its eastern provinces, an incident which aroused the curiosity of Mr Henderson, their representative in Dubai and Muscat. The British took Aramco's report seriously, regarding it as having been the basis for the Sa'ūdī claim of October 1949. It was at once arranged for Henderson to visit Rentz in Dhahrān, where he discovered the vast investigation upon which the latter had embarked. In Rentz's house he saw a copy of the English version of the Eastern Approaches of al-Ḥasā and a copy of Lorimer's Gazetteer, which was not available even to British civilians of the British Petroleum Concession. This soon stimulated more energetic studies, not only by the representatives of Petroleum Concession Limited, but also by the Foreign Office in London, on the hinterland of Abū Dhabī. Thenceforth, energetic mutual co-operation began between the British Company and the Foreign Office in collecting data. Rentz's report was translated into English in October 1952. Buckmaster, Assistant Political Officer in Shārjah (1951–3), began his wide investigation of the *dirah* of the tribes and their loyalties, and visited Līwā oasis for the first time. Unlike Rentz, Buckmaster travelled freely through vast areas and met local personalities easily.

In 1952 Rentz and his colleagues in Aramco's research branch finished their second work, 'Oman and the Southern Coast of the Gulf', copies of which can now be found only on microfilm or in a few printed versions in the larger universities.

Whilst Aramco's first report relied upon interviews and oral material, the data collected for the second book, a scholarly group work of two years' duration, was mainly based on official documents from the India Office, Arabic and Turkish sources. Somehow Rentz had managed to procure a copy of Lorimer's confidential Gazeteer of the Gulf, written in 1905 and restricted to British official circles for more than four decades. Access to this new and rich source of material strengthened Rentz's hand in discussing the affairs of this unknown region.

The second work comprised six chapters and included a comprehensive bibliography. In the introduction Rentz stated that the book was complementary to the first report as it dealt with the adjacent areas of the Sa'ūdī eastern province of al-Ḥasā. He hoped that this study might throw light upon the facts regarding the disputed area, information which he hoped would enable the officials to solve the frontier dispute. In Chapter One the book dealt with the Imamate of 'Omān (which was then to a certain extent exercising internal autonomy) and its boundaries, the northern part of which extended only as far as 'Ibrī; also its history during medieval times up to the revival of the Imamate in 1913. The chapter ended with a study of the existing Imam, Moḥammad b. 'Abdullah al-Khalīlī, who began his rule in 1921, and the two important personalities of the Imamate, Sulaimān b. Ḥimyar, the Lord of the Green Mountain, and Shaikh Ṣāliḥ b. 'Īsā al-Ḥarithī, the head of Sharqiyyah province. Then followed a study of the tribes of the Imamate and their different loyalties, Hināwī and Ghāfirī, and their sects, Sunnī or Ibādhī. Mention is made of the expedition of Ṣāliḥ b. 'Īsā and Sulaiman b. Ḥimyar in 1925 to subdue al-Buraimī to the Imamate, which succeeded in including only 'Ibrī in its domain. Therefore the al-Dhāhirah area remained independent, beyond the power of both the Imamate and the Sultan.

In Chapter Two the authors studied the al-Dhāhirah area, its villages and its tribes, mentioning Thesiger, who had travelled through it. They noted its strategic position and recorded that the Shaikh of Abū Dhabī had authority over some of the Buraimī villages. Al-Buraimī, the centre of al-Dhāhirah, was the main theme for Chapter Three. As the Buraimī oasis was the centre of the Sa'ūdī influence in 'Omān during the nineteenth century, the history of this oasis and Sa'ūdī relations with 'Omān, to which they had given only a few pages in their first report, was the next subject for a detailed and comprehensive study, recording that the al-Buraimī area had been independent since the Sa'ūdī departure of 1871 and making reference to Miles who visited it in 1875, the Reverend Zwemer who visited it in 1901, and Lorimer who in 1950 regarded it as independent. The authors also drew upon two British works, the first by Eccles, a captain in the Indian Army, who in 1925–6 became Commander of the new Levies of the Sultan of Muscat, and the second by Bertram Thomas, the Minister of Finance in Muscat from 1925 to 1930, who both visited the surroundings of Buraimī, the first British visits to the interior since those of Cox in 1903.

In Chapter Four a study is made of the Abū Dhabī Emirate, its history, boundaries, tribes, economy and relations with Britain. The authors consider that the Banī Yās is the only tribe in the Abū Dhabī Emirate and that the Manāṣīr are Sa'ūdī subjects. The coast between the small port of al-Mirfa' and al-'Udaid, which was claimed by the Sa'ūdīs in October 1949, is the theme of Chapter Five, while Chapter Six is devoted to a study of Qaṭar, its land, tribes and modern history. The book's seven maps are very important and helpful to an understanding of the region, as they set out clearly the facts regarding the tribes, their *dirah*, their political loyalties and religious sects.

The failure of the Dammām Conference in February 1952 put an end to the frontier negotiations and the unstable situation in al-Buraimī set the stage for later events. In July Rāshid b. Ḥamad, the chief of the Āl Bū-Shāmis in Ḥamāsā, went on pilgrimage. On his return on 31 August, he brought with him Turkī b. 'Utaishān as the representative of the Sa'ūdī Government, accompanied by forty retainers. Turkī established himself in Ḥamāsā village, where the Sa'ūdī flag was raised.

Although the arrival of Ibn 'Utaishān at Ḥamāsā was more a political act than military, it soon inflamed the situation. The Sultan of Muscat, who regarded it as an occupation of his land, immediately gathered a force at Ṣuḥār, and a detachment of the Trucial 'Omān Levies was hastily moved to al-Jāhilī fort in al-'Ain. During these difficult days the strong and popular figure of young Zāyed, the brother and representative of Shaikh Shakbūṭ at al-'Ain, played a vital role in keeping stability and loyalty among Abū Dhabī tribes in the area. On 14 September the British protested to the Sa'ūdī Government and demanded Turkī's withdrawal. The Sa'ūdīs refused to withdraw and reinforced Turkī with men and vehicles. Finally, partly perhaps as a result of American intervention, the British advised the Sultan of Muscat to abandon his attack on the al-Buraimī area, which they greatly regretted three years later. On 26 October a standstill agreement was signed at Jeddah by British and Sa'ūdī representatives. It was agreed that the British should lift their restrictive measures around Ḥamāsā, the Sa'ūdīs should refrain from provocative acts, both sides should remain in their positions in al-Buraimī for the time being, and negotiations for a solution of the frontier problem should be renewed.

Negotiations were renewed in November 1952 but it took seven months to get the British and the Sa'ūdīs to agree to submit the dispute to arbitration, which was signed in July 1954. Both sides now accelerated their efforts to gather documents and collect new sources of information.

In August 1954, Ṣālīḥ al-Mutawwa', an intellectual from Shārjah, completed his manuscript *'Uqūd al-Jumān Fi Sirat Al-Sa'ūd Fi'Omān* (Necklace of Pearls in the History of Al Sa'ūd in 'Omān), a title which reveals the author's approach and concept of the history of the area. The work reflects a sympathy towards the Unitarians among the advocates of the reform movement on the Trucial Coast, and the heroic story of King 'Abd al-'Azīz and the growth of his power in the early twentieth century was followed with enthusiasm and revived religious feeling among the Unitarians on the Coast. It is an intelligent accumulation from Arabic and translated sources and reveals its author's wide reading. Its real value is in the last chapters concerning the tribal history of al-Dhāhirah and the interior of the Trucial Coast in the last three decades, and it is frequently quoted anonymously in the Sa'ūdī 'Memorial' of 1955.

During these years the 'Aḥmad b. Hilāl Papers', the most important official documents on the internal affairs of the Trucial Coast, were found. 'Alī al-Tājir had visited Muscat in search of documents and although he received no response from the Sultan, Aḥmad b. Ibrāhīm (the Minister of the Interior) was very co-operative; 'Alī al-Tājir was able to copy some documents and return them. Moreover, Shaikh Hazzā', brother of Shaikh Shakbūṭ, found in the former home of the late Aḥmad b. Hīlāl several sacks of old official correspondence covering Aḥmad's long service at al-'Ain from 1890 to 1940, written between himself and the rulers Zāyed b. Khalīfah, his sons Ṭahnūn, Ḥamdān, Sulṭān and his grandson Shakhbūṭ, as well as neighbouring rulers and tribal shaikhs. As the India Office archives are rich in papers relating to external affairs but poor in those relating to internal matters of the Trucial Coast, one can imagine the real value of the documents discovered, which revealed for the first time the actual jurisdiction practised in the hinterland. 'Alī al-Tājir translated these Arabic letters into English and an extensive report was prepared by him and Mr Henderson; all of which were sent to the Foreign Office in London.[107] In fact the 'Aḥmad b. Hīlāl Papers' form an important element in the evidence presented in the Abū Dhabī and Muscat Memorials of 1955.

On 13 August, after the signing of the arbitration agreement, Turkī b. 'Utaishān and his men left al-Buraimī and were replaced by a small Sa'ūdī police detachment. The arbitration tribunal met for the first time on 23 January 1955 in Nice. Subsequent sittings took place in Geneva, where the two huge Memorials of both sides were presented. Although much research had been done and many reports produced during the previous five years, the two Memorials were written in their entirety by the Sa'ūdī Foreign Ministry and the Research Department of the Foreign Office in London respectively. However, there were continued accusations on both sides of violation of the terms of the arbitration agreement in the al-Buraimī area. Finally, in September 1955 Sir Reader Bullard, the British representative at the tribunal, resigned and thus the arbitration conference failed.

Meanwhile in May 1954 the old Imam, Muḥammad b. 'Abdullah al-Khalīlī, who had been co-operative with the Sultan, died and a new Imam, Ghālib b. 'Ali, was elected and proclaimed the sovereign independence of the interior of 'Omān. The Sultan of Muscat, Sa'īd b. Taimūr, took the opportunity to unify 'Omān under his rule and his forces occupied 'Ibrī in September. Following the collapse of arbitration in Geneva, the forces of the Sultan seized Nīzwā in September 1955, and in October the Sultan and the ruler of Abū Dhabī, supported by the Trucial 'Omān Scouts, moved into the Buraimī oasis. The Sa'ūdī police force, accompanied by Rāshid b. Ḥamad, the head of Āl Bū-Shāmis, and Ṣaqr b. Sulṭān, the head of the Na'īm, were eventually allowed to leave for Sa'ūdī Arabia. On 26 October, with the British still maintaining their supremacy in the area, Eden, the Prime Minister, declared that his Government would acknowledge only the 'Riyadh Line' of 1937 as the accepted boundary between Abū Dhabī and Sa'ūdī Arabia and this would be the basis for any further negotiations.

On 15 December the Sultan's Levies occupied Nizwā and Imam Ghalib fled to the mountains, preparing for a revolt which took place a year and a half later. From Salālā Sa'īd b. Taimūr made his first tour in the interior of his country after thirty-three years of rule; he arrived in Nizwā on 19 December and ended his tour at Buraimī on the 28th, where the next day he met Shaikh Shakhbūṭ.

In February Eden visited Washington and had talks with Eisenhower at which he explained recent events in Buraimī. A communiqué followed in which Britain declared her readiness to renegotiate with the Sa'ūdīs, but the Suez crisis put an end to this first stage of the frontier problem when the Sa'ūdīs in November 1956 broke diplomatic relations with Britain. Anti-colonialism which dominated the Arab countries following the Suez crisis and the 'Omāni revolt of 1957, in addition to the lack of information about the history of the frontier problem, directed Arab sympathy towards the Sa'ūdīs. More than a decade passed before the Arab world took a neutral stand and realised that the origin of the Buraimī was a frontier demarcation between neighbouring brother countries.

During the second period of the frontier dispute, between 1956 and 1963, there was no progress. Events, however, created new alliances and a new political atmosphere helped to reconcile the British and the Sa'ūdīs. Relations between the two countries were resumed in 1963, which contributed to the solution of the frontier dispute. At the same time, in Abū Dhabī, Shaikh Zāyed b. Sulṭān, anxious to reach an understanding with the Sa'ūdīs, encouraged his brother Shakhbūt to go on pilgrimage in 1964. They went to Dammām together with a large number of Abū Dhabī's notables where they were warmly received. 'Abd al-Raḥmān al-Bassām, a Sa'ūdī citizen who had visited Abū Dhabī several times in the preceding few years, accompanied them in the royal plane to Jeddeh. The cordial meeting between the new King Faiṣal and Shaikh Shakhbūt and his brother Zāyed was the first step in establishing friendly relations between the two states.

The third and last stage, which brought the dispute to an end, witnessed the appearance of new leaders in Sa'ūdī Arabia and Abū Dhabī. Fundamental international and local changes also took place in the area. In 1964 King Faiṣal assumed power in Sa'ūdī Arabia and began his great work in his own country as well as in the Arab and Islamic world. He accelerated internal development and laid the foundations of modern Sa'ūdī Arabia within the Islamic traditions. Because of his personality, wisdom and long experience in international affairs, he played a constructive role in the Arab world after the defeat of 1967 and made a large contribution to the victory of 1973, actions which gained great respect for himself and his country. Since 1967, Sa'ūdī Arabia as the major Arab country in the Gulf has assumed responsibility for Arab interests there. In April 1967, Shaikh Zāyed b. Sulṭān paid a friendly visit to Faiṣal, who believed that peaceful negotiation and contact would solve the long-standing frontier dispute.

The great achievements by which Shaikh Zāyed built modern Abū Dhabī, and the generous help he gave to the nationalist cause and to the Arab world, gained a great reputation for both Abū Dhabī and her leader; Zāyed became the symbol of stability at this time and the probable leader for the expected union of the Trucial Coast. In fact, mutual friendship, admiration and respect between the two leaders helped greatly in opening direct negotiations for the first time.

During the 1960s British interest in Sa'ūdī Arabia as well as in Abū Dhabī increased. In 1968, after deciding to withdraw from the Gulf, the British became even more keen for a quick settlement of the frontier dispute and encouraged direct negotiations, as did the Americans and the friendly Arab countries, too, urging the two states towards an understanding.

The creation of the United Arab Emirates in 1971, the energetic activities of Aḥmad Suwaidi, the Foreign Minister, the establishment of stable government and a speedy start to the development of the area, as well as the efforts of Prince Fahd b. 'Abd al-'Azīz were all factors helping to further friendly relations and mutual co-operation between Sa'ūdī Arabia and the new state. Finally in 1975 a frontier agreement was signed by both heads of state, which put a satisfactory end to the problem.

VI Settlement of the Maritime Boundaries of Abū Dhabī and Qaṭar

In the angle formed by the western part of the Abū Dhabī coast and the east coast of Qaṭar lies a group of islands, including Hālūl, Dās, Shirā'ūh, Dayyīnah, 'Arzanah, Dalmā, Sīr Banī Yās, al-Yāsāt, Ghāghah, al-Qaffāy and al-Mihayyimāt, Makāsib and al-Asḥāṭ. The frontier between Abū Dhabī and Qaṭar extends not only inland from the coast but outwards into the sea, dividing the numerous islands which lie among the rich pearl fisheries off the coast of both emirates, from which they derive their significance. Some of them, such as Sīr Bāni Yās, al-Yāsāt, Ghāghah and particularly Dalmā, were inhabited during the winter months by groups of the Bāni Yās (the Qibaisāt, Maḥāribah and Mazārī'), while during the summer they became overcrowded by the influx of pearl fishermen coming usually from the Trucial Coast, Qaṭar and Baḥrain. The Shaikh of Abū Dhabī had a permanent representative in Dalmā. Even many of the small uninhabited islands had some importance because the fishermen took refuge there in stormy weather. The majority were acknowledged, as is clear from their names, as belonging to Abū Dhabī, and the inhabitants of Sīr Bāni Yās, Dalmā and al-Yāsāt, and Ghāghah, especially, which lie near the mainland, were in the habit of making settlements and camps on the coast, a fact which constituted one of the strong arguments in favour of Abū Dhabī's claim to the coast of al-'Udaid peninsula, al-'Uqal, al-Mijann and Sabkhat Maṭṭī.

Before World War I there was no recorded dispute over the ownership of these islands, presumably because the pearl fisheries were considered common property and the Shaikhs of Abū Dhabī made no difficulty over the use of the islands by Qaṭari fishermen. An early indication of the ownership of Hālūl, later one of the disputed islands, occurred in 1913 when the British implicitly recognised Abū Dhabī's ownership by officially informing the Shaikh of the erection of a cairn on the island. It was not until the 1930s, when oil concessions necessitated the precise demarcation of all frontiers in the Gulf, inland or maritime, that the ownership of some of the islands became a matter of dispute between Qaṭar and Abū Dhabī. In 1931 Major Holmes mentioned to Colonel Dickson that the island of Hālūl was one of the places in the Gulf where oil might be found. On 23 May 1933 Fowle wrote a private and confidential letter to E. H. O. Elkington, Director of APOC, suggesting a geological survey of Hālūl, in view of the past reports of oil seepages in its vicinity. Fowle recommended that, in view of the indeterminate status of the island and the undesirability of exciting comment, this would have to be done as discreetly as possible, for instance by an apparently casual visit by the tanker *Khuzistan.* When in the early 1930s the British opened their air route along the Arab coast, the islands of Dalmā and Sīr Bāni Yās were chosen for the establishment of landing grounds and stores.

The islands under dispute between Qaṭar and Abū Dhabī were Hālūl, Dayyīnah, al-Asḥāṭ and Shirā'ūh. Between 1936 and 1938 considerable investigation of the ownership of these islands is recorded in British official archives. However, there was no open dispute until after World War II, when oil was produced and the determination of their ownership became a matter of urgency. In 1961 the British recognised Hālūl as belonging to the Shaikh of Qaṭar, after a report by Mr Charles Gault and Professor Norman Anderson. A decision about the islands of Dayyīnah, al-Asḥāt and Shirā'ūh was reached in the treaty of 1969 between Qaṭar and Abū Dhabī regarding their maritime frontiers: Dayyīnah was considered to belong to Abū Dhabī while the other two islands were recognised as owned by Qaṭar.

Notes

1. Sa'ūdī Arabia, *Memorial of the Government of Saudi Arabia*, Cairo, 1955, I, pp.11–29.
2. Lorimer, I, Part I B, op.cit., pp.799–803, 839.
3. OA, Irade 1288H (1891), Dahiliyye, 44930, Report from Midhat Pasha to the Sublime Porte.
4. Kelly, *Britain*, op.cit., pp.756, 768.
5. Kelly, ibid., pp. 769–72, 813, 825–8, 842–51.
6. IOR, R/15/1/6/181, Hostilities between Shaikh Zāyed and Shaikh Jāsim. Jāsim to Shaikh Tahnun and Khalīfah, sons of Zāyed, 16 November 1880; Jāsim to Ross, 11 May 1881; Ross to Jāsim, 19 May 1881; Ross to Jāsim, 30 June 1881; Hājjī 'Abu al-Qāsim to Ross, 22 July 1881.
7. IOR, L/P & S/18/B19, Turkish Jurisdiction along the Arabian Coast IV, pp.2–3.
8. IOR, ibid., pp.5–10.
9. IOR, ibid., pp.13–15.
10. IOR, R/15/1/0/178, Intention of Shaikh Jāsim to settle his people at al-'Udaid, Turkish Captain to Zāyed, 26 June 1886, and Zāyed to Ross, 8 July 1886.
11. IOR, R/15/1/0/181, Zāyed to Ross, 2 May 1888; Residency Agent to Ross, 10 May

1888; Aḥmad 'Abd al-Rasūl, Baḥrain, to Ross, 16 May 1888 and 28 May 1888; Residency Agent, Shārjah, to Ross, 2 June 1888.
12. IOR, R/15/1/0/189, Qaṭar and Abū Dhabī, William White, Ambassador to Constantinople to Salisbury, 9 May 1889.
13. IOR, op.cit., Hājjī 'Abu al-Qāsim to Ross, 26 May 1888, and letters from Residency Agents in Baḥrain on 11 June 1888 and in Lingah on 11 June 1888.
14. IOR, R/15/1/0/189, Ross to SGI, 18 February 1889 (enclosed letter from Jāsim to Abdullah b. Thaniyyān, 9 June 1888).
15. IOR, op.cit., Residency Agent, Baḥrain to Ross, 14 September 1888; Mīrzā 'Abu al-Qāsim at al-Bid' to Ross, 5 October 1888; Hājjī 'Abu al-Qāsim to Ross, 8 September 1888; Residency Agent, Lingah, to Ross, 21 October 1888; Jāsim to Ross, 13 June 1888 and 17 July 1888; Hājjī 'Abu al-Qāsim to Ross, 20 July 1888; Ross to Jāsim, 8 July 1888; Ross to Residency Agent, 1 August 1888; Ross to Zāyed, 10 August 1888.
16. OA, Meclis-i Vukelā, Defter 37, 2 November 1888; OA, Irade, Dahiliyye 86689, 18 September 1888. Letter from Ibn Rāshid to the Sultan and report of presents.
17. IOR, op.cit., Precis of a conversation between Pol. Res. and Jāsim on 5 October 1888.
18. IOR, R/115/1/189, William White, Ambassador at Constantinople, to Salisbury, 9 May 1889; Ross to SGI, 18 February 1889; Residency Agent, Baḥrain, to Ross, 19 March 1889; Residency Agent, Baḥrain to Ross, 7 January 1889; Sultan Faiṣal b. Turki to Ross, 13 January 1889.
19. IOR, ibid., 'Abd al-Latif to Ross, 31 January 1889; Ross to GI, 8 March 1889; Ross to SGI, 18 February 1889.
20. IOR, ibid., Report from 'Abd al-Latif to Ross, 8 March 1889; Jāsim to Ross, 12 April and 15 April 1889.
21. OA, Meclis-i Vukelā, Defter 42, 13 Saban 1306H, 15 April 1889; IOR, op.cit., Residency Agent, Baḥrain to Ross, 6 May 1889.
22. IOR, ibid., SGI to Ross, 14 March 1889; Ross to SGI, 15 March 1889; 'Īsā, Shaikh of Baḥrain, to Ross, 11 March 1890.
23. OA, Husui, No. 67, 3 Receb 1315H, 29 November 1897; OA, Meclis-i Vukelā, Defter 87, 1313H, (1896), Report on Qaṭar, 4 December 1895.
24. IOR, L/P & S/4, FO to IO, 18 July 1904.
25. IOR, L/P & S/10/4, Persian Gulf, Kemball to SGI, 8 April 1904.
26. Hurewitz, I, op.cit., pp.269–72.
27. H. C. Armstrong, *Lord of Arabia, Ibn Saud, An Intimate Study of a King*, Beirut, 1966, p.16.
28. IOR, L/P & S/18/B437, Historical Memorandum on Ibn Sa'ūd, pp.27–34.
29. IOR, ibid., pp.28–31.
30. IOR, ibid., pp.32–9.
31. H. St. J. B. Philby, *Arabian Days*, London, 1948, pp.140, 153–4, 164, 167, 172.
32. At this critical point in his career, Amīn al-Riḥānī visited Ibn Sa'ūd in 1922. Riḥānī was a Lebanese and a liberal Arab nationalist writer of some repute. The Near Eastern Affairs Division of the US Department of State was at this time much concerned to collect reliable information on Arabia. In opposition to the British and French, the Americans were strongly advocating an 'open door' policy in the Middle East, particularly as regards oil concessions. Riḥānī's 1922 tour of the Arabian peninsula had a dual purpose. He was collecting material for a book and also preparing a general report on Arabia at the request of the Near Eastern Affairs Division. He was received with much caution in British circles at Aden and the Gulf, being suspected of instigating anti-British feeling or representing American oil companies' interests. At first he was refused permission to go from Baḥrain to Riyādh to visit Ibn Sa'ūd, but Cox in Baghdād wisely invited Riḥānī to accompany him on an urgent visit he was making to Ibn Sa'ūd.
33. Dickson, op.cit., pp.266, 270, 271, 276, 281–2, 284–5; IOR, L/P & S/10/938, IO to FO, 20 October 1922.
34. Two years later Cox expressed Ibn Sa'ūd's feelings at a lecture in London when he said, 'The great Wahhābi ruler Ibn Sa'ūd was and is a very dear friend and I have discussed his ambitions with him many times . . . practically he thinks that he is justi-

fied in principle in regaining any territory that his forefathers had a century ago, whether as territory or as a sphere of influence . . . after the war, however, we had to reduce expenditure . . . one of these reduced was that of Ibn Sa'ūd . . . but what he felt was "up to now I have been under specific obligations not to annoy the British Government by any policy that I pursue but now that they have felt obliged to stop my payment to me, I think I am entitled to pursue my own policy and work out my own destiny as I think best." ' G. J. Eccles, 'The Sultanate of Muscat and Oman', *JRCAS*, XIV, I, 1927; Comment of Cox, p.40; A. J. Toynbee, *Survey of International Affairs, 1925*, London, 1927, p.273.

35. Dickson, op.cit., pp.284, 285.
36. Hurewitz, op.cit., II, pp.149–50.
37. Dickson, op.cit., pp.285–7.
38. Wahbah, op.cit., pp.119–20, 129; Dickson, op.cit., pp.330–32.
39. DSA, Box 7066, Wallace Murray to Secretary of State, 27 January 1931.
40. US Government Printing Press, *Foreign Relations of the US*, Washington, 1939, IV, pp.824–5; and 1942, IV, pp.559–61.
41. Wahbah, op.cit., pp.95, 96, 104, 105–6; CAB, 51/4, Meeting No. 52, 29 June 1937.
42. H. St. J. B. Philby, *Arabian Oil Adventures*, Washington, 1964, pp.86–9, 119–27. Philby, *Arabian Days*, p.296.
43. UK Memorial, I, op.cit., pp.74–9.
44. IOR, L/P & S/18/B/437, pp.28, 42; Graves, op.cit., pp. 104–5.
45. IOR, op.cit., 30–4.
46. IOR, R/15/3/XXV/4, Arabian Politics, Prideaux to SSC, 9 June 1929.
47. IOR, op.cit., p.34.
48. IOR, R/15/3/XXV/1, Memorandum of an Interview with the Ibn Sa'ūd, 15–16 December 1913, & enclosure to Memorandum, 18 December 1913.
49. IOR, L/P & S/18B 437, pp.38–9, 42, & R/15/1/14/34, Arab Coast and Islands, Hamdan to Knox, 4 October 1914.
50. IOR, R/15/3/XXV/4, Arabian Politics, Pol. Agent, Baḥrain to Pol. Res., 7 April 1920, Pol. Agent to Pol. Res., 4 April 1920.
51. Sa'ūdī Memorial, op.cit., pp.53–8, 321–2; IOR, L/P & S/11/924, Thomas' Report, 13 June 1927, pp.27–8.
52. IOR, L/P & S/10/1165, Fowle to CO, 8 June 1926, and Foreign Secretary to Viceroy, 21 August 1926.
53. IOR, R/15/1/14/40, Arab Coast, 'Īsā to Pol. Res., 31 March 1926.
54. IOR, L/P & S/10/1271, The Trucial Chiefs, 1908–28, p.3.
55. IOR, L/P & S/18/B 437, pp.43–4.
56. CAB, 16/94, PG Sub-Committee, Memorandum by GSI, 18 October, 1928, p.4.
57. IOR, R/15/14/40, SNO to Pol. Res., 20 June 1926.
58. IOR, L/P & S/12/2136, Tribal History of Trucial Oman 1918–34.
59. CAB, 51/7, Rendel to IO, 16 March 1934.
60. IOR, L/P & S/12/2136, Laithwaite Memorandum on 'The Southern Boundary of Qatar and the Connected Problems', 26 January 1934.
61. CAB, op.cit., Ryan to FO, 14 February 1934.
62. IOR, L/P & S/12/2136, Memo.B., 430. 'The Southern Boundary of Qaṭar', 27 February 1934, and Appendix LV, re Cox's comments.
63. CAB, 51/3, Meeting No. 29. OME Sub-Committee, 23 February 1934.
64. CAB, 51/7, Fowle to IO, 28 February 1934, and FO to Ryan, 27 March 1934.
65. CAB, 51/3, Meeting No. 30, 23 March 1934.
66. CAB., op.cit., Rendel to IO, 16 March 1934, and Ryan to FO, 21 March 1934.
67. UK Memorial, I, op.cit., pp.146–9.
68. CAB, 51/3, Meeting No. 33, OME Sub-Committee, 13 September 1934.
69. CAB, 51/7, Ryan to FO, 30 July 1934; Memorandum respecting Anglo-Saudi Relations by Ryan, 30 July 1934; Note by Ryan, 12 September 1934.
70. CAB, 51/3, Meeting No. 33, OME Sub-Committee, 13 September 1934.
71. IOR, L/P & S/18/B437, 'Historical Memorandum on the Relations of the Wahabi Amirs and Ibn Sa'ūd with Eastern Arabia and the British Government'. 1800–1934, IO, 26 September 1934.

72. CAB, 51/3, Fowle to SSI, 30 March 1934, and Meeting of 13 September 1934.
73. UK Memorial, I, op.cit., pp.86–7.
74. CAB, 51/8, Report on Thomas' Meeting, 19 October 1934; Rendel to Laithwaite, 23 October 1934.
75. IOR, R/15/3/11/60, Rendel to Laithwaite, 7 November 1934.
76. CAB, 51/3, Meeting No. 37, OME Sub-Committee, 8 November 1934.
77. IOR, L/P & S/12/2134, Fowle to Laithwaite, 1 November 1934.
78. IOR, R/15/3/11/60, FO to Ryan, 16 January 1935.
79. CAB, 51/3, Meeting No. 37, OME Sub-Committee, 8 November 1934.
80. IOR, L/P & S/12/2136, IO Laithwaite report, 3 January 1935.
81. Hunter's map, which was considered at the time to be the most reliable for this area, was first compiled for Lorimer's Gazetteer and was revised in 1924. As British surveys of this region were concentrated mainly on the coast, Hunter's map was not always reliable regarding the exact position of places in the interior, such as Bunayyān and Sufq wells, and indicated only a few places. The more recent maps made by Thomas and Philby, though authoritative to a great extent, could not fill the gap completely. This lack of accurate geographical information about the interior was to create problems during these frontier negotiations.
82. IOR, R/15/3/11/60, FO to Ryan, 16 January 1935; Secretary of State Foreign Affairs, to Ryan, 21 January 1935.
83. Saudi Memorial, op.cit., pp. 383–5.
84. CAB, 51/8, Ryan to FO, 6 April, 1935.
85. CAB, 51/3, Meeting No. 40, OME Sub-Committee, 15 April 1935.
86. IOR, L/P & S/12/2136, Baggally, FO, to Under-Secretary of State, CO, 18 April 1935.
87. Saudi Memorial, op.cit., pp.385–8.
88. CAB, 51/8, Memorandum of OME Sub-Committee, Records of Meetings, 24 June, 25 June, 2 July, 8 July 1935.
89. CAB, 51/3, Meeting No. 42. OME Sub-Committee, 24 September, 1935, pp.15–25.
90. IOR, L/P & S/12/2/2135, Hoare to Ryan, 23 October 1935.
91. CAB, 51/8, OME Sub-Committee, Loch to Pol. Res., 4 November 1935; Fowle to SSI, 7 November 1935; Loch to FO, 18 November 1935.
92. CAB, 51/3, Meeting No. 43, OME Sub-Committee, 11 November 1935.
93. CAB, 51/8, Ryan to FO, 8 December 1935.
94. CAB, 51/13, Meeting No. 45, OME Sub-Committee, 24 February 1936.
95. CAB, 51/9, OME Sub-Committee, Bullard to FO, 29 December 1936.
96. CAB, 51/3, Meeting No. 49, OME Sub-Committee, 1 February 1937.
97. CAB, 51/10, OME Sub-Committee, FO to the Secretary of the Sub-Committee, 10 June 1937; record made by Mr. Rendel, 20 March 1937; Bullard to Eden, 27 March 1937.
98. CAB, 51/3, Meeting No. 52, OME Sub-Committee, 29 June 1937.
99. CAB, 51/4, Meeting No. 53, OME Sub-Committee, 8 November 1937.
100. UK Memorial, II, op.cit., pp.173, 174–5.
101. CAB, 2/7, CID, Minutes of Meeting, 19 July 1938; CAB, 51/19, Cabinet Meeting, Conclusion 5(C), 22 December 1937.
102. Saudī Memorial, op.cit., pp.394–5.
103. CAB, 51/10, OME Sub-Committee, Memorandum by FO, 3 February 1938; Memorandum by IO, 7 February 1938; CAB, 51/4, Meeting No. 56, OME Sub-Committee, 8 February 1938.
104. Henderson left the company in March 1956 and entered the Diplomatic Service. He was appointed First Secretary to the Political Resident in Baḥrain and afterwards Political Officer in Abū Dhabī between 1958 and 1960. Then he spent three and a half years in Jerusalem, to be followed by two and a half years in the Information Department of the Foreign Office. He came back to Baḥrain in 1966 and remained there until 1969, when he became the Political Agent in Qaṭar. He was the first British Ambassador to independent Qaṭar in 1971 and left the Diplomatic Service in December 1974.
105. It took more than a decade to draw an aerial map of this interior region, a strenuous task which the British Department of Survey of the War and Air Ministries undertook in 1957 and which developed into the comprehensive detailed aerial map of 1963.

106. For the first time, in 1969, Rentz visited the area he had studied two decades before. He went to Abū Dhabī and also visited both al-'Ain and Rās al-Khaimah, having had a friendly audience with Shaikh Zāyed.
107. In 1971 'Ali al-Tājir joined the Centre for Documentation and Research at the Presidential Court in Abū Dhabi. He adopted the idea of recovering these original documents for the Government of Abū Dhabī and in 1975 they became part of the Centre's collection after they had been well preserved and technically treated in the Foreign Office. Their historical value is great, as they are the most extensive original collection in the possession of the Government of the United Arab Emirates, whilst all their other documents are photocopies of the originals which are still in the possession of the India Office Library in London.

4 Britain, Persia and the Trucial States

4 Britain, Persia and the Trucial States

I The Qājār Period

Arab Migration to the Persian Coast in the Eighteenth Century

Migration between both shores of the Gulf has been recorded many times in the history of the area. One of the most important of these movements took place from the Arab side during early Islamic expansion, and thenceforth the Persian coast was predominantly Arab in population and culture. In fact, throughout the centuries the Gulf has never been a barrier but a link strengthening the social and economic ties between both sides.

The fall of the Safavid dynasty in Persia at the beginning of the eighteenth century was followed by disorder and political vacuum. This situation further encouraged the migration from the Arab coast to the Persian shore that continued throughout the century. The area of our study of the migration extends along five hundred miles from Bushire to Bandar ʻAbbās, where the coastal plain is between only one and five miles deep, but contains many villages and small ports surrounded by date groves, and some larger towns with fortified defences. The mountains which separate the coast from the main plateau reach between 3,000 and 7,000 feet above sea level, and there are only three passable tracks through them: Bushire to Shīrāz, Lingah to Lār, and Bandar ʻAbbās to Kermān. The main navigable channel of the Gulf lies close to the Persian coast and this was the cause of the past prosperity of many of its ports.

The Persian coast is divided into three main areas. The first area lies between Bushire and Nābānd and includes the Dāshtī and Tangistān coast. Here a low range of mountains divides the coastal plain into two valleys: the Dāshtī plain which lies between the maritime range and the sea, and the Tangistān, a well cultivated inland valley between the maritime range and the main Zagros mountains. According to Lorimer's estimate the population was 30,000 excluding the port of Bushire, and composed of Persians and Arabs, the former being cultivators and the latter fishermen and sailors. The main towns are Khurmūj, Kangūn, Ṭahirī, Asīlūh and Nābānd. The second area, between Nābānd and Lingah, called the Shibkūh coast, is notable for its distinctively Arab inhabitants. The main islands off this coast are Shaikh Shuʻaib, Hindurābī, Qais and Farūr. Gābāndī, Shīvūh, Muqām, Nakhīlūh, Shīrū, Chārak, Mughūh, ʻAramkī, Dawwān and Bustānah are the most important towns. Lorimer estimated the population at 42,000. The third coastal area stretches between Lingah and Bandar 'Abbās; its population, including these two towns, amounts to 30,000. Numerous salt marshes divide the coastal track, on which the main village is Khamīr. The most important Persian islands are situated off this part of the coast, dominating the entrance to the Gulf, Qishm, Hormuz, Hanjām and Lārak.[1]

The Arab tribes who migrated to the Persian coast were isolated from the main population of Shī'ī Muslims on the inland plateau, not only geographically, by the high Zagros mountains, but also because of their adherence to the Sunnī sect of Islam. Niebuhr, the German traveller who visited the Gulf in 1765, has given a vivid description of the towns and villages inhabited by Arab tribes who had recently settled on the Persian coast. One of the principal tribes to migrate from the Arab coast was the Maṭārīsh, who came from 'Omān and became rulers of Bushire; another was the Qawāsim, whose main centre was Lingah. The Arab tribes who mastered the coast from Bandar 'Abbās to Bushire were called *Houle* by Niebuhr.[2]

At the beginning of the twentieth century Lorimer listed the distribution of the Arab inhabitants of the Persian coast as follows:

Qawāsim	at Lingah, Dawwān, Bustānah and Shīvūh.
Banī Ḥammād	at Nikhīlūh, Muqām, Mirbāgh Qala'āt and Shaikh Shu'aib island.
Āl-Alī	at Shārak and Qais island.
'Ubaidlī	at Shibkūh, Shivūh, 'Aramkī, Chīrūh and Shaikh Shu'aib and Hindurābī islands.
Marāzik	at Mūghūh, Bustānah and Farūr island.
Sūdān	at Mūghūh and Farūr island.
Nasūr	at Ṭāhirī and Kangūn.
al-Ḥaram	at Asīlūh and Nāband.
Āl-Bū-Flāsah	at Hanjām island.
Āl-Bū-Ṣumaiṭ	at Lingah.
Banī Mu'īn	at Qishm island.

Lorimer noted that the Arabs, and the majority of the few Persians settled along the coast, were of the Sunnī sect of Islam, a point Niebuhr also had mentioned two centuries earlier. As the political concepts at the beginning of the twentieth century were religious rather than nationalistic, the Sunnī Persians had a feeling of brotherhood for the Arab Sunnīs, whereas they felt no affinity with the Shī'ī Persians. Moreover, the Arab inhabitants of the Persian coast kept in close economic and social contact with their families and tribes across the Gulf, due to Lingah's role at the end of the nineteenth century as the main trading depot for the Trucial States, and in particular as a flourishing pearl market. Further cultural and religious relations continued between both sides of the Gulf, since some of the religious teachers in the

Trucial States were educated on the Persian side in schools financed by the wealthy Sunnī merchants, notably at Lingah.[3]

The Extension of Tehran's Authority over the Persian Coast

It was during the long rule of the Qājār dynasty (1796–1923) that the Shāhs of Persia, from their new capital at Tehran, were able to regain a great measure of government control over the Gulf coast and islands from the semi-independent Arab tribes. The main resistance came from the Āl Bū-Sa'īd rulers of Muscat who occupied Qishm and Hormuz islands, the Qawāsim at Lingah, the Maṭārīsh at Bushire, and the shaikhs of the Ka'b tribe in 'Arabistān at the northern end of the Gulf. Persia's continuous and successful efforts against the Āl Bū-Sa'īd, Maṭārīsh and Qawāsim during the Qājār period paved the way for the last consolidating action taken by Rezā Shāh against the head of the Ka'b tribe, Shaikh Khaz'al, in 1924, which brought the whole coast and its islands under the complete authority of the strong central government in Tehran.

At the beginning of the Qājār dynasty, Sulṭān b. Aḥmad, the Ruler of Muscat, took the island of Qishm from his enemies, the Qawāsim, who had been exercising control there since 1779. The Shāh of Persia, who at that time was unable to exercise any real authority over his southern coast, leased Bandar 'Abbās and its dependencies for twenty-five years to Muscat, with which he was on friendly terms owing to their mutual enmity towards the powerful Qawāsim federation.

In 1832 the Persian Government took a major step when it appointed a Persian governor at Bushire and put an end to the hereditary rule of the Maṭārīsh tribe. In 1854 Persia decided to restore direct control over Bandar 'Abbās; her troops clashed with those of Muscat and after lengthy negotiations a settlement was reached in the spring of 1856. This treaty was restricted to Sa'īd and his sons for a period of twenty years, after which it was renewable only with Persia's approval. Its main articles provided that the annual rental should be increased threefold to 16,000 tumans.[4]

In 1860 Prince Mas'ūd Mirzā, third son of the Shāh of Persia, who belonged to the pro-Russian party in Tehran, was appointed to the vice-royalty of Fars, a significant step in the development of Persian ambitions in the Gulf. The erection in 1863 of telegraph lines through Persia, connecting India with London, provided the Persian Government with an effective instrument with which to achieve her policy of centralisation.[5] At the same time, the British India Steam Navigation Company began mail services to the main Persian ports in the Gulf, and Indian postal services to large inland towns were inaugurated. When Sayyed Salīm, a grandson of Sayyed Sa'īd b. Sulṭān, became Ruler of Muscat in 1866, the Persian Government took the opportunity to cancel the lease of Bandar 'Abbās, under the pretext that it had been granted only to Sayyed Sa'īd and his sons. It was only after energetic efforts by Colonel Pelly, the Political Resident in the Gulf, that the Persian

Government agreed on 4 August 1868, to renew the lease for a period of eight years only, at an annual rental of 30,000 tumans; but in 1871 a revolution in Muscat gave the Persian Government a second opportunity to cancel it and the Shāh was adamant in his refusal to allow Bandar 'Abbās to revert to Muscat control.[6]

As a result of increases in central government expenditure, caused by a policy of centralisation and modern reform, Tehran now demanded a larger sum of money from the Governor of Fars for farming out her Gulf ports, which had prospered immensely after the opening of British steam navigation in the area. He in turn imposed higher taxation on the inhabitants. After 1872, when many Arab shaikhs began to resist the new levies, they were detained and replaced by Persian governors, as happened to the Shaikh of Kangūn in 1880. In fact, owing to their internal feuds, the Arab shaikhs were powerless to resist the extension of Persian authority, which had been pushed forward in those regions with uncompromising vigour.[7]

In 1882 a vital step was taken when the administration of the Gulf ports was withdrawn from the Governor-General of Fars and entrusted to Amīn al-Sulṭān, a former Prime Minister and a court favourite at Tehran. He appointed Ḥājjī Aḥmad Khān as his representative in Bushire, and Malik al-Tujjār, a very wealthy merchant of Tehran, as his tax collector. The arrival in the Gulf in 1885 of the two warships *Persepolis* and *Susa*, ordered by Persia from Germany, enabled Ḥājjī Aḥmad Khān to exercise more control over the Gulf ports. In 1887 a decree was issued establishing the Gulf ports as an independent administrative unit under the supervision of a 'Derya Begi', the Governor-General of the Gulf ports, who reported directly to the palace in Tehran.[8] This administrative change, inspired by the Amīn al-Sulṭān, in addition to the presence of the warship *Persepolis* encouraged the central government to direct an audacious attack on the Qawāsim emirate of Lingah, an unprecedented outburst of Persian political activity on her southern coast. As a result of such a vigorous policy the Arab inhabitants felt themselves oppressed and two successive waves of migration were precipitated from the Persian coast and islands to the Trucial States and the Arab littoral: the first in 1887, when the Persians imprisoned the Qāsimī ruler of Lingah, and the second in 1899, particularly when the Persian Government put an end to the Qawāsim rule at that town.

British Relations with Persia during the Qājār Dynasty

This is not a detailed history of Anglo–Persian relations, but in order to understand the relationships involved in the Trucial States it is necessary to have an outline of the periods of friendship and conflict between the two countries.

By 1892 Britain had succeeded in gaining several major political, economic and naval privileges in Persia, particularly in the Gulf ports. After 1907, however, these privileges were bitterly resented by the Persian nationalists who associated them with a humiliating past. Britain had a Political Resident at Bushire who looked after British interests, not only on the Persian coast, but also on the Arab side of the Gulf. Sepoy guards, seconded from the Indian army, protected the Residency in Bushire, and the Resident was escorted on his travels in Persia by a large detachment of Indian cavalry. One of the several warships which belonged to the East India Squadron of the Royal Indian Navy and remained at anchor in Bushire was permanently at the disposal of the Resident. Owing to Persia's weakness and her lack of naval units in the Gulf, British warships entered Persian ports without hoisting the Persian flag and without any Persian control.[9]

The Treaty of Paris in 1857, which followed Persia's defeat by Britain, gave the British the same capitulatory privileges granted to the Russians in 1828. By the terms of the treaty, the Political Resident was empowered to intervene judicially in the affairs of the British-Indian subjects who had been settling in the Gulf ports. British privileges were extended to the postal, quarantine and telegraph services in Persia. Furthermore, in accordance with the treaty of 1882, which Britain concluded with Persia to suppress the slave trade in the area, British warships were entitled to search Persian vessels.

At the end of the nineteenth century rivalry developed between Britain and Russia over their respective influences at Tehran. Following the assassination of Nāsir al-Dīn Shāh in 1896, the Russians fulfilled their pledges to his son Mudhaffar al-Dīn, Governor of Azarbayjan and the Crown Prince of Persia, who under their protection peacefully proceeded from Tabrīz to his new throne in Tehran. Thus, the Russians had secured overwhelming influence in the capital. In response the British reasserted their position at the top of the Gulf by immediately establishing friendly relations with Shaikh Khaz'al (1897–1924), the new ruler of Moḥammarah. Furthermore, in 1901, as a result of prudent negotiations by Britain and despite the unfavourable situation in Tehran, William D'Arcy was able to obtain an oil concession from the Persian Government.

Security in Arabistān was the main problem faced by the D'Arcy company at the start of its operations, for this area, where the central government's authority was nominal, was semi-independent under Shaikh Khaz'al.[10] In 1901 British prestige in Tehran was overshadowed by the Russians after a second Russian loan, by the terms of which the Shāh promised that he would revise Persian tariffs. M. Naus, the Belgian Director of Customs who later became a Minister, drew up the terms of a new commercial convention in the same year, favouring the Russians and their trade in the north at the expense of the British and their trade in the Gulf ports. The new tariffs came into effect in 1903 and were directed mainly against Britain.

The British, having lost ground in government circles, were prompted by this to strengthen their ties with the leaders of the emerging popular movement in order to maintain their position in Persian politics. In the early spring of 1905 Persian merchants were refusing to clear their goods at Bushire owing to the severity of the new tariffs, so they sent a telegram to the Shāh in which they threatened not to forward goods up country until the new regulations had been withdrawn. At first the Shāh paid very little heed to their complaints, but their resentment continued, culminating in the revolution of 1905.[11] In December of that year a large number of merchants took sanctuary in the Shāh's mosque, where they were shortly joined by many of the chief Mullās and popular leaders. The British, who now identified themselves with the progressive movement, permitted a crowd of 14,000 demonstrators, who were demanding a constitution, to take sanctuary in the large garden of their legation in Tehran, a step which at last compelled the Shāh to dismiss the Prime Minister and grant a constitution. On 7 October 1906, after a general election, the new Majlis (National Assembly) was opened amid popular enthusiasm and rejoicing. However, Britain's close relations with the nationalist movement did not last long.

The Anglo-Russian agreement of 1907, which in Europe was regarded as a victory for British diplomacy, came as a shock to the pro-British nationalists in Persia, to whom the agreement seemed a prelude to the partition of their country. Thenceforward the British were associated with the traditional enemy, Russia, and the immediate result of this ill feeling, aggravated by an internal power struggle between the Shāh and the constitutionalists, was harmful to British interests. On 15 December 1907 Muḥammad 'Alī, the new Shāh, began his attack upon the constitutionalists, concentrating the Cossack division in the capital.[12]

On 23 June 1908 the Shāh ordered the Cossacks to fire on the Majlis building. This aroused furious anger against him in all the big towns, where the constitutionalists began to seize control of administration. In October Tabrīz revolted against the Shāh, refusing to recognise him as the legitimate ruler, and this was followed early in 1909 by similar uprisings at Isphahān, at Resht, at Bushire and Bandar 'Abbās. Seyyed 'Abd al-Ḥusain, a revolutionary from Shīrāz, incited the inhabitants of Bandar 'Abbās to seize the customs house, which they did, and in the same month, Seyyed Murtazā, a Mullā, led the nationalists against the Customs House in Bushire, where he became the *de facto* Governor. Since the customs receipts in the Gulf ports had been pledged as security for a British loan to the Shāh, Cox asked Seyyed Murtazā and Seyyed 'Abd al-Ḥusain to be reasonable and recognise British financial claims, but the former, with whom Wassmus, the new German Vice-Consul at Bushire (appointed in 1909), had established friendly relations, rejected those claims. On 7 April 1909 a British ultimatum was sent to Seyyed Murtazā, demanding that he should keep order in the town, and this was followed three days later by a naval force which occupied the Customs House and the port. Although these forces left on 19 May their landing created intense animosity against the British among the nationalist groups.

Defeated in his efforts to suppress the revolution Muḥammad 'Alī Shāh fled his palace to seek sanctuary at the Russian Embassy, where the Cossack squadron guarding the Shāh was soon joined by Sepoys from the British Legation. At last the constitutionalist cause had triumphed and on 16 July 1909 the Shāh was formally deposed and his twelve-year-old son, Aḥmed Mīrzā, proclaimed Shāh.

In April 1909, after the discovery of oil at Masjid Sulaimān, the Anglo–Persian Oil Company was established. The company reached an agreement with the Bakhtiārī chiefs, who were now in power in Tehran. Simultaneously, on 16 July 1909 a further agreement was concluded with Shaikh Khaz'al, negotiated by Cox on behalf of the oil company, by which the Shaikh agreed to let an area on Abadan island for building a refinery. Furthermore, Khaz'al, in October the following year, received a renewed assurance from the British Government that they would not merely safeguard him to the best of their ability against unprovoked attack by a foreign power, but would support him by diplomatic activity in the event of an encroachment by the Persian Government on his recognised rights.[13]

At this critical juncture, with faith in Britain on the wane, the activities of Imperial Germany, now emerging as a great power, had unfavourable repercussions for the British in Persia. The sympathy which German representatives showed towards the nationalists in their recent struggle against the Shāh and foreign interference created a close relationship. Wassmus cultivated friendly relations with the Tangistānī tribes, who were severely affected by the British arms blockade.[14] Aware of this new menace, the Government of India established a British Vice-Consulate at Lingah in 1909, to be followed by another at Moḥammarah in 1910, where the consul appointed was A. T. Wilson, chosen for his past experience and intimate friendship with Shaikh Khaz'al.

After deposing Muḥammad 'Alī Shāh, the new Government was unable to restore order. In October 1910 the British Legation in Tehran, after consultation with the Russians, presented the Persian Government with an ultimatum, stating that if order were not restored in the south Britain would act on her own. Then at the end of the month, when the Warāvī tribe raided Lingah, 160 sailors were landed at Cox's request and remained in the town for a month. Confusion in the south continued and once again, in September 1911, four British squadrons landed at Bushire to strengthen the Consular guards at Shīrāz and Isphahān. The Persian nationalist authorities regretted the action of the British at such a critical moment and informed Cox that, as they understood it, this landing was a preliminary step to establishing an independent state in the south friendly to Britain. The tribes in Fars, for their part, reacted fiercely and the Qashqāi tribe attacked two Indian detachments which were escorting Mr Smart, the British Acting Consul, to Shīrāz, and imprisoned him temporarily.[15]

Meanwhile, on 25 February 1912 the Admiralty established a coal depot on Hanjām island, ostensibly to aid the arms blockade, but mainly for its strategic position at the entrance to the Gulf, and with the object of establishing a wireless station there. The Admiralty's measures soon received the support of the Foreign Office.[16] At the beginning of 1912 the Government of India was pressing for Bushire to be occupied as a punitive measure for the attack on Acting-Consul Smart. The Persian Government protested at British attacks on their ports in the Gulf. Eventually it was decided by the Government of India and the Foreign Office that owing to vigorous opposition in Persia, Indian forces should be evacuated from Bandar 'Abbās, Shīrāz and Isphahān; also that the Persian Government would be requested to appoint a strong governor in Fars to restore order, and a loan granted towards establishing the new gendarmerie regiment, to be trained by Swedish officers recently arrived. In April 1913 the Indian troops were withdrawn from Shīrāz and Isphahān.

In 1913 the British Government became directly involved in the oil industry, when an agreement was concluded between the company, the Admiralty and the Treasury, by which the Government became the controlling partner, appointing the directors and having the power to veto. During 1913 the British paid more attention to the strategic island of Hanjām and began to establish a wireless station.[17]

On 1 November 1914, soon after war in Europe broke out, Mustawfī al-Mamālik, the Prime Minister, proclaimed Persia's neutrality, despite which Persian soil was violated by the entry of Russian, Turkish and British troops. A regiment of 8,000 Persians was recruited in Bandar 'Abbās during May 1916, trained by British Officers, led by Percy Sykes, and was known as the South Persia Rifles. It was well equipped with modern British arms. The regiment forged its way, slowly but steadily, towards the town of Shīrāz, which it occupied on 16 November the same year. Two squadrons of Indian cavalry were despatched to the Afghānistān and Balūchistan frontiers of Eastern Persia to prevent German missions from crossing over to India.

Following the Russian Revolution and the commencement of the evacuation of Russian troops from Persia, another force, under Colonel Dunsterville, left Baghdād for the Bākū oilfields on the Caspian Sea. In April 1918 the Persian Government, influenced by nationalist sentiments, declared that the despatch of British troops to Persia was a violation of her neutrality and denounced the South Persia Rifles as a menace to Persian independence, demanding that it be placed under Persian control; but this and the Persian demands for a withdrawal of British troops were both rejected. When both notes were made public by the Persian Government in the big cities, further resentment developed, stirred up by the Mullās, who preached a *jihâd* against Britain; but with the return in August of a Prime Minister of pro-British leanings, Vussuq al-Dawlah, the British hoped for a more favourable policy.[18]

Early in 1918 Curzon regarded the Bolsheviks as a threat to Persia and to British India. With the elimination from Persia of Britain's chief rivals, Germany, Turkey and Russia, Curzon sought an appropriate moment to establish a virtual protectorate and in 1919 Percy Cox became Minister to Tehran, entrusted by Curzon with the task of concluding a closer agreement with Persia. On 9 August 1919, after lengthy and secret negotiations with Vussuq al-Dawlah, a treaty was signed and proclaimed, which Curzon regarded as a personal triumph and the culmination of British influence in Persia.

Contrary to Curzon's expectations, the treaty provoked immediate and strong opposition from the powerful nationalist parties in Persia, as well as from the American, French and Bolshevik governments, who denounced both its terms and the secrecy with which it had been concluded, considering that it had given Britain virtual tutelage over Persia. Unable to gain support for the ratification of the Anglo–Persian treaty, Vussuq al-Dawlah resigned on 24 June 1920.[19]

The collapse of the old régime, together with its complete failure to ratify the treaty prompted Britain to devise an urgent alternative solution. Prevailing opinion in British political circles was that the rise to power at this time of a strong Persian military government, friendly to Great Britain, would be the only way of meeting the interests of both countries. Soon the need for the emergence of a stable nationalist government, which could turn Persia into a buffer state between Bolshevik Russia and both India and the Middle East, regardless of the small sacrifices the British would have to tolerate, was to overcome all traditional British policies between the two world wars.[20]

Fall of the Qawāsim's Emirate at Lingah, 1887–99

Lingah, largely a Sunnī Arab town, was the most attractive port in the Gulf. It extended for over a mile along the shore, surrounded by date groves. A large fortress, capable of offering effective resistance to any enemy not provided with modern artillery, defended the town. This fortress was the seat of the Qawāsim rulers on the Persian coast. The town was divided into two quarters: the larger eastern quarter was inhabited by Arabs of the Qawāsim, Āl Bū-Ṣumait, 'Utūb and Dawāsir tribes, together with their slaves and dependants, all of whom were Sunnī, and the western quarter, which was populated by Persians who were mainly Shī'ī. The total population of both quarters was estimated at 12,000 in winter, when they were gathered together after the pearl fishing season. In 1863 Colonel Pelly, the Political Resident, visited the town and reported that its trade was starting to flourish owing to the regular visits of the new steamers on their way from Bombay to Bushire. Lingah's dhows were easily able to transfer goods from them to the quays in the shallow harbours of the Trucial States, which were practically beyond the reach of the deep-draught steamers. Because of Lingah's significant development in the second half of the nineteenth century, the British in 1865 decided to appoint a local agent who would look after the interests of one hundred Hindu merchants recently settled in the town.[21]

In 1874 Shaikh Khalīfah b. Sa'īd, the Qasimī Ruler of Lingah died, and as his son 'Alī was not of age, the Persian Government saw the opportunity to extend its authority and immediately appointed a Director of Customs in Lingah. The imposition of heavy taxes that year prompted the first wave of the migration of wealthy traders to the Trucial States and many others were to follow shortly.

Shaikh Khalīfah, before he died, had appointed Shaikh Yūsuf b. Muḥammad, a distant member of the Qasimī family, as guardian of his young son 'Alī, but in November 1878 Shaikh Yūsuf assassinated the boy and the Persian Government found in this a further opportunity for interference. Shaikh Yūsuf, they discovered, was hated by the people; he would be ready to co-operate with the Government, however, and was appointed Deputy Governor of Lingah. Antagonism between the Persian authorities and the Arabs of Lingah then intensified and the Sunnīs of Lingah, both Arabs and Persians, attacked the Persian Shī'ī quarter in 1880. In April 1885 Yūsuf himself was murdered by one of the Qasimī ruling family, Shaikh Qaḍīb b. Râshid, who once again assumed the position of an independent ruler in Lingah, a situation which created further unrest. Shaikh Qaḍīb applied to his relative, the Qawāsim of 'Omān, for armed assistance. Finally, in September of the same year, the Persian Government of Bandar 'Abbâs, Shahzādah Muḥammad Huṣain Murtazâ, arrived at Lingah to mediate a settlement, by which Shaikh Qaḍīb was confirmed as Governor and the yearly revenue fixed at 190,000 tumans.[22]

Although Lingah continued with an independent government under Qasimī rule, it had been nominally within the jurisdiction of Amīn al-Sulṭān since 1882, and particularly since the 'Derya Begi' decree of 1887. The people of Lingah were in favour of the Arab government of Shaikh Qaḍīb, but Amīn al-Sulṭān, newly appointed Derya Begi, decided to put an end to Qaḍīb's rule, instructing his admiral, Ḥājjī Aḥmad Khān, and Malik al-Tujjār, to capture the Shaikh. On 11 September 1887 a group of Malik's men stormed Qaḍīb's house; Qaḍīb was imprisoned in the Diwān and badly treated.

On 15 September 1887 Ḥājjī Aḥmad Khān sent messengers to all the governors of the villages around Lingah appointed by Shaikh Qaḍīb, and reassured them concerning their positions. Qaḍīb was sent to Tehran and died in prison. Barracks were immediately erected at Lingah and a body of 200 regular Persian infantry placed there, much to the disgust of the inhabitants, some of whom prepared to leave. Another wave of migration to the Arab coast took place.[23]

In the summer of 1898 Muḥammad b. Khalīfah, a descendant of former Qasimī shaikhs at Lingah, made a swift attack on the town and established himself there. The Qasimī partisans rejoiced at this victory and poured into Lingah to join the Shaikh, and he was now able to defend the town effectively. The suddenness and boldness of the attack, together with the high morale of the Qasimī followers, made it difficult for the Persian authorities to take immediate action. Finally, in February 1899 Ḥājjī Aḥmad Khān, now the new Derya Begi, proceeded there in his warship *Persepolis*, but as he found the Arabs on the alert he postponed taking action until a more favourable occasion. Shaikh Muḥammad b. Khalīfah was thus lulled into a false sense of security and rashly dismissed most of his followers. The Derya Begi went to 'Asīlū with the avowed intention of collecting more troops for the proposed attack, but meanwhile despatched the *Persepolis* to Lingah in order to discover the Arab strength. The captain of the *Persepolis* pretended that he was bound for Bandar 'Abbās, relieved the Shaikh of 12,000 tumans and told him that as long as he complied with the Derya Begi's wishes he would be left in peace. But the speedy return of the *Persepolis* to 'Asīlu made the Shaikh suspicious and he began to muster his defences. Anticipating a lengthy blockade, he stocked his fort with ammunition and food.[24] The *Persepolis* having returned at about three in the morning of 2 March and landed 700 troops about seven miles west of Lingah, the Shaikh shut himself up in the fort with a force of around 2,000 men. Shortly after daylight the warship appeared before the town. Fighting continued for two days, during which time the Shaikh managed to escape by ship. According to the *Bombay Gazette* correspondent, as soon as the fort fell, looting began; there was rejoicing in the Shī'ī quarter whilst wailing was heard from the Arab side. The Derya Begi's declaration that he intended to leave after organising the customs and installing a new governor was received with anxiety by the Shī'ī Persians. They believed, incorrectly, that the Shaikh had not fled, but was rallying his scattered forces to attack the town.[25]

The fall of the Qawāsim Emirate at Lingah in 1899 enabled the central government to exercise real authority in the south. Customs houses administered by Belgian officials were established in the Gulf ports. These new measures prompted a mass wave of emigration from the Persian to the Arab coast, in particular to Dubai, which had long-term economic, social and political effects on the history of the area. In 1901, instigated by Russia, a new customs tariff was issued which severely affected British trade in the Gulf ports. It was reported that in March 1902 some 15,000 sacks of merchandise destined for the Trucial Coast were held up at Lingah and lay neglected on the quayside. The Customs Department, to increase its force in the Gulf, ordered six small patrol ships from Bombay. The merchants of Lingah and other Persian ports found their interests directly threatened and their goods subjected to heavy duties. At last some leading merchants, mainly Sunnī Persians, found no alternative but to close down their stores in protest and to emigrate to Dubai. There they began to establish agencies and ordered their big trading ships to come from India direct, by-passing Lingah. In addition, they arranged with the Bombay & Persia Steam Navigation Company for a direct and regular service of steamers to Dubai.[26]

In 1902, steamers began to call at that port for the first time, amounting by the end of the year to twenty-one vessels. At the beginning of 1904 the important British India Steam Navigation Company also began to make Dubai a regular port of call. Consequently, the role played by Lingah as an entrepôt for transit trade at the end of the nineteenth century began to shift to Dubai and thus began the flourishing trade this port has enjoyed in modern times. Kemball, the Political Resident, visiting Dubai in January 1903, reported

> When I visited Arab Coast I saw one of the steamers of the Bombay Persia Company at Dubai, and I was told that steamers of the British India Navigation Company make Dubai a port of call. It may be taken for granted that the trade which has now been diverted from Lingah will not return there, and that the importance of this port will continue to decline as a result, which is entirely due to the short-sighted policy of the Belgian Customs Administration.[27]

Furthermore, the fall of the Qawāsim Emirate at Lingah had immediate effects on the island of Hanjām, which was inhabited by the Āl Bū-Flāsah tribe, and now became the focus of new strife between the Arabs and the Persian authorities. The former had traditional relations with the Sultan of Muscat, whose ancestors had governed the island several decades earlier, and also with the Ruler of Dubai, whence they had emigrated. The Persian Government attempted during 1904 to alter the *status quo* by levying customs duty from them and stationing soldiers on the island, a step which alarmed the Arabs: Owing to the Government of India's recognition of Persia's sovereignty over the island at that time the Persian Government relaxed its policies and left the Arabs alone. At the beginning of 1905 the people addressed an appeal to the Sultan of Muscat, asking for his protection on the grounds of their past friendship. In October 1905, Lieutenant Shakespear, visiting the island of Hanjām, found the feelings of the local population towards the Persians much exacerbated. On 13 November 1905 the Sultan of 'Omān, returning to Muscat from a visit to Abū Dhabī, called at Hanjām in order to despatch telegrams to his capital. The Arab inhabitants naturally took the opportunity of calling on him, reiterating their grievances against the Persians, to whom the Sultan then protested about their aggressive policies.[28] At the beginning of 1914, the Shaikh and some of his relatives had imported various goods by mail steamers from Bombay; the Director of Customs naturally demanded duty and after negotiations a small sum was agreed upon. Since the mail steamers had started calling at Hanjām, many merchants from the neighbouring island of Qishm then began importing their merchandise from Hanjām instead of Bandar 'Abbās, where there was strict customs control. When it became evident to the authorities that a good deal of smuggling had been taking place, the Persian Government decided to establish a customs house in Hanjām and levy duties by force, but these plans were interrupted by the outbreak of World War I.[29]

II Ṣirrī, Ṭanb and Abū Mūsā Islands until 1921

Early History of the Islands in the Nineteenth Century

The issue of sovereignty over the islands of Ṣirri, Abū Mūsā, Ṭanb Kubrā and Ṭanb Ṣughrā, brought about the fundamental dispute between the Trucial States and Persia at the end of the nineteenth century. These are four small islands lying near the entrance to the Gulf; though small, their significance lay in their strategic position on the deep navigable route separating them from the Persian shore, and in their importance as a port of call for the sailing dhows running between the two shores of the Gulf. They were also important as a refuge in stormy weather, and were used by the Qawāsim shaikhs as pastures for their animals in spring.[30]

In 1763 the Qawāsim controlled Qishm island, Lingah, Luft and Shināṣ on the Persian coast, besides their main bases on the coast of 'Omān. Since the beginning of the nineteenth century the Qasimī ruling branch of Lingah had been descended from Shaikh Qaḍīb, the uncle of Shaikh Sulṭān b. Ṣaqr. After the British expedition of 1820, close relations between the main branches of the Qawāsim on the Persian and 'Omān Coasts became difficult; thus, prior to 1835 they reached an understanding whereby Qasimī islands in the Gulf were apportioned between different branches of the family to be used by each exclusively. Within this agreement a specific assertion was made by Shaikh Sulṭān b. Ṣaqr, which he communicated in writing to Colonel Pelly in December 1864. This letter constituted the first recorded evidence regarding the ownership of these islands among the Qawāsim. The text is as follows:

> Last year, I informed you of the interference of the Dubai people in regard to Abū Mūsā island. This island belongs to me. Tanb, Abū Mūsā and Ṣīr [Bu Nair] belong to me from the time of my forefathers, but you did not reply to my letter. It is well known from olden times that the islands, Abū Mūsā, Ṭanb and Ṣīr belong to me. Sirrī belongs to the Qawāsim of Lingah, Hanjām to Seyed Theweini and Farūr to the Marāzīk. If you make enquiries about my statement, you will find it correct.[31]

During the reigns of Shaikh Ṣālim b. Sulṭān (1868–83), Shaikh Ṣaqr b. Khālid (1883–1913) and Shaikh Khālid b. Aḥmad (1913–24), two separations occurred in the Qawāsim Emirate of 'Omān between the towns of Shārjah and Rās al-Khaimah. Due to Ṭanb's close proximity to Rās al-Khaimah, Shaikh Ḥumaid b. 'Abdullah took possession of the island of Ṭanb Kubrā for himself for the same reason as Shaikh Sālim b. Sulṭān in Shārjah held the island of Abū Mūsā.[32] Until the 1870s the Government of India held no carefully considered opinion as to the ownership of the Qawāsim islands in the Gulf, which was to the British authorities a completely local matter. The British attitude towards their ownership was influenced by their policy towards the Qawāsim, coupled with the personal relations between their representative, the Residency Agent, and the Qasimī ruler.

During the controversial period before 1887, the reports of two Residency Agents provided the Political Resident at Bushire with the information upon which the British based their policies and all their future correspondence and memoranda. Both Ḥajjī 'Abd al-Raḥmān (1866–80)[33] and Ḥājjī Abu al-Qāsim (1880–90) held the post of Residency Agent at Shārjah.[34] An example of the British attitude took place in 1870, when the first edition of the *Persian Gulf Pilot* appeared as a British Admiralty publication. It contained the statement that the islands of Ṣirrī, Ṭanb, Nabiyū Ṭanb and Abū Mūsā belonged to the Shaikh of Lingah. On 14 September 1875 a memo prepared by Lieutenant Fraser, First Assistant Resident, tells us that he was informed by Mīrzā 'Abū al-Qāsim that the Qawāsim family had entered an agreement forty years previously to divide their islands, and that those of Ṭanb Kubrā, Ṣirrī and Farūr had been ceded to the Lingah branch.

Shaikh Sālim b. Sulṭān informed the Residency Agent in December 1871 that he was going to exercise his sovereignty and prevent anyone using the island of Abū Mūsā. On 13 December 1871 'Abd al-Raḥmān advised the Political Resident that this should not be allowed and Shaikh Sālim was informed of the decision. The infringements continued in successive years. In 1872 the offenders were Dubai, 'Ajmān and Umm al-Qaiwain; in 1873 it was Dubai yet again and two boats from Lingah.[35]

A final incident at the end of that year proved crucial in the sovereignty of the Qawāsim of Shārjah over Abū Mūsā, particularly after 'Abd al-Raḥmān's decision in February 1873 that Ṭanb belonged to Lingah. Shaikh Sālim b. Sulṭān sent fifty armed men of the Shiḥūḥ tribe, who fired upon the boats from Dubai and Lingah, an incident which caused Ross to enquire in June 1875 to whom the island of Abū Mūsā really belonged, and on 17 December 'Abd al-Raḥmān gave Ross an answer: 'The Joasmee chiefs claimed the island of Abū Mūsā and Moonshee Abool Kasim says the island belongs to the Joasmees so that both Shārjah and Rās al-Khaimah chiefs can place their men there'. This answer being an issue of controversy to Ross, he asked 'Abd a-Raḥmān to: 'Await any further comments on the subject.'

At the start, Shaikh Khalīfah b. Sa'īd, Ruler of Lingah, acknowledged

Shaikh Ḥumaid b. 'Abdullah's sovereignty over Ṭanb after the latter had declared his independence at Rās al-Khaimah. In the autumn of 1871, in accord with Shaikh Sālim b. Sulṭān at Shārjah and his firm policy towards the island of Abū Mūsā, Shaikh Ḥumaid b. 'Abdullah prevented the tribe of Āl Bū-Ṣumaiṭ, dependants of the Qawāsim at Lingah, from entering the island of Ṭanb and complained to Shaikh Khalīfah b. Sa'īd about their unauthorised visit, and he, on 25 November 1871, in reply sent to Shaikh Ḥumaid the first important communication regarding the ownership of Ṭanb. He wrote:

> As regards your last letter in which you mentioned the visits of Āl Bū-Ṣumaiṭ to Ṭanb, oh brother, know that the Bu Sumaitis are your followers and are obedient to you, but you should prohibit such people as the chief of Dubai, Ajman and Umm al-Qaiwain, as all of these go to that place. Otherwise, the Āl Bū-Ṣumaiṭ as mentioned, are in obedience.[36]

However, Shaikh Ḥumaid continued to adopt the same firm policy with the followers of the Qawāsim of Lingah without distinction between them and the dependants of the neighbouring chiefs, a policy against which Shaikh Khalīfah b. Sa'īd reacted vigorously in the autumn of 1872, encouraging his people, the Āl Bū-Ṣumaiṭ, to go to Lingah without Ḥumaid's permission. A dispute began and Ḥumaid on 10 February 1873 sent a complaint to Ḥājjī Abū al-Qāsim, the Residency Agent at Lingah. The latter communicated with Khalīfah, who claimed the island for himself. Both sides of the question were then reported to the Political Resident, Ross, and he on 12 February 1873 wrote to 'Abd al-Raḥmān at Shārjah, to 'inquire and report as to whom the Tanb island was supposed to belong'. 'Abd al-Raḥmān, fearing that the situation would lead to disturbances at sea between the Persian and Arab coasts, instead of investigating and reporting only to the Political Resident, enabling him to decide, himself decided that the island belonged to the Shaikh of Lingah and followed it with action, trying to impose the decision upon the Shaikh of Rās al-Khaimah. He was probably influenced by his feeling that the British still harboured anti-Qawāsim sentiments and would welcome a decision against them; he was probably influenced also by his own commercial interests at Lingah. At the end of February 1873 he wrote to Shaikh Ḥumaid, ordering him to 'keep clear of the island', but Ḥumaid replied unsuitably the same month, asserting that Ṭanb, Abū Mūsā and Ṣīr were under the authority of the Qawāsim of the Trucial Coast, whilst the islands of Ṣirrī and Nabiyū Ṭanb belonged to the Shaikh of Lingah. This letter of protest is significant for its explanation of the differing ownership of the two Ṭanb islands, as seen at this stage by the Qawāsim of the Trucial Coast, complementing Shaikh Sulṭān b. Ṣaqr's letter of 1864. It also shows how important it is to consider each of the four islands individually because of differences in their history. The letter stated that Ṭanb Kubrā was owned by the Qawāsim of ‘Omān and Ṭanb Ṣughrā by the Qawāsim of Lingah. ‘Abd al-Raḥmān then took the forceful step of visiting Rās al-Khaimah and the island of Ṭanb on 10 March 1873 and ordering the Shaikh to write a letter of apology to the Shaikh of Lingah, explaining that if the chief of Lingah accepted his apology, well and good; otherwise he should remove his horses and camels from the island.

On 30 March 1873 ‘Abd al-Raḥmān sent his answer to the Political Resident's enquiry of 12 February, embodying his decision that the island of Ṭanb was a dependency of Fārs and under the chief of Lingah, and informed the Political Resident of his proceedings at Rās al-Khaimah. As Ross found ‘Abd al-Raḥmān's opinion and action in accordance with the old conception at the Residency, he sent his sanction for all that he did on 19 April 1873.[37] However, it seems that the death of Shaikh Khalīfah b. Sa‘īd in 1874 re-established friendly relations and the old understanding over Ṭanb between the young new Ruler of Lingah, Shaikh ‘Alī b. Khalīfah (1874–8), and his old relative, Shaikh Ḥumaid b. ‘Abdullah, Ruler of Rās al-Khaimah. On 8 January 1877 ‘Alī b. Khalīfah sent the second of the three important letters recorded during this period between the rulers of Lingah and the Shaikh of Rās al-Khaimah, which read as follows:

> You write about the Al Bu-Sumait, that you wanted me to prohibit them from going to the island of Tanb, where they do various damages because the said island was your territory and that there has been a copious correspondence between you and my father. This is a fact, and I am satisfied that the island of Tanb is a dependency of the Qawasim of Oman, and we have no property there and no interference except with your consent; since I considered the subjects and territories as one, I assumed the authority of giving them permission to go there, but now as you are displeased, and you want they should be prohibited I will prohibit them, and I hope that God may preserve you as a proper representative of all who has passed away.[38]

These disputes made Ross consider once again the need for a detailed study of the subject. On 21 June 1879 he commissioned Ḥājjī ‘Abū al-Qāsim to visit the Trucial Coast to prepare a study of the dependencies of the Trucial chiefs, noting particularly those claimed, acknowledged and otherwise. On 16 July Ḥājjī Abū al-Qāsim submitted his report, in which he listed the island of Abū Mūsā as part of Shārjah. Although he judged that the island of Ṭanb belonged to Rās al-Khaimah and added that it was also owned by the chief of Lingah in part, as he too was of the Qawāsim tribe, Ross noted in the margin: ‘considered Persian’. In accordance Ross commented in a letter of 1881 concerning it that there was common ownership between Rās al-Khaimah and Lingah.

During 1881 correspondence and talks took place between Ḥājjī 'Abū al-Qāsim, now the Residency Agent at Shārjah (1880–90), and Shaikh Ḥumaid b. 'Abdullah over the ownership of Ṭanb. After instructions from Ross the former presented copies to Shaikh Ḥumaid of the previous decisions and correspondence of Ḥājjī Abd al-Raḥmān and further informed him about Ross's wish to be on friendly terms with the chief of Lingah. Ḥumaid was exceedingly surprised at these decisions and gave Ḥājjī 'Abū al-Qāsim copies of the letter he had received in 1871 from Shaikh Khalīfah b. Sa'īd and of the letter received in 1877 from his son, 'Alī b. Khalīfah, in which both rulers acknowledged the right of the Qawāsim of 'Omān over the island of Ṭanb. As these two letters came to British knowledge for the first time and their contents were contrary to the opinion the British held, Ḥājjī Abū al-Qāsim sent copies to Ross on March 1882, together with an important letter from Ḥumaid to the Political Resident. Ḥumaid, sensing the dangers of Persian encroachment on the Qawāsim Emirate of Lingah in the dispute over Ṭanb, particularly when Shaikh Yūsuf b. Muḥammad (1878–85) became a Persian vassal, explained in his letter to Ross that the British Government would not agree to the Arab territories being considered Persian. Moreover, he expressed his fear that the matter would become very much graver if changes in the Government of Lingah took place and the island were included as a part of Fārs. On 17 March Ross replied that it was his wish that the arrangement about Ṭanb should continue as hitherto until he himself visited the Coast and discussed the subject with Shaikh Ḥumaid.

In 1884, however, the dispute over Ṭanb was renewed when Shaikh Yūsuf, who usurped the rule of Lingah by murdering his ward, 'Alī b. Khalīfah, planted some date trees on the island without Ḥumaid's previous consent. Ḥumaid reacted forcefully: he destroyed the trees, sent a letter to Yūsuf and complained to Ḥājjī Abū al-Qāsim. On 29 March 1884, therefore, Yūsuf sent his last important letter to Ḥumaid:

> I have received your letter. Hajji Abu al-Qasim, the Residency Agent, came to me and informed me of your complaint about the island of Tanb. In reality, the island belongs to you the Qawasim of Oman, and I have kept my hand over it, considering that you are agreeable to my doing so. But now when you do not wish my planting date offsets there, and the visits of Al Bu-Sumait to cut grass there, God willing, I shall prohibit them and our mutual relations shall remain friendly.[39]

This significant letter was the third to be received by Ḥumaid from successive rulers of Lingah acknowledging the ownership of the island of Ṭanb by the Qawāsim of 'Omān. Whilst the British authorities in the Gulf began to obtain new documents and consequently formulate a new opinion regarding the ownership, other British departments contrived to hold the established but inaccurate concept that Ṣirrī, Ṭanb and Abū Mūsā belonged to the

Qawāsim of Lingah, who had become Persian officials. In 1886 the Intelligence Branch of the War Office prepared a map of Persia in which, as in the *Pilot* of 1870, the three islands were shown in the same colour as Persian territory.[40]

Persian Occupation of Ṣirri in 1887

The occupation of Ṣirrī was closely connected with the Persian seizure of the Qawāsim government of Lingah and coincided with vigorous Persian political activity at Baḥrain, Qaṭar and the Trucial Coast. It was one of the major plans of the newly appointed Dery Begi, Amīn al-Sulṭān, carried out jointly by his representatives at Bushire, Ḥājjī Aḥmad Khān, and his tax collector, Malik al-Tujjār. At the beginning of August 1887, Ḥājjī Aḥmad Khān visited the Trucial Coast and returned to Lingah on 13 September, two days after the capture of Shaikh Qaḍīb, the Qasimī ruler of the town. At that time two eminent Qāsimīs, 'Abdullah b. Sālim, Wazir of Shaikh Qaḍīb and brother of the Shaikh, had succeeded in fleeing to Rās al-Khaimah, where they took refuge. On his arrival Ḥājjī Aḥmad sent a letter to the Sultan of Muscat apologising for the delay in visiting him and explaining that this had been caused by unrest at Lingah. During his stay at Dubai, Ḥājjī Aḥmad wrote a letter to its ruler containing four articles of an agreement which he wished the Shaikh to sign: first, renewal of friendly relations with the Persian Government; secondly, anyone from the Persian Coast who took refuge under the Shaikh's protection should be surrendered to the Persian Government if it had claims against him; thirdly, the Shaikh should not forbid readings about Ḥusain during 'Āshūrā; fourthly, the Shaikh should accept a Persian agent who would take care of any Persian claims against Persian subjects, in the same way as had been arranged with the British Government.

In reviewing the agreement proposed by Ḥajjī Aḥmad Khān and his talks with the Shaikh of Dubai (see Chapter 1, p. 25), two main purposes become apparent: the extension of Persian authority over the Arab Coast, and the wish to prepare a suitable atmosphere for Persia's termination of the independence of the Qawāsim at Lingah. Indeed, the probable effect on the Arab coast of the seizure of power at Lingah and the imprisonment of the Shaikh of the Qawāsim was a problem which preoccupied Ḥājjī Aḥmad Khān and Malik al-Tujjār. Ḥājjī Aḥmad found it prudent to visit Hināwī, Abū Dhabī, Dubai and Muscat while the attack against Ghāfirī Shaikh Qaḍīb at Lingah was being well prepared. From the itinerary of his visit it seems clear that he intended to ally himself with the Hināwīs, whom he considered to be the rivals of the Qawāsim.

On 15 September 1887, as soon as Persia had established her control over Lingah, Ḥājjī Aḥmad summoned Shaikh Ḥasan b. Muḥammad, Governor of Qishm Island, to the town. Under orders from Ḥājjī Aḥmad, Ḥasan proceeded from Lingah in native vessels with an armed party of thirty men and two small cannons to erect a flagstaff for the Persian flag on the island of Ṣirrī. According to a telegram of 18 September 1887 from the Residency Agent at Lingah, Ḥasan should have proceeded to the island of Ṭanb to inspect it and to erect a flagstaff, thus bringing it under Persian sovereignty. The British authorities in the Gulf were very disturbed by the occupation of Ṣirrī and the accompanying rumours about Ṭanb. Their annoyance was greater since the Residency Agent in Shārjah had failed to gather any accurate information about Ḥājjī Aḥmad's talks with the Shaikhs of Abū Dhabī and Dubai.

On 27 September Ross sent the Government of India a summary in which he began to review British policy in the light of the latest events. He wrote that the Qawāsim shaikhs domiciled on the Persian Coast had now acquired the status of Persian subjects, which led Persia to consider the islands as Persian territory. Ross stressed that as the Qawāsim shaikhs on the Trucial Coast had an undisputed joint ownership of these islands, they would strongly object to recent Persian possession. He went on to say that he thought it probable that some of the Qawāsim shaikhs might demand the intervention of the British Government, or failing that would ask to be allowed to eject the Persian officials themselves.[41]

In fact, although Persia intended to encroach on the four islands—Ṣirrī, Ṭanb Kubrā, Ṭanb Ṣughrā and Abū Mūsā—it was prudent of 'Amīn al-Sulṭān to confine his first move to Ṣirrī alone, which was acknowledged by the Qawāsim of 'Omān as belonging to their relatives at Lingah. The rumours did not mention Abū Mūsā, as this island was recognised by all sides as the property of the Qawāsim of 'Omān, whilst Ṭanb during the last years of Shaikh Khalīfah b. Sa'īd, Ruler of Lingah, was a matter of dispute with the Shaikh of Rās al-Khaimah. When Mockler, the Political Agent in Muscat, obtained a copy of the letter from the Shaikh of Dubai to the Sultan concerning Ḥājjī Aḥmad's visit to the Trucial Coast, he set out for Bushire. His hasty departure caused the correspondent of the Bombay *Pioneer* to report on 3 October 1887 that Mockler had proceeded to Bushire to confer with Ross about intrigues which Persia, at the instigation of Russia, had lately been carrying on with the chiefs along the coast of the Persian Gulf.

The Persian authorities at Lingah encouraged the spread of reports to the effect that British maritime supremacy in the Gulf was about to cede to that of Persia, who would assume the responsibility of keeping order at sea. The reports led the Qawāsim on the Trucial Coast to believe that Persia also intended to raise flagstaffs at Rās al-Khaimah and 'Ajmān, and that Shaikh Zāyed b. Khalīfah, the Ruler of Abū Dhabī and the head of the Hināwī party in the Trucial States, would be appointed Imam for the 'Omānī Coast. Although the Residency Agent told the two Arab chiefs that these rumours were false, they were not satisfied, especially as the Persians had actually erected a flagstaff at Ṣirrī.[42] The Shaikh of Shārjah informed the Residency Agent on 2 October 1887 that he had received a threatening letter from Ḥājjī Aḥmad saying that the Persian subjects at Shārjah should be treated with kindness, and on 15 October he expressed his anxieties to the Residency Agent and said he could not help but join with Rās al-Khaimah against any Persian designs. On 16 October Shaikh Ḥumaid b. ʻAbdullah protested to the Political Resident about the Persian occupation of Ṣirrī and asked for British protection for Ṭanb island. Furthermore, on 17 October the Shaikh of Shārjah in the name of the Qawāsim family appealed to the British Government about the hoisting of the Persian flag on Ṣirrī, which belonged to his family, and requested that the reported intention of the Persian authorities to hoist their flag on Ṭanb be prevented. Ross sent instructions to Ḥājjī Abū al-Qāsim on 31 October to calm the Arabs and told him to quieten their apprehensions over Persian rumours.[43]

The British Minister to Tehran informed the Political Resident on 10 October 1887 that he understood from unofficial sources that the hoisting of the Persian flag on the island of Ṣirrī had been carried out under orders from Tehran. On 30 October Ross sent to the British Minister at Tehran a copy of the agreement which Ḥājjī Aḥmad had presented to the Shaikh of Dubai and explained that although Ḥājjī Aḥmad's proposals fell short of what was rumoured, the presence of a Persian agent and the conclusion of a treaty between the Trucial chiefs and Persia would materially alter Britain's relations with those chiefs. Ross also sent a letter to the Government of India recommending that the British Minister to Tehran should be moved by the Government of India to take diplomatic action with a view to causing the Persians to lower their flag at Ṣirrī and refrain from hoisting it on Ṭanb. He explained that in the meanwhile he would take measures to prevent the Arab shaikhs concerned from undertaking hostilities for the recovery of their rights. Two months after the occupation of Ṣirrī, and following repeated demands from Ross, the Government of India finally took diplomatic action. On instructions from the Viceroy of India, Nicolson, the British Chargé d'Affaires in Tehran, took up the question of Ṣirrī with the Persian Prime Minister on 17 November 1887 and on 22 November Nicolson cabled that the latter expressed ignorance of the matter. However, on 10 December the Prime Minister made it known that both Ṣirrī and Ṭanb had paid taxes to the Persian Government during the preceding nine years and that documents in support of this assertion were at Bushire with Malik al-Tujjār. When approached by the Political Resident, Malik declared he had none and that he had telegraphed to Amīn al-Sulṭān excusing himself from discussing the question with Ross. On 14 December Amīn al-Sulṭān promised that he would shortly communicate the Persian case to the British in full. Ross meanwhile informed the Shaikh of Shārjah of the statement he had received from Amīn al-Sulṭān about collection of taxes from Ṣirrī and Ṭanb.[44]

On 2 January 1888 Amīn al-Sulṭān gave the British Legation five official letters from Shaikh Yūsuf to the Governor of Bushire during a period of one month in the year 1885. Only two of these letters mentioned Ṣirrī, one of which stated that Yūsuf visited Ṣirrī to inspect the island and recover

Government dues. The other three letters mentioned Ṭanb and one letter showed that Yūsuf had corresponded with the inhabitants there about receiving the Shaikh of Qishm. Nicolson sent the letters to Ross on the same day and asked his opinion. On 14 January, before Ross had answered, the Shaikh of Shārjah, giving his opinion on Amīn al-Sulṭān's statement, informed Ross that the island of Ṭanb was uninhabited and that there was no village and no fishermen to pay any taxes. The Shaikh again sent copies of the three letters of 1871, 1877 and 1884, which Shaikh Ḥumaid had received from the rulers of Lingah acknowledging his sovereignty over Ṭanb. The last of these letters had been written by Shaikh Yūsuf himself.[45]

In January 1888, Ḥājjī Aḥmad Khān, having supplied himself with a number of Persian flags, left Bushire and proceeded in a native vessel to the promontory of Rūs al-Jibāl. On landing at Khaṣab he was warned off by the inhabitants. Subsequently, accompanied by the Shaikh of Qishm and some armed men, he visited Umm al-Qaiwain, causing much excitement among the Arabs. Ḥājjī Aḥmad induced the ruler to accept the Persian flag, and was also reported to have announced that the British had no rights whatever in the Gulf and that at the request of the Government of Persia a Russian man-of-war would shortly arrive there. Ḥājjī Aḥmad left the Trucial Coast and returned disappointed to Bandar 'Abbās, where he declared that he had visited 'Omān only for personal reasons. Coinciding with Ḥājjī Aḥmad's latest activity on the Trucial Coast the Persian authorities tried to correspond directly with the Qawāsim rulers there. The Residency Agent reported to Ross on 18 January that the Deputy Governor of Lingah had written a letter to Shaikh Sālim b. Sulṭān, ex-ruler of Shārjah, requesting the extradition of an inhabitant of Ṣirrī island, who had taken refuge on Abū Mūsā. Ross instructed the Shaikh to reply that he was not in a position to exercise authority in such matters. Moreover, he observed to the Government of India that it was necessary to establish close supervision over the correspondence between Persian authorities and the Trucial chiefs.

Under instructions from the Government of India, Nicolson presented a memo to the Persian Minister for Foreign Affairs on 6 March 1888, stating that some time previously the Persian flag had been hoisted on the island of Ṣirrī and that the British Legation would be glad to know on what grounds the Persian Government had annexed the island which was the property of the Qawāsim chiefs, who were under British protection and who had asked for British help in this matter. On 10 March, in the first Persian note on the subject, the Minister for Foreign Affairs expressed his surprise that the British Legation, which had full knowledge of the Gulf, thought it right to entertain the ill-founded claims of the Qawāsim chiefs, and that the Persians should be asked for proof of their claims. The island of Ṣirrī was, he stated, a dependency of the port of Lingah. Nicolson replied on 19 March that it was quite true the Rulers of Lingah exercised jurisdiction over the island of Ṣirrī, but not in their capacity as Persian Governors of Lingah, but as

Qasimī shaikhs. The Qasimī family had traditional rights over the island of Ṣirrī which had never been disputed and were generally recognised. The hoisting of the Persian flag altered the existing status, and it was on that ground a request had been made for the reasons for this change. Nicolson emphasised that both the Government of India and HM Legation wished to treat the question in a friendly and conciliatory spirit.[46]

On 19 April 1888 Sir Drummond Wolff, British Minister to Tehran, informed the Marquis of Salisbury that Ross had discovered an intrigue by the Persian Prime Minister, Amīn al-Sulṭān, to promote Russian influence in the Persian Gulf to the extent of ceding an island to Russia as a coaling station. However, on 24 April Sir Drummond cabled London and Delhi that the Shāh, with whom he had had an interview that day, repudiated most emphatically the report of the cession of an island to Russia. At the end of the month Ross privately obtained a report prepared for Amīn al-Sulṭān by the Persian General, Ḥājjī Aḥmad Khān, who summarised certain passages from the first edition (1870) of the *Persian Gulf Pilot*, but Ross commented that this book was a nautical and not a political compilation and statements in it about the status of various places on the Gulf could not be considered authoritative. The British diplomatic attack on Amīn al-Sulṭān and the complaint to the Shāh caused some embarrassment for Ross and Wolff in Persian official circles and this had repercussions on the discussions regarding Ṣirrī. No reply was sent to Nicolson's communication of 19 April 1888, but Ross pressed the British Legation in Tehran for an answer from Persia, particularly when on 9 June Shaikh Ṣaqr b. Khālid repeated his anxiety about the Persian occupation of Ṣirrī. On 20 July the Persian Government eventually replied with a dismissive statement to the effect that as the Qasimī shaikhs of Lingah were Persian governors and also rulers of Ṣirrī no further proof was needed that the island was part of Persia.[47]

An event in July 1888 greatly influenced the talks concerning Ṣirrī. The British Minister in Tehran, on the instructions of the Marquis of Salisbury, during discussions about Perso-Afghan frontiers, presented to the Shāh a copy of the map prepared by the War Office. Sir Drummond subsequently reported that this map had produced 'certain results which were hardly contemplated'. The Shāh pointed out that in this very map both Ṣirrī and Ṭanb had been painted in the Persian colour. The Foreign Office, who did not share the enthusiasm of Ross and the Government of India over Ṣirrī, found it prudent to shelve the issue for the time being in order to prepare a friendly atmosphere for arbitration of the Persian–Afghan frontier dispute, which it considered more important. The Foreign Office's attitude for the time being was well summarised in the words of Churchill (Chargé d'Affaires) during his audience with the Shāh:

> The Arab tribes who claim these islands as theirs are within the radius of our jurisdiction and influence, and have appealed to us against the

action of the local authorities in the Gulf in hoisting a flag on their island. We, on our part, have communicated this complaint to the proper quarter and have simply asked for an answer to be given to the Arabs. We have never said that this or that island belongs to this or that tribe. We are simply the proper channel for the transmission of their complaints . . . it has never been desired that this question should assume an official aspect, nor that it should become the subject of official correspondence between us.[48]

Persian Claims to the Islands up to 1921

During this period a new and important factor intervened: the conclusion of the treaty of 1892 whereby Britain was charged with a much more definite obligation than previously to defend the Trucial Coast, and was empowered to represent the Trucial chiefs diplomatically. On 11 September 1894 the British Minister to Tehran sent the Persian Government a further note concerning Ṣirrī at the instigation of Colonel Wilson, the new Political Resident. The Persian Government replied on 6 November, trying to justify its occupation on the grounds that Ṣirrī had always been administered from Lingah.[49]

A sign of Shârjah's sovereignty over the island of Abū Mūsā at this time was the granting of mining concessions for the red oxide deposits (see Chapter 1, p. 31) which began to attract the attention of European businessmen. During 1898 Colonel M. J. Meade, the new Political Resident, continued research into the islands with a view to achieving a settlement of the Ṣirrī problem and on 13 December 1898 sent a study to the British Minister to Tehran which clearly formed the basis of much of the thinking of the British authorities in the 1930s. Meade recognised that the problem arose from the gradual assertion of Persian authority over the independent Arab tribes on the Persian Coast during the nineteenth century, but repeated the misconception which was by that time common amongst British officials, drawing no distinction whatever between the historical status of the various islands, whereby Abū Mūsā and Ṭanb, unlike Ṣirrī, were not governed by the Rulers of Lingah. The Resident's theory was that the Rulers of Lingah had had dual capacities, enabling them in one capacity to exercise authority in Lingah as Persian officials and in the other to govern Ṣirrī as Qawāsim shaikhs. Meade concluded that the Qawāsim chiefs on the Arab coast, who were under British protection, had an actual claim to the island and deserved British support against the Persian Government whose occupation was a distinct case of usurpation.[50]

On 14 October 1899 the Persian Government informed the British Minister that the Shāh feared that the Arab leaders of Lingah might return and hoped that the Government of India would take steps to prevent the assembling of men on the Arab coast with a view to attacking Lingah. The Government of

India cabled the Political Resident on 21 October to warn the Trucial chiefs not to assist any schemes for an attack on Lingah.

Once again, in January 1900, the Persian Government complained that Shaikh Muḥammad b. Khalīfah had taken refuge at Rās al-Khaimah, whose chief intended to aid him. The Persian Government were prepared to take measures to subdue the Arab chief of Rās al-Khaimah, but asked the British Government to intervene. Colonel Meade told the Government of India that the Trucial chiefs had been warned in October 1899 and that this warning had been repeated when he visited the Arab coast in December; however, he sent the *Melpomene*, a British man-of-war, with a renewed warning to Shaikh Ḥumaid to abandon all idea of making a descent on Lingah and the vessel's commander was instructed to prevent any such attempt.[51]

The Persian occupation of Abū Mūsā and Ṭanb at the end of March 1904, which lasted only until 14 June of the same year, was quite different in circumstances and results from the occupation of Ṣirrī in 1887. The British, who had become aware of the sensitivity of the problem raised by these islands, predicted the incident a year in advance. On 12 January 1903 Colonel Kemball reported the desire of certain immigrant merchants from the Persian coast that the island of Abū Mūsā should be substituted for Lingah as a port of call for the steamers of the Bombay and Persia Steam Navigation Company. Kemball suggested that the chief of Shārjah should fly his flag on the island as a sign of ownership; on 10 March the Government of India desired that the chief of Shārjah should fly his flag not only on the island of Abū Mūsā but on the sister island of Ṭanb, which came under his sovereignty after Shaikh Ḥumaid's death in 1900. On 30 April Kemball informed the Government that during his last visit to Shārjah the Shaikh had sent some of his men to Abū Mūsā to fly his flag. Although in this letter Kemball was discussing the different points to be considered regarding the advisability of flying an Arab flag on Ṭanb island as well as on Abū Mūsā at that time he made it clear that after investigation he had found that the Shaikh of Shārjah's claim to sovereignty over Ṭanb was stronger than his claim to Ṣirrī. British responsibilities to the Shaikh therefore obliged them to defend his claim to Ṭanb. Kemball expected that flying the Arab flag on Ṭanb as well as on Abū Mūsā could provoke the Persians into occupying the island, but he thought that further protest, as in the case of Ṣirrī, would be fruitless and that Britain should this time assert the rights of the Shaikh of Shārjah to the extent of forcibly removing the Persian flag from the island.

In fact the positive policy expressed by Kemball reflected the firm attitude now adopted by Britain in the Gulf in a period of international challenge. At the end of March 1904 the Persian customs authorities removed the Arab flags from the islands of Abū Mūsā and Ṭanb, hoisted the Persian flag in their place and left some Persian guards on both islands. After this occupation Sir Arthur Hardinge, the British Minister to Tehran, explained that he had very little doubt in his own mind that the instructions to occupy the two islands were connected with the Viceroy of India's recent cruise in the Gulf and that the Persian Government had been advised by the Russian Legation to anticipate, while there was still time, any seizure of islands or other strategic points in the area.

In a telegram to the Foreign Secretary dated 13 April 1904, the Viceroy of India proposed that a gunboat should be sent with a representative of the Shaikh of Shārjah to haul down the Persian flag, replace the Arab colours and remove the Persian guards to Persian territory. During a tour in the Gulf, Cox visited Ṭanb island on 14 April. Hardinge, who was consulted by the Foreign Office, cabled on 20 April his opinion that before taking action as proposed by the Viceroy, it would be advisable to afford the Persian Government the opportunity of removing the flags. On 23 April Lansdowne concurred with Hardinge's view. On 24 May Hardinge telegraphed to the Government of India that the Persian Government, while reserving its right to discuss with the British Government their respective claims to Abū Mūsā and Ṭanb, had agreed to send orders to Bushire to remove the Persian flags and guards.

This immediate success prompted Cox to raise the Arab claim to Ṣirrī island also, which had been shelved in 1888. On 31 May he urged the Government of India to seize the opportunity for some action. In his letter of 11 June Cox repeated that the British Government should press the question of Ṣirrī with Persia and suggested a request to the British to do so could be made by the Shaikh of Shārjah.

On 14 June the Persian Foreign Minister replied to Hardinge that the Persian Government considered Abū Mūsā and Ṭanb as their own property, and the steps taken by the customs authorities there had been for that reason. However, owing to their previous conversation a Royal command had been issued that for the present the measures should be abandoned. He expressed the wish that neither party should hoist flags on the two islands pending settlement of the question. It should be noted that this was the first official challenge by Persia to the Qawāsim's ownership of Abū Mūsā. In pursuance of the orders issued from Tehran the Persian flags were removed.

After a few days the Arab flags were hoisted on both islands. Britain's energetic action earned for her the deep gratitude and appreciation of the Arab tribes on 'Omān Coast. The SNO in his report to the Government of India on 28 June 1904 underlined the opinion of Hardinge and Cox about the significance of Ṣirrī, stating that the island was as important to the British as were the islands of Ṭanb and Abū Mūsā, and suggesting that similar steps be taken there. The Government of India informed Hardinge on 15 July that owing to the delay which had occurred in urging Arab claims to Ṣirrī, the British case was not strong; however, if the Persians were to advance further claims to Abū Mūsā and Ṭanb, the Arab claim to Ṣirrī could then be revived.[52]

The British Chargé d'Affaires warned the Persian Government in 1908 against any attempt to renew the Persian claim to Abū Mūsā during the Wonkhaus dispute over the cancellation of the red oxide mining concession on the island. In the same year Persia granted a British company a concession to mine red oxide on Ṣirrī island. Meanwhile, particularly in relation to the Wonkhaus issue, Cox was preparing a detailed study of the islands based on the previous studies and reports in the archives of the Residency, and sent it to the Government of India at the end of 1908. The British protested to the Persian Government about the granting of the concession on Ṣirrī, a disputed island, and informed the company that sovereignty there was still unsettled.[53]

At the beginning of 1912 the British authorities decided to establish a lighthouse on Ṭanb. With the approval of the British Government no communication on the subject was made to Persia, but Cox was authorised to obtain the consent of the Shaikh of Shārjah, Ṣaqr b. Khālid, in his capacity as Ruler of Rās al-Khaimah, who granted his permission on 22 October 1912, subject to an assurance that his rights of sovereignty would not be affected. Cox also wrote to Shaikh Ṣaqr that while it was desirable that the Shārjah flag should always be in evidence on Ṭanb, 'now at all events this island will be preserved for you by the mere presence of the lighthouse'. In October 1912, in reply to an enquiry by the Derya Begi, Cox stated that with the concurrence of the Shaikh of Shārjah a lighthouse was about to be erected on Ṭanb. On 13 February 1913 the Persian Foreign Minister raised the question with the British Minister to Tehran. A reply was given by Cox that he had recently made it clear to the Governor of the Gulf Ports that the ownership of Ṭanb was not open to question, and added 'since the correspondence of 1905, the subjects of the Shaikh of Shārjah and his flag have remained established on the island; that if the question was now re-opened, HM Government would no doubt revive the question of Ṣirrī; but that a flat refusal to discuss it would probably be best'.[54] On 15 July the lighthouse was first put into use.

III Britain's Attitude towards Persian Policy during the Rezā Shāh's Reign

Rezā Shāh's Dominance over the Persian Coast and Islands

In 1921 Rezā Shāh came to power in Persia and established a central government of a strength without parallel in modern Persian history. He reorganised the Cossack division and successfully built a well-equipped modern army, with which he subdued the border provinces, most of which were ruled by local hereditary chiefs, one of whom was Khaz'al in 'Arabistān, an Arab shaikh prominent in Gulf politics. By November 1923 Rezā Shāh had decided to collect taxes from 'Arabistān and subject it to the central government, and a settlement was eventually reached with Khaz'al by which he agreed to pay the Government all future taxes, in addition to half a million tumans of his tax arrears, and made an immediate payment in cash of 100,000 tumans.

However, Rezā Shāh's successful campaign against the Lur tribesmen in August 1924 seriously alarmed Khaz'al, their immediate neighbour, who rashly sent a rebellious telegram to the Ministry of Finance renouncing his previous settlement. His defiance went further with his refusal to recognise Rezā Shāh as Prime Minister, calling him a usurper who had driven the real Shāh out of the country. At the same time he incited other Arab chiefs in his territory to demand from the Majlis the return of the real Shāh from Europe. To his disappointment the Majlis supported the Shāh, as did the Mullās. Rezā Shāh sent four divisions of his new army to 'Arabistān and in November 1924 left for Isphahān, where he received a telegram of apology from Khaz'al, though he insisted on Khaz'al's unconditional surrender. A few days later, after Khaz'al's forces had been defeated, the Shāh's demands were satisfied. 'Arabistān was occupied by the army and the Shaikh was exiled to Tehran, where he spent the rest of his life in confinement.[55]

The most urgent problem facing the new Shāh was to secure adequate sources of income to finance the reconstruction of his country. In order to link the Caspian Sea with the Gulf, he built the Trans-Iranian Railway, begun in October 1927 and completed in December 1938. He established a number of textile factories and constructed a great many miles of modern roads. In securing revenue for these ambitious projects he refused to ask for external loans, thus avoiding the risk of foreign interference, and relied instead on internal sources. He depended mainly upon the high taxes on tea and sugar and the government monopoly of foreign trade. These measures affected substantially the inhabitants of the southern coast, who were the principal importers of these items through the Gulf ports. Smuggling, which had begun on a small scale some decades earlier, now flourished and in order to prevent this loss of revenue, a key obstacle to all his reforms, and to gain control of the Gulf shores, Rezā Shāh had to build a navy. In July 1930 Persia signed a contract with Italy for the supply of six warships. In October 1932 these ships entered the Gulf, and although they were not wholly successful in ending the smuggling, they caused great annoyance to the British Navy and to the Arab dhows.[56]

The Persian military and naval authorities ruled the southern coast and islands with a firm hand and this, together with the government monopoly of trade caused further waves of emigration to the Arab coast during the thirties. Moreover, the enforced unveiling of women in 1936, considered heretical by the devout among both the Sunnī and Shī'ī inhabitants, precipitated heavy waves of emigration at the end of the same year, of which the monthly reports of the British Political Residency at Bushire provide evidence. In October 1936 the police on the island of Hindurābī tried to force the female population to discard their veils, but the islanders seized the guards, together with the Director of Customs, bound them hand and foot, placed them in confinement and then emigrated to the Arab coast. Their number was calculated at three hundred. Another report stated that in

Tumbâq, Kushkanār and other small towns in the Shibkūh region, a Persian officer shaved the beards of some thirty old Mullās and Qādīs who had resisted westernisation reforms. Finally, compelled to emigrate, the people of these towns went to Baḥrain, Qaṭar and the Trucial States. In a letter from Colonel Fowle at Bushire to the British Minister in Tehran on 7 December 1936 we learn that the Banī Ḥammād tribe on Chīrūh had emigrated to the port of Kalbā out of dissatisfaction with the Government of Iran and it was understood that their particular grievance concerned the unveiling of women. Fowle added that some thousands of individuals from Iranian coastal tribes had also emigrated to the Trucial Coast in recent years for more or less similar reasons.[57] The *Persian Gulf Pilot* of the 1930s reported that the town most affected was Lingah and that its population had dwindled from 12,000 at the beginning of the century to 3,000 in 1939.[58]

Rezā Shāh and Britain

At the beginning of 1921 Sayyed Ziā al-Dīn Ṭabāṭabā'ī, a young former editor of the Tehran newspaper *Ra'd* who had recently become immersed in politics, approached Rezā Khān, a general in the Cossack division who was also deeply involved in the nationalist cause, and together they agreed to carry out a *coup d'état*. Ziā was known to look to Britain for support in Persia's struggle for independence and reform and was in frequent contact with the British Legation in Tehran. In contrast, Rezā Khān, who was both suspicious towards and sensitive about foreign interference, believed that Persia's future had to be secured independently. A few days after the *coup*, Sayyed Ziā, responding to popular nationalist feeling, made public the official cancellation of the Anglo-Persian treaty of 1919, and on 26 February 1921 he signed the treaty of friendship with Russia which had already been negotiated and accepted before the *coup*. This gave Russia the right to despatch troops in the event of a Persian failure to check military intervention by a third party threatening the frontiers of Russia. This was one of the reasons which restrained Britain's use of force despite considerable provocation on occasions.

The 1921 *coup* which had been expected to restore British influence in Persia, in fact had the opposite effect, bringing about an antagonistic attitude towards Britain that continued throughout Rezā Shāh's reign. As Persia began to assert her sovereignty in the 1920s, numerous clashes occurred between Britain and Rezā Shāh over military and economic issues, reaching a climax in 1928. One of the initial differences arose when the Persians asked for British instructors and ammunition to be seconded to their army from the British forces in Persia, but the Foreign Office, influenced by the cancellation of the treaty of 1919, refused this request unless it were incorporated in a treaty. Rezā Khān was trying to induce the British to transfer the South Persia Rifles to the Persian army in fulfilment of the agreement made between the two governments in 1916, but Britain, on the pretext of wishing to maintain the high efficiency of the force, insisted on the regiment preserving its present organisation under the command of British officers. Consequently, the Persian Government refused the British demand and the Government of India disbanded the regiment.[59]

Another early clash of interests occurred with the Anglo-Persian Oil Company. To Rezā Khān the existence of a powerful foreign company with Arnold Wilson, a prominent soldier of well-known imperialist convictions and a personal friend of Shaikh Khaz'al, as General Manager was alarming.[60] Moreover, Persia's policy towards the oil company was determined by her immediate need of money. When Rezā encouraged American oil companies and granted them concessions in areas claimed by the APOC, the British Government protested vigorously.

Rezā Khān's principal worries in his early relations with Britain were over the submission of Shaikh Khaz'al. In fact, in their dealings with Khaz'al the British were torn between their desire to see a strong central government in Persia and their earlier commitments to this shaikh who, when he publicly attacked Rezā Khān in 1924, had hoped to receive help from the British because of earlier mutual friendship. To his astonishment, the British authorities explained to him the uselessness of resistance, leaving him no alternative but to surrender. It was nevertheless difficult for the British Legation and the directors of the oil company to allow the total defeat of Khaz'al without vigorous diplomatic protest. The Persian Government was suspicious of the oil company's intrigues and Rezā Khān was informed by his military intelligence that cases of rifles and ammunition had been conveyed to the Shaikh in the company's barges. As Rezā Khān moved further south, the British protested more sharply and tried to act as mediators, but Rezā Khān insisted that the problem of Khaz'al was entirely a domestic matter in which the British had no right to interfere. With Khaz'al's submission in 1924, 'Arabistān and APOC were brought for the first time into direct relation with the central government,[61] but the abandonment of this Arab Shaikh, who had long enjoyed British friendship, did not pass unnoticed by the rulers of the Trucial States.

Another important dispute between Britain and Persia during these years concerned the war debt, which amounted to approximately £3½ million. Whilst the British Treasury was very much averse to waiving any part of it, the Persians contended that no obligation rested on them to repay a debt which had been illegally incurred without the sanction of Parliament. Moreover, the money had been spent primarily for the benefit of the Allies and should therefore be regarded as British war expenditure. Eventually the British Government, in order to arrive at a satisfactory all-round settlement, decided to forgo a portion of the debt.[62]

In 1927 the two main sources of disagreement were over the cancellation of foreign capitulations, and Persia's renewal of her claim to Baḥrain. On 10 May 1927 Rezā Shāh declared the abolition of capitulations, to take effect in one year's time. Rezā Shāh's decision was directed particularly against Britain, since by the early 1920s Russia had relinquished her privileges. The Baḥrain controversy provides another example of the upsurge of anti-British nationalist feeling. Since 1922 the Persians had revived the question of passports and British protection of Baḥrain's subjects visiting the Gulf ports. The Anglo–Sa'ūdī Treaty of 20 May 1927 precipitated a renewal by Persia of her historical claims to Baḥrain island, since Article 6 of this treaty bound Ibn Sa'ūd to refrain from interference with the chief of the island. On 22 November Persia protested against the British Government's claim to exercise protection over Baḥrain and circulated a note to this effect in the League of Nations. On 18 January 1928 Britain rejected Persian demands, but Persia reiterated her claim and on 5 January 1929 protested against a British regulation requiring Persian citizens to produce passports in order to visit the Baḥrain islands.[63]

The year 1928 witnessed several serious crises which obliged the Persian Gulf Sub-Committee to consider the possible courses of action open to them. The attack which Teymourtāche, the Minister of the Court, made in this year on the validity of the D'Arcy concession seriously affected APOC. He declared that the Persian Government could be neither legally nor logically bound by the provisions of a concession granted prior to the establishment of the constitutional rēgime, arguing that the concession had been obtained under duress and that it did not sufficiently protect the interests of the Persian people.[64] The 'Dubai dhow' incident (see p. 257) presented a new challenge to British naval supremacy in the Gulf and had a harmful effect upon British prestige among the Arabs.

Following upon this, in 1928, after seven years' achievement, the Government felt confident enough to challenge British traditional privileges acquired during the nineteenth century on the Persian coast and islands. In August 1928 the Persian Government requested British withdrawal from the naval bases at Hanjām and Bāsīdū and erected a flagstaff at the former, which gave rise to a British complaint. There were rumours of an imminent Persian occupation of both bases, and a permanent British guard was established at Bāsīdū to forestall any such attempt. Finally, in September 1928, a formal request for evacuation was presented on the grounds that the anchorage would be needed for the new Persian Navy.[65] Thus, during the tense year of 1928 the continuing problems arising from the Political Residency in Bushire and the naval bases at Hanjām and Bāsīdū came under serious discussion at the Meetings of the Persian Gulf Sub-Committee. The Government of India, the Admiralty and the Political Resident in Bushire adopted the traditional pre-war policy. In several telegrams to the Government of India during August 1928 the Political Resident discussed the Persian demands with feverish anxiety and obstinacy, clearly influenced by recent Persian aggressiveness towards Arab dhows, whose owners were under British protection. He advised that it was dangerous for the British to withdraw from any naval bases they held on the islands, as Persian policy was without question one of edging the British out not only from her own territory but also from the whole of the Gulf. If the British gave way at all, he warned, they would by degrees lose their dominant position altogether and thus be reduced to mere equality with Persia. He suggested that the Indian Government should inform the Persian Government that the Gulf lay within the area of a kind of British Monroe Doctrine.[66]

However, despite the views of the Political Resident, there were early signs of a conciliatory policy. At the meeting of CID on 17 October 1928 the Secretary of State for India presented a note on the separation of the functions of the Political Resident in the Persian Gulf and those of the Consul General of Fārs at Bushire, together with the removal of the Residency from Persian soil. As the international climate prevented members of the League of Nations resorting to military measures in the settlement of disputes, it was the decision of the Persian Gulf Sub-Committee that negotiations with Persia would be the best means of arriving at a settlement.[67] Accordingly, to encourage Persia to accept negotiations and reach a settlement, it was agreed in December 1928 to waive a further substantial part of her debt should she sign a general Anglo–Persian agreement in addition to an undertaking to purchase her naval requirement from British shipyards. Persia responded favourably to this new gesture from the Foreign Office and in February 1929 the British Legation in Tehran offered a draft treaty for discussion.[68]

Negotiations for the proposed Anglo–Persian treaty lasted six years but came to an abortive end in 1935 due to the uncompromising attitudes of the Government of India and the Admiralty on the one hand and nationalist ambitions of Persian policy on the other. The main articles in the draft of the proposed treaty of 1929 were concerned with British naval facilities, particularly at the base at Hanjām. Britain requested Persia to renounce her claims to the islands of Baḥrain, Ṭanb and Abū Mūsā and to repay the capital of her pre-war debt; in return Britain was prepared to offer certain important financial concessions. The Foreign Office offered in the draft to cede British rights on the island of Hanjām on condition that the base was leased to them for twenty years. After this draft had been presented Sir Frederick Johnson, the Political Resident, accompanied by Captain Boyes, the Senior Naval Officer, came by plane to Tehran on 12 February 1929 and held friendly talks with Teymourtāche, the Minister of the Court, to discuss the naval bases at Hanjām and Bāsīdū, Persia's new quarantine laws, and various urgent questions concerning the Trucial Coast.[69]

Although the negotiations began in a favourable atmosphere, the question of the Persian Navy soon created difficulties. In order to establish a small but strong fleet to patrol her long coastline, Persia, suspicious of British attempts to limit her naval development, sought to obtain assistance from Italy as well as England. Early in 1929 Major de Jeurme and Captain Delbrateau, Italian naval experts, were engaged in the Persian Government's service and twenty young Persians were sent for training at an Italian naval school at Leghorn. However, on 2 August 1929 Teymourtâche informed Sir Robert Clive, the British Minister in Tehran, that Persia would prefer British help in building a small fleet of armed patrol vessels, four of 1,000 tons and six of 200 tons, and in the supply of naval officers for their command. He added that Persia was prepared to abandon her claim to the Baḥrain islands and to recognise Britain's hegemony in the Gulf, on condition that she herself was enabled by Britain to become the second power there. The Foreign Office received these proposals with sympathetic attention and referred them to an interdepartmental committee in September 1929. On 7 November the Admiralty and the Government of India made it clear that the new Persian naval forces must be kept as small as possible. The Senior Naval Officer reported that two sloops of 600 tons and four motor launches of 150 tons would be sufficient to deal with the contraband trade which was annoying Persia. He estimated the capital cost of this proposal at £140,000, whilst the cost of the ships requested by Teymourtâche amounted to £500,000.[70]

An answer was sent to Teymourtâche on 14 January 1930. As proof of goodwill the British Government was prepared to remit an additional amount of the debt to cover the cost of these ships, on the condition that Persia accepted the Admiralty's recommendations regarding their size and number. On 31 March 1930 Teymourtâche wrote to Clive that he had expected the British Government to provide ten ships not six, and that these should be free of charge in part compensation for abandoning claims to Baḥrain. Moreover the Persian Government would not pay any part of the debt for reasons that had been repeatedly explained; negotiations on this basis would therefore be useless.[71] Clive informed the Persian Government that although it had agreed to buy Ṭanb island in return for leasing Hanjâm to Britain, the Arabs refused to allow the sale and the British found themselves unable to put pressure on them. Disappointed by Britain's attitude, Teymourtâche gave a definite order for ships to Italy.[72]

The atmosphere deteriorated and communications exchanged in August and September 1930 made it apparent that deep-rooted differences did exist. Conflict arose mainly over territorial questions: Britain's insistence on keeping naval privileges at Hanjâm, and Persia's claims to the islands of Baḥrain, Abū Mūsā and Ṭanb. The most crucial point in Teymourtâche's discussion with Clive was his insistence on Britain's withdrawl from Hanjâm, and this was to become a major obstacle in Anglo–Persian negotiations. Since Baḥrain was gaining considerable political weight in British strategy in the Gulf, as a possible alternative position for the Political Residency, an airport on the Arabian air route and a naval base, the Foreign Office answered on

18 September 1930 that Persia had no rights there whatsoever. Persian demands for compensation were therefore considered absurd. The discourtesy with which the British Government felt it had been treated by Persia in arranging to buy ships from Italy without informing Britain that assistance was no longer required was also pointed out.[73] Teymourtâche's sudden change of policy over Hanjām resulted from the British failure to put through the sale of Ṭanb by the Shaikh of Rās al-Khaimah. The September note from the Foreign Office therefore reiterated Britain's request for the lease of Hanjām for at least fifty years and unless Persia was willing to comply with this demand, it seemed to Britain useless to continue negotiations for the proposed treaty of friendship.

Although 1931 was an uneventful year for Anglo-Persian negotiations, storm followed the calm in 1932. In March that year Persia finally refused renewal of the Imperial Airways agreement, which Britain had been desperately seeking for the past three years. In May 1932 Persia reacted further against Britain by tightening quarantine regulations for British ships. Teymourtâche suggested for the first time that Persia's new warships, expected at the end of the year, would themselves require the use of Hanjām and asked for British withdrawal from the base.[74]

The oil negotiations which began in 1929 reached deadlock in 1932. On 7 August 1931, after two years of discussions between Sir John Cadman and Teymourtâche, the former informed the Minister of the Court that the revision of the concession could no longer be contemplated as the demands of the Persian Government were greatly in excess of anything the company could accept. The Government's revenue from the oil company had actually been decreasing. The Persian Government protested to the company and refused to accept the royalty in June 1932.

On 20 September 1932 the Persian Government formally requested the evacuation of Hanjām, to which the Admiralty objected strongly. The official British reply in October 1932 was that negotiations on the draft Anglo–Persian treaty would be broken off if the demand were not withdrawn. This adamant refusal to make way for the Persian naval force expected in the Gulf during that month made Persia furious, and she directed her anger against the British oil enterprise.[75] On 27 November 1932 the Persian Minister of Finance notified APOC of the cancellation of the d'Arcy concession but expressed the Government's willingness to negotiate another. A day later the British Government protested, reserving the right to take all legitimate measures to protect British interests. On 23 January 1933 both governments submitted written memoranda to the League of Nations and the next day M. Benes of Czechoslovakia was appointed Rapporteur. During February 1933 direct negotiations began between the two governments and a new convention was signed on 19 April 1933, which Benes announced to the League Council as an effective disposal of the dispute.[76]

During this year the Foreign Office, after finding that Britain's status on

Hanjām and Bāsīdū was weak, developed a new policy towards Persia. Whilst it agreed that voluntary evacuation would mean a decline in prestige, it would be much less than the loss suffered through a forced withdrawal. However, on 31 July 1933 Major Bayander, Commandant of the Persian Navy, approached Rāsīdū and landed a party which hauled down the Union Jack and substituted the Persian colours. From the outset the Shāh and the Persian Government repudiated the Commandant's action and gave assurances against the repetition of such incidents. When written communication was received from Persia it was vague and unsatisfactory.

The British authorities were shocked, but as no legal ground existed for their presence at Bāsīdū they felt unable to use force and had to acknowledge the accomplished fact. However, the flag incident aroused antagonism to Persia among British naval officers, and it had not settled down when an even more serious crisis arose over the arrest at Bāsīdū on 9 October 1933 of the Persian Director of Customs who had examined a dhow lying off the British area.[77] Persia retaliated with a vigorous counter-protest, denying that the British possessed any rights whatsoever at Bāsīdū. Still anxious to reach a settlement, the British Government instructed the Admiralty in November 1933 that British naval forces in the Gulf must for the time being turn a blind eye to the activities of the Persian Navy. The Admiralty, although it implemented these instructions, described them as not only damaging to the prestige of the Royal Navy, but placing naval personnel in a very difficult and indeed false position.[78]

Anglo–Persian relations at the end of 1933 and the beginning of 1934 were dominated by mutual suspicion. In his two memoranda of May and August 1934, Rendel, Head of the Eastern Department, advocated the transfer of the British naval base from Hanjām to Baḥrain as the final and definitive answer to Persian pretensions there. In his May memorandum he pointed out that Persia had to be treated on terms of equality, and the traditional idea of the Persian Gulf as a British lake would have to be abandoned. His opinion was that however obstinately Persia asserted this equality, her goodwill was still necessary to protect the interests of APOC as well as to ensure that Persian friendship was not transferred to Russia by default.[79] Despite this, the Admiralty adhered to its firm traditional policy to maintain Bāsīdū and Hanjām and on 4 June 1934 suggested that an ultimatum should be sent to Persia. It also demanded that the November 1933 instructions be modified. However, by telegram on 4 July the Foreign Office informed its Minister to Tehran that the decision of the Middle East Committee at its meeting of 11 June was that no action of a challenging nature should at present be taken *vis-à-vis* the Persian Government.[80] At the subsequent meeting of 12 October the OME Sub-Committee reached an agreement for the evacuation of Hanjām and Bāsīdū and the establishment of a base at Baḥrain was accepted as an alternative. Among the factors influencing the Admiralty's acceptance of this was the announcement in

May 1932 of a large oil strike on the island of Baḥrain.[81] However, the evacuation was delayed and took place between 5 and 11 April 1935; the Persian Navy was to establish a small detachment at Hanjām in early May.[82] In 1935 Persia changed her name to Iran, a step which added her present pride and sovereignty to her past glories.

Persia and the Trucial States during the 1920s

Waves of immigrants from the Persian coast, whether of Arab or Persian origin, continued during Rezā Shāh's reign as a result of his strong policy of centralisation. This migration, and the development during the late 1920s and the 1930s of a complicated system of smuggling into Persia, formed the background to many important issues, particularly in 1928, between Persia and the Trucial States, which therefore involved Britain as the protecting power, responsible for external relations. The competition offered by Japanese cultured pearls, together with the world economic depression which began to be felt at the end of the 1920s, severely damaged the pearl trade of the Trucial States and provided major incentives for widespread smuggling. The formation of stable governments in Sa'ūdī Arabia, Iraq and Persia saw the introduction of high tariffs as the only possible means of revenue, whilst the rulers of the Trucial States, particularly Dubai, felt that low tariffs would attract more trade. The extensive development of smuggling dated from Persia's imposition in 1925 of a monopoly tax on all tea and sugar imported from abroad, so that the smuggling of these commodities had become a source of income for groups of unemployed pearl divers and adventurers, providing substantial profits; this traffic replaced the trade in arms which had flourished between the beginning of the century and the outbreak of World War I. The Persian authorities felt that the formidable British Navy turned a blind eye to smuggling and that it was too lenient in accepting the flow of immigrants to the Trucial States and to Baḥrain and Qaṭar. These two issues embittered Anglo-Persian relations.[83]

In 1921 Britain recognised the independence of the Rās al-Khaimah emirate, allowing Ṭanb island to remain in its possession, while Abū Mūsā island was to be retained by Shārjah. Early in 1921 Shārjah granted a mineral concession to a British company, an action which prompted a protest from Persia. In April of that year, Sir Percy Loraine, the British Minister to Tehran, learned that the Persian Government was being urged by Mu'īn al-Tujjār, the holder of the Hormuz red oxide concession, to refer their claims to Baḥrain and Abū Mūsā to the League of Nations. On 16 May 1921 Sir Percy denounced these claims and reminded the Persians of the forceful measures Britain had adopted in 1904 and were willing to use again. This threat was followed on 23 May 1921 by a Persian note which insisted on her rights to the islands of Abū Mūsā and Ṭanb. In the autumn of 1925 the Persian customs authorities sent a launch to Abū Mūsā where its personnel inspected the red oxide mined on the island and removed one bag. Following a protest against this action Persia reasserted her claims to Abū Mūsā but British diplomatic pressure in Tehran brought about the withdrawal of the Persian note in 1926. Persian customs officials were instructed to take no active steps in Abū Mūsā or Ṭanb pending a statement from the Ministry of Foreign Affairs on the status of the two islands.[84] However, from that year on the Persians annoyed the Arabs by threatening confiscation of their dhows. This aggressive attitude was to cause wide political repercussions in 1928.

During January 1928 the Persian authorities repeated that to take effective measures against smuggling British co-operation was necessary. Sir Robert Clive, the new British Minister to Tehran, then suggested to the Foreign Office that it might be possible to dispose of the Persian claims to the islands of Baḥrain, Ṭanb and Abū Mūsā in exchange for British co-operation in preventing smuggling to the Persian coast from Baḥrain, Kuwait and Dubai. The Government of India and the Admiralty objected to such co-operation, partly because of its general political character and partly for reasons of impracticability. Sir Lionel Howarth, the Political Resident, explained that the greater part of the smuggling was carried out from Persia in Persian ships and that the real difficulty lay in the fact that all the Persian khāns had interests in the smuggling, that the Persian customs officials were bribed, and that the province of Tangistān was not within Persian control. He stated that to force the rulers affected to adopt preventive measures would be difficult at Baḥrain and Kuwait and impossible at Dubai without altering the whole policy of HMG on the Trucial Coast and without increasing the British naval force in the Gulf, as had been done in the case of the arms traffic twenty years earlier. In a report later that year he went on to explain that it would be an act of political folly for Britain to take such expensive measures while Persia was attempting to drive her out of the Gulf and while Britain was therefore becoming dependent on Arabs for her position in those waters. If, however, Britain's paramount position in the Gulf were recognised by Persia, it would be worthwhile to take measures which, even if unsuccessful, would at least demonstrate British goodwill towards Persia. He wondered how the Persians could endeavour to drive the British from the Persian coast and still expect to use British influence on the Arab coast for their own ends. The Government of India, in expressing agreement with the views of the Political Resident, added that 'it is not our business to control harmless exports like sugar from our Arab protectorates'.[85]

At the beginning of 1928 an acute problem arose concerning the Āl Bū-Flāsah clan on Hanjām island, which was to bring to the surface the latent questions concerning British protection of the Trucial States, the nationality of the Persian immigrants living on Arab soil and central Persian authority over the Arab inhabitants of Persia. The clashes between the Arabs of Hanjām and the Persians, which had increased before the war, continued during the 1920s. The Shaikh of Hanjām, 'Ubaid b. Jum'ah, feeling that Muscat could no longer offer any effective help, appealed for protection from the Ruler of Dubai, asking to become his dependant and the Shaikh of Dubai raised the question of the nationality of the Āl Bū-Flāsah Arabs of Hanjām with the British authorities in the Gulf.

In May 1928 Shaikh 'Ubaid b. Jum'ah became involved in a fierce new dispute with the local Persian authorities, during which the Director of Customs on the island was murdered and the Shaikh was forced to flee with his supporters to Bukhā on the Arab coast to the north of Rās al-Khaimah. The Persian authorities did not wish the Arabs of Hanjām to vacate the island, so in an attempt to persuade those who had fled to return they prevented the women from following their husbands to Bukhā, but this action only further aggravated the already mounting tension between Persians and Arabs. The Shaikh of Dubai, nephew of the Shaikh of Hanjām, was at this time on a pilgrimage to Mecca and the British restrained the Arabs from retaliating, promising to solve the problem themselves.

In July 1928 a Persian customs launch, which had been operating off the south of Ṭanb for two months, seized an Arab dhow approaching the island on its way from Dubai to Khaṣab. The dhow was carrying twenty-two persons, eight women and seven men as passengers, and seven crew, including the captain, and was taken to Lingah where the provisions of sugar and dates were confiscated as contraband and those on board detained. Four days later the news of the incident reached Dubai, where it caused great agitation, increasing the hostility against Persia that had been felt since the Hanjām issue in May. The Arabs of Dubai, more especially the husbands of the kidnapped women who were at the mercy of the Persians at Lingah, demanded the despatch of three armed dhows to rescue the seized vessel. More extreme opinion was for waging war at sea against all Persian ships.[86]

The Shaikh of Dubai, having returned from his pilgrimage, informed the Residency Agent of the strong desire among his people for revenge and retaliation. Such hasty action was forbidden by the Residency Agent, and he advised the Shaikh to restrain his people. The Shaikh commented bitterly on Britain's tolerance of Persian aggression at sea, for which in the past she had always severely punished Arabs and bombarded their ports. In these circumstances the Shaikh felt he could control his people for no more than ten days, and then only if the British sought the immediate release of the dhow and its passengers and compensation for the seizure. On 28 July the SNO heard the news on his arrival in Dubai. He supported the advice given by the Residency Agent and promised that the British themselves would find a satisfactory solution, but asked that the Arabs should wait patiently for definite news until 11 August. He then hastened on board HMS *Triad* to Hanjām, where he cabled the British authorities.

On 2 August the British Chargé d'Affaires, on instructions from the Foreign Office in London, made urgent representations to the Belgian chief of customs, and an official note of protest to the Persian Minister followed two days later, asking for the immediate release of the dhow, its passengers and their belongings. The limited attitude of the British Legation at Tehran was at odds with that of the Political Resident, who himself took a different view of the case. The seizure, carried out under direct orders from the Persian authorities, in the territorial waters of an Arab island of a dhow belonging to subjects of an Arab shaikh protected by the British was to him an incident of international dimensions. The Political Resident proposed that the British should press not only for complete repudiation by the Persian Government of any claim to the island of Ṭanb, mentioned in the British Legation note, but also for compensation to persons wrongfully arrested and to the shaikhs whose territory had been violated. The Government of India in its letters of 5 August agreed with the Political Resident generally that the British must secure full restoration and ample compensation. It found in the very audacity of the incident an opportunity to teach the Persians a salutary lesson.[87]

Despite the Shaikhs' efforts to calm their people, they were finding it difficult and matters became worse with each day's delay. The SNO had already ordered HMS *Lupin* to Dubai as a patrol vessel with strict instructions to contain any Arab attempt against the Persians at sea, and its arrival on 5 August was effective in preventing an intended Arab outbreak. There was in Dubai at that time a party, the number of whose adherents was growing steadily, that was adopting a strongly anti-British attitude.

Meanwhile, the Shaikh of Dubai had received a message from the Director of Customs at Lingah asking for an interview in connection with the dhow incident; the Shaikh, however, refused. On 8 August 1928, having received news that the Chief of Customs, after another British protest, had ordered the release of the dhow and passengers, but not the confiscated sugar, the SNO set out for Dubai, arriving on 9 August. There the Shaikh anxiously questioned him about the release of the dhow and of his uncle's women detained on Hanjām. The SNO said that the first problem had been settled and he himself was going straight to Lingah; about the latter he promised to remind the Political Resident. On his way to Lingah he received information that the dhow had been released and had already sailed direct to Khaṣab; this fact he telegraphed to HMS *Lupin*, to be communicated to the Shaikh. ʻĪsā informed the Shaikh that the Political Resident intended to ask compensation from Persia to the extent of Rs. 300 for each passenger and Rs. 1,000 for the captain, in addition to Rs. 5,000 to the Shaikh of Dubai and Rs. 10,000 to the Shaikh of Rās al-Khaimah for the violation of their sovereignty within their territorial waters by the Persian customs officials. The news of the release and proposed compensation was received with joy in Dubai. Shaikh Jumʻah, the Ruler's brother, on a visit to the Captain of the *Lupin*, informed him of the letter the Shaikh had received from the Director of Customs at Lingah. The report of Persia's correspondence with the Shaikh of Dubai was cabled immediately to the SNO, who found in it support for the rumour that Persian officials had instructions to open direct negotiations with the Shaikhs of the Trucial Coast without the mediation of the British authorities.[88]

In response to the situation on the Trucial Coast, which was still difficult even after the release of the dhow, and to the strong reaction from the Government of India, the Political Resident and the Admiralty, the Foreign Office agreed on 11 August that the Minister to Tehran should not be content with the mere release of the dhow and passengers, but requested him to submit to the Persian Government a pecuniary claim on account of goods confiscated and general compensation for illegal detention of the dhow. Annoyed by the repeated aggression of the Persian customs authorities, which it described as 'piratical activities', the Foreign Office concluded that 'seizure of the dhow off Ṭanb, and confiscation of its cargo, appears indeed to be indefensible, as transportation of a cargo of sugar is in itself no crime'. When these views were put to the Persian Foreign Minister he was eager in his assurances that Persia had not the slightest intention of occupying Ṭanb, or behaving aggressively towards the Arabs. It was agreed that the *status quo* in the area should be maintained and problems of disputed sovereignty should be negotiated in a spirit of amity.[89]

Aware that two issues, the detention of the women at Hanjām, and the expected compensation for the dhow incident, were still arousing much heat and causing doubt about Britain's power in the Trucial States, the SNO maintained continual patrols off Dubai. On 14 August HMS *Cyclamen* replaced *Lupin* and on the 18th cabled the SNO that the Shaikh of Dubai wished to visit his uncle at Bukhā, as they had not met since the Shaikh's return from pilgrimage, and he wished to find out for himself the true situation of the exiles from Hanjām. The SNO offered to take the Shaikh on HMS *Triad*, not only as a compliment, but also so that he could provide himself with up-to-date information on this crucial issue. Initially the Shaikh accepted the offer and the SNO arrived at Dubai on 20 August; but the next day, accompanied by two members of his family and the Residency Agent, the Shaikh boarded the *Triad* and explained that at a Council held late the previous night there had been serious discussion and the Council had insisted that he should not travel in a British warship. The SNO reported that one of the headmen had expressed the opinion of the Council as a whole as follows:

> We have had British warships anchored off Dubai now for three weeks; the people are expecting an answer about the inhabitants of Hanjām, and about [compensation for] the captured dhow. They see the warships continually changing but always there is one here; they come and go but never do we get any answer from them; the Shaikh goes off to the ships but never brings any answer back; the people are getting tired of it all and are beginning to doubt; either the Shaikh is telling lies or else

> the British Government is unable to do anything for us; if the people see the Shaikh go away in the British man-of-war, the people will at once say he has been sent for to make a formal settlement of both matters, and then when he comes back with no answer the patience of the people will give out and there will be riots and all sorts of trouble.[90]

The Shaikh left for Bukhā in his own boat after requesting that British ships be withdrawn for several weeks to avoid arousing the expectations of the people and that they should not reappear for some time unless there was good news to communicate. Describing the unrest which he had witnessed during his visit to Dubai the SNO reported that the extremist party might engineer an outbreak in about a fortnight. Anti-British feeling was growing owing to the delay in finding a solution to the Arabs' problems, and rumour was spreading on the Trucial Coast that the British flag at Bāsīdū had been taken down by Persians and the pole broken, and that the British there were afraid to fly it again.

As Britain had made an official protest, stating that Ṭanb was an Arab island, the Persian Minister of Foreign Affairs replied that he felt compelled to assert Persia's sovereignty there. On 31 August 1928 the British Minister sent Persia's note to London with a letter recommending that the Persians be provided with a copy of the treaty of 1892, under which Britain was responsible for the conduct of the external relations of the Trucial States with Persia and other foreign powers. This must be presented to Persia immediately, since it appeared from her direct correspondence with the Shaikh of Dubai early in this month that she refused to recognise Britain's position in the Trucial Coast.

As a result of a Reuter telegram reaching the Trucial Coast early in September, the Arabs began to believe that compensation for the dhow incident was no longer under consideration in Tehran, because of the tolerant attitude of the British. Arab anger was further inflamed by the rumour that the Persian military officer at Hanjām had forced his way into the Shaikh's house, and when this story reached Bukhā the women there began to urge the men to go to Hanjām to release by force the women still detained. The Shaikh of Dubai, despairing of British help for the Shaikh of Hanjām and his people, intended to inform the Persians directly that if they considered his uncle a Persian subject because he had lived on Persian soil, then he too could now decide the nationality of the immigrant Persians residing in Dubai. Since the Shaikh of Dubai's departure to Bukhā on 23 August the focus of events had moved from Dubai to Rās al-Khaimah, where the three shaikhs of Dubai, Rās al-Khaimah and Hanjām were met together. On 2 September the Residency Agent left Shārjah for Rās al-Khaimah to collect more details about the dhow incident, in particular all letters and other proof of the Qawāsim's ownership of Ṭanb, Abū Mūsā and Ṣirrī. On 4 September he met the Shaikh of Dubai there, who informed him of Persian overtures to Rāshid. The Shaikh went on to say that the Arabs, too, were tired of waiting for the British to move, and as he did not think he could restrain his people any longer he proposed to go to Hanjām in an attempt to settle matters. The Residency Agent, however, advised him not to go, but to put his case in a letter to be sent to the Political Resident in Bushire. This suggestion did not content the Shaikh, but he returned to Bukhā, promising to write later.[91]

On Monday 10 September the SNO arrived at Rās al-Khaimah to notify 'Abd al-Laṭīf, the Residency Agent, of an urgent message from the Political Resident, to the effect that any reports that the dhow incident was closed were false, and that the Political Resident hoped to settle all outstanding matters within a month; the delay was due to the Persian claim to Ṭanb island. The question of the nationality of the Shaikh of Hanjām was still unsettled because of the murder which had been committed on Persian soil, but it was undergoing careful examination by British legal officers. The British Government could not allow any direct mediation by the Shaikh of Dubai. This matter and the nationality of the other Persians in Dubai, would have to wait until the Shaikh's case was decided. In accordance with the wishes of the Political Resident this message was relayed in strict confidence. 'Abd al-Laṭīf agreed that these delicate matters must indeed be kept secret, explaining that if they became known to the people of the Trucial Coast their faith in Britain would be lost and the lives of all British subjects there, including his own, would be in danger.

When the SNO explained that Britain had fought and won the last war but that her policy now was one of patience in order to prevent bloodshed, the Shaikh's reaction was that this policy, although aiming at peace, was really inspired by fear. This became particularly clear when the Shaikh openly put the question: 'How much more of the Gulf will you give up to the Persians?' Before the SNO left the Trucial Coast he sent his answer to the Political Resident's enquiries about smuggling from Ṭanb; the Royal Navy, stationed at Hanjām, he said, had had Ṭanb under close observation for a long time and had found no trace of smuggling. His investigations had shown that all smuggling was carried out by Persians, not Arabs. His opinion was that if the Persians were allowed ownership of Ṭanb, their proximity to the Trucial Coast would be a thorn in the side of the Arabs.[92]

However, in a communication of 14 September the Foreign Office found it advisable to restrict the demand for compensation to the sum of Rs. 5,000 for the seizure of the dhow and detention of the captain, passengers and crew and to drop for the present any demand regarding the Shaikhs' sovereignty, which was totally denied by Persia. On 20 September the Persian Foreign Minister sent his reply to the British Chargé d'Affaires, emphasising the Persian attitude previously laid down in a note of 21 August 1928. Regarding the treaty of 1892, he pointed out that any agreement which might be against the rights or interest of Persia, or might limit those rights and interests, could not be recognised as valid and could not be used as legal justification for measures taken against Persia.

On 2 November the Director of Customs at Lingah himself went to the port of Dubai, on the pretext that his launch required emergency repairs, but the Shaikh refused him permission to land. The Residency Agent cabled the news immediately, after warning all the shaikhs of the coast to receive no Persian officials. He asked in his report of 10 November that British warships should visit the Trucial Coast every two weeks during this critical period.[93] Three days later, as a precaution, the Persian Gulf Sub-Committee issued instructions to the Commander-in-Chief, East Indies, which were repeated to SNO Persian Gulf, to the effect that occupation by Persia of Ṭanb and Abū Mūsā would be an infringement of the agreement that the *status quo* was to be maintained in the Gulf pending decision on outstanding questions, and that if necessity arose and as a last resort it was to be prevented by force.[94]

The Trucial States in Negotiations for an Anglo–Persian Treaty

The disputed ownership of the islands of Ṭanb and Abū Mūsā, and Britain's obligations to the Trucial States arising out of the treaty of 1892, were major obstacles to the conclusion of the Anglo–Persian treaty presented for negotiation on 4 February 1929. In his meeting with the Political Resident at Tehran on 12 February Teymourtâche raised three main questions: Persian emigrants to the Arab Coast, the smuggling of sugar and tea, and Persia's territorial waters. He enquired whether it would be possible for the Persian Government to have a consular agent at Dubai, where, he understood, there was a Persian colony of about four thousand people. The Political Resident pointed out that these Persians, who had over the years emigrated from Lingah, probably had a greater strain of Arab than Persian blood, and he added that there was no British consular agent there because it had never been considered safe to send one; therefore he thought it most unlikely that a Persian agent would be allowed.[95]

On 1 May, after three months of negotiation, the Government of India had found that the island of Ṣirrī was not mentioned in the draft treaty and suggested that the British might claim this island as well but recognise its occupation by Persia if Persia in turn recognised Arab rights to Abū Mūsā and Ṭanb.[96] During talks between Clive and Teymourtâche on 27 August the Minister of the Court explained that Ṭanb was more important to Persians than Abū Mūsā, because it was nearer their coast and was believed to be the centre of the smuggling operations. He proposed striking a bargain whereby Persia kept Ṭanb and left Abū Mūsā to the Shaikh of Shārjah. Clive explained to Teymourtâche that no British government could agree to hand over territory belonging to Arab rulers under British protection against their wishes. However, Clive felt that if the Persians' demand for Ṭanb were acceded to the conclusion of the treaty might be greatly facilitated. On 16 September he therefore suggested to Henderson, the Foreign Secretary, that if the Persian Government were prepared to offer a sum of money acceptable to the Shaikh of Rās al-Khaimah for the outright purchase of the island this might afford a solution, and asked to be informed of the views of the Government of India as soon as possible.[97]

Between 1930 and 1932 three main issues affected Persian relations with the Trucial States: the activities of the new Persian Navy, the sale or lease of Ṭanb island, and the question of passports and visas. The Government of India's attitude, and the Admiralty's answer to Teymourtāche's request for help in building a Persian fleet to deal with the contraband trade, were influenced by British obligations and interests on the Arab Coast. The Government of India insisted that the new Persian Navy should be limited in size so as to avoid, as far as possible, any trouble with the British Navy or the Arabs.

The year 1930 began in a spirit of optimism over the issue of Ṭanb. The Persians paid the compensation of Rs. 5,000 on 20 March and this was distributed to the passengers and crew in Dubai; the Residency Agent found it advisable to give the Ruler, Shaikh Sa'īd b. Maktūm, Rs. 1,000 from the total amount for the expenses he had incurred. The Ruler sent a letter of recognition to the Political Resident on 27 March and the compensation was joyfully received.[98] Subsequently, in April, Teymourtāche suggested that Persia would renounce her claims to Baḥrain and Abū Mūsā on condition that the British Government made arrangements with the Shaikh of Rās al-Khaimah for the sale of Ṭanb and for Persian control of the lighthouse. Clive sent this proposal to the Foreign Office on 29 April, supporting the idea, but only if the lighthouse remained under absolute British ownership.[99] The Shaikh of Rās al-Khaimah was asked for his reactions in May but after discussions with his relative, the Shaikh, he replied that he would not agree to sell the island for any sum whatever.[100] The Persian Government was immediately informed of the Shaikh's answer. Clive was instructed by the Foreign Office on 8 May to tell Teymourtāche that, with the refusal of the Shaikh of Rās al-Khaimah, on whom the final decision rested, the only possible course of action was for Persia to abandon her claim.[101] As the fulfilment of this claim had become an absolute condition of any settlement with Britain, negotiations over the Anglo–Persian treaty were suspended until the end of the year, by which time the Persian customs authorities committed another act of aggression against an Arab dhow and problems had arisen over the passports and identities of travellers from the Trucial Coast to Persia.

In July 1930 two dhows from 'Ajmān were seized by Persian customs authorities at Farūr Island for examination. The Residency Agent sent the Political Resident an urgent report on the incident, pointing out that all the shaikhs on the Trucial Coast were repeating that if Britain did not protect them they would carry arms to defend themselves.[102]

Since January 1928, when new regulations were issued in Baḥrain requiring Persian subjects to be furnished with passports and to obtain visas for visiting the island, new Persian restrictions on Arabs visiting Persia had been enforced. Persia insisted that no passports would be issued to Persians travelling to Baḥrain, and that she did not recognise the validity of the new Baḥraini passport. In his reply, on 23 September 1930, to a letter dated 10 September from the British Chargé d'Affaires regarding Arab travellers from the Trucial Coast to Persia, the Persian Minister of Foreign Affairs explained the attitude of his government, announcing that as it was not possible for the Persian Government to recognise the passports of the Trucial Coast and issue visas on them, instructions had been given to the frontier officials to issue exit and entry passes to travellers coming from the Trucial Coast on their entry into Persian territory against payment by them of statutory fees. Outlining the background to this new procedure, which created a major problem between Persia and the Trucial States, he said that Persia had never recognised the form of government of the States on the Trucial Coast and had no diplomatic relations with them; on the other hand no census had ever been made of the large number of Persians who were living on that coast and had no identity papers or passports. Moreover, it had often been observed that the holders of the passports or identity papers issued by the coastal Shaikhs were Persians, who, being unprotected, had been compelled to take out travel papers from them.[103] In response to the Persian restrictions the Foreign Office issued an administrative circular in March 1932 to the effect that all foreigners visiting the coast of 'Omān had to obtain a visa in advance from the appropriate British authorities.[104]

In 1930 discussions also took place on a proposal that the Arab shaikhs should be induced to request the British Government to inform Persia on their behalf that they did not wish Persian warships, which were commanded by Italian officers, to visit them without notification. This year ended without reaching conclusions on the issue of the visits of the Persian Navy to Arab ports. The debate continued during 1931 and a decision was approved that if a Persian warship visited the Trucial Coast it would be permitted but not officially received, and an ensuing protest would be made, stressing the necessity of advance notification in future. Any case of aggression would be met with retaliation from the British Navy. As the arrival of the first Persian warships was expected in October 1932, formal letters from the shaikhs of the Trucial Coast were obtained in March requesting the British Government to inform the Persians on their behalf that they expected formal notification through the British authorities.[105]

Negotiations for the Anglo–Persian treaty were reopened in conversations on 4 and 28 October between Clive and Teymourtâche, who repeated the importance of Ṭanb to Persia. When Clive refused even to discuss it,

Teymourtâche changed his ground, saying that Persia would be content with a fifty-year lease of the island. He mentioned that Persia would permit the Shaikh to keep his guards on the island and would grant him exemption from customs duties. He declined to believe that the British Government could not induce an Arab shaikh, however obstinate, to accept some such fair and reasonable arrangement. Teymourtâche indicated that a long lease of Ṭanb was one of the conditions which must be met before he could contemplate a treaty. Then he spoke at length about the necessity for saving Persia's face over Baḥrain. Obtaining Ṭanb would satisfy the Persian public when the treaty came up before the Majlis for ratification. When Clive, in a letter on 4 November reported this change in Persia's attitude, he advised that Britain should try to obtain the Shaikh of Rās al-Khaimah's acceptance; he was in favour of the suggested solution, which the British Government might be able to turn to its own advantage by associating the lease of Ṭanb with negotiations for the lease of Hanjām.

C. W. Baxter of the Foreign Office, in a memorandum of 14 November concerning Persia's proposed lease, agreed with Clive that a lease of Ṭanb would greatly improve Britain's position with regard to Hanjām. If the Persian Government, for example, wanted to lease Ṭanb for fifty years, it would be difficult for them to refuse to lease the British a part of Hanjām for fifty years, which they had hitherto refused to do on the ground that the period was too long.[106] The Political Resident was instructed to attempt to discuss the question with the Shaikh of this emirate, a task on which he commented on 6 January 1931, as the Shaikh was in his opinion the most difficult of all the Trucial rulers to deal with. He pointed out that the Arabs entertained a deep suspicion of the Persians, and that such an arrangement would undermine Arab confidence in Britain. However, on 11 May the Shaikh indicated his willingness but laid down conditions which the British Government found very harsh and restrictive. They were:

1. His flag should continue to fly and his representative should remain.
2. His subjects should not be interfered with without reference to himself.
3. Persian customs vessels should not visit 'Omān waters to search Arab dhows and offend his neighbouring shaikhs.
4. Absconding divers who were in debt should be handed over.
5. Merchandise imported into the island for his personal requirements should be free of duty, as also foodstuffs imported by the inhabitants.
6. The annual rental to be paid in advance.
7. Any flagstaff erected by the Persian Government should be over a building and not on the ground.
8. The conditions should be enforced by the British Government.[107]

Britain felt that Persia could not agree to such restrictions and because of a rupture in the treaty negotiations the Shaikh's answer was not communicated to the Persian Government.

In 1933 Persia's hostility towards British naval bases, especially evident in July in the Bāsīdū incident, was also directed against Britain's special position on the Trucial Coast. On 23 July a party which included the Commander of the Persian Navy and a French lighting expert landed at Ṭanb island to inspect the lighthouse. Their first visit lasted about ten minutes, during which time they drew a sketch map and gave the lighthouse supervisor a signed certificate that all was in order.[108] After this audacious visit, Britain sent her First Destroyer Flotilla to the Gulf on 31 July to restore confidence on the Arab coast. In spite of Britain's insistence that Persia should negotiate the lease of Ṭanb only through British diplomatic channels, the Persians, after receiving no answer from the British for a year to their demand of a lease for Ṭanb, made direct contact with the Shaikh of Rās al-Khaimah. Mallet, the British Minister to Tehran, protested vigorously on 22 August and 23 September about the Persian visit to the island and about her direct communication with the Trucial Coast.[109] In September the SNO heard from the Residency Agent that he had heard from the Shaikh of Rās al-Khaimah that he had received a letter from Tehran asking him to lease the island of Ṭanb, but the Shaikh was not willing to produce this letter when called to do so. Although the Residency Agent thought that the letter was probably mythical and that the Shaikh was trying to intimidate the British into paying, the story nevertheless disturbed the Political Resident at Bushire and he asked the SNO to investigate it further. On 7 October the Political Resident enquired of the Shaikh Sulṭān b. Sālim, concerning this letter and reminded him of his obligation not to negotiate directly with the Persians, as laid down in the treaty of 1892. On 21 October the SNO went to Rās al-Khaimah, but, although the Shaikh's brother visited him, Shaikh Sulṭān himself refused to board the *Triad*. The SNO then left for Shārjah; he called at the Residency Agent's house, where his meeting with the agent was interrupted by the arrival of Shaikh Sulṭān, accompanied by his bodyguards. Although the SNO initially ignored the Shaikh's presence, conversation was held between them through 'Īsā b. 'Abd al-Laṭīf, and the SNO was given to understand the Shaikh's complaints were that the British had used the island of Ṭanb for a long time without paying any rent; he asked for compensation for Persia's confiscation of his ships inside his territorial waters, and a reasonable amount for Britain's use of his land and inlets for the emergency landing of Imperial Airways. He showed willingness to board a British warship only if a court of high officials, not the Political Agent, listened to his case and judged it. The Shaikh declined to give an answer to enquiries by the SNO about the letter from Tehran and the Residency Agent advised the SNO to leave this matter to him. Ḥājjī 'Īsā b. 'Abd al-Laṭīf, who knew that Persian propaganda had been at work in Rās al-Khaimah, considered that Persia had taken advantage of the Shaikh's grievances and cupidity.[110]

In mid-November the Political Resident reported that no letter had been sent from Persia to the Shaikh of Rās al-Khaimah, and that the story had been a device aimed at alarming the British into leasing the island themselves to provide revenue for the Shaikh. On 21 October 1933 the Persian Foreign Minister had presented the reply he had promised two weeks previously to the British notes, alleging that the Persian Government considered the island of Ṭanb to be its property *de jure* and *de facto*. Regarding Ṣirrī island, Persia had always considered, and still did, that this island was also her property *de jure* and *de facto*.

Regardless of British wishes, Ṭanb occupied the same position in Anglo–Persian relations during 1934 as Rāsīdū had done in 1933. Persia was still concentrating all her attention on the island and increased her attempts to make direct contact with the Shaikh of Rās al-Khaimah. At the end of March 1934 a Persian customs launch landed a party on Ṭanb island, which proceeded to the house of Maḥmūd, representative of the Shaikh of Rās al-Khaimah, and asked him how much he earned and whose was the flag flying on the island. They then told him that the Persian Government would reward him highly if he would lower the Shaikh's flag and replace it with the Persian colours, which they would give him. To this he replied that he was not able to do this, since it would be treason. He was asked what rent British warships paid the shaikhs, but he replied that he did not know.[111]

On 26 April 1934 another Persian Government launch called at Ṭanb island and four men disembarked; the Governor, the Head of Police, the Director of Customs of Bandar 'Abbās, and Ṣālih, an inhabitant of Qishm island who was accompanying them as interpreter. Maḥmūd was again asked how much he earned, either from the Shaikh or from the British Government. The Persian Officials remained on the island for four hours, but were prevented from visiting the lighthouse by its supervisor. The Governor told Maḥmūd that if the island became Persian property he would be retained in his present position and the Persian Government would pay him double the wages he was then receiving from the Ruler of Rās al-Khaimah.[112] No British protest was made over these two incidents since it was the policy of the British Government to avoid anything in the nature of a needless challenge to Persia.

On 4 May the Persian Government asserted that it could not admit any sort of intervention on the part of Britain in its relations with the Arab rulers on the opposite shore of the Gulf. Moreover, on 18 June the Majlis passed a law defining the limits of Persian territorial waters at twelve miles, six miles of offshore waters in addition to a further six of adjacent waters under Persian sovereignty. The British Minister was at once instructed to make a formal declaration to the Persian Government on behalf of his Government and the Arab emirates that no claim to territorial waters outside the three-mile limit could be recognised.[113]

Persia continued her studied policy towards Ṭanb with a further two visits which were considered by the British Government too serious to be overlooked, the first on 28 August and the second on 11 September. The Persian warship *Palang* was sighted by HM ships *Shoreham* and *Bideford* anchoring for the night at Ṭanb. Lieutenant-Colonel Bayander, the Admiral of the Persian Navy who had hauled down the British flag at Bâsīdū the previous year, was informed that the island belonged to the Shaikh of Rās al-Khaimah and that the Shaikh wished for advance notification of visits. However, on 11 September the Captain of the Persian warship *Chahrokh* visited the island and denied all knowledge of the intimation given to Bayander of the need for notification, although it was later discovered that he had met Bayander on his way to Ṭanb.

Expecting that Persia would raise the question of her claim to Ṭanb and Abū Mūsā during the September 1934 meeting of the Council of the League of Nations in Geneva, Lascelles of the Foreign Office had on 4 September presented the Memorandum he had prepared on the history and legal position of these islands for the use of the British representative at Geneva. Lascelles assured Rendel that the Persian claim to Ṭanb and Abū Mūsā was similar to, but much weaker than, their claims to Baḥrain. The Arab case rested on the fact that Persia had not exercised effective dominion in these islands for at least 184 years, as against 151 years in the case of Baḥrain. It was doubtful whether even before 1750 she had exercised dominion at Ṭanb and Abū Mūsā, whereas it was certain that she exercised dominion over Baḥrain for a period before 1783.

In summary, he said that the Persian case was based on the following two points: (1) Ṭanb and Abū Mūsā were shown as Persian on a War Office map presented to the Shāh in 1888; (2) the 'Jowāsimī' Arab shaikhs of Lingah who administered Ṭanb and Abū Mūsā for a long period before their final expulsion from Persia in 1887, were for a part of that period Persian subjects, governing Lingah as Persian officials. However, his study was based on the traditional misapprehension that for many years prior to 1887 the management and jurisdiction of the two islands was by common consent vested in the chief 'Jowāsimī' Shaikh of the Persian coast, that is the Shaikh of Lingah. So although the shaikhs of Lingah who administered Ṭanb and Abū Mūsā were at one period Persian vassals and even Persian officials, this fact was in no way whatever responsible for their connection with the two islands. The 'Jowāsimī' owned Ṭanb and Abū Mūsā long before any of their number established themselves on Persian soil; the dominant Shaikh of the clan never ceased to reside on the Trucial Coast; the rights of the Lingah shaikhs, which were in any case derived from their family connection and not from their position in Persia, were at all times shared with, and subordinate to, the rights of the shaikhs on the Trucial Coast; when the Lingah shaikhs had been finally driven from Persia, any shadow of connection between their rights and Persia went with them.

On 17 September 1934, after several meetings at the Foreign Office, new instructions were issued to the British Navy in the Gulf regarding its behaviour towards Persian warships. The Minister at Tehran was told to inform the Persian Government of Britain's change of policy at sea. Britain was now beginning to lose hope of concluding any treaty with Persia. Persia's repeated defiance of Arab rights on the islands of Ṭanb and Abū Mūsā, in particular the right to be previously notified of any visit, had lowered British prestige on the Arab coast, while strengthening Persia's. The new instructions laid down that if a Persian naval vessel visited Abū Mūsā or Ṭanb without proper notification, the British Navy were to secure its withdrawal as soon as possible by such means as were deemed necessary, including force. On 8 October the Persian Minister in London visited Sir Victor Wellesley in the Foreign Office and informed him that his government regarded Ṭanb and Abū Mūsā as Persian territory and therefore could not but regard the British communications as an unfriendly gesture.[114]

Meanwhile the Shaikh of Rās Khaimah wrote a letter on 3 September 1934 congratulating Fowle, the new Political Resident, on his appointment. The Shaikh, whose financial position was very weak owing to the decline in the pearl trade, informed Fowle that he would prefer Britain to lease his island, but if she did not wish to do so he hoped she would grant him permission to exercise his rights in the matter. However, on 31 December the SNO reported to the Admiralty that a visit by HMS *Bideford* to Ṭanb had revealed the fact that the Shaikh of Rās al-Khaimah had withdrawn his flag from the island. It was rumoured that the Persian authorities were in communication with him concerning a lease.

The situation became even more serious at the end of 1934, particularly after ʻĪsa b. ʻAbd al-Laṭīf had received a letter from Maḥmūd, complaining that he had not received his last salary from the Shaikh of Rās al-Khaimah. He was therefore in a difficult position and asked either for permission to leave Ṭanb or for the payment of his salary by the British Government. This latest news regarding Ṭanb was greatly disturbing not only to British authorities in the Gulf and the Government of India, but also the Foreign Office in London. The Foreign Office was prepared to depose the Shaikh of Rās al-Khaimah on the grounds of treason in handing over national property. It believed that it would be better to have the island under direct British control, rather than in the hands of an unreliable shaikh or in the hands of the Persians, without any promise of a general Anglo-Persian treaty. The India Office, although agreeing that the island should be taken from Rās al-Khaimah, preferred it to go to Shārjah as a piece of Qawāsim tribal property, and was firmly opposed to any suggestion that the island might end up in Persian hands.[115] The Political Resident on 5 January 1934 recommended that if the Shaikh did not replace the flag, the Shaikh of Shārjah, having shown himself ready to hoist his own flag, should be allowed to do so. Any change in the ownership of Ṭanb at that time was opposed by the British Minister to Tehran and by the Government of India, as they felt it would weaken the British and Arab position *vis-à-vis* the Persian Government. On 8 January the British Minister to Tehran stated that the Ṭanb issue would be an important one in any future Anglo–Persian negotiations and British control over it should therefore not be relaxed. He recommended that the Shaikh of Rās al-Khaimah be given some payment for the lighthouse as an inducement to him to rehoist his flag.[116]

The SNO at once landed a small guard on Ṭanb island; this was later withdrawn, though for some weeks a sloop visited the island at frequent intervals. However, enquiries made by the Political Resident during January showed that the Shaikh of Rās al-Khaimah's motives were pecuniary; his aim was to receive a rent for the lighthouse, similar to that received by his relative the Shaikh of Shārjah for the British aerodrome on his territory. He ascertained that the Shaikh of Rās al-Khaimah had not actually offered the island to the Persians but was acting in the belief that Britain would step in and lease the island. Whilst the above matter was under consideration by the British Government, the Political Resident reported at the end of January that a native of Ṭanb had been approached by the Governor of Bandar 'Abbās with a request to deliver official papers to Ṭanb from Tehran, but that the man had refused. It was a purely local initiative by Persian Officials in an attempt to take advantage of the opportunity by the removal of the Shaikh's flag, and there was no evidence to show that the Persian Government was behind the manoeuvre.[117]

These new rumours upset the Political Resident and persuaded him to write a detailed letter on 4 February demanding an immediate hardening of policy towards Shaikh Sulṭān b. Sālim. As the British could neither keep a sloop indefinitely stationed at Ṭanb nor allow the island to remain without a flag, he recommended that the Shaikh be informed that if he agreed to replace his flag on Ṭanb within a certain period, the British Government would then be prepared to consider paying him rent for the lighthouse. If he did not, the Political Resident now felt the only alternative was to allow the Shaikh of Shārjah to take over. However, the Political Resident made it clear that from the local point of view he would not himself recommend the offer of rent for the lighthouse since it was in the nature of a concession to a Shaikh who had behaved badly.[118] Eventually a decision, taking into account the Political Resident's recommendations, was made at a meeting of the CID on 8 March 1935 that the Shaikh of Rās al-Khaimah should be given ten days to replace his flag and that he should be told that failure to do so would result in the transfer of the island to the Shaikh of Shārjah. On 19 March this ultimatum was communicated to the Shaikh by the Political Resident, the Shaikh receiving it nine days later. Moreover, to settle any problems arising from personal contact, Lieutenant-Colonel Fowle himself flew to Rās al-Khaimah to discuss matters with the Shaikh, who proved to be absent in the interior.

The Shaikh immediately explained the whole story in a comprehensive letter, sent on 29 March, in which he stated that the only reason for

Maḥmūd's leaving the island and for the lowering of his flag was his own lack of money. In the past, when Rās al-Khaimah had enjoyed a considerable income from pearl fishing, he had not asked the British for rent for the lighthouse in order to pay his employees on Ṭanb, but now his financial position had changed completely. Although he had informed 'Īsā b. 'Abd al-Laṭīf about this the previous December no help had been forthcoming. However, the Shaikh complied with the ultimatum he had received from the Political Resident and agreed to restore his flag to the island and he concluded his letter with an apology for not having been available to meet him, having had no knowledge of his arrival. 'Īsā reported that one of the Shaikh's dhows had arrived at Ṭanb on 2 April and on the 3rd his flag had been rehoisted.

At the beginning of 1935, particularly after Britain's decision the previous year to evacuate the naval bases at Hanjām and Bāsīdū, both parties hoped for a revival of Anglo–Persian negotiations, but the hope soon vanished and all prospects of a treaty came to an end in May. Although Britain had yielded to Persian nationalist aspirations at Hanjām and Bāsīdū, the islands of Ṭanb and Abū Mūsā proved insurmountable obstacles. With the breakdown of negotiations Britain adopted a much tougher policy towards Persian visits to the islands, leaving the League of Nations as the only possible channel for discussion of the dispute. This period marked the beginning of the re-evaluation of British legal evidence in regard to the islands, and the different British departments were henceforth occupied with detailed studies and with the collection of more data in order to provide the British representative at the League with a consistent and authoritative policy. In October 1934 Baggallay, one of the Foreign Office's legal advisers, had given his superior, Rendel, a brief note commenting on the Lascelles report of the previous month. Baggallay's conclusions differed fundamentally. His main point was that in fact the Arabs had a stronger title to Baḥrain than to Ṭanb; for this reason, and because Ṭanb was nearer to the Persian coast, it was expected that in the coming sessions at the League Persia would concentrate her case on Ṭanb. Baggallay asserted that the 'Jowāsimī' shaikhs of Lingah, who were not only resident in Persia but were Persian subjects and Persian officials, might easily prove very damaging to the British and Arab case. Baggallay suggested that any official information about the Arab custom by which a family such as the Qawāsim held property in common might be particularly useful. Rendel put this new line of enquiry to the India Office, which asked the Government of India on 13 October for a study of the Arab tribal system of ownership.[119]

Interdepartmental correspondence followed at the beginning of 1935 on the earlier history of the ownership of Ṭanb and Abū Mūsā islands. On 11 January Laithwaite declared that the India Office did not agree with the revised views of the legal advisers in the Foreign Office, and told Rendel that comprehensive studies of the manner in which Arab tribes held land were expected soon from the Political Resident. Laithwaite sent to the Foreign

Office what information he had already received from Fowle on the ownership of Ṭanb, and this supported the views laid down by Lascelles. The theory of common tribal ownership which Baggallay had enquired about was favoured by the British officials in the Gulf, who were endeavouring to transfer the sovereignty of Ṭanb to the Shaikh of Shārjah in the event of the Shaikh of Rās al-Khaimah abandoning the island to the Persians. On 11 March the Political Resident sent his answer, enclosing with it two interesting notes, one prepared by Dickson, the Political Agent at Kuwait, dated 6 February, and the second by Captain Loch, Political Agent at Baḥrain, dated 2 March.[120] Dickson explained in his comprehensive note that land was held in the Arabian Peninsula under two main systems: that of private ownership and that of tribal ownership. Dickson asserted that a tribe always owned its grazing and tribal lands including wells jointly and never individually. The shaikh, as the head of the family and its trustee, would be quite unable to cede the whole or part of it without first obtaining the consent of the other members of the family. Loch's study was in its conclusions similar to Dickson's.

Meanwhile on 8 March Rendel had transferred all reports and evidence for legal advice to Beckett, who once again laid down that the Shaikh of Lingah, who ruled a portion of the Persian mainland, also ruled over the three islands of Ṭanb, Abū Mūsā and Ṣirrī. His considered opinion was that there was nothing in 1880 to show him that, though the Shaikh of Lingah had become a Persian vassal as regards the territories of the mainland, he ruled the three islands in a different capacity, i.e. still as a representative of the head of his family on the other side of the Gulf. Moreover, the first period of separation between Shārjah and Rās al-Khaimah from 1869 to 1900 would not make it any easier to show that the Shaikh of Lingah had continued in this period to rule the islands as the representative of his now completely separate family across the Gulf. The very likely conclusion in his view was that during this period the Shaikh at Lingah ruled all his territories, including the islands, as a Persian vassal. Becket's final opinion was that, unless further evidence was forthcoming to prove that during the period 1880–87 the Shaikh of Lingah had ruled the islands under some title different from that under which he had ruled the mainland, the Persians did possess sovereignty over Ṭanb and Abū Mūsā during these years. However, he added that the Shaikhs of Shārjah and Rās al-Khaimah respectively now had a prospective title against Persia of about forty-eight years' duration, and that it was this title and this alone on which the British or the Shaikhs must rely.[121]

On 4 May the Persian Foreign Minister, at a meeting with Knatchbull-Hugessen, the British Minister to Tehran, revived the dispute over Ṭanb and mentioned that he would like to reopen discussion with the British Foreign Minister at Geneva at the coming session of the Council. He put forward a tentative suggestion that HM Government should recognise the

Persian claim to the islands of Ṭanb and Abū Mūsā and give Persia certain assistance in the Shaṭṭ-al-'Arab, in return for which the Persian Government would recognise the independence of Baḥrain and the treaty relations of HM Government with the Arab rulers of the Trucial Coast. Knatchbull-Hugessen made it known that there was no hope of reopening such negotiations. However, Lambert of the Foreign Office prepared a brief note on 17 May for the British representative at that month's meeting at Geneva. Rendel commented on this report that it was impossible to give the Persians any encouragement for their suggestion, due to British commitments to the Arab rulers of the islands in addition to the fact that none of the other British departments concerned would even contemplate such a possibility.[122]

Although Britain did not welcome reopening negotiations, Persia continued to consider Abū Mūsā as Persian territory. When the Shaikh of Shārjah granted a red oxide concession on the island to a British company towards the end of 1934 the Persian Government protested on the grounds that this was a violation of the gentleman's agreement of the *status quo*.[123]

From 1936 to the beginning of World War II, the years following the end of negotiations for an Anglo–Persian treaty, the *status quo* was observed and few incidents of direct conflict were recorded.

IV The Search for a Settlement to the Islands' Dispute after 1945

In the post-war period the main issue influencing relations between Iran and the Trucial States was their dispute over the ownership of Abū Mūsā and Ṭanb islands. Although the issue now involved pressure from the Arab countries and attracted attention from the major powers, it remained, as it had been before, a matter of concern to Iran, Shārjah, Rās al-Khaimah and Britain. The fundamental change in relations between the disputants was in Britain's approach to the problem; she now played an active role as mediator due to her friendship with, and her growing interest in, both Persia and the Arab countries. For a few years the Abū Mūsā and Ṭanb dispute remained dormant and finally emerged in 1970 as an urgent issue, a year after the British decision to withdraw from the Gulf. We must therefore study the wide and complicated dimensions of this problem along four lines; first, the emergence of contemporary Iran under the leadership of Muḥammad Rezā Shāhanshāh as a dominant regional power and her intensified activities in Gulf politics in the post-war period; secondly, Iran's relations with the Trucial States in the context of her relations with the Arab countries; thirdly, Anglo–Iranian relations with the major powers; finally, the development of events in this dispute between 1968 and 1971.

Muḥammad Rezā, who succeeded his father in 1941, after Rezā Shāh's forced abdication by Britain and the Soviet Union, continued the mission his father began of building an independent and modern Iran. Although Muḥammad Rezā was faced in the early days of his rule with strong internal opposition, he was finally able in 1953, with the support of the army, to regain his absolute rights as monarch and was crowned Shāhanshāh in September 1967.

The renaissance which Iran has witnessed in the last two decades is the product of various factors, among the most important of which is the success of the Shāh in maintaining since 1953 a stable and strong central government through the loyalty of his army officers and by his own wise leadership and social reforms. He distributed his family lands during the 1940s and in 1962 succeeded in enforcing the same procedure on the big landlords. In his 'White Revolution' in the early 1960s he gave material expression to his ideas of a welfare state. In the last decade he has opened six universities in addition to the University of Tehran, given women the right to vote and extended medical care.[124]

The Iranian renaissance is due also to the enormous growth of the Iranian armed forces. The Shāh paid much attention to the building of sophisticated naval and air forces, and spent a great proportion of the national income on them. It is remarkable that the Arabs, who were the only strong sea power in the Gulf when the British entered the area, had completely lost this supremacy when the British left in 1971, by which time Iran had acquired the only effective and well-trained local naval force in the Gulf.

Last but not least in the Iranian renaissance is the growth of the economy and the country's successful move towards industrialisation. In the late 1940s Iran started to plan its economy, and the first 'Seven-Year Plan' came into effect between 1949 and 1955. Although the nation faced bankruptcy in the early 1950s, the Shāh's new agreement with the 'Consortium' in 1954, which replaced the nationalised AIOC, supplied Iran with a continuous and increased income from the expansion of oil production and from better financial terms. This enabled the Shāh in the mid-1960s to finance his plans independently, the fourth of which began in 1968 and ended in 1972. In 1970 Iran completed the establishment of her iron and steel complex at Isphahān, built the gas pipeline from the Gulf to the Soviet frontier, and constructed major chemical fertiliser and petrochemical plants.[125]

In the post-war period Iran's activities in the Gulf have increased and her role has become more important. The improvement in relations between Iran and the Soviet Union in 1962 gave the Shāh ample opportunity to concentrate more attention on Gulf problems. Thenceforth Iran has given concrete expression to her increased interests in the area in many fields—military, administrative, economic and political. In 1962 the Ministry of Economics established a special department for the Gulf trade. Local administration in this area has been improved and considerable salary increases have been offered as an inducement to Iranian officials to move there. The volume of trade between Iran and other countries was greatly influenced by the two projects to convert Bandar 'Abbās in 1964 and Bushire in 1965 into modern ports for handling ocean-going freighters. Roads linking these two ports to the hinterland were constructed and the most important of these was the one begun in 1969 along the Persian Coast between Bandar 'Abbās and Ahwaz.[126]

During the 1950s Iran's army was mainly directed northwards, but in the late 1960s the new *rapprochement* with the Soviet Union facilitated a change in the placement of its forces. In a speech reported in March 1965 the Shāh stated that Iran's military concentration was now focused on the Gulf. In 1967 the Second Army Corps was withdrawn from the north to Tehran and a new Third Army Corps was formed, complete with paratroop units, and based in the south of Shīrāz. Huge army barracks were built, and naval bases established in Bandar 'Abbās and Bushire. The announcement of British withdrawal intensified Iran's drive towards the Gulf. As an example of the amount spent on air defences, Iran in 1968 ordered two squadrons of F4 Phantoms from the United States, and in 1970 she purchased a high-powered mobile radar defence system for the south to complete the established northern radar umbrella. Meanwhile, Iranian waters and islands in the Gulf witnessed many military exercises in which units from all three services took part.[127]

There are several main reasons which could explain the intensification of Iranian interest in the Gulf, and the concentration of her forces towards the south during the 1960s. It was oil and its associated problems, together with its increasing role in the Iranian economy, which drew the Shāh's attention in that direction. By 1968 Iran had nine out of twenty-two sea concessions in the Gulf, which provided Iran not only with one eighth of her oil production but also with her most profitable arrangements with oil companies. As oil revenues amounted during the 1960s to 50 per cent of all government revenue and provided 75 per cent of Iran's hard currency, the Shāhanshāh had to pay much attention to his country's oil problems. During the 1960s the Shāh's objective was to regain Iran's previous superiority in oil production, achieved before the 1951 nationalisation crisis and Musaddaq's period, when Iranian production was equivalent to the combined production of Baḥrain, Iraq, Sa'ūdī Arabia and Qaṭar. However, all Shāhanshāh's efforts made Iran in the early 1970s only the second largest oil-producing country in the Gulf after Sa'ūdī Arabia, and it eventually became apparent that his insistent demands on the oil companies would never materialise.[128]

The second reason for Iran's intensified interest in the Gulf was the challenge that the Shāh felt there from Egypt, and the spread there of Arab nationalism. This point will be covered later in more detail. The third reason was British withdrawal from the Gulf. As Iran possessed no pipeline to the Mediterranean, the security of the Gulf had become of great importance. Between 1968 and 1971 the Shāh frequently expressed his anxiety about the stability of his Arab neighbours, and his worry that guerilla activities in

Dhofār might extend into the area. The Shāh, confident in his country's military effectiveness, therefore considered her the sole guardian of stability and order in the Gulf.[129]

The post-war migration from Iran to the Arabian littoral, which acquired political dimensions and has become a controversial issue, coloured by Iranian expansionist policy and creating suspicion among the Arabs, is a matter of importance to this study. It was not the first migration in that direction, for there had been an earlier one in the late nineteenth century and another in the 1930s. Then, during the 1950s and early 1960s, while the attention of the Iranian Government had been concentrated northwards, the Persian coast suffered from government neglect and there had been much misunderstanding between officials, military and civil, and the coastal population. Simultaneously, the town development schemes and free health, education and social services initiated in Kuwait and Qaṭar during the 1950s and in the Trucial States in the 1960s, drew a steady stream of migrants from Iran seeking work and the privileges of modern life along the flourishing Arab coast. The elements of the first migration, in the late nineteenth century, had been the rich Arab and Persian merchants who contributed to the rise of Dubai port, and the second migration of the late 1930s had been prompted by religious feelings and as a protest amongst Arabs and Persians against Rezā Shāh's unveiling of women. Both waves of immigrants had been easily absorbed. The third migration, in the post-war period, was composed entirely of Iranian elements, difficult to integrate and thus a completely new phenomenon. These immigrants were unskilled labourers and shopkeepers, and they entered in enormous numbers, generally illegally over a short period of time. Although they were badly needed on the Arabian shore, the time of their arrival coincided with a period of confrontation between Arab and Iranian nationalism; they were therefore viewed with suspicion and their influx assumed political significance.[130]

The new Iranian policy of the mid-1960s, with its southward turn of interest, and the attention given by the Shāh to the reform and reorganisation of the Persian coast, had its influence on this migration. The immediate effect of the construction of roads and ports along the Persian coast, creating new opportunities for Iranian workers, was to decrease the number of emigrants to the Arabian shore and there were signs in 1975 that the tide of migration was dying down, and that some Iranians, for the first time, were returning to their homes. The Ministry of Education in Tehran, during the mid-1960s and in accordance with the new policy, expanded its activities on the coast: Iranian schools were opened in the principal ports, still mainly inhabited by Arabs, but the imposition of an Iranian curriculum and the Iranian language on these schools was viewed by the Arab inhabitants as the final liquidation of their identity and culture, and in the early 1970s it caused many Arab tribes and families to leave for the Arabian coast. Tehran's interest intensified when the Iranian emigrants to the Arab coast, formerly neglected, became a matter of concern; Iranian schools were opened to maintain their culture whenever they were to be found in sufficient numbers, the first in Dubai in 1962 and the second in Abū Dhabī in 1972. Passports were also issued to the emigrants to encourage them to retain their Iranian identity.

In the post-war period Iran's relations with the Trucial States were influenced by her relations with the Arab countries, where serious efforts were made with a view to achieving a union of Arab states from the Atlantic Ocean to the Arabian Gulf, which disturbed the Shāh. During this period Iran's relations with some Arab countries deteriorated, particularly those with Egypt. Many factors account for the hostility between Nasser and the Shāh which to some extent clouded the relations between Iran and the Arab coastal states in the Gulf. While the Shāh's principal fears in the early 1950s were Soviet imperialism and subversion, which encouraged him to acquire his arms from Washington, Nasser's fears were Western imperialism and the Western pacts, which led him to arm himself with the aid of the Eastern bloc. It was the Baghdād Pact of 1965 which inaugurated disagreement between the Shāh and Nasser, who became, after the Suez War in 1956, the champion and spokesman of Arab nationalism and extended his propaganda and activities into the Gulf, asserting the Arabism of Baḥrain, Abū Mūsā, Ṭanb, the Gulf itself and 'Arabistān too. The involvement of Egypt in Gulf affairs was viewed by the Shāhanshāh as illegitimate and unnatural, and increased his worries about Nasser's aims and ambitions.

Iran's dispute with Iraq in 1950–60 over the Shaṭṭ-al-'Arab waterway, causing both sides to alert their armed forces and fortify their frontiers, also had a serious effect on the Shāh and his plans to strengthen his army in the Gulf. But it was the question of Iran's relations with Israel, the *de facto* recognition of Israel since 1950 and the flow of Iranian oil to that country that caused Nasser, in July 1960, to break off relations and persuade other Arab states to follow his example. Differences between Egypt and Iran took on the appearance of an Arab–Iranian dispute, with Nasser attempting to isolate Iran from all the Arab countries, describing the Shāh as imperialist and expansionist. Nasser's involvement in Yemen's civil war in 1962 was viewed with much alarm by the Shāh, who was convinced that his next move would be direct intervention in the Gulf. Although the Yemeni war created a division in the Arab world, the Shāh continued to feel Nasser's challenge in the Gulf to the extent of justifying his increased defence expenditure at home, in Washington and in the CENTO meetings, asserting that Nasser's threat was a reality and that Egypt's armament necessitated an equal increase in Iranian armed forces. Only Syria at that time moved to Nasser's side and provoked a breach with Iran in 1965.[131]

Although Iran's relations with Egypt, Iraq and Syria had deteriorated the Shāh was keen to establish friendly ties with his Arab neighbours in the Gulf and since 1957 he has regularly invited the Trucial shaikhs to visit Tehran, to which they have responded. However, when in 1957 the Shāh again announced Iran's claim to Baḥrain, Sa'ūdī Arabia strongly opposed him.

During the Yemeni war Nasser's accepted leadership among the Arabs was shaken and he lost the sympathy of some Arab governments—Sa'ūdī Arabia and Jordan particularly—who aided the royalists as did the Shāh, who denounced Nasser's acts as aggression. Two distinct attitudes then developed in Arab relations with Iran. The first was that of Egypt, Syria and Iraq, who regarded Iran as an expansionist and imperialist monarchy, and expressed suspicion of her activities, particularly regarding the Iranian migration to the Arab coast which could, in their opinion, develop into another Palestine. The second attitude was that of the states on the Gulf coast; although they agreed with Cairo, Damascus and Baghdād in principle, they differed in their approach, and influenced by historical and Islamic ties as well as by proximity, believed that to open a dialogue with Iran would greatly facilitate a solution. This attitude found expression in the frequent meetings between the Shāh and the heads of the Gulf states. In 1965 the Islamic Conference at Rabat, called together by King Faiṣal and the Shāh, greatly strengthened this emerging attitude.[132]

The Arab defeat in the June war of 1967 had a direct effect on Iranian relations with the Arab countries, as well as on Gulf politics. After that war Nasser withdrew his troops from Yemen and became deeply involved in the Sinai front. Thus Egypt's role in the Gulf, previously an important one, gradually diminished and a turning point was reached in Iranian–Egyptian relations, which soon began to improve.[133] The immediate result of these changes in Gulf politics was that Kuwait and the growing Kingdom of Sa'ūdī Arabia, under King Faiṣal, took their responsibilities for protecting Arab interests in the region more seriously. Although Iraq, which remained hostile to Iran, also now played an important role in Gulf politics, the easier atmosphere offered an opportunity for more effective dialogue.

During these events oil played an important role in Iran's relations with her Arab neighbours in the Gulf. In 1949, after the Truman Proclamation, the Gulf shaikhdoms proclaimed their rights over their continental shelf.[134] Between 1957 and 1958 Iran inaugurated her own oil activities in the Gulf and granted three oil concessions at sea. As the entire Gulf, because of its shallowness, had become continental shelf, these concessions overlapped at certain points with the Arab concessions on the other side and legal problems regarding maritime boundaries emerged. Negotiations started with Iraq in 1963, with Kuwait and Sa'ūdī Arabia in 1964, and finally with Britain, on behalf of Qaṭar and the Trucial States in 1966. At the beginning these were fruitless, due to Iran's insistence on using her islands as a baseline, and the Arabs determination to use the Persian Coast. The stumbling block in the negotiations for a dividing line between Iran and the Trucial States constituted, first, Iran's consideration of the island of Qishm as part of her coastline, and secondly, her claims to Abū Mūsā and Ṭanb, which complicated agreement with Shārjah and Rās al-Khaimah.[135]

The third important issue to influence the search for a settlement between Iran and the Trucial States was Iran's relations with Britain. After 1941 Anglo-Iranian relations passed through three stages: from 1941 to 1953, from 1954 to 1962, and from 1962 to 1971. During World War II occupation by British and Russian troops and the forced abdication of Rezā Shāh not only injured the pride and dignity of the people of Iran, but also influenced the young Shāh's attitude towards Britain. During the first period the powers of the Shāh were greatly decreased as the country was governed by a quasi-parliamentary régime with a multi-party system, dominated by the well-organised communist Tudeh Party. The collapse of the Soviet-supported régime in Azarbayjan in 1947 directed the Tudeh Party's energies against the British. The Tudeh Party joined forces with the nationalist group and greatly influenced the Iranian Government in its decision in 1951 to nationalise the Anglo-Iranian Oil Company. The numerous British consulates which were the last manifestation of their previous privileges in Iran were now closed by Dr Musaddaq, the Prime Minister (1951–3), and diplomatic relations with Britain were broken off. At the height of the dispute, Musaddaq considered invading Baḥrain. Britain's failure to face up to the Soviet Union in Iran after World War II obliged the United States to increase her aid, replacing Britain in her traditional role as the dominant western power seeking to check Russian expansion and influence.[136]

After the downfall of Musaddaq's Government in 1953, the 'Consortium' agreement of the following year, which gave Britain only 40 per cent of the new concession, ended British economic monopoly in Iran. But in 1955, the Shāh, who had now regained his full powers as a monarch and sought to increase American aid for his bankrupt country as well as maintain her sovereignty in the face of Soviet threats, found it prudent to enter the 'Baghdād Pact' with Britain. Although this pact ameliorated the relations between the two countries, the Shāh in 1957 reasserted his country's claim to Baḥrain, and in so doing was responding to pressure from the right-wing Pan-Iranist party, which four years later called for an invasion of Baḥrain. In 1962, however, Britain re-established firm relations with the Shāh as a result of their common attitude towards Nasser's campaign in Yemen and propaganda in the Gulf, and the Shāh suspended his claim to Baḥrain for the time being in order not to disturb this new relationship. A fundamental change in the Shāh's foreign relations with his powerful neighbour, the Soviet Union, also took place in 1962. Confident in Iran's internal economy and stability, particularly after his land reform, and discontented above all with the United States' recognition of republican Yemen, the Shāh turned towards the Soviet Union. Trade between the two countries soon expanded and included some military equipment and a projected gas pipeline from the Gulf to Soviet borders and the iron and steel works at Isphahān.

The British withdrawal from Aden and Britain's decision the following year to withdraw from the Gulf at once re-established strong ties between

Iran and the United States, who again provided Iran with sophisticated weapons. Thus in 1968 Iran was on cordial terms with all the great powers, particularly Britain, and the Shāh was most successful in convincing them that the dominant position of Iran in the Gulf would secure to a great extent their main interests in that region.[137]

Finally, the sequence of events after January 1968, when Britain announced her intention to withdraw, in addition to the Shāh's diplomatic handling of the Baḥrain question, greatly influenced the dispute over Abū Mūsā and Ṭanb. After the announcement of withdrawal Arab–Iranian co-operation became the cornerstone of British policy for security in the Gulf as well as for international trade. In January 1968, at the suggestion of Britain and the United States, the Iranian Government proclaimed its support for Arab–Iranian co-operation in a 'Gulf Pact', but this was attacked immediately by Cairo, Damascus, Baghdād and Moscow, who regarded it as western and imperialist. For their part, the Arab coastal states in the region received the projected 'Gulf Pact' with little enthusiasm, for three reasons. First, there were the long-standing differences between Iran and Iraq, and two incidents at sea in January between Sa'ūdī Arabia and Iran, which caused their relations to deteriorate: in this month, a major oilfield was discovered in the vicinity of the median line between Sa'ūdī Arabia and Iran, and Iran used its navy to protect her oil operations, seizing an Aramco oil rig in the area, against which action Sa'ūdī Arabia protested. The second reason was Iran's claim to Baḥrain, which conflicted with Sa'ūdī Arabia's adoption of the Arabism of the island; on 17 January the Shaikh of Baḥrain paid a visit to Sa'ūdī Arabia, where the Government declared its full and effective support for Baḥrain in all circumstances. Faiṣal's policy and leadership in the Gulf was immediately supported by Cairo. Iran reacted by postponing a scheduled visit of the Shāh to Riyādh and adopting a harder line regarding the division of the continental shelf. The third reason for the lukewarm reaction of the Arab States towards a 'Gulf Pact' was the military imbalance between Iran and her Arab neighbours, through which Iran would extend and legitimise her influence on the Arabian side.[138]

On 26 February the announcement, endorsed by Britain, of a proposed Federation of Arab Emirates, including the seven Trucial States, Baḥrain and Qaṭar, was immediately welcomed by the Arab countries. Britain's support for this Federation, besides her diplomatic activities during 1968, clearly demonstrated to the Shāh the British attitude on the Baḥrain question. However, in April Iran denounced the Federation because of Baḥrain's inclusion and again asserted her claim to the island. Sa'ūdī Arabia and Kuwait actively supported the Federation and Iran's relations with her Gulf neighbours became strained. A solution for the Baḥrain dispute had now become essential to the British, for it would help Iran to accept the Federation and thus ensure Arab–Iranian co-operation in the projected 'Gulf Pact'.

However, Iranian opposition to the Federation did not interrupt her endeavours to strengthen her relations with the Trucial States and did not interfere with the continuing dialogue between herself, Britain and the neighbouring Arab States.[139] It should be noted that Britain's good relations with the Shāh at this time greatly increased her ability to play an active and effective role as mediator during 1968. With Sa'ūdī Arabia and Kuwait she increased her efforts to find a solution to the Baḥrain problem. During the summer and autumn of this year, shaikhs from the Trucial Coast and the Ruler of Qaṭar visited Tehran to discuss the future of the Gulf. The *rapprochement* between Iran and Egypt in June created a better atmosphere in the area, and in October an agreement was reached, with the help of foreign mediators, between Iran and Sa'ūdī Arabia, regarding the median line. Consequently, the Shāh's postponed visit to Sa'ūdī Arabia took place in November, and from there he went on to Kuwait.

British sponsorship of the Federation of nine emirates, and the unanimous backing of the Arab world for the Kuwait and Sa'ūdī Arabian stand regarding Baḥrain, directed the Shāh towards a more realistic strategy concerning Iran's traditional claims in the Gulf. In a speech at New Delhi in January 1969, the Shāh said that Iran would not use force to reclaim Baḥrain and that she would listen sympathetically to the wishes of the inhabitants of the island in determining their future, a decision which was welcomed at once in Britain, Sa'ūdī Arabia, Kuwait and all the Arab countries. This courageous proclamation made clear that the Shāh was determined to relinquish the traditional Iranian claim to the island and encouraged Britain to pursue her endeavours with Iran. The desire of the Baḥrainis was ascertained by a representative of the Secretary-General of the United Nations, and on 11 May 1970 the Security Council endorsed their wish for independence.[140]

Early in 1970, as Baḥrain was progressing towards independence, the dormant dispute over Abū Mūsā and Ṭanb became the centre of attention in Arab–Iranian relations in the Gulf. Iran, Britain and the Arab countries all had different attitudes to this dispute. The Shāh adopted the Iranian attitude of the 1930s when Teymourtāche had been ready to relinquish his country's claim to Baḥrain in order to obtain a foothold in either Abū Mūsā or Ṭanb. He now emphasised the strategic position of the islands at the entrance to the Gulf and his anxiety about their possible seizure by subversive elements, an event which would interfere with oil traffic and the stability of the region. As Iran had shown tolerance in the Baḥrain issue, the Shāh thought it was now the turn of Britain and the Arabs to abandon their earlier attitudes regarding the islands; in fact he expected Britain to put pressure on the Arabs to accept a solution satisfactory to Iran. Meanwhile, between May and August 1970 full diplomatic relations between Cairo and Tehran were restored and Iran as a consequence abandoned her earlier policy of neutrality in the Arab–Israeli dispute, siding with the Arabs in their demands, particularly for the Palestinians' right to a national home and opposing Israeli policy in respect of Jerusalem. On the other hand relations between

Iran and Iraq deteriorated during this period, due to a renewal of their dispute over the Shaṭṭ-al-'Arab waterway.[141]

In April 1970, in order to give weight to the Iranian case, the Shāh made the first of his offers of economic assistance to Shārjah and Rās al-Khaimah on condition that a settlement was reached. At the same time, he took a hard line with the Trucial States. In May 1970 Iran threatened to use force against the Occidental Petroleum Company of Shārjah if the company did not cease operations off the island of Abū Mūsā; in October Iran reasserted opposition to the Federation until a settlement could be reached over the ownership of Abū Mūsā and Ṭanb; finally, in February 1971, and in response to Arab reluctance to negotiate, the Shāh proclaimed that if necessary his country would resort to force to take possession of the islands. This proclamation was followed by a press campaign to mobilise public opinion and heighten emotions over this dispute.

Although Britain was still representing Shārjah and Rās al-Khaimah in external matters, in this dispute Sir William Luce, the British special envoy to the Gulf, acted as a provider of good offices between Tehran and the two Emirates rather than as a negotiator. In May 1970 the British directed the Occidental Petroleum Company to stop their operations in order to prevent an Arab–Iranian confrontation. However, the Shāh's behaviour over the Baḥrain dispute, which the British considered was of more importance than Ṭanb and Abū Mūsā in Arab–Iranian relations, gained him the admiration of British officials, and they were prepared to use their influence on the Arabs in order to reach a settlement concerning the two islands.

On the other hand, the Arab countries, and in particular the Trucial States, did not view the independence of Baḥrain as part of a package deal and thought to solve the Abū Mūsā and Ṭanb dispute through international arbitration. The Trucial States insisted on their complete rights over these islands and this was expressed bluntly in their press, particularly in the journal *Shurūq* and by articles in the daily *Gulf Journal*, written by young graduate editors in Shārjah. Shaikh Khālid b. Muḥammad, the Ruler of Shārjah in 1971, prepared a well-documented legal and historical study of the Abū Mūsā question.

During the lengthy and exhausting negotiations all Iranian proposals were rejected by the Shaikhs of Shārjah and Rās al-Khaimah, who insisted on a declared statement of their sovereignty over the islands. However, Iran and Shārjah finally came to an ambiguous agreement over Abū Mūsā in which neither party acknowledged the other's sovereignty, but under the terms of which Iran would annually provide $3.75 million of aid to Shārjah until the oil revenue from the island, or its offshore waters, reached $7.5 million. Thereafter oil revenues were to be divided equally. The Shaikh of Shārjah agreed to allow Iranian troops to camp on half the island. The Shaikh of Rās al-Khaimah totally refused to sign such an agreement. The Shāh had decided from the beginning to confine this dispute to Iran, Britain and the two emirates concerned, so as to avoid a confrontation with the forthcoming United Arab Emirates (UAE), and so, on 30 November 1971, the last day of British protection, Iranian troops landed on Abū Mūsā and occupied their half of the island, while the two Ṭanb islands were attacked and taken by force.[142]

Iran's occupation of the islands, following an action which differed strongly from her previous policy in respect of Baḥrain, had wide regional repercussions. The people of the Trucial Coast, particularly in Rās al-Khaimah and Shārjah, reacted angrily and Iranian properties were attacked in the main towns along the coast. In the first statement of the Supreme Council of the recently established UAE they expressed their deep regret at the forcible action taken by Iran. The Shaikh of Rās al-Khaimah sent a letter of protest through Iraq to the Security Council of UNO, and on 9 December the representative of the UAE who attended a special session of the Security Council declared his country's protest. All the Arab countries rejected the Iranian action, but because of their preoccupation with the dominant matter of Israeli withdrawal from occupied lands, their condemnation took different forms. However, Iraq severed diplomatic relations with Iran; Britain accused Iran of violating her international obligations since the occupation took place on the eve of British withdrawal; and Libya nationalised the British Petroleum Company in retaliation for what she considered Britain's conspiracy with Iran. Had the occupation taken place a week later, Britain would not have been technically responsible for the defence of the islands, and would therefore, in all probability, not have had her assets in Libya and Iraq nationalised. Furthermore, Algeria, the Republic of South Yemen, Libya and Iraq joined together and requested an 'urgent meeting of the Security Council to consider the dangerous situation in the Gulf area arising from the occupation, by the armed forces of Iran, of the islands', and they adopted severe measures against Iran at a meeting of the Arab League. In fact, Iranian occupation of the islands put the Arab countries, particularly Egypt and Sa'ūdī Arabia, who had been concentrating on the Israeli question, in an embarrassing situation; although in the Arab League they condemned Iranian behaviour, they did not agree with the extremist measures designed to isolate Iran.[143]

Improved relations between Iran and the Soviet Union, and well-established co-operation with Britain and the United States, besides the interests of the Great Powers on the Arab side, greatly influenced them to take a neutral stand in this dispute. They openly avoided taking sides both during and after the discussion in the Security Council meeting, and on 9 December the Security Council finally agreed to shelve the subject temporarily and allow third parties to reach, by quiet diplomacy, a settlement between the disputants.[144]

Although Iran on the same day recognised the UAE, her occupation of the islands created a dangerous situation for the Federation in the earliest days of its existence. Since that time the Arab countries have remained consistent in insisting at every available opportunity on the Arabism of the islands. On 18 July 1972 they presented a note to the President of the Security Council stressing that 'the islands are Arab and constitute an integral part of the UAE and of the Arab homeland'. It is noticeable however, that this dispute has not interrupted the development of friendly relations between Iran and the Arab countries, particularly the UAE, for the preservation of Gulf security. Therefore, the islands dispute remains quiescent, awaiting a suitable opportunity to be reopened and discussed. Nevertheless, Iran's action to a great degree has, for the time being, alienated her Arab neighbours from her projected Gulf Pact, which would have to be based on complete respect for her neighbours' sovereignty and the finding of a peaceful solution for the islands acceptable to the UAE.

Notes

1. Lorimer, op.cit., II B, p.1455–66.
2. C. Niebuhr, *Description de P. Arabie*, Copenhagen, 1972. II, pp.270–74. The word *Houle* used by Niebuhr seems to be derived from the Arabic word *Mutaḥawwilah*, meaning 'those who change their original dwelling'. At the beginning of the twentieth century Lorimer describes those Sunnī immigrants who had recently come back from the Persian coast to the Arab side as *Houle*. This makes it clear that *Houle* is a descriptive word for immigrant people and distinguishes them from the established inhabitants in the area to which they came, and confirms that it is not the name of a specific tribe.
3. Lorimer, op.cit., II B, pp.1097, 1782; op.cit., I Part I A, pp.410, 631.
4. Kelly, *Britain*, pp.530–32.
5. P. Sykes, *History of Persia*, London, 1930, II, p.369.
6. Kelly, *Britain*, pp.656–61, 742.
7. Curzon of Kedleston, *Persia and the Persian Question*, London, 1892, II, pp.288, 399, 409.
8. Lorimer, op.cit., I Part II, p.2054.
9. H. Arfa, *Under Five Shahs*, London, 1964, pp.284–5; Graves, op.cit., pp.110–11.
10. F. Kazemzadeh, *Russia and Britain in Persia, 1864–1914*, New Haven & London, 1968, pp.259, 296–300, 355–7, 428–31.
11. Graves, op.cit., pp.108–9, 116–17; GA, Persien 7, bd. 5, Listemann to Bülow, 5 February 1905.
12. E. G. Browne, *The Persian Revolution of 1905–1909*, Cambridge, 1910, pp.110, 112–13, 119, 123–4, 172–3.
13. Graves, op.cit., pp.117, 121–3, 124–6. GA, Turkei 165, bd. 28, Listemann to Bülow, 30 January 1908.
14. Martin, op.cit., pp.156, 160, 165, 171, 182; GA, Persien 12, bd.2, German Legation, Tehran to Bülow, 11 April 1909.
15. Graves, op.cit., pp.124, 139–41, 159, 163–4, 166–8; FA, Asie Oceanie, NS, Mascate XIV, Légation de France à Tehran au Ministre, Paris, 19 Janvier 1909.
16. IOR, L/P & S/10/230, Sir E. Grey to British Minister, Tehran, 18 March 1912.
17. IOR, ibid., Slade to Commander-in-Chief's Office, Bombay, 15 February 1912, and Henjam Wireless Station 1913–18.
18. Sykes, op.cit., pp.451–62, 487–91, 517–20.
19. Graves, op.cit., pp.253, 256–8.
20. R. K. Ramazani, *The Foreign Policy of Iran, 1500–1941*, Charlottesville, 1966, p.161.

21. Lorimer, op.cit., II B, pp.1097–8, 2101.
22. Lorimer, ibid., II B, pp.2063–5.
23. IOR, P/3276, Residency Agent, Lingah to Pol. Res. 18 September 1887. Lorimer, op.cit. II B, 2065.
24. FA, Asie Oceanie, NS, Mascate XVIII, L'Agent-Consulaire de France à Lingah, au Vice-Consul de France à Mascate, 8 Mars 1899.
25. GA, Turkei 165, bd. 7 Consul, Calcutta, to Minister, Berlin, April 1899 (enclosed cuttings from Indian newspapers).
26. IOR, L/P & S/20, C 248. Saldanha, Precis of Affairs of the Persian Coast & Islands, 62.
27. IOR, R/1/14/15, Abū Mūsā & Ṭanb, Kemball to SGI, 12 January 1903.
28. Lorimer, op.cit., I Part II pp.2148–9.
29. IOR, L/P & S/10/230, Henjam Coal Depot, Biscoe, Bandar 'Abbas to Pol. Res., 15 January 1915.
30. Lorimer, op.cit., II B, pp.1275, 1830, 1909.
31. IOR, R/15/14/8, Arab Coast, Sulṭān b. Ṣaqr to Pol. Res., 28 December 1864.
32. Government of Shārjah, *Shārjah's Title to the Island of Abū Mūsā*, by M. E. Bathurst & Messrs. Coward Chance, September 1971, I.
33. Ḥājjī 'Abū al-Qāsim, an elderly and experienced man, well-informed in local affairs, was held in high regard by the Political Resident at Bushire and played an important role in providing the British with more accurate information, a major factor in reviewing their old unconsidered attitude.
34. Hawley, op.cit., p.328.
35. GS, op.cit., I, pp.26, 36.
36. GS, ibid., II Documents, pp.67, 78–9.
37. GS, ibid., pp.58–60.
38. GS, ibid., p.88.
39. GS, ibid., pp.68–71, 76–80, 348.
40. FO, 371/13009, Ṭanb, FO Minute, 21 September 1928.
41. IOR, P/3276, Ross to Nicolson, Tehran, 30 October 1887 & Pol. Res. to SGI, 26 September 1887 and Pol. Res. to SGI, 27 September 1887.
42. IOR, ibid., Extract from *Pioneer*, 3 October 1887, Residency Agent to Ross, 18 October 1887, and Ross to SGI, 8 October 1887.
43. IOR, ibid., Residency Agent to Ross, 15 October 1887, Ḥumaid b. 'Abdullah to Ross, 16 October 1887; Ṣaqr b. Khālid to Pol. Res., 17 October 1887; Ross to Residency Agent, 31 October 1887.
44. IOR, ibid., Nicolson, Tehran, to Ross, 10 October 1887; Ross to Nicolson, 30 October 1887; Ross to SGI, 16 November 1887; HM *Durand*, Viceroy's Camp to Nicolson, 17 November 1887; Nicolson to Viceroy's Camp, 22 November 1887; Nicolson to Viceroy's Camp, 10 December 1887; Ross to HM Chargé d'Affaires, Tehran, 10 December 1887.
45. IOR, ibid., Nicolson to Ross, 2 January 1888; Ross to SGI, 18 February 1888.
46. IOR, ibid., Residency Agent to Ross, 18 January 1888; HBM Legation, Tehran to the Persian Minister for Foreign Affairs, 6 March 1888; the Persian Ministry for Foreign Affairs to HBM Legation at Tehran, 10 March 1888; HBM Legation Tehran, to the Persian Ministry for Foreign Affairs, 19 March 1888.
47. IOR, ibid., Drummond Wolff to the Viceroy, 19 April 1888; Drummond Wolff to the Viceroy, 24 April 1888; Shaikh Ṣaqr to Ross, 6 June 1888; Minister, Tehran, to Ross, 26 July 1888.
48. IQR, L/P & S/3/292, Drummond to Salisbury, 27 August 1888 (enclosure 5, meeting of Mr. Churchill, Chargé d'Affaires with the Shāh).
49. OOR, ibid., Churchill to Persian Minister, 11 September 1888; Memo of Persian Minister to Churchill, 6 November 1888.
50. IOR, R/15/1/14/8, IO to FO, 8 June 1904. Enclosure 2, Meade to Durand, 13 December 1898.
51. Saldanha, op.cit., p.19.
52. Saldanha, ibid., pp.62–5.
53. IOR, L/P & S/10/127, Telegram British Minister to FO, 6 January 1908; IOR, L/P & S/10/1267, Status of the Islands of Ṭanb, Abū Mūsā and Ṣirrī, 5.
54. IOR, L/P & S/18/B 397, Status of the Islands of Ṭanb, Abū Mūsā and Ṣirrī (1928), 6.

55. Ramazani, op.cit., pp.200–01, 210.
56. R. M. Burrell, '*Britain, Iran and the Persian Gulf: Some Aspects of the Situation in 1920s and 1930s*', *The Arabian Peninsula*, edited by D. Hopwood, London, 1972, pp.161–2.
57. IOR, L/P & S/30/145, Fowle to British Minister, Tehran, 7 December 1936; Bushire Diary for the Month of October 1936.
58. Admiralty, Naval Intelligence Division, *Iraq and the Persian Gulf*, 1944, pp.161–2.
59. Arfa, op.cit., pp.110–12.
60. R. Bullard, *The Camels Must Go*, London, 1961, pp.218–19.
61. Arfa, op.cit., pp.167, 169–70.
62. IOR, L/P & S/30/59, Clive, Tehran to Hunderson, 19 April 1930.
63. Ramazani, op.cit., pp.243–8.
64. Shwadran, op.cit., p.42.
65. FO, 371/16967, Annual Report 1932, p.34.
66. IOR, R/14/1/13/41, Dubai Dhow Incident, Pol. Res. to SGI, 14 August 1928.
67. CAB, 16/93, PG Sub-Committee, Meeting No. 4, 22 October 1928 and Meeting No. 5, 24 October 1928.
68. IOR, L/P & S/30/59, Clive to Hunderson, 19 April 1930.
69. IOR, L/P & S/10/1045, Baḥrain, Clive to Chamberlain, 16 February 1929.
70. IOR, L/P & S/30/59, *Shafaq al Sharq* Magazine, 21 August 1929; Clive to Hunderson, 21 August 1929; Rendel to IO, 24 September 1929.
71. IOR, ibid., FO to Clive, 14 January 1930; Teymourtâche to Clive, 31 March 1930.
72. FO, 371/144678, FO Memorandum re 'Suggestion that the Island of Ṭanb might be leased to Persia', 14 November 1930.
73. IOR, L/P & S/30/59, Clive to Hunderson, 21 August 1929; FO to Clive, 18 September 1930.
74. IOR, L/P & S/10/1267, FO to Clive, 8 May 1930; FO Memorandum to Hoare, CO September 1930; FO to IO, 16 March 1932.
75. FO, 371/16967, Annual Report 1932, p.34.
76. Shwadran, op.cit., pp.42–51.
77. FO, 371/17909, Annual Report 1933, p.7.
78. CAB, 51/1, Note of the First Lord of the Admiralty, 4 June 1934.
79. CAB, 51/7, OME Sub-Committee, Memoranda; Burrell, op.cit., pp. 163–4.
80. CAB, 51/1, Minutes of MME Sub-Committee, 11 June 1934; IOR, L/P & S/12/30/75, Telegram FO to Hoare, Tehran, 4 July 1934.
81. CAB, 51/3, Meeting No. 35, OME Sub-Committee, 12 October 1934.
82. Burrell, op.cit., p.168.
83. IOR, L/P & S/18B p.408, Persian Complaints of Smuggling in the Persian Gulf, 1 October 1928.
84. IOR, L/P & S/18/B 397, pp.6–7.
85. IOR, L/P & S/18B 408, op.cit., 1 October 1928.
86. IOR, R/15/1/14/41, Capture of Dubai Dhow, SNO to Pol. Res., 10 September 1928; SNO to Pol. Res. 5 August 1928; 'Īsā to Pol. Res., 27 August 1928.
87. IOR, ibid., SNO to Admiralty, 5 August 1928; 'Īsā to Pol. Res., 27 August 1928; Parr to Pakrevan, 4 August 1928; GI to SSI, 5 August 1928.
88. IOR, ibid., SNO to Pol. Res. & Admiralty, 5 August 1928, SN to Pol. Res. 13 August 1928; 'Īsā to Pol. Res., 27 August 1928; Acting Secretary of State for Foreign Affairs, London to Minister at Tehran, 11 August 1928.
89. FO, 371/13009, Acting Minister for Foreign Affairs to Parr, 21 August 1928; IOR, R/15/1/14/9, Ṭanb Island, Bagher Kazemi to Mallet, 21 October 1933.
90. IOR, ibid., SNO to Pol. Res., 23 August 1928.
91. IOR, ibid., M. Pakrevan to Parr, 21 August 1928; SNO to Pol. Res., 10 September 1928; 'Īsā to Pol. Res., 9 September 1928.
92. IOR, ibid., SNO to Pol. Res., 10 September 1928.
93. IOR, ibid., FO to British Minister, Tehran, 14 September 1928; M. Pakrevan to Parr, 20 September 1928; 'Īsā to Fowle, 10 November 1928.
94. FO, 371/13721, Admiralty to FO, 13 November 1928.
95. IOR, L/P & S/10/1045, Clive to Chamberlain, 16 February 1929.
96. IOR, R/15/1/14/34, SGI to Pol. Res., 1 May 1929; Pol. Res. to SGI, 4 May 1929.

97. IOR, L/P & S/10/1267, Clive to Hunderson, 31 August 1929.
98. IOR, R/15/14/41, 'Īsā to Pol. Res., 20 March 1930; Shaikh Sa'īd to Pol. Res., 27 March 1930.
99. IOR, L/P & S/10/1267, Clive to Hunderson, received 28 April 1930.
100. IOR, L/P & S/12/467, Telegram from Pol. Res. to SGI, 10 May 1930.
101. IOR, L/P & S/10/1267, FO to Clive, 8 May 1930.
102. IOR, R/15/1/14/32, Pol. Res. to British Minister, Tehran, 8 August 1930.
103. IOR, L/P & S/12/30/75, Persian Minister for Foreign Affairs to Clive, 23 September 1930.
104. IOR, L/P & S/30/145, FO Circular, 10 March 1932 (included in a letter from Br. Minister Seymour to Fowle, 28 January 1937).
105. FO, 371/16967, Annual Report, 1932, p.37; FO, 371/16077, Annual Report, 1921, pp.41–2.
106. IOR, L/P & S/12/467, Memorandum on lease of Ṭanb by C. W. Baxter, 14 November 1930.
107. FO, 371/16077, p.43.
108. CAB, 24/243, Memorandum on the Incident at Bāsīdū, 2 September 1933.
109. FO, 371/17909, Annual Report, 1933.
110. IOR, R/15/1/14/10, Ṭanb (1912–34), Pol. Res. to Sulṭān b. Sālim, 7 October 1933; 'Īsā to Loch, 8 November 1933.
111. IOR, R/15/1/14/9, Baghaer Kazemi to Mallet, 21 October 1933; 'Īsā to Pol. Agent, Baḥrain, 19 April 1934.
112. IOR, op.cit., Report from 'Īsā.
113. CAB, 51/1, Relations with Persia, Note by the First Lord of the Admiralty, 4 June 1934.
114. IOR, L/P & S/12/467, SNO to Pol. Res., 15 October 1934 and Persian Claim to Ṭanb and Abū Mūsā, Memorandum by Mr. Lascelles, 4 September 1934; Report on Ṭanb Incidents 1934; FO to Hoare, 12 October 1934.
115. IOR, R/15/1/14/9, Ṭanb (1912–34), Sulṭān b. Sālim to Loch, 3 September 1934; Maḥmūd to 'Īsā, 4 June 1934; Fowle to Sulṭān b. Sālim, 1 July 1934.
116. IOR, R/15/1/14/10 Fowle to SSI, 4 February 1935; HM Minister, Tehran, to FO, 19 February 1935.
117. IOR, L/P & S/12/467, Fowle to GI, January 1935.
118. IOR, R/15/1/14/10, Fowle to SGI, 4 February 1935.
119. IOR, R/15/1/14/10, Fowle to Sulṭān b. Sālim, 19 March 1935; Sulṭān b. Sālim, to Fowle, 29 March 1925; 'Īsā to Fowle, 10 April 1935; Rendel to FO, 13 October 1934.
120. FO, 371/18901, Laithwaite to Rendel, 11 January 1935; IO to FO, Transmits copy letter of 11 March from Fowle enclosing copy of Dickson, 6 February 1935.
121. GS, I, op.cit., p.58.
122. FO, 371/18901, The Brief for the Br. Delegation to the League of Nations on 'The Persian Claim to the Islands of Ṭanb and Abū Mūsā, 17 May 1935.
123. FO, 371/10052, Annual Report, 1935, p.18.
124. D. N. Wilber, *Iran Past and Present*, Princeton, 1975, pp.224–35, 240–5; M. R. Pahlavi, *The White Revolution*, Tehran, 1967, pp.86–134; R. Sanghvi, *Aryamehr: The Shah of Iran*, London, 1968, pp.204–10.
125. A. K. S. Lambton, *The Persian Land Reform*, Oxford, 1969, pp.87–118; J. Bharier, *Economic Development in Iran 1900–1970*, London, 1971, pp.89–100, 189–93; Zabih, op.cit., pp.103–107.
126. Zabih, ibid., pp.199–200.
127. Zabih, ibid., pp.69–70, 196, 202.
128. Zabih, ibid., pp.274–9.
129. R. K. Ramazani, *Iran's Foreign Policy 1941–1973*, Charlottesville, 1975, pp.397–9, 410, 437.
130. Ramazani, ibid., pp.405–6; Zabih, op.cit., pp.212–13.
131. Zabih, ibid., pp.140–54; Ramazani, op.cit., pp.397–406.
132. Ramazani, ibid., pp.406; Zabih, op.cit., pp.202–3, 236. It was during one of these Islamic Conferences in Algiers in 1974 that Iraq and Iran began negotiations to discuss their disputes and reached an understanding in early 1975.
133. Sadat, the new President of Egypt, has promoted very friendly relations between

Iran and his country and these have greatly influenced the recent politics of the Middle East.

134. The continental shelf was defined as land at less than 100 fathoms beneath the sea and adjacent to the mainland.
135. Zabih, op.cit., pp.282–3, 289–94; Ramazani, op.cit., pp.412–14.
136. Marlowe, op.cit., pp.127, 129, 141–64, 208–9.
137. Ramazani, op.cit., pp.254–8, 330–7, 359–70.
138. Zabih, op.cit., pp.240–55.
139. Branches of the Sadirat Bank of Iran were opened in 1968 in Dubai, and in 1969 in Abū Dhabī; Iranian Airways inaugurated their early services between Dubai and Bandar 'Abbas in 1969, and the Arya Shipping Company, the newly established maritime line, in 1970 began its fast passenger services across the Gulf.
140. Ramazani, op.cit., pp.413–16.
141. Zabih, op.cit., pp.222–6.
142. Zabih, ibid., pp.226–8.
143. Zabih, ibid., pp.228–31.
144. UN Security Council, Provisional Records, 9 December 1971.

5 Britain, Muscat and the Inter-State Boundaries

5 Britain, Muscat and the Inter-State Boundaries

I A Historical Review of the Political Map

The coastal part of the frontiers between the Trucial States and the Sultanate of Muscat and 'Omān was mainly established and recognised by the Government of India at the turn of the nineteenth century. They represented a British solution to territorial doubts and disputes which had continued throughout the century, a solution which was accordingly influenced by consideration of British interests as well as by the geographical and historical facts. The early boundary decisions of the Government of India were officially recorded in Lorimer's *Gazetteer*. However, although the *Gazetteer* is historically and ethnographically exhaustive, its method is descriptive and unillustrated; no boundaries are shown in the map which Hunter made for it, and the frontier lines remained imprecise.

In contrast, the inter-state boundaries did not emerge until the 1930s. Before then the concept of a state with clearly defined boundaries was totally alien to the political notions of the rulers and the tribes of the area. Political boundaries were dependent on tribal loyalties to particular shaikhs and consequently were subject to frequent change. Therefore, the frontier between the Trucial States and the Sultanate of Muscat and the inter-state boundaries changed frequently during the nineteenth and twentieth centuries as it was based on the *dirah* of the tribes. *Dirah* in Arabia at this time was a flexibly defined area, changing in size according to the strength of the tribe which wandered within it. In addition, a tribe's loyalty was determined by its own interests and could, and at this time often did, alter: the Banī Ka'b, for example, who were originally members of the Qawāsim federation, were found by Lorimer to be divided, a minority having transferred its allegiance to Muscat, whereas by Julian Walker's time (Assistant Political Agent, Dubai, 1953–5), the whole tribe could be regarded as subjects of the Sultan.

The awareness of a need among the shaikhs for a recognised and stable boundary had its origin in 1935 with the advent of oil concessions. At this time, with revenue from a dying pearl industry shrinking, the power of the shaikhs diminished and a feeling of independence from their previous masters prevailed among the tribes of the hinterland. This state of affairs was well illustrated by Captain Hickinbotham, Political Agent in Baḥrain, on 10 July 1937:

> Petroleum Concessions Limited quite naturally are anxious to know exactly for what amount of territory they are buying concessions and at the same time the Trucial Shaikh is anxious, especially in the event of oil being discovered, to claim as much territory as he possibly can. The present boundaries between the states are not demarcated with any accuracy and I am doubtful if any of the Trucial Shaikhs themselves can accurately describe where their territorial boundaries run . . . The advent of oil has made these [barren] areas potentially as rich as areas where there is water and grazing and now the individual shaikhs are anxious to claim as much land, however barren, as they possibly can. This will give rise to boundary disputes between the Shaikhs, even along boundaries which are fairly clearly defined . . . some of the Shaikhs have been gradually losing control and what was considered an integral part of the Shaikhdom ten years or more ago has now become separated and under the rule of the Shaikh of one of the nomadic tribes.

The Shaikh of Dubai commented that negotiations for oil concessions in 1935 were accompanied by the emergence of territorial disputes between his emirate and her neighbours.[1] When the Company of Petroleum Development concluded agreements with the Shaikhs of the Trucial Coast in the late 1930s the question of boundaries became crucial, as Article I of these agreements shows: 'If the Shaikh agrees that when the territorial limits of the State of .... have been determined, the area covered by the concession will be coterminous with the limits so determined.'[2]

The conclusion of oil agreements and the payments to the shaikhs according to the extent of their lands provoked claims in Umm al-Qaiwain, now a small emirate based on historical rather than actual sovereignty. When the Shaikh of Umm al-Qaiwain in January 1937 refused to grant oil options to the d'Arcy Exploration Company, his explanation was that he was not offered money according to his territory, which he considered equal to Abū Dhabī.[3]

The problem was apparent in the difficulties which faced the geological teams of the d'Arcy Exploration Company which initiated oil activities on the coast and was granted options in November 1935 to last for two years. Petroleum Concessions which followed in 1937 concentrated their activities in two main areas in the interior, Jabal Fayah and the Buraimī area, which they were unable to reach. The exploration teams were met with harassment from the Banī Qatab, the Na'aīm and Āl|Bū-Shāmis, who did not at that time recognise the authority of either their traditional rulers on the coast or the Sultanate of Muscat. For example, in January 1937, Shaikh Rāshid b. Ḥumaid of 'Ajmān informed the Ruler of Shārjah and the Residency Agent that the Qasimī Shaikh Khālid b. Aḥmad, who was now under his protection, had a written document of 1927 stating that Dhaid belonged to him, and that geological teams wanting to visit this area needed permission from him and not from the Shaikh of Shārjah.[4]

The directors of the oil company suggested that they would give presents to the petty shaikhs in the interior in order to be able to carry out their exploration, a policy with which Fowle disagreed. Fowle thought that this policy would involve the company in a series of expensive concessions and undermine the power of both the Trucial Shaikhs and the Sultan of Muscat. He insisted that the hinterland belonged *de jure* to the Trucial Shaikhs or to the Sultan of Muscat. In his subsequent discussions with the company he stressed that it would be better in the long run to stop exploration and give the Political Agent in Baḥrain and the Residency Agent in Shārjah time to study the situation in the interior. This area was unknown to the British as no British Political Officer had penetrated beyond Buraimī since Percy Cox went there in 1905. Fowle's proposal to recognise and strengthen the power of the shaikhs over the interior was to constitute the cornerstone of British policy on the coast a decade later.

Until the question of demarcation could be settled and the rulers could maintain practical authority over the tribes, the British found it prudent to establish good relations with the tribes of the interior directly. On 18 November 1936 the Political Agent instructed 'Abd al-Razzāq to visit the Buraimī area and to cultivate friendly relations with its shaikhs.[5] As a result, in June 1938 Shaikh Muḥammad b. Raḥma Āl-Shāmis visited the Political Agent in Baḥrain and outlined the *dirah* of his tribe, that of the Shaikh of Āl Bū-Khribān in Buraimī and that of the Shaikh of Abū Dhabī.[6]

The first negotiations in this early period to solve the problem of frontiers peacefully were conducted between Abū Dhabī and Dubai and began in December 1936. On 16 November 1936 Shaikh Sa'īd b. Maktūm accompanied by his brother Jum'ah and a notable, Muḥammad b. Ḥiraiz, went to see Shaikh Shakhbūṭ, who claimed that Jabal 'Alī belonged to his emirate whilst Shaikh Sa'īd demanded Khūr Ghanāḍah. Through the mediation of Aḥmad b. Hīlāl both shaikhs agreed to put the question to arbitration. On 9 December 1936, Aḥmad b. Khalaf al-'Utaibah and Aḥmad b. Hīlāl came from Abū Dhabī and informed Shaikh Sa'īd that Abū Dhabī agreed that Ḥaṣaṭ Umm al-Jibaib, ten miles southwest of Jabal 'Alī, should be the point of demarcation. A council of Āl Bū-Flāsah over which Shaikh Sa'īd presided agreed to respond to this new proposal, but they offered Ḥiṣyān, which is three miles southwest of Abū Dhabī point, claiming that they needed the jetty at Ḥiṣyān for their pearling boats. A year of slow but fruitful interchange passed and on 1 November 1937, after a long meeting between Shaikh Shakhbūṭ and Shaikh Sa'īd at Khūr Ghanāḍah a verbal agreement was reached, establishing that the area west of a line running from Bandar Ḥiṣyān southwards should be Abū Dhabī country and that the area east of this line should belong to Dubai.[7]

In keeping with Fowle's policy, the Political Resident instructed Hickinbotham, with the help of Captain J. B. Howes, the British Political Officers and 'Abd al-Razzāq the Residency Agent at Shārjah, to study the loyalties of the tribes in the hinterland and the territorial claims of the Trucial shaikhs. On 12 August 1938, Hickinbotham informed Fowle that he had drawn the first sketch map marking the boundaries of the Trucial shaikhdoms.[8] After the war in 1946, Colonel Galloway, with the help of Jāsim Kazmāwī, the Residency Agent, translated all this information and the sketch into the first real map of the frontiers of the Trucial States.[9] This map constituted the final effort of the local representatives of the Government of India to find a solution to the frontier problem.

One of the main obstacles which the British faced in demarcating the boundaries was the vagueness of information on the geography of the interior and consequently the lack of a precise physical map. Early in 1945 a joint project was undertaken by the United States Army Survey Department in conjunction with Brigadier Papworth of the British Survey Department, Cairo, to make a map of the area between Qaṭar and Shārjah, using aerial photography.[10]

Such was the extent of geographical knowledge in this area in 1947 when the Foreign Office took over the responsibility for the affairs of the Trucial States in solving the frontier question. It was at this time that the bitter dispute of 1946–8 between Abū Dhabī and Dubai over Khūr Ghanāḍah was in progress. The British authorities intervened as mediators and succeeded in 1948 in obtaining the agreement of both shaikhs to abide by their decision. When the British gave their judgement the following year, however, designating Ḥiṣyān as the frontier coastal point, Dubai was not satisfied.

The increasing activities of the oil companies during the 1950s and the need for safe conduct for the exploration teams in the interior made it vital that a comprehensive solution should be found to the protracted frontier problem of the whole area. The Foreign Office detailed Julian Walker to delineate on sketch maps the inter-state boundaries within the Trucial States and the frontiers between the latter and the Sultanate of Muscat. He began the task in 1954 and worked on it at intervals until 1960.

Unwilling to involve themselves in these internal disputes, the British explained to the shaikhs at the beginning that they would act only as intermediaries and arbitrators, and in January 1955 the Trucial Shaikhs agreed to abide by the decision of the Political Officer. In May of that year, Julian Walker presented a massive frontier report, including his recommendations on frontier lines and indicating the basis of his decision. Accordingly, during 1956 and 1957 official letters were sent to the shaikhs of the Trucial Coast from Mr Tripp, the Political Officer in Dubai, informing them of their frontiers between the Trucial States and the Sultanate of Muscat, the result of which was the agreement in 1959 between Shaikh Shakhbūṭ b. Sultān, the ruler of Abū Dhabī and Sa'īd b. Taimūr, the Sultan of Muscat.

In February 1963 an authoritative map was prepared and drawn up by the Research Department of the Foreign Office. Although the shaikhs showed willingness to accept British arbitration, some of them expressed discontent with Julian Walker's decision in some areas. The difficulty of imposing formal boundaries on an area inhabited by tribes unused to the whole concept can be seen from the distinction made in the legend of the Foreign Office map between settled, unsettled and presumptive frontiers. Walker's lack of authenticated maps—there were no aerial maps of the whole region at the time and the maps prepared for Lorimer had hardly been able to concern themselves with the interior—increased the magnitude of the task, as did the intensity of the disputes among the parties concerned.

To find a solution to the unsettled areas and to follow up the investigations of Julian Walker the Foreign Office sent Mr Buckmaster out at intervals between 1963 and 1967. He was able to give some recommendations, the most important of which concerned the Wādī Madḥah and Umm al-Zamūl areas. Also in the last few years before withdrawal, the British agreed to and tolerated direct relations between the Trucial Shaikhs and the Sultan of Muscat to solve their own problems. Shaikh Zāyed b. Sultān, the new ruler of Abū Dhabī, whose aspirations went far beyond the territorial limits of Abū Dhabī, succeeded in February 1969 in concluding a satisfactory agreement with Dubai. Abū Dhabī gave Dubai ten miles west of Ḥiṣyān, a tolerance which played a decisive role in establishing the federation of the Trucial States two years later.

Looking at the map of the boundaries of the Trucial States prepared and drawn by the Foreign Office in 1963, one sees that only Abū Dhabī and Umm al-Qaiwain form integral areas, whilst the remaining five emirates comprise many units—Dubai two, 'Ajmān three, Rās al-Khaimah two, Fujairah two and Shārjah four. In a small area containing numerous tribes with different political alignments and a background of shifting loyalties and constant feuds, this state of affairs is inevitable. It is evident that the demarcation between the Trucial States as a unit and the Sultanate of Muscat was much easier to define than the boundaries between the Trucial States themselves.

Referring to the map of the political boundaries between the Trucial States and Muscat, it may be seen that the areas which could be discussed here are the frontiers of Rūs al-Jibāl, Wādī Madḥah, Muscat's border with Shārjah, Dubai and Ajmān in the south, and finally its boundaries with Abū Dhabī. Muscat's frontiers with Dubai and Abū Dhabī, with whom Muscat enjoyed friendly relations, presented relatively few problems and these were considered by the British to be completely internal matters in which they had no interest. We shall, however, have to study the disputes in connection with the borders between Muscat and the Qawāsim, in Rūs al-Jibāl and the Shimailiyyah district, as most of the points of dispute which arose involved British interference and arbitration.

II The Frontiers between Muscat and the Trucial States

The Frontiers in the Rūs al-Jibāl Area

Rūs al-Jibāl district forms the northern tip of the promontory of the Trucial States, defined to the southwest by an approximate line between Dabā on the Gulf of 'Omān and the headland of Al-Qīr, north of Sha'am on the Gulf. It is inhabited mainly by the Shiḥūḥ tribe, the settled members of which live in Dabā al-Bay'ah, Līmā, Kamzār and Khaṣab. Khaṣab is the seat of the Sultan of Muscat's representative. These Shiḥūḥ are Hināwī in politics and Shāfi'ī in sect. However, the Shiḥūḥ who live outside Rūs al-Jibāl so defined, in Dabā al-Ḥiṣn, Sha'am and Ghalilah, are Ḥanbalī (Wahhabī) in sect, a fact which had a direct effect on demarcations in the area. The northernmost part, Rās Musandam, a peninsula indented by numerous deep-water inlets, is inhabited by the Dhahūriyyīn tribe, who live in the villages of Ḥablain, Film and Maqāqah. Although they are surrounded by Shiḥūḥī country, they are Hanbalī and Ghāfirī, a trace of the former Qawāsim sovereignty in the area. In the spring, the Dhahūriyyīn migrate in a body to Khūr and Dabā to work in the date groves, an economic tie which attached them closely to the Qawāsim.[11]

At the opening of the nineteenth century Rūs al-Jibāl was an important part of the Qawāsim federation. In discussions about the future of the area in connection with the British expedition to Rās al-Khaimah in 1819, Nepean, the Governor in Bombay, expressed the view that the Rūs al-Jibāl and Shimailiyyah districts should be placed under the immediate control of the Sultan of Muscat. The essence of his plan was that the peace of the Gulf could best be maintained by extending the power of the Ruler of Muscat and establishing a British base in a commanding position near the entrance to the Gulf. Francis Warden, the Chief Secretary to the Government, objected that Sa'īd b. Sulṭān was probably not strong enough to subdue the tribes in these areas, pointing out that time and again the Qawāsim had overrun, not only the Rūs al-Jibāl and Shimailiyyah, but also Shināṣ on the Bāṭinah Coast. Finally, the commander of the expedition, General Keir, received instructions to subdue the whole of the 'Pirate Coast' and keep it under strict surveillance, to depose Shaikh Ḥasan b. Raḥman, the Qawāsim leader, and to put the area under Sa'īd b. Sulṭān's control if Ḥasan refused. Sa'īd b. Sulṭān was, in fact, far from eager to take over the territory of the troublesome Qawāsim: he had plans to extend into East Africa which seemed to him more profitable and less hazardous.[12] In 1836, after Sa'īd's return from one of his expeditions to East Africa to deal with a revolt in Ṣuḥār and Qawāsim attacks on Muscatī ships on the Shimailiyyah coast, he said in reply to British approaches that the Shiḥūḥ of Rūs al-Jibāl were dependants of the Qasimī Shaikh Sulṭān b. Ṣaqr. However, the Shiḥūḥ themselves were in favour of becoming dependants of the Sultan of Muscat, under whose distant and nominal sovereignty they would enjoy practical independence. Being Hināwī, they were the first to respond to the decline in the fortunes of the Qawāsim, against whom they revolted in 1839. Shaikh Sulṭān b. Ṣaqr blockaded Khaṣab and Kamzār, but a peaceful settlement was reached. However, before the end of his long reign Shaikh Sulṭān was to experience graver risings from the Shiḥūḥ in 1855.

As the Shiḥūḥ controlled the land route from Rās al-Khaimah to Dabā, Sulṭān blockaded their ports and sent armed men to Dabā by boat. Captain Felix Jones, the Political Resident, who had come to the conclusion that the Shiḥūḥ of Rūs al-Jibāl owed their allegiance to the Ruler of Muscat, ordered Shaikh Sulṭan, in January 1857, to stop sending troops by sea. In 1858 the latter protested to the Government of Bombay, saying that the Shiḥūḥ were his rebellious subjects, whom he must be allowed full liberty to coerce. The Government of India supported the Political Resident's attitude, and Shaikh Sulṭān was ultimately obliged to submit to British orders. In 1863 Colonel Pelly, the new Political Resident, following his predecessor's line, referred a maritime incident at Khaṣab to the Political Agent in Muscat, and reported to the Government of Bombay that both Khaṣab and Kamzār belonged to the Sultanate of 'Omān.

During the first quarter of 1864 the question of the ownership of Rās al-Jibāl became urgent. In January Colonel Disbrowe, the Political Agent in Muscat, visited the Rās Musandam peninsula to prepare for the landing of the telegraph cable there and its necessary security. The Dhahūriyyīn tribe at Ḥablian insisted that they must be fairly paid for the concession, and also that the project required the permission of Sulṭān b. Ṣaqr, to whom they declared their allegiance. On 21 February 1964, Colonel Disbrowe obtained from Thuwainī b. Sa'īd, the Sultan of Muscat, a written document stating that Rās Musandam and the rest of Rūs al-Jibāl were part of his Sultanate, and granting the telegraph company the right to cross the isthmus and all the facilities they required. By this authority, underlined by the presence of a gunboat sent from Bombay, the cable was successfully landed. In reality, the Qawāsim no longer had the strength to control Rūs al-Jibāl; although in 1871 Turkī b. Sa'īd granted them rights over the whole coast from Khūr Kalbā to Shārjah, with the single exception of Khaṣab, in the hope that they would help him claim the Sultanate, they could not help him, and they could not enforce the document either, in so far as it related to Rūs al-Jibāl. Around this time the revolt of the Shiḥūḥ spread to the Sharqiyyīn of Fujairah, in the Shimailiyyah district, and it was this new problem which absorbed the attention of the Qawāsim for the rest of the century.[13]

The first recorded instance of the Government of India's attitude towards the extent of Qasimī territory on the western coast of Rūs al-Jibāl was an incident occurring in 1889. There was an uprising among the Shiḥūḥ of Sha'am, and the British authorities not only allowed the Shaikh of Rās al-Khaimah, Ḥumaid b. 'Abdullah to send troops by sea, but also sent a warship to help him restore his authority. At the turn of the nineteenth century, Rūs al-Jibāl, and in particular Rās Musandam with its natural harbours, occupied a central role in British strategy for the escalating rivalry of the great powers in the Gulf. Among Curzon's energetic designs against the challenge of the Russians and the French was the establishment of a naval base on the Musandam peninsula. He agreed with the remark of Admiral Bosanquet, early in 1902, that the Musandam promontory is for naval war purposes the most important strategical position in the Gulf and could never be allowed to fall into the hands of an enemy. The military view had immediate repercussions on the British diplomatic attitude towards the status of Rūs al-Jibāl. At an interdepartmental meeting at the India Office in July 1902 it was recommended that the local shaikh should be recognised as independent, rather than under the Sultan of Muscat, who it was thought might be difficult over the question in the light of his association with the French during the late 1890s. This is an example of the British willingness to manipulate frontiers in accordance with needs arising from the internal situation and attitude of individual rulers.

In 1902, when Cox sailed from Muscat to Abū Dhabī to begin his first journey inland, one of his assignments was to stop at Rūs al-Jibāl and test local opinion on the subject of jurisdiction. The most significant change which he reported was that the Dhahūriyyīn no longer objected to being ruled by Muscat. His opinion therefore was that it was open to the British Government to regard Rūs al-Jibāl either as a district of the 'Omān Sultanate or as an autonomous tract.[14] Britain's strategic interest in the area was emphasised when Curzon, on his tour in the Gulf in November 1903, devoted a day to an examination of the coast and inlets in Rūs al-Jibāl. Following this, and in response to the visits of Russian warships, the British in 1904 chose three prospective bases from which to fly the British flag in the Musandam peninsula. However, this plan was abandoned as a result of Russia's naval defeat in the Far East. In Shārjah, in March of the same year, Lorimer discussed sovereignty over Rūs al-Jibāl with the Shaikh of Shārjah and an elder of the Shiḥūḥ. Lorimer recorded a unanimous decision that all places upon the sea between Sh'am and Dabā, in other words the whole coast of Rūs al-Jibāl, belonged to Muscat, adding that no difference of status in the interior was suggested. Julian Walker, in his 1960 decision, took from Lorimer the coastal extremities of the boundary of Muscatī Rūs al-Jibāl. The details of the line inland, however, he had to establish by his own investigations on the ground. As Dabā al-Bay'ah is inhabited by Shāfi'ī Shiḥūḥ, loyal to the Sultan of Muscat, and Dabā al-Ḥiṣn by Ḥanbalī Shiḥūḥ, loyal to the Shaikh of Shārjah, the line follows the watercourse which divides the two villages. It then turns west along the route from Dabā via Khatt to Rās al-Khaimah, which is generally regarded as the boundary between the country of the Shiḥūḥ to the north and that of the Sharqiyyīn to the south. At the point where the route reaches the *dirah* of the Ḥabūs the line leaves it and turns north. The Ḥabūs live in the southwestern part of the mountains of Rūs al-Jibāl, overlooking the cultivated valley of al-Sīr between Mi'airiḍ and Digdāgah, in the hinterland of Rās al-Khaimah. They are a part of the Banī Hadiyyah branch of the Shiḥūḥ, and are a good example of the way that a sub-group, separated from its parent tribe over a long period, could become what was effectively an independent tribe. Living on the slopes above al-Sīr, and developing dominant economic ties with it, the Ḥabus became Hanbalī and Ghāfirī. Leaving the Ḥabūs to the west, therefore, the line continues directly northward, traversing the slopes above Rams, Khūr al-Khuwair, Ghalīlah and Sha'am, then turns west, enclosing in the angle a group of the Dhahūriyyin, to reach the Gulf at the headland of al-Qīr. Rams is inhabited by the Ṭinaij tribe, who are Ghāfirī and Ḥanbalī, traditionally loyal to the Qawāsim. Khūr al-Khuwair, Ghalīlah and Sha'am are inhabited by Shiḥūḥ, but these are also Ḥanbali and have economic links along the coast with Rās al-Khaimah, and so are loyal to the Qawāsim. These coastal connections do not extend north of al-Qīr: beyond this point the Shiḥūḥ are Ḥināwī and Shāfi'ī. Hence the line's abrupt westward turn to leave these Shiḥūḥ under the sovereignty of Muscat.

The Wādī Madḥah Tract

The Wādī Madḥah is a small enclosed valley running northeastwards from the Ḥijr mountains towards the bay of Khūr Fakkān, and inhabited by the Banī Sa'd tribe, whose main villages are Ghūnah and Madḥah.[15] They are Hināwī and Shāfi'ī. Their origin is uncertain: some authorities connect them with the Shiḥūḥ of Rūs al-Jibāl, some with the Dhawāhir of al-Buraimī. In their secluded valley, without political significance, they were unaffected by the vicissitudes of the Qawāsim, and maintained an unchanging loyalty to the Sultan of Muscat. Thus the Government of India's decision of 1903, that the whole of the Shimailiyyah district, from Dabā al-Ḥiṣn to Khūr Kalbā, belonged to the Qawāsim, put the Madḥah tract in an anomalous position. Julian Walker's map shows the line around the enclave claimed by Muscat, making clear that this is an unsettled frontier. However, in 1967 an agreement was reached between the Sultanate of Muscat, Shārjah and Fujairah fixing the boundaries.

Muscat's Frontiers with the Qawāsim, Dubai and 'Amjān

The line between the southern Qawāsim territories and the Sultanate of Muscat underwent many changes during the late nineteenth and the twentieth centuries. The definitions in this area are far more delicate and complex than in Rūs al-Jibāl; the frontier is much longer, running through the mountainous wastes of the interior, and so involves a large number of tribes whose relative strengths were subject to alterations which were reflected in the size and extent of their respective *dirah.* Tribal loyalties were also liable to change, and such a change could involve the transfer of an entire *dirah* from one state to another.

In 1871 Sultan Turkī b. Sa'īd gave the Qawāsim a document recognising their rights over the coast from Khūr Kalbā to Shārjah, with the exception of Khaṣab. However, Turkī repudiated the document in 1879 when Shaikh Ḥamad b. 'Abdullah, the headman of Fujairah, sought his help and protection (see Chapter 2, pp.92–3). Colonel Miles, Political Agent in Muscat, and later Acting Political Resident in the Gulf, advised the Sultan after instructions from Ross, not to interfere in the Shimailiyyah district. Turkī did not finally abandon his interest in the district, and in June 1886 the question was reopened when the Governor of Ṣuḥār reported to him that the people of Khūr Fakkān and Dabā were appealing for the protection of Muscat. Turkī consulted Miles, who replied that interference in the Shimailiyyah was inadvisable and that it would probably in the end prove injurious to the interests of the Sultan himself.

The legal right of the Qawāsim to the Shimailiyyah district was unequivocally stated by Britain in 1903, and it was decided by the Government, in accordance with recommendations by the Government of India, that the Shimailiyyah district from Dabā to Khūr Kalbā should be regarded as belonging to the shaikhdom of Shārjah, and not as an independent principality, nor as connected with the Sultanate of 'Omān. Lorimer took immediate point between Khūr Kalbā and Murair as marking the southern limit of the Shimailiyyah district of the Trucial States. However, speaking more precisely in connection with the Bāṭinah Coast, he gave Khaṭmat Milāḥah, a spur of the Ḥijr mountains which comes down almost to the sea, as the boundary with Shimailiyyah. He mentioned that at the time of writing the border was marked by a stone wall running between the end of the spur and the sea, a distance of a quarter of a mile.[16] Bertram Thomas, accompanying Sultan Taimūr b. Faiṣal, visited Khaṭmat Milāḥah in 1930, and confirmed that from there north to Dabā the country was Qasimī in affiliation.[17] Julian Walker took Khaṭmat Milāḥah as the starting point for the Muscat-Qawasim border.

The line from Khaṭmat Milāḥah inland is influenced by the position of the tribes, whose *dirah* are divided between the mountains, the valleys and the coastal plain of al-Bāṭinah. The main geographical feature of the area is the two narrow valleys, Wādī al-Qūr and Wādī Hattā, which pass through the mountains and connect al-Bāṭinah with the inland plains of Gharīf and Mudām.

From the western end of Khaṭmat Milāḥah inland across the mountains Lorimer's definition of the boundary is vague, owing to the paucity of his information about the inland area, which was not a matter of interest to the British. He stated a line which leaves the Gulf between Khūr Kalbā and Murair and, after partially crossing the promontory in such a way as to exclude the Maḥḍah (the capital of Banī Ka'b tribe on the inland side of the mountains) and Jaw districts (the centre of which is Buraimī) to the south, is eventually lost in Khatam. However, from his demarcations between Muscat and Trucial 'Omān in Wādī al-Qūr and Wādī Hattā, and from his analysis

29. Shaikh Zāyed presents awards during the 'Day of Learning'.

30. Shaikh Zāyed visiting the Religious College, Rās al-Khaimah.

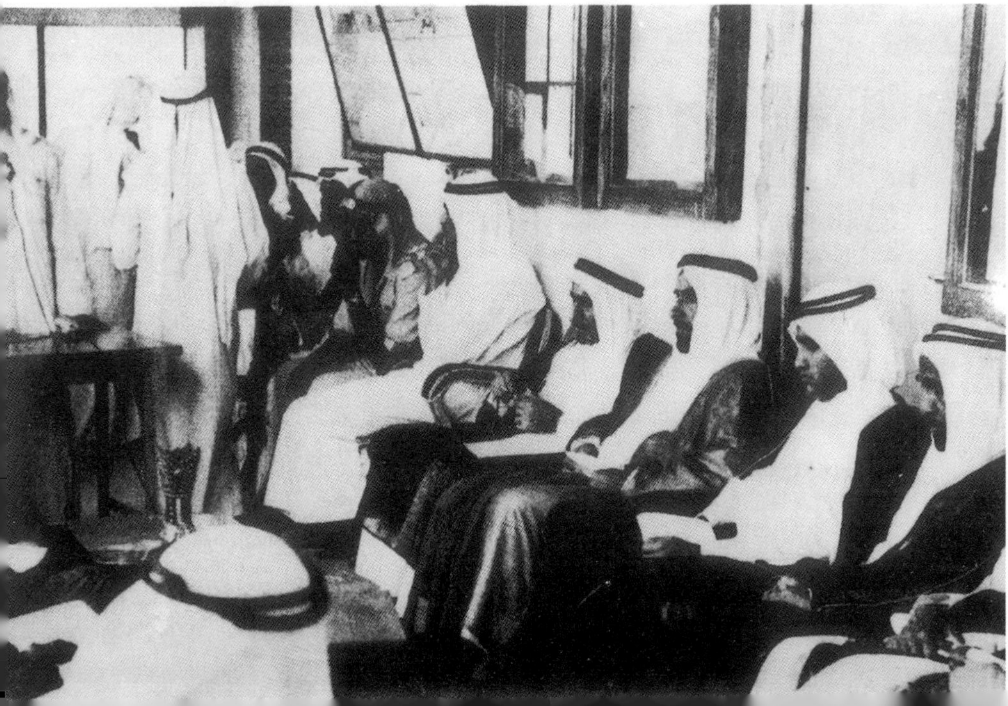

31. The late Saif b. Ghubāsh, Minister of State for Foreign Affairs, one of the pioneers of modern education during the 1960s.

32. The unification of Security For in the Emirates in the last few years marks a significant development of Union.

33. Much attention is given to educating wives in the special schools opened by the Women's Organisation in the UAE headed by Shaikhah Fāṭimah b. Mubārak, Shaikh Zāyed's wife.

34. The first group of girls to join the United Arab Emirates University at Al-'Ain in October 1977.

35. Digging an irrigation canal as part of the agricultural development of the UAE.

of tribal loyalties to the Qawāsim in the area, it is possible partially to reconstruct a line that represents his opinion, which was also the opinion of the Government of India at the time. Since his list of tribes belonging to Trucial 'Omān includes the Sharqiyyīn, the line would run first of all southwards, parallel to the coast, including Waḥalah in Trucial 'Omān. As he regarded the Washāhāt tribe in Aswad as belonging to the Sultanate of Muscat, as well as Dahāminah in the mountain section of Wādī al-Qūr, the line then turns gradually westwards, through the mountains south of Wādī al-Qūr, to enter the catchment area of Wādī Hattā.[18]

Here the line turns first southwest and then west, leaving Ḥirjrain and Maṣfūt villages in Wādī Hattā[19] to Dubai and Ajmān respectively, and afterwards turns northward towards the *dirah* of Banī Ka'b and Banī Qatab. It is at this point that the border becomes involved once again with the Qawāsim and the complex question of the loyalties of the Banī Qatab and the Banī Ka'b.[20] As mentioned above, the British at this time did not involve themselves in the question of the boundary between the Qawāsim and the Sultanate of Muscat from Khaṭmat Milāḥah inland. However, after 1938, when the security of British geological teams engaged in the interior became a matter of interest to them, the British were obliged to settle the disputed question of the allegiance of the Banī Qatab and the Banī Ka'b tribes. In order to reach a decision in this matter the British found it necessary to study the history of the changing loyalties of the two tribes in the period before the Second World War.

By the agreement of April 1906 between Shaikh Zāyed b. Khalīfah and Shaikh Rāshid b. Aḥmad, the Ruler of Umm al-Qaiwain, the Banī Qatab were recognised as being under the protection of Shaikh Rāshid. After the death of Zāyed b. Khalīfah, and particularly after World War I, the Banī Ka'b gave their allegiance to the Sultan of Muscat. Sālim b. Dayyīn, the shaikh of this tribe, accompanied Thomas on his trip in the interior in 1927 and showed his loyalty to the Sultan.[21] Although the Banī Qatab tribe had changed its attachment again, its loyalty to the Trucial Rulers in general was never in doubt, and its *dirah* continued to be a part of Trucial 'Omān. In 1909 the Banī Qatab renewed their understanding with Abū Dhabī, to the concern of Rāshid b. Aḥmad,[22] and this dual association with the rulers of Umm al-Qaiwain and Abū Dhabī continued into the 1920s. In 1927 the Banī Qatab demonstrated their hostility to the legitimate ruler in Shārjah by co-operating in a plot against him by his uncle, Khālid b. Aḥmad, who afterwards established himself as independent ruler of the inland village of Dhaid, ruling there only under the control of the Banī Qatab, who continued to be the effective power in the village even after it was handed back to Shārjah two years later.[23] The 1930s saw a general loss of control by the Shaikh of Shārjah over the Banī Qatab and the question then assumed serious dimensions in connection with oil concessions.

In January 1937 the Banī Qatab tribe refused to countenance a visit to

Jabal Fāyah, south of Dhaid village, by Abdullah Williamson and some geological engineers who were proceeding from Shārjah accompanied by Shaikh Muḥammad b. Ṣaqr, claiming that it was their own land. The team was forced to return.[24] The ruler of Shārjah found it necessary late in 1938, after he had granted an oil concession, to make a settlement with the Banī Qatab, the biggest tribe in his emirate. As the survey team attached great importance to the area of Jabal Fayāh, the Shaikh of Dubai was asked by the British to mediate, and in October 1938 he concluded an alliance with the Shaikh of Umm al-Qaiwain, who still had good relations with the Banī Qatab, to give British geologists access to the area. In the later 1940s the Banī Qatab finally returned to the Shaikh of Shārjah, whose authority over them was restored by an agreement which guaranteed them some revenues.[25]

Accordingly, when Julian Walker came to consider the question, he concluded that the Banī Qatab belonged entirely to Shārjah, and the Banī Ka'b to Muscat, a decision in which he differed from Lorimer.

The Abū Dhabī–Muscat Frontier

The frontier between the Sultanate of Muscat and Abū Dhabī beginning in the north at Wādī Simainī, which lies south of the Mudām plain and west of Jabal Simainī, first runs southwards, makes a semicircle round Buraimī, and continues southwards to end at the wells of 'Umm al-Zamūl.[26] Over 300 kilometres in length, this is the longest of the Trucial States' borders with Muscat. Its most important feature is the Buraimī area, inhabited by the Na'īm, Dhawāhir and Banī Yās tribes.

The Na'īm occupy Buraimī, Ḥamāsā and Sa'rā villages, and their pasture lands lie to the east and northeast of the central oasis. The distribution of the Dhawāhir in the remaining six villages is as follows, listed in order of their size: al-'Ain was inhabited by Najādāt, Kuwaitāt, al-Nawāsir, al-Maṭāwi'ah and Āl-'Arār; Qaṭṭārah and Hīlī by Al-Darāmikah; Mu'tariḍ by Āl-Sūrūr; and al-Jīmī by Āl-Humūdah, Al-Hilāl and Āl-Sūrūr. Some Banī Yās were also living in al-'Ain and on the two estates of al-Jāhilī and Ma'sūdī. The *dirah* of the Dhawāhir forms a broad circle around al-Buraimī, complete except for the sector in the east and northeast which is occupied by the Na'īm. The northern pasture lands of the Najādāt are bounded by the route from al-'Ain to Khatm al-Shiklah, where it enters the mountains towards Wādī al-Jizī. Its eastern and southern lands are bounded by a line that runs southwards from Khatm al-Shiklah, passing Jabal Zarūb, Tawī 'Uwayyir, Jabal Mindassah, Jabal Mathmūmah and then follows Wādī Miraikhāt westwards, including Tawi Mazyad. The *dirah* then turns northwest across Jabal Ḥafīt, passes to the south of Shi'b al-Ghāf, and then runs westwards into al-Khatam, keeping to the south of the wells of Mundafinah, Bu-Samrah, Umm al-Da'ālī and Sannūtah.[27]

The Āl Bū-Shāmis group of the Na'īm, who live in the village of al-Qābil under the southern end of Jabal Ḥafīt, took as their *dirah* an area to the south of the Dhawāhir which extends both east and west from their village, its western extremities penetrating into the southeast corner of al-Khatam. Al-Khatam tract, a rich pasture land east and southeast of Abū Dhabī, and southwest of al-Buraimī, is the meeting ground of the Bedouins of the Manāṣīr, Banī Yās and 'Awāmir tribes, all of them Hināwī and Shāfi'ī.

South of al-Khatam lies Manādir al-Rabbāḍ, which ends at the Umm al-Zamūl wells. This tract is one of the main *dirah* of the 'Awāmir. The Na'īm *dirah* extends south of al-Qābil, including al-Sinīnah, as far as Wādī Samhān, south of which begins the *dirah* of the Bedouins of the Durū tribe, who are Ibādhi and Ghāfirī.[28]

During the Ya'āribah dynasty in the seventeenth century, the Buraimī oasis, then known as Tawām, was an important part of its territory. When the Ya'āribah period ended the split into Hināwī and Ghāfirī factions took place, which affected political life throughout 'Omān. This was felt in the oasis too; the Dhawāhir became Hināwī and the Na'īm became Ghāfirī, and a prolonged rivalry ensued. Although the Dhawāhir were more numerous than the Na'īm, the latter dominated the big forts in the oasis and extended their power beyond their traditional boundaries, north to the Gulf and south towards 'Ibrī. Traces of this period of expansion can be found in the towns they colonised on the coast, in Ḥīrah, 'Ajmān and Ḥumriyyah. The Khawāṭir tribe in the hinterland of Rās al-Khaimah is an isolated branch of this big tribe. At the beginning of the nineteenth century, the Na'īm lost their position on the coast of 'Omān and were succeeded by the Qawāsim. When the Sa'ūdīs occupied Buraimī in 1800 the Na'īm strengthened their position by becoming devout Wahhābīs.

The fall of the first Sa'ūdī state in 1818 had far-reaching political consequences in the oasis. The Sultan of Muscat, Sa'īd b. Sulṭān, extended his authority over the area, but for various reasons Āl Bū-Sa'īd's sovereignty soon became merely nominal, leaving the Na'īm semi-independent. The intermittent occupation of Buraimī by the Sa'ūdīs and the continual rebellions in Ṣuḥār, which was the administrative base of the Sultan, were main causes of this situation. Faced with the dominance of the Na'īm, and the ineffectiveness of the Sultan's government, the Dhawāhir resorted to Abū Dhabī for their protection, where the Banī Yās began after 1818 to emerge as a strong Hināwī power. The successive shaikhs of Abū Dhabī made themselves the rulers of the Dhawāhir's villages and at the same time attracted the loyalty of the Banī Yās into the Buraimī area and Manādir al-Rabbād.

In 1871 Sultan Turkī, whom the Na'īm had helped to seize power in Muscat, made their shaikh his representative in the oasis and presented him with the village of Maṣfūt in Wādī Hattā, and though the privileged status of the Na'īm was thus recognised, this action worked in effect to re-establish Muscat's sovereignty over them. In 1875, when Colonel Miles visited the oasis, he found that the Na'īm owed allegiance to the Sultan and were involved in a feud with the Bāni Yās. However, after 1888 Sultan Faiṣal b.

Turkī entrusted the administration of his territory in al-Dhāhirah area to Shaikh Zāyed, a decision which consolidated Zāyed's authority over Abū Dhabī's section of the interior, and placed the Na'īm within Zāyed's sphere of influence. Moreover, Zāyed attempted to resolve the hostility between the Na'īm and the Banī Yās by his own marriage to the daughter of one of the Na'īm shaikhs. Zāyed's loyal and able governor in the area, Aḥmad b. Muḥammad b. Hilāl, who represented him, his sons and his grandson from 1897 to 1936, further strengthened his master's influence there by his marriage with the Āl Bū-Shāmis, the other branch of the Na'īm. In the agreement of 1906 between Shaikh Zāyed and Shaikh Rāshid b. Aḥmad of Umm al-Qaiwain, Zāyed was recognised as governing the Na'īm of Buraimī and their other groups to the south.[29]

Lorimer, in his description of the boundaries of Abū Dhabī says: 'Inland the frontiers of Abū Dhabī are not defined: it is asserted that on the east they reach to the Buraimī oasis but without taking it in; and on the south they may presumably be placed at the margin of the Rub-al-Khali'. Explaining the political position of the Buraimī oasis he says that

> the influence of the Shaikh of Abu Dhabi in the district is strong and increasing. The ruins of the fort of Maraijib bear witness to the hereditary connection of his family with Buraimi, and he has recently acquired an estate at al-Jahili, while Masudi is being formed into a village by his eldest son. Moreover, a regular tribute is paid him by the Dhawahir, who are numerically a majority in the oasis. At the present time the Shaikh could probably seize Buraimi if he wished to do so, but his policy appears to be one of pacific penetration.

The Buraimī oasis itself Lorimer describes as 'a tract situated between the 'Omān Sultanate and the Trucial 'Omān, which may be described as independent 'Omān'.[30] When Lorimer says that the boundary of Abū Dhabī reached to Buraimī but without taking it in, this can be taken to mean that Abū Dhabī's territory includes only that part of the oasis which is inhabited by the Dhawāhir. 'Independent 'Omān' must therefore be the Na'īm area of the oasis.

On Shaikh Zāyed's death in 1909, Sultan Faiṣal b. Turkī appointed Shaikh Sulṭān b. Muḥammad, the head of the Na'īm, as his representative in Buraimī. In the following year the arrangement by which Zāyed had administered the Sultan's possessions in al-Dhāhirah was slightly modified. It was agreed that the previous allowance should be paid jointly to Shaikh Taḥnūn b. Zāyed and Shaikh Sulṭān b. Muḥammad al-Na'īmī, who now shared responsibility for maintaining law and order on behalf of the Sultan. In 1913, when the Imamate was proclaimed in Nazwā, Sultan Taimūr b. Faiṣal summoned Shaikh Sulṭān b. Muḥammad to Muscat and was able, by cultivating good relations with the Na'īm to stop the movement from spreading northward into the Dhāhirah and Buraimī.[31]

Between the two World Wars the balance of tribal power in the interior was transformed. Shaikh Zāyed b. Khalīfah had died in 1909, and in 1922 the death of Shaikh Rāshid b. Aḥmad of Umm al-Qaiwain, the other signatory to the tribal settlement of 1906, signalled the end of his town's pretensions to internal power. By now the Na'īm found themselves without the protection of Abū Dhabī, and the Banī Ka'b no longer claimed the protection of Umm al-Qaiwain, so the two tribes formed an alliance.

Confronted by the local independence of the Imām in the interior, and by the general decline of Āl Bū-Sa'īd's authority, the British decided to interfere in the internal affairs of the Sultanate; to modernise the administration, to give aid and to make security effective throughout the territory, in order to prepare the country for the discovery and exploitation of its oil. Two British experts were contracted out to Muscat, Eccles, a Captain in the Indian army, who in 1925–6 became the commander of the new levies, and Bertram Thomas, who was the Minister and financial adviser from 1925 to 1930. In 1925 the Sultan signed an agreement with the D'Arcy Exploration Company, and in the same year Eccles accompanied a survey team on their visit to Wādī al-Jizī and the interior. This was the first time for many years that an official representative of the Sultan had appeared in these areas, and this constituted the first assault on the semi-autonomy of the Sultanate's remote possessions in the interior.[32]

At this time Buraimī was the focal point for the activities of three conflicting groups, the Sultan's government, the Imām in Nazwā, and the Sa'ūdī agents. This confused situation worked to the advantage of the Na'īm who exploited the rivalries of the three powers to preserve their own local independence. However, the weakening of central control made Buraimī an easy target for Sa'ūdī activities. In 1925, in response to the emerging power of Ibn Sa'ūd in Arabia, and in particular to the activities of his agents and *zakat* collectors in Buraimī, the Imām sent an expedition to assert his authority over the oasis; however, the expedition for some reason turned back at Ḍank. Alarmed by this threat to his tribe's independence, the shaikh of the Na'īm turned to the Sa'ūdīs for manpower and arms. The Na'īm showed themselves to be equally unwilling to give up their independence to the Sultan of Muscat. When Eccles was invited to Maḥḍah and met Shaikh Sālim b. Dayyīn, the paramount shaikh of the Banī Ka'b, he found him unhappy about the correspondence which his allies, the Na'īm, were conducting with the Sa'ūdīs. Sālim said that he ought to have been consulted before so important a step was taken. This informal conversation, and the hospitality which Eccles received in Maḥḍah, were signs of a shift of allegiance by the Banī Ka'b towards the Sultan of Muscat.[33]

Although Bertram Thomas served five years in the role of financial adviser to the Sultan of Muscat, his main achievements lay outside the political sphere. It is noteworthy for our study that Thomas's intended journey to Buraimī in the interior in 1927 was under the auspices of the Banī Ka'b, whom he considered to be loyal to the Sultan. He began this trip at Ṣuḥār, where he was taken by a British naval vessel, and was to proceed through Wādī al-Jizī to Buraimī.

However, at the western end of the wādī he was stopped by members of the Na'īm who gave him a letter from their shaikhs, informing him that Buraimī belonged to themselves and to the Ibn Sa'ūd, and that he should have obtained prior permission from these authorities. At this time the position of Shaikh of Buraimī was held jointly by the brothers Muḥammad and Ṣaqr b. Sulṭān, whose father had recently died and who were much under the influence of his slave, bin Sindah. It was bin Sindah who had instigated this policy of non-co-operation in response to the presence of Sa'ūdī tax collectors in the area. When Ṣaqr became the principal shaikh of the Na'īm a year later, he re-established cordial relations with Muscat.[34]

Sa'īd bin Taimūr, who succeeded his father as Sultan in 1932, was energetically concerned with the matter of his authority over the Na'īm and the Banī Ka'b. This was exemplified by an incident in 1936, when a representative of the Shaikh of Abū Dhabī accompanied a geology party from Petroleum Concessions Ltd, which had included the southern part of the Jabal Ḥafīt area in their tour. The Sultan complained that this party had penetrated into his territory. In 1937 the Sultan granted an oil concession in his territory to the same company, and his efforts to centralise the Sultanate increased. In 1938 Shaikh Ṣaqr b. Sulṭān, the paramount Shaikh of the Na'īm, visited Muscat, and arrangements were made for the despatch of an exploration party to Buraimī. In 1945 the Sultan's brother, Ṭāriq, toured the Dhāhirah, visiting the oasis.[35]

While the Sultan of Muscat was thus building up his administrative control over the Banī Ka'b and the Na'īm, the Shaikhs of Abū Dhabī were consolidating their authority over the Dhawāhir, the Manāṣīr and the 'Awāmir in the eastern region of their emirate. Shaikh Zāyed b. Sulṭān, who represented his brother Shaikh Shakhbūṭ in the eastern region in the post-war period, commanded considerable respect among his tribes, and this contributed greatly to Abū Dhabī's authority in its traditional lands. He lived in his fort in the new village of Muwag'ī and established a new fort and a modern market in the village of al-'Ain. Wilfred Thesiger, the British traveller who crossed the Empty Quarter in 1948, described him at a meeting in the oasis:

> He was a powerfully built man of about thirty with a brown beard. He had a strong, intelligent face, with steady, observant eyes, and his manner was quiet but masterful . . . I had been looking forward to meeting him, for he had a great reputation among the Bedu. They liked him for his easy, informal ways, and his friendliness, and they respected his force of character, his shrewdness, and his physical strength. 'He knows about camels, can ride like one of us, can shoot, and knows how to fight.'[36]

In the 1950s, and particularly after the Buraimī dispute of 1955, the oil companies were active, both in Muscat and Abū Dhabī on a scale which made increasingly pressing the need for definitive boundaries between the neighbouring states. In May 1959 a frontier agreement was signed by Sultan Sa'īd b. Taimūr and Shaikh Shakhbūṭ b. Sulṭān, which settled the boundary between the two countries. The preamble states categorically that the Na'īm, Āl Bū-Shāmis and Banī Ka'b tribes belong entirely to the Sultanate of Muscat, and mentions that the boundary agreed on is based on the maps of Julian Walker. The most fundamental difference between these maps and Lorimer's description fifty years earlier is the change in the allegiance of the Banī Ka'b, described and explained above. In this agreement, north of Buraimī the line begins west of Jabal Simainī and runs south, dividing the *dirah* of the Banī Ka'b from those of the Banī Qatab and the Dhawāhir. It passes between the two wells of Jifār, so that the eastern well is the property of the Banī Ka'b and the western well the property of the Dhawāhir. In the Buraimī area, according to the agreement, the line divides the *dirah* of the Dhawāhir, which is on the Abū Dhabī side, from those of the Na'īm and Āl Bū-Shamis which fall in Muscat. South of Buraimī the border extends far enough west to include the southeast corner of al-Khatam as part of the *dirah* of Āl Bū-Shāmis. Then it turns south, dividing the *dirah* of the 'Awāmir, first from Āl Bū-Shāmis and further south, in Manādir al-Rabbaḍ, from the Durū'.[37]

III The Inter-State Boundaries

Movements towards Independence within the Qawāsim Emirate

During the period of our study (1892–1971), with the decline of the Qawāsim Emirate many of her towns became the centres of movements towards independence, particularly Rās al-Khaimah, Fujairah, Ḥamriyyah and Kalbā. Independence is a major issue in understanding the changing boundaries of the Trucial Coast. Although the majority of the towns in the Qawāsim Emirate enjoyed intermittent *de facto* independence, the British before World War II recognised only Rās al-Khaimah and Kalbā as independent states. The British were, however, to recognise the independence of Fujairah in 1952.[38] Besides analysing these movements, the intention here is to explain British policy and outline the factors that influenced Britain to recognise the independence of Rās al-Khaimah in 1921, Kalbā in 1936 and Fujairah in 1952.

In Julian Walker's map the Sharquiyyīn are shown as centred upon two separate areas, divided from one another by a strip stretching westwards into the interior from Lūliyyah, Zubārah and Khūr Fakkān on the coast. Fujairah is the capital of the Sharquiyyīn tribe and they occupy all the coastal ports of the Shimailiyyah district except for Zubārah, Lūliyyah and Khūr Fakkān in the north and Kalbā and Ṣūr in the south. The most important geographical feature affecting the history of the Sharqiyyīn tribe was their dominance of the main pass through the al-Ḥijr mountains to the Shimailiyyah district, Wādī Ḥām, the entrance to which, at Sījī, they controlled as well as the exit at al-Bithnah. Furthermore, their village of Waḥalah in the south controls the road from Wādī al-Qūr to Kalbā, the main centre of the Qawāsim in this area. The Sharqiyyīn, being Hināwī in political matters, different from the Qawāsim, were inclined towards revolt at the decline of the emirate.

Shaikh Ḥamad b. ʻAbdullah (1870–1930), who led the successive revolts of the Sharqiyyīn tribe from 1870 until the turn of the century, was the founder of the Fujairah independence movements. After the Government of India's decision in 1903 that Fujairah belonged to the Shaikh of Shārjah a long period of peace ensued during which Shaikh Ḥamad b. ʻAbdullah strengthened his ties with his allies. In 1914 he visited Umm al-Qaiwain, which the British resented as a sign that Ḥamad was, in establishing a firm ally, preparing himself for future conflict with the Qawāsim. With the same consideration in mind he gave Manāmah village, a family possession, to the Shaikh of ʻAjmān as a present. He also established a bond with the Qawāsim branch of Kalbā and Rās al-Khaimah when he married the daughter of Shaikh Saʻīd b. Ḥamad, and also the sister of Shaikh Sālim b. Sulṭān. It soon became clear that the balance of power between the Qawāsim, on the offensive in the past, and the Sharquiyyīn, who had been obliged to look to Muscat, Dubai or Abū Dhabī for succour, had moved in favour of the Sharquiyyīn.[39]

In 1925, after two decades of undisturbed calm between the Shaikh of Fujairah and the Shaikh of Shārjah, a minor incident became a political crisis. The Political Resident, Lieutenant-Colonel Prideaux, received a complaint at the beginning of the year, through the Political Agent at Muscat, from a Balūchī woman residing in the Sultan's dominions that her daughter had been kidnapped, taken to Fujairah and sold to Shaikh Ḥamad. As the British Government recognised Shaikh Ḥamad as feudatory of the Shaikh of Shārjah, he was asked through the latter to restore the girl to her parents. The British attitude aggravated Shaikh Ḥamad's pretensions to independence, and he failed to give a satisfactory explanation. The Political Resident, in the course of his tour of the coast, visited Kalbā on 17 April 1925, where he informed Shaikh Ḥamad that he expected to meet him the following day on board ship off the coast of Fujairah to discuss the matter. Prideaux proceeded to Fujairah on board HMS *Lawrence*, but after two days of unsuccessful negotiations the Shaikh insisted that they meet on shore, though he expressed his willingness to pay a fine for the girl.[40]

In his letter to the SNO the Political Resident said that the British had been willing to allow Shaikh Ḥamad to continue quietly with his insubordination to the Shaikh of Fujairah so long as British interests had been unaffected, but this disrespectful reception, together with the Shaikh's claim that 'customs and regulations imposed by long usage of the Trucial chiefs and their subordinate officials' did not apply to him brought the Resident to the view that to give way to Shaikh Ḥamad over the matter of his visit on board was to undermine very materially the Resident's authority over the inhabitants of the Trucial Coast. He was convinced that the British Government could not condone Shaikh Ḥamad's claims, which would remove from the Resident's control a district containing eight villages on the Shimaliyyah coast, so Prideaux asked for prompt naval intervention and the Naval Commander-in-Chief gave permission to bombard the fort of Fujairah and seize and destroy Shaikh Ḥamad's property. Shaikh Ḥamad, expecting British antagonism to his claim of independence, had had the thick-walled fort built on a hill away from the shallow coast where British fire could not seriously damage it. On the morning of 20 April 1925 the fort was bombarded for an hour and a half and the seaward faces of the three towers were knocked down. Shaikh Ḥamad paid the fine of Rs. 1,500 imposed on him.[41]

The Shaikh of Fujairah suspected that the Shaikh of Kalbā was responsible for bringing the wrath of the British Government upon his town, and this rekindled old feuds and created an atmosphere of mutual distrust. At the beginning of 1926 the situation between Kalbā and Fujairah became tense, particularly when the Shaikh of Kalbā built a wall around a garden on the road to Fujairah. As the Shaikh Ḥamad insisted that Kalbā had no *haram* territory, and was without rights to adjacent territory, hostilities broke out in March 1926. Soon Khūr Fakkān and Dabā al-Ḥiṣn were attacked and Kalbā besieged. As Kalbā was the weaker, Shaikh Sa'īd b. Ḥamad secretly solicited the intervention of Sayyid Ḥamad b. Faiṣal, the Wālī of Ṣuḥār and brother of the Sultan of Muscat. Sayyid Ḥamad despatched a deputy to the scene and arranged a forty-five-day truce. On 22 May Sultan Taimūr b. Faiṣal visited Kalbā and on 23 May Fujairah, and a written agreement was concluded between the two shaikhs, but in September hostilities were renewed and Shaikh Sa'īd was obliged to flee to Shārjah to ask for help.

The Political Resident, completely exasperated with the situation, devised a radical plan. He asked the Political Agent in Muscat to discuss with Bertram Thomas the advisability of presenting this proposition to the Sultan and his council. As the Shaikh of Fujairah was friendly with the Shiḥūḥ tribes, who were subjects of Muscat, Kalbā should be given to the Shiḥūḥ of the west coast of Rūs al-Jibāl and that their territories at Rams, Tibāt and perhaps Bukhā should be added to Rās al-Khaimah. There was little response and the idea was considered impractical.

In January 1927 hostilities once again reopened. The Shaikhs of Shārjah and Rās al-Khaimah were again asked for permission to send reinforcements to Kalbā by sea, but the British refused. The British authorities were not only annoyed with the feud between Kalbā and Fujairah but viewed it as an internal matter, involving no British interests; they therefore preferred not to intervene. Finally, ten months later, on 10 November 1927, HMS *Triad* arrived at Kalbā; the captain found both parties suffering from exhaustion.

On 12 November another new settlement was reached in which both parties accepted the arbitration of the Residency Agent in the event of future disputes, but when the SNO visited Kalbā in July 1928 he found the Shaikh complaining of the continual aggression of Fujairah; he also discovered that the Sharqiyyīn tribe's power had developed to the point that it threatened the Qawāsim in the area. He came away with the impression that the Shaikh of Kalbā was a poor man with little property, who could not afford to finance a war against Fujairah; consequently he relied upon the British Government to defend him against his powerful neighbour. On the other hand, it was well known on that part of the coast that Shaikh Ḥamad b. 'Abdullah was more powerful and more wealthy, that he recognised no overlord, regarding the British with contempt. The SNO strongly recommended that when a suitable opportunity arose this shaikh should be dealt with in a really effective manner.[42]

During the 1930s the Sharqiyyīn tribe, who now completely dominated the mountains, increased their power to the extent that they were able to take the offensive against the territories of Rās al-Khaimah and Shārjah. Between 1930 and 1932 continual raids between the Sharqiyyīn and the Banī Qatab tribe, the Bedouin power of Shārjah, were recorded. Furthermore, between 1932 and 1935 the Sharqiyyīn moved against the Khawāṭir tribe in Rās al-Khaimah territory and occupied Ḥabḥab village, less than twenty miles from Rās al-Khaimah itself, taking it as a base for further attacks.[43] When the British in 1936 recognised the independence of Kalbā they gave it protection, giving rise to Sharqiyyīn's hope for similar treatment. In 1951 the young Shaikh of Kalbā died and the British, finally accepting the reality of the Fujairah position, acknowledged its independence; to equalise the situation they found it prudent to recognise Kalbā as a part of the Shaikh of Shārjah's dominion.

British Recognition of the Independence of Rās al-Khaimah

Between the two World Wars two independent emirates emerged, Rās al-Khaimah in 1921 and Kalbā in 1937, and both were recognised by the British authorities. Britain's recognition of these two states not only explains the *de facto* acceptance of dismemberment within the Qawāsim Emirate but also exhibits some aspects of British strategy and British policy in internal affairs.

In 1869 Shaikh Ḥumaid b. 'Abdullah governed Rās al-Khaimah and enjoyed independence until he died in 1900, but the British withheld official recognition, although the conclusion of the treaty of 1892 with Shaikh Ḥumaid implied it. In 1900 the Government of Rās al-Khaimah was re-incorporated in the Emirate of Shārjah, and Shaikh Ṣaqr b. Khālid sent his son Khālid to rule as his deputy. In March 1908 Khālid died, and the Ruler of Shārjah deputed his old uncle and adviser, Sālim b. Sulṭān, to replace the deceased son. Since the British remembered Sālim as one of the principal figures in the Abū Mūsā 'drama' in connection with the Wonkhaus Company, they viewed his appointment as unwise. As the British expected, Shaikh Sālim, supported by the elders of the Qawāsim family, soon made pretensions which his nephew, the Ruler of Shārjah, strongly resented, expressing his firm intention of ousting him. The Residency Agent, aware of the sensitive situation, accordingly did not provide Sālim with British treaties, the usual procedure at the accession of a ruler, and asked for permission to do so, but Cox found it inexpedient to accord British official recognition because it seemed to him that the Germans might make use of the Shaikh's independence and advance claims to share in the income of Abū Mūsā and Ṭanb islands, which the Shaikh had previously been unable to put forward when in 1905 he was adviser and henchman to the Shaikh of Shārjah. However, Shaikh Sālim b. Sulṭān, aged eighty, was able to gain the sympathy of the elders of the Qawāsim family, who frequently showed resentment to Shaikh Ṣaqr b. Khālid for his failure to suppress the revolts of Fujairah and the fact that he had recently deprived them of their allowances.

As Sālim b. Sulṭān unexpectedly consolidated his hold on Rās al-Khaimah, the issue of British recognition of his independence was renewed in 1912. In his answer to the Government of India on 4 August 1912 Cox found it convenient for the purpose of the Abū Mūsā dispute to let things remain as they were and to withhold specific official recognition of Sālim's independence. He added that in the meantime the Shaikh was acting in accordance with the spirit of treaty engagements, so that no local inconvenience might arise from his non-recognition.

In October 1914 the Residency Agent repeated in a letter that in view of the prohibition on the trade in arms and slaves it was desirable to give Shaikh Sālim copies of the treaties. On 12 May 1915 Colonel Trevor, the Acting Political Resident, found that it would be advisable during the war, and particularly since the circumstances had changed that had prevented Cox from agreeing to Shaikh Sālim's recognition as an independent Shaikh. He wrote to Cox explaining that Shaikh Ṣaqr b. Khālid had died and that the Shaikh of Shārjah, Khālid b. Aḥmad, was more or less subservient to Shaikh Sālim, who became the dominant figure in the Qawāsim family. He wrote further that because of the war the Abū Mūsā case had lost a good deal of its importance. Bearing these circumstances in mind Trevor asked Cox for his opinion, and Cox recommended that copies of the treaties be sent to the Residency Agent without giving recognition of independence, preferring to hold this issue in suspense until the end of the war, when they would know definitely that the Abū Mūsā case was finished.

In December 1917 Shaikh Sālim had suffered a paralytic stroke and his eldest son Muḥammad took charge of the government. In July 1919, shortly before his father's death in August, Muḥammad abdicated in favour of his younger brother Sulṭān, who ruled for nearly thirty years from 1919 to 1948.

In December 1920, during the second visit to Rās al-Khaimah, Colonel Trevor found Sulṭān b. Sālim in a strong position, acting in the spirit of his treaties with the British and ready to accept all undertakings entered into by his predecessors. In these circumstances, particularly in the post-war period, Trevor felt that British recognition should not be withheld from the new Shaikh, who had proved co-operative in the matter of British interests. His recommendation to the Government of India that Shaikh Sulṭān b. Sālim be recognised as independent ruler of Rās al-Khaimah, which meant official separation from the Emirate of Shārjah, was accepted. On 27 June 1921 he asked 'Īsā to inform Sulṭān of the government's recognition, subject to the proviso that he confirm his formal assurance to abide by the treaties which existed between the government and his predecessors. On 10 July 'Īsa visited Sulṭān and obtained a signed statement to this effect.[44] The new Emirate of Rās al-Khaimah emerged, gaining British recognition; thus Shaikh Sālim succeeded, even after his death, in establishing his branch of the Qawāsim family in authority over the new independent state.

The Independence of Kalbā

The independence which Kalbā achieved in 1936 and maintained until 1951 was not the product of a successful revolt against the Shaikh of Shārjah. It was merely the outcome of the British need during the 1930s for air facilities in that area, which the Shaikh of Shārjah could not guarantee.

Kalbā had been governed semi-independently by the branch of Mājid b. Sulṭān of the Qawāsim family since 1871, but the Shaikh of Shārjah retained nominal authority, particularly when the Government of India decided in 1903 that the Shimailiyyah district belonged to the Shaikh of Shārjah. The administrative area of Kalbā includes the port of Khūr Fakkān, inhabited by the Naqbiyyīn tribe, and Kalbā, inhabited mainly by the Za'āb tribe. Shaikh Sa'īd b. Ḥamad ruled over Kalbā between 1903 and 1937 and during the 1930s enjoyed *de facto* independence because of his age and his status among the elders of the Qawāsim family.[45] Thus, Sulṭān b. Ṣaqr, the Shaikh of Shārjah, who was young by comparison, had no real authority over Sa'īd b. Ḥamad. Between the two World Wars Kalbā suffered greatly from the attacks of the Sharqiyyīn tribe, under the nominal sovereignty of the Qasimī ruler of Shārjah, who extended their semi-independence in the Shimailiyyah district and the mountains of al-Ḥijr.

The background to the establishment of the independence of Kalbā began in 1932. Early in May that year an agreement was concluded between the British and the Shaikh Sulṭān b. Ṣaqr to construct an airport at Shārjah. The Air Ministry, after insistent demands from the Air Force in Iraq, asked for an emergency landing ground at Kalbā. An Air Force officer, Captain Alban, lost no time in visiting the Shaikh of Kalbā in August 1932, accompanied by the Political Agent in Muscat. Loch and Fowle later complained bitterly about Alban's 'hustling tactics' and of the fact that he received a complete rebuff from the Shaikh. Furthermore, Fowle pointed out the possible long-term implications of this failure, which made further negotiations more difficult and gave the Shaikh a precedent, 'in that he had been able to turn down a British officer'.[46] In October 1932 Shaikh Muḥammad b. Ṣaqr, brother of the Shaikh of Shārjah, was taken by a British sloop to Kalbā to open negotiations with Sa'īd b. Ḥamad and the very fact that he arrived in a British warship further aroused the suspicion of Sa'īd and reinforced his reluctance to consider the proposals.[47] After some correspondence between the Government of India and the Air Ministry it was agreed in December 1932 to entrust the negotiations for a landing ground entirely to the Political Resident in the Gulf.[48]

Four years passed, during which Fowle addressed various letters to the Shaikh of Shārjah, requesting him to arrange air facilities at Kalbā. At the beginning of 1936 the Air Ministry urgently repeated its demands. On 21 March a meeting took place between Fowle and Sulṭān b. Ṣaqr at which the Shaikh explained that his relative the Shaikh of Kalbā had definitely refused, adding that Sa'īd b. Ḥamad was anxious about possible aggression by the Shaikh of Fujairah, with whom he had always been on bad terms, and the safety of the aerodome, for which the British might hold him responsible. Sulṭān b. Ṣaqr explained that, although Kalbā was a part of his Emirate, his respect of Sa'īd of Kalbā prevented him enforcing the project; moreover, he had not the arms or the men to enforce the British demands in Kalbā, which lay beyond the mountains. In addition, Wādī al-Qūr, the sole pass to Kalbā, was under the sovereignty of Rās al-Khaimah. Fowle understood that the Ruler of Shārjah was unable to persuade the Shaikh of Kalbā to listen to what should have been his orders, but was in practice his advice. When Fowle suggested that the British could send him by sloop to aid his negotiations with the Shaikh of Kalbā, no satisfactory answer was given.[49]

Fowle then decided that any endeavour to approach Kalbā through Shārjah was futile and that the British would have to deal direct with the Shaikh of Kalbā from then on. Aḥmad b. Ḥasan, the head of Rams in the Emirate of Rās al-Khaimah and a close relative of Shaikh Sa'īd b. Ḥamad, was the man chosen by the British to begin secret overtures. Aḥmad achieved his mission quickly and successfully when he persuaded the Shaikh to deal directly with the British authorities. Captain T. Hickinbotham, the Political Agent in Baḥrain, after a favourable reply from the Shaikh of Kalbā, visited him and opened negotiations. When the Foreign Office received notice of these negotiations they expressed doubts regarding the possible infringements of Paragraph 2 of Lieutenant-Colonel Dickson's letter to the Shaikh of Shārjah of 22 July 1932, which bound the British to defend the Shaikh's rights over his territories and dependants in return for his granting facilities in Shārjah. Accordingly, on 19 June 1936 the Secretary of State for India telegraphed Fowle for his views on the situation and on 22 June Fowle replied that he considered, as a general principle, that the Shaikh, who had ceased to exercise control or accept responsibility for an area under the *de facto* rule of another Shaikh, had forfeited any claims that he might once have had to the area in question.[50]

On 8 December the British accepted, for the strategic reasons explained by Fowle, the absolute independence of Kalbā; consequently Shaikh Sa'īd b. Ḥamad entered into an understanding with HM Government identical to those of the other Trucial States. Sa'īd was recognised by Britain as ruler of Kalbā and was granted a personal salute of three guns. For administrative purposes his emirate was included in the jurisdiction of the Political Agent in Baḥrain. On 30 April 1937 Sa'īd b. Ḥamad died, and as his son Ḥamad was a minor, the three heads of the Qawāsim branches in Dabā, Rās al-Khaimah and Shārjah showed a tendency to interfere in the government of Kalbā. The elders of the Naqbiyyīn and Za'āb tribes of Kalbā appointed the young Ḥamad as their Shaikh, and Bārūt, a trusted and responsible slave, as his guardian, notifying the British of their decision.

The Shaikh of Shārjah, who was not officially informed by the British of the independence of Kalbā, received a warning from the Political Agent on 4 May 1937 not to interfere in the question of the successor to Shaikh Sa'īd, who must be chosen, they insisted, by the people of Kalbā themselves. On 8 May Sulṭān b. Ṣaqr, in answer to this warning, claimed that Kalbā was an integral part of his domain and that he could not tolerate Khālid b. Aḥmad's interference in its affairs.

After Sulṭān b. Sālim's dramatic interference in the affairs of Kalbā in June 1937 Fowle was convinced that Bārūt, as a slave, was not a suitable regent to Ḥamad. He agreed with Loch in August that the most satisfactory solution of the problem might be for Khālid b. Aḥmad, ex-ruler of Shārjah, now resident at Dhaid, to establish himself as regent. On 24 August 1937, whilst 'Abd al-Razzāq was instructed by the Political Agent to remind the Shaikh of Shārjah of his treaty with Britain of 1820, Paragraphs 2 and 7, and to inform him that any interference in Kalbā would not be tolerated, 'Abd al-Razzāq encouraged Khālid to proceed to Fujairah, from whence he opened negotiations with the inhabitants of Kalbā and Khūr Fakkān.

On 2 September Sulṭān b. Ṣaqr sent a bitter reply to 'Abd al-Razzāq, mentioning the letter he had received from Colonel Dickson on 22 July 1932, and the Political Agent's letter of 22 December 1935, which assured him that the British Government undertook to recognise his rights over his dominions and not to interfere in his internal affairs. As to Paragraphs 2 and 7 of the treaty of 1820, the Shaikh of Shārjah claimed that they had no relevance to the present dispute. As the British expected, Sulṭān b. Ṣaqr, a man perhaps with stronger literary than military inclinations, was satisfied with the mere fact of having sent the letter. After a visit to Kalbā by 'Abd al-Razzāq on 13 September 1937 the elders of Khūr Fakkān and the regent Bārūt invited Khālid b. Aḥmad to Kalbā, and he was accepted by them as the new regent.

At the end of October, after Khālid gave pledges to respect their treaties and agreements, he was officially recognised by the British.[51]

During the reign of Khālid b. Aḥmad as regent in Kalbā he extended his authority over Dabā after the death of her ruler, his brother Rāshid b. Aḥmad, in December 1937. It was reported that in April 1938, in addition to his influence over Dhaid, he encroached on the authority of Rās al-Khaimah, taking the pass of Wādī al-Qūr on al-Ḥijr mountain.[52] This however, was an ephemeral state, for after the death of Khālid b. Aḥmad in the later 1940s, and of the young Shaikh, Ḥamad b. Sa'īd in 1951, the British, influenced by post-war changes, came once again to recognise Kalbā as part of the Shārjah Emirate.[53]

Notes

1. IOR, L/P & S/12/3767, Baḥrain News and Intelligence Report, October 1935, January 1937, October 1938.
2. IOR, L/P & S/18/B 467, Petroleum Concession Limited.
3. IOR, R/15/1/675, Petroleum Concessions 1936–37, Residency Agent to Pol. Agent, 15 January 1937.
4. IOR, R/15/1/14/38, Shārjah Residency, Shaikh Rāshid b. Ḥumaid to Residency Agent, 13 January 1937.
5. IOR, R/15/1/674, Pol. Res. to Pol. Agent, 18 November 1936.
6. IOR, L/P & S/12/3767, Report of 16–30 June 1938 and Report of 1–15 December 1936 and 1–15 October 1937.
7. IOR, ibid., Report of 1–15 November 1937.
8. IOR, R/15/3/425, Muscat Frontiers, Hickinbotham to Fowle, 12 August 1938.
9. IOR, Map of the Trucial States, boundaries by Col. Galloway.
10. IOR, L/P & S/12/3967, survey of Trucial States, Telegram from Political Resident to Political Agent, Muscat 21 August 1945.
11. Lorimer, II B, op,cit., pp.1605–14.
12. Lorimer, I Part I A, op.cit., p.622; Kelly, *Britain*, pp. 141, 157.
13. Lorimer, I Part I A, ibid., pp.622–6, 635, 762.
14. IOR, L/P & S/10/23, British Flagstaffs, IO to Governor General of India, 19 May 1905; Cox to SGI, 29 January 1905; Lorimer, I Part I A, op.cit., p.627.
15. Lorimer, II B, op.cit., p.1806.
16. Lorimer, II A, op.cit., p.283.
17. Thomas, op.cit., p.198.
18. Lorimer, II A & B, op.cit., pp.931, 963, 1386, 1428.
19. In the earlier part of the nineteenth century the middle of Wādī Hattā, inhabited by the Bidaiwāt—whose main villages were Ḥijrain and Maṣfūt—belonged to the Sultan of Muscat. Although the two villages were inhabited by members of the same tribe, a feud was in progress between them. In recognition of the help given him in 1871 by the Shaikhs of Dubai and Buraimī, Sultan Turkī gave Ḥijrain to Shaikh Ḥashr b. Maktūm and Maṣfūt to the Shaikh of Buraimī. During the 1930s, a time of disorder throughout the Trucial States, when Bedouin tribes were raiding settled places near their areas, the inhabitants of Maṣfūt appealed to the Shaikh Sa'īd b. Maktūm of Dubai for protection and Shaikh Sa'īd advised them to ask Shaikh Rāshid b. Ḥumaid of 'Ajmān instead, since he was related to the Shaikh of Buraimī. They did this, and after discussing the question with the elders of Āl Bū-Khirībān of 'Ajmān, who belonged to the same branch of the N'aīm as those in Buraimī, it was decided that Shaikh Rāshid had to defend them. Shaikh Rāshid went there himself and took over the area.
20. IOR, R/15/1/14/35, Wādī Hattā village, Residency Agent to Pol. Res., 31 August 1914.
21. Thomas, op.cit., pp.178, 181.

22. IOR, R/15/1/14/28, Khālid b. Aḥmad to Pol. Res., 7 May 1914 and Res. Agent to Pol. Res., 28 June 1909; IOR, R/15/1/14/12, Res. Agent to Cox, 28 June 1909.
23. IOR, R/15/1/14/37, Arab Coast, Res. Agent to Pol. Res., 30 June 1927.
24. IOR, R/15/1/675, Pol. Agent, Baḥrain to Pol. Res., 21 January 1937.
25. IOR, L/P & S/12/3767, Baḥrain News and Intelligence Report, January 1937 – October 1938.
26. Frontier Agreement between Sultan Sa'īd b. Taimūr (Muscat) and Shaikh Shakhbūṭ b. Sulṭān (Abū Dhabī) on 13 May 1959.
27. Map of the United Arab Emirates by the author in 1972.
28. A survey made by the author and accompanied by Nasir b. Mizkir al-Hajiri.
29. See Chapter 2, p.102.
30. Lorimer, II A, op.cit., pp.264, 405.
31. UK Memorial, I, op.cit.
32. Eccles, op.cit., pp.19, 28–9.
33. Eccles, ibid., pp.36–7.
34. IOR, L/P & S/11/294, Bertram Thomas's Report to Pol. Res., 13 June 1927.
35. UK Memorial, I, op.cit.
36. W. Thesiger, *Arabian Sands*, London, 1960, p.250.
37. Frontier Agreement between Muscat and Abū Dhabī, 1959.
38. Lorimer, II B, op.cit., pp.1694–9.
39. IOR, R/15/1/14/37, Khālid b. Aḥmad to 'Abd al-Laṭīf, 7 April 1914.
40. IOR, R/15/1/14/39, Kalbā and Fujairah, Pol. Res. to SNO, 20 April 1925; Pol. Res. to SGI, 2 May 1925; Pol. Agent, Muscat, to Pol. Res. Bushire, 4 June 1926; 'Īsā to Pol. Res., 30 June 1926.
41. On 22 May 1925 the Political Resident, reporting the incident to the Government of India, exaggerated the effect of the bombardment. The Senior Naval Officer wrote three years later: 'As a matter of incidental interest, it may here be remarked that the affair of 1925 in which the Shaikh of Fujairah had his town bombarded and was forced to pay a fine of Rs. 1,500, ended with the laugh definitely on his side, for the bombardment did neither him nor his army material damage and he forced his poor neighbour of Kalbā to pay the fine.' IOR, R/16/1/278, SNO to Pol. Res., 16 August 1928.
42. IOR, ibid., Telegram Pol. Res. to Pol. Agent, Muscat, 5 November 1926; 'Īsā to Pol. Res., 6 February 1927; SNO to Pol. Res., 14 November 1927; SNO to Pol. Res., 16 August 1928.
43. IOR, R/15/1/14/39, 'Īsā to Pol. Res., 26 September 1932; Pol. Res. to Pol. Agent, Baḥrain, 20 June 1924.
44. IOR, R/15/1/14/6, Arab Coast, Trevor, Pol. Res. to Cox, 12 May 1915; Cox to Trevor, 14 May 1915; Trevor to SGI, 22 December 1922; 'Īsā to Pol. Res., 26 July 1921.
45. IOR, R/15/1/14/45, Res. Agent to Pol. Agent, 5 May 1937.
46. IOR, L/P & S/12/30/37, Fowle to SGI, 11 February 1933.
47. IOR, L/P & S/12/474, News Summaries, October 1932.
48. IOR, op.cit., Air Ministry to IO, 1 December 1932.
49. IOR, R/15/1/14/45, Pol. Agent to Pol. Res., 5 October 1937.
50. IOR, R/15/1/14/45, Kalba Affairs, Pol. Agent Baḥrain to Pol. Res., 5 October 1937.
51. IOR, R/15/1/14/38, Sharjah Residency, Pol. Res. to Pol. Agents at Kuwait, Baḥrain, Muscat, SNO and the Air Officer Commanding in Iraq; Muḥammad b. Matar Zaabi to Pol. Res., 12 May 1937; Pol. Res. to Res. Agent, 4 May 1937; Res. Agent to Pol. Agent, Baḥrain, 12 May 1937; Pol. Res. to Pol. Agent, 17 June 1937; Residency Agent to Shaikh Sulṭān b. Ṣaqr, 24 August 1937, and 21 August 1937; Shaikh Sulṭān b. Ṣaqr to Residency Agent, Shārjah, 2 September 1937; Pol. Agent to Pol. Res., 5 October 1937; Res. Agent to Shaikh Sulṭān b. Ṣaqr, 24 August 1937.
52. IOR, L/P & S/12/3767, 16–30 April 1938.
53. Hawley, op.cit., p.224; Hay, op.cit., p.123.

6 Conclusion

6 Conclusion

By the 1890s one era in the relations between Britain and the Trucial States had ended and another had begun. Although the British had concluded a number of treaties with the Trucial States during this century, the nature of the relations was that of a dominating power enforcing order at sea and abolishing the slave trade by imposing fines under threat of bombardment. The British imposed by force what they thought was good for the people, but their complete disregard for the reactions of the local inhabitants earned them considerable hatred. As the British had very little economic interest in the Coast, they practised to the letter their traditional policy of non-interference in internal affairs.

At the close of the nineteenth century British policy in the Trucial States was influenced by three main factors. First, the activities of the neighbouring countries; second, the rivalry of other big Powers; and third, internal changes within the States.

To counteract the growing British influence in the Gulf in the second half of the nineteenth century, the Qājār dynasty and the Ottomans paid great attention to their own influence in the area. The Ottoman extension to al-Ḥasā and Qaṭar in 1871 brought them into direct confrontation with the British over al-'Udaid which Britain regarded as an integral part of the Abū Dhabī Emirate. The Persian takeover from the Qawāsim of the Government of Lingah, their seizure of the island of Ṣirrī in 1887, their intention to occupy Ṭanb island and to establish direct relations with the Trucial shaikhs were felt by the British as a real threat. To face these challenges, in addition to the French activities in 'Omān in the early 1890s, the British concluded the 'Exclusive Treaties' with the Trucial shaikhs to isolate the area from foreign intervention, and this treaty became the cornerstone of British supremacy in the Trucial Coast until December 1971. The prudence and vigilance of the authors of this treaty were soon to be proved when at the turn of the century other major powers began to challenge British supremacy in the area and found it closed to them by the shaikhs' treaty obligations.

Although the Trucial Coast, unlike Muscat and Kuwait, was not the stage for any international rivalry towards Britain before the First World War, it was indirectly affected by this challenge. This can be seen in Britain's realisation in 1902 of the Musandam peninsula's strategic importance to the Admiralty, Cox's role in the cancellation by the Shaikh of Shārjah in 1906 of the red oxide concession to the German Wonkhaus Company, and the clash of December 1910 between a squad of British marines and the inhabitants of Dubai during a search for arms.

At the beginning of the twentieth century the British were faced politically with a crucial problem resulting from the growth of the power of Zāyed b. Khalīfah, Ruler of Abū Dhabī, and the weakness of the Qawāsim Emirate, both the product of Britain's own policy throughout the nineteenth century. The British were forced to reconsider their previously hostile attitudes towards the Qawāsim on a number of issues. The recent friendship between France and Sultan Faiṣal b. Turkī required a review of the ownership of the disputed area of Rūs al-Jibāl, the Musandam peninsula and the Shimailiyyah district between Muscat and the Qawāsim. The Persian occupation of the island of Ṣirrī and Persia's claims to Ṭanb in 1887, an action which the British felt had been inspired by Russia, precipitated a lengthy study of the sovereignty of these islands and the adoption at the turn of the century of a firm positive policy that Ṭanb and Abū Mūsā islands belonged to the Qawāsim of Shārjah and Rās al-Khaimah. During his two visits in 1902 and 1904 to the hinterland of the Trucial Coast, Cox was surprised at the extension of Abū Dhabī's influence in the interior, a situation which he regarded as potentially explosive, for the oppressed Ghāfirī group might appeal to Ibn Sa'ūd, then a growing power in inner Arabia. The new British policy of interference in internal affairs could be seen in Cox's rejection of Shaikh Zāyed b. Khalīfah's project at Zūrā and his intervention in order to release Shaikh Aḥmad b. Rāshid, the young Ruler of Umm al-Qaiwain from detention. In 1903 the Government of India acknowledged the Shimailiyyah district as part of Shārjah and ignored the attempts of Fujairah to achieve independence. When in 1904 Persia hoisted their flag on Abū Musā island, the British obliged them to evacuate it and the Shaikh of Shārjah replaced his flag. As Shaikh Sālim b. Sulṭān was accused of having dealings with the German Company of Wonkhaus the British refused to grant recognition to his claim for the independence of Rās al-Khaimah from Shārjah in 1908; recognition was delayed till the end of the war and granted to his son Sulṭān b. Sālim in 1919.

At the beginning of our period new economic ties between India and the Trucial States started to emerge, changing the character of the previous relations of the nineteenth century. Peace at sea, which the British had established, now allowed the pearl industry to flourish, and Indian traders, who were British subjects, migrated and were able to live safely in the towns of the Trucial Coast under imperial protection. The situation developed further with the emergence of the port of Dubai and the establishment of a regular service of British steamships there from 1902. These new and growing economic links caused a fundamental change in British policy. At the time of Cox, the Political Resident from 1904 to 1914, it was decided to establish a British Officer instead of the local Residency Agent and to erect a wireless station at Dubai. Cox also adopted on occasions a new policy of interference in internal affairs to safeguard the new interests.

During the first four decades of our period (1890–1928) the pearl trade reached its zenith. The opening of the Suez Canal and the call at Dubai by steam navigation lines ended a period of complete isolation for the Trucial Coast. Contacts with Bombay, representing British progress and civilisation, and Cairo, a centre of Islamic and Arab culture, created an awareness of current local and world events and awakened a desire for reform. Schools were established by philanthropic pearl merchants in the main towns of the Trucial Coast, particularly in Dubai and Shārjah. The new British policy of interference in internal affairs was viewed with suspicion on the Coast and we have seen that the Shaikh of Dubai and his people firmly rejected Cox's attempted imposition of a British political officer and the proposal for a wireless station. During the 1930s the educated young generation were greatly influenced by the nationalist magazines of Cairo and Iraq. British policy in Palestine was much resented by them.

The world economic depression of 1929 had an immediate effect on the Trucial Coast. Schools were closed and many rich pearl merchants became bankrupt. Oil concessions in the late 1930s secured for the Rulers a comfortable and independent source of income which made them for the first time richer than the pearl merchants who were now in a particularly miserable state. They were thus in a position to buy the military support of tribesmen to overthrow their opponents. The shaikhs' new power was soon encouraged by the British, who favoured strong rulers who would be able to maintain security and order.

In the inter-war period significant changes in international rivalry and local powers in the Gulf influenced British relations with the Trucial Coast. Russian, German and French rivalry disappeared completely after the First World War, but American competition over oil concessions proved serious to British interests in the area. The Americans, taking advantage of the Foreign Office's agreement to an 'open-door' policy, succeeded in acquiring a share of 23½ per cent in the IPC in 1928, the exclusive concession in Baḥrain also in 1928 and al-Ḥasā in 1933, and 50 per cent in Kuwait in 1934. These successes, achieved in a comparatively short period, were caused by the unpopularity of APOC in which the British Government was the major shareholder. Other factors in this success were the British belief, contrary to the American idea, that there was no oil on the Arabian Coast—hence the absence of a serious desire to extend their concessions into the area—and further the lack of unity between the various British interests involved.

These American gains caused a strong reaction at the Admiralty, at the India Office and with Fowle, the Political Resident in the Gulf (1932–9). These favoured a policy of interference, giving support to British companies in order to gain the major share in future oil concessions. This policy grew with the increase of British activities after the inauguration of Imperial air routes along the Gulf and the Coast and the acquisition of oil concessions in the area. Proof of this can be seen in the minutes of the Persian Gulf Sub-Committee and the Standing Official Middle East Sub-Committee (established by the Committee of Imperial Defence, the first between 1928–9, and the second between 1930 and 1939) both of which gave a high proportion of their time to the growing British interest on the Trucial Coast.

This policy was immediately implemented in May 1935 and Qaṭar was given a guarantee of protection in return for the granting of a concession to APOC acting for IPC. In October of the same year Petroleum Development (Trucial Coast) was established and started negotiations with the Trucial shaikhs. It was only through the energetic intervention of Fowle that an oil concession was concluded with Dubai in May 1937.

As these interests relied on the friendship and co-operation of the rulers, Britain found it necessary to make great efforts to gain the general goodwill of the shaikhs. The nineteenth-century gunboat diplomacy therefore began to diminish gradually.

Besides American economic rivalry, Britain found herself faced between the wars by the growth of two local powers, the nationalist state of Persia under Rezā Shāh and the Islamic Sa'ūdi Kingdom under King 'Abd al-Azīz b. Sa'ūd. Relations between Rezā Shāh and Britain deteriorated for a number of reasons: the establishment of Persian naval units in the Gulf, which created trouble for the Arab dhows in 1928; Persia's refusal of air facilities along its coast for Imperial Airways after 1932, and her insistence that the Political Resident should be moved from Bushire and that the Admiralty should hand over the naval base of Henjam; and Persian territorial claims. One of the main reasons for the failure to reach a settlement during the negotiations for an Anglo–Persian treaty between 1929 and 1935 was British support for the Qawāsim rights to Ṭanb and Abū Musā. It is worth noting here Persia's willingness to drop its claim to Baḥrain, but her determination to secure Ṭanb, an omen of what was to happen in 1971.

The oil concession in al-Hasā granted to the California Oil Company by Ibn Sa'ūd in May 1933 opened the question of the frontiers between Sa'ūdi Arabia and Abū Dhabī. After long and tedious negotiations which they began in an adamant manner, the British became more generous, influenced by the deterioration of the international situation before the Second World War and their urgent need to satisfy Ibn Sa'ūd, who was playing a leading role in the Palestine question which was at that time causing great resentment in the Arab world. In 1938, in order to reach a settlement, Britain agreed to concede al-'Udaid to the Sa'ūdi Kingdom and compensate the Shaikh of Abū Dhabī from the British Treasury. However, the war intervened and the British attitude differed completely in the post-war period.

As regards Fujairah and Hamriyyah, the British continued to refuse recognition to their attempts to achieve independence. However, when in

1936 the Shaikh of Kalbā granted them air facilities which the Shaikh of Shārjah could not offer, the British imposed on the Shaikh of Shārjah the independence of this area, an interesting example of how British policy reacted to the developing expediencies rather than following rigid traditional principles.

After 1945 fundamental and far-reaching changes took place in the area. The Foreign Office, which replaced the Indian Government in handling British interests in the area after 1947, adopted a new policy of involvement in the internal affairs of the Trucial States. In 1949 a British Political Agent was appointed for the first time in Shārjah, replacing the local representative who had looked after British interests since 1823. Three years later the Political Agency was transferred to Dubai, the growing economic centre of the area. In 1952 also, Britain recognised the independence of Fujairah and decided to consider Kalbā as part of the Emirate of Shārjah. This was followed by a demarcation of the inter-state frontiers.

In internal affairs, modern education developed, particularly in Shārjah, with the help of some Arab countries. The accession of Shaikh Zāyed to power in 1966 marked the beginning of a period of great progress in Abū Dhabī and internal political developments on the whole Coast.

Although the British increased their activities in the area, they were obliged, largely because of economic pressures at home to announce their withdrawal from the Gulf in 1968 and this was put into effect in 1971. This year marked the end of the century and a half of British supremacy. It also marked the emergence of the United Arab Emirates, under the leadership of Shaikh Zāyed b. Sulṭān, and a new page in the history of the area.

Bibliography

Unpublished Material

India Office, Library, London

R/15	Persian Gulf Residency Records.
R/15/1	Bushire Residency Records, 1763–1947.
R/15/2	Baḥrain Agency Records, 1920–50.
R/15/4	Trucial Coast, 1937–50.
L/P/ & S	Political and Secret Department Records.
L/P & S/10	Political and Secret Department Subject Files, 1902–31.
L/P/ & S/12	Political and Secret Department External Collections, 1931–49.
L/P & S/18(B)	Political and Secret Department Memoranda (Arabia and the Persian Gulf).
L/P & S/20	Political and Secret Department Library.
P	Proceedings of Government of India & Bombay.
	Government of India, Saldanha, J.A. Precis of the Affairs of the Persian Coast and Islands, 1854–1905, Simla, 1906.

Public Records Office, London

CAB 2	Committee of Imperial Defence, Minutes and Meetings, Vol. 1–9 (between 18 December 1902–1 September 1939).
CAB 9	CID Colonial and Overseas Defence Committee, Remarks.
9/20	September 1929–March 1933.
9/21	June 1933–August 1939.
CAB 16	Committee of Imperial Defence, Ad Hoc Sub-Committees of Enquiry, Proceedings and Memoranda.
16/93	Persian Gulf Meetings.
16/94	Memoranda.
16/95	Political Control, Persian Gulf Sub-Committee.
CAB 51	Committee of Imperial Defence, Middle East Questions.
51/1	Ministerial Sub-Committee.
51/2–51/11	Official Sub-Committee.

FO	371	General Correspondence, Political Annual Reports on Persia between 1928–35.
FO		Confidential Prints.
	406	Eastern Affairs—Arabia.
	407	Persian Gulf.
	416	Persia.
FO		Research Department, Boundaries of the Trucial States, prepared from sketch maps and information supplied by Julian Walker, February 1963 (Map).

Politisches Archiv des Ausweitigen Amts, Bonn

Turkei 165 Nr. 1	Kuiet 1901–16, 9 Boden.
Turkei	Arabien 1889–1920, 43 Boden.
Persian 7	Beziehungen Persiens zu England 1886–1918, 5 Boden.
Persien 13	Beziehungen Persien zu Deutschland 1889–1920, 10 Boden.
Politik, Arabien	Von 10.8.1936 bis 17.3.1939.

Archives du Ministère des Affaires Etrangères, Paris

Asie Océanie, Nouvelle Série, Mascate 1891–1916, 35 Volumes.
Correspondence Commerciale, Bouchir, 1889–1901.

Basvekâlet Arşivi, Istanbul

Irâde 1288H(1871), Dâhiliyye, 44822 and 44930.
Irâde 1300H(1882), Dâhiliyye, 70899.
Irâde 1304H(1886), Dâhiliyye, 79724.
Irâde 1305H(1887), Dâhiliyye, 82789.
Irâde 1306H(1888), Dâhiliyye, 86689.
Irâde Receb 1319H (October 1901), Dâhiliyye, 42.
Irâde 1294H (1877) Hâriciyye, 16634.

MecLis-i VukeLâ, Defter 37, Safar 1306 H (October 1888).
MecLis-i VukeLâ, Defter 42, Sabân 1306 H (April 1889).
MecLis-i VukeLâ, Defter 71, Safar 1310 H (September 1892).
MecLis-i VukeLâ, Defter 74, Sabân 1310 H (Mars. 1893).
MecLis-i VukeLâ, Defter 78, 1311 H (1894).
MecLis-i VukeLâ, Defter 84, 1312 H (1895).
MecLis-i VukeLâ, Defter 87, 1313 H (1896).

Husûsî, No. 67 & 68 Receb 1315 H (November 1897).
Husûsî, No. 117, Safar 1317 H (June 1899).
Hususî, No. 97, Cumâzî el-evvel 1317 H (September 1899).

Taltifât, Defter 134, Receb 1325 H (1907).

Department of State Archives, National Archives and Records, Washington

Record Group 59

Decimal Files, 1910–39

890A	Internal Affairs of Oman.
890B	Internal Affairs of Arabia.
890F4	Internal Affairs of Saudi Arabia.
891	Internal Affairs of Persia.
890G	Internal Affairs of Iraq.
811	Near East.

Decimal Files 1930–39

From 890A 001/16 – 890B 60/1 Box No. 7055.
From 890E 041/3 – 890F 01/292 Box No. 7066.
From 890F 01/20 – 890F 927/10 Box. No. 7067.

Record Group 84

Consulate

Bushire	1924–5, Vols. 3 & 5.
Basrah	1869–1926.
Baghdād	1880–1935.
Aden	1880–1939.
Muscat	1888–1914.

Diplomatic

Iraq	1931–6.
Iran	1883–1915.

Missionary Board Reports, The Reformed Church in America, New Brunswick

Board of Foreign Missions, The Arabian Mission Annual Reports, 1891–1925.

The Arabian Mission
  Quarterly Letters No. 1–40 (1892–1901).
  Neglected Arabia, No. 41–186 (1902–39).

Government of Shārjah

Government of Shârjah, Shârjah's Title to the Island of Abū Musâ, by M. E. Bathurst, Northcutt Ely & Messrs. Coward Chance, 3 Vols., September 1971.

Published Material

Admiralty, Naval Intelligence Division, *Iraq and the Persian Gulf*, 1944.
Anthony, J. D., *Arab States of the Lower Gulf*, Washington, 1975.
Antonius, G., *The Arab Awakening*, London, 1938.
Aramco, *Oman and the Southern Shore of the Persian Gulf*, Cairo, 1952.
Arfa, H., *Under Five Shahs*, London, 1964.
Belgrave, C., *Personal Column*, London, 1960.

Bentley, G. W., 'The Development of the Air Route in the Persian Gulf', *JRCAS*, 20 (1933), 173–189.

Bharier, J., *Economic Development in Iran* 1900–1970, London, 1971.

Ibn Bishr, U.A., '*Unwān al-Majd Fī Tarik Nejd*, Beirut, 1967.

Browne, E. G., *The Persian Revolution of 1905–1909*, Cambridge, 1910.

Bullard, Sir Reader, *The Camels Must Go*, London, 1951.

Burchall, H., 'The Air Route to India', *JRCAS*, 14(1927), 3–18;
——, 'The Political Aspect of Commercial Air Routes', *JRCAS*, 20, January 1933.

Burrell, R. M., 'Britain, Iran and the Persian Gulf: Some Aspects of the Situation in 1920s and 1930s', in *The Arabian Peninsula*, edited by D. Hopwood, London, 1971.

Busch, B. C., *Britain and the Persian Gulf 1894–1914*, London and California, 1967.

Curzon, of Kedleston, *Persia and the Persian Question*, 2 Vols., London, 1892.

Darby, P., *British Defence Policy East of Suez, 1947–1968*, London, 1973.

Dickson, H. R. P., *Kuwait and Her Neighbours*, London, 1956.

Eccles, G. J., 'The Sultanate of Muscat and 'Omân, with a description of a journey into the interior taken in 1925', *Journal of the Central Asian Society*, XIV, a, 1927.

Gooch, G. P. and Temperley, H., *British Documents on the Origins of the War, 1898–1914*, London, 1926–1938, 11 Vols. in 13.

Graves, P., *The Life of Sir Percy Cox*, London, 1941.

Hansard, IV series 121 (1903), HoL.; V series 64 (1926), HoL.

Hawley, D., *The Trucial States*, London, 1970.

Hay, R., *The Persian Gulf States*, Washington, 1959.

Hurewitz, J. C., *Diplomacy in the Near and Middle East: A Documentary Record*, 2 Vols., Princeton, 1956.

Institute of International Affairs, *Political and Strategical Interests of United Kingdom*, London, New York and Toronto.

Kazemzadeh, F., *Russia and Britain in Persia*, 1864–1914, New Haven and London, 1968.

Kelly, J. B., *Britain and the Persian Gulf*, London, 1968;
——, *Eastern Arabian Frontiers*, London, 1964.

Klebanoff, S., *Middle East Oil and US Foreign Policy*, New York, 1974.

Kumar, R., *India and the Persian Gulf Region, 1858–1907*, 1956.

Lambton, A. K. S., *The Persian Land Reform*, Oxford, 1969.

Longrigg, S. L., *Oil in the Middle East*, London, 1954.

Lorimer, J. G., *Gazetteer of the Persian Gulf, Oman and Central Arabia*, Calcutta 1908 and 1915, 6 Vols., republished by Gregg International, Westmead, England, 1970.

Mann, C., *Abu Dhabi; Birth of an Oil Sheikhdom*, Beirut, London, 1962.

Marlow, J., *The Persian Gulf in the Twentieth Century*, London, 1962.

Martin, B. C., *German-Persian Diplomatic Relations, 1873–1912*, 'S-Gravenhage, 1959.

Ministry of Education, Abū Dhabī, Annual Report.

Ministry of Education, Qaṭar, Annual Report.

Ministry of Education, UAE, Annual Report.

Monroe, E., *The Changing Balance of Power in the Persian Gulf*, New York, 1972.

Morsy, M., *Oman and the First Sa'ūdi Dynasty*, Cairo, 1978;

——, *Two Glorious Years in the History of Abu Dhabi*, Beirut, 1968.

Newton, Lord, *Lord Lansdowne*, London, 1929.

Niebuhr, C., *Description de l' Arabie*, 2 Vols., Copenhagen, 1772.

De Novo, John A., *American Interests and Policies in the Middle East 1900–1939*, Minneapolis, 1963.

Nowfal, S., *Imarat Sāḥil Oman*, Cairo, 1972.

Al-Otaibah, M. S., *OPEC and the Petroleum Industry*, London, 1975.

Pahlavi, M. R., *The White Revolution*, Tehran, 1967.

Philby, H., *Arabian Days*, London, 1948;

——, *Arabian Oil Ventures*, Washington, 1964.

Ramazani, R. K., *The Foreign Policy of Iran*, 1500–1941, Charlotteville, 1966;

——, *Iran's Foreign Policy, 1941–1973*, Charlotteville, 1975.

Rendel, G., *The Sword and the Olive*, London, 1957.

Rihani, A., *Around the Coasts of Arabia*, London, 1930.

Rimaihi, M. G., *Oil and Social Change in the Gulf*, Kuwait, 1975.

Ronaldshay, Earl, *The Life of Lord Curzon*, 3 Vols., London, 1928.

Sadik, M. T. and Snavely, W. P., *Bahrain, Qatar and the United Arab Emirates*, Lexington, 1972.

Said, R. J., 'The 1938 Reform Movement in Dubai', *Al-Abhath*, XXIII, Beirut, December 1970.

Sanghvi, R., *Aryamehr: The Shah of Iran*, London, 1968.

Sassoon, P., 'Air Power in the Middle East', *JRCAS*, 20(1933), 394–405.

Saudi Arabia, *Memorial of the Government of Saudi Arabia*. Arbitration for the settlement of the territorial dispute between Muscat and Abu Dhabi on one hand and Saudi Arabia on the other. 3 Vols. (Arabic), Cairo, 1955.

Shwadran, B., *The Middle East, Oil and the Great Powers*, London, 1956.

Staley, E., 'Business and Politics in the Persian Gulf; the Story of the Wonkhaus Firm', *Political Science Quarterly*, 48 (1933).

Stanton-Hope, W. E., *Arabian Adventurer, The Story of Haji Williamson*, London, 1951.

Sykes, P., *A History of Persia*, 2 Vols., London and New York, 3rd edition, 1930.

Thesiger, W., *Arabian Sands*, London, 1960.

Thomas, Bertram, *Alarms and Excursions in Arabia*, Indianapolis, 1931.

Toynbee, A. J., *Survey of International Affairs, 1925*, I. The Islamic World since the Peace Settlement, London, 1927.

The Government of the United Kingdom of Great Britain and Northern Ireland, *Arbitration Concerning Buraimi and the Common Frontier Between Abu Dhabi and Saudi Arabia*, 2 Vols., 1955.

UN Security Council, *Provisional Records*, 9 December 1971.

US Government Printing Press, *Foreign Relations of the US*, Washington, 1939, Vol. IV and 1942, Vol. IV.

Wahbah, H., *Khamsun 'Āma Fī Jazīrat al-'Arab*, Cairo, 1960.

Wilber, D. N., *Iran Past and Present*, Princeton, 1975.

Wingate, R., *Not in the Limelight*, London, 1959.

Zabih, S. and Chubin, S., *The Foreign Relations of Iran*, Berkeley, California, 1974.

Maps and Appendices

Map 1

Sheikh Sh
BAHRAIN
Al-Zubārah
Hālul
QATAR
DOHA
Al-Wakrah
Dās
Sherā'ūh
Dayyinah
Al-Jāfūrah
Salwā
Al-Aṣhāṭ
Al-Udeid
Al-Qaffāy
Dalma
Ghāghah
Al-Uqal
Ṣīr Banī Yās
Al-Yāsāt
Al-Mijann
Ba'yā
Al-Sil'
Sabkhat Maṭṭī
Al Safq
Baynūnah
SAUDI
UNITED
ARA

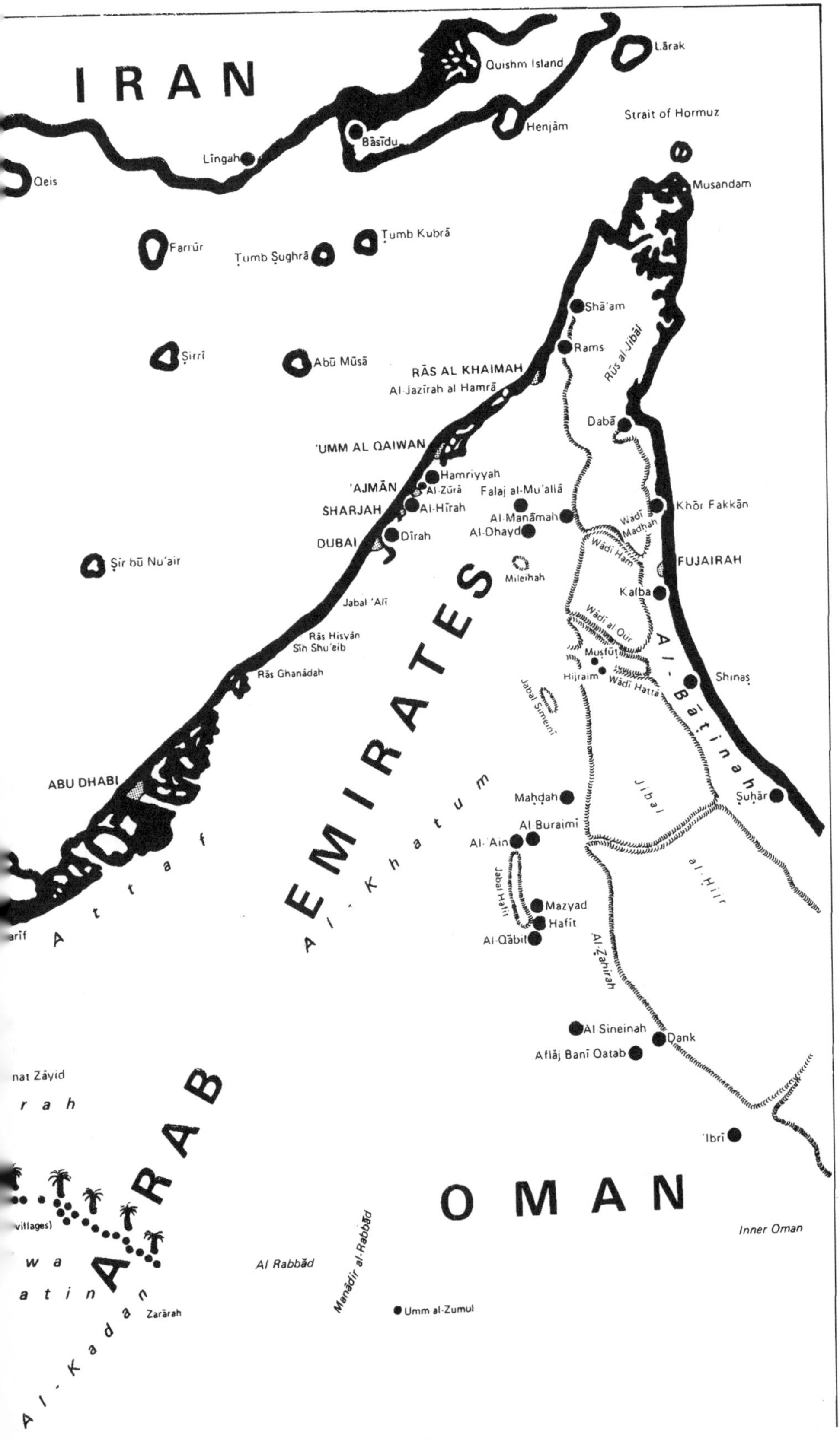

IRAN
Lārak
Quishm Island
Strait of Hormuz
Henjām
Bāsīdu
Līngah
Qeis
Musandam
Farrūr
Ṭumb Ṣughrā
Ṭumb Kubrā
Shā'am
Rams
Rūs al-Jibāl
Ṣirrī
Abū Mūsā
RĀS AL KHAIMAH
Al-Jazīrah al Hamrā
Dabā
'UMM AL QAIWAN
Hamriyyah
'AJMĀN
Al-Zūrā
Falaj al-Mu'allā
SHARJAH
Al-Hīrah
Khōr Fakkān
Al-Manāmah
Al-Dhayd
Wādī Madhah
DUBAI
Dīrah
Wādī Ham
FUJAIRAH
Ṣīr bū Nu'air
Mileihah
Kalba
Jabal 'Alī
Wādī al-Qūr
Rās Hisyān
Sīh Shu'eib
Musfūt
Rās Ghanādah
Hijraim
Wādī Hattā
Shinaṣ
Jabal Simeini
Al-Bāṭinah
ABU DHABI
Mahḍah
Jibal
Ṣuḥār
Al-Buraimi
Al-'Ain
EMIRATES
Al-Khatum
Attaf
Jabal Hafit
al-Ḥijr
Mazyad
Hafīt
Al-Qābil
arif
Al-Ẓahirah
Al Sineinah
Dank
Aflāj Banī Qatab
nat Zāyid
rah
ARAB
'Ibrī
OMAN
villages)
Inner Oman
wa
Al Rabbād
Manādir al-Rabbād
atin
Zarārah
Umm al-Zumul
Al-Kadan

Map 2 (Chapter 3)

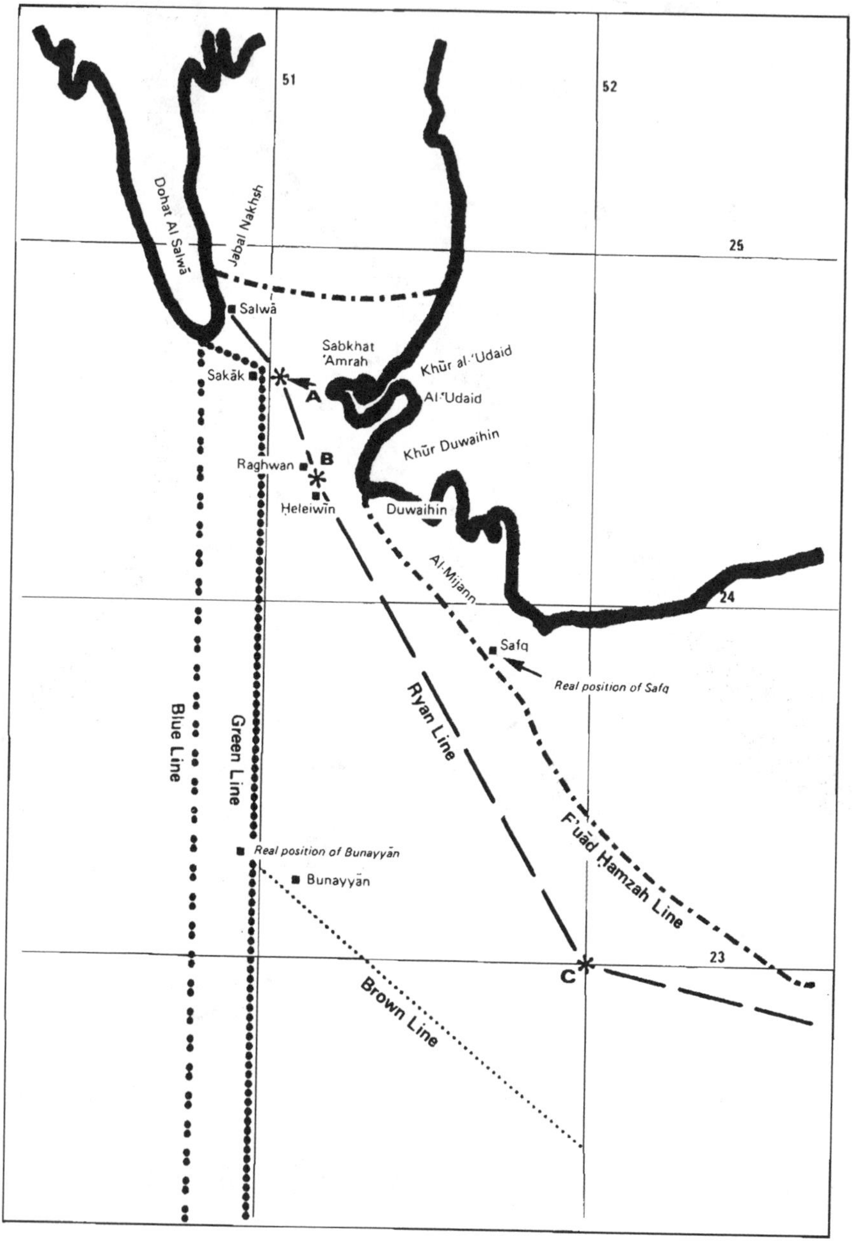

Map 3 (Chapter 3)

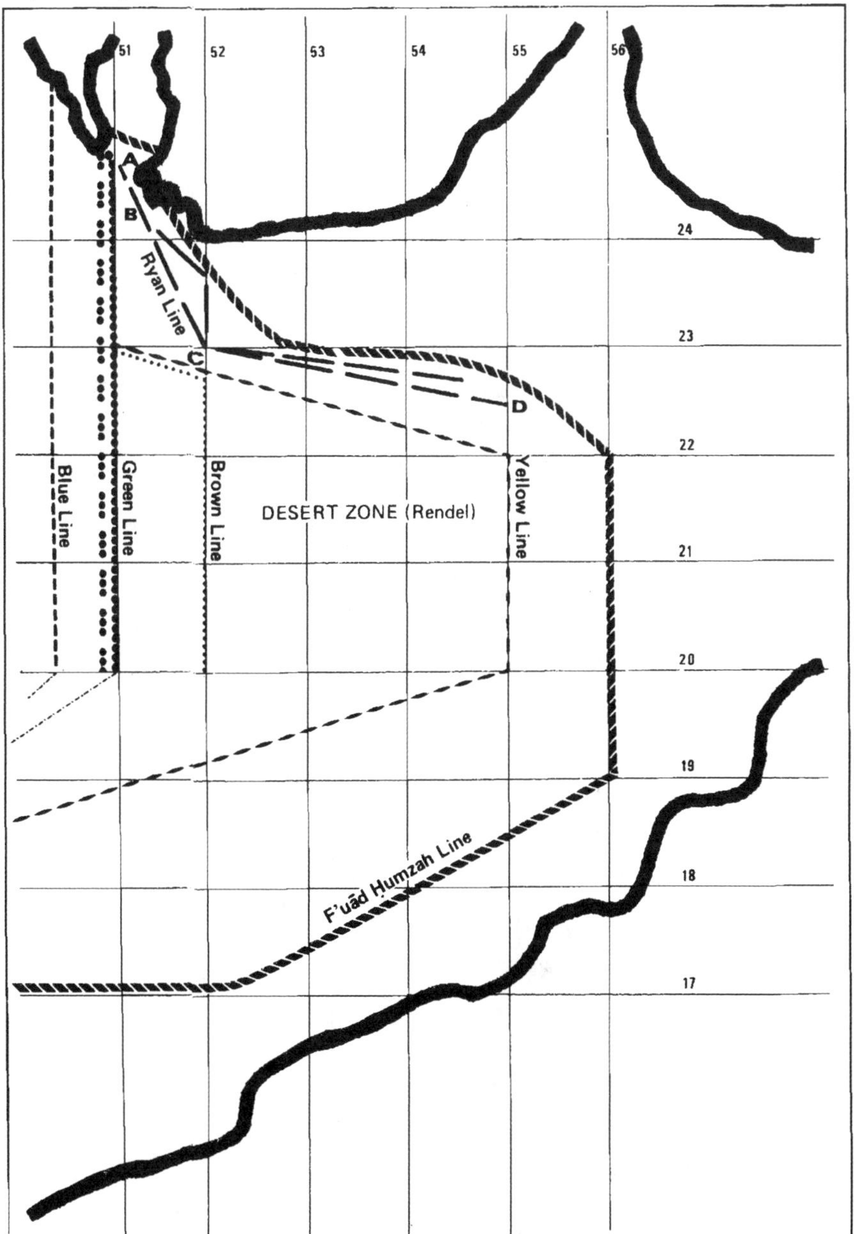

Map 4 (Chapter 2)

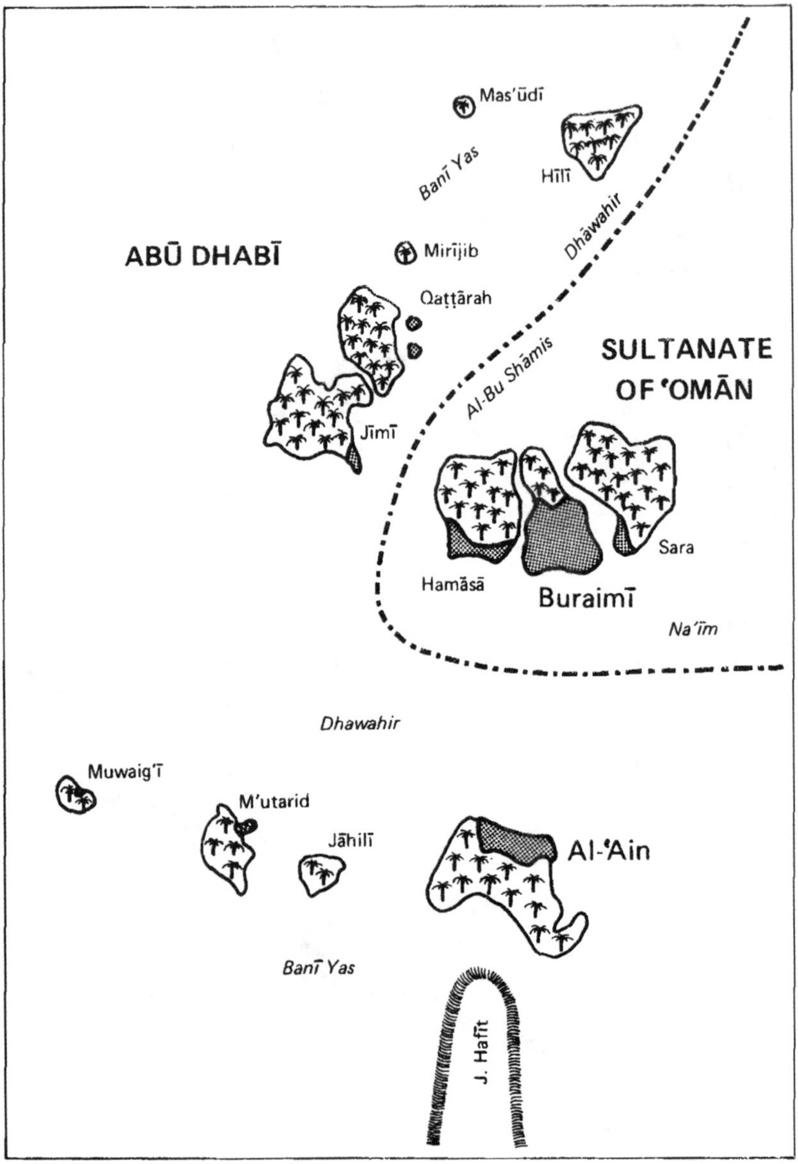

Map 5 (Chapter 5)

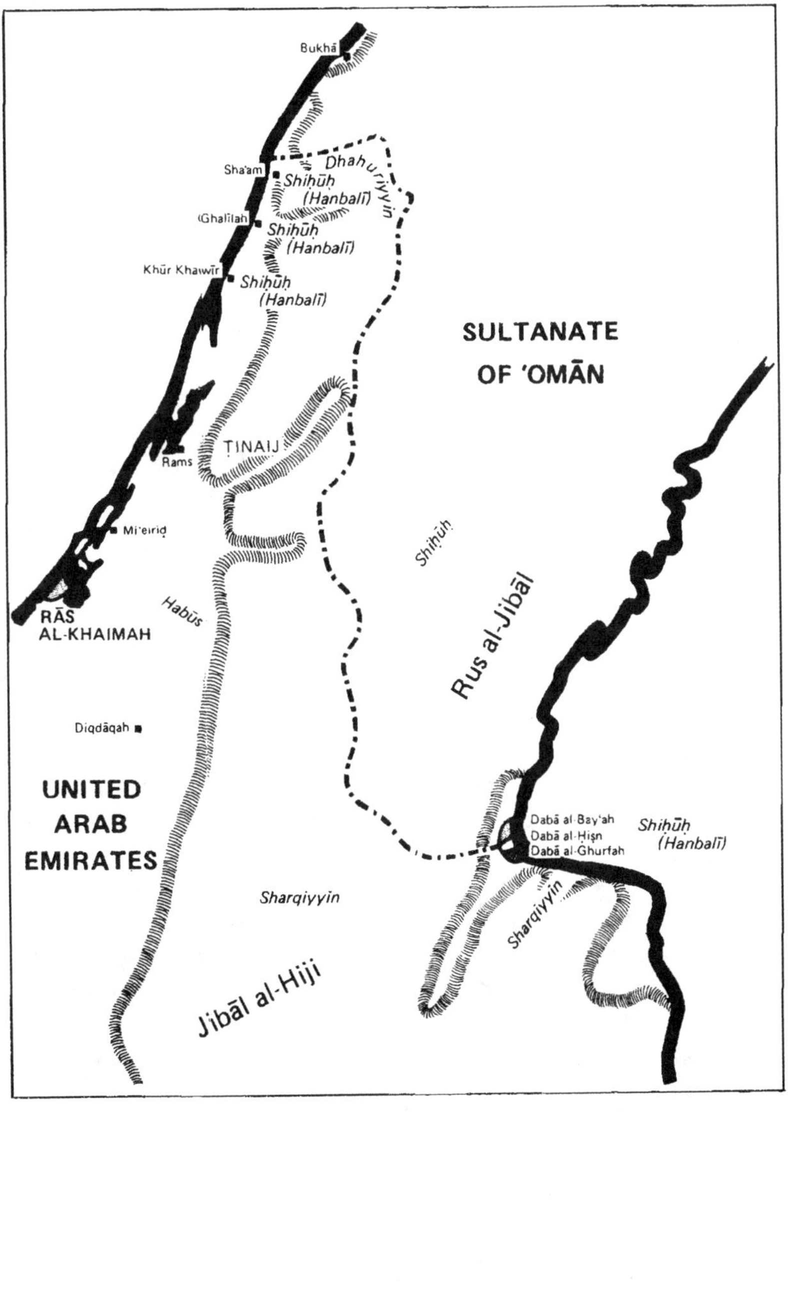

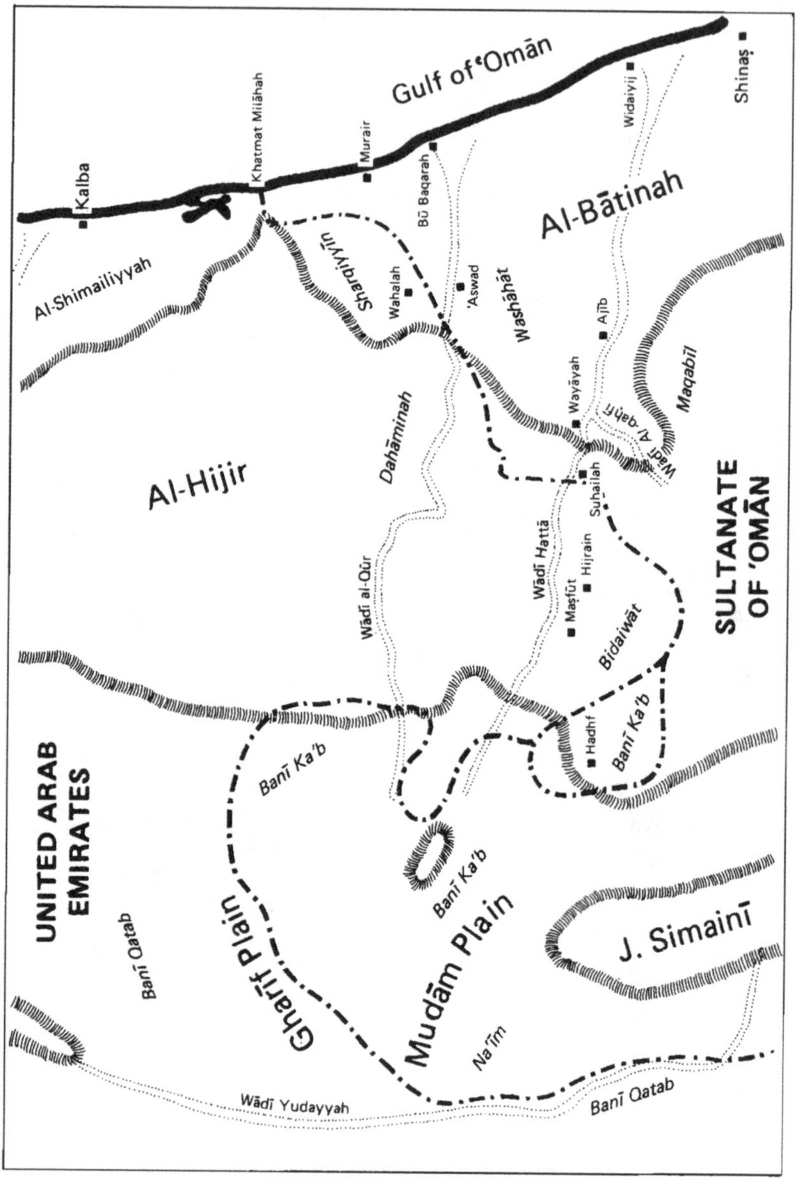

Map 6 (Chapter 5)

Map 7 (Chapter 5)

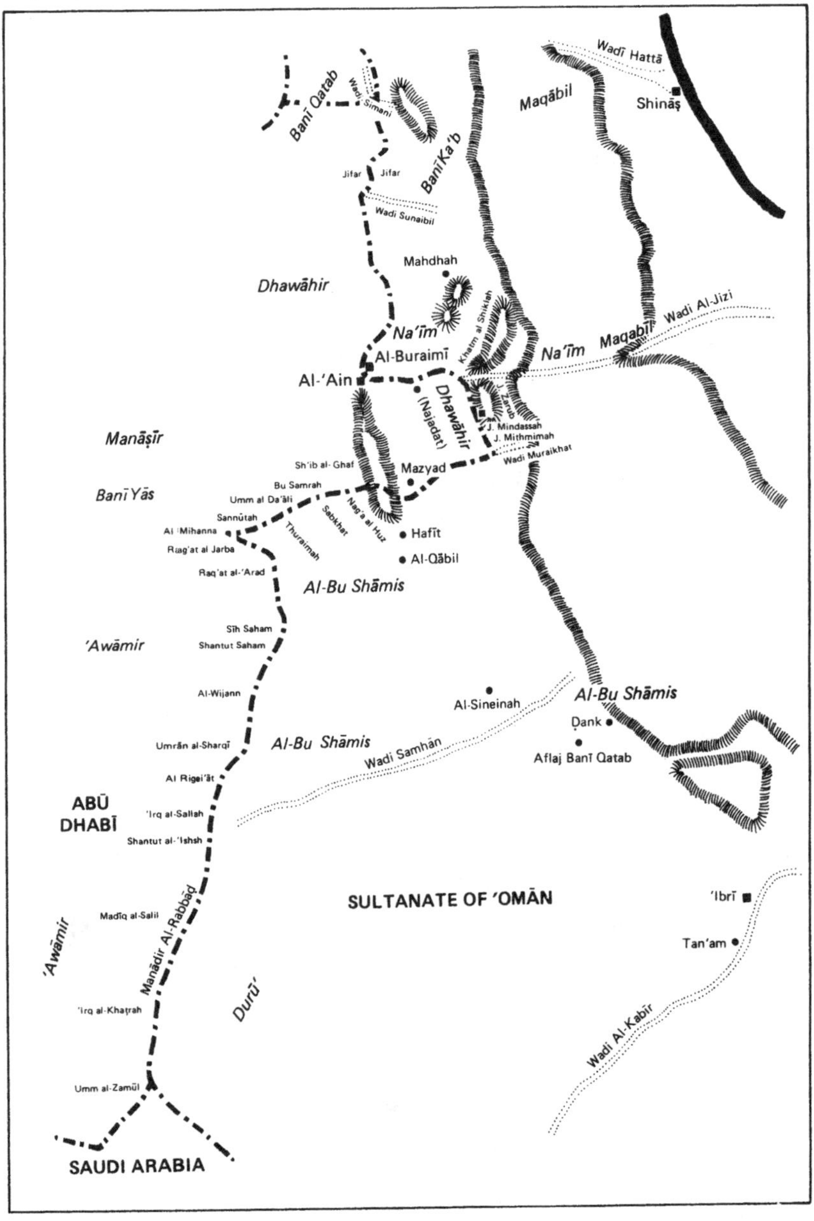

Map 8 (Chapter 5)

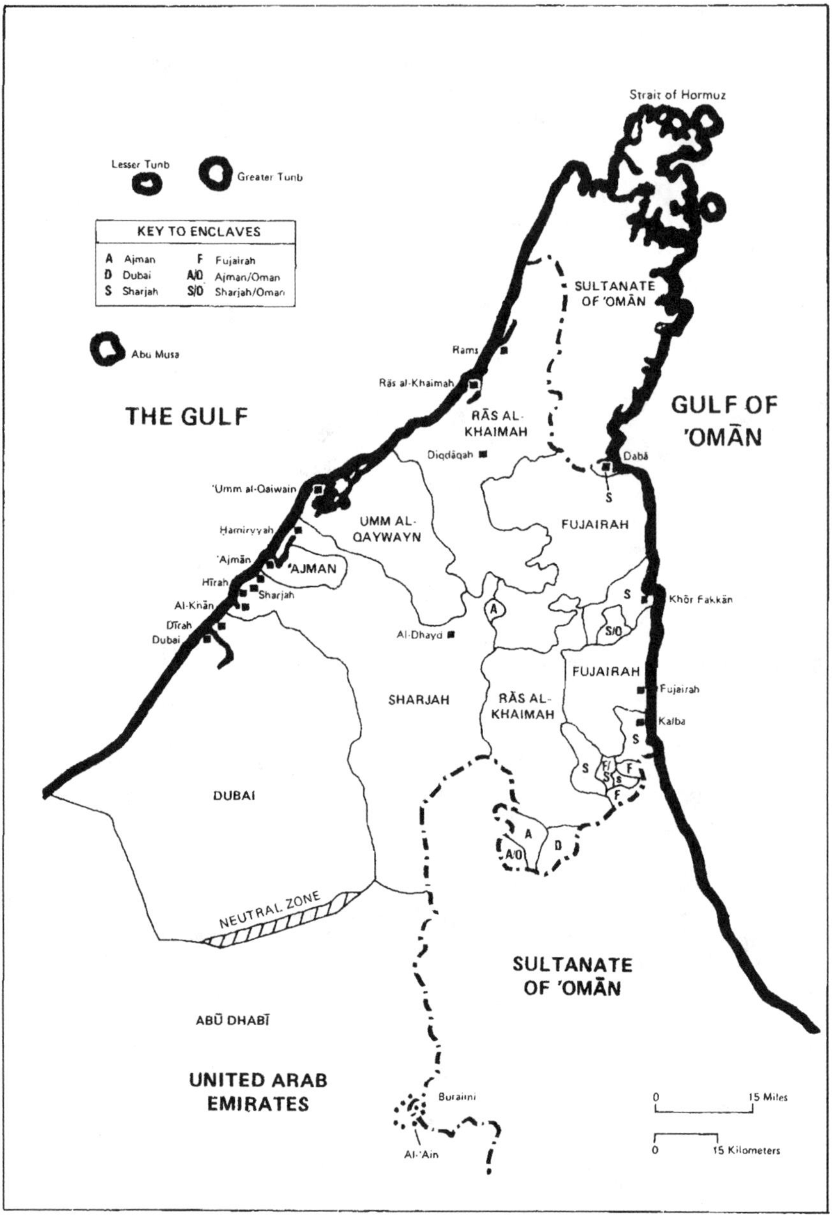

The Qawāsim Family

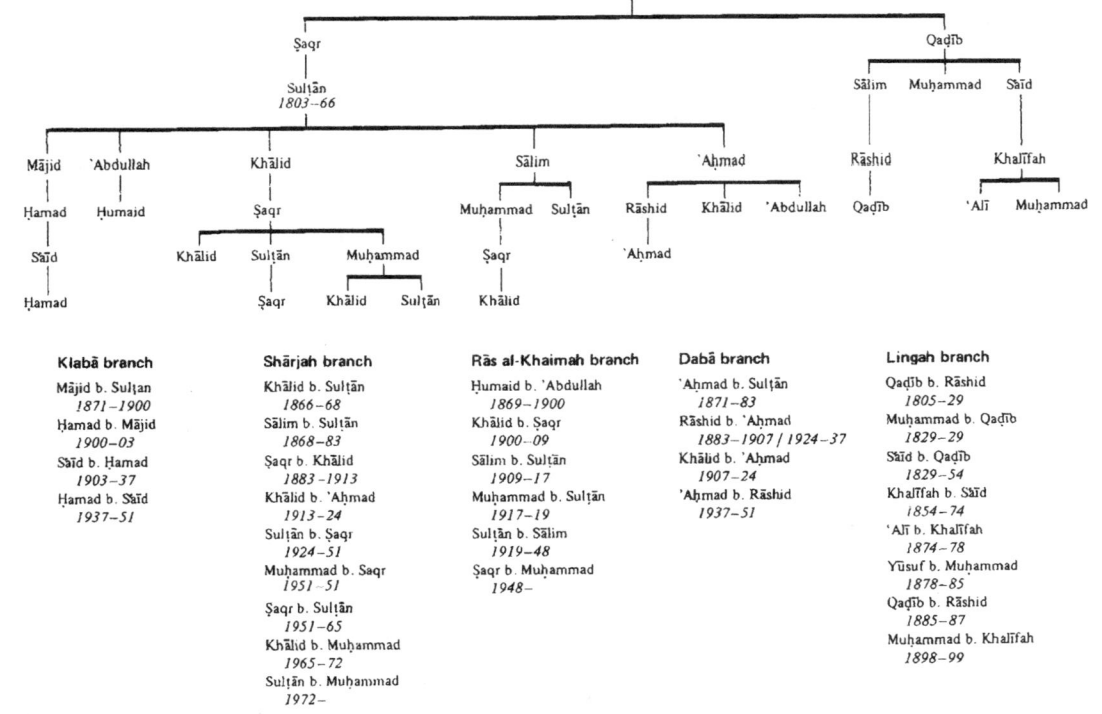

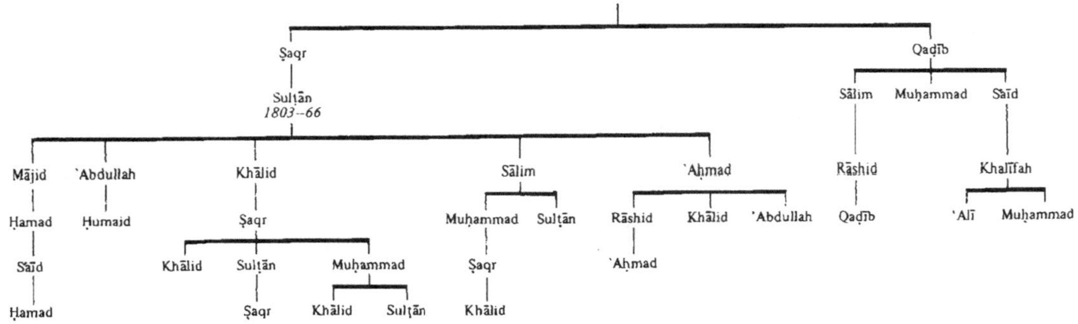

Klabā branch

Mājid b. Sulṭan
1871–1900
Ḥamad b. Mājid
1900–03
Saʿīd b. Ḥamad
1903–37
Ḥamad b. Saʿīd
1937–51

Shārjah branch

Khālid b. Sulṭān
1866–68
Sālim b. Sulṭān
1868–83
Ṣaqr b. Khālid
1883–1913
Khālid b. ʿAḥmad
1913–24
Sulṭān b. Ṣaqr
1924–51
Muḥammad b. Saqr
1951–51
Ṣaqr b. Sulṭān
1951–65
Khālid b. Muḥammad
1965–72
Sulṭān b. Muḥammad
1972–

Rās al-Khaimah branch

Ḥumaid b. ʿAbdullah
1869–1900
Khālid b. Ṣaqr
1900–09
Sālim b. Sulṭān
1909–17
Muḥammad b. Sulṭān
1917–19
Sulṭān b. Sālim
1919–48
Ṣaqr b. Muḥammad
1948–

Dabā branch

ʿAḥmad b. Sulṭān
1871–83
Rāshid b. ʿAḥmad
1883–1907 / 1924–37
Khālid b. ʿAḥmad
1907–24
ʿAḥmad b. Rāshid
1937–51

Lingah branch

Qaḍīb b. Rāshid
1805–29
Muḥammad b. Qaḍīb
1829–29
Saʿīd b. Qaḍīb
1829–54
Khalīfah b. Saʿīd
1854–74
ʿAlī b. Khalīfah
1874–78
Yūsuf b. Muḥammad
1878–85
Qaḍīb b. Rāshid
1885–87
Muḥammad b. Khalīfah
1898–99

Genealogical Tree No. 1

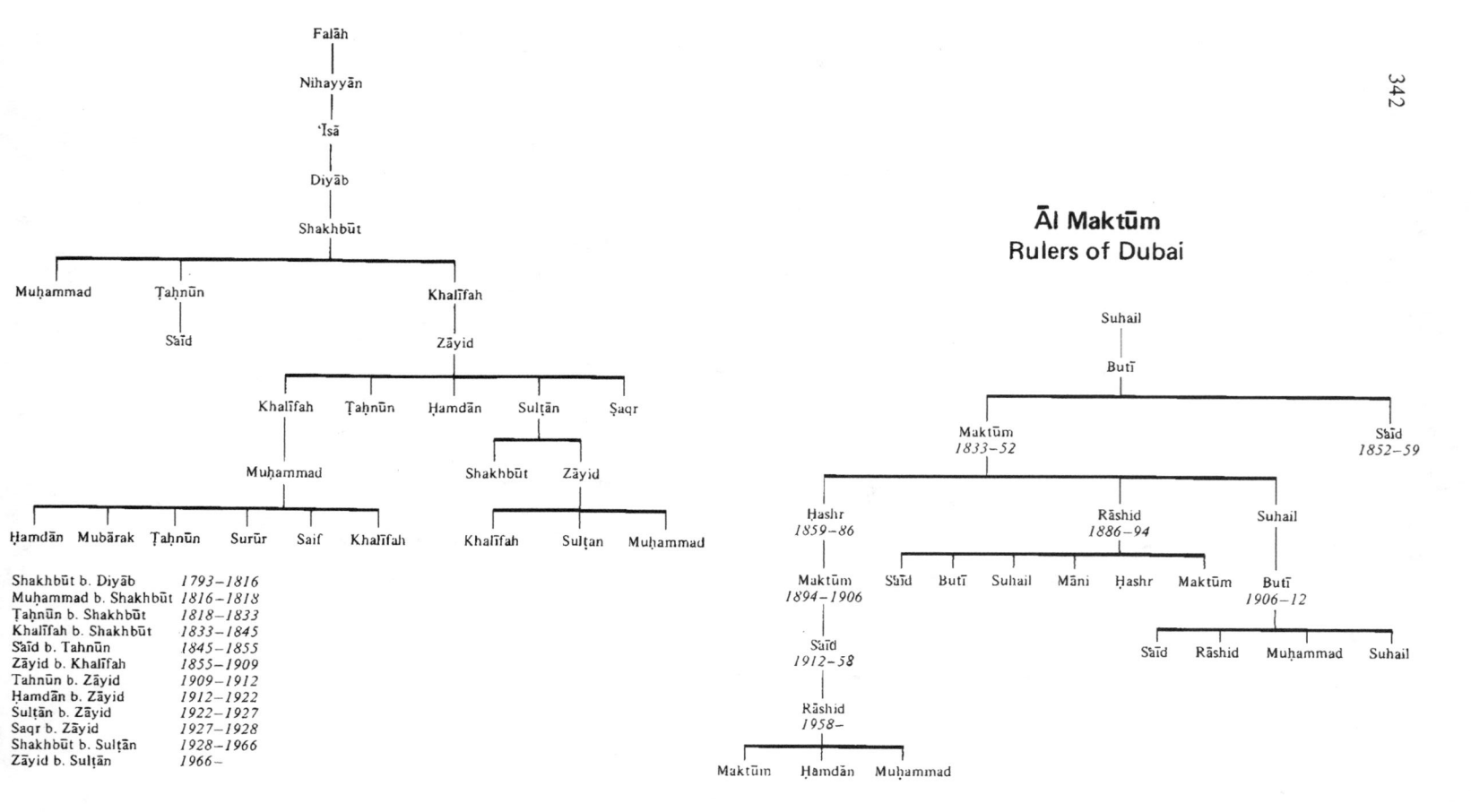

Āl Nihayyān
Rulers of 'Abū Dhabī

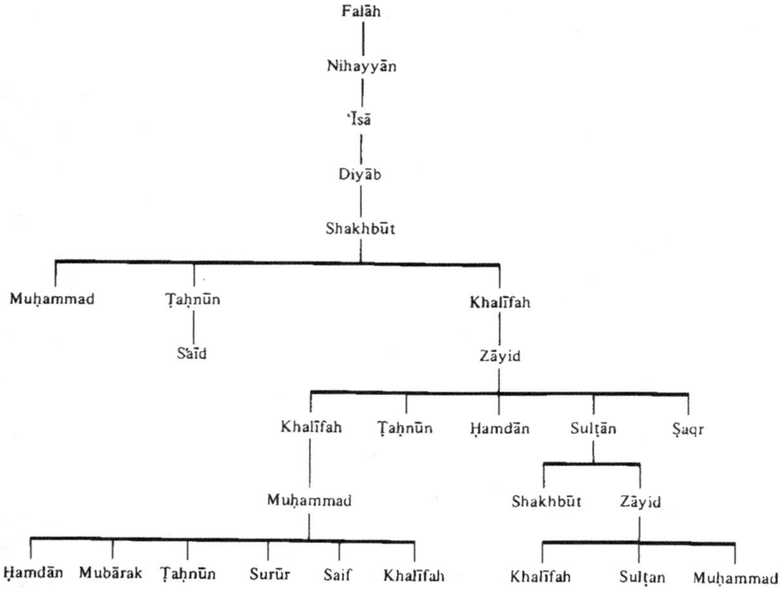

Shakhbūt b. Diyāb	*1793–1816*
Muḥammad b. Shakhbūt	*1816–1818*
Ṭaḥnūn b. Shakhbūt	*1818–1833*
Khalīfah b. Shakhbūt	*1833–1845*
Saʿīd b. Tahnūn	*1845–1855*
Zāyid b. Khalīfah	*1855–1909*
Tahnūn b. Zāyid	*1909–1912*
Ḥamdān b. Zāyid	*1912–1922*
Sulṭān b. Zāyid	*1922–1927*
Saqr b. Zāyid	*1927–1928*
Shakhbūt b. Sulṭān	*1928–1966*
Zāyid b. Sulṭān	*1966–*

Genealogical Tree No. 2

Āl Maktūm
Rulers of Dubai

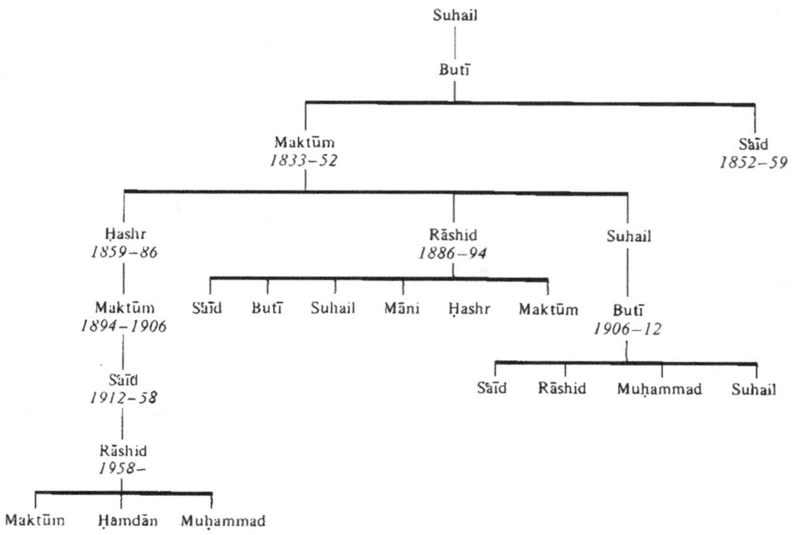

Genealogical Tree No. 3

Āl Mu'allā
Rulers of 'Umm-al-Qaiwain

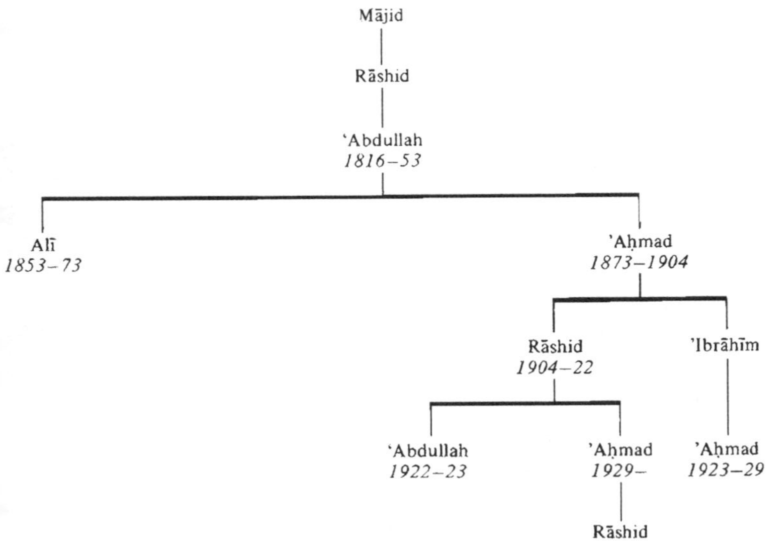

Genealogical Tree No. 4

'Āl Bū Khribān
Rulers of 'Ajmān

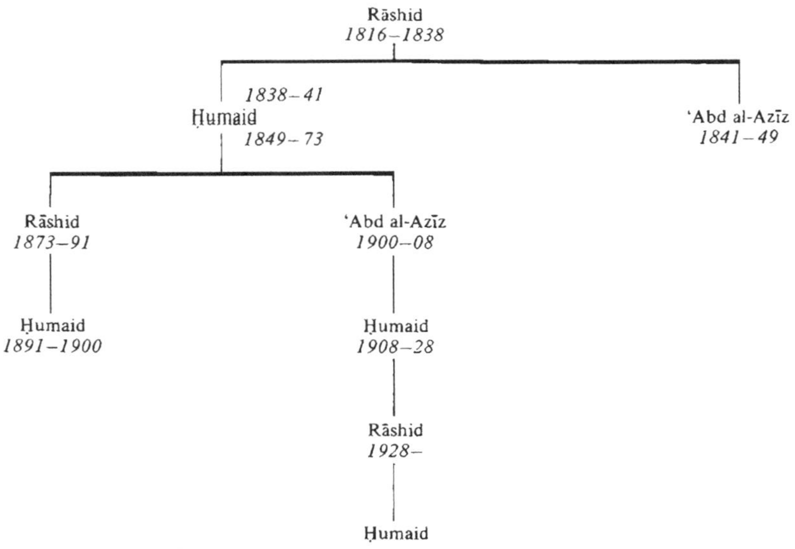

Genealogical Tree No. 5

The Ruling Family of Fujairah

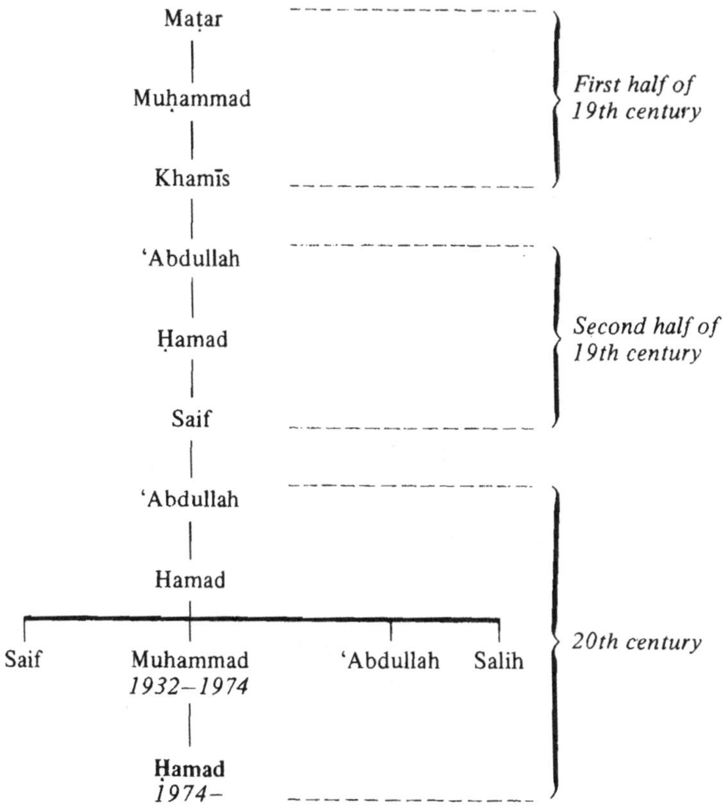

Genealogical Tree No. 6

The Hināwī and Ghāfirī Parties on the Trucial Coast

Ghāfirī	Hināwī
Qawāsim	Banī Yās
Āl 'Alī	Manāṣīr
Banī Qatab	'Awāmir
Banī K'ab	Shiḥūḥ
N'aim	Sharqiyyīn
Āl Bū Shāmis	Dhawāhir
Naqbiyyīn	Z'aāb
Ṭinaij	
Ḥabūs	

British Administration in the Gulf relating to the Trucial States, 1892 – 1939

Residency Agents in Shārjah	Political Agents in Bahrain	Political Residents in Bushire
'Abd al-Raḥmān 1866–80		E. C. Ross 1872–91
		A. C. Talbot 1891–93
		F. A. Wilson 1894–97
		M. J. Meade 1897–1900
	G. Gaskin 1900–4	C. A. Kemball 1900–4
Ḥājjī bū al-Qāsim 1880–90	F. B. Prideaux 1904–9	P. Z. Cox 1904–13
	C. F. Mackenzie 1919–10	1914–20
	S. G. Knox 1911	
	D. L. R. Lorimer 1912	
'Abd al-Laṭīf b. 'Abd al-Raḥmān 1890–1919	A. P. Trevor 1913–14	J. G Lorimer 1914
	T. H. Keyes 1915–16	
	G. Loch 1917–18	
	G. A. G. Hungavin 1919	
	A. G. Philips 1920	A. P. Trevor 1920–4
'Īsā b. 'Abd al-Laṭīf 1919–35	H. R. P. Dickson 1921	
	C. K. Daly 1922–6	F. B. Prideaux 1924–7
	C. C. J. Barrett 1927–9	L. B. Haworth 1927–9
		F. Johnston 1929
		C. C. Barrett 1929–30
	C. G. Prior 1930–2	H. V. Biscoe 1930–2
Ḥusain 'Amād 1935–6	G. Loch 1933–7	T. C. W. Fowle 1932–9
'Abd al-Razzāq 1936–45		
Captain J. B. Howes 1937–40	W. Weightman 1938–40	

Political Residents in Bahrain, 1946–71

1946–52
Lt. Col. (later Sir) W. R. Hay
1953–8
Mr B. A. B. Burrows
1958–61
Sir G. H. Middleton
1961–6
Sir W. H. T. Luce
1966–70
Sir S. Crawford
1970–1
Sir C. Arthur

Professionally qualified members of HBM's Court Dubai

W. P. R. Maudsley, Assistant Judge	1953–?
A. H. Hijazi, Assistant Judge	1956–?
P. J. Davis, Registrar	1959–?
Assistant Judge	1960–?
H. C. N. M. Oulton, Assistant Judge	1962–4
W. H. Pridmore, Assistant Judge	1964–7
W. J. Palmer, Assistant Judge	1965–9
Judge	1969–71
A. R. P. P. K. Cameron, Assistant Judge	1967–71
A. E. Otto, Assistant Judge	1967–9
B. A. Miller, Assistant Judge	1969–71

The Political Agents Trucial Coast

Political Officers in Sharjah (resident in the cold weather only)

1945–6
Capt. R. C. Murphy
1946–7
Capt. J. E. H. Hudson
1948–9
Mr G. H. Jackson

(permanantly resident)

1949–51
Mr P. D. Stobart
1951–2
Mr A. J. Wilton
1952–3
Mr M. S. Weir

(20 May 1953 post raised to status of Political Agency)

Residency Agent (the last)

1945–9
Jasim Kazmawi

Political Agents in Dubai

1953–5
Mr C. M. Pirie-Gordon
1955–8
Mr J. P. Tripp
1958–9
Mr D. F. Hawley
1959–61
Mr E. R. Worsnop (Acting)
1961–4
Mr A. J. M. Craig
1964–6
Mr H. G. Balfour-Paul
1966–8
Mr D. A. Roberts
1968–70
Mr J. L. Bullard
1970–1
Mr J. F. Walker

Political Officers in Abū Dhabī

1955–8
The Hon. M. S. Buckmaster

1958–9
Mr E. R. Morsnop
1959–61
Mr B. F. Henderson

Political Agents in Abū Dhabī

1961–5
Col. (later Sir) Hugh Boustead
1965–8
Mr A. T. Lamb
1968–71
Mr C. J. Treadwell

Table 1: Five Year Development Plan, 1968-72 (in Thousand Dinars)

	Chapters	Total Cost	ANNUAL ALLOCATIONS					Plan Appro-priations
			1968	1969	1970	1971	1972	
1	Education	12,140	4,228	1,803	2,057	2,588	1,464	12,140
2	Public Health	6,510	830	2,465	2,040	845	330	6,510
3	Agriculture	13,969	880	1,769	2,560	4,130	4,050	13,389
4	Industry	63,100	11,270	14,460	9,970	8,220	15,420	59,340
5	Communications	82,870	17,260	16,990	17,370	11,060	8,350	71,030
6	Municipalities	54,260	8,725	12,925	11,650	9,520	7,490	50,310
7	Housing	16,700	2,750	4,700	3,150	2,400	2,800	15,800
8	Labour	2,785	260	930	640	550	375	2,755
9	Tourism	5,916	850	1,170	1,325	1,571	1,000	5,916
10	Public Buildings	9,720	2,220	3,715	2,375	830	580	9,720
11	Loans and Investment	49,000	3,000	4,250	11,750	14,500	15,500	49,000
	Total	316,970	52,273	65,177	64,887	56,214	57,359	295,910

Table 2: General Educational Statistics for the Gulf City States for the Academic Year, 1969 - 70

Country	No. of Schools			No. of Students			No. of Teachers						
							Local			Foreign			
	Male	Female	Total	Male	Female	Total	Male	Female	Total	Male	Female	Total	Grand Total
Baḥrain	62	45	107	27,376	20,290	47,666	1,107	691	1,798	262	253	515	2,313
Qaṭar	48	40	88	10,122	7,101	17,223	84	23	107	490	359	849	956
Abū Dhabī*	14	8	22	4,128	1,968	6,096	2	2	4	218	98	316	320
Dubai	6	4	10	3,357	2,270	5,627	3	1	4	145	82	227	231
Shārjah	6	6	12	2,856	1,973	4,829	–	1	1	116	97	213	214
Ajman	2	1	3	483	313	796	–	2	2	29	11	40	42
Umm al-Qaiwain	1	1	2	267	198	465	–	–	–	16	13	29	29
Rās al-Khaimah	5	5	10	1,161	846	2,007	–	–	–	80	65	145	145
Fujairah	1	1	2	265	117	382	–	–	–	13	9	22	22
	145	111	256	50,015	35,076	85,091	1,196	720	1,916	1,369	987	2,356	4,272

Note: Some schools have more than one level.
* Kindergartens were not included.
Sources: Government of Baḥrain, Education Department (unpublished material);
Government of Qaṭar, Ministry of Education (unpublished material);
Government of Abū Dhabī, Education Department (unpublished material);
Kuwait office in Dubai (interview with Education Officer, June 1970, and unpublished material).
Source: Sadiq, op. cit., p. 90.

Table 3: Government Hospitals and Number of Beds in the Gulf City States, 1970

Country	No. of Hospitals	Total No. of Beds
Baḥrain (1)	6	929
Qaṭar (2)	3	621
Abū Dhabī (3)	2	300
Dubai (4)	2	164
Shārjah (4)	1	18
Ajman (4)	–	–
Umm al-Qaiwain (4)	–	–
Rās al-Khaimah (4)	1	20
Fujairah (4)	–	–

Sources: (1) Government of Baḥrain, *Statistical Abstract, 1970*, p. 16;
(2) Government of Qaṭar, Ministry of Health, 1970 (unpublished material);
(3) Government of Abū Dhabī, Department of Health, 1970 (unpublished material);
(4) Kuwait Office in Dubai, July 1970 (unpublished material).
Source: Sadiq, op. cit., p. 100.

Table 4: Expenditures and Revenues of the Government of Abū Dhabī, in 1967 and 1968 (Baḥraini Dinars)

Department		1967	1968
Agriculture		33,320	122,505
Civil Aviation		20,116	125,752
Civil Service Commission		7,453	33,756
Customs		94,023	125,567
Defence Force		1,218,762	5,606,892
Development Headquarters		20,432	98,674
Education		129,442	657,905
Electricity		146,220	462,693
Finance		36,510	156,344
Guest House		99,322	112,171
Health		319,996	1,289,197
Justice		35,171	71,085
Labour		22,959	103,706
Municipalities		168,808	1,155,871
Petroleum Affairs		36,962	131,664
Planning and Co-ordination		7,672	29,267
Police and Public Security		642,285	1,503,015
Post Office		66,213	86,584
Public Works		215,675	842,187
Water Supply		155,988	346,834
Privy Purse		12,691,827	18,324,511
Miscellaneous		9,546,081	10,522,072
Development		16,037,659	30,512,225
Intelligence		–	39,031
Labour and Social Affairs		–	27,807
London Office		–	11,364
Palace Office		–	811,156
Ports and Harbours		–	225,782
Telecommunications		–	6,056
Total Expenditure		41,752,896	73,512,864
Source of Revenue		**1967**	**1968**
Customs		275,639	534,299
Civil Aviation		21,360	46,435
Interest on Public Account and Investment Income		804,205	830,276
Electricity Supply		25,249	38,399
Health		–	5,229
Justice		4,998	28,826
Labour		1,177	1,374
Municipality		100,686	155,807
Post Office		80,077	115,412
Police and Traffic Fees		16,256	34,302
Water Supply		44,297	31,915
Petroleum Royalties and Taxes		45,592,865	71,607,972
Miscellaneous		19,924	337,118
Donation by HH the Ruler		2,007,000	–
Total Revenue	B.D.	52,993,733	73,767,362

Note: All items are given to the nearest B.D.
Source: Sadiq, op. cit., pp. 178–9; Government of Abū Dhabī, *Statistical Abstract*, Vol. I, July 1969, pp. 47–8.

Table 5: Trucial States Council Development Expenditures for Various Periods by Major Development Programmes

Major Programmes	Total to end 1968 BD	Expenditures in BD 1969	1970	Total to end 1970 BD	% of Grand Total[1]
1. Technical Education	232,836	35,089	144,000	411,925	5.37
2. Health	192,829	348,919	588,500	1,130,248	17.74
3. Agriculture	541,829	240,803	247,000	1,029,632	13.43
4. Fisheries	–	142,515	119,000	261,515	3.41
5. Harbours	229,055	3,270	96,200	328,525	4.28
6. Trunk Roads	732,905	228,157	745,000	1,706,062	22.25
7. Town Roads	145,308	2,876	30,000	178,184	2.32
8. Town and Village Water Supplies	636,660	137,751	422,000	1,196,411	15.60
9. Electricity	680,130	280,480	168,000	1,196,411	15.60
10. Housing	62,600	13,436	23,000	99,036	1.29
11. Urban Development	93,333	35,424	12,000	140,757	1.84
12. Telecommunications	49,465	2,429	–	51,894	0.68
13. Miscellaneous	2,683	–	3,000	5,683	0.07
Grand Total	3,599,633	1,471,149	2,597,700	7,736,283	100

[1] Percentage figures do not add to 100 because of rounding.
Source: Development Office, Trucial States Council, Round-Up News for the month ending 28 February 1970, n.d. (unpublished material).
Source: Sadiq, op. cit., p. 188.

Table 6: Trucial States Development Office Income, 1965 - 1970

Contributions	1965 BD	1966 BD	1967 BD	1968 BD	1969 BD	1970 BD	Total BD
The Ruler of Abū Dhabī	266,625	666,600	1,819,762	337,662	1,700,000	2,500,000	7,290,649
The Ruler of Qaṭar	333,250	–	–	–	–	–	333,250
The Ruler of Baḥrain	53,298	–	–	–	–	–	53,298
Britain – Annual Grant	322,720	266,600	196,768	278,597	114,000	–	1,178,685
Initial Capital	399,900	533,199	85,725	257,175	171,000	–	1,446,999
Grand Total	1,375,793	1,466,399	2,102,255	873,434	1,985,000	2,500,000	10,302,881

Source: Unpublished Report, Development Office, Trucial States Council, n.d., p. 43;
Unpublished Material, Development Office, Round-Up of News for 1969 and 1970; Sadiq, op. cit., p. 188.

Table 7: Military Strength of the United Arab Emirates and Individual Member States

Name of Military Unit	Total Armed Forces	Army		Navy	Air Force
		Manpower and formations	Equipment	Manpower and equipment	Manpower and equipment
Union Defence Force	1,700	5 companies	Land-Rovers	–	–
Abū Dhabī Defence Force	10,000	6,000 2 inf bns 1 armed regt. 1 support regt.	75 *Saladin* armed cars; some *Ferret* scout cars; (*Vigilant* ATGW on order); field guns	12 patrol craft (under 50 tons)	12 *Hunter* FGA 6 tpts 3 hel *Mirages*
Dubai Defence Force	1,000	paramilitary	–	Nil	–
Rās al-Khaimah Defence Force	250	mobile force	6 *Ferret* scout cars	4 powered dinghies	Nil

Source: Adapted from *Strategic Survey, 1972* (London: 1973), p. 36. See also *Military Balance, 1973–4* (London, 1974) and *Strategic Survey, 1974* (London, 1975); Anthony, op. cit., p. 105.

Index

'Abd al-'Azīz b. Ḥamad 108
'Abd al Laṭīf b. Ibrāhīm (Shaikh) 108
'Abd al-Laṭīf b. 'Ibrahīm Āl Mubārak (Shaikh) 111, 169
'Abd al-Raḥmān b. Muḥammad 15, 113–20, 132, 179
'Abd al-Razzāq 48, 69–70, 128, 130
'Abd al Wahhāt al Wuhaibi 108
'Abdullah b. 'Abd al-'Azīz 100, 108, 114, 204
Abdullah b. Faiṣal 205
'Abdullah b. 'Ali b. Hiwaiden 116, 130
'Abdullah b. Jilwī 177–8, 179
'Abdullah b. Ṣāliḥ al-Mutawwa' 106, 209
'Abdullah al Muzayyin 109
'Abdullah b. Jāsim 64, 108
Abū Dhabī 14, 15, 16; administrative reform in 139; aid from 143; air route and 57; boundaries of 293–5, 301, 302–7; British court in 80; development of 137–9; dispute with Sa'ūdī Arabia 73, 78; education in 151–2; growth of under Zāyed b. Khalīfah 96–103; maritime boundaries with Qatar 212–3; oil in 66, 74; relations with Britain 98–9; relations with Qatar 98, 160–68; relation with Sa'ūdī Arabia 173, 180–212; union with Dubai 141
Abū Dhabī Marine Areas Ltd 73, 76
Abū Dhabī Petroleum Company 75
Abū Dhabī village 96
Abū Mūsā island 42, 78, 94, 95; air routes and 53; ownership of 122–4, 233–46 *passim*, 255–62 *passim*, 262–84; Sharjah and 243–6
Ad Hoc Persian Gulf Sub-Committee 40
Admiralty 40, 41, 321; air routes and 53–4
Aḥmad b. 'Alī (Shaikh) 135
Aḥmad al-Raḥbānī (Shaikh) 108
Aḥmad Biṭār 80
Aḥmad b. Ḥāmid (Shaikh) 138
Aḥmad b. Ḥasan 313
Aḥmad b. Hilāl 209–10, 304
Aḥmad b. Ibrāhīm 209–10
Aḥmad b. Sulayyim 112, 134, 136
Aḥmad Suwaidī 138, 212
Aḥmed Mīrzā 227
aid, Arab 76, 143
air communication and power 48–57, 74, 119, 172, 322; Gulf's importance in 72; importance of, for Britain 14; negotiations for 119, 122, 173–4; Russian 42; Admiralty and War Office attitudes to 44
Air Force *see* Royal Air Force
Air Ministry 40, 41–3; advocates intervention policy 47; presses for landing facilities 46–57 *passim*
'Aishah al-Sayyār 146
'Ajīb Khān 67
'Ajmān 110, 239, 299, 303; dhows seized 263–4
'Ajmān, Shaikh of 66, 98, 100
al-'Ahrām 29
al-'Ain 98
Āl-Āli 222
al-Asḥāt 213
Āl Bū-Falāh 194
Āl Bū-Flāsah, the 129–30, 222, 256–7
Āl Bū-Sa'īd, the 223
Al Bū-Shāmis, the 292, 302–3, 307
Āl-Bū-Ṣumait tribe 222, 229, 235
al-Buraimī *see* Buraimī
al-Dhāhirah 98, 203, 208, 209
Al Fatḥ 107, 112, 120, 176–7
al-Ḥaram 222
al-Ḥasā 108, 169, 176; boundary of 170; oil in 58, 59, 61, 173, 183, 199, 203, 321
'Alī b. Khalīfah (Shaikh) 236–7
'Alī al Muhmūd 107
al-Jāhilī 98
'Alī b. Sa'if 121
al-Khalij 148
'Alī al-Tājir 202, 209–10, 217n
al-Liwa 32, 111
Allyne, Captain, J. M. 126–7
al-Manār 176
al-Mijann 192
al-Mu'ayyad 32, 111
Āl Murrah tribe 159, 177, 181, 186, 189, 191, 192

al-Shūrā 112
al-Shuruq 148
al Sil' 167
al-'Udaid 97, 159, 196–7, 319; dispute over 160–68
al-'Uqal 192, 193
al-Yaqazah 147–8
'Amad, K. S. 68
Amīn al-Riḥānī 59, 112, 173, 214n
American Gulf Oil Co. 64
Anderson, Norman 213
Anglo–French Entente (1904) 28, 30
Anglo–Iranian Oil Co. 73
Anglo–Japanese treaty (1902) 30
Anglo–Persian Oil Co. 58–90, 180, 191, 227, 249, 253, 254, 321; Trucial Coast explorations 62–71 *passim*
Anglo–Persian treaty (proposed, 1919) 229
Anglo–Russian treaty (1907) 30, 42, 226
Anglo–Turkish Convention (1913) 162, 168, 170, 171, 182, 205
Arab–Israeli dispute 281
Arab League 137, 143
Arab nationalism 15, 72, 73–5, 77, 112–13, 140; effect of education on 144
Arabistan 225, 277
Aramco 16, 73, 200–203, 204, 207
arms trade 32–8, 129, 255–6; French 28
'Awāmir tribe 110, 160, 205, 303, 306
'Azzān b. Qais 97

Bacter, C. W. 265
Baggally, Mr 190, 271
Baghdād Pact 277
Baghdād Railway 30
Baḥrain 42, 78; declares independence 141; oil concessions in 58–9, 60, 62, 255; Persian claim to 249–50, 264, 265, 277, 279, 280; Political Residency in 43–4
Baḥrain Oil Company 67
Baḥrain Political Agent 45
Bākū oilfields 228
Bandar 'Abbas 223, 228, 233, 274–5
Banī Hājir 189
Banī Ḥammād 222
Banī Ka'b, the 301–2, 305
Bani Mu'īn 222
Banī Qatab tribe 101–2, 110, 292, 301–2
Banī Yās federation 14, 96, 98, 110, 160, 167, 208, 212–13, Qawāsim and 89–90, 91–2
Banians 105–6
Barr al-Qara 181, 183
Barrett, Lieutenant-Colonel 43
Barry, Captain 179
Bāsīdū 250–55; incident 266
Baṣrah air base 51–2
Bayander, Major 254
Beckett 184–5, 272
Bedouins 104, 105–6, 125, 127, 206; Abū Dhabī and 97, 100
Benes, M. 253
Biscoe, Lieutenant-Colonel 53–6 *passim*
Bombay 106–7, 301
Bosanquet, Admiral 298
Bosworth, Frederick 74
boundaries 291–2
Briggs, Major 136
Britain: abandons landing ground plan on Trucial coast 51; administration and political control of Gulf 78–81; administrative and political machinery 40–48; aid to Trucial states 137; change from negative to positive policy 14; concludes air agreement with Persia 51; effect of attitudes of Arabs on 15; effect of Foreign rivalry on 26–38; end of the Empire 71–81; growth of interests (1918–1939) 40–71; increasing involvement in Gulf politics 51, 114; imperial interests and the Trucial States 21–85; military position of 77; oil concessions and 57–61, 62–71, 228; opposition to, in Trucial States 120; origins of presence in the Gulf 23; relations with Dubai 126–33 *passim*; relations with Persia 219–84; relations with Rezā Shāh 248–55; relations with Sa'ūdī Arabia 16, 72, 74, 75, 168–212; relations with the Turks 161–8 *passim*; relations with Trucial States (1914–18) 39; Round Table conference (1952) 206–8; tightens control 32–8; trade interests of 23; withdrawal of 77–8, 140–41, 275, 279–80
British Petroleum Concessions 267
Buckhardt 104
Buckmaster, M. S. 79, 80, 295
Bullard, Sir Reader 195–8, 210
Bunayyān 191, 192
Buraimī 16, 50, 97, 98, 104, 160, 302–7; oil in 292; Sa'ūdī–British conflict over 74, 174, 176, 203–4, 208, 210
Bushire 274–5
Buṭi b. Suhail (Shaikh) 33, 34–5, 37, 75

Cadman, Sir John 253
Cairo 106
California Oil Co. 69, 174, 183, 200
Churchill, W. 242–3
Clauson 192
Clayton, Sir Gilbert 172, 173
Clive, Sir Robert 252, 256, 262–5
Colonial Office 40, 41, 42; India Office and 45–6

Committee of Imperial Defence 44; boundaries of Qatar and 182; discussion of Musandam peninsula 29; oil concessions and 65; Persian Gulf Sub-Committee 42–3, 44, 250–51
construction 137
Consul-General for Fars 43
Courtney, Air Vice-Marshall, 47
Cox 27, 39; Abū Dhabī and 100–103; Dubai incident and 33–8 *passim*; pearl fishing and 103–4; Persia and 226, 227, 229, 246; Rās al-Khaimah and 311; red oxide concession and 30–31, 320
cultural clubs 147
cultural development 106–9
Cunningham, Captain 53
Curzon, Lord 26–7, 95; Persia policy 229; proposes protection over Qatar 168; Rūs al-Jibāl and 298; *status quo* policy 99
customs duties 231, 255–6; in Dubai 131

Dabā 90, 92, 300
Dalmā 96, 103
Dame, Dr 61
Dammam Conference 206–8
D'Arcy, William 225
d'Arcy exploration Co. 292
Dawāsir tribe 229
Dayyīnah 213
Dhāhirah province 101, 102
Dhahūriyyīn tribe 296–9
Dhawāhir tribe 97, 160, 302, 306
Dhaid 90, 103
Dickson, Colonel H. R. P. 56, 64, 187–8, 191–2, 272, 313–14
dirah 291, 299
Disbrowe, Colonel 297
Dōḥaḥ 194
Dubai 135; boundaries of 293–5, 299–302; British political representative transferred to 79; education in 134, 135–6, 148–9; oil in 66, 139; relations with Sa'ūdī Arabia 174–80; schools in 109; the Majlis 126–33; union with Abū Dhabī 141
Dubai, Shaikh of 33, 37, 38, 134, 263, 321; air route negotiations with 54–5, 57; Dubai dhow incident and 257–62; Ḥīrah and 117–18; oil concessions and 66, 67, 68–71; Ṣirri island and 238; support for 46–7; the Majlis and 126–33
Dubai dhow incident 257–62
Dubai Incident (1910) 28, 32–8
Dubai Municipality 15, 134–5
Dubai Oil Co. 76–7
Dubai port 103, 104–5, 134, 231, 276, 320
Dubai village 96

Eccles, Captain 208, 305
economic change 103–6
Eden, Sir Anthony 74, 210
education *see* schools
Egypt 76, 106–7, 277–84 *passim*
Exclusive Treaty (1892) 14, 23–6

Faiṣal, Emir 173, 206–7
Faiṣal, King 16, 199, 211
Fars 224, 228
Fath al-Basayer 28
Fāṭimah b. Mubārak (Shaikah) 142
Fisher, Sir Warren 43
flying boats 51, 52
Foreign Office 26, 40–48; India Office and 45–6; made responsible for Gulf 78, 232; Sa'ūdī Arabia's boundaries and 180–99 *passim*
Fowle, T. 45, 64, 321; advocates policy of non-interference 47; boundaries of Qatar and 182–90 *passim*; Dubai and 128–33; importance of his appointment 45; Kalbā and 312–13; oil concessions and 64–72 *passim*, 293; Persia and 269
France 23, 26, 27–8, 94; slave trade and 38
Fraser, Lieutenant 234
Fu'ād Ḥamzah 183, 184, 185, 189, 195, 196
Fujairah 17, 90, 92–5, 96, 102, 297; independence of 307–10, 320, 322–3

Galloway, Colonel 294
Galpin, B. W. 54
Gamal Abdel Nasser 74, 75, 144, 277, 278
Gault, Charles 213
Germany 23, 26, 30–32, 42; relations with Peris 227
Ghafalah 102
Ghāfirī party 14, 109–10, 140, 208, 299
Ghāfirī tribes 97, 99
Ghālib b. 'Ali 210
Goguyer 28, 102
Gulf Aviation Co. 74
Gulf Pact (proposed) 280, 284

Ḥabbāniyyah 49
Ḥabūs, the 298–9
Hajji 'Abd al-Raḥmān 234
Ḥajjī Abu al-Qāsim 25, 163, 234–8, 285n
Ḥājjī Aḥmad Khān 24, 25, 224, 230, 238–42
Ḥamad b. 'Abdullah (Shaikh) 92, 93, 94, 95, 300, 309–10
Ḥamad b. Majid 94
Ḥamāsā 74
Hamdām b. Zāyed (Shaikh) 176
Hamdā (Shaikn) 103, 136
Ḥamdān b. Muḥammad (Shaikh) 137, 151

Hamilton, Lloyd 67, 173–4
Ḥamriyyah 90, 94, 303, 307–10, 322–3
Ḥanbalī 299
Hanjām 228, 232–3, 250–55, 256–62, 265
Hardinge, Sir Arthur 244–5
Ḥasan b. Muḥammad (Shaikh) 238–9
Ḥasan b. Raḥman (Shaikh) 296
Ḥasan Sumaiḥ 31, 32
Haworth, Colonel 127; proposes increased interference 41, 43, 178
Hay, Sir Rupert 206–7
Hearn 64
Heath, Edward 77–8
Henderson, E. F. 202, 207, 210, 216n
Hickinbotham, Captain 69, 70, 291–2, 293–4, 313–14
Hijaz 171
Ḥimūdah 'Alī b. 141
Hināwī party 109–10, 140, 160, 167, 296–9 *passim*, 303, 308; attitude to Ibn Sa'ūd 174
Hināwī tribes 91, 92, 96, 97, 165, 208
Hīrah 90, 114–20, 303
Ḥissah bint al-Murr 126
Ḥiṣyān 293
Hoare, Sir Samuel 193
Holmes, Dr R. 66–7
Holmes, Major 59, 61–72 *passim*, 181
hospitals 136
Houle 284n
Howarth, Sir Lionel 256
Howes, Captain J. B. 48, 128
Hudson, Captain J. E. 79
Ḥumaid b. 'Abdullah (Shaikh) 234–8, 310
Husain b. 'Ahmād 46
Ḥusain Yatīm 68

Ibn Mānī' 111–12
Ibn Rashid 164–7
Ibn Sa'ūd 39, 40–41, 43, 65, 214–15n; his influence on Bedouins 51; objects to aircraft 49, 56; oil concessions granted by 60; *see also* Sa'ūdī Arabia
Ibri 96
Ikhwān, the 50, 171–3, 176
Imperial Airways 49, 253, 322
India, Government of 29, 41; Trucial coast's importance for 26, 42–3, 72, 320
India Office 26, 321; end of its role in Gulf 78; frontiers of Sa'ūdī Arabia and 184, 185, 190, 197; policy on Ṭanb 269–72; takes control of the Gulf states' affairs 46
Indian Steam Navigation Co. 223, 232
Inter-Departmental Committee 40
Iran 16; armed forces 274–5; Baḥrain and 78; development of 274; oil and 275, 278; relations with Britain 72, 73, 75; relations with Egypt 277–84 *passim*; relations with Iraq 277, 280, 283; relations with the Soviet Union 274, 279; relations with Trucial Shaikhs 277–8; the Islands' dispute and 273–84
Iraq 75, 277, 280, 283; defence of 41, 49; American oil exploration in 58; boundaries of 171–2
Iraq Petroleum Co. 64, 65, 174
'Isā b. 'Abd al-Laṭīf 179; Dubai and 126–133 *passim*; Ḥirāh and 116–20; Rās al-Khaimah and 122, 269; role of 114
Isphahān 228
Italy 192, 195

Jabal 'Alī 293
Jabal Duckhān 196
Jabal Fahūd 203
Jabal Fāyah 203, 292, 301–2
Jabal Hafīt 203
Jabal Nakhsh 192, 196
Jabal Shammar 164–5
Jackson, J. N. 79
Japan 61–2
Jāsim b. Thānī (Shaikh) 161–8, 169
Jazirat al-Hamrā 90
Jeddah, Treaty of (1927) 172
Johnson, Sir Frederick 251
Jones, Captain Felix 91

Ka'b tribe 223
Kalbā 90, 124–5; independence of 307–10, 312–15; oil concessions in 67
Kamāl Hamzah 136
Kamzār 297
Keir, General 296
Keith, C. H. 49–51
Kelly, J. B. 13
Kemball, Colonel 232, 244
Khādim, B. 177
Khādim b. Buṭī 98, 161, 162
Khājah 'Abd al-Raḥīm 111
Khalaf Alī al-Zamānī 129
Khalaf b. 'Utaibah 108
Khālid b. Aḥmad (Shaikh) 96, 114–20 *passim*, 124, 292, 311, 314–15
Khālid b. Khālid b. Ṣaqr 121
Khālid b. Muḥammad (Shaikh) 147
Khalifah b. Sa'īd (Shaikh) 230, 234–6, 239
Khalīfah b. Zāyed (Shaikh) 137, 139, 141, 194
Khān Bahādur 'Abd al-Latīf 26, 31, 33, 38–9, 45, 68; Abū-Dhabī and 99; air route and 55; Qawāsim and 95
Khaṣab 297
Khatmat Milāhah 300–301

Khawānij, the 102
Khawāṭir tribe 110, 303
Khaz'al (Shaikh), 223, 225, 246–7
Khūr al-'Udaid 189, 192, 196–9
Khūr Fakkān 90, 300, 312
Khūr Ghanādah 293
Knatchbull-Hugessen 272–3
Knox, Captain 176
Kuwait: Baghdād Railway and 30; educational development and 143–52 *passim*; independence 75; oil concessions in 58–9, 61, 64; relations with Iran 278
Kuwait Political Agent 56
300

Laithwaite, G. 44, 180, 182, 187, 271–2
Lamington, Lord 41
Lansdowne, Lord 26–7, 245
Lascelles 268, 272
League of Nations 268, 276
Lebanon 107
liberation movements *see* Arab nationalism
Lingah 23, 94, 108, 238, 244, 319; fall of Qawasim Emirate and 299–300; population of 248; port 104, 222; Shaikhs of 268, 272; Vice-Consulate proposed at 33, 227
Līwā 96, 103, 153n, 160, 193, 195
local government 136
Loch, Lieutenant Colonel 45, 46, 66, 69, 193–5, 272, 312
Longrigg, Major Stephen 66, 71, 174
Loraine, Sir Percy 255
Lorimer, V. G. 13, 24, 27, 28, 90, 221, 284n, 298, 300, 304–5, 307; his Gazeteer of the Gulf 207, 216n, 291

McMahon 39
Maḥdah 50
Mahdī-al Tājir 134, 136
Maḥmūd 267, 270–71
Majlis (Persia) 226
Maktūm b. Rāshid 129, 141, 148
Malik al Tujjār 24, 224, 230, 238
Mālikī Sunnī sect 160
Manāsīr tribe 110, 159, 160, 186, 191, 205, 208, 303, 306
Mānī'al- 'Utaibah 138
Mānī' b. Rāshid (Shaikh) 25, 69, 106, 113, 119
Marāzīk 222
Masfūt 101
Mas'ūd Mirzā (Prince) 23
Mas'ū ī 98
Maṭārīsh, the 223
Maus, M. 225
Māzim 101
Meade, Colonel M. J. 243–4
Memorials, the 200
migration 134, 221–3; from abroad 135, 140; from Persia 247, 255, 276–7
Miles, Colonel 300, 303
Mockler 239
Moḥammarah 227
Mubārak al-Nākhī 112
Mubārak b. Khalaf al-Hināwī 109
Mubārak b. Muḥammad (Shaikh) 138, 141
Mudhaffar al-Dīn 225
Muḥammad 'Abd al'Azīz b. Mānī' 108
Muḥammad b. 'Abdullah al-Khalīlī 208, 210
Muḥammad 'Alī al-Maḥmūd 145, 179
Muḥammad al-Mānī' 65
Muḥammad 'Alī al-Ṭāhir 112
Muhammad 'Alī Zainal 109
Muḥammad b. Aḥmad b. Dalmūh 107–8, 126
Muḥammad b. Ghubāsh 108, 109
Muḥammad Ḥabrūsh al-Swaidī 138–9
Muḥammad 'Ismā'īl 37
Muḥammad b. Khādim 179
Muḥammad b. Khālid (Shaikh) 138, 231, 244
Muḥammad Khalīfah al-Kindī 152
Muḥammad b. Manṣūr 206
Muḥammad b. Nāsir al-Ghāfirī 109
Muḥammad b. Raḥma Al-Shāmis (Shaikh) 293
Muḥammad Rezā Shāhanshāh 16, 273–4; relations with Britain 248–55
Muḥammad b. Thānī (Shaikh) 161
Muḥammad Yatīm 62
Mu'īn al Tujjār 255
Mullās, the 228–9
Murphy, Captain R. C. 79
Murshid al-Albab 28
Mūsā Island 16–17
Musaddaq, Dr 279
Musandam peninsula: strategic importance of 29
Muscat 91; France and 28, 29; frontier of 17, 291 - 315; Qawāsim and 92–3; relations with Abū Dhabī 100; relations with Britain 99; relations with Persia 223; relations with Sa'ūdī Arabia 174–6
Muscat, Sultan of 97, 203, 209, 294
Mustawfī al-Mamālik 228

Na'īm tribe 292, 302–7; Abū Dhabī and 97, 98, 100, 101–2
Naṣir b. Mubārak 166
Nāṣir at Nuwais 143
Nasūr 222
National Oil Co. of Abū Dhabī 142
naval bases, Gulf 29

Nejd: blue line of 180–88, 199; boundary of 168, 170–71, 180–99; Sa'ūdīs and 101; teachers from 107
New, Mr 33, 35
Nicolson 240–42
Niebuhr, C. 222, 284n
Nizwā 110, 210
Noakes, Lt 34

OPEC 76
O'Brien, T. V. 49–51
O'Connor, Sir Nicholas 169
Odessa Maritime Line 29
Official Middle East Sub-Committee 40; Arabian air route and 52, 53, 55; boundary of Qatar and 180–99 *passim*; oil exploration and 63, 64; Persia policy 254
oil concessions and industry 15, 16, 106, 191, 213, 321; American 44, 58–61, 173; boundaries and 291–2, 294; British 72, 77, 125, 197, 228; in Abū Dhabī 136; in Dubai 131; on the Trucial Coast 62–71; Persia and 275, 278; profit sharing in 73, 76
Oman 89; civil war in 14, 109–10; frontier 17; relations with Britain 110; resentment over arms trade 32; revolt against 74; Sa'ūdī policy in 168–80; the Imamate in 203, 205, 208, 210
Ottavi 38–9
Osborne, Major 190
Ottomans, the 23, 319; Arab attitudes to 111; dispute with Qatar over al-'Udaid 160–68; opposition of, to Britain 23–4; propaganda 39

Palestine 107, 112, 204; revolt in (1936) 195
Parkes, Ernest O. 71
Parry, Captain M. 117–18
passports, Persian 263, 264
pearl fisheries 96, 103–4, 105, 212–13, 255; effect of on education 109, 110
Pelly, Colonel 161, 224, 229, 233
Permanent Resident 79
Persia 23, 322; air routes and 49, 253; antagonism towards Britain 24–6; British attitude to 121; claims to the Islands 233–46; development of 247; navy 251–5, 263, 269; oil revenues 253; relations with Britain 224–9, 233–84; relations with Germany 227; relations with Russia 225–249; relations with Trucial States 255–62; Russian influence in 30; trade 105; war debt 249–50, 252; weakness of 42; *see also* Iran
Persia, Shah of 223–4, 226, 246–84 *passim*; *see also* Iran
Persian Gulf: British withdrawal from 72; importance of, for Britain 72; Tehran's authority over 223–4
Persian Gulf Pilot 234, 248
Petroleum Concessions Ltd 66, 67, 69, 85n, 202, 292
Petroleum Development (Trucial Coast) Co. 66, 73, 74
Philby 206, 216n
Philips, Captain 48
Pirie-Gordon, C. M. 79
Political Agent (Bahrain) 119, 125, 129, 170, 179
Political Agent (Dubai) 79
political attitudes 109–13
political change (1918–1939) 113–33
Political Officer (Sharjah) 48, 79, 128, 204
Political Resident 25, 26, 45, 77, 78–9, 86n; air routes and 53–4, 55; Dubai and 132–3; Persia and 250–55; relations with government departments 40; relations with Ibn Sa'ūd 169; transfer of, discussed 43–4, 48; Rās al-Khaimah and 125; refuses to allow oil exploration 63; role of 225, 251; Tanb and Abū Mūsā islands and 234–38, 269–70
Porte, the 166, 175
press, Arab 128, 130, 147–8; *see also specific newspapers*
Prideaux, Lieutenant Colonel F. B. 63, 161–2, 308–9

Qadīb (Shaikh) 233, 238
Qadīb b. Rāshid (Shaikh) 230
Qajār dynasty 221–33
Qashqāi tribe 228
Qatar 78, 135, 322; Abū Dhabī and 98; boundary with Sa'ūdī Arabia 180–99; declares independence 141; dispute with Ottomans over al-'Udaid 160; education in 109, 134, 143, 145, 147; importance of for Britain 65; maritime boundaries with Abū Dhabī 212; oil concessions in 64–5
Qawāsim, the 222, 223, 233–8, 296–9, 320; Banī Yās and 89–92; claim to the islands 233–46 *passim*, 260–61; frontiers of 299–302
Qawāsim Emirate 81n; change in British attitude to 94–5; conflict with Britain 91; dismemberment of 14, 16, 90–96, 229–33; frontier 17; independence movement within 307–10; navy 91; Sa'ūdīs and 91
Qibaisāt, the 98, 159, 161, 162
Qishm 223, 241, 278

Rās al Khaimah 90, 110, 120–26, 239, 297–9; air base at 52–4; Abu Musa and 273–84; education in 137; government of 95–6; independence of 255, 307–12; oil exploration in 66–71 *passim*; relations with Britain 121–5; Tanb islands and 234–8, 273–84
Rāshid b. Aḥmad (Shaikh) 101–2, 301, 304
Rāshid b. Ḥamad 209, 210
Rāshid b. Ḥumaid (Shaikh) 292, 315n
Rāshid b. Māni' (Shaikh) 112, 127–33 *passim*, 155n
Rāshid b. Sa'īd al-Maktūm (Shaikh) 15, 98, 126–33 *passim*, 164–5, 293; *see also* Dubai, Shaikh of
Rāshid b. Sa'īd (Shaikh) 141
Rayyis Muḥammad Rasūl 129
red oxide concession 3, 102, 243, 246, 255, 273, 320
reformers, social 111–12, 133
religion 114
Rendel, G. 44; air route and 53, 54, 55; oil concessions and 64; Sa'ūdī Arabia and 173, 182–99 *passim*; Persia and 254, 272; supports intervention policy 48
Rentz, George 201–2, 205–6, 207–8, 217n
Roosevelt, President 201
Ross, Colonel 24–5, 93, 235, 239–41; al-'Udaid and 162–8
Royal Air Force 40–41, 48–9; becomes responsible for Gulf defence 51; control of Arabian coast by 43; establishment of bases for Imperial defence by 48–57
Royal Dutch Shell Co. 58
Rūs al Jibāl 91, 296–9
Russia 23, 26, 28–30, 42, 94, 320; relations with Persia 225, 242, 249
Ryan 181–99 *passim*

Safq 194, 196
Sa'īd b. Buṭī (Shaikh) 128–9
Sa'īd b. Ḥamad 124
Sa'īd b. Sulṭān 96, 303
Sa'īd b. Ṭaḥnūm 96, 103
Saif b. 'Abd al-Raḥmān 94, 95
Saif b. Muḥammad (Shaikh) 138
Ṣāliḥ b. 'Alī (Shaikh) 97
Ṣāliḥ b. 'Īsā al-Ḥarithī (Shaikh) 208
Ṣāliḥ b. Muḥammad al-Khilaifī 108
Sālim b. 'Abdullah 124
Sālim b. Dayyin (Shaikh) 50, 51, 305
Sālim b. Miṣabbah Āl-Ḥimūdah 108
Sālim b. Sulṭān (Shaikh) 31, 92, 93, 97, 234–5, 320
San Remo petroleum agreement 58
Ṣaqr b. Khālid b. Sulṭān 92
Ṣaqr b. Muḥammad (Shaikh) 81, 137
Ṣaqr b. Sulṭān (Shaikh) 203–4, 210
Ṣaqr b. Zāyed (Shaikh) 50
Ṣaqr b. Khālid (Shaikh) 31–2, 93–4, 95, 97, 246, 311; *see also* Sharjah, Shaikh of
Sa'ūdī Arabia 16, 322; dispute with Abū Dhabī 73, 78, 305; oil industry 200–203; policy in Oman 168–80; Qawasim and 120; relations with Abū Dhabī 180–212; relations with Britain 72, 74, 75, 168–212; relations with Iran 278; relations with United States 200–201, 204
Sayyed Nādir b. Faiṣal Āl Bū Sa'īd 50
Sayyed Salīm 223
Sayyed Ziā al-Dīn Ṭabāṭaba'ī 248
schools 15, 107–9, 110, 134, 135–7, 143–53, 276–7, 321, 323
Senior Naval Officer 118–19, 179; Dubai and 127; Dubai dhow incident 257–62; Fujairah and 308–10, 316n; Ḥirāh and 117–19; Rās al-Khaimah and 121; Sirrī and 245; Tanb and 266
Seyyed 'Abd al Ḥusein 226
Seyyed Murtazā 226–7
Sha'am 90
Shāfi'ī 299, 303
Shaikh b. Buṭī b. Suhail 33, 34–5, 57, 75
Shakespear, Lieutenant 29, 169–70, 175–6, 232–3
Shakhbūṭ b. Diryāb (Shaikh) 110
Shakhbūṭ (Shaikh) 57, 73, 130, 150–51, 194, 204
Shakhbūṭ b. Sulṭān (Shaikh) 307
Shanzādah Muḥammad Husain Murtāza 230
Sharif Ḥusain 39, 171
Sharjah 90, 95–6, 98, 320; Abū Mūsā and 243–6, 255–62 *passim*, 273–84; air agreement with 45, 54–71; airport 103, 106, 113, 312; as a cultural centre 107; British base in 14; education 134, 136–7, 146–7; modernisation in 140; oil exploration in 66; Ṭanb and 269–70, 273–84
Shārjah, Shaikh of 31, 351, 50, 55, 106, 301–2; Abū Dhabī and 96, 100; air route agreement with 55–7; Ḥirāh and 114–20 *passim*; Kālba and 313–15; oil concessions and 68–71; Ṣirrī island and 239–40
Sharjah Residency Agent 23, 26, 48, 66, 323
Sharqiyyīn tribe 91, 92, 125, 297, 301, 307–10, 312
Shaṭṭ-al-'Arab waterway 277
Shawāmis tribe 110
Shiḥūḥ tribes 102, 112–13, 296–9, 309
Shī'ī, the 222
Shimāiliyyah 90, 91, 93, 299, 300, 320
shipping, Japanese 62

Shirā'uh 213
Shīrāz 228, 275
Simon, Sir John 182
Sir 103
Ṣīr Banī Yās 57, 96, 212
Ṣirrī island 94, 233–46 *passim*, 262, 267, 319, 320; Persian occupation of 238–43
Slade, Rear Admiral 33, 35
slave trade 38–9, 129
Sloan, Alexander 60
Smith, Sir James Masterton 40
smuggling 255–6
social change 113, 133–43; Britain's role in 135
sport 144, 146
Standard Oil Co. 60, 61, 65, 67, 69, 180, 197
Stobart, P. D. 79, 204
Sūdān 222
Suez crisis 74, 144, 211
Sulaiman b. Ḥimyan 208
Sulaimān Masjid 227
Sulṭān b. Aḥmad 223
Sultan Faiṣal b. Turkī 28, 97, 98, 303–4, 320
Sulṭān b. Muḥammad (Shaikh) 100, 146, 304
Sulṭān b. Muḥammad al-Na'īmī (Shaikh) 304
Sulṭān b. Muḥammad al-Qāsimī (Shaikh) 147, 148
Sultan b. Nāsir 99–100
Sulṭān Sa'īd b. Taimūr 211, 294, 306–7
Sulṭān b. Sālim (Shaikh) 52, 54, 113, 116, 120–26, 130, 311–12; Ṭanb island and 265–72
Sulṭān b. Ṣaqr (Shaikh) 110, 233, 296–7; education and 145–6; Ḥirāh and 115–20; Kalbā and 312–14
Sulṭān b. Shakr (Shaikh) 55–6, 75, 76, 90–91
Sulṭān Taimūr b. Faiṣal 304
Sulṭān Turkī b. Sa'īd 300
Sulṭān b. 'Uwais 147
Sulṭān b. Zāyed (Shaikh) 141, 179
Sunnī sect 222, 230
Superior Oil Co. of California 73
Surūr b. Muḥammad (Shaikh) 138, 141
Switzer, C. W. 49–51
Syria 107

Taḥnūm b. Muḥammad (Shaikh) 138, 142
Taḥnūn b. Zāyed (Shaikh) 304
Ṭālib al Naqīb 111
Talbot, Major 25
Ṭanb islands 16–17, 42, 79, 319, 320; lighthouse on 246, 263, 266–71; ownership of 121, 122–4, 233–46, *passim*; 252–3, 255–62, 262–84
Tangistānī tribes 227
Tehran 225
Telegraph Island 29–30
Texas Oil Co. 201
Teymourtāche 250–54, 262–5
Tha 'ālibī 112
Thesiger, W. 206
Thomas, Bertram 49–50, 60, 112–13, 177–8, 187, 208, 216n, 300, 305–6, 309
Thomas, Dr 65–6
Thuwainī b. Sa'īd 297
Times of India 35
Trans-'Omān Expedition 49–50
Tredwell, C. J. 80
Trenchard, Sir Hugh 49
Trevor, Lt Colonel A. P. 59, 62, 115–16, 170, 175–6, 311
tribal influences 110–11
Tripp, J. P. 79
Trucial 'Omān Levies 80
Trucial States: administration of 80–81; Arab nationalism in 75–6; between 1891 and 1918 90–103; British withdrawal from 72–81; fear of British interference 49; first maps of 205–6; frontier map 17, 80; importance of, for Britain 72; oil concessions and 62–71; protectorate proposed for 42; relations with Britain (1914–18) 39; relations with Persia 255–62
Trucial States Council 135
Turkī b. 'Utaishān 209, 210
Turkish Petroleum Co. 58

'Ubaid b. Jum'ah (Shaikh) 126, 257
'Ubaid b. Nabūdah 109
Ubaidlī 222
'Umm al-Qaiwan 90, 96, 110, 176, 241; oil concessions in 66, 67
'Umm al-Qaiwan, Shaikh of 25, 35, 66, 292, 302; Abū Dhabī and 101–2
unification (of the emirates) 15
United Arab Emirates: formation of 78, 140–43, 212, 280, 284, 323; education in 142; *see also* Trucial States
United States Army Survey Department 294
United States of America 321; balance of power and 279; diplomatic representation in Sa'ūdī Arabia 173; economic activity 57; relations with Britain 72–3; relations with Sa'ūdī Arabia 200–201, 204; State Department 183, 214; support for American oil companies 73, 183
university education 139, 143, 147, 149, 150

'Utūb tribe 229

Vussuq al-Dawlah 229

Wādī Ḥattā 101, 315n
Wādī Madḥah 299
Wahhābis, the 176, 178, 179, 303
Walker, Julian 17, 204–5, 298, 299, 302, 307
Walker, J. F. 80
Walton, J. C. 44
Warāvī tribe 227
Warden, Francis 296
Wassmus, Mr 266–227
Wazīr b. Kāmil 55
Weightman 129, 130
Weir, M. S. 79
Wellesley, Sir Victor 269
Williamson, 'Abdullah 63, 66–7, 68, 70–71, 84–5n, 302
Wilson, A. T. 227, 249
Wilson, Colonel 243
Wilson, Harold 77
Wilton, A. J. 79
wireless station 45
Wolff, Sir Drummond 242
women: education of 146–7, 149; position of 142
Wonkhaus, Robert (company) 30–31, 246, 311

Yemen 75, 277, 279
Yūnis Baḥarī 112
Yūsuf Kanū 62, 68
Yūsuf b. Muḥammad (Shaikh) 230
Yūsuf Sirkāl 109

zakat collection 177, 179–80, 185, 187, 205
Zāyed b. Khalīfah (Shaikh) 24, 28, 38, 92, 95, 239, 301, 304–5, 320; al-'Udaid dispute and 161–8; growth of Abu Dhabi and 96–103
Zāyed b. Sulṭān (Shaikh) 15, 81, 136–9, 306, 323: relations with Sa'ūdī Arabia 199–212
Zuhdī al-Khaṭīb 149
Zūrā 92, 99–100